LIMERICK
THE RICH LAND

Sean Spellissy
John O'Brien

SPELLISSY/O'BRIEN PUBLISHERS

First published in 1989 by
Spellissy-O'Brien Publisers
68 Parnell St., Ennis, Co. Clare.

ISBN   0 9512474 1 7   (Pbk.)
ISBN   0 9512474 2 5   (HB.)

Text	Sean Spellissy
Photography & Design	John O'Brien
Design, Artwork, Setting & Origination	Alphaset Ltd.
Map & Drawing	Gerard Dore
Printed by	Kilkenny People Ltd.

CONTENTS

Cover Picture:
An aerial view of Adare Manor, County Limerick.

Back Cover:
Evening tranquility. Swans on the river Shannon with King John's Castle in the background.

PREFACE

The history of Limerick, City and County, has been well documented by Rev. John Begley, Sir Bernard Burke, Rev. P. Fitzgerald, James Frost, P.W. Joyce, Maurice Lenihan, Samuel Lewis, John O'Donovan, George Petrie, T.J. Westropp, Rev. P. White, and Rev. Patrick Woulfe.

This book is, in part, a compilation of their works augmented by information gleaned from the more recent publications of, amongst others, J. Grene Barry, T.B. Barry, Mark Bence-Jones, William Smith Clarke, Robert Cussen, Brian de Breffny, Michael Dolley, Thomas Fanning, Pat Feeley, J. Anthony Gaughan, Willie W. Gleeson, Aubrey Gwynn and R. Neville Hadcock, Rev. G.F. Hamilton, Kevin Hannan, Peter Harbison, Robert Herbert, Louis Hyman, Dr. Robert Wyse Jackson, M.J. and C. Kelly, Seán Kelly, Lord Killanin and Michael V. Duignan, Marie Leo, Phil Lovett, Paddy Lysaght, Colonel J.M. MacCarthy, Edward MacLysaght, Tom McNamara, Máire MacNeill, Gearóid Mac Spealáin, T.W. Moody and F.X. Martin, Mary Mulcahy, Charlotte M. Murphy, Dr. Jeremiah Newman, Ivar O'Brien, John O'Connor, Patrick J. O'Connor, Máirtín O Corrbuí, Michael O'Dwyer, Padraic O'Farrell, Michael J. O'Kelly, Seán P. O'Riordáin, John O'Sullivan, Michael O'Sullivan, Thomas F. O'Sullivan, Seán O Tuama, A.J. Otway-Ruthven, P.J. Ryan, Mainchín Seoighe, Elizabeth Shee-Twohig, Alfred P. Smyth, Rev. M.J. Talbot, Rev. Mark Tierney, Patrick F. Wallace, Larry Walsh, Hugh W.L. Weir and Frank Whelan.

The North Munster Antiquarian Journal and *The Old Limerick Journal* proved to be extremely valuable sources of information, a fact which could be attributed to the quality of the published articles and the editorial skills of Etienne Rynne and Jim Kemmy. Other material used in *Limerick, The Rich Land* is derived from some of the, as yet, unpublished works of Niall Behan, Tony Browne, Joseph S. Honan, Liam Irwin, Hank Jones, Denis Leonard, Brian O Dálaigh, Yann Philippe MacBradaí, Eamon O'Flaherty, Chris O'Mahony, Walter Ruttle and Nicholas Sheaff.

In this book we have tried to emulate Samuel Lewis's *A Topographical History of Ireland* (1837) and present a portrait of various places, highlighting the historical, archaeological, and architectural heritage of both city and county. Unlike *A Topographical History of Ireland, Limerick The Rich Land* provides a unique pictorial record of present-day Limerick as most of the photographs used in illustration, date from September 1988 to May 1989. The text is based on secondary rather than primary sources and is presented under a series of easy to read headings and sub-headings. There are references to the old civil parishes, which remained in use from the reign of Henry VIII (1509-1547) until 1898, and the baronies of Shanid, Glenquin, Connello Upper, Coshma, Coshlea, Small County, Coonagh, Owneybeg, Clanwilliam, Pubblebrien and Kenry, which were formed for purposes of civil jurisdiction. Each chapter deals with a specific place, lists other places in the vicinity of the one first mentioned, and finishes with a series of reference numbers which can be linked to sources detailed in the bibliography. Some of the sub-headings are in no particular sequence and, in several cases, can be found under more than one main heading, but all people and places are indexed.

A special word of thanks is due to Pat Flynn, Dr. C.D. O

Murchadha, Dr. Patricia Lynch, Bill McInerney and Michael Meaney who proof-read *Limerick, The Rich Land*. Thanks are also due to Mary Moroney of the Clare County Library, Fred Bourke of Yardfield, Clonlara, Celie O'Rahilly, Limerick City Archaeologist, Erin Gibbons of Clifden, Risteárd Ua Cróinín of Dysert O'Dea, Tom Donovan of Glin, Kay Sheehy of Granagh, Michael Clarke of Ennis, Pat Costello of Shannon, Aine Thornhill and Deirdre O'Dea of the Limerick City Library, Gerry Dore of Glin and Raheen Cross, Colonel Seán O'Driscoll of Castle Matrix and Thomas Coffey, Gerald O'Connell and Leslie McCrum, all of Ennis, who suggested various sources, and in most cases also procured the relevant material. We would also like to take this opportunity to thank Monica O'Brien and Mary Spellissy, whose invaluable assistance and encouragement throughout the entire production of the book are especially appreciated. Thanks are also due to Tony Hartnett of Alphaset Ltd. for his professionalism and patience and his design ideas which help to make the book distinctive; Tim Crowley, our advertising representative and our advertisers whose sponsorship subsidised the production costs and enabled us to publish *Limerick, The Rich Land* at a reasonable price; Chris Walsh of Alphaset Ltd. who managed to decipher the handwritten text; and Breandán O Ciobháin of the Irish Placenames Commission who explained how *Hlimrek* was a Norse corruption of *Luimneach*.

Seán Spellissy.
John O'Brien.

Acknowledgements

This book could not have been written without the help we received from so many people encountered during our forays into both city and county, and without the assistance of the people who checked the final proofs of the book. We would like to express our gratitude by thanking the following people:

Seamus O Cinnéide.
Eddie Doherty, Derry and Shannon.
P.J. O'Connell, Knocklong and Ennis.
Mattie McDonagh, Ennis.
Sineád Spellissy, Ennis.
Pat Costello, Shannon.
Therese Gorey, Ennis.
Yann Philippe MacBrádai, Limerick.
Lal Quinn, Ennis.
Monica O'Brien, Drumline.
Tony Browne, Limerick.
Carol Gleeson, Coore, Doonogan.
Noel Crowley, Clare County Library.
Pauline and Bridie Brennan, Castleroberts.
Jim Mackessy, Castleroberts.
Margaret Mullane, Adare.
Chris Oakes, Adare.
John Canty, Gortnagluggin, Feenagh.
Mary Fraser, Galbally.
Kitty Conway, Ballingarry.
Jack Allan, Aherlow.
John McEniry, Bruff.
Michael Mitchell, Knockainy.
Gwendoline Pearson, Scarteen.
Thady Ryan, Scarteen.

Roy and Patricia Shireby, Hospital.
Bernie Mulcahy, Limerick City and Ennis.
Margaret Rowlandson, St. Mary's Cathedral, Limerick.
Robert O'Neil, St. Mary's Cathedral, Limerick.
Dean Maurice Sirr, St. Mary's Cathedral.
Joe Lynch, Limerick City.
Mick Kelly, Castle Quarter, Kilbeheny.
Patrick Quish, Duntryleague.
Michael and Hilda Jackson, Shannon.
Margaret O'Connor, Monasteranenagh.
Donal Duggan, Ennis.
Michael Collins, Ennis.
Tony Kelly, Ennis.
Freda O'Brien, Dublin.
Mary Fitzgerald, Limerick County Council.
Dick Tobin, Limerick Corporation.
Louis Fine, Limerick.
Mary Moore, Ardcanny.
Dr. Frank Counihan, Ennis.
Katherine Geoghegan, Listowel and Ennis.
Joe and Phil MacNamara, Hunt Museum, Plassey.
Finbar Crowe, St. Mary's Cathedral, Limerick.
Munchin Kelly, Limerick City.
Jim Reid, Kilkeedy.
The MacNamara Family, Pallaskenry.
Michael Deere, Pallas Grean.
Declan Hayes, Pallas Grean.
The Bradshaw Family, Cullen.
Kim Hutchinson, Castleconnell and Ennis.

Cian O'Carroll, Limerick.
Jacinta McGowan, Mohill.
Tuohy Family, Ennis.
Geraldine McHugh, Limerick.
Michael Mitchell, Knockainy.
John Carroll, Knocklong.
Elizabeth Stanley, Doonvullen South, Caherconlish.
Paddy O'Reilly, Ferry Bridge.
Patrick Mangan, Tory Hill.
Mark Lynch, Ferry Bridge.
Michael Lynch, Ferry Bridge.
Joe Ryan, Moanrue, Killeedy.
Con Dunleavy, Glenquin, Killeedy.
Brendan O'Brien, Churchfield, Clarina.
Seán Elder, Limerick City.
Casey Family, Grange.
Tiny Fitzgerald, Bruree.
Cathal O'Regan, Bruree.
Dermot O'Sullivan, Pallaskenry.
The MacNamara Family, Pallaskenry.
Cornelius & Oliver Irwin, Athlacca.
Terry Lynch, Kilfinnane.
Eddie Lenihan, Crusheen.
Mary Lane, Rathcannon.
Tony Fitzsimons, Shanagolden & Kilkishen.
Jean Mulholland, Shannon.
Andrew Hendrix, Limerick.

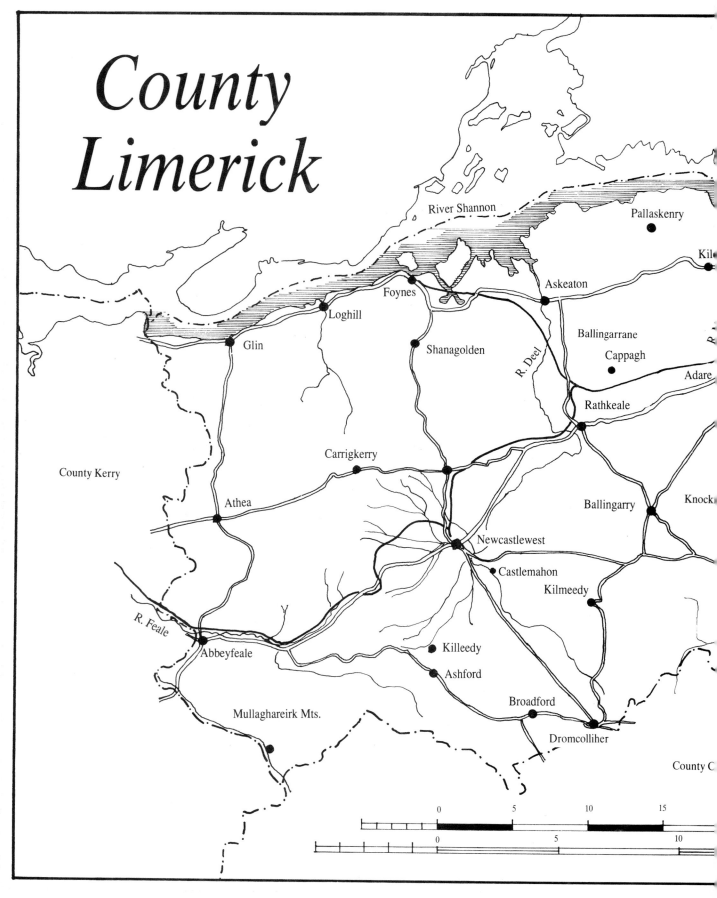

County Limerick

River Shannon

Pallaskenry

Kil

Askeaton

Foynes

Loghill

Ballingarrane

Cappagh

Shanagolden

R. Deel

Adare

Glin

Rathkeale

Carrigkerry

County Kerry

Ballingarry

Knock

Athea

Newcastlewest

Castlemahon

Kilmeedy

R. Feale

Killeedy

Abbeyfeale

Ashford

Broadford

Mullaghareirk Mts.

Dromcolliher

County C

| 0 | 5 | 10 | 15 |

| 0 | 5 | 10 |

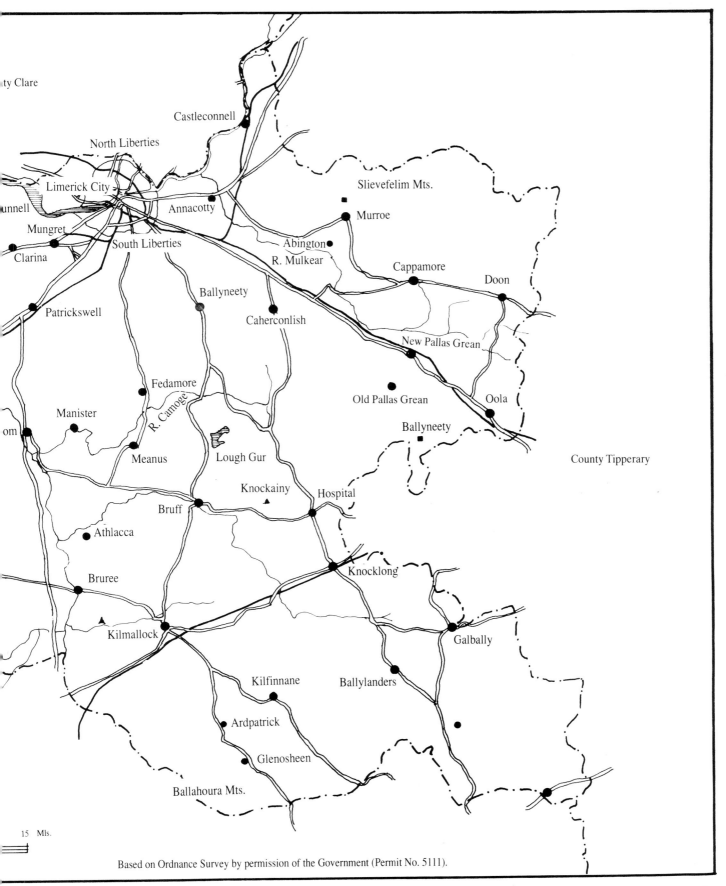

ty Clare

Castleconnell

North Liberties

Slievefelim Mts.

Limerick City

Murroe

Annacotty

unnell

Abington

Mungret

South Liberties

R. Mulkear

Cappamore

Doon

Clarina

Patrickswell

Ballyneety

Caherconlish

New Pallas Grean

Oola

Fedamore

Old Pallas Grean

R. Camoge

Manister

Ballyneety

County Tipperary

Meanus

Lough Gur

om

Knockainy

Hospital

Bruff

Athlacca

Knocklong

Bruree

Galbally

Kilmallock

Kilfinnane

Ballylanders

Ardpatrick

Glenosheen

Ballahoura Mts.

15   Mls.

Based on Ordnance Survey by permission of the Government (Permit No. 5111).

LIMERICK

The Viking City

LIMERICK, *Allymrick, Hlimrek,* or *Laemrich,* was founded by Vikings in the early ninth century as they established settlements around the Irish coastline at *Vikingsalo* (Wicklow), *Veiksfjord* (Wexford) and *Dyflin* (Dublin).

LAEMRICH, the Rich Land, Rich Soil, or Rich Loam, is a Norse term which describes the countryside in which both city and county are located. Pryce Maunsell advocated *Laemrich* as the origin of the word Limerick at the turn of the century. T.J. Westropp disputed this interpretation and claimed *Laemrich* was a Norse corruption of *Luimneach* just as *Dyflin* was a debased version of *Dubhlinn,* The Black Pool. Breandàn `O Ciobhàin of the Irish Placenames Commission supports T.J. Westropp's view as he believes Limerick is a Norsification of the much older *Luimneach,* a name, that once applied to the Shannon Estuary. *Luimneach Beag* is also the name of a place opposite Poulnasherry Bay, near the mouth of the Shannon.

LUIMNEACH is often written as *Lom an Eich,* meaning the place cropped bare by horses. Other accounts claim that it derived its name from a tribe, the *Tuath Luimnigh.* It was also called *Ros da Nochoilledh* in the ninth or tenth century and was considered as the southern boundary to the influence of the ruling race of *Gamanraighe* in north-west Mayo.

LUIMNEACH LIATHGHLAS was another name applied to this area where, according to legend, in ancient times, the warriors of Connaught and Munster met on the banks of the Shannon to indulge in war games under the gaze of their mythically-named kings, Sword and Spear. The champions threw off their *Luimneach Liathghlas,* Grey-green Cloaks, to play and became so engrossed in the sport they never noticed the tide rising until their cloaks had been swept away.

LUIMNEACH has also been translated as The Steed's Leap and commemorates a folk tale which tells of a horseman who coaxed his mount to jump the Abbey River. A more prosaic version of *Luimneach* may be *Loimeanach,* the Bare Marsh.

MYTHOLOGY AND FOLKLORE date the city to 155 when it was founded by the legendary *Immar,* Yvorus or Yuorus. Ptolemy may have known it as Regia, and the *Annals of Multifernan* refer to it as *Ross-de-Nailleagh.* Cormac Mac Airt fought a battle near here in 221; St. Patrick baptised the Dalcassian chief Carthann the Fair and his infant son, Eochaidh Bailldearg in Singland, Saingeal's Fort, in 434; the battle of *Luimneach* was fought in 567; and when St. Cuimin Fada of Clonfert died nearby, his body was carried up the *Luimneach* in a boat.

THE VIKINGS are generally credited with the foundation of Limerick. They arrived as raiders in 812, plundered a small settlement they found on an island off the east bank of the Shannon, and remained to become traders, mercenaries and bishops.

KING'S ISLAND, *Inis Sibtond* or *Inis Uibhtonn* may even have been known as Odin's Island in Viking times, although if this were so the name *Odensey* might have survived. By the middle of the ninth century the Vikings had made it one of their principal maritime stations and surrounded it with walls and towers. Their earlier way of life, that is the killing of clerics, the burning of churches and seizure of church valuables was later copied by the Irish chieftains when they realised such transgressions did not inspire supernatural vengeance.

LIMERICK proved to be a perfect site for handling the Viking trade from Atlantic Europe; for controlling the Shannon Basin; and for defying the Vikings of Dublin when disagreements erupted among themselves. After 881 Viking raids became fewer. Those who had settled on King's Island had lost rapport with their kinsmen at home and in Dublin; they were surrounded by hostile Irish; their resources were overstretched; but they were a strong powerful group who resented any attempts to curb their independence.

THORMODR HELGASON, Tamar Mac Ailche, the "king of an immense fleet", established a permanent stronghold on King's Island in 922. In 924 he defeated a rival fleet sent against him by the Vikings of Dublin, under Gothfrith, as he was unwilling to share his spoils.

THE VIKINGS OF LIMERICK operated quite independently from their Dublin compatriots. Their raiding parties devastated the ancient monastic settlements of *Inis Cealtra, Muc Riagaill,* Lorrha, Terryglass, Clonfert, Clonmacnoise and elsewhere on the islands, or along the banks of the Shannon. The falls on Ireland's mightiest river did not deter these hardy marauders. They carried their longships overland to avoid obstacles when they sailed upriver as far as Lough Ree. They also journeyed inland from the river to plunder Meath and Connaught for treasure, or captives whom they could hold, sell or trade as slaves.

LIMERICK OF THE SWIFT SHIPS or Limerick of the Riveted Stones rivalled Dublin under Viking rule. The Limerick Vikings had settlements scattered over what are now the counties of Limerick, Kerry and Tipperary, they organised themselves in the same way as the Irish tribes, and gave an Irish form to their names as they stopped raiding and began to integrate with the natives.

OLAFR CENNCAIREACH Olafr Scabby-Head, dominated the midlands from Limerick in 933. In 934 he led his men on a rampage through Roscommon and transported his fleet from the Shannon to Lough Erne. During the depths of winter, in 936, he had his longships carried from Lough Erne via Breifne to Lough Ree - an unimaginable feat.

OLAFR GOTHFRITHSSON, the Viking King of Dublin, raided Clonmacnoise in 936. Olafr Cenncaireach resented this intrusion into what he considered his own preserve, and in August 937, the Viking fleets of Dublin and Limerick met in battle on Lough Ree. The Limerick Vikings were defeated, Olafr Cenncaireach was captured, and the losers' longships were broken up - the deadliest insult such raiders could be offered.

HARALDR SIGTRYSSON, Aralt Mac Sitric, was a cousin of Olafr Gothfrithsson while his father, Sigtryggr Caech, was a brother-in-law of King Athelstan, King of both York and Dublin. Under his rule Limerick joined a loose federation of Scandinavian towns whose rulers were kinsmen of the Dublin overlord. He died in 940.

THE BATTLE OF SINGLAND in 943 was a momentous victory for the men of Munster who drove the Vikings into the city and forced them to pay a heavy contribution. The earliest Viking coin-hoard dates from about this time and was discovered in Tipperary in 1843, the exact site was never recorded. Ceallachan the Munster king who had defeated the Vikings with the aid of Brian Boru's father, Kennedy, was as much an Irish folk-hero as Brian, despite the fact that he destroyed as many churches, killed as many people, and took as many slaves as the most infamous of the Viking raiders. He was also notorious for forming alliances with the Vikings whenever he found it convenient to do so. He died in 954.

THE CONCEPT OF COINAGE was alien to the Irish tradition. The Vikings introduced coins in the ninth century and imported a considerable number of them during the tenth century. By the eleventh century coins passed fairly freely amongst the Viking colonists, but most of the Irish were reluctant to use coinage until almost into the sixteenth century.

BRIAN BORU (c. 940-1014) attacked the city in 967, plundered it and drove out its occupants. The survivors returned and re-occupied it soon afterwards.

LIMERICK was thoroughly sacked in 968. On this occasion its occupants were not slaughtered as in previous raids. They were forced to part with some of their accumulated treasures to the besieging Irish and were allowed to remain, on payment of an annual tribute to Brian Boru, who seemed more anxious to curb their power than to expel them from the country. Brian exacted a levy of 365 tuns (32-gallon casks) of wine annually from

the Vikings. He had proved how easily he could take their city and they had no desire to see him do so again.

THE IRISH admired the Vikings as merchants and mercenaries; fought or allied with them as circumstances dictated; imitated their vessels; and traded with them in their own ports for overseas goods.

MUNSTER OF THE SWIFT SHIPS or Munster of the Great Riches became a reality as an uneasy trading alliance between the two different races blossomed into uncertain friendship. Limerick prospered, and so too did its inhabitants, Viking and Irish alike.

DANISH ALE was one of the city's earliest products as the Vikings were the first Limerickmen to brew beer - a custom which had originated in the Middle East five thousand years before. Water was often unsafe to drink, but the sterilising effects of fermentation in the beer-making process rendered it safe. Over the intervening centuries weak, or "small" beer, was consumed as drink and most beer was home-brewed until its manufacture became a commercial proposition in the eighteenth century.

SCATTERY ISLAND was raided by the Vikings in 816 and 835. By 954 it had become an important Viking base, second only to Limerick. It was sacked by rival Vikings under the leadership of Magnus in 974, and in 975 Brian Boru "violated" the island, killing from 600 to 800 of its inhabitants. Brian returned in 990 to negotiate with the Vikings who had returned to Scattery which even though it was over sixty miles west of the city, was a strategic point controlling the entry into the mouth of the Shannon River. The Vikings did not embrace Christianity until the eleventh century when one of them, Gilbert or Gilla Easpuig, was consecrated Bishop of Limerick in 1106 or 1107. Scattery Island was united with the Bishopric of Limerick in 1195. It formed part of the Parish of St. Mary and remained within the jurisdiction of the Limerick Corporation until they relinquished their control to the Limerick Harbour Commissioners in more modern times.

THE ANNAGHBEG FORD, over a mile above Athlunkard Bridge, may have been the earliest crossing point over the Shannon. As such, it would have been utilised by Vikings and Irish alike even though it was considered a rapid and dangerous ford. In 1690 the Williamites used it when its water level had dropped to its lowest point in years.

THE LAX WEIR can trace its name back to the Viking occupation of the city. The Danish word for salmon, *lax*, still survives more than eleven centuries later. The Irish must have known this place as *Cora na mBradàn*, The

Salmon Weir, and the Weir Castle was remembered as *Caisleàn na Corann*. Fisheries in tidal waters were vested in the Crown from the time of the Norman Conquest. In 1200 King John granted William De Braose Limerick's "appurtenances in waters and mills, in fish ponds and fisheries". In 1215 John agreed to pay the Bishop of Limerick and his successors £10 annually, forever, as the church had a prior claim on "the mill-seats" and fisheries of Limerick. Maurice Fitzgerald, as Justiciary of Ireland, gave a three-year-lease to the citizens of Limerick for the sum of £66.66 1/2 in 1247. The lease expired but succeeding Lord Lieutenants refused to accept a surrender of the lease even though the Corporation was unable to pay the rent. The matter came to a head in 1274, and in 1282 Edward I gave the weir to Robert De St. Edmund. Robert, like the Corporation, was unable to meet the rent. In 1308 Edward II granted the Lax Weir to David, Bishop of Killaloe, for a rent of £10.66 1/2, but he had returned it to the Corporation by 1312. The rent was not paid during 1317-1320. During the reign of Richard II (1377-1399) Patrick Fox held the weir on condition that the profits were used for repairing the city. The Corporation got possession of the weir in 1414, and later got a separate grant of the fishery. After the Cromwellian Siege in 1651, Robert Pawsey, Robert Playstead and Joshua Bennett leased the weir for £165 a year. After the Restoration, Charles II (1660-1685) granted the weir and fishery to Sir George Preston in 1662. He soon found himself in dispute with the Corporation who let the fishery to Sir William King and Gerald Fitzgerald for £160 a year. The Corporation eventually bought out Preston's interest but the entire affair cost them £1200 between purchase, court costs and legal fees, in 1685. In 1719 a company was formed by George Roche, John Vincent, John Higgins, Rowley Colepoys, Francis Sargent, David Davis and David Bindon which took a 100-year lease from the Corporation at an annual rent of £325. This expired in 1818. The fishery was leased to Messrs. McAdam and Little who were obliged to surrender it soon after they had re-built the weir with cut-stone and erected twelve piers. In 1834 Poole Gabbett leased the fishery for £300 a year. In 1885 the Corporation sold their interest in the Lax Weir to Alexander Bannatyne, in the Landed Estates Court for £5,050.

THE VIKING SURNAMES OF LIMERICK perpetuate its Scandinavian past.

Aerial view of King's Island

COSTELLOE is derived from *Oisdealbhach*, the God-shaped. Rev. Patrick Woulfe believed the family was a branch of the Nangles in Dublin.

COTTER from *Mac Oitir*, the son of Oitir. The Earl Oitir Dubh, or Oitir the Black, laid Munster waste in 916. The Cotters descended either from him, or his grandson, another Oitir. Other variants of the name include *M'Cottir, M'Cotter* and *MacCoitir*.

DOYLE OR O'DOYLE is derived from *O'Dubhghaill*, the Dark Strangers. The Irish differentiated between the Vikings. Norwegians were called the *Fionn-Ghaill* or Fair Strangers, whereas the Danes were called the *Dubh-Ghaill* or Dark Strangers. Variants of the name include *O'Doagill*, O'Dowell, *MacDubhghaill, M'Dougall, M'Dugald, M'Doile*, MacDowell, Dowell, *M'Cowgall, M'Cougald, M'Cowell, M'Coyle* and Coyle.

GODFREY is derived from *O'Gothfraidh*. *O'Goherie*, O'Gogherie and MacCaffrey are variants of the name.

HALLY is derived from Ailche or *O hAilche*.

HAROLD OR O'HAROLD is derived from *O hArailt*, the grandson of Aralt the only surviving son of Imar or Ivor, the Viking leader slain by Brian Boru on Coney Island in the Fergus Estuary. Aralt's two brothers *Amhlaoibh* (cf. MacAuliffe) and *Dubhceann* were killed on the same occasion in 977.

HASTING is derived from *O hOistin*, after Oistin, a Viking slain in 874. Variants of the name include *O Hustyne, O Hustin*, Histon, Heston, Hestion, Hestings and Hastings.

HOWARD is a derivation of Imar, Ivor, Ifars or Imrs which passed into Irish as *Iomhar* or *O'hIomhair*, the grandson of Imar. Variants of this name in Thomond include *O'Hawrde, O Hyver, O Hewer, O Huar, O Huare* and *O Hure*. Versions of the name found in Sligo are O'Heiver, Eivers, Ivers, *MacIomhair, MacIvor*, MacKeever, MacGeever and MacKeevor.

KENRICK derives from the Irish *MacEanraic*, the son of Eanrac, the Danish form of Henry. Variants of the name include *O'Henrick, O hEanraic* and Henrick.

MacAULIFFE, is a derivation of *MacAmhlaoibh* (cf. Harold), the son of Anlaf or Olaf. Variants include MacAuley, MacAulay and, somehow in West Munster it was Anglicised to, Humphrey.

NIHILL derives from *O Neighill*, the son of Nigel. It is much the same surname as O'Neill insofar as the Vikings borrowed the form *Nihill* from the Irish name *Niall* and returned it as Nigel. Variations include *O'Nihill* and *O'Nyhill*.

O'BROUDER from *O'Bruadair*, the grandson of Bruadar. Variants of this name are Broderick or Broder.

O'LOUGHLIN or MacLoughlinn is a derivation of the Irish name for the Lakeland or Fiordland, of Norway, *Lochlainn*. *Lochlannach* was the name for a lakelander, a name synonymous for Viking in Irish history, myth and folklore. Variants of this name include Laughlin, Loughlin, MacLoughlin and *O'Melaghlin*.

SETRIGHT is derived from *Sitreac, Sigtrygge* or *Sihtric*. Variants of the name incude MacKittrick and Kittrick.

VIKING SURNAMES found elsewhere include variants of the following, Corless, MacManus, Reynolds, Sugre, Toner and Thorkell.

SOURCE REFERENCE NUMBERS
48-62-63-65-70-74-110-120-129-165-213-216-233-244-245-246-255-260-264-271-279-281

Aerial view of the probable location of the Viking stronghold.

Limerick: The Norman City

THE O'BRIEN FAMILY tolerated the Viking settlement of Limerick, traded with it, and protected it to a certain extent. Turlough O'Brien became King of Munster in 1064 but maintained his Dalcassian capital at Kincora until he died in 1086. Shortly after his succession to the throne of Munster he accepted the homage of *Donsleibhe*, King of Ulidia, here.

MURTAGH MOR O BRIEN reigned as King of Munster from 1086 until 1114 when illness reduced him to the condition of a skeleton. His brother, Dermot, assumed control until the sick but more warlike Murtagh wrested power back.

LIMERICK became the seat of Munster royalty, the residence of the O'Brien Kings of Thomond, when Murtagh gave his former capital of Cashel to the church in 1106. Murtagh died in 1119. His brother Dermot died in 1118. Murtagh's successors were indiscriminately styled kings of North Munster, Thomond or Limerick and they retained the city as their capital until the advent of the Anglo-Normans.

TURLOUGH O'CONNOR, King of Connaught, besieged the city in 1153 and compelled its Viking inhabitants to renounce the authority of Turlough O'Brien, and drive him west of the Shannon.

DOMHNALL MOR O'BRIEN came to power in 1168. His first action was to blind his brother, Brian, to prevent him from claiming the throne. He conducted a feud with the Connaughtmen and eventually swore homage and allegiance to Henry II in order to obtain much-needed allies. Robert FitzStephen came to his assistance with a troop of Anglo-Norman adventurers in 1171. With their help O'Brien succeeded against his Irish enemies but allowed the Anglo-Normans to gain their first foothold in Munster. In 1175 Raymond Le Gros and the King of Ossory forded the Shannon under fire and invaded the city which they were allowed to enter without opposition. Their bravery impressed the hostile Irish and the resident Vikings welcomed their arrival. They obtained booty in the city and then secured it with a garrison. Domhnall Mòr O Brien turned on his erstwhile allies, killing 1700 of them in battle near Thurles, before returning to Limerick where he drove the Anglo-Normans out of the city and burned it, declaring that Limerick would no longer be a nest for foreigners.

HERBERT FITZHEREBERT received a grant of the Kingdom of Limerick from Henry II, according to Lewis, but he appears to have resigned his uncertain inheritance in favour of Philip De Braose.

THE COUNCIL OF OXFORD in 1177 granted the Kingdoms of Limerick and Thomond to Philip De Braose.

THE LORDSHIP OF IRELAND was granted to John, Henry II's youngest son, in 1177. He held this lordship during the reigns of Henry II (1177-1189), Richard the Lionheart (1189-1199) and his own (1199-1216), with possible exceptions in 1194 and 1195, when he was deprived of his Norman and English lands for trying to usurp his crusading brother's throne. He also held the title Count of Mortain from 1189 to 1199.

DOMHNALL MOR O BRIEN defeated Prince John's forces in 1185. He then resumed his attacks on Connaught by invading Galway, only to have his own territory beset by the men of that province. Despite his tempestuous and contentious career he felt secure enough to donate his former palace in Limerick to the church. He died in 1194. His kingdom was left in dispute as various factions of the O'Briens fought for the throne, and in 1195 the Anglo-Normans entered the city again. MacCarthy of Desmond drove them out for a while but they soon returned.

PRINCE JOHN had little interest in his Irish fief. The Pope was technically its owner, not the English Crown. Richard I was reluctant to involve the Papacy in what was essentially a family dispute so it was probably on his orders that de Courcy and de Lacy moved against John's representatives in 1194. John renewed the grant of the Kingdom to Philip De Braose with the exception of the city, the cantred of the Ostmen (Vikings), and the Holy Island, which he committed to the custody of William de Burgo.

LIMERICK received its first charter in 1197 and installed its mayor and corporation under John's stewardship, ten years before London installed its own mayor and corporation. During John's reign the constitution of the first shires or counties began with the intention of making English law effective in Ireland.

WILLIAM DE BURGO founded an Anglo-Norman enclave here which defied all Irish efforts to dislodge it. A strong castle and bridge were erected and Anglo-Norman settlers congregated here in great numbers. They established amicable relations with the inhabitants of the surrounding countryside, and Irish names appeared amongst the names of the chief magistrates, even though these were generally of Anglo-Norman, Flemish, Italian, and, later, English descent.

LIMERICK did not become an Anglo-Norman possession until Domhnall Mor O Brien died. Until then the foreign grip remained insecure although the new invaders cultivated its Ostmannic population, the descendants of the Vikings.

WILLIAM DE BRAOSE received a grant of the city from King John in the summer of 1203. John later regretted his magnanity and tried to reclaim it but de Braose upheld his right to it and it was recognised formally in 1205. John regained Limerick in 1206. He besieged William's castle in Meath in 1210 and captured William's wife, his son, another William, and his daughter-in-law. These captives were sent to England "laden with cruel chains" and were imprisoned in Windsor.

KING'S ISLAND was the base from which Limerick developed. The city was captured by Richard, Earl Marshall of England after a four-day siege in 1234 but it survived the bloody strife of the O'Briens, de Burgos, de Clares and FitzGeralds to become a county in its own right as the county system came into operation. Meath and Kildare were constituted counties in 1297, before then Limerick, Cork, Kerry, Tipperary, Dublin, Waterford, Louth, Roscommon and Connaught were the only recognised counties. Clare did not became a county until 1569 when Connaught was divided into Sligo, Mayo, Roscommon, Galway and Clare, a partition which left Clare and the North Liberties of Limerick City within the Province of Connaught until 1660. Edward II reigned from 1298 until he was murdered in Berkeley Castle in 1328. He made grants available for enclosing the suburbs and repaired King John's Castle as the prevailing climate rendered additional military defences necessary.

COMMERCIAL PROGRESS was hampered by violence throughout the thirteenth and early fourteenth centuries. Piers Gaveston, the Viceroy, passed through Limerick in 1308 and compelled the O'Briens to submit for a while; de Clare burned the suburbs in 1314; Edward Bruce finished his career of conquest to the south of the city in 1316 and maintained his court here until Easter of the following year; the Earl of Desmond became Marshall of Limerick in 1331 only to fall foul of the O'Briens who resented his unbounded authority and the Anglo-Norman presence in the city; open hostilities erupted between Galway and Limerick in 1337, despite the intervention of the Lord Justice, when the merchants of both cities had a dispute in respect of toll payments; and Sir William Windsor, the Chief Governor had his headquarters here in 1340, for a brief period, when he marched against the O'Briens.

DONNCHADH CAIRBREACH O BRIEN was educated in *Cairbreach Aova*, now Kenry. He allied himself with the Anglo-Normans and protected his territory by paying homage to King John at Waterford. He purchased the lands of Carrigogunnell, and its lordship, for himself and his heirs forever, for a yearly rent of £40. At the same time the Kingdom of Thomond was granted to him, and other claimants, such as his older brothers were declared usurpers and enemies of John, the Supreme Lord of Ireland. As the third son of Domhnall Mòr O Brien he had successfully outwitted his brothers and succeeded to his father's crown. He had a lot in common with John but this did not help him to retain his capital at Limerick which he lost soon afterwards to the Anglo-Normans. To protect his Kingdom of Thomond he moved his residence to Clonroad, Ennis, thereby ensuring the survival of his line as Kings and Earls of Thomond, Viscounts Clare and Lords Inchiquin. He died in 1242, the most perceptive of the O'Briens. The word *Cairbreach* may mean the ruddy, or rough-complexioned although it is also believed that Donnchadh's association with *Cairbreach Aova* may have resulted in his being called Donnchadh Cairbreach.

King John's Castle

King John's Castle

KING JOHN'S CASTLE is said to have been built on the orders of that monarch to keep watch over Thomond and the O'Briens. It may have been erected as early as 1185 and is similar in style to one built in Framlingham, Suffolk in 1190. The castle may have been completed by 1200, as a reference was made to its bawn in that year; it was mentioned in 1202; castle repairs were noted in 1207, 1212, 1216 and 1227; and the Bishop of Limerick complained about the fortress encroaching on church lands in 1216. Other repairs were recorded in 1272, 1326, 1417, 1423, and throughout the centuries. On 3 August 1988 Michael Noonan, Minister for Defence, outlined an international tourist development scheme for the entire area, including the castle.

THE CASTLE was built without a keep. The layout plan consisted of a powerful curtain wall with towers surrounding a roughly rectangular enclosure, an idea much favoured by the Anglo-Normans during the thirteenth century and used in other royal castles like those established in Dublin, Roscommon and Kilkenny. The bottom of the walls was curved to deflect missiles dropped from the battlements outwards; round towers jutted out from the walls to enable archers to catch enemies in a cross-fire and prevent them from undermining the walls; and the entire structure was encircled with a moat fed by the River Shannon. The inner bailey of the castle contained the great hall, kitchen, private rooms, chapel and stables, most of which were removed to make way for a military barracks at a later stage. In 1935 Limerick Corporation breached the walls and erected 22 houses in the castle courtyard. Areas outlined with brick, near the gatehouse, indicate where some of the barracks' buildings stood. By 1988 only one of ten such structures remained.

THE GATEHOUSE Faces north-north-west and is still protected by two flanking towers. A temporary iron grill is set into the centre of each tower's wooden floor, and a moveable glass skylight is situated in the middle of either roof, reminders of the castle's imperial military past when munitions had to be supplied to gun-crews on the roofs. Stone steps leading up to the pointed doorway replace a drawbridge, but the slots in the stonework through which a portcullis descended can still be seen. A murder-hole, in this case a long narrow slit now covered by a large flagstone still protects the original entrance between the two d-shaped flanking towers.

THE NORTH-WESTERN TOWER, the one nearest to Thomnd Bridge, is the oldest of the three remaining towers while the two d-shaped flankers are of a later period than the thirteenth century. The marks of Ginkel's bombardment of 1691 can still be seen on its facade, especially where brickwork was inserted to replace damaged stone. All of the towers had their roofs removed to accommodate artillery as methods of warfare changed, and the south-eastern tower was demolished and replaced with a new bastion which could accommodate "five or six pieces of ordnance" in 1611. The roofs of this and the north-eastern tower are slightly conical; their floor levels were raised when the area was converted into an armoury. In 1988 only the base floor of this north-eastern tower remained and it was kept closed to the public. The third tower to the south-west is also closed, but the walls by the river and the gatehouse are still intact although the battlements were demolished at the end of the eighteenth century.

KING JOHN'S CASTLE dominated Limerick for over 700 years. It was neglected under the rule of King John's son, Henry III, who succeeded to the throne at nine years of age in 1216, and ruled until 1272. In 1224 the king's goods in Limerick were scarcely worth eighteen pence, yet in 1226 it was the only castle in Ireland which was not fortified against the king. It was then defended by Richard de Burgh, its constable, one of an uninterrupted line of such incumbents who held that post, stretchng from the appointment of Godfrey Roche, or de Rupe, in 1216 and finishing with the death of Viscount Gort in 1942. The Earl of Desmond's followers took the castle in 1332 but were unable to hold it against the Crown forces.

THE O'BRIENS AND MACNAMARAS captured the castle in 1369 but lost it soon afterwards. In 1417 Henry V (1413-1422) granted monies for repairs while his successor gave the charge of the castle to the Mayor and citizens of Limerick on the condition that it should be kept in repair.

FR. WOULFE compiled a report, in 1574 on the city: "There is a castle in the said city built by John son of King Henry II an for many years it is disused, and the houses and roof of said castle in ruins, and a part of the wall is already down, but with little expense it can be repaired, and it is in a most beautiful place above the city which it can keep in check, although the people of that city have been always loyal to the Princes of England ..... Artillery. Limerick has none save two very small pieces, and no other munitions of war save a few arquebuses, bows and crossbows. I may truly affirm that in all the city there is not half a pipe of powder for the artillery".

THE CASTLE remained in a state of disrepair until the end of the sixteenth century. Its condition was noted in 1585 and it would have been unable to resist an attack in 1588 if any ships of the Spanish Armada had sailed into the pool of LImerick.

SIR GEORGE CAREW, Lord President of Munster, ordered its restoration in 1600. Sir Josias Bodley fulfilled his instructions over the succeeding years. The building was modified and its defences strengthened; two tower bases and the curtain wall were reinforced; a long storehouse was erected by the riverside wall; and a large bastion complete with sally port was built in 1611. A 1633 map of the castle shows the bastion; three round towers that "beare ordinance"; a drawbridge over the moat, or ditches; and fortifications on either end of Thomond Bridge.

LORD MUSKERRY forced the city to surrender to his Confederate Irish forces in 1642. Captain George Courtenay resisted and defended King John's Castle with 60 of his own men, 28 warders and 100 others until the Confederates bombarded his position from St. Mary's Cathedral, breached his walls with cannon and ignited mines.

GENERAL IRETON forced the Confederate garrison to surrender to the Cromwellian forces in 1651 when he bombarded the castle from the foot of Thomond Bridge and succeeded in breaching its walls.

PATRICK SARSFIELD surrendered King John's Castle to the Williamites under Ginkel in 1691.

THE CASTLE BARRACKS was built within the ruins of the castle in 1751 and was capable of accommodating 400 men. Over the eighteenth and nineteenth centuries the buildings were altered and renovated to cater for the military. The angle-towers were reduced in height and reinforced to bear heavy guns, while the flanking gate-towers lost their rectangular projections.

LIMERICK'S MOTTO describes its history very accurately: *Urbs Antiqua Fuit Studiisque Asperrima Belli,* an ancient city well-studied in the arts of war. The City arms are represented by a gate-tower complete with portcullis, flanked by two towers, an apt depiction of the entrance into the castle or the city.

THE TOURIST DEVELOPMENT PLAN for Limerick centres on the restoration of the castle. Work has since commenced on an integrated and innovative 13-acre heritage precinct project within the medieval quarter of the city, which should be ready for the tercentenary commemoration of the Siege of Limerick in 1991.

THE CASTLE DEVELOPMENT PROJECT will start with the demolition of 22 municipal houses erected in the courtyard in 1935, to make way for a medieval style tavern-restaurant and tourist-craft outlets. The Department of the Environment have approved the plan, and the families now resident there will be rehoused within the new King's Island medieval quarter if they so desire.

THE LIMERICK CIVIC TRUST was inaugurated at a public meeting on 17 February, 1983, Ireland's first Civic Trust, although others had long since been established throughout England, Scotland and Wales. The Trust exists to aid the social and economic regeneration of the Limerick communities and has identified the need for action in three ways: to strengthen community awareness through its programme of activities; to create a better understanding of the area through information, advice and education; and to assist the economic life of the area through the provision of work schemes, by the re-use of redundant historic buildings and derelict sites. The projected plans for the revitalisation of Limerick's inner city have been spearheaded by the Civic Trust, Shannon Development, Limerick Corporation, and the Government.

THE INNER CITY DEVELOPMENT PLAN designates the following areas for special attention; Arthur's Quay; the old City Gaol and John's Castle area; and Charlotte Quay and the John's Gate areas. In all, a total of 39 acres, of which the Corporation owns 20, are due for development, and it is hoped that the new Government incentive will inject new life into the city centre. Developers investing in these areas will enjoy a special status with rates relief, capital allowances, double rent allowances, and incentives for owner occupiers and owners of multiple dwellings.

THOMOND BRIDGE may have been erected as early as 1185 to lead from King John's Castle, in the Englishtown, to Thomondgate, on the Clare side of the Shannon. Like the castle, the bridge was reputedly built on the orders of King John and erected for £30. Other accounts state that the bridge was built in 1210, the real date hardly matters as this first structure collapsed about 1292, drowning 80 men.

WILLIAM DE PRENE became "Carpenter of the King's houses and castles in Ireland" in 1284 at the rate of 5p a day for his sustenance with an allowance of £2 a year for his robes. By 1290 he had been appointed "Keeper of the King's works in Ireland" — one of the highest administrative positions a skilled craftsman could reach during the late thirteenth century. He was arrested in 1292 and charged with stealing £3 worth of nails from Roscommon Castle and selling them in Dublin; taking £20 in wages due to others; embezzling £300 by falsifying the accounts of workmen he employed; and of causing the deaths of 80 men who drowned when Thomond Bridge collapsed. He was dismissed from the King's service and imprisoned until he could find pledges for £200.

THOMOND BRIDGE was rebuilt with fourteen arches of unequal size which were turned on wicker-wick, the marks of which Samuel Lewis noted in 1837. In 1790 Charles Etienne Coquebert de Montbret, appointed French Consul to Dublin by Louis XVI in 1789, noted that this bridge of fourteen arches, all different, was astonishingly flat and solid. One of the disadvantages of using the bridge was that it was often covered by the waters of the River Shannon, and despite the fact that it was subsequently widened, the surface level was never raised. Gate-towers controlled access to both ends of the bridge until Limerick was no longer a walled city.

THE PRESENT THOMOND BRIDGE was designed by James and George Pain. Its foundation-stone was laid in 1836 although work on it did not commence until 1838. It is a plain strong structure, somewhat out of keeping with the rather ornate gothic-style toll-house designed and built for it on the city side, opposite the castle. The commemorative plaque states that work on the bridge was completed in 1840.

SHAWN-A-SCOOB, John of the Brooms, an industrious broom-maker from Cratloe Woods, used to sell his merchandise in the city markets. Tradition relates how the Limerick Burghers were unable to select a major and eventually decided to appoint to the office the first man to cross Thomond Bridge, on a certain morning.

To his surprise *Shawn-a-Scoob* was given the office. Some time elapsed before his worried wife came looking for him, only to discover him living in the lap of luxury and, apparently, unable to recognise her. "Shawn, Shawn", she cried, "Don't you know me?" "Get home out of that, woman", he replied, "sure I don't even know myself".

SOURCE REFERENCE NUMBERS
24-28-44-63-86
120-126-127-129-131
141-176-178-180-199
222-246-249

Thomond Bridge, the Toll House and St Munchin's Church

St. Mary's Cathedral

THE CATHEDRAL CHURCH OF THE BLESSED VIRGIN MARY is not the first edifice erected for Christian worship within the walls of Limerick City but it is the oldest surviving building still serving its original purpose. 1168 is the date generally accepted as the date of its foundation, although Rev. J. Dowd believed 1172 to be a likelier choice. Other sources trace its beginnings to a period between 1180 to 1190 or to 1192.

DOMHNALL MOR O'BRIEN founded the church more familiarly known as St. Mary's Cathedral on the site of his former palace, some time before 1192-1194. This can be proved from a document granting lands at Mungret to "Brictius, Bishop of Limerick, and to his successors, and to the clergy of St. Mary's of Luimneach" which was witnessed by Matthew, Archbishop of Cashel. As Mathew Henry did not become Archbishop of Cashel until 1192, this updated land grant mentioning St. Mary's clergy dates from 1192 to the time of Domhnall Mor's death in 1194.

THE THINGMOUNT, or *Thing-Mote*, a Viking council chamber and court of justice, was one of the earliest recorded buildings on the site of St. Mary's Cathedral. Pagan temples dedicated to Thor and Freya stood close beside the *Thingmount* , making this area the civic and religious centre of Viking Limerick until the O'Briens deserted their ancient capital of Kincora to establish a royal residence where the cathedral now stands.

THE ORIGINAL STRUCTURE may not have been cruciform in design but developed from subsequent rebuilding, modification and renovation over a period of time. Brian De Breffny believed otherwise and wrote that the original floor plan was cruciform with an aisled nave, a short chancel not much deeper than the transepts, and was strongly influenced by the Cistercians. The aisles had arches, no vaulted bays and simple diaphragm walls which supported the roof. Construction of the original building was completed in 1207. Brian De Breffny believed this took place between 1180-1195 while T.J. Westropp thought that the nave, side aisles, transepts and choir assumed the shape of a Latin cross between 1172-1207. Between 1891-1897 T.J. Westropp traced the development and growth of St. Mary's over the centuries. His floor plan, reproduced here, shows the cathedral's main architectural features and their locations. Modern additions not shown on this plan are mentioned in the relevant text.

THE GREAT ROMANESQUE DOORWAY in the western face is flanked at either angle by projecting buttresses, one of which contains a stone staircase. This impressive entrance is now open only on formal occasions. The usual entry today is through a porch on the southern side. The western doorway was partly sculptured under Bishop O'Dea's episcopate, "Not in a spirit of vain glory, but in order that others hereafter should imitate the memorials of their piety". Tradition claims that this was once the origi-nal entrance to the O'Brien palace and it was "restored" in the nineteenth century.

THE CHANCEL was built, or enlarged, by Donoh O'Brien, Bishop of Limerick and a member of the Royal House of Thomond, in 1207. His name, Donoh, is inscribed over an escutheon bearing a chevron between three lions, on a small slab of stone positioned high above the doorway on the north wall. He also established a chapter consisting of Dean, Archdeacon, Precenter, Treasurer, and six Canons. He died in 1209. The present chancel dates from the fifteenth century, as do a number of chapels whch were added to the aisles, and one added to the south transept. James and Edmond Harold were responsible for decorating or enlarging the chancel in 1529. This part of St. Mary's was almost destroyed by cannon fire from the great battery at Corbally during the siege of 1691. The present east window was installed in 1860 and replaced a much larger one which was not in keeping with the style of St. Mary's. Most of the windows are later insertions modelled on fifteenth-century styles.

KING DOMHNALL MOR O'BRIEN died in 1194. He was succeeded by his eldest son Murtagh Dall who lost his kingship after being blinded by the Anglo-Normans. Conor Roe, his brother, assumed power but was dethroned in 1198, and murdered by his nephew in 1201. Between 1194 and 1201 the political instability amongst the feuding O'Briens allowed the Anglo-Normans to gain

Earls of Thomond memorial

FLOOR PLAN OF
ST. MARY'S CATHEDRAL

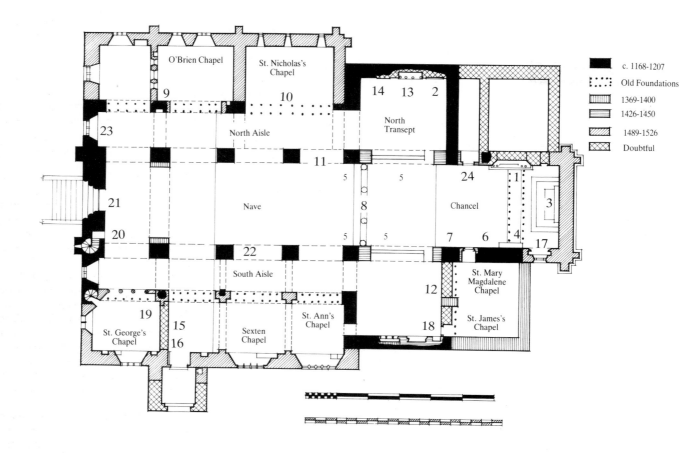

■	c. 1168-1207
⬚	Old Foundations
▦	1369-1400
▤	1426-1450
▨	1489-1526
▩	Doubtful

O'Brien Chapel

St. Nicholas's Chapel

North Aisle

North Transept

Nave

Chancel

South Aisle

St. Mary Magdalene Chapel

St. Ann's Chapel

St. James's Chapel

Sexten Chapel

St. George's Chapel

1 The Earls of Thomond Memorial with Domhnall Mor's Coffin Lid at its base.
2 The leper squint and John ffox mural slab.
3 The high altar, reredos and surrounds.
4 Bishops O'Dea and Adams memorial.
5 Black Oak Misericords.
6 Earl of Limerick's stalls.
7 Bishop of Limerick's stalls.
8 Choir screen.
9 Probable location of Murrough The Burner O'Brien's burial.
10 Bishop Jebb's statue.
11 Caen stone pulpit.
12 Pre-Reformation stone mensa with the Westropp Memorial overhead.

13 Archer triple-arched sedilia.
14 The Harold Tablet.
15 World War I Memorial.
16 World War II Memorial.
17 Credence Table.
18 Bultingfort - Galwey - Stritch Memorial.
19 Viscount Glentworth Memorial.
20 Entrance to tower and monks' walks.
21 Romanesque Doorway.
22 Eyre Lloyd Memorial.
23 Cleeve Memorial.
24 Donoh O'Brien Memorial, 1207.

Main altar and rerodos

control of Limerick City.

DOMHNALL MOR'S COFFIN LID is encased in black marble at the base of the Earls of Thomond memorial on the northern wall. This oblong stone, less than five feet long, is the oldest monument in the cathedral. It is narrower at one end and bears the O'Brien arms, a lion rudely carved, ornamented by a border with ancient Irish characters.

THE EARLS OF THOMOND MEMORIAL occupies all of a large Gothic arch in the north wall. It consists of three tiers of black marble with side columns and divisions of grey and pink Dean Mamarble and composite pillars of Limerick marble. An effigy of Donough, fourth Earl of Thomond, who died on 5 September 1624, lies on the lowest tier or shelf. The next shelf contains the effigy of his wife, Elizabeth Fitzgerald, second daughter of Gerald, eleventh Earl of Kildare. Both effigies are damaged as the tomb was "defaced in ye time of ye late rebellion of Ireland". It was repaired by Henry, the seventh Earl of Thomond, mistakenly identified as the "second Earl" on the inscription, in 1678. Little else remains of the original tomb. Henry died in 1691.

HORSES were stabled in the cathedral during the Cromwellian occupation of the city. Account books of the time recorded a payment of £6.91 to "Cap. John Ffreind for horse guard kept in ye church of Limericke". St. Mary's was wantonly vandalised during this period by the soldiery.

THE HIGH ALTAR, REREDOS AND SURROUNDS demonstrate the continuity of O'Brien patronage. The translated inscription reads "To God be the praise. By means of this work the O'Brien family give thanks to God for the founder and benefactors of this church. To God be the praise. Erected in 1907".

M. PEARSE, the stone-mason who executed the reredos and stone surrounds was the father of Patrick and Willie Pearse, architects of the 1916 Rising.

BISHOP CORNELIUS O'DEA was connected to the O'Briens by fosterage. When he died in 1426 he was buried under a monument of black marble adorned with a recumbent effigy of the robed and mitred bishop which has long since vanished. Part of his monument still survives, beneath that of Bishop Adam's, on the south wall of the chancel. Cornelius O'Dea founded a library in what is now the Chapter Room (over the Chapel of St. George) which was completely destroyed in 1691.

BISHOP BERNARD ADAMS (1566-1625) was born in Middlesex; educated in Trinity College, Oxford, where he became a Fellow in 1588; and was nominated Bishop of Limerick by King James I in 1603. He was consecrated in this role in 1604, and was also Bishop of Kilfenora from 1606 to 1617. His inscription — in Latin and English, contains the following;

"... sufficient God did give me, which I spent;

I little borrowed, and as little spent;

I left them whom I loved enough in store,

Increased this Bishopric — relieved the poore ..."

THE CREDENCE TABLE dates from the thirteenth century.

THE BLACK OAK MISERICORDS, or choir stalls, were carved between 1480 and 1500, possibly out of oak from Cratloe Woods. Sitting was prohibited in the early church but the clergy were allowed to support themselves by leaning upon staffs or crutches placed under their arm-pits. This concession led to the introduction of the *Misericordia* or

Act of Mercy which resulted in seats designed to tip up vertically revealing a shallow ledge, three or four inches deep, on the underside upon which the clerical posterior could be rested while the occupant of the choir stall appeared to be standing rather than sitting.

There are 23 of these fifteenth-century misericords in St. Mary's. The decoration is mainly on the underside of each seat, and the carved motifs include depictions of human and animal figures as well as those of legendary and imaginary creatures. These pieces of furniture are unique isofar as they are the only examples of their kind preserved in Ireland.

LORD LIMERICK is the hereditary Grand Prior of the cathedral, an honour bestowed on his ancestor Edmund Sexten, by King Henry VIII. His carved stall commemorates this fact today.

THE CHOIR SCREEN was designed by Conor O'Brien of Foynes. His niece, Brigid, posed as a model for the two angels carved on it. Conor was at sea when the screen was put in place. In his absence the builder erected it back to front, a mistake that may be rectified at a later date.

THE BRONZE RAILINGS AND GATES were added in 1929 in memory of Thomas Aylmer Pearson, Dean from 1913 to 1928.

THE OAK SANCTUARY DOORS were donated by the members of the Limerick-Shannon Rotary Club in 1968 to commemorate the cathedral's 800th. anniversary, which was celebrated that year. The organ console was installed, for the same reason, in the same year.

THE NAVE has four plain pointed arches resting on massive piers, over which run "monks' walks" or lintelled passages through the walls and windows. The unbroken vault of the roof over the nave and choir is an unusual

Section of Misericords

feature while the ground level rises by 3'6" in a series of seven steps from the Romanesque doorway to the east window. Thomas Arthur and his wife Johanna Morrough built the eastern end of the nave, and installed a window, in 1410. The oak beams in the roof came from Cratloe Woods while the two brass chandeliers, and another in the choir, were made by Daniel Crosbie of Dublin and presented by the Corporation and other worthies in 1759.

THE SAMUEL BARRINGTON MEMORIAL dating from 1693 can be found in the nave where there is also a bust on the southwestern pillar dedicated to Robert Maunsell.

THE NORTH TRANSEPT was added in 1360. In 1860 some of the stonework around the five-light window was renovated and a few years later it was filled with stained glass as a memorial to Samuel Caswell who died in 1874. Three Canadian sisters, Jessie "Ruby" Michie, Helen Rowland Wilson, and Gladys Skellaton Cleeve restored the transept of the Chapel of the Holy Spirit during the early twentieth century.

THE LEPER SQUINT derived its name from its use. Lepers were not allowed into the medieval churches but were permitted to hear Mass and receive Communion through openings like this. Part of the organ now obstructs the view of the squint.

JOHN FFOX, the Prior of Holy Cross, died on 28 August, 1519. His mural slab is located beneath the leper squint.

GEOFFREY ARCHER, the fifth recorded cathedral treasurer, died in 1519. He is commemorated with a stone slab set into a triple-arched sedilia (a wall-seat used for those celebrating Mass) recess, upon the bottom of which a decorative cross is inscribed.

THE HAROLD TABLET was originally placed elsewhere but moved here during later

The Westropp memorial

renovations. James Harold became Mayor of the city in 1525. Edmund Harold was bailiff in 1519 and Mayor in 1531.

THE CAEN STONE PULPIT at the corner of the north transept and the chancel was erected by Foster of London, in memory of Archdeacon Maunsell who died in 1860.

THE SOUTH TRANSEPT may have been the Lady Chapel in the earlier cathedral. The arch corbels date from 1420 and the west pier is built against the old arcade. This transept, with the chapels along the south aisle, was extensively repaired by the Galweys, Sextens and others about 1489. Anne Westropp restored this transept and rebuilt its five-light window some time around 1862 while the Barringtons restored the chapels along the south aisle in 1866. It was restored again in 1962 and re-dedicated as the Chapel of St. James and St. Mary Magdalene.

THE STONE MENSA, a pre-Reformation altar, was restored to its original site in 1962. It weighs 3 tons and is 13 feet long, 2 feet 9 inches wide and 9 inches thick. The altar contains a celtic-designed frontal donated by the Gelston family in 1962.

THE WESTROPP MEMORIAL, a triple arcade, depicting the Agony in the Garden, the Entombment, and the Resurrection, was erected by Anne Westropp in memory of her son Thomas Johnson Westropp who died in 1839. His middle name was mis-spelled and the incorrect date of his death was given on the carved inscription of this ornate monument, which was crafted by James Redfern of London and displayed at the International Exhibition of 1862. His body was supposedly brought home to Cheltenham for burial, he had died in Madiera, but on his mother's death the chest was opened and found to contain no human remains.

THE CROSS on the wall behind the altar and

Dean Maurice Sirr, at the pre-Reformation stone mensa

beneath the Westropp memorial is the original cross of consecration of the chapel.

THE MURAL TABLET on the wall at the entrance lists family tombstones of the Arthurs, 1439 and 1729; Creaghs, 1632; Fannings, 1634; and Rices, 1709 and 1924.

THE SEDILIA in the south wall consists of a triple recess with trefoil arches resting on four slender spiral-fluted shafts. It dates from about 1400 and was erected by John Budstone, or Budston, bailiff of the city in 1401.

THE GALWEY-BULTINGFORT-STRITCH MONUMENT is a low cinque-foil arch resting on octagonal piers, two on each side, with an angular hood. This was erected by Edmond Galwey, in memory of his father, Geoffrey Galwey, and his grandfather, Richard Bultingfort, both of whom died in 1414.

RICHARD BULTINGFORT, or Bullingfort, may have derived his name from a place of that name in Hertfordshire. He married Catherine Roche by whom he had a daughter, Margaret, who married Geoffrey Galwey, and a son, John, who succeeded to some of his estate. Richard owned several tenements in the city and suburbs, one near the Tholsel, one near St. Mary's Cemetery, one near Thomond Bridge, a large selection of silver plate, and other property in Cork. He appears to have been a typical hard-working, God-fearing, Church-loving medieval burgess, respected by his peers and loved by his wife, family, friends and servants. He was Mayor of Limerick in 1357, 1367, 1376, 1380, 1386 and 1390. Between 1369 and 1405 he helped Bishops Peter Creagh and Cornelius O'Dea to restore a large section of the cathedral and, at some undefined date allowed Nicholas Stritch a right of burial in the same tomb.

MURROUGH THE BURNER O'BRIEN, the Sixth Baron and First Earl of Inchiquin, was a talented survivor, one of Ireland's greatest generals, a political opportunist and the most hated man in the country. The morning after his burial, in 1674, the citizens of Limerick stormed into St. Mary's Cathedral, removed his body and threw it into the Shannon. Two centuries later his empty coffin was found in the North Aisle. His unoccupied grave was marked only by the letter "I" cut into the pavement.

THE ARTHUR CHAPEL the burial place of the Arthur family, is also known as the Chapel of St. Nicholas and St. Catherine. In 1439 Catherine, the widow of Nicholas Arthur, was buried beside her husband "in the ancestral monument near the altar of St. Catherine." At one stage King Domhnall's coffin lid and the pre-Reformation altar were stored here. The tendency to use this chapel

as a store continued into the 1980's as the stone font now kept here came from the church in Newcastle West to which it had been presented by the Earl of Dunraven.

THE CURIOUS CORBELLING evident in the Arthur Chapel and the clumsy way in which it was built against the north transept has led some people to suggest that this chapel probably incorporates part of the O'Brien palace within its fabric.

T.J. WESTROPP wrote that every chapel appeared to have been built without any intention of having the levels or shapes of its

windows conforming with those of the adjoining fabric.

JOHN JEBB (1775-1833) became Bishop of Limerick in 1823. He was a native of Drogheda and is commemorated in the white marble statue of a seated bishop, which was executed by E.H. Baily of the Royal Academy, London, in 1836.

ANDREW CREAGH was Dean of St. Mary's, twice, first in 1505 until he was deprived of his living for some reason now unknown. He was reinstated after receiving

Below: The Galwey-Bultingfort-Stritch Monument

the King's pardon. In 1543 he resigned and was succeeded by Andrew Stritche. The stone slab marking his grave is on the western side of the chapel near that of Thomas FitzDavid Creagh who died in June 1497. Thomas's wife is also commemorated on the slab, as well as his son, Peter Creagh, who died in May 1546.

WILLIAM FRASER (1700-1753) was buried here. He was the only son of his namesake who served as a captain in Schomberg's Company in 1689-1691. After the surrender of the city William Snr. married Maria Lloyd of Drumsallagh and continued to live in Limerick. William Jnr. is buried on the east side of the vestry. Anne Fanning died in 1634. Her memorial slab bears two coats of arms. One of the two two-light windows was installed by the widow of James Fitzgerald Bannatyne, the other by the clergy of the diocese in memory of Rev. James Dowd.

THE VESTRY is also known as the O'Brien Chapel, the Napier Chapel or St. Mark's Chapel. Murrough the Burner was reputedly buried in its north-western corner but it may only have been his memorial slab which was placed here, as T.J. Westropp stated that he was buried in the north aisle. The chapel is generally considered to be the fifteenth-century burial place of the O'Brien family. Its vaulted ceiling is considered one of its more interesting features.

THE LONG PRAYER DESK was constructed out of fifteenth-century black oak removed from Listowel Church. Sir Arthur Vickers presented the timber to St. Mary's and a local craftsman completed the desk. The heraldic carvings may date from the fifteenth century.

SIR ARTHUR VICKERS was Ulster King of Arms and in charge of the Irish Crown Jewels when Edward VII visited Ireland in 1908. Sir Arthur became the scapegoat to cover someone else when he was unable to produce the jewels, his keys to the vaults in Dublin Castle had mysteriously disappeared, and he was dismissed from his post.

THE DUKE OF TYRCONNELL, Richard Talbot, became Lord Lieutenant of Ireland under James II, the first Catholic viceroy appointed in over a century. He died in Limerick in 1691 and tradition relates that he was buried secretly, at night, under the west wall of the vestry.

THE BAPISTRY with its ancient font is the burial place of Catherine Plunket. Her husband Walter was appointed a commissioner of the Limerick Mint by King James II in 1689. She died in 1752. Her memorial slab is on the floor, as is that of Piers O'Morony of Cloonenagh, County Clare, who died in 1723. He was a landowner in Killard, West Clare, in 1659, and was married to Margaret Creagh.

THE SOUTH AISLE contains the only perpendicular order window in the cathedral. It was donated by Croker Barrington and depicts the Talents, the Good Samaritan and the Husbandman. The light stained-glass window at the western end was donated by the Rev. Arthur Williams in memory of his wife, Isabella (1822-1849). The south aisle formed three of the cathedral's thirteen chapels during the fifteenth century and was later used as the Consistory Court.

THE CRUCIFIXION CARVING set into the central pillar of this aisle has been dated to the tenth century.

THE CHOIR ROOM was originally erected as a chapel dedicated to St. Mary Magdalene by John Budstone some time about 1400.

St George's Chapel

Until the south transept was rededicated in 1962 the Choir Room had still been known as the Chapels of St. Mary Magdalene and St. James and the plain Gothic arches of the conjoined chapels remain closed in its western wall. These two chapels were considered by some to be the first structural alterations and were carried out under the episcopate of Stephen de Valle (or Wall) between 1360 and 1369. During the siege of 1691 the chapels were damaged. In 1866 the Choir Room was restored.

ST. GEORGE'S CHAPEL, or the Pery Chapel, contains the Glentworth memorials which include two windows dedicated to Edmond Viscount Glentworth in the south wall, and the Hartstonge family memorials in memory of Elizabeth Hartstonge who died in 1663 and Henry Hartstonge (1789-1834), Viscount Glentworth, son of the First and father of the Second Earl of Limerick.

THE RECUMBENT EFFIGY is dedicated to Edmond Henry, Lord Glentworth (1809-1844), Viscount Limerick, Baron Glentworth of Mallow and Baron Foxford of Stackpole Court in County Clare.

THE CATHEDRAL ORGAN was presented by Bishop Adams in 1626. It has been rebuilt and added to throughout the years. Lawtons of Aberdeen carried out a major overhaul and added the solo organ and a new console in 1913. It was cleaned and overhauled in 1958 while electrical action and a new console were added in 1966.

THE SQUARE TOWER, located over the western facade of the church, is 120 feet high. Access to it, and to the "monks' walks", is through a stone staircase in the buttress at the south-western corner. A narrow damp worn staircase in the east wall of the tower, and over the arch which supports it, gives access to the bell-ringers' room. The outer door on the south side of this room allows entry to the battlements, from which an excellent view of the city and county to the south can be obtained. Entry to the northern battlements can be obtained through another door at the top of the staircase.

THE BELL CHAMBER is reached by a steep window staircase. Tradition relates how the friars carried off thirteen silver bells which they concealed in the Abbey River at the time of the Reformation. The hiding-place of these bells was forgotten over the centuries. Another folk tale says that the bells were stolen from an Italian church during political disturbances. Their founder searched Europe for them and his quest finally extended to Ireland. As he sailed up the Shannon he recognised the familiar chime of his long-sought bells, only to drop dead before he could reclaim them.

A PEAL OF EIGHT BELLS is the poetic expression used by campanologists, or bell-ringers, to describe the eight bells installed in the bell-tower. In 1673 six bells were presented to the cathedral by William Yorke. Two more, cast by Tobias Covey, were added in 1703. Later on three new bells were cast, two in 1829 and one in 1859. Bells were also re-cast in 1703, 1873, 1907, 1930 and 1938. The ropes attached to the bells average an overall length of 40 feet with a tail end of 13 feet 6 inches. The chief campanologist of St. Mary's is called the Captain of the Bells.

WILLIAM YORKE was three times Mayor of the seventeenth-century city. He died in 1679 and his black marble memorial can be seen on the west side of a pillar on the north

One of St Mary's unusual central heating radiators.

side of the nave. William Perdue, the craftsman whose family cast the bells, died in 1673. His memorial may have been on the floor of the main aisle, near the west door.

WILLIAM EVERARD GARDINER HEWSON, Ballyengland, was the son of John Hewson of Castle Hewson. He was a keen campanologist who rang the changes in many English cathedrals, as well as Irish. He was responsible for re-casting and re-hanging five of the bells. He died, nearby, in Barrington's Hospital, and is buried in the cathedral grounds.

THE 1914-1918 WAR MEMORIAL was erected in memory of the men of Thomond who perished in that war, especially those whose names were inscribed on the wall tablet inside the south-western doorway.

THE 1939-1945 WAR MEMORIAL was erected by the parents of those whose names are inscribed on the roll of honour. Many Irish families have had a tradition of service in the British Army. Limerick's imperial past can be traced through the memorials of her dead in St. Mary's Cathedral. Limerick men served in their own, and other regiments, throughout the world, in France, Egypt, Palestine, South Africa, India, the East Indies, Spain, Afghanistan, Turkey, the Crimea, the Americas and wherever the English flag was flown. Some of the battles in which they fought have passed into history.

The regiments in which they served formed the backbone of the British army. These included the Royal Munster Fusiliers, the Connaught Rangers, the Coldstream Guards, the Inniskillings, the Prince of Wales' Own West Yorkshire Regiment, the King's Light Infantry, the Prince of Wales' Dragoon Guards, the North Gloucestershire Regiment on foot, and many more whose names can be found on the floor and walls of St. Mary's.

The Royal Navy also features in the Cathedral's memorials as well as some brief references to those who served in the fledgling Royal Air Force. The roster of officers included Bannatynes, Campbells, Crokers, Gabbetts, Glentworths, Glosters, Ievers, Lloyds, MacAdams, Maunsells, Napiers, O'Briens, Powers, Russells, Shaws, Summerfields and Wallers, Limerick's nineteenth-century elite.

ST. MARY'S CATHEDRAL contains many architectural features, too numerous for individual mention. In this account only the more prominent memorials are mentioned but there are several more worth looking at. The cathedral's silver plate is rarely put on public display as bank-vaults are now the only places in which such treasures can be considered safe. One of St. Mary's least mentioned but unique features is its vintage central heating system with its massive radiators and ultra-thick pipes, an industrial archaeologist's dream and a curator's nightmare. During the Cromwellian occupation General Ireton lived in a house in the cathedral grounds and James Craven was paid £5 "for mending and setting up the clocke in Mary's church" with materials valued at £15.77. During renovations in 1893-1895 the western porch was removed; "Ireton's House" and "Galwey's Castle" were demolished with other old houses; and the chapels of the south aisle were re-roofed.

THE EPISCOPAL SEE OF LIMERICK was founded by St. Munchin but little mention was made of it until after the Vikings converted to Christianity. One of them, Gille or Gilbert, was consecrated by the Archbishop of Canterbury and governed the see until 1140. The Charter of Domhnall Mòr O'Brien refers to the bishops of the diocese as the *Lumnicenses* or *Lumnicani.* They lost some of their see to the bishops of Killaloe and Emly until Gerald Le Mareschal recovered it for them in 1284. By the time of the Reformation the property was extensive and valuable, but was afterwards so much diminished by grants to the Fitzgerald family that the see of Ardfert and Aghadoe was added to it in 1660.

DEAN TALBOT OF ST. MARY'S wrote extensively on the history and monuments of St. Mary's. The epilogue he wrote to his *The Monuments of St. Mary's Cathedral, LImerick* (1976) is worth repeating. It terminated with a thought and a prayer for both the living and the dead; "We salute them, one and all: the founder, King Donal Mòr O'Brien, kneeling at the altar: Edward the Bruce praying before he marched to Faughart to disaster and to death: Cardinal Rinuccini, joining in a solemn Te Deum, receiving the English standards captured by Owen Roe O'Neill at

Benburb: General Ireton asking forgiveness for his own misdeeds and those of his father-in-law, Oliver Cromwell: Terence O'Brien, Bishop of Emly, listening to his death sentence pronounced by court martial in the cathedral: Patrick Sarsfield singing a hymn of thanksgiving for the victory which his famous 'ride' brought on reaching Ballyneety, and not long afterwards, praying for guidance as he led the 'Flight of the Wild Geese' to the continent, and so to the unlucky, lonesome Tyrconnell and the anti-clerical Murrough O'Brien (Murrough of the Burnings): to the Scottish historian Thomas Carlyle, who, so overpowered by emotion, whispered 'That lovely big dark brown edifice'; and then to more modern times, that Englishman, William Thackeray, as he entered the shrine exclaimed (God help him) 'The old cathedral, a barbarous old turretted 14th century building'. And so we salute them all ... pilgrims travelling to eternity.

THE CHURCHYARD contains many interesting tombstones and memorials with epitaphs ranging from the eloquent to the prosaic.

SAMUEL JOHN JONES is buried in the new plot near the Potato Market. His inscription reads;

> "I said to the man who stood
> at the gate of the year
> Give me a light
> that I may tread safely
> into the unknown".

CHARLES GRAVES, Bishop of Limerick, is remembered with a celtic cross inscribed with the symbols of the Paschal Lamb and the four Evangelists. His epitaph was written in Latin by R.G. Tyrrel (later Vice Provost of Dublin University); in Irish by Douglas Hyde (President of Ireland 1938-1945); and in English by A.P. Greaves (author of *Father O'Flynn*).

THE CROKER ARMS can be found on a stone slab inserted in the churchyard wall at the southern end of the old Exchange wall.

WILLIAM JOHN SHAW died on 2 December, 1869. He is remembered with a cenotaph erected by the pig buyers of Limerick and his employees, inscribed twice to ensure its benefactors' generosity was not overlooked. South of the cathedral's south-western doorway is another Victorian "masterpiece", the block-like tomb of James Butler Boyd.

THE BLUE SCHOOL is remembered by means of a plaque on the northern wall of that part of the cathedral where it was housed. It took its name, the Blue School or the Blue Coat Hospital, from the blue and yellow uniform worn by its pupils. Rev. J. Moore founded the school in 1717 and bequeathed some property in Dublin for its support. In 1724 Mrs. Alice Craven conveyed her house on the corner of Nicholas Street and Bow Lane to the Dean and Chapter for the same purpose, a school in which boys were taught a trade while they sang in the cathedral choir. The school supported fifteen boys. It fell into decay in 1748 but was revived by the Bishop and Dean in 1772.

SOURCE REFERENCE NUMBERS
43-49-52-65-70-86-89
129-161-173-183-246-254-255
264-271-274-276

Above: St Mary's Cathedral.
Left: Aerial view of St Mary's Cathedral and surrounding area.

Limerick:The Englishtown

THE ENGLISHTOWN is the oldest part of the city and occupies the southern end of King's Island, a tract formed by the Shannon, here divided into two streams, of which the narrowest and most rapid is called the Abbey River. Both are tidal, with tides of over fourteen feet. The term, Englishtown, came into use as the original inhabitants who were unwilling, or unable, to assimilate English culture, customs and language were squeezed out by the invading Anglo-Normans. This was the earliest part of the city to be walled in, first by Vikings, secondly by Anglo-Normans. The island's natural features, the surrounding water and the dependable water supply ensured the security of its inhabitants. By 1450 the surrounding countryside was in a state of unrest due to the prevailing power of the "Irish enemy and English rebels". The loyal, but beleagured, citizens of the Englishtown survived because supply ships, protected by Henry VI (1422-1455), brought the provisions they needed, sometimes from as far away as France.

THE FORTIFICATIONS, which had included the Englishtown alone, were extended to enclose part of the ground on the southern bank of the river between 1450 and 1495. Richard Stanihurst wrote in 1577; "The town is planted in an island, which plot in old time, before the building of the city was stored with grass ... yet the river is so navigable, as a ship of 200 tons may sail to the quay of the city [which was both] sumptuous and substantial". In an old map of the city displayed in the Hunt Collection in Plassey, the part of the island on which the Englishtown was located is shown as being completely walled in and surrounded by water. A moat or secondary channel of water separated the town from the upper two-thirds, or so, of the island. This map can be dated to some time before 1611 as it pre-dates the building of the bastion in King John's castle. Another fortification is shown on the west side of the island, north of St. Munchin's Church as well as tower-house on the east bank of the Abbey River, in Corbally.

THE LIMERICK MINT may have come into operation between 1195 and 1199, possibly under the direction of Siward, the first recorded Limerick moneyer. King John tightened up the administration of his Irish Lordship, in 1200, by reserving to himself all Irish pleas regarding the Crown, the exchange and the mint. During the Scottish wars of Edward I (1272-1307) the Irish economy was bankrupted by his Justiciar, Sir John Wogan, in an effort to mobilise Irish resources. In 1467 another mint was established in the city. Until then the Irish chieftains had been reluctant to adopt the use of coinage. But when a monetary economy came into play with the "surrender and re-grant" policies of the English Crown, they discovered the benefits of turning their followers into cash-paying tenants.

THE EXCHANGE WALL forms part of the eastern boundary of St. Mary's Church. This facade of hewn stone with its seven blocked-in Tuscan columns, linked by a handsome balustrade, faces Nicholas Street although the rest of the building has been demolished and now forms part of the churchyard. The Exchange was erected as a local administrative centre in 1673, was rebuilt in 1702 and 1777, and eventually fell into disuse when the Town Hall was opened in Rutland Street in 1846.

THE NAIL, a brass table standing on a short pillar, was set up in the Exchange by Robert Smith, Mayor of Limerick, in 1685, at his own expense. His name was engraved on it and the Limerick saying "To pay on the nail" originated with this monument. After the closure of the Exchange it was moved to the Town Hall in 1866 and is now in the Limerick Museum.

THE CITY COURTHOUSE, or the Gerald Griffin Memorial School, is located on the site of the Augustinian Abbey founded by the O'Briens during the thirteenth century. The City Court-house was built on the same site in Quay Lane or Bridge Street in 1640. This was later replaced by the present edifice erected between 1763-1765 at a cost of £700. The Quay Lane facade of this structure follows the curve of the street. The most spectacular of the cases tried here was that of John Scanlan who was executed on 20 March, 1820, for the murder of the *Colleen Bawn*. Fr. Brahan, the Catholic parish priest of St. Mary's Parish, bought the old court-house for £200 on 3 September 1845.

THE CHRISTIAN BROTHERS spent £500 on renovating the building before opening it as a school on 2 February, 1846. Initially four brothers taught 560 pupils in this converted court-house in which Gerald Griffin had witnessed the trials of John Scanlon and Stephen Sullivan for the murder of Ellen Hanley, the *Colleen Bawn*.

GERALD GRIFFIN (1803-1840) was born in a house that stood on the corner of Old Dominic Street and Love Lane on 12

The Exchange wall.

December 1803. His family moved out of the city, to Fairy Lawn, in 1810, until his parents eventually decided to emigrate to Pennsylvania. Gerald was reared in Adare and Pallaskenry, the ninth son of a large family. Originally he had intended to study medicne and had been left, with two sisters and a brother, to the care of an older brother who was a doctor in Pallaskenry. He moved to Limerick where he worked as a reporter and helped in the formation of a dramatic society before moving to London in 1823. John Banim (1798-1842) encouraged him to write and he worked as a reporter, book reviewer, parliamentary reporter and translator. The publication of *Holland Tide; or Munster Popular Tables* established him as a successful writer in 1827, and in 1829 he published *The Collegians* which was based on the *Coleen Bawn's* story. At the height of his fame he burned his manuscripts and joined the Christian Brothers. From 1825 he had been troubled by rheumatism and recurrent illness. He succumbed to typhus, in Cork, on 12 June, 1840.

THE COUNTY COURTHOUSE, on Merchant's Quay, still serves its original, and the city court-house's purpose. It was designed by two local architects, Nicholas and William Hannan, and was completed at a cost of £12,000 in 1810. It replaced an older county court-house which had been erected in 1732 on the site of the ancient Franciscan Abbey. The present structure is a quadrangular building with a portico supported by four tall pillars which was designed to contain civil and criminal courts, jury-rooms and other offices concerned with the dispensation of justice.

THE CITY JAIL was demolished in 1988. It had been completed in 1813 in an area formerly known as the Dean's Close. Public

hangings had taken place in front of the jail which had been designed with a stage, or drop, in front to facilitate spectators. Elizabeth Fry, the prison reformer, visited here. Both city and county prisoners were kept in the city jail in 1821. Before its eventual demolition the building served as a sweet-factory.

THE THOLSEL, in Mary Street, was founded in 1449. This was the city's earliest town hall, or court, and at one stage served as a jail. When John Howard, the prison reformer, visited here in 1788 he pointed out various defects which probably resulted in the erection of a newer city jail. In 1837 it was the chief civil court with the mayor and sheriffs presiding as judges, assisted by the recorder, when present, as assessor, and the town clerk as protonotary. This court was held under the Charter of Henry V, which gave pleas, real and personal, to any amount arising within the county of the city. The court sat every Wednesday; the process was either by attachment against goods; action against the person; or the issuing of a writ to summons someone who was in hiding. The Tholsel was demolished over half a century ago but a small portion of the structure remains behind the shop of the same name built on its site.

FANNING'S CASTLE, in the grounds of the Technical Institute, Barrington's Quay, is a late-sixteenth or early-seventeenth century house built by a merchant of that name. It was the home of Dominick Fanning, the Mayor of Limerick, executed by the Cromwellians for his part in the defence of the city in 1651. Thirty years later, in 1681, it was occupied by another mayor, Francis Whitamore, and tradition relates how Patrick Sarsfield stayed here during the Williamite siege. The windows are unusually large for a fortified residence. Another building was added to the original fabric at a later stage.

PETER'S CELL takes its name from an ancient nunnery built by Domhnall Mòr O'Brien for the Canonesses of St. Augustine in 1171. The foundation was dedicated to St.

The Gerald Griffin Memorial School

Peter and was encompassed by the north-eastern walls enclosing the fortified Englishtown. Peter's Cell survived as an area name despite the disappearance of the nunnery and the walls; but today it applies only to a lane leading into Bishop Street. The Augustinian Convent of Killone, in County Clare, became the mother-house of Peter's Cell after 1189.

THE PETER'S CELL THEATRE was established some time before 1760 when some entrepreneur converted part of the ruined convent into a playhouse complete with a stage, boxes, a pit, one gallery, and a few dressing rooms. Spranger Barry, manager of two theatres, one in Dublin, the other in Cork, instituted a regular summer season here in 1760. Seats cost fifteen pence for the boxes, ten pence in the pits and five pence in the gallery. Audience participation was a feature of the performances as the Limerick bucks and dandies vied with each other, even by walking onstage, to display their finery. Fruit-sellers sold peaches at one fifth of a penny each (one old half penny), an unusual refreshment for that time and place. This theatre was still in use as late as April, 1770.

ST. SAVIOUR'S DOMINICAN FRIARY may have been founded by Donnchadh Cairbreach O'Brien in 1227 on land donated by the English King. Edward I made a grant in 1285 in which he mentioned the affection

St Munchin's Church of Ireland Church.

he bore for the friars of Limerick whose house was founded by his ancestor. Donnchadh Cairbreach was buried here in 1242. In 1462 the Earl of Desmond rebuilt the priory. It was suppressed in 1541. In 1644 Pope Vincent X established a university in St. Saviour's for the Catholic Confederation. Only one wall and some fifteenth-century, and later, carvings survive. The latter have been placed in two grottoes. In 1837 "a nunnery had been established: attached is a large school for girls, who are gratuitously instructed by the ladies of the convent". The convent is now known as St. Mary's.

ST. MUNCHIN, or St. Mainchìn, an early bishop, is said to have been the nephew of Bloid, King of Thomond, and a disciple of St. Patrick, who asked him to convert the inhabitants of Connaught to Christianity. In later years he became Prior of Mungret and is generally accepted as the first Bishop of Limerick, where he built a church upon the river island on which the city was established. When the local people refused to help Munchin build his church he is said to have laid a curse upon them to the effect that strangers would flourish while the natives perished.

ST. MUNCHIN'S CHURCH OF IRE-LAND CHURCH was erected in 1827 almost on the same site as an older edifice said to have been built in 561. Tradition claims that the older structure was burnt by the Vikings. This was borne out by a stratum of ashes discovered when the foundations of the present building were being built.

The ancient parish church of St. Munchin may have served as a cathedral long before St. Mary's was built. Despite all the renovations and re-buildings over successive centuries one of the unique features of this church, as late as the nineteenth century, was

its retention of an episcopal throne, a link predating Domhnall Mòr O'Brien's foundation. St. Munchin is supposed to be buried in the churchyard. The church, was disused, neglected and vandalised until recently. Carved memorials had been ripped from the tombs, the graveyard was badly littered, the church roof was in poor condition, holed in places, and the entrance and windows were sealed off. St. Munchin's was restored by the Civic Trust over a six month period. On 13 March 1989 the renovated structure was leased to the Island Theatre Company by the Civic Trust but an exclusion clause in the lease prohibits its use for public performances. The present church, designed by the Pain brothers and erected for £1,460 in 1827, is a handsome edifice with a square tower embattled and crowned with pinnacles. St. Munchin's was also the burial ground of the Smyth's, Lord Gort's family.

METHODISM was introduced into the city by Robert Swindells who preached his first sermon on the parade of the Castle Barracks in 1748 or 1749. Soon afterwards John Wesley visited Robert Swindells. They formed the Methodist Society and rented the old church of St. Francis's Abbey where the Methodists remained until they spent £600 on erecting "a handsome edifice near the city court-house". In 1812 they built a new Wesleyan Chapel in George's Street but in 1815 a religious controversy split the congregation in two. The Wesleyan Methodists kept possession of the George's Street preaching house and the Primitive Wesleyan Methodists retained the old one. The dispute arose concerning the expediency of the original group's preachers administering the sacraments of Baptism and the Lord's Supper.

THE VILLIERS' ALMS HOUSES, and schools, were endowed by Mrs. Hannah Villiers in her will which was established in the Court of King's Bench in 1815. In 1826 an

Villiers' Alms Houses.

Elizabethan-style building, designed by the Pain brothers, was erected in the Bishop's Garden, by Mrs. Villiers' trustees. The structure "consists of a centre and two projecting wings, the former being surrounded by a cupola; it contains apartments for 12 poor widows, each of whom receives £24 Irish per annum; and there are two school-rooms". Despite some modernisation the building remains basically unchanged. The garden wall in front of the alms houses is part of the old city wall. It extends to, and includes, some of St. Munchin's Churchyard.

THE BISHOP'S HOUSE, in Church Street, may have been designed by Francis Bindon (1698-1765), the architect who pioneered pal-

The Bishop's House.

ladian-style Irish architecture, although the Civic Trust dates it back to the seventeenth century and claim it is the oldest standing domestic dwelling in the city. The Civic Trust re-roofed the building, quite recently, and intend to restore it completely to provide themselves with a permanent base. This was the residence of the Church of Ireland Bishops of Limerick until they moved to Park House in the early nineteenth century. Its most famous resident was, or is, the *Bishop's Lady*, Limerick's most famous ghost, immortalised in the Bard of Thomond's poem, *Drunken Thady and the Bishop's Lady*. There were only four carriages in use around the city between 1740 and 1750. These were "the Bishop's, the Dean's, and one other clergyman's and one neighbouring gentleman's". By 1776, with the growth of Newtownpery, there

were 183 four-wheeled carriages in the district.

ST. MARY'S COURT was originally known as the Doctor Hall's Alms Houses. In 1761, under the terms of his will, "the present neat and convenient edifice was erected, which contains apartments for thirteen men and twelve women, who receive each five pounds a-year, school rooms, with apartments for the teacher, and a chapel, where the clergyman of the Established Church celebrates divine service twice a-week". The buildings were restored in the mid 1970s.

THE CITY BREWERY, near the Golden Mills, was located in Newgate Lane, between the Old City Jail and King John's Castle. This was also known as the Newgate Brewery and was one of the earliest established in the city to make beer for public, rather than private, consumption. It was founded, and owned, by the Fitt family in 1739. Ale, pale ale and porter were brewed here in 1866.

ANDREW CHERRY (1762-1812), songwriter, dramatist, playwright, comic actor and wit was born in what is now the post office in Bridge Street. *The Dear Little Shamrock of Ireland* was his best-known song and he is also remembered for a letter he wrote to a former manager; "Sir- I am not so great a fool as you take me for! I have been bitten once by you, and I will never give you an opportunity of making two bites of

A. Cherry."

QUAY LANE was mentioned by the playwright, John O'Keefe, in his *Recollections* which were published in 1826; "I knew Mr. Ferrar of Limerick, a printer, bookseller and author; he wrote an excellent *History of Limerick* which a few years ago I read with pleasure. His little shop was at the corner of Quay Lane. Ferrar was very deaf, yet had a cheerful, animated countenance, thin, and of middle size."

ST. FRANCIS ABBEY was founded before 1279. the year a Franciscan of Limerick, Br. Malachy, was postulated to the See of Tuam. He was rejected by Pope Honorious IV in 1286. The exact date of its foundation is unknown but T.J. Westropp suggested that it could have been founded by Donnchadh Cairbreach O'Brien before 1241 or by William Fion de Burgo who had died by 1287. He also gave a third date and founder, 1350, by Mary, Countess of Desmond, which has been disproved by the 1279 appointment. This first Franciscan Friary was located between Sheep Street and Sir Harry's Mall, north-east of Jail Lane. It was known as St. Francis Abbey, and even though its buildings have all long since disappeared, it is still remembered in local names like those of the Abbey River, Chapel Lane and St. Francis' Abbey Lane. Fion de Burgo, Thomas de Clare and Richard de Clare were buried here. St. Francis Abbey stood outside the city walls, to the east. After the Reformation its lands were parcelled out and many of its buildings put to profane use. The church, dormitory, cloister and hall were demolished, only buildings useful to a farmer were retained. The choir was turned into a court-house and Edmond Sexten received a grant of the property in 1543. He kept the friars here, as his tenants, until 1548. The Franciscan Order was re-established elsewhere in the town in 1615 and a chapter was held there in 1629. On 23 June 1636 all but one of the Sexten tenements in St. Francis Abbey, Richard Coynes, were burned. The friars returned to the area for a while in 1687 but were forced to leave soon afterwards, in 1691. The old county hospital was built on its site in 1765. The Franciscans erected a well-built spacious chapel in Newgate Lane where they remained until they moved to Henry Street where they had "an elegant structure in progress" in 1827.

EDMOND SEXTEN was Mayor of Limerick in 1535. His grandson, and namesake, managed to get legal title to freedom from rates and taxes on St. Francis Abbey in 1603. In 1609 a grant of King James I certified that the former choir was suitable for holding assizes and sessions for the county, as a result of which Edmond Sexten enjoyed two votes in the Corporation, and the Mayor and Corporation were obliged to present him with the first salmon taken in the sea weir each year.

THE COUNTY INFIRMARY was opened by Sylvester O'Halloran and Giles Vandeleur, two noted surgeons of the day, as a four-bed hospital in 1759. It was located in three small houses on Little Island and was conducted as a charity. Other people soon became involved in the project and additional finance was required for expansion.

THE COUNTY HOSPITAL developed from the infirmary but used the former title to benefit from an act in favour of county hospitals. Edmond Sexton Pery conveyed some ground, with the ruins of a former work-house on it, in St. Francis Abbey, to the trustees, Charles Smyth and Dean Hoare, at the yearly rent of one peppercorn in 1765. Lady Hartstonge contributed heavily to the erection of a new hospital capable of holding upwards of forty beds. Sylvester O'Halloran was retained as the officially appointed surgeon: he had given his services free in the infirmary; but Giles Vandeleur did not live long enough to see the new hospital, as he had died within sixteen months of opening the infirmary.

BARRINGTON'S HOSPITAL was endowed by Joseph Barrington in 1830. For over a century and a half the hospital served the medical and surgical needs of the city, county, and neighbouring counties extremely well, only to become the victim of economic recession and medical cut backs in 1988.

THE BARRINGTON FAMILY have been

Barrington's Hospital Entrance.

associated with the city since Francis Barrington arrived from Engand in the 1640s. Samuel Barrington survived the Williamite siege of 1691. He was a clock-maker who died in 1693 and was buried in St. Mary's Cathedral. His epitaph reads; "Little Samuell Barinton that great undertaker of famous cittis clock and chime maker ...:

JOSEPH BARRINGTON was an enterprising man with a philanthropic flair. He was disliked by Caleb Powell who described him as a "Pewterer dwelling in a very small shop" who had "rais'd himself to eminence" and acquired extensive landed property in Limerick. Joseph owned, amongst other possessions, a pewter works under the sign of the Copper Globes on Charlotte Quay. Ironically, soon after Caleb Powell wrote that description of Joseph in 1858, Powell's ownership of

Clonshavoy passed into Barrington hands. Joseph became a baronet in 1831, the year after he had founded Barrington's Hospital. His first cousin, William Canter, of Ballyvarra was a skillful bone-setter. Joseph died in 1846.

SIR MATTHEW BARRINGTON was a solicitor with practices in Limerick and Dublin. He was Crown Prosecutor in Munster during a very disturbed period and his son, William H. Barrington was a Grand Juror selected by Caleb Powell in 1858. Matthew is best remembered as the instigator of the Barrington's *Mont De Pieta* or pawnshop.

BARRINGTON'S MONT DE PIETA was the first of eight such establishments opened in Ireland in 1837. It operated as a type of pawnshop in which an interest rate of less than two new pence to the pound was charged, and there was no charge for the ticket of pledged articles. In 1840 it made a profit of £1,357 which was used to fund Barrington's Hospital. By 1841 the *Montes De Pietas,* or *Mons Pietas,* had started to lose money. By 1843 ony three remained, and the last one, in Portadown, closed at the end of that year.

THE FRANCISCANS of Perugia founded the first *Mont De Pieta* in 1461. The idea proved so successful that Pope Leo X had to issue a bill in their defence, in 1515, to silence the vested banking interests who had objected to religious orders getting involved in financial affairs.

SIR FITZWILLIAM BARRINGTON lived in Glenstal House as a child. He returned to Limerick for the closure of Barrington's Hospital, of which he had been honorary secretary, on Wednesday, 30 March, 1988.

BOURKE'S HOUSE, on Athlunkard Street, was also known as Castle Friary because Franciscan friars lived here from 1732 to 1766. This is not a typical Irish tower-house although the machicolation proves that it was built as a fortified structure. A Gothic-style drinking fountain was inserted in the stone facade of this late medieval dwelling in 1860. This was a presentation to the people of Limerick by the Malcolmson family, founders of the Limerick Shipping Company. The inscription reads, "Protect what is erected for your benefit". The fountain no longer serves its original purpose but is used instead as a lit-

Bourke's House.

ter-bin, despite the inscription.

ATHLUNKARD STREET developed after the demolition of the old city walls in 1760, part of the general clearance that presaged the building of Newtownpery. Salvaged material from the demolished walls and buildings was used to build the quays. Athlunkard street, itself, was built in 1824.

ATHLUNKARD BRIDGE was designed by the Pain brothers. Work on the five large elliptic arches was started in 1826 and completed at a cost of £16,000 in 1830.

ST. MARY'S CATHOLIC CHURCH was erected on the Sluice or Little Island between 1746 and 1749. It was cruciform in design; had no external decorations; and contained a handsome altar donated by a merchant, John Kelly, in 1760. This church was demolished when the newer church, designed by Mesrs. Ashlin and Coleman, Dublin, and erected by Messrs. Maguire and Shortt, Dublin, was opened on 31 July, 1932. The foundations of the older structure remain, forming an attractive feature within the garden.

THE CELL OF ST. MARY HOUSE or Priory, was located on the bank of the Abbey River, on King's Island, east of Baal's Bridge.

THE SANDMEN of the *Parish* carried on their arduous, often hazardous trade, from the earliest days of the city's foundation until the completion of the Shannon Hydroelectric Scheme in 1929 changed the river so completely that most of them were forced out of their ancient profession.

THE SAND from which most of the older parts of the city was built had been washed into the river-bed from the catchment areas of the Shannon, Mulcair, Newport and Clare rivers. It was deposited in several places along the Shannon's bed but the three most important locations were where the Mulcair river entered the Shannon; the deep waters below Plassey Bridge; and between the Lax Weir and the Island Point. The sandmen used an ugly but versatile craft, known as a sand barge, to recover and transport the sand. This was thirty feet long by five wide; sloped fore and aft; had a small jib; a hand-winch in the stern for raising dredges filled with sand from the river bottom; could be loaded from the gunwale by one man but needed a crew of two; carried ropes, anchors, grapnels and a *skeef*, a wooden bailer; and was powered and steered from the stern, over which a heavy sweep was set in a socket.

SOURCES USED

1-13-30-39-48-49-52
54-55-63-64-76-78-80
81-83-84-86-96-110-120
123-127-129-130-131-170-171
176-220-227-246-250-256-264
261

Below: Aerial view from Corbally over the Abbey and Shannon rivers.

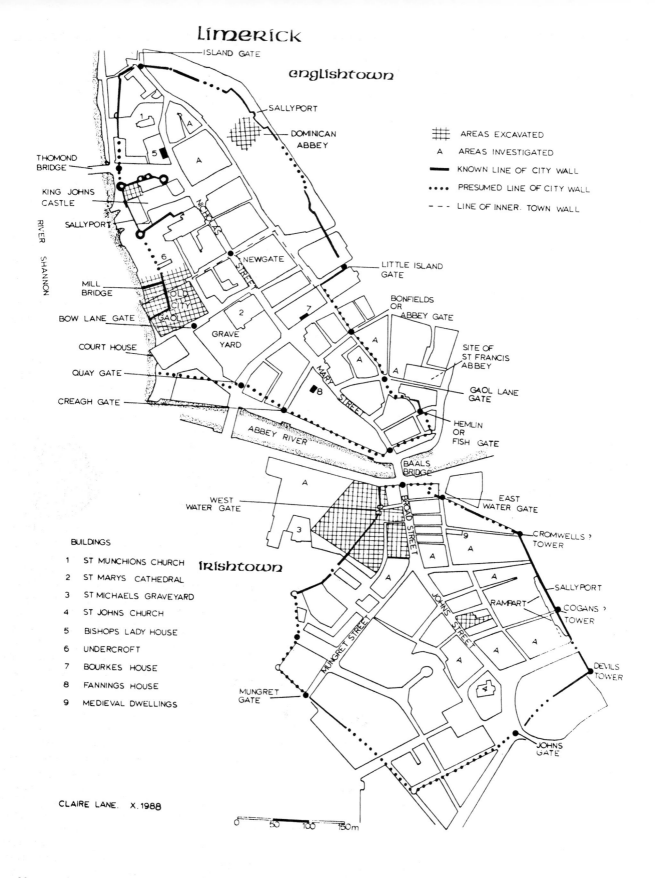

Limerick

englishtown

⊞	AREAS EXCAVATED
A	AREAS INVESTIGATED
▬	KNOWN LINE OF CITY WALL
••••	PRESUMED LINE OF CITY WALL
– – –	LINE OF INNER TOWN WALL

ISLAND GATE
SALLYPORT
DOMINICAN ABBEY
THOMOND BRIDGE
KING JOHNS CASTLE
SALLYPORT
RIVER SHANNON
NICHOLAS STREET
NEWGATE
LITTLE ISLAND GATE
MILL BRIDGE
BOW LANE GATE
OLD CITY GAOL
COURT HOUSE
GRAVE YARD
MARY STREET
BONFIELDS OR ABBEY GATE
SITE OF ST FRANCIS ABBEY
GAOL LANE GATE
QUAY GATE
CREAGH GATE
HEMLIN OR FISH GATE
ABBEY RIVER
BAALS BRIDGE
WEST WATER GATE
EAST WATER GATE
BROAD STREET
CROMWELLS ? TOWER
SALLYPORT
RAMPART
COGANS ? TOWER
JOHNS STREET
DEVILS TOWER
MUNGRET STREET
MUNGRET GATE
JOHNS GATE

irishtown

BUILDINGS

1. ST MUNCHIONS CHURCH
2. ST MARYS CATHEDRAL
3. ST MICHAELS GRAVEYARD
4. ST JOHNS CHURCH
5. BISHOPS LADY HOUSE
6. UNDERCROFT
7. BOURKES HOUSE
8. FANNINGS HOUSE
9. MEDIEVAL DWELLINGS

CLAIRE LANE. X. 1988

0   50   100   150m

Map reproduced by kind permission of Celie O'Rahilly, Limerick Corporation Archaeologist. Originally published in Archaeology Ireland.

Limerick: The Irishtown

THE IRISHTOWN came into existence as the Anglo-Norman invaders of the old city forced the earlier inhabitants out of their island homes, across to the opposite bank of the Abbey River. This second settlement dates back to the days of King John. The streets were wider and some of the houses more modern but it became part of the walled city even though it retained a separate identity. From about 1450 the fortifications were extended to enclose the Irishtown, work that was completed with the erection of St. John's Gate in 1495. In 1654 only one Irishtown landlord, Christopher Sexton, was considered to be acting in the "English interests", as the others, landlords and tenants alike, were classed as "Irish papists". When the old city walls were knocked in the mid 1700's Mungret Street and St. John's Square became elite residential areas. The development of Newtownpery led to the downgrading of the Irishtown; formerly fashionable houses were turned into tenements; the more prosperous inhabitants moved away; and even today some sites remain cleared, but undeveloped, for over sixty years. Urban renewal schemes have halted the decline in recent years; older historic buildings have been restored; and the people of the area are more aware of their heritage.

BAAL'S BRIDGE or Ball's Bridge was built about 1340. This was a bridge of four arches with a range of houses on one side. The original Baal's Bridge was replaced by a single-arch structure built in 1831 by the Limerick Navigation Company, at a cost of £3,000, as it interrupted the communication between the canal and the tide-water of the river. The name may be a derivation of *Droichead Maol*, the Bald Bridge, meaning a bridge without parapets, or a corruption of Boyle's Bridge, part of a grant made to the Earl of Shannon whose family name was Boyle. It was known as the Tide Bridge in Elizabethan times, was "disgraced by a row of houses" as late as 1827, and the silversmiths of Limerick used a picture of its gateway tower as their hallmark, or mark of origin device. It was taken down in November 1830 and replaced with the present structure, designed by the Pain brothers, the following November.

THE SYLVESTER O'HALLORAN (1728-1807) FOOTBRIDGE is named after the distinguished surgeon, historian, antiquarian, patriot and genius who was born in Caherdavin, educated in London, Leyden and Paris, practised in his native city, and died in his house near St. Mary's Cathedral. As a surgeon Sylvester O'Halloran specialised in brain and eye surgery, developing a new method of treating cataracts, in the latter half of the eighteenth century. In 1774 he wrote *A General History of Ireland*. Six years later he became an honorary member of the newly-formed Dublin College of Surgeons. His *A History of Ireland* was published in 1803 but did not find favour with the establishment as it contained too many details which the Anglo-Irish ascendancy would rather had been forgotten. His brother, Fr. Joseph Ignatius O'Halloran, a Jesuit priest, was successfully professor of rhetoric, philosophy, and divinity in Bordeaux, before returning to Ireland. Dr. Sylvester O'Halloran was buried in the family vault in Kilteely grave-yard in 1807 but he has not been forgotten. In 1987 the new footbridge over the Abbey River was named after him.

THE MATHEW BRIDGE was originally known as the New Bridge and connected Englishtown with Newtownpery. It consisted of three irregular arches erected at a cost of £1,800 in 1762. There were two lamp-posts set opposite each other, in the centre of the bridge, which were used as impromptu gallows in 1798. In 1844 John Duggan was awarded the contract for a new bridge which was officially opened in June, 1846. This was designed by W.H. Owen and named after Fr. Theobald Mathew (1790-1861), the Capuchin friar who launched a national temperance movement at about the same time as Daniel O'Connell was urging the repeal of the Union. Fr. Mathew was known as the Apostle of Temperance and is said to have obtained 180,000 disciples in Limerick in 1846 (the population of city and county in 1831 was 248,201).

THE O'DWYER BRIDGE was erected in 1931 to replace Park Bridge, a lofty bridge of five irregular arches which had been built in 1835 to replace "a mean structure". This bridge was dedicated to the Catholic Bishop of Limerick, Dr. E.T. O'Dwyer (1886-1917). The Athlunkard Boat Club is located on its north-western end, behind an old iron gate containing decorative scrollwork representing the city arms, round towers and other Celtic-style motifs.

THE TUDOR CITY was a prosperous place. Gerald, the Earl of Kildare, held a parliament here in 1484, the year before Henry VII (1485-1509) came to the English throne. In 1495 the Brotherhood of the Guild of Merchants was formed. Commercial jealousy between Limerick and Galway erupted into open hostility by 1524. In 1536 peace was restored with a formal treaty and by an injunction from Henry VIII (1509-1547) stating that he required a better demeanour from the men of Galway. Henry was declared King of Ireland in 1542. Alderman Sexten was his greatest proponent in Limerick, and in 1543 Sir Anthony St. Leger convened a parliament here in which many important acts were passed. The Earl of Thomond and his followers swore fealty to the Crown when Lord-Deputy Sussex arrived to help him "suppress a revolt of some inferior branches of the O'Brien family against their chief" towards the end of Queen Mary's reign (1553-1558).

FR. DAVID WOULFE, Apostolic Commissary in Ireland from 1561, was persuaded, by Hugh O'Donnell, to give his allegiance to Queen Elizabeth. Despite his pledge, he was imprisoned in Dublin Castle by Sir Henry Sydney until he escaped in July 1572 after an incarceration of five years. He sailed for Spain in September, 1573. In 1568 and 1574 he prepared two reports on his homeland for the benefits of the Spanish Ambassador and King Philip of Spain. The 1574 *Description of Ireland* begins with; "Touching the City of Limerick. Limerick is stronger and more beautiful than all the other cities of Ireland, well walled with stout walls of hewn marble, and is an island city in the middle of that rapid Shannon river, and there is no entrance except by stone bridges, one of the two of which has 14 arches, and the other 8 ... for the most part the houses are of square stone of black marble and built in the form of

Sylvester O'Halloran Memorial Footbridge.

towers or fortresses. The suburb of the city is even better walled ... and there are ten towers or bulwarks, most beautiful and strong about it, which allow no one to come near the wall". The walls extended round a circuit of about three miles. Despite the many wars that devastated the whole of the surrounding province Limerick maintained the most unshaken loyalty to Elizabeth I and was made a centre of civil and military administration. Sir Henry Sydney, Lord-Deputy of Ireland visited here in 1567, 1569 and in1576. He stated that he was received with greater magnificence than he had hitherto experienced in Ireland. In 1579 Sir William Pelham arrived here as Lord-Deputy. The Mayor appeared before him attended by 1,000 well-armed citizens. The city militia amounted to 800 men in 1584, double that of Cork and a third more than that of Waterford, making Limerick the most important city in Ireland, next to Dublin. During the Earl of Desmond's rebellion Limerick became the headquarters of the English army.

THE SPANISH WINE TRADE sparked off intense rivalry between the merchants of Limerick and Galway. The Galway traders held a virtual monopoly on this business but were unable to prevent the Limerick men from competing. Limerick exported the products, and especially corn, of the rich neighbouring districts known then as Kennory and Conelogh. Payne states that they were called "The gardens of the land for the varietie and great plentie of venison, fish and foule than elsewhere in Ireland, although in every place there is great store". Travellers were usually impressed with the town's natural advantages. William Body wrote to (Thomas) Cromwell in 1536 that it was "a wondrous proper city" standing environed by the River Shannon, and might be called "Little London for the

situation and the plenty". Stanihurst admired the navigable properties of the Shannon which made it possible for a ship of 200 tons burden to sail right up to the quays sixty miles from the sea. As in Galway, the buildings were fine; Stanihurst calls them "sumptuous and substantial", but, again like Galway, Limerick suffered at the end of the century. Despite its strategic position the city's defences were in a poor state of repair with "its cannon resting on rotten wooden frames" by 1588, the year of the Spanish Armada. When Sir John Davies saw it in 1606 it was still "a town of castles, compassed with the fairest walls that ever I saw", but the plenty which made Body compare it to London was no longer there, "the fair structures", contained nothing but "sluttishness and poverty within".

THE MERCHANTS of the city sometimes sent their goods via Waterford during the mid 1500s. One cargo sent by Nicholas Wolf of Lymbrick, a "native merchant" contained 300 linen cloths, £3.; 12 marten skins £2.; 6 otter skins, 60p.; and 200 sheepfells, £1.33.The towns of Munster supplied the majority of animal hides exported. In 1578 the shoemakers of Limerick were licensed to tan "as well for the maintenance of their trade as for the benefit of their neighbours and town dwellers". John Stacboll and James Creagh of Limerick are mentioned as business partners in the patent rolls "concerning a certain carvell laden with wines to the number of 6 score butts", while in another account the Mayor and Corporation complained to Lord Deputy Bellingham that a Limerick boat "laden with wines" had been wrecked on the Wexford coast and its goods plundered by the inhabitants. As relations worsened between England and Spain in the latter half of the sixteenth century the government of the day kept

a watchful eye on ships trading in Spain. The State Papers contain numerous references to the wine trade as merchants were frequently consulted and examined about the preparations they had observed along the Spanish coast, especially the Andalusian coast. On 27 September, 1575, Queen Elizabeth granted the Corporation of Limerick certain privileges, one of which was "that no ship coming within the river there do sell or discharge any munition, shot, powder, wines of other wares to any other than to the said corporation".

TWO ACCIDENTAL FIRES in 1618 and 1620 led to considerable improvement in the construction of buildings and the undertaking of major public works. The reign of King James I (1603-1625) was a tranquil one for the city; a quiet prosperity prevailed. Luke Gernon wrote, in 1620, that the lower town was surrounded by a wall a mile in compass, in which three men might walk abreast. The quay wall, which extended from the town wall into the middle of the river and was made for a defence harbour for the shipping was about 200 paces in length. It was actually a double wall. "There is within it a long gallery arched overhead, and with windows most pleasant to walk in, and above that a terrace to walk upon with fair battlements; at the end of it there is a round tower with 2 or 3 chambers, one above the other, and a battlement above". In 1636 Lord-Deputy Wentworth was splendidly entertained by the Mayor for nine days and he presented the Corporation with a valuable silver-gilt cup on his departure.

THE CONFEDERATE IRISH ARMY laid a boom of tree-trunks linked with iron across the Shannon, in order to prevent ships from bringing provisions upriver to the Water Gate of the city, when they marched against Limerick in 1642, under the command of

Lord Ikerrin, Lord Muskerry and General Barry. The citizens of the city welcomed them by throwing the gates open although the 200-man garrison in the castle resisted until they were forced to surrender after a stubborn defence. Later on the Confederates used a 32-pounder cannon captured within the city to reduce castles around the county. The fortifications were repaired and strengthened by the magistrates who also sent representatives to the Confederation at Kilkenny.

STONEY THURSDAY CORNER was named after an incident, in 1646, in which the Mayor, John FitzThomas Bourke, was almost stoned to death on this site when he attempted to proclaim the details of the pacification that had been concluded between King and Parliament. Shortly afterwards, the Supreme Council headed by the Papal Nuncio, Cardinal Rinuccini, moved into the city to encourage the Confederate forces who were besieging the Parliamentarians at Bunratty Castle, County Clare. In 1650 Rinuccini's party deprived the Marquess of Ormond, the man who had secured Limerick for Charles I, of all power. After Ormond's departure the Earl of Castlehaven persuaded the magistrates to let him defend the city against Ireton's forces who were marching to attack it.

THE CROMWELLIAN SIEGE OF LIMERICK commenced in the spring of 1651 and was protracted until the approach of winter. Major-General Hugh O'Neill, the defender of Clonmel, was governor of the besieged city, while General Henry Ireton, Oliver Cromwell's son-in-law, commanded the Parliamentarian army. The Cromwellian forces had prepared for the siege in advance; ships had ferried tents, beds, arms, ammunition, cannon and provisions up to the Shannon; garrisons were placed in the castles of Kilmallock and Castleconnell; outposts were located at various strategic points, including a fort that stood in the middle of the Shannon, on the Lax Weir; Henry Ireton had made himself the master of O'Brien's Bridge and Killaloe, by treachery; while an attempt to make the Shannon fordable by diverting the water was later abandoned by his men.

FAMINE, MISERY, AND DEATH made life in the besieged city miserable for inhabitants and attackers alike. The attempts of the Confederation to relieve Limerick were defeated, although a sally by Hugh O'Neill nearly proved fatal to the Cromwellians. Eventually the inhabitants of Limerick were compelled to turn out all "useless persons" to prevent them from spreading the plague which then raged amongst them. Ireton whipped these involuntary refugees back to the besieged city, and hanged some of them to deter others from trying to pass through his

lines. As the death toll rose within the city dissensions broke out amongst the besieged as to the propriety of capitulating. Fennel, the man suspected of having betrayed the pass at Killaloe to Ireton, had somehow managed to be placed in charge of St. John's Gate which he threatened to give up to the Parliamentarians if the garrison would not surrender. Two hundred Cromwellian soldiers were admitted to the Irishtown, by Fennel, to garrison another fort called Price's Mill. Soon afterwards the East Gate was delivered up to Ireton's forces by some officers in favour of capitulation. This was a crucial move as the East Gate separated the Irishtown from the Englishtown and its possession placed the Cromwellians in a strong position. This position was further strengthened when Ireton's bombardment of King John's Castle, from Thomond Bridge, made a breach in the castle wall which was secured by twenty dragoons supported by infantry.

THE CITY SURRENDERED. Hugh O'Neill met with Henry Ireton to negotiate terms. Twenty-four people were excluded by name from the benefit of this treaty; 2,500 soldiers were allowed to march out unarmed; those willing to reside in the city were promised protection of life and property while a similar promise was made to those who wanted to move elsewhere; and the city, castle and places of strength were surrendered to the Cromwellians on 29 October, 1651, two days after the Articles of Surrender were signed.

5,000 PEOPLE DIED in the course of the siege. Ireton's council of officers demanded, and received, a pardon for Hugh O'Neill, one of the twenty-four excluded from the benefits of the treaty. Ireton wanted to hang him but facing the near-mutiny of his officers had little choice but to let him go. Bishop O'Dwyer was also pardoned but was believed to have made a private deal with the Cromwellians for his own safety. The other twenty-two were executed, mainly for their active roles in the defence of Limerick. These were Major-General Purcell; Sir Geoffrey Galway; Lieutenant-Colonel Lacy; Captain George Woulfe;Captain-Lieutenant Sexton; Terence O'Brien, Bishop of Emly; John Quin, a Dominican friar; Captain Laurence Walsh, a priest; Francis Woulfe, a friar; Philip Dwyer, a priest; Alderman Dominick Fanning; Alderman Thomas Stritch; Alderman Jordan Roche; Burgess Edmond Roche; Sir Richard Everard; Doctor Daniel O'Higgin; Maurice Baggot of Baggotstown; Geoffrey Barron; a Welsh soldier named Evans and three other people, including a deserter from the Cromwellian army. Ireton did not savour his victory for long. He died on 26 November, 1651, of the plague or of a heavy 'flu or pneu-

monia which developed during his stay in Clarecastle, County Clare.

AFTER THE SURRENDER the city was left with 4,000 men still capable of bearing arms. The emblems of royalty were removed, the magistrates displaced, and for five years the city was subjected to a military government. Under Cromwellian rule house-rents were collected not only from the Irish inhabitants of Limerick, but from their own soldiers and adherents. Under an Act passed in 1653, English adventurers, officers and soldiers has been allowed to buy forfeited houses within the city and county. In the account books of this period, house-rents were seen to fall off and abatements were made as families were transplanted out of the city; doors were built to keep intruders off the deserted streets; and as damaged houses collapsed, their timbers were salvaged and sold off. The Cromwellian government repaired the old castle for £661.401/2 and demolished some of the surrounding houses in order to secure it against attack. During Ireton's siege the great salmon weir, the Lax Weir, was damaged. This too was repaired but in September, 1655, a "flood of waters" destroyed the "great ffishing weare" and its tenant was granted an abatement in compensation. In 1653 a charter was granted giving the citizens of this city the same privileges and franchises as those enjoyed by the citizens of Bristol. In 1656 the municipal government was restored with the election of a Mayor and twelve English aldermen. Sir Ralph Wilson declared in favour of the King when he was Governor of Limerick at the time of the Restoration. He was succeeded by the Earl of Orrery.

THE PENAL LAWS were not enforced too stringently, within the city, during the Vice-Royalty of Lord Berkeley (1679-1672). A Catholic, John Halpin, was elected Mayor in September 1672, but was deposed after four weeks when he refused to take the required oath of office. A fanatical Protestant, the Earl of Orrery, was appointed Governor of Limerick and President of Munster soon after the Restoration. He was responsible for terminating the more tolerant Earl of Ormond's appointment to the Vice-Royalty in 1669, and in 1672 he had Lord Berkeley removed from the same office. In 1671 he banned the Catholic clergy from saying Mass in the cities of Cork and Limerick. The discovery of the Popish Plot in England, in 1678, gave the Earl of Orrery an opportunity to issue a proclamation banning all Catholics from the city, as "multitudes of loose Irish papists" had moved into the city during the previous three months. Despite issuing this proclamation Orrery confessed to the Earl of Ormonde that it was unlikely to have any effect, as any attempt to implement such legislation would fill all the prisons, drive many from their homes, send unemployment soaring, and destroy the economy. Dr. James Dowley, or Duley, was appointed Vicar Apostolic in 1657 although he did not take up office until 1669. In 1676 he became Catholic Bishop of Limerick. In 1678, he surrendered himself to the authorities. He was neither imprisoned or transported but was released and kept under surveillance. In 1680 he appeared in court. Four years later, in 1684, he was still working in his diocese despite being old and infirm.

JOHN FREND, a Cromwellian captain, was one of many Cromwellian officers who acquired a considerable amount of confiscated land in the county. In 1858 Caleb Powell described his descendant, Ben Frend of Boskell, as having an iron leg which was "the softest part of him".

THE EARL OF ORRERY was instructed to endeavour to procure "good English and Dutch merchants" to inhabit the city — good in this case meant of the right persuasion and politics. It was hoped that this influx of businessmen would cause the city to flourish with trade. Orrery also restored the banished merchants of Limerick to their freedom and privileges, on their entering into recognizances to keep the peace. The city prospered under his rule. The inland trade increased so rapidly under his instruction that the tolls of the gates were let for upwards of £300 per annum in 1672. In the same year, the Mayor and citizens were able to perambulate dry-shod out-side the walls of the Englishtown as the waters of the Shannon fell to an unprecedented level during a considerable drought. The following year a great storm and high tide caused great damage to the city. Thomas Dineley described Limerick in 1680; "It is one of the fairest cities of the Province of Munster upon the River Shannon, distinguished thus, the English Town and the Irish Town. The English Town is an island and hath a wall distinct; in this is kept the main guard and is seen the King's Castle. The Thomond Gate and the Balls Bridge Gate are the two chiefest gates thereof. That part of the city going by the name of the Irish Town is also walled in. Here is seen the Citadel; the chiefest gates of the Irish Town are the St. John's Gate and the Mongrett Gate". The accession of James II (1685-1689) caused an alteration in the religious ascendancy of the Corporation.

THE FIRST WILLIAMITE SIEGE took place soon after the Battle of the Boyne when the French and Irish forces regrouped here and used the city as a major rallying point. The occupying armies spoke disparagingly of old and decaying fortifications which could be knocked down with roasted apples, although the Williamite accounts treated the fortifications more respectfully. The Jacobites strengthened the defences; a trench with a covered way was constructed outside the walls; redoubts were erected; and suburban houses demolished to prevent besiegers using them. King William had expected the city to surrender by the time he reached Caherconlish on 7 August 1690. He had left his heavy siege artillery in Dublin and had brought only his light field guns with him. His siege train was despatched from Dublin. In the early hours of 11 August the Williamites saw "a great light in the air and heard a strange rumbling noise", Patrick Sarsfield had crossed the Shannon and destroyed the siege train at Ballyneety. The 20,000 besiegers were hampered by the loss of their heavier guns and battering ram whereas the city's occupants had an abundance of the munitions of war and were able to obtain supplies of every kind from Connaught, and by sea, where the French fleet rode undisturbed.

THE BRAZEN HEAD was the name of a young red-haired woman beheaded in the fighting of 26 August 1690 when King William's Brandenburg Regiment, Saxon and Dutch mercenaries, made an almost suicidal frontal attack on the city walls near the Black Battery where they managed to get into the Irishtown through a gap in the south wall near today's St. John's Hospital. Despite heavy losses they almost succeeded in reaching Baal's Bridge. The women of Limerick fought alongside their men and managed to repel the invaders killing 500 of them near St. John's Mount, now John Street. It was during this encounter that the Brazen Head was killed, some accounts say she was involved in the fighting while others state that she was merely an innocent bystander. She died near the principal inn which was named in her honour *The Brazen Head*. Simon Kent rebuilt the original inn at 23 John Street in 1794 and had a commemorative plaque placed on the building's facade between the first floor windows. This plaque was removed to O'Connell Street and re-inserted outside another building in the 1960s. The Williamites battered their way into the city on two other occasions but were driven out each time by the Jacobites. William was forced to raise the siege and withdraw towards Waterford and England. He left Limerick to the combined Irish and French Jacobite army of 14,000 infantry and 2,500 cavalry under the command of General Boiseleau, the Duke of Berwick and other distinguished leaders, including the Earl of Tyrconnell who had established his vice-regal court here after the battle of the Boyne on 12 July 1690. The Earl of Tyrconnell and the French troops went to France after the siege, leaving Patrick Sarsfield in charge of the city until he returned, the following year, with the French commander, St. Ruth, but no French soldiery.

THE SECOND WILLIAMITE SIEGE started in August 1691. This time General

The Treaty Stone

Ginkel invested the city in William's name. After the disastrous battle of Aughrim, Limerick became the last major Jacobite stronghold to hold out against William. The siege became a protracted and sanguinary affair as French officers urged the Irish leaders to continue the struggle with promises of aid from Louis XIV. Thomond Bridge was the scene of one of the city's bloodiest encounters when 850 of its defenders were trapped outside the walls because the gates had been closed too quickly, 600 were slain, 150 were drowned and 100 were taken prisoner. When the Earl of Tyrconnell died Patrick Sarsfield had assumed control. After the slaughter on Thomond Bridge he sued for peace as the French reinforcements he had expected had failed to arrive. With a Scottish general named Wauchope he arranged an interview with General Ginkel to propose a three day cease fire prior to signing a treaty. That evening General Ginkel entertained Limerick's most prominent citizens to dinner and the following day both sides exchanged hostages.

THE TREATY OF LIMERICK was arranged after a long and angry debate to finalise the terms. Patrick Sarsfield, Lord Galmoyle, Colonel Nicholas Purcell, Colonel Nicholas Cusack, Sir Toby Butler, Colonel Garret Dillon and Colonel John Browne were chosen to act as commissioners for the Jacobites. General Ginkel acted as his own commissioner but called all of his officers above the grade of brigadier-general to his assistance. On 1 October 1691 the Lords-Justices, Coningsby and Porter, arrived. On 3 October 1691 this historic treaty was signed. Two days later French reinforcements arrived with fresh troops and 30,000 stands of arms. Patrick Sarsfield was urged to continue the war but he insisted on abiding by the terms of the treaty, a treaty which was ratified by William of Orange but later repudiated by the English Parliament.

THE IRISH JACOBITE SOLDIERS were allowed to march out of the city with full military honours. 19,000 of them embarked for France, to found the Irish Brigade, while 3,000 joined the Williamite army. Limerick became known as the "City of the Broken Treaty" because the terms of the treaty were repudiated almost as soon as the last shipload of Irish soldiers sailed away. *Remember Limerick* became the battle-cry of the Irish Brigade as they swept all before them on the battlefields of Europe. Patrick Sarsfield, the Earl of Lucan, was killed at the Battle of Landen in 1693, fighting for France. His last words are said to have been, "Would to God this was shed for Ireland".

THE WILD GEESE, a word that later became synonymous with mercenary, was coined by ships' captains to describe their illegal cargoes of young recruits travelling abroad to join the Irish Brigades of France and Spain. Between 1691 and the time of the French Revolution, over 100,000 Irishmen left their native country to serve in the armies of Europe.

AFTER THE SIEGE the entire city was a scene of desolation. The inhabitants had been compelled to quit their dwellings by the bombardment, only to return and find their effects destroyed. While everyone was engaged in repairing their losses, the poorer by erecting small huts under the walls, the richer by re-edifying their houses, and the soldiers by restoring and enlarging the fortifications, a new and unthought of casualty nearly involved the whole in a second destruction. One of the towers on the quay suddenly fell, and 250 barrels of gunpowder which it contained blew up with a tremendous explosion; 240 people were crushed to death or dreadfully maimed, some being struck dead by stones which fell a mile from the town.

THE GATES of the walled city starting with the Englishtown and travelling clockwise were Thomond Gate, Thomond Bridge Gate, Island Gate, St. Peter Cell Gate, Abbey North or Little Island Gate, Gaol Lane Gate, Fish Lane Gate, Baal's Bridge North Gate, Creagh Lane Gate, Bow Lane Gate, Castle Water Gate and New Gate. The gates of the Irishtown, starting at Baal's Bridge, were Baal's Bridge South Gate, East Water Gate, St. John's Gate, Mungret Gate and West Water Gate.

THE PENAL LAWS passed by William's Parliament ordered all Catholic clergy to depart from his kingdom by 1 May, 1698. They were forbidden to return and heavy penalties were introduced to prevent the populace from harbouring priests. After 29 December 1697 burials were forbidden in any suppressed monastery, abbey or convent not used for the Protestant liturgy. Catholics were barred from the legal profession as Catholic solicitors were considered "common disturbers" engaged in evading the law to secure the landed properties of their fellow-Catholics for their rightful owners rather than the Protestant usurpers. Protestant heiresses had to receive special permission to marry Catholics while Protestant men who married reputed Catholics without such permission were not allowed to act as guardians, executors, sit in the House of Commons or hold any civil or military office unless they could prove that they had converted their wives to Protestantism within a year of marriage. If the son of a Catholic became a Protestant, the father could not sell or mortgage his estate or dispose of any portion of it by will; nor could a Catholic father become his own child's guardian if that child, no matter how young, had become a Protestant. Catholics were rendered incapable of purchasing landed property, or rents, or profits arising out of land. They were not allowed to hold leases of more than thirty-one years. In such cases the reserved rent had to be one third of the improved annual value but any Protestant who discovered a flaw in the agreement became entitled to the lease. A Catholic was not allowed to inherit from a Protestant, and if he did not have a Protestant heir to inherit his lands they had to be divided equally amongst his sons. Catholics were also completely debarred from taking part in social or political life, while any defects in the administration of the law in favour of Catholics was usually rectified by new Acts. The Marquess of Winchester and the Earl of Galway visited the city on a tour of inspection as Lords Justices in 1698.

WILLIAM OF ORANGE never opposed the anti-Catholic laws introduced after the Treaty of Ryswick in 1697. With peace restored between England and France, William and his advisers revised the Treaty of Limerick to their own satisfaction. After William's death in 1702, Anne, the second daughter of James II, succeeded to the English throne. No Roman Catholic strangers were allowed to reside in the city or suburbs under an act passed in 1703. The same act stated that the Catholic inhabitants of the city would be expelled from it unless they gave sufficient securities for their allegiance. These restrictions were removed in 1724. During the Scottish rebellion in 1745 similar restrictions were used, but no symptom of disaffection was discovered. Later in the eighteenth century the Penal Code was relaxed. Catholics were allowed to possess property under favourable terms and invest in land. They were allowed to take fifty-year leases on bogland in 1771, and if the bog was too deep to sustain a house foundation they were allowed to take an acre of ground for this purpose, on condition that it should not be within a mile of any city or town. Catholics were allowed to inherit and take a 999-year lease of property under an act passed in 1778 which also repealed the earlier act giving the entire property of a Catholic to his eldest son in the event of the son becoming a Protestant. The 1778 Act also repealed another act under which Catholic priests and schoolmasters were liable to prosecution and transportation.

TOXETH ROCHE was the leader of the Orange faction who ruled Limerick City after 1691. This group was so corrupt that sixty years later Parliament declared them unfit to govern, and all of their illegal acts were declared void. George Roche may have been a relation of Toxeth's but this has never been proved. George became Mayor in 1702; his son, David, was Mayor in 1749; and his grandson, another David, married Frances Maunsell of Limerick.

THE GRANARY was built for "an enormous sum" after Philip John Roche purchased a site on the Mardyke in 1787. Philip was a mer-

the city or county of Limerick. Copies of all extant pre-twentieth century church records, Roman Catholic, Church of Ireland, Presbyterian, Methodist and Quaker, are housed here. Land surveys from about 1830 to 1850 are used to place families accurately in the townland they lived in, while the 1901 Census is available to check if any members of the family remained in the area.

at *Beall na Corrie* (Ballinacurra), a few thatched cabins, the prior's mill near the churchyard and a few gardens. Today only the graveyard remains. Once again it is an island, this time in a sea of tarmacadam, within the Charlotte Quay car-park. This is a small neat recently-renovated graveyard containing mainly late-eighteenth century and nineteenth century tombstones, many of which show

The Granary

chant prince, an adventurer, a major exporter of flax, cereals and seeds, and one of the most successful businessmen in the south of Ireland. He died in 1797 and was buried nearby in St. Michael's graveyard. His nephew, Thomas Kelly, rented the Granary to the customs authorities as a bonding warehouse for spirits, wines and tobaccos during the nineteenth century. The building remained in use as a bonding warehouse into the 1970s. In 1980 the Shannon Free Airport Development Company bought the Granary from Michael Harkin and developed it at a cost of £3,000,000. Its original structure was retained intact. A concrete-framed office wing, a hanging garden and a water-fountain were added, while the old edifice and the new were linked by a glass-enclosed service area which houses the main staircase. Within the old Granary two intermediate floors were removed and replaced with a single floor, the windows were renovated and the entire building was re-roofed. Today's Granary accommodates the Limerick City Library, Limerick Corporation's Planning and Personnel Departments, the Shannon Free Airport Development Company's Field Office, the Limerick City Tourist Information Office and several flourishing businesses and services.

THE MID-WEST ARCHIVES are located within the Granary. This office offers a comprehensive genealogical research service to people whose ancestors emigrated from either

THE MARDYKE took its name from a new quay Limerick Corporation developed in 1715. This includes the area known today as Charlotte Quay and Michael Street. Part of the old city wall can be seen on the Charlotte Quay car-park while a considerable amount of old foundations were revealed, but covered again, during excavations near the north-eastern corner. Ten feet below the surface was a large stone wheel with a toothed edge which was part of an apparatus for drawing up water containers, a twelve-foot length of wooden conduit or piping, old weapons and cannonballs. These finds confirmed that there was a well in use on this site in 1691 when the city was under siege. The well may have been closed because of seepage from St. Michael's graveyard, a short distance away.

ST. MICHAEL'S CHURCH has been attributed to the Vikings, but it is more likely to have been an Anglo-Norman foundation as the latter people had a great veneration for St. Michael. This church was positioned on a division of the Abbey River, and maps of a later period show its location outside the West Water Gate. Henry Ireton saw this old church in 1651 although other accounts claim it was in ruin by then and had been dismantled before the Cromwellian siege to prevent the soldiery using it as a base from which to attack the West Water Gate. By 1654 the church had disappeared as the *civil survey* mentioned only a ruined castle and mill seat

signs of repair. It is located on the western end of the car-park, near the Granary, and there are entrances to the east and west. Philip Roche was interred here but his memorial has disappeared, as have those of other prominent citizens of the past. The last burial took place here in 1945.

ST. MICHAEL'S CATHOLIC CHURCH in Denmark Street opened on 29 September 1781 although work on the building commenced in 1779. It was enlarged in 1805. This was a large edifice without any external ornament, with an adjoining house and garden for the clergymen. Daniel O'Connell held some of his rallies within this church and William Bardwell, the architect, designed a fifteenth-century-style wall memorial for St. Michael's in 1839. Edward Thomas O'Dwyer was the curate here in 1881. At a later stage in his career when he became Bishop of Limerick he denied responsibility for the demolition of the older St. Michael's which was replaced with the present structure in the early 1880s. This last building was designed by M. Morris who, because of restricted space, was forced to conceal its facade in a small yard off Denmark Street.

REV. EDWARD THOMAS O'DWYER was consecrated Bishop of Limerick on 29 June 1886. He once stood on Isaac Butt's platform when he sought election but on another occasion he told the Irish Party that their public policy was stupid while the Plan of Campaign was morally wrong. In 1915 he condemned English attempts to recruit Irishmen into the ranks during World War I. On 17 May 1916 he wrote to General J.G. Maxwell, Commander-in-Chief of the British Forces in Ireland who had asked him to remove two of his clergy, Fr. Tom Wall and Fr. Michael Hayes "to such employment as will prevent them having intercourse with the people", as General Maxwell considered them "a dangerous menace to the peace and safety of the realm". The Bishop replied that he did not "see in them any justification for disciplinary action" on his part as "they are both excellent priests, who hold strong national views, but I do not know they have violated any law, civil or ecclesiastical". He continued to castigate Maxwell for "altogether your regime has been one of the worst and blackest chapters in the history of the misgovernment of the country". He was a staunch nationalist although he disapproved of the Easter Rising; "Was I to condemn them! Even if their rebellion was not justifiable theologically ... in my humble judgement there is deep down in the heart of Ireland the sacred fire of nationality." Edward Thomas O'Dwyer never bowed to public opinion. On 19 August, 1917, he died at home after returning from his summer holidays in Kilkee. He was seventy-five years old.

THE CITADEL was the Irishtown's main fortification. It was not shown on the 1590 map of the city in the Hardiman Collection, Trinity College, Dublin, but can be dated to either the early or middle years of the seventeenth century. In 1690 it was the scene of a heroic Jacobite defence, the Battle of the Breach, which was fought nearby on the site of the Devil's Battery or the Black Battery. The gate-building, or sallyport, of the original stronghold has been incorporated into the structure of St. John's Hospital, as have parts of the old city walls. Other parts of the city walls and some remains of the famous battery can still be seen within the hospital grounds. The Citadel remained in use as a military barracks until 1752. St. John's Gate was located on the main roadway, nearby, but no trace of it now remains.

ST. JOHN'S HOSPITAL, or the Fever Hospital of St. John's, was originally known as the Fever and Lock Hospital, John Street. In 1781 Lady Hartstonge obtained the use of the old St. John's Barracks. She set up two or three beds, and the hospital developed from this meagre beginning. The old buildings were demolished in 1787 and a new structure, from which the present building evolved, was built on the site. This was the first fever hospital, founded as such, in the British Empire.

THE ARTILLERY BARRACKS in the Irishtown was adapted for 6 officers, 194 men, and 104 horses with an hospital for 35 patients in 1837.

ST. JOHN'S CHURCH OF IRELAND CHURCH stands on the site of an earlier one dating from about 1200. Thomas Dineley sketched the older building in 1680. A Latin-inscribed plaque in the churchyard wall makes only a passing reference to the damage caused by the Williamite sieges as it reads in translation; "John Foorde being Mayor and promoter of this work the parishioners of St. John of the Holy Cross after the havoc of the war procured the building of these walls of the cemetery at their own expense AD 1693. John Paterson, vicar; Edward Uncles and Robert Kemp, churchwardens; and John Barry, Sculptor." In 1843 John Norris Russell laid the foundation stone of the present building during his term of office as Sheriff. This was designed in the popular round-arched Anglo-Norman style church architecture of the period by Joseph Welland (1798-1860). The church fell into disuse but in recent times both church and churchyard were renovated. A folk tale of the area claims that Brian Merriman may have been buried here but this story has been discounted by Limerick historians.

ST. JOHN'S SQUARE is a three-sided "square" facing St. John's churchyard. It dates back to 1751 and, prior to the formation of Newtownpery, was one of the city's earliest Georgian developments. John Purdon of Tinerana may have been the entrepreneur who thought up St. John's Square, but Davis Ducart is generally believed to have been its architect. The houses were sold for £630 each, and proved to be a popular investment with county families such as the Perys, Vere Hunts and Monsells who purchased townhouses here in which they could while away the winter months. The square was restored in the 1970s. Two of the restored houses now contain the Limerick Museum, founded in 1916, which was transferred here in 1979.

LIMERICK MUSEUM came into existence almost accidentally. In 1906, Limerick's Carnegie library was opened, and, after a short time, the maximum library rate allowed, 2/5 of a new penny in the pound, was found inadequate to run it. To provide further library funds, the Museum Acts were adopted by the local authority, and an additional 1/5 new penny in the pound was levied on the rates. It was not until 1916 that the museum opened to the public. Successive librarians acted as

St Michael's graveyard

St John's Square.

curators, and had differing levels of interest in the museum. One Robert Herbert, (1939-1957) had both the knowledge and the interest to develop the collections, but at no time were adequate records of accessions kept, or the collection properly indexed. The city library lacked a reference section, so, in 1974, the museum was dismantled to provide the space. Partly as a result of pressure from local historical and archaeological societies, the position of part-time temporary curator was advertised in 1977. This became wholetime later that year, and permanent and pensionable from 1982. The present premises at St John's Square, always regarded as temporary, was partially opened in 1979, and fully in 1980. It consists of the ground floors and basements of two interconnecting houses. New civic offices for the city local authority are at present under construction at Merchant's Quay, on the site of the old city jail. The museum will be incorporated in the new building behind a retained facade of the prison. The building is due for completion by April, 1990, and the museum should re-open there in 1990. The museum is a general local history museum, aiming to collect and display objects relating to all aspects of the past of Limerick city and surrounding areas. It does not collect works of art or archives, these being catered for by the City Gallery of Art and the Regional Archive.

THE CHURCH OF IRELAND RECTORY, number three, is easily identified because of its elaborate doorway, with composite pillars and a fanlight, which was mod-

elled on those doorways favoured by the builders of Newtownpery. Canon Frederick Langbridge (1849-1922), novelist, poet, dramatist and rector of St. John's Parish lived here.

ST. JOHN'S CATHEDRAL was a commodious edifice built in the form of a cross and completed in 1753. Between 1856 and 1861 a new Gothic-Revival-style church was erected to replace the old eighteenth-century one. Philip Charles Hardwick (1820-1890) was the architect responsible for this edifice. The design of the tower with its 280-foot high spire, however, was the work of two Limerick men, Maurice and S. Hennessy. The cathedral was not considered complete until a large richly-gilded cross was placed on its apex stone on 4 August 1883, and the building was consecrated by Cardinal Logue in July 1894.

THE O'DEA MITRE AND CROZIER were once considered the cathedral's greatest treasures but they have not been placed on public display in recent years. They were made by Thomas O'Carryd in 1418 for Bishop Cornelius O Dea, Bishop of Limerick.

THE ARTHUR CRUCIFIX was made to house a fragment of the true cross for Bishop Arthur in 1625. The maker, Phi Lyles (possibly Philip Leyles or Lawless) seems to have had an earlier cross of about 1400 from which the figured plating on the stem was derived. Laurence Walsh wrote that "the front of the cross bears repeated scenes of the Nativity and the Flight into Egypt, in Gothic style, out of keeping with a 1625 date. The technique of manufacture appears superficially to be

repoussè on thin plates which would be fixed to a wooden core, but the cross is actually formed of thick cast plates held by screws. The scenes on the cross are obscured by the seventeenth-century settings of the relic, in the form of a cross above, the figure of Christ, the skull and crossbones and the jewels. The settings of the jewels on the pedestal are identical to some of those on the O'Dea mitre, and could be products of the same workshop. The central setting of the pedestal front bears the Arms of France, ancient, which dates from the fourteenth or early fifteenth century. The craftsman appears to have had an early cross from which he made a mould, and re-used the jewel settings from it". The Arthur Cross and the Arthur Cup are no longer kept in the Cathedral, for security reasons.

THE VIRGIN AND CHILD STATUE was designed by Benzoni. The cathedral's stained-glass windows were installed in the apse by Dr. Butler, the Bishop of Limerick, in 1867; and in the transepts by Thomas and Harriet O'Brien of South Hill, in 1881, to commemorate "their dear friend, Dr. George Butler".

PATRICK SARSFIELD (1644-1693), the product of a French military academy, commanded by virtue of his bloodline rather than his considerable ability as a soldier. Yann Philippe Mac Bradai explained to me how Patrick Sarsfield, Lord Lucan, was descended from the royal houses of both Ireland and England. Through Lady Margaret Butler, the grandmother of Rory O Moore (1641), he was related to the Boleyns and the Ormondes and was a cousin of Black Thomas Butler — the man Queen Elizabeth I called "My black husband", and by whom she was nebulously believed to have had an illegitimate son. Diana Spencer, the wife of England's Crown Prince, Charles, is a descendant of Patrick Sarsfield's brother, William. Sarah Ferguson, the wife of Prince Andrew, is a descendant of William Sarsfield's in-laws, the Monmouths. Both ladies are descended, illegitimately, from the House of Stuart. Patrick Sarsfield, like many other men of his time, was a Catholic in Ireland and a Protestant in England. He had a distinguished military career in England, Ireland and France. Today he is commemorated with a statue designed by John Lawlor of Dublin; cast in Young's London Art Foundry; and placed in the garden of St. John's presbytery since 1881.

THE CATHEDRAL FOUNTAIN was erected in Cathedral Square by the Pery and Jubilee Committee in 1865. Iron goblets were attached to two of its spouts to provide on-the-spot drinking facilities for the public at large and help them to fill small containers easily; while larger vessels were filled at the other two spouts.

THE OLD DISPENSARY, in Lower Gerald Griffin Street, has been repaired and restored by the Jehovah's Witnesses who now use it as a Kingdom Hall for their local congregation. This large red-brick building is similar in design to other such structures erected in the late-nineteenth century.

THE JEHOVAH'S WITNESSES had a turbulent history in Ireland throughout the 1940s and 1950s. In 1956 Stephen Miller and another Witness were attacked by a group of people, led by a priest, near Clonlara, County Clare. The two were beaten and their literature burned. When the case came to court their nine attackers were exonerated, and Stephen Miller and his companion were bound over to keep the peace on sureties of £200 each. Later in the same year a Limerick newspaper appealed to its readership to have nothing to do with the Witnesses or "their propaganda and to refuse firmly to enter into any discussions with them. Any copies of their publications which readers may have acquired should be destroyed immediately. So strongly does the church wish us to shun their evil doctrines that any Catholic who reads publications of the Society leaves himself open to excommunication". In 1966 there were 268 Witnesses in the Republic and 474 in Northern Ireland. This total of 742 in 1966 had risen to 2,021 Witnesses by 1982. By May 1987 there were 2,661 Jehovah's Witnesses in Ireland.

CHARLES ETIENNE COQUEBERT DE MONTBRET enjoyed his visit to Limerick in 1790, particularly the fresh salmon which fetched from 2½ new pence to 5 new pence a pound during the winter, but could be purchased for less than 1 new penny in the summer. Fish was procured from the Shannon by the inhabitants of West Clare and North Kerry who fished in, and off, the mouth of the river, and by the native fisherfolk of the city who fished for trout, eels, perch and pike. The Corporation leased a salmon fishery while, farther down-river, all kinds of shell and flat fish were caught along the neighbouring coasts. In May of each year numerous temporary causeways were formed several yards into the river on each side, by the poor, on which they fished with nets for eel fry; the quantities taken were so great that each individual filled a couple of washing tubs with them at every tide. The Corporation still claimed an exclusive right to all fishing from the city to Scattery Island. Limerick remained prone to flooding, and storms accompanied by high tides did great damage in 1698 and 1751. Charles Etienne enjoyed his visit here although he recorded that the city's upper class "eat and drink too much, wasting their time". He found the company convivial; claimed he had never met so many men of learning in such a short period; and was delighted to discover so many of them spoke French. While staying here he often visited Ralph Ousley's house where a collection of newspapers from all over the world, and a wide range of archaeological artifacts were stored.

THE PALMERSTOWN BREWERY was located in an area enclosed by Mungret Street, Palmerstown, Old Francis Street and Benson's Lane. After its demolition the site became a scrap-yard until the Sean Heuston housing scheme was built there. St. Mary's Park was used for the re-housing of people from the area uprooted during the slum clearances of the 1930s. Part of the old Palmerstown Brewery site was later occupied by Newsom's Ltd., St. John's Brewery was located where St. John's Girls' School now stands while Miss Tucker's Brewery was situated in a building behind No. 5 North St. John's Square. In 1820 there were twenty tanneries and one pawnbroker in the city but by 1865 there were only two tanneries, over twenty pawnbrokers, and three breweries.

CHALK SUNDAY took its name from an old custom, no longer practised, of children putting chalk marks on the backs of bachelors who were unwed by the first Sunday in Lent. Clampett's Bow, a narrow laneway off John Street, was the scene of a minor siege on Chalk Sunday night, 2 March, 1879 when John Moran, his two daughters, and a man named Halloran resisted constabulary attempts to arrest them for an assault which was sparked off by a chalking incident.

CLAY PIPES were manufactured in Merrit's factory in Broad Street which employed over twenty Merrit relations in the process. Clay for the pipes was imported twice a year, in fifty-ton cargoes, from Liverpool.

THE LANE NAMES of the Irishtown are all but forgotten as so many of these old thoroughfares have disappeared over the years with their histories unrecorded. The following list includes only their names, not their locations: Scabby Lane, Mass Lane, Scott's Lane, Bushy Lane, Goat's Lane, William's Lane, Ball Alley Lane, Monaghan Lane, Father Quin Lane, Sheehy Lane, Garvey's Lane, Black Bull Lane, Town Wall Lane, Jones's Lane, Magdalen Lane, Moloney Lane, Curry Lane, Barrack Lane, Hatter's Lane, Pencil's Alley, Purcell's Lane, Joshua's Lane, Moore's Lane, Repeal Alley, Forker's Lane and White Wine Lane.

THE FORTIFICATIONS were restored after the siege of 1691. For over sixty years afterwards the walls, defensive structures and gate-towers were kept in complete repair. A garrison and several companies of city militia maintained a strong army presence and every precaution of an important military station was observed. In 1760, Limerick was declared to be no longer a fortress, and the dismantling of its walls and other defences was immediately commenced and completed by slow degrees, as the extension of the various improvements rendered it necessary.

SOURCES

9 39 44 47 56 63 64 65 72
75 80 84 85 99 103 104 110 116
119 120 123 127 129 130 131 136 150
170 173 176 178 204 211 222 227 244
246 250 256 263 264 271 274 279

Overleaf: Aerial view of Newtownpery.

Newtownpery

and the South Liberties

NEWTOWNPERY was developed by Edmond Sexton Pery and the independent citizens of the city in an attempt to break the strangle-hold the Roche-Vereker-Smyth-Prendergast clique had acquired over the old municipality. The developers of the new town, called after Edmond Pery the principal landowner, moved their businesses, services and residences outside the old municipal boundaries, where the corrupt clique were unable to operate. Two of the major factors that contributed to the growth of the new town were legislation enacted in 1759 lowering the rateable valuation on land outside the city walls, and secondly the way in which the citizens of Newtownpery manipulated St. Michael's Vestry in order to circumvent the jurisdiction of the Corporation. The new town expanded rapidly. George's Quay was built in 1763. This was followed by the erection of the South Mall (now Charlotte's Quay) in 1766 and Sir Harry's Mall in 1767. The Custom House was erected in 1769 and the Assembly House went up in 1770. All of this earlier development took place on the fringe of the Pery properties, but as Newtownpery expanded new brick residences and shops radically changed the appearance of the city to an extent only equalled by Dublin during the eighteenth century.

The aerial photographs in this book illustrate how neatly the broad straight streets cut across one another to form spacious blocks. From the air one can see noticeable differences in the street-scapes of the older and newer parts of the city.

EDMOND SEXTON PERY spearheaded the Newtownpery development, the main growth of which was over his own land, when the city walls were demolished. He was a clear-sighted city planner, an astute businessman, and pioneered the Georgian architecture of which Limerick can be so proud. In 1768 he was Speaker in the Irish House of Commons but was raised to the peerage as Viscount Pery, Earl of Limerick, in 1786. His grandfather, Colonel Edward Pery, married Dympna, the daughter of Bartholomew Stacpoole who was a merchant, and recorder, of Limerick in 1651 when he signed the capitulation of the city to Cromwell's forces.

DAVIS DUCART was born Daviso de Arcort, in Sardinia. He was both an engineer and an architect and is believed to have worked on the Newry-Lough Neagh canal (1730-1741). His exact role in the formation of Newtownpery has never been clearly defined, but, with Edmond Sexton Pery, he is generally credited as co-founder of Limerick's Georgian heritage. Newspaper advertising of 1769 extolling the virtues of Newtownpery could almost have been written by an auctioneer of today. "An extensive view up and down the river, commanding a full prospect of many agreeable objects ... the county Clare mountains ... spacious basin ... shipping ... several Quays and the Pool ... in short the most elegant town residence in the Kingdom, or perhaps in the World, cannot boast such rural beauty or so fine a landscape, and the Variety is daily increasing". The once-fashionable districts of St. John's Square, Mungret Street and Quay Lane were gradually deserted by their former occupants. These people moved on to the elevated ground parallel to the river, which was once known as the South Prior's Land before it became the property of the Pery family. It later became known as Newtownpery.

THE CUSTOM HOUSE is an elegant, Palladian-style building designed by Davis Ducart and finished under the superintendence of Christopher Colles in 1769 at a cost of £8,000. It consists of a hewn-stone centre with two wings facing a small quay-side park where the Abbey River rejoins the Shannon, and replaced an older structure on Merchant's Quay which was described as a plain brick building supported with four rusticated pillars. The customs' duties in 1633 came to a total of £1.619.07 so Limerick could afford to build an imposing custom house from an early period. Such a building could also become a "legitimate target" in wartime. On 3 April, 1920, a group of I.R.A. men under the command of Joe O'Brien set fires in the Custom House in an attempt to set it ablaze. After they left the premises, civilian and military fire brigades extinguished the flames. The building was located here because of its accessibility to the quays, particularly Merchant's Quay and the city's famous Long Dock.

SARSFIELD HOUSE is built on the site of Reuben Harvey's carrier-pigeon terminus. Reuben, the son of Joseph Massey Harvey of Cork, used the birds to communicate between Plassey and his stores and granary in Francis Street. Carrier-pigeons were also used by other merchants in the city to keep themselves informed of whatever ships and cargoes were approaching Limerick along the Shannon, or from outside ports. Reuben Harvey refused to meet his workers' demands for payment, for time spent travelling from the canal harbour to the mill in his barges, and became one of the earliest city employers to face strike action. The dispute was never resolved and eventually led to the closure of his works. The income tax offices were originally located in the centre of O'Connell Street where they were raided by the I.R.A. on the night of 3 April, 1920 under the command of Davy Dundon. Staff were held up, offices ransacked, and mail was taken away for assessment by I.R.A. intelligence officers. The income tax authorities are now based in Sarsfield House.

ROCHE'S STORES was founded by Philip Roche in 1787. As a Catholic he was not permitted to buy land, but by purchasing the ground he required in the name of his friend and kinsman, Dr. Pery, the Church of Ireland Bishop of Limerick, he acquired the sites on which he built his stores, a range of houses on the south side of Rutland Street, and another range of houses on the south side of Patrick Street. His religion was no bar to commercial success. He carried on an enormous trade with Holland in rape seed, flax and other materials and was a major supplier of government provisions until his death in 1797.

WILLIAM ROCHE'S HANGING GARDENS were one of the wonders of Limerick in the early 1800s after William Roche erected a series of store-houses behind his house in

The Custom House

George's Street for £15,000 in 1808. The gardens were located over the vaulted storehouses, which were protected from the damp by flags cemented together, with channels of lead to draw the moisture away through tubes of the same metal concealed in the arches. The facade of these elevated terraced gardens, the highest of which was 70 feet above the street, was about 200 feet in length. The top terrace contained hot-houses in which grapes, pineapples, peaches and oranges were grown; vegetables and hardy fruit trees were produced on the middle terrace; while the lower terrace was turned over to flowers of every form, scent and hue. The government of the day leased the store-houses from William at a fine of £10,000 and at an annual rent of £300 in 1826, a rent which had increased to £500 per annum in 1837. The gardens extended from what is now No. 99 O'Connell Street as far as Henry Street.

THE TOWN HALL was originally known as the Commercial Buildings, and was erected for £8,000 in 1806. This edifice was owned by one hundred shareholders and consisted of a large and well-supplied newsroom on the ground floor, above which was a library and apartments which were used by the Chamber of Commerce after its incorporation in 1815. According to Brendan Woods, the current manager of Limerick Chamber of Commerce, his society let this building to Limerick Corporation in 1846, after they had moved to their present premises in O'Connell Street.

THE LIMERICK CHAMBER OF COMMERCE was incorporated by Royal Charter in 1815 to protect the city's trade and control the pilotage of the Shannon River. Their funds were financed with fees paid by their members on the import and export of goods, while surplus money was used to promote Limerick's commercial interests, develop markets, aid manufacturers, improve navigation, maintain buoys to warn shipping of rocks, and pay for salvage services. Under an act passed in 1834 the President of the Chamber of Commerce, the Mayor, and a Commissioner of St. Michael's Parish were appointed as Limerick Bridge Commissioners. In January 1983 the Chamber of Commerce minute books were transferred into the care of Dr. O'Mahony of the Mid West Archives.

THE LIMERICK SAVINGS BANK, "The Stone Jug", is a Doric-temple-style building with four fluted columns, designed by W.H. Owen soon after the Earl of Limerick leased land in Upper Glentworth Street to the bank in 1839. This was one of several banks established in the city in the opening decades of the nineteenth century. It was founded in 1820 to encourage and facilitate savings by the less affluent members of society, and in the year ending 25 December, 1823, a total of £17,000 was lodged.

MAUNSELL'S BANK was founded by Robert Maunsell (1745-1832), his brother Thomas, and Sir Matthew Blackstone in 1789. Robert was born in Limerick and reared in India where he joined the Indian Civil Service. He became Chief of the Council of Gangham and Member of the Supreme Council of Madras before he retired to Limerick where he established the banking firm of Maunsell and Company. When the bank, in Bank Place, failed in 1820, Robert had already withdrawn from it, with the fortune he had made in India still intact.

FURNELL'S LIMERICK BANK was located in a building close to the corner of O'Connell Street and William Street. It was founded by Michael "The Banker" Furnell in 1804 but failed a few years later. Michael was a descendant of Thomas Furnell who arrived into the county during the Confederate wars of the 1640s and established the Furnell name in Ballyclough and Cahirelly. George Evans Bruce founded another bank, Bruce's Bank, at No. 6, Rutland Street in 1806, which also failed, and closed, in 1820.

THE ROYAL MAIL COACH HOTEL, the Bianconi Coach Station or Cruises Hotel, was established in 1791 to cater for the expanding stage coach services of the day. In 1828 Prince Herman Ludwig Heinrich von Puckler-Muskav stayed here during his memorable trip to Limerick — in which he was mistaken for an illegitimate son of Napoleon Bonaparte. William Thackeray was a guest here in 1842. He described George's Street as a handsome one "with plenty of idlers, you may be sure, lolling in the portico; likewise you see numerous young officers, with very tight waists and absurd brass shell-epaulettes to their absurd little frock coats, walking the pavement — the dandies of the street .. the houses are bright red — the street is full and gay, carriages and cars in plenty go jingling by — dragoons in red are every now and then clattering up the street, and upon every car which passes with ladies in it you are sure (I don't know how it is) to see a pretty one ... After you get out of the Main Street the handsome part of the town is at an end, and you suddenly find yourself in such a labyrinth of busy swarming poverty and squalid commerce as never was seen — no not in St. Giles's where Jew and Irishman side by side exhibit their genius for dirt. Here every house almost was half a ruin and swarming with people ..." An old picture of Cruise's Hotel shows a four-horse coach — with roof passengers and postillions, outside the main entrance to the hotel, beside which an archway leading into the coaching yard could also be seen. In more recent times Sean Bourke, the man responsible for the "springing" of George Blake from an English prison, was a regular customer in the hotel's Round Bar. Sean died while on holiday in Kilkee, the manuscript he was working on at the time of his death has never been found.

THE STAGE COACH appears to have operated as a summer-only service between Dublin and Limerick from 1751 to 1756. It left the Hog in Armour Inn, James Street, Dublin at 7.00 a.m. on Mondays and returned on Saturdays. From 1772 onwards the stage departed from Francis Jenkinson's, 7 Bolton Street, Dublin on Thursdays and from

Limerick on Mondays. Francis Jenkinson referred to his coach transport as the Limerick Stage Coach from 1783 onwards but reduced his trips to once weekly in each direction from 1787. His vehicle was described as an elegant post coach capable of carrying four inside and two outside passengers in 1794.

THE LIMERICK-DUBLIN MAIL COACH went into competition with the Limerick Stage Coach in 1794. Between then and 1806 the mail coach operated six days of the week while its rival did the same journey only three times a week. After 1806, Sundays excepted, the service became a daily one. The two day Dublin Stage Coach was inaugurated in 1815, while a "Caravan for Passengers" ran between the two cities in 1824 covering the entire journey in 30 hours. Tierney's caravan had a terminus at Patrick Coleman's, Francis Street, and another caravan operated from Limerick's Mail Coach Office in George's Street. Both caravans had offices in Ennis, the former in Chapel Lane, the latter in Church Street.

STAGE WAGGONS owned by Andrew Buchanan of Limerick competed for business with those of Foster and Osborne of Dublin in 1784. These waggons were used for transporting second-class passengers such as poorer merchants, traders and craftsmen. Foster and Osborne went into partnership with Benjamin Meredith of Limerick but by the end of 1784 the three had closed down, leaving the market to Andrew Buchanan. During the mid 1830s the competing mail and stage coaches were able to complete the journey between Limerick and Dublin in about fourteen hours. By 1849 the railroad had arrived and the trip could be done in seven hours and twenty minutes.

THE ENNIS FLY COACH was first linked to Dublin through the Galway-Dublin route rather than through Limerick. The Limerick-Ennis stage coach operated from 1809 while William Bourne's Limerick-Ennis mail coach service commended officially on 5 July 1815 although it was listed in *Watson's Almanack* in 1813. This became part of the Bianconi network when the Bianconi coaches spread throughout Munster and most of Ireland in the 1820s, 1830s and 1840s. By then Limerick was connected with Cork (from 1815), Waterford (from 1819) and all the major towns and cities. Charles Bianconi operated the Limerick-Tralee run by stage coach until 1853; and by mail car until 1866.

CHARLES BIANCONI (1786-1875) was born in Northern Italy and apprenticed to a print-maker who took him to Dublin. When his apprenticeship ended in 1804 he continued his education through the offices of two friends, Fr. Theobald Mathew and Edmond Ignatius Rice. In 1809 he opened a shop in Clonmel selling prints and mirrors before he started speculating in gold, reselling guineas purchased from the peasantry to the government. He ran his first jaunting car from Clonmel to Cahir in 1815 and by the end of that year had linked Clonmel to Limerick. By 1834 he had acquired the Limerick-Galway mail coach and several other Limerick-linked enterprises such as the Limerick-Killarney car (1839-1853), the Limerick-Tipperary car (1851-1861), the Limerick-Ennis mail car (1852-1865), the Limerick-Ennis day car (1854-1865) and the Limerick-Tralee car which was established in the 1830s. In later years he purchased shares in the railway companies with whom he refused to compete. Instead he used his coaches to connect with the rail services until an accident in 1865 persuaded him to retire. On doing so he sold off his interests, mainly to his former employees, on generous terms.

THE ROYAL GEORGE HOTEL was once visited by Queen Victoria. Rev. Robert Wyse Jackson, former Church of Ireland Bishop of Limerick wrote, in 1973, that "in its original form it fitted handsomely into the Georgian facade of O'Connell Street. The last function before it was demolished and rebuilt was one which I organised for the Archbishop of Canterbury, Dr. Ramsey, when he came to Limerick to dedicate a window in St. Mary's Cathedral to the memory of his kinsman, Major Stafford O'Brien of Cratloe".

THE LIMERICK CHAMBER OF COMMERCE PREMISES was surveyed by the Irish Architectural Archive in 1984. Located at 96 O'Connell Street, this terraced house, comprising four storeys over a basement, dates from around 1800. The interior has been restored and renewed rather than renovated as many of the original internal features, woodwork, and plasterwork, were intact. About 1875 the front facade was re-faced in a plaster of lime and fine sand (stucco), the cast-iron balcony was inserted at first-floor level, the gate piers and cast-iron railings were built over the basement area and the door screen was moved forward towards the front door to form an inside porch when the building was re-modelled. The main reception rooms were, and still are, on the first floor. They are connected by the original pair of panelled doors, cleverly designed to slide laterally on castors into wall cavities on either side, creating a spacious opening between both rooms. The front room was originally the principal drawing room and contains a white statuary marble chimney piece, french-style casement windows, a distinctive plaster ceiling and two oil paintings, one of Sir Alexander Shaw (President of the Limerick Chamber of Commerce 1899-1905) and another of Lord Monteagle (Member of Parliament for Limerick 1820-1832). The first floor rear room contains its original tripartite Wyatt window and a fine Irish breakfront bookcase of mahogany dating from circa 1830. The rear facade is virtually unaltered except for the addition of a ground-floor wing containing service rooms and toilets. The former coach-house has been modified to provide vehicular access to parking in the former garden which is now metalled over. A dovecot on the wall facing the rear of the house has been retained. The Limerick Chamber of Commerce have occupied this building since they left their former premises in Rutland Street almost a century and a half ago. The organisation's proudest possession is a painting *The Chairing of Thomas Spring Rice* (in 1820) which was executed in oils by William Turner of London. William Turner painted in the Clare, Limerick and Dublin areas and signed many of his pictures under the name of W. Turner *De Lond*. Brian O'Dàlaigh did not know whether Turner used the pseudonym *De Lond* to confuse himself with, or distinguish himself from, the great English landscape painter Joseph Mallord William Turner, R.A.. This picture was last restored by James Gorry in 1945 but it is now stored away until further restoration work can be carried out in the near future.

THE AUGUSTINIAN CHURCH is built on the site of an old theatre which the Augustinian Prior purchased for £400 in 1822 — although the Limerick Theatre building had originally cost the public £5,000 to construct. After purchasing it the Augustinians spent £600 on improving it and the original structure remained in use as a church until 1939. The foundation stone of the present church was laid in March, 1939. Designed and built by two Dublin firms, respectively Messrs. Jones and Kelly and Messrs. George Walsh and Sons, the Augustinian church cost £42,000 to erect, can hold a congregation of 2,000 and was opened on 20 December, 1942. An inscribed stone on its facade draws attention to an adjoining stone, part of a lintel taken from a chapel the Augustinians had founded in Fish Lane in 1633. In 1778 the Augustinians erected a neat chapel in Creagh Lane where they stayed until 1823.

THE UNITED LONDON GAS COMPANY contracted to light the city with gas in 1824. The original engagement was confined to Newtownpery but the Corporation had the gas extended to the Irishtown, Dublin Road and parts of the Englishtown. Public lighting was not new to Limerick, however, as Alderman Thomas Rose erected the first street lamps in 1696.

Early twentieth century George's Street.

A WATER-WORKS to supply Limerick was commenced in 1834 by a London company who placed two tanks, about a mile from the city, at Cromwell's Fort, near Gallows Green, one of the forts erected on the high ground of Singland Hill during the Cromwellian siege. The second fort, Ireton's Fort, was constructed to the east, above the Penny Well. The tanks' elevation was 50 feet above the highest part of the city, and 72 feet above the river, from which the water was raised through a metal pipe 12 inches in diameter by two steam-engines, each of twenty horse-power. During the process of excavating a foundation for the tanks, several skeletons, cannon, musket balls, armour and a selection of old military weapons were found. The water-works near Cromwell's Fort was later known as the Garryowen Reservoir.

THE DANIEL O'CONNELL STATUE was erected in the Crescent during Dr. Thomas Kane's second term of office, as Mayor, in 1857. Originally £1040 had been subscribed to erect a statue of Lord Fitzgibbon on this site, but when five members of the Corporation objected, the idea was abandoned and the O'Connell Monument, sculpted by John Hogan, was placed on its present site at a total cost of £1,300. Daniel O'Connell (1775-1847), known as the Liberator, or the King of the Beggars, is generally credited with achieving religious freedom for the Catholic majority.

THE CATHOLIC EMANCIPATION ACT was passed in 1829. This was celebrated with a procession through the city on 5 July, 1830, in which every sector of the community took part, regardless of class or creed. For the first time since the Jacobite forces left Limerick in 1691 Catholic clergy appeared on the streets wearing surplices, soutanes, stoles and birettas. The participants assembled at the Exchange where the various bodies were marshalled into order, and marched through the main streets to a second assembly point, at Bank Place, where the town clerk read out the proclamation. The military led the parade, followed by the members of the Corporation, the Freemasons' Lodges, the Chamber of Commerce and both Protestant and Catholic clergymen.

CRESCENT HOUSE was purchased from Richard Russell by the Jesuits who also acquired the adjoining houses in order to erect a new church dedicated to St. Aloysius on the site.

THE JESUIT CHURCH was dedicated to the Sacred Heart rather than to St. Aloysius on 27 January, 1869. The original plans may have been drafted by Charles Geoghegan, according to Charlotte Murphy, who credits William Corbett with the overall design of the church completed in 1868. The present facade dates from 1900.

HOBSON'S CHOICE is a phrase that found a second home in the city of Limerick. Timothy O'Brien of the Crescent was a large landowner with extensive properties in Limerick, Clare and Tipperary. He had two beautiful daughters, Emma and Mary Jane, both of whom were courted by a young man called Hobson who was unable to decide on which sister to marry. He eventually married Emma. Both sisters died in 1907.

ST. JOSEPH'S CHURCH was designed by William Corbett, built by J.J. Ryan and Sons, and opened on 24 April, 1904. This church's greatest treasure is a chalice used by Cardinal

Present day O'Connell Street.

Rinuccini when he celebrated the victory of Benburb (1646) in St. Mary's Cathedral.

THE BELLTABLE ARTS CENTRE is located in a building now owned by the Arch Confraternity Credit Union who accept only a nominal rent from their tenants. The Gough family were the original owners during the last century. When one of the Gough daughters demonstrated that she might have enough talent for a career as an opera singer, her indulgent father, a prominent building contractor, had the Belltable erected in the garden. The acoustics were, and still are, excellent. It was known as the Coliseum Cinema from the silent-film era until its closure in the early 1950s. On occasion its patrons amused themselves by tossing *crubeens* (pigs' toes or trotters) from the balcony into the stalls. This former opera-house cum-cinema was opened as the Belltable Arts Centre on 21 April 1981. Its small theatre is known as Peter's Cell, after an older theatre of the same name. [cf. Peter's Cell].

WILLIAM TODD AND CO. occupied about four-fifths of a large city block fronting O'Connell Street with William Street to the north and Thomas Street to the south. On Tuesday, 25 August, 1959, at 11.00 a.m. a fire was first noticed in the Todds building. The building was in flames within the hour. By 12.30 the block was a blazing inferno and, at 1.00 p.m., the army was called in to cordon off the area and assist the firemen. The Limerick Fire Brigade brought the fire under control with the help of the E.S.B. Fire Service, the Ranks Auxiliary Fire Service and outside fire brigades from Ennis, Shannon, Ardnacrusha, Charleville, Rathkeale, Tipperary, Cork and Fermoy. This was the biggest fire disaster in the city since the eight-acre site of MacMahon's timber yard was destroyed by flames in 1906. Todds, Burtons, Liptons, Goodwins and Cesars were completely gutted; Gaywear, Cromer's and Nicholas's were badly damaged; and Michael Gleeson's licensed premises and Jack Flanagan's were badly affected when Todd's collapsed across Little William Street.

SARSFIELD BRIDGE was originally known as the Wellesley Bridge. The overall design was based on that of the Pont Neuilly in Paris, by its architect, Alexander Nimmo.

The foundation stone was laid on 2 October 1824 and the work was completed, at a cost of £89,000, when it was officially opened by the Lord Lieutenant of Ireland on 5 August, 1835. The expansion of Limerick, stemming from the Newtownpery development of the 1760s, had extended mainly to the west and downriver, so a bridge had to be constructed before further growth could take place. John Grantham surveyed the Shannon for the city fathers who eventually decided on a suitable site; "Said bridge shall be built over the said river, adjoining or near to the end of Brunswick Street in the parish of Saint Michael in the suburbs of the said city, to the north strand on the opposite side of the said river". The bridge consists of five large and elegant elliptic arches crossing the Shannon from Newtownpery to the northern, or county Clare, shore. The structure is basically unchanged since 1837 when the roadway was described as level with a parapet formed of a massive open balustrade. The swivel bridge on the city side is no longer functional but some of its heavy machinery is still intact underneath the roadway. This bridge could once swing aside to allow vessels through the lock, on their way to, or from, the upper basin and quays. Sarsfield Bridge was the main bridge into Limerick, from Clare, for over a century and a half.

THE POOR MAN'S KILKEE is the name bestowed on the small jetty-cum-park extending from Harvey's Quay into the Shannon. This was once part of the swivel bridge lock but is now used by the general public as a recreation area. Kilkee, on the west coast of Clare, was a popular vacation centre for the citizens of Limerick from the early nineteenth century onwards, those who were unable to afford a seaside holiday had to be satisfied with the city's parks and public places. The man-made island on which the boating clubs are located was constructed as a buttress to support the outer wall of the lock. Michael Clarke explained how a weir extended from this lock wall to the Clare side of the

Shannon, parallel with the bridge, to retain water of a certain level within the basin. The demolition of this old weir, and construction of car parks on the old quays, deprived the city of what had been one of its greatest assets.

THE WAR OF INDEPENDENCE MEMORIAL at the north-eastern side of Sarsfield Bridge consists of four stone seats, a fountain and two inscribed commemorative plaques enclosed within a tiny park at the corner of the Ennis Road and O'Callaghan Strand. One plaque inscribed in English is located on a small monument above ground level while the Irish-inscribed plaque is mounted on the wall behind the park. This reads:

Tógadh an leacht seo mar chuimhneachán ar cheannairí mhuintir chathair agus chontae Luimní a thug a n-anam ar son na saoirse sna blianta 1919 go dtí 1921

Micheál O Ceallacháin méara Luimní 1920

Seoirse Mac Fhlanncadha méara Luimní 1921

A dúnmharaíodh ina dtithe féin óiche an 7ú Márta 1921

agus

Seán De Báll Cathaoirleach Chomhairle Chontae Luimní a thit sa ghleo in 'Ath na Cairte an 6ú Bealtaine 1921

Is cuimhneachán an leacht seo freisin ar an óglach Seosamh O Donnchú ar dúnmharaíodh freisin leis óiche an 7ú Márta 1921.

Agus ar na fir go léir ó chathair agus ó chontae Luimní a maraíodh de linn chogadh na saoirse.

THE SARSFIELD BRIDGE MONUMENT now commemorates the Irish War of Independence in which Limerick, city

and county, played an important role. This is flanked by two small Russian cannon captured during the Crimean War. The original monument on this site was a statue of Viscount Fitzgibbon who was posted as missing, presumed dead, after the Charge of the Light Brigade at Balaclava, on 25 October, 1854. During the second Afghan War (1878-1880) a "bowed and tattered figure" approached a British officers' mess. His English appeared to be rusty from disuse but he was entertained by the officers who discovered he was familiar with their customs and those other regiments. In the course of conversation he mentioned that he had been living in Siberia and they, the officers, assumed that he had once served in the 8th Hussars. Some time afterwards when a roster of that regiment was checked it was discovered that the only officer, or ex-officer, of that mysterious approximate age, had been Viscount or Lord Fitzgibbon. Kipling based a short story, *The Man Who Was*, on this incident. The statue was blown up by the Irish Republican Army during the Troubles.

THE OLD HARBOUR was located up-river from Sarsfield Bridge at the junction of the Abbey and Shannon rivers from which it extended downstream for 1600 yards. By the 1750s it had become a roadstead, rather than a harbour, where ships could ride at anchor until low tide left them lying aground on the rocky river-bottom. This situation led to a spate of harbour reconstruction from that period onwards which resulted in the erection of quays named after their founders, Meade, Harvey, Russell, Spaight, Kelly and Arthur. The Inland

Aerial view from the north of Sarsfield Bridge.

Steam Navigation Company opened up the Shannon communication from here with Athlone, Banagher, Portumna, Killaloe and Kilrush. They opened a terminus here which was linked with the east coast in 1804. Another entrepreneur, James Patterson, went into shipping in 1812. By 1817 he owned one of the first steam-boats, Lady of the Shannon, to ply regularly between Limerick and Kilrush. In the 1820s two boats operated this route twice weekly "on days uncertain".

THE SHANNON RIVER was, and still is, Limerick's most important natural resource. The city, later embodied in the Corporation, claimed an exclusive right to all fishing from here to Scattery Island from the days of the Vikings, and developed as a port despite being over sixty miles from the sea. In 1837 navigation was obstructed and intricate with insufficient water for larger vessels in the upper reaches of the channel. Samuel Lewis noted that "no funds are applied to the maintenance of the navigation, which is almost entirely neglected: ships may discharge ballast in any part without restriction, and the proprietors of adjoining lands may create any obstruction they please. At each side of the narrow arm of the Shannon that encircles the English town are several quays accessible only to boats; and at Merchants' Quay is the Long Dock, where the turf and fish boats unload. From the custom-house, at the mouth of the Abbey River, various detached quays, erected by private individuals, extend along the united channel, but they are in a very bad condition; the ground around them is rugged and hard, so that vessels lying there are frequently damaged ... the Chamber of Commerce, consisting of opulent and most respectable merchants, has supreme interest in the navigation of the port, and from its funds has been defrayed the greater portion of the expense that has been incurred by whatever improvements have been made, although it has no right or control over the river. The commissioners appointed by Act of Parliament, in 1823, have power to levy certain taxes for the erection of the Wellesley Bridge, and of docks to accommodate vessels frequenting the port."

THE PORT OF LIMERICK was revitalised by commercial interests intent on making the city a major maritime port. In 1822 the Limerick Chamber of Commerce, Mayor and Corporation decided that a new bridge and wet dock were essential if Limerick was to expand. A civil engineer, employed by the

Government to survey the Shannon, was persuaded to help in 1822. His name was John Grantham. He submitted his report with plans, drawings and estimates for a new bridge and wet dock, on suitable sites, in May 1822. On 17 June 1823 "An Act for the Erection of a bridge across the river Shannon and of a Floating Dock to accommodate sharp vessels frequenting the port of Limerick" was passed. The Wellesley/Sarsfield bridge was built first but because there were insufficient funds left to finance the rest of the project, the wet dock, pier, quays, gates, walls and other works were not constructed for over twenty years. The Limerick Bridge Commissioners were empowered, by Act of Parliament in 1834, to borrow up to £200,000 to compensate mill-owners at Corbally and Curraghour; to make compulsory purchases of private quays and areas necessary for the proposed development; and to levy a charge on imported coal. Russell's Quay was constructed for £3,356, Spaight's Quay for £622, Harvey's Quay for £1,628.75 and, in all, a total of £50,000 was spent on the development of the port before the Treasury sanctioned a £50,000 loan for the erection of a wet dock on 5 October 1846. Customs paid in the port amounted to £6.90 in 1277; £5.33 in 1337; £9.04 in 1485; £6.37 in 1521; £9.42 in 1537; £15.73 in 1607; and £1619.08 in 1633. Customs receipts dropped during the Confederate wars but rose to £1,906.98 in 1672 when tolls at the city gates rose to £310.62. By the eighteenth century Limerick had recovered from the Williamite wars. In the 1830s agricultural produce, corn, provisions and butter were exported to London, Liverpool, Bristol and Glasgow from here, as this was the main shipping point for Kerry, Tipperary and Clare, as well as the county of Limerick. In 1835 the customs paid amounted to £146,222.89.

EXPORTS IN 1835, for the year ending 1 September, amounted to 1,364 tierces (42-gallon casks) of beef; 14,263 tierces of pork; 72,360 firkins (56lb-casks) of butter; 81,839 cwts of bacon; 9,697 cwts of lard; 117,874 barrels of wheat; 32,847 barrels of barley; 285,623 barrels of oats; 22,728 cwts of flour; 16,320 cwts of oatmeal; 26,214 crates of eggs; and over £1,000,000 sterling worth of hams, tongues, spirits, porter, ale, flax, linen, wool, feathers and salmon. During that year 51 vessels entered inwards from foreign ports and on 5 January, 1836, there were 71 vessels of 5,008 tons belonging to the Port of Limerick. The chief imports in 1835 were timber, coal, iron, flax-seed, tallow, pitch, tar, hoops, staves, wine and fruit.

CANNIBALISM saved the captain and crew of a Limerick ship from death by starvation in

1835. The *Francis Spaight* had sailed for St. John's, New Brunswick, on 25 November, 1835, when it was upended by strong gales during a snowstorm. Three of the crew of eighteen were drowned, two of these being Ben Cusack and "Griffin, our first mate"; provisions were washed away; water fouled; and only the cargo of timber kept the wrecked ship afloat until eleven survivors were rescued by the brig *Agenora* on 23 December. Patrick O'Brien had worked on the Limerick docks before joining the crew of the *Francis Spaight*. On 18 December 1835 the remaining crewmen of the ill-fated ship realised that the only way they might survive their ordeal was by eating human flesh. They decided to draw lots in order to select who would die. Fifteen-year-old Patrick O'Brien lost. He was killed and eaten by his shipmates. Three more of the crew shared his fate before the others were rescued. The captain and crew were later tried for murder, and acquitted, after their return to Limerick. This incident was commemorated in a ballad, *The Sorrowful Fate of O'Brien*, part of which is as follows;

"... A bandage o'er O'Brien's eyes they quickly then did tie
For the second lot that was pulled up said O'Brien was to die.

He said unto his comrade boys: 'Now let my mother know
The cruel death I did sustain, when you to Limerick go'.
Then John O'Gorman he was called to bleed him in the vein
Twice he tried to take his blood, but it was all in vain.

Our captain cries: 'Cheer up, my boys, this work will never do;
O'Gorman you must cut his throat, or else you will die too.'
The trembling cook, he took the knife, which sore did him confound.
He cut his throat and drank his blood as it flowed from the wound."

FRANCIS SPAIGHT was the main Limerick agent involved in the timber and emigrant trades, a successful merchant, town councillor, magistrate and owner of the craft on which Pat O'Brien was killed. When a public collection was held for the survivors and relatives of those who died aboard the *Francis Spaight* he contributed £10.

EMIGRATION, particularly to Canada, was a major business in the 1830s and later. Limerick ships brought a steady stream of emigrants to the Gulf of St. Lawrence and usually returned to their home port with cargoes of timber. Cost was a major factor in selecting a Canadian passage — a steerage passenger could travel from Limerick to Quebec for between £2.10 to £2.25 whereas the trip to New York cost from £3.25 to £3.50. In 1831 emigrants were advised to take 4st. of oatmeal; 4st. of cutlings for gruel; 4st. of biscuits; 1/2st. of sugar; 1/2lb. of tea; 4st. of butter; 20st. of potatoes; "a few dozen eggs, which should be well greased, to exclude the air, and consequently preserve them fresh"; and a quart or two of whiskey for emergencies on the voyage. On 23 June 1841, 300 vessels were waiting for the ice to break up in the St. Lawrence River before sailing for Canada from here.

THE LIMERICK HARBOUR COMMISSIONERS

was a new title applied to the former Limerick Bridge Commissioners under an act passed in Parliament on 9 July, 1847, which allowed them to borrow up to £50,000 for the construction of new harbour works, including a wet dock.

THE WET DOCK,

built of native limestone, covers an eight-acre area, and was built for a total cost of £54,000, £39,000 for labour and £15,000 for materials. The foundation stone was laid by Mayor John Boyce on 26 September 1849, and the dock was formally opened by Earl St. Germans, Lord Lieutenant General, and General Governor of Ireland, on 26 September 1853. The depth of water within it is 20 feet at neap tide and 25 feet at spring tide. The entrance is 70 feet wide to admit vessels, and the dock measures 1,385 feet in length by a width of 463 feet. Between 6000-8000 tons of shipping can be accommodated here, while cranes are available for the discharging of cargoes. Other vessels, of up to 600 tons, can berth at the quays where there is a depth of up to 16 feet of water at ordinary tides. Work on a repair dock began in December 1867. On 17 February, 1868, there was a one-day strike. Despite labour unrest throughout the entire project the repair, or graving, dock was formally opened by Earl Spencer, the Lord Lieutenant, on 13 May, 1873. Despite modifications and renovations over the intervening period the docks remain basically unchanged since Victorian times. The Harbour Commissioners still control the port and are responsible for the docks and the 3,300 feet length of quays. An article in the *Evening Press* on 17 December, 1987, referred to Captain John "Chalkie" White, a native of Cornwall, as the longest-serving master coming into the port. For the previous twenty-six years he had brought refined oil from Milford Haven and Stanlow, in England, to Limerick City. Despite his experience of the Shannon waters, which he knows extremely well, he would not negotiate the channel without the aid of a Shannon pilot.

THE RIVER PILOTS

contribution to the development of Limerick port cannot be over-estimated. Pilots boarded from yawls, usually ketch-rigged, or currachs which were known as canoes until motor boats came into use. The Western Pilot Division was based in Cappa, County Clare, opposite Scattery Island and the Eastern Division maintained a base on Cain's Island opposite Bunratty. Until World War II erupted the Western Pilots usually brought vessels only as far as Grass Island where they relinquished control to the Eastern Pilots.

MICHAEL JOYCE, Squarerigger, Pilot, Harbour Commissioner, Alderman, Member of Parliament, Mayor of Limerick, President of the U.K. Pilot's Association, and a founder and first Chairman of Garryowen Rugby Club, was the most remarkable of the Shannon pilots. He became involved in politics when he was elected to the Corporation in 1899. The following year he was elected M.P. for Limerick for the Irish Parliamentary Party and retained the seat until 1918. His nautical background was valued highly in Westminister and he was one of the principal architects of the Pilotage Act of 1913 which still governs pilotage in Ireland. Michael was shipwrecked four times. The last occasion was while he was an M.P. travelling on the *S.S. Leinster* when she was torpedoed in the Irish Sea in 1918. His marine background enabled him to take charge of a lifeboat. He died at his home, The Moorings, O'Connell Avenue, Limerick in 1941 in his 90th year.

THE EXPORT AND IMPORT OF GRAIN

was one of the most important functions of the harbour. In the 1890s Bannatyne's Mill (later Ranks) employed a special floating grain elevator to discharge large cargoes. The author of *The Cape Horn Breed* whose fully-rigged ship *British Isles* brought a cargo of grain from Tacoma in 1909 was impressed enough to write: "The cargo was discharged by shore labour with an up-to-date labour-saving technique which was proof of the progressive spirit of the local flour millers, who imported large quantities of grain from overseas, and sold flour, pollard and bran, not only throughout Ireland, but also for export to Britain and the Continent of Europe". His remarks about the city are interesting "The berth resembled a promenade rather than a wharf, as there was a bandstand and gardens, and many people strolling to and fro along the river bank which formed one side of the dock. The City of Limerick, with its castle and cathedral, its cobbled streets, and busy market place where cattle and pigs are sold directly by the farmers, its bacon factories, butter-factories and flour mills, and its people light-hearted and witty, and friendly to strangers, was a pleasant place in springtime when we arrived there on 18th April 1909".

LIMERICK STEAMSHIP COMPANY

dated from 1893 but its roots were in the London & Limerick Steamship Company dating from the 1850s. The Limerick Steamship Company served the west and southwest ports of Ireland for six decades, trading mainly to the U.K. and near continent with general goods, livestock, coal and fertilizers. At one time they had "puffers" on the estuary trade and large seagoing vessels on world-wide trading. During World War II the Limerick Steamship Company was appointed with the Wexford Steamship Co. and Palgrave Murphys as managers of the new Irish Shipping Ltd. In addition to their own seven vessels they were assigned the *Irish Popular,* the *Irish Pine* and the *Irish Oak.* The *Irish Pine* was torpedoed in the Atlantic in 1942 with the loss of all 33 hands, the *Irish Oak* was torpedoed in 1943. Of their own vessels the *Maigue* and the *Rynanna* were both lost in January 1940. In September of the same year, the *Luimneach* was sunk by U-boat gunfire. The *Clonlara* was torpedoed in August 1941 in Biscay. February 1943 saw the loss of the *Kyleclare* with all 18 hands. After the war the company built up its fleet again. The familiar red and white banded funnels were seen again in Liverpool, Rotterdam, Antwerp and the Irish West Coast ports. In May 1969 the Limerick Steamship Company amalgamated with the Palgrave Murphys to form Hibernian Transport. It was an unfortunate move. By the end of 1970 the new company was in liquidation and a colourful chapter of Limerick port history was closed. Fortunately an enthusiastic local marine historian, Mr. Dick Scott has recorded the full story of the Limerick Steamship Company for posterity.

THE CARGO

throughput in Limerick did not vary greatly up to the late 1960s. It was based entirely on the Wet Dock and Quays at Limerick with an occasional grain vessel lightened at Beagh Castle anchorage. The most common cargoes were grain, loose timber, coal, fertilizers, petroleum and general cargoes. 350 independent casual dockers busied themselves sorting and cessing timber, charging recklessly about with generals on handcarts and even bagging coal in the hold. "Car men" with their horse drawn drays transported most of the cargoes. Loose timber covered seven or eight acres of the docks and often stretched along the quays as well. Oil tanker movements were confined to daylight hours and the greatest attraction for the curious onlookers was the swinging of partly laden 10,000 ton grain vessels supervised by the late Captain Carlo Hanrahan with whistle and booming voice. Two significant events adversely affected port trade about this time. The Limerick Steamship Company collapsed following an unwise partnership when packaging revolutionised the traditional handling of timber. With a huge excess of casual dockers it was feared that restrictive practices would drive away the remaining trade. Good sense prevailed and a successful Docks Rationalisation Scheme was introduced by the Harbour Commissioners resulting in a slimmed down stevedoring company with equipment and practices suitable for the changing times.

SINCE THE 1960s with the increasing size of vessel, the attention of the Harbour Commissioners was diverted downstream where the estuary offered the greatest development potential. Various physical and economic surveys were undertaken to ascertain the potential of the estuary and the infrastruc-

ture required. The first breakthrough came in January 1967 with the opening of a tanker terminal for Cement Limited at Foynes Island for vessels up to 60,000 tons deadweight so that fuel oil could be bought on the world market. By 1969 the E.S.B. had established an oil fired electricity generation station at Tarbert where vessels up to 80,000 tons dwt could berth. 1972 saw the construction by the Harbour Commissioners of an oil jetty off Shannon Airport so that jet fuel could be imported directly into the airport. This project bore fruit some years later when the jetty attracted the attention of the Russian airline, Aeroflot, and enabled them to use the airport for refuelling with oil imported from the Russian Baltic. Possibly the greatest breakthrough in the history of the port since the building of the Wet Dock was the establishment of the Alumina Extraction Plant at

Aughinish. This was a major international industry importing bauxite in 60,000 ton vessels, fuel oil and liquid caustic in tankers up to 30,000 tons dwt and exporting alumina in many classes of vessels. The first bauxite vessel arrived in November 1982. Before this plant came into operation construction had begun on the giant electricity generating station at Moneypoint. This came on stream in 1985 and immediately doubled the size of the largest vessel handled in the Shannon to 150,000 tons deadweight. In 1962 the largest vessel visiting the Shannon was just over 9,000 tons dwt. Throughput was 0.43m tonnes. In 1988 the largest vessel was 150,000 tons dwt and throughput had increased to 5.55m tonnes. Thus in a quarter of a century the size of vessel has increased 16 fold and the volume of cargo 12 fold while investment has been in the region of £2Bn.

Limerick Docks

THE WHINING BRIDGE was the name bestowed on Limerick's newest bridge before it was officially opened, and unimaginatively named the Shannon Bridge. On Tuesday, 9 February, 1988 a storm passed through the country and the bridge emitted a whistling sound as gale force winds swept across it. Because of this piercing noise, it soon became known as the Whiner, the Singing Bridge, the Banshee Bridge or the Whistling Bridge. The Taoiseach, Charles J. Haughey, opened it formally, on 30 May 1988. Two plaques located on each end commemorate the event and name some of the dignitaries involved. A railway bridge of the same name is located upriver, north of the Island.

THE SAILORS' MEMORIAL is a tasteful modern monument located on the small jetty-cum-park which juts into the Shannon from Bishop's Quay, at the eastern side of the new Shannon Bridge. This consists of a cut-stone plinth with an old anchor embedded on one side and carries the following inscription: "In proud memory of merchant seamen from Limerick and the Shannon Estuary who were lost at sea in the course of duty. *Brat Dè ar a n-anamacha.*"

THE DOCK CLOCK was designed by the harbour engineer, William J. Hall, and erected in 1880.

SPILLANE'S TOWER, a small Gothic-style round tower cum harbour light or marker-buoy, dates from the days when the ship owners of Limerick had to fund their own requirements. It is now visible from the new approach road into the city from the Clare side and is known locally as the "Snuff Box". The Spillane family were the largest tobacco importers in Munster.

LIMERICK LACE was once one of the city's most famous products. An Oxford man, Charles Walker, arrived in Ireland in 1824. He purchased a store at Mount Kennett and by 1829 had established a lace-factory there. Ten young girls whom he had brought over from England worked as instructors for the 300 children and young women employed at weekly wages ranging from 5 pence to 25 pence to produce running and tambour lace. His produce was sold through Henning's of London, initially, until he opened his own store there at a later stage. By 1837 his lace was known as Irish Blonde, and up to 400 young women were employed in its manufacture. After Walker's death the business continued to flourish under the title of Lambert and Bury, and at one point employed up to 900 young women. William Lloyd established a lace-factory in Clare Street in 1836. Within a year he was employing 250 young women and exporting lace to London. Coincidentally, the only lace-factory still operating today is run by the Good Shepherd Convent in Clare Street. In 1914 Limerick Lace was manufactured at Mrs. Vere O'Brien's Lace School and Depot at No. 48 O'Connell Street, which was managed by a Miss Dunne. At the same time as the lace industry was being developed, 100 boys were employed in a muslin-factory in the Abbey parish.

THE LIMERICK FLOUR-MILLS were extensive and mainly located within the city liberties in 1837, when upwards of 50,000 barrels of flour were ground annually. By the end of the nineteenth century Limerick had the largest flour-milling industry in the south of Ireland, and could be listed as one of the country's largest exporters of provincial harvests, and importers of foreign wheat, a role maintained by the flour-millers throughout the days of the Great Hunger. Limerick contained five large mills in 1913. Working conditions were brutal. The Bard of Thomond worked in a mill for three years and later said: "It was like three years penal servitude". People worked twelve hours a day on six days of the week. The grain had to be turned continuously, as a result of which workers continually toiled in dust and darkness. People's lungs were affected by the dust; they were not permitted to take breaks, had to eat while they worked, and were not allowed to rest.

THE BANNATYNES' BUILDING is one of several six-storied grain stores which still survive from the nineteenth century when men like James Bannatyne, who made his fortune importing wheat from Montreal, dominated the commercial life of the city. This building was erected on a six-foot-deep concrete foundation which was laid, in 1873, on a solid rock strata, thirteen to twenty-five feet below the surface of the ground. William Sydney Cox, the architect, designed the building to hold 300 tons of cereal in each of eight large bins extending from the basement to the top floor. Cereal was delivered to the ground floor from where it was distributed throughout the store by machinery. Built by Messrs. MacCarthy and Guerin in 1874, the Bannatyne's building is as impressive a structure today as it was then. A Victorian architectural report commented on the aspect of its blank windows; the appearance of part of the roof which was broken up by gables and dormers; its length of 135 feet by a breadth of 60 feet; the materials used in its construction, limestone, rubble, masonry with chiselled limestone strings and dressings, white Scotch fire-brick in its external arches, and Killaloe slates on the roof; and the first floor and basement, vaulted and groined in brick, with cast iron pillars, and iron tongueing connecting the planking. A short distance away is the massive Ranks' complex which dwarfs Bannatyne's building in size. The facades of other vanished structures can also be seen nearby, along the Dock Road. The only grain store now serving its original purpose, in the city, is O'Neill's Mill in Upper William Street.

THE TRADESMEN at the turn of the century included auctioneers, bootmakers, bellow-makers, brassfounders, basket-makers, blacksmiths, brush-makers, cage-makers, candlemakers, car-makers, coachmen, coffin-makers, chandlers, crockery repairers, clock-menders, coopers, carpenters, dyers, dairy men, dockers, fiddlers, furniture-makers, fishermen, grave-diggers, glaziers, labourers, lime-burners, lace-makers, last-makers, mill-wrights, nailers, pipe-makers, pavers, pipers, rag gatherers, soldiers, slaters, stage-keepers, snuff grinders, stonemasons, tinmen, thatchers, tailors, varnishers, weavers, wheelwrights, whip-makers, weightmasters, and wool card-makers.

THE TRANSPORT UNION HALL on O'Connell Street became the headquarters of the Mid Limerick Brigade of the I.R.A. during the War of Independence. This was "an open secret", as the I.R.A. presence within the building could not be kept from all of the workers who used the place for meetings and other activities. The I.R.A. quarters were located in the attic, access to which was through a cunningly-concealed trap door, and in the event of a police or military raid on the premises a bell-push was used to sound an alarm which the I.R.A. staff would heed. Their usual shelter at such times, while the building was being searched by their enemies, was the roof-top, close to the adjoining building where the British Crown Solicitor had his office.

THE LIMERICK SOVIET came into existence soon after the city was proclaimed a special military area on 9 April, 1919. Organised labour supported Sinn Fein's nationalist aspirations. At 11.30 p.m. on Sunday, 13 April, the Limerick Trades and Labour Council called for a complete work stoppage commencing the following Monday morning, 14 April, 1919. Proclamations were printed calling on the workers to declare a cessation of all work from 5.00 a.m. on that Monday morning, as a protest against British government plans to place them under military law. A special strike committee was set up to oversee the general strike, print and issue their own money, publish their own proclamations, draft their own permits, and control food prices. Two other committees handled propaganda and the issue of permits. The former group produced a citizens' news sheet and prepared daily reports for the many foreign correspondents who had gathered in the city to report on a proposed trans-Atlantic aeroplane flight which a Major Woods had intended to undertake. The permits committee, which was staffed by four city councillors, issued permits allowing people to carry out essential works, maintain selected services, make necessary sales or purchases, and, despite the closure of all businesses, inconvenience the citizens as little as possible while making the city intolerable for the military. On 19 April the Limerick Chamber of Commerce demanded the abolition of martial law, strange partners for the Limerick Trades and Labour Council. Martial law was rescinded on 26 April, 1919, and the strike committee ordered everyone back to work.

JEWISH HISTORY does not date back very far in Limerick. Bobby (Abraham) Genese died on 30 May 1847. He was buried in a Christian cemetery but later exhumed and reinterred in a Jewish cemetery at Ballybough, Dublin. The 1861 census listed only one Jew living in the city while the 1871 census listed two in the county ·borough. By 1881 this figure had risen to four in the county borough but considerably more in the city. Lithuanian Jews arrived in Ireland in 1878.

Twenty families settled in Edward Street, Limerick. These were quiet reserved people who traded mainly in books and pictures. They formed an acceptable, but not integral, part of Limerick's retail trade. A few of them were wholesalers who supplied their co-religionists with the necessary trade goods.

AN ANTI-JEWISH DEMONSTRATION occurred on Easter Sunday, 1884. A hostile group of Limerick people surrounded the house of Lieb Siev after his maid-servant complained of the cruel way in which she had seen him slaughter fowl, she had not realised that animals had to be killed in ritual fashion before their meat could be considered fit for consumption. Lieb Siev's windows were broken with stones and his wife and child injured. Two of the riot's ringleaders were sentenced to a month's imprisonment each, with hard labour. People tried to avoid paying petty debts to the Jews by instigating other incidents. Life became intolerable for the small Jewish community, and many of them moved to Cork in May 1884. The incidents continued. Two Jews were beaten up in August 1892 and the house of Moses Leone

was damaged by stone-throwing on 24 November, 1896. There were 130 Jews living in the city in 1896. From 1897 until 1904 they lived in peace with their Gentile neighbours. Most of Limerick's Lithuanian Jews had settled in Collooney Street by the 1890s. They held prayer meetings in a private house in Emmet Place, initially, and later moved to No. 18 Collooney Street, until they eventually opened a synagogue at 63 Colooney Street. On 14 August 1888 Rev. Dr. Hermann Adler, Delegate Chief Rabbi, addressed a congregation of thirty-five Jews in Limerick. By 1 December, 1892, there were ninety in the congregation. On 17 February 1902, the Jews bought a site in Newcastle, Kilmurray Parish, from William Nunan for £150. This was purchased, and used, as a Jewish cemetery.

THE CHURCH OF ST. ALPHONSUS LIGUORI and the adjoining residence were designed by Philip C. Hardwick, in Gothic-style, for the Redemptorist Fathers, who first arrived in Ireland in 1850. Known also as the Missionary Fathers of St. Alphonsus, they preached at a mission held in the old St. John's Cathedral in 1851, and were invited back the following year to speak at St.Michael's. Dr. Ryan, the Catholic Bishop of Limerick, gave them a foundation in 1853, and they opened a small oratory in Bank Place. In 1854 they acquired a large field in Courtbrack, at the top of Henry Street, where they erected a temporary chapel. They resided near it until they built their own residence, the foundation stone of which was laid in August, 1856. The foundation stone of the church was laid on 30 May, 1858. Both buildings were constructed by a builder, named Wallace, under the supervision of William Corbet. George Goldie (1828-1887) of London designed the high altar, which was unveiled on Sunday, 15 October, 1865, although the tower was not completed until 1879. The chief building material is magnesium limestone, imported from France, with horizontal strips of pink granite used to enliven the facade. Clare and Sicilian marble were used in decorating the interior, the former in the columns supporting the apse arch, and the latter in the altar rail.

THE LIMERICK CONFRATERNITY was founded by the Redemptorist Fathers soon after their full development as a community in Mount St. Alphonsus, in 1867. They spent the last three days of 1867 celebrating a solemn *triduum* to Our Lady of Perpetual Succour, and on New Year's Day, 1868, they opened a mission for men and boys. When this mission ended, 8,000 men had received communion and 1,400 boys had been confirmed. The Confraternity was founded and directed by Fr. Bridgett, who laid the foundations of a movement which dominated the religious and social life of Limerick for well over a century, earning it a reputation as a city of nothing but churches and "piety upon piety'. Year after year, street by street, and house by house, the male members of the Limerick Confraternity trooped off to their meetings. Attendance was compulsory; excuses were checked and recorded by two officers of the association; social pressure was exerted to boost attendance but non-membership was tolerated, though not quite approved, amongst one's Catholic peers. By 1880 the Confraternity had 4,200 members. This figure had climbed to 7,000 by 1918, and the movement continued to flourish into the early 1960s.

FR. JOHN CREAGH was born at Thomondgate on 19 August, 1870. He was educated by the Redemptorists, in Limerick and in England, before his ordination on 1 September 1895. He taught history at Teignmouth, England, and at Clonard, Belfast, before returning to Limerick where he was director of the Holy Family Confraternity in 1904. On 12 January, 1904,

he delivered a sermon from the altar of the Redemptorist Church castigating the Jews of Limerick. He indicted their business methods, accused them of shedding Christian blood, and stated that they would "kidnap and slay Christian children" if they dared. This tirade was probably sparked off by a type of hire-purchase system operated by the business people of the city in which weekly payments were collected from various debtors within the locality. Fr. Creagh held the small Jewish enclave in Colooney Street responsible for this state of affairs. In fact, the few Jewish dealers involved in this *gombeenism* formed only a small percentage of the business community which was more than predominantly Christian.

THE JEWISH COMMUNITY was insulted, assaulted and threatened after Fr. Creagh's sermon, according to a report of the Rabbi, Rev. Elias Bere Levin, on 18 January, 1904. Worse was to come. Fr. Creagh preached a second sermon, in which he urged Catholics "not to deal with the Jews" after he had further maligned them. This sermon may have been inspired by the expulsion of Redemptorist priests from France, an incident for which Fr. Creagh held the Jews responsible.

THE LIMERICK POGROM was an economic boycott waged against Limerick's small Jewish community for two years. Life was made intolerable for the Jews. Rabbi Levin and some of his flock were assaulted, their businesses boycotted, their livelihoods destroyed, their homes attacked, and they were subjected to abuse and slander. They were never given a chance to defend themselves or place their case before the public. The Protestants of Limerick tried to support the Jews throughout this troubled period, but their sponsorship only deepened the animosity of the Redemptorists and the Confraternity of the Holy Family. Eventually the Jewish community were forced into asking the Protestants to desist, thus depriving themselves of essential funds and allies, in the hope that the Catholics would attempt a reconciliation. Despite this gesture the boycott continued. Standish O'Grady (1832-1915) wrote on 23 April that "it is difficult to believe that the priests and the Bishop of Limerick could not put an end to it if they tried ... These Limerick Jews seem to be a very harmless body, neither money-lenders nor extortioners; just traders trading in clothes, and selling the same at no more profit than is permitted". Arthur Griffith (1872-1922), the Sinn Fein leader, supported Fr. Creagh in the *United Irishman,* demanding freedom for the Irish peasant from the international moneylenders (the Jews). He was

reprimanded by Frederick Ryan, co-editor of *Dana,* who wrote that Irishmen who were claiming freedom for themselves could ill afford to refuse it to others. Dr. Bunbury, the Church of Ireland Bishop of Limerick, spoke to the Church of Ireland Synod. He defended the Jews, claiming that they charged no more than the other shopkeepers in the city. His speech was condemned at a special meeting of the Corporation, in which the Mayor, Michael Donnelly, denied that the Jews had been subjected to violence.

JOHN RALEIGH, a fifteen-year-old youth, was sentenced to one month's imprisonment, without hard labour, for assaulting Rabbi Elias Bere Levin, with a thrown stone, on 4 April 1904. In court, Raleigh was defended by an anti-semitic solicitor, Nash, who stated that as far as he was concerned, any reported assaults on the Jews were just fabrications by which the Jews hoped to enrich themselves. The resident magistrate, Hickson, said it was quite clear that Raleigh was guilty of the charges. It was not his first time to cause trouble or annoy the Jews, and although he, and several other children, had been involved in various incidents concerning the Jews, it was obvious that "other parties" should bear the responsibility for such actions. Raleigh served his sentence in Mountjoy Jail. He was released in May and received a hero's welcome on returning to Limerick. He was carried home, shoulder-high, from the railway station by enthusiastic supporters who also presented him with a silver watch and chain. Rabbi Elias Bere Levin (1862-1929) had settled in the city in 1882 where he was appointed Reader and Shochet to the single congregation placed under the jurisdiction of the Chief Rabbi.

THE COLLOONEY STREET OUTRAGE is another term used to describe the *pogro m* which is usually defined as an organised massacre or the preaching which culminates in such an event. Fr. John Creagh left Limerick in May 1906. He worked as a missionary in the Phillipines, New South Wales, Western Australia and New Zealand. He returned to Australia where he was appointed Rector of the Redemptorist House in Perth from 1914 to 1916. He was Vicar-Apostolic of the Kimberleys from 1916 to 1923, and from 1923 to 1925 he was acting parish priest of Bunbury. From 1926 to 1930 he was in Pennant Hills and after that he was stationed at Waratah and Wellington, New Zealand, where he died in the Lewisham Hospital on 24 January, 1947. He was buried at Karori. Controversy followed him even after he had left Limerick. When a white stock drover, Jackie Parks, was accused of murdering an Aboriginal stockboy, Fr. Creagh attended

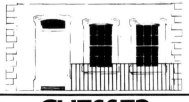
Parks's trial in Perth to give evidence. He claimed that it had long been the practice, amongst drovers, to fire a charge of buckshot at the stockboys' legs to encourage them to work if they were slacking off. His seven years in the Kimberleys were described by a friend, Sister Ignatius, as "lonely, poor and frustrated'. She also referred to his "flashing" temper but admitted that he could be very kind.

SEAN SOUTH (1930-1957), of Garryowen, was a fervent Catholic who established a branch of *Maria Duce* in the city during the early 1950s. He is best remembered, in song and in story, as a Republican hero killed during an abortive paramilitary raid on an R.U.C. barracks, at Brookeborough, County Fermanagh. Lord Mayors, county and urban councillors, city Corporation members and Catholic clergy from all over Ireland extended sympathy to his family and friends at the time of his funeral. During his brief paramilitary career Sean South, or Sabhat, had visited many of the R.U.C. barracks along the border to assess their armaments. In Brookeborough he had seen only pistols and sten-guns in the R.U.C. arsenal which was on open display, so he did not realise that a bren-gun was kept in the married quarters, upstairs. Sean advised his comrades to use a county council lorry, which sten-gun bullets would not penetrate, for their raid. As the truck pulled up opposite the barracks the sergeant realised what was happening and opened fire with the bren-gun, the bullets of which "tore through the truck as if it were made of paper". Sean South's last words were, "They've got a bren-gun", as its bullets literally cut him in two. Several of the Republicans were wounded. Fergal O Hanlon bled to death from a wound in his thigh but some of his companions were luckier and received competent medical treatment.

MARIA DUCE was a right-wing Catholic association founded by Fr. Denis Fahey of the Holy Ghost Missionary Order, in the early 1930s.

THE PRESBYTERIAN CHURCH had its foundation-stone laid by the Moderator, Rev. D.A. Taylor, on 16 October, 1899. Prior to then the Presbyterians had occupied a "commodious edifice of hewn stone" in Glentworth Street which they had erected about 1817. The earlier history of Limerick's Presbyterian congregation is rather vaguely detailed, but it is probable that some members of the Church of Scotland settled in the city about 1649. They rented the old chapel of the Augustinian Nunnery in Peter's Cell from Lord Milton until 1765 when they built the Dissenters Meeting House in Pump Lane, at the north end of the Englishtown. This building was considered "plain and handsome", with a

house for the minister adjoining. Both were erected for £500. The Glentworth Street church proved to be too small. It was enlarged in 1829 and had a gallery added in 1846. When the present church and lecture hall was built, the old building was sold to George McKern & Sons Ltd., Printers, on 18 August, 1904. When the foundation-stone was laid Archibald Murray gave a historical sketch, and a bottle was deposited at the right-hand corner, bearing the names of the ministers of the church from the reign of Charles I to October 1899, as well as a copy of the *Limerick Chronicle*, and current coins of the realm from a sovereign to a farthing. This building was erected for £8,000 and was opened on 3 October, 1901, by Prof. Heron D.D., Moderator of the General Assembly. Constructed mainly of red brick, with dressings of Portland stone for the arches and windows, the first system of lighting used was gas lighting until, in 1915, electricity was installed. The most unusual feature is the church's lecture-hall which is located underneath the church. The Presbyterians now worship in a smaller church building, Christ Church, on O'Connell Street.

VILLIER'S SCHOOLS were founded soon after the will of Mrs. Hannah Villier was established in the Court of King's Bench on 12 December 1815. Samuel Lewis reported that very large schools for males and females were in course of erection in 1837. In 1866 Maurice Lenihan stated that £7,507.90½ had been spent by Mrs. Villier's trustees on acquiring a site, building schoolhouses in Henry Street and Nicholas Street, and on the Villier's Alms Houses. There were 50 boys and 44 girls in attendance in the Henry Street school in 1866, but fewer attended the Nicholas Street school which was run in connection with the National Board of Education. In more recent times, Villier's Schools were relocated in the North Liberties, off the North Circular Road.

THE LEAMY FREE SCHOOLS, in Hartstonge Street, were established by William Leamy in 1814, when he left £13,300 for the education of the children of the poor, especially those in the neighbourhood of Limerick. In 1841 the Court of Chancery in Ireland decided that the pupils were to be taught gratuitously, and to receive a good English education; members of the Church of Ireland were to be instructed in the scriptures; and Roman Catholics in the Scripture Lessons in the National school books. £3,940 was spent on the schools and site in Hartstonge Street while the interest on the £10,000 balance maintained the school. This building now houses the Crescent Clothing factory.

THE   PRIMITIVE   WESLEYAN

METHODIST PREACHING HOUSE was founded in Bedford Row in 1821. This had been built in a Gothic style, with a handsome entrance, an elegant balustrade and apartments for the preacher. Next door to it was the Independent Meeting House. Both have long since closed but their locations can still be traced.

THE FRANCISCAN CHURCH is a neo-Classical building designed by William Corbett and erected by Messrs. McCarthy and Guerin. The foundation-stone was laid on 28 May, 1876. It was extended and renovated in 1931. All traffic leaving the city by Sarsfield Bridge has to pass its facade.

THREE BLACK AND TANS were attacked on Henry Street, by a group of I.R.A men, on 22 June, 1920. Constable Oakley was shot dead and his two companions, E.T. Jones and H. Jones, disarmed. One of the I.R.A. men got rid of his revolver by dropping it into a nearby post office pillar-box, from which the I.R.A. recovered it the following morning.

COLLOONEY STREET was named after an engagement in which the Limerick militia distinguished itself under the command of Colonel Vereker, on 5 September, 1798, some time after the English forces had run from the French in the "Races of Castlebar". City tradition claims that Vereker lied about his exploits and that the Corporation supported his claim, turning his defeat into a triumph. In 1803 the military commandant of the city foiled a surprise attack by "those engaged in Emmett's conspiracy". The prompt and decisive measures he adopted prevented a revolution. Limerick remained a staunch garrison town. In 1821 symptoms of subordination in the Liberties led to a proclamation declaring the county to be in a state of disturbance, and to require an extraordinary establishment of police, which was accordingly sent. The Castle Barrack accommodated 17 officers and 270 non-commissioned officers and privates, with an hospital for 29 patients in 1837. The new barrack at the western side of Collooney Street, behind the small Spellacy Square, was adapted for 37 officers, 714 infantry and cavalry, and 54 horses in 1837. It also contained an hospital for 60 patients and a recently-constructed six-cell military prison. Today the latter barrack is known as Sarsfield Barracks. At the start of the twentieth century these two barracks were still in use as well as the Ordnance Barracks in Mulgrave Street (now Heiton's premises) and the Militia or Strand Barracks. Most of the officers lived in the Georgian houses in the Crescent or Clare Street. The various regiments were composed of Irish, English, Welsh and Scottish soldiers although Welsh and Scottish regiments were never allowed to share the same barracks

because of some long-rooted animosity between them. The Royal Irish Constabulary also maintained a heavy presence in the city at the turn of the century, with barracks at Edward Street, John Street, William Street, Mary Street, O'Curry Street (then known as Frederick Street), Mulgrave Street, Thomondgate, Caherdavin, Corbally, and on the outskirts of the city at Cratloe Castle, Castletroy, Mungret and Clarina. In the early nineteenth century the Revenue Police used the city as a headquarters with other stations located at Ennis, Gort and Cashel.

THE JEWISH SURNAMES OF LIMERICK between 1847 and 1904 were Arinon, Blonde, Clein, Cropman, Fine, Genese, Goldberg, Gould, Graff, Greenfield, Jaffe, Jerome, Leone, Levin, Moizel, Shochett, Siev, Toohey and Weinronk.

SPELLACY SQUARE is the smallest square in Limerick city. It derives its name from a member of the Spellacy family of Cratloe.

THE SPELLISSY SURNAME has been described as a rare Thomond surname by Rev. Patrick Woulfe in *Sloinnte Gaedheal is Gall, Irish Names and Surnames* (1923). Variations of the name include Spellacy, Spelessy, Spillessy, and Spilacy. The name appears in Irish as `O Spealghusa, `O Spilgheasa and `O Speallassa and has been translated as *Speal-Ghusa,* Scythe-Choice or Strong Scythemen. P.J. Spellissy of Islington, London, and the late George Spellissy of Tirmaclane, County Clare, claim the Spellissys were descended from a man who "came in from the water", either through the

Fergus Estuary, or through Miltown Malbay. Family tradition, in Clare, states that the name was originally *Spoleto* and that the family originated in the north of Italy. I have found nothing to corroborate this. The name is mainly found throughout counties Clare and Limerick, in Tirmaclane, Ennis, Kilmaley, Cratloe, Raheen Cross and Limerick City.

The Spring Rice Memorial and the People's Park.

THE BAPTIST CHURCH was built in red brick with limestone dressings. It contained a fine lecture-room, several classrooms and other apartments, and could seat up to 300 people. P. Kennedy, 3 Military Road, was the builder, and the design was by George P. Beater of Dublin. While it was being constructed in 1894 it was estimated that the edifice would cost over £2,000 to complete.

THE WOLFE TONE CLUB was a legal front organisation for the illegal Irish Republican Brotherhood. On 25 January, 1914, the club organised a meeting in the Athenaeum Hall in Cecil Street to recruit members for the Irish Volunteer Movement. Padraig Pearse and Roger Casement addressed the large audience, out of which practically every man enlisted. On Whit Sunday, 23 May, 1915, volunteers from Dublin, Cork and Tipperary marched through the streets of the city with their Limerick comrades, led by men such as Padraig Pearse, Tom Clarke, Willie Pearse, Liam Mellows, Tomàs McCurtin, Eamon de Valera, Terence McSwiney, George Clancy, Ned Daly and Sean McDermott. World War I was in progress, so the marchers had to suffer a barrage of insults from the soldiers and the "separation women" of the city whose husbands had enlisted in the British Army. Wolfe Tone Street is now the name of Collooney Street.

THE SOCIETY OF FRIENDS, the Quakers, arrived in Limerick in 1655. They were persecuted by the Cromwellians and were unable to set up a regular establishment until after the Restoration. In 1671 they erected a meeting-house in Creagh Lane. This was rebuilt in 1735 and remained in use until they moved to another meeting house in Cecil Street, which they built for £1,242.45 in 1809. This building is now owned by the Red Cross, but one room has been refurbished, at the back, for the use of today's Society of Friends. During the *Great Hunger* the Quakers set up auxiliary relief committees throughout Ireland. Their reputation for involvement in charitable works is legendary, and they are the most respected Protestant sect in both the Rpublic and the six counties. The Quaker cemetery is located in Ballinacurra.

THE PEOPLE'S PARK, or New Park, is enclosed by iron railings on three sides. The Earl of Limerick granted Pery Square and the surrounding grounds to the Corporation on certain conditions. He gave them a 500-year lease when they agreed that no political or religious meetings would be allowed in the free park; bands would not be allowed to play there on Sundays; and the Corporation would make a new street extending from Mallow Street to the park. The People's Park was for-

mally opened by Mayor Spaight on 20 August 1877.

THOMAS SPRING RICE (1790-1866) is commemorated in the centre of the People's Park, where his statue is mounted on a Doric column designed by Alexander Nimmo in the early 1830's. Thomas Spring Rice coined the term *West Briton*. Lalor Shiel believed Thomas was a political schizophrenic; "He sees the poor laws from the Shannon as he sees the Repeal from the Thames. He takes a Treasury view of the one, and a Mount Trenchard view of the other ... He designates himself as a West Briton. He does himself an injustice for he is more than English. All the mud of his native Shannon has not only been washed off by his ablutions in the Cam, but he comes more fresh and glossy from the academic water than those who at their birth were immersed in the classic stream". Thomas Spring Rice was Chancellor of the Exchequer from 1835 to 1839 and was created 1st Baron Monteagle of Brandon in 1840.

THE DRINKING FOUNTAIN in the People's Park was erected by the employees of Russell's Mills.

ST. MICHAEL'S CHURCH OF IRELAND CHURCH was designed to blend with the surrounding architecture. It was consecrated in 1844 and replaced an older church, St. Georges, which was founded and endowed by the Pery family. This older edifice was opened on 14 June 1789 and contained an east window which was "a beautiful antique of the thirteenth century, and was formerly in the old Franciscan Abbey". The height of the tower which rises directly above the main doorway, was increased when the present building was reopened, after major renovations, on 18 November 1877. The stained-glass windows, brass plaques, and church fittings and furniture from the now-disused parish church of Kilkeady were sent here for storage, almost a century later.

THE PERY SQUARE TONTINE BUILDING was completed in 1838. This is the most notable example of Georgian architecture in the square, most of which dates from the 1840s. The doorway, complete with fanlight, has supporting Doric columns on either side.

THE CARNEGIE LIBRARY is now an art gallery. The Romanesque-Celtic doorway and arches reflect the taste of a period which has since become known as the Celtic Twilight. George Sheridan designed the building in 1903. It opened in 1906.

THE CENOTAPH, in Pery Square, is a link with the city's military past. It is dedicated to the Limerick men who died in both World Wars, particularly the Munster Fusiliers.

DURING THE WAR OF INDEPENDENCE an I.R.A. unit under the command of

Michael Hartney captured two detectives, near the People's Park, on the night of 15 August, 1920. On the same evening two R.I.C. sergeants, Dunphy and Harty, were shot by three members of the I.R.A. in Mallow Street. The two events combined to send the Crown Forces on a rampage through the city. R.I.C. and military personnel raided the homes and work-places of suspected Sinn Fein sympathisers. In High Street the home and stores of the Foley brothers were emptied with volleys of rifle-fire, and several other places were burned throughout the city including the home and business premises of Matthew Griffin, a Sinn Fein member of the Corporation.

THE TAIT CLOCK in Baker Place was erected as a tribute to Sir Peter Tait, a Scotsman, who pioneered the manufacture of ready-made clothing in an era when even army uniforms were all made by hand. In 1850 he introduced power-driven machinery and mass-production methods to the city. Within a few years his factory was producing uniforms for the entire British army. During the American Civil War, Limerick was an important maritime and industrial centre which supplied both North and South with military uniforms. Uniforms for the British, American, European and other armies were manufactured here and helped Limerick to develop into a major city. Sir Peter Tait was Mayor three times between 1866 and 1868. He lived in South Hill House. During his own life-time a 65-foot-high clock-tower was designed by J. Corbett, a civil engineer. It was completed, on its present site, for £750, in 1867. Today this four-faced clock is worked by electricity.

THE TAIT BUSINESS CENTRE is a modern industrial development named after Limerick's most successful Victorian businessman, who would have appreciated such a memorial. Purpose-built factory units, workshops and offices are provided for small manufacturing and other related businesses.

ST. SAVIOUR'S DOMINICAN CHURCH was designed by the Pain brothers soon after the friars moved from Fish Lane to Baker Place in 1815. A new chancel was built in 1863 and the main body of the church was considerably altered in 1870. In 1898 the Sacred Heart Chapel was erected as a memorial to Fr. Carberry, the prior. This chapel and that of St. Martin de Porres on the opposite side of the church were later joined by the Terence Albert O'Brien Memorial Chapel of 1982 with its modern stained-glass windows.

TERENCE ALBERT O'BRIEN (1600-1651), Bishop of Emly, encouraged Irish resistance within the walls of the besieged city, in 1651. At one stage the Cromwellians offered him £10,000 and safe passage to any country outside of the kingdom. He refused the bribe. Ireton excluded him from amnesty and had him hanged. Terence Albert O'Brien was a master of sacred theology, an alumnus of the Limerick Convent of St. Saviour, and was elected Prior of the Province of Ireland, at Kilkenny, in 1643. After the death of James O'Hurley in 1644 he was created Bishop of Limerick.

OUR LADY OF LIMERICK, an oak statue of the *Madonna and Child* preserved in the Dominican Church, dates from the second quarter of the seventeenth century. The Dominicans believe that this life-sized statue and a silver-gilt chalice were given in 1640, as an act of reparation, by Patrick Sarsfield of Limerick and his wife, Eleanor White. This Patrick Sarsfield, not to be confused with his namesake, the Jacobite General, lost his rich lands around Shannon and Bunratty under the Act of Settlement, in 1653, and was forced to start a new life in Burren and Corcomroe. Patrick was a nephew of Judge Dominic Sarsfield, the man who sentenced Sir John Burke to death, and the statue was presented to the Dominicans because of Sir John Burke's long association with their church. The Madonna's fifteen-decade silver rosary beads date from the late eighteenth or nineteenth century but her crown is modern.

THE GLENTWORTH HOTEL was the home of James Pain (1779-1877), a noted architect, who, with his brother, George Richard Pain, studied architecture as pupils of John Nash. They later collaborated in the building and renovation of some of Ireland's finest houses. James eventually decided to live in Limerick while George continued to live in Cork.

TRINITY CHURCH was built by Rev. Edward Newenham Hoare who collected funds for its erection in 1834 or 1844 when he decided the adjoining asylum for blind females should have its own place of worship. The building is occupied since the 1960s by the Mid-Western Health Board. The rectory was at one side of the church and the asylum for the blind on the other. The church gallery was accessible from either house as both had doors leading on to it.

THE BAHA'I FAITH was founded by a Persian aristocrat, Baha'u'llah (1817-1892), who is regarded, by his followers, as the most recent in a long line of Messengers of God. Abraham, Moses, Buddah, Zoroaster, Christ and Muhammad are amongst the earlier Messengers of God accepted by the Baha'is who believe that humanity is one single race and are working towards its unification in one global society. Baha'u'llah was sent to Israel, as a prisoner, in 1868. He died at Bahji, north of Acre, and is buried there. His shrine is visited by thousands of pilgrims every year. The Baha'is, like the Jews, Christians, and Muhammadans regard Israel as the Holy Land. Unlike other religions the Baha'i faith has no clergy but the spiritual and administrative affairs of the entire Baha'i community are directed by a nine-member body, The Universal House of Justice, situated on Mount Carmel, Haifa, elected at five year intervals.

The Baha'i faith was established in Limerick in the late 1960s. The community is small and members congregate in each others' homes for worship. There are now over 20 local spiritual assemblies administering the Baha'i faith in Ireland overseen by the National Spiritual Assembly which is centred in Dublin. Limerick has its own spiritual assembly which is elected annually.

THE SEXTON STREET AREA was once the seat of Limerick's mineral water industry. Wells were sunk to a depth of over fifty feet, at times, to extract bacteria-free mineral waters with a unique preservative quality. These mineral waters were utilised by the Limerick bacon factories and were responsible for the distinctive flavour and world-wide reputation of Limerick ham. The Russell family were involved in both the milling and bacon industries. Grain-stores built by John Norris Russell can still be seen in Limerick and Ennis. During the Civil War, July to August 1922, O'Meara's Bacon Factory and a large section of William Street were destroyed.

WILLIAM STREET, Ellen Street and Patrick Street were named after various members of the Arthur family. Catherine Street was named after Catherine Unthank and Nicholas Street was called after the long-vanished church of St. Nicholas. In 1837 the city supported four newspapers, three published twice a week, and one weekly. Social gatherings were moved from the Assembly House which had been built for £4,000 in 1770 to Swinburne's Hotel and the Limerick

St. Saviour's Dominican Church and the Tait Clock.

Institution, formed in 1809, could boast of a library containing over 2,000 volumes.

THE LINEN AND COTTON INDUSTRY had declined by the 1830s despite the efforts of the Limerick Chamber of Commerce to halt the deterioration by erecting a new linen-hall and holding a weekly market every Friday and Saturday. The adaptation of new designs did little to help the faltering market, so the problem was eventually turned over to the agricultural association. This body tried to promote the linen, woollen, cotton and other trades among the poor with a fund of £7,000 allocated to them by the association's board of directors in London. At the same time the glove trade was in trouble, and most of the "Limerick gloves" on sale were actually manufactured in Cork.

HAY AND STRAW MARKETS were held on Wednesdays and Saturdays in 1837. The large wheat market had sheds all around its enclosure and the butter market, a spacious and lofty building, was opened daily throughout the year. There were two potato markets, one in the Englishtown, the other in the Irishtown; as well as two meat markets, plentifully supplied with butchers' meat and poultry, but the supply of fish and vegetables was often deficient. The smaller of these markets, called the Northumberland Buildings, had attached to it large apartments for public buildings, a bazaar, and commercial chambers. Four annual fairs were held in the city on Easter Tuesday, 4 July, 4 August and 12 December. The August fair carried a curious privilege as no person could be arrested in the city or Liberties on process issued out of the Tholsel Court for fifteen days after it.

THE BLACK AND TANS were given this derogatory title by Christopher O'Sullivan, proprietor and editor of *The Limerick Echo* when he described the "strange type of individual wearing the black cap and tunic of the Royal Irish Constabulary and khaki trousers of the British soldier" with whom he had travelled in a train from Limerick Junction to Limerick City. He later remarked, in a leading article, in his own newspaper that "this puny creature resembled something one would associate with the Scarteen Hunt (the Black and Tans) of Pallasgreen judging by his strange attire". Mike Nono, the Ennis comedian, perpetuated this nick-name shortly afterwards from the stage of Limerick's Theatre Royal when he used Christopher O'Sullivan's quip to describe the new occupying force set up by the British.

JOHN FERRAR, the grandson of a Williamite cavalry officer and a descendant of Nicholas Ferrar who founded the Little Gidding community, published a short sketch of Limerick's history in 1766. He established

The Limerick Chronicle in 1768, and in 1787 produced a substantially enlarged version of his history. Denis Fitzgerald Mahony (1773-1840) was a part owner of *The Limerick Chronicle*. He lived in the Tontine Buildings on what is now O'Connell Street and was a successful stockbroker, alderman, magistrate and philanthropist. His son, Andrew Watson Mahony, (1817-1839) was drowned on the Night of the Big Wind, 6 January 1839, when the schooner *Undine* was swamped in the Shannon.

THE RECORD PRINTING WORKS, at No. 6 Cornmarket Row, published seditious material, *Bottom Dog* and the *Factionist*, during the War of Independence. The proprietor was usually warned of impending R.I.C. raids by Sergeant McCarthy of Clare Street who used to give three taps on the window pane nearest to the door of the premises.

GERALD GRIFFIN STREET was the site of Tottenham Heaphy's Theatre, the New Theatre Royal. This was located at the south western corner of Gerald Griffin Street and Little Gerald Griffin Street which were then known as Cornwallis Street and Playhouse Lane. Heaphy built his theatre for £600 in 1770. It was 80 feet long by 40 feet wide, awkwardly designed, and lacked a proper facade as the front part was used by a coach-builder, named Edward Gubbins, for both business and domestic purposes. In fact, access to the playhouse boxes was through Edward's kitchen and the entry to the pit was through Playhouse Lane. A site next to the Assembly House, at the eastern end of Charlotte's Quay, was given to Tottenham Heaphy, by Thomas Smyth, in August 1774 but there is no record of this being used for theatrical purposes. In 1771 Tottenham Heaphy complained of counterfeit admission tickets, unruly audiences, backstage romeos, heating, light, air-conditioning and maintenance. He often let his theatre to other entrepreneurs such as Richard Daly who leased it from him in 1781. Sir Vere Hunt of Curragh Chase formed the Limerick Theatrical Society with Major Alcock of the 47th Regiment and Captain Trevor Lloyd Ashe, a skilled instrumentalist, on 17 January 1785. The society then leased the Theatre Royal from Richard Daly who sub-let to them. In 1790 Sir Vere Hunt turned the ballroom of the Assembly House into a "beautiful" theatre and established a touring theatrical group which operated with some success until a disagreement with his manager led to its closure. By then the city had a population of about 50,000. In 1858 Charles Dickens appeared on stage in Limerick to give a dramatised public reading. On 4 September a correspondent for the *Limerick*

Market scene.

Chronicle, disappointed with the famous man's performance, acknowledged his ability as a writer but stated that as a "general reader we cannot give him unqualified praise, for though he undoubtedly possesses dramatic talents of a first rate order for personifying characters, yet he recited several passages of a descriptive nature in a sing-song, schoolboy style that was below par."

THE MULGRAVE STREET HOSPITAL was erected for £7,100, in 1811, on what was then called the New Cork Road. In 1827 Fitzgerald described it as the New County Hospital. Elizabeth Fry, the prison reformer, visited here with a Mr. Gurney and the Protestant Bishop of Limerick and they were gratified with the good order, cleanliness and comfort of the hospital. The lower floor was occupied by the hall, board-room, surgery, kitchen and other apartments. Two upper floors contained ten wards for male patients and six for female patients. The building contained a resident surgeon and served the city and county until the 1950s when the Regional Hospital opened at Dooradoyle. The Limerick School of Commerce then occupied the old infirmary.

ST. JOSEPH'S PSYCHIATRIC HOSPITAL opened for the reception of patients in 1826. It was constructed for £30,000 over a period of two years. The design was by Messrs. Johnson and Murray and the construction was carried out by a Dublin builder, Williams. This limestone edifice was lined with brick and extended 429 feet in front and 314 feet in depth. The centre formed an octagon from which four wings diverged with cells for patients from Limerick, city and county, as well as the counties of Clare and

Tipperary. Eugene O'Curry (1794-1862) worked as a warder here before joining the Ordnance Survey Office in 1835.

MOUNT ST. LAWRENCE CEMETERY is the burial-place of Maurice Lenihan (1811-1895) and the Bard of Thomond, Michael Hogan (1832-1899).

LIMERICK PRISON was designed by James Pain, an architect more renowned for his work on the big houses of Ireland. In 1816 three acres of ground on the New Cork Road were purchased for £958.33. In 1817 work commenced on the "New County Jail" which was completed in 1821 at a cost of £23,000. A further £2,000 was expended on the erection of a kitchen, laundry, tread-mill-house, and sheds for fuel, straw and other materials. The building was described in 1827 as castellated in appearance. The basic structure seems unchanged from the exterior but because of the prevailing political climate and the need for security a more complete description of the building cannot be given here. The grand, or main, entrance is formed of very fine cut stone. "In the centre is a polygonal tower", wrote Samuel Lewis in 1837, "60 feet high, containing on successive stories the governor's residence, the committee-room, a chapel, and an hospital, and having round the second story an arcade commanding the several yards. Five rays of building diverge from this tower, forming ten yards, each communicating by a cast-iron bridge with the chapel, and containing in the whole 22 apartments for debtors, and 103 cells for criminals. Between the wall immediately surrounding these and the outer wall is a space containing two tread-wheels, the female prison, various offices, and some ornamented plots. The whole is supplied with excellent water from the springs".

THE CONSTABULARY, or Peace Preservation Police, consisted of a chief magistrate, one chief officer of the second class, 49 men and four horses in 1836. Of these 37 men were stationed in the city barracks, and the remainder in the Liberties. Their maintenance amounted to £1,852.071/2 for the year ending on 1 June 1836, two-thirds of which was paid from the Consolidated fund and the balance by Grand Jury presentment. This force was occasionally employed beyond the limits of the civil jurisdiction. In 1836 the Peace Preservation Force and the county constabulary were amalgamated into a centralised police force under an inspector general. From 20 May 1867 they were known as the Royal Irish Constabulary. Their main role is fulfilled today by the Gardai Sìochana, who were established in 1922, as Guardians of the Peace.

THE JOHN O'GRADY MONUMENT at the top of Mulgrave Street was erected in the

Market scene.

shape of a large weight. This commemorates John O'Grady (1892-1934), a world's champion weight-thrower who was born in Ballybricken.

THE FAMINE forced the Mayor, E.F.G. Ryan, to lead a deputation to Dublin on 23 March 1846 in order to urge the Relief Commission to provide the city with relief works before the population resorted to violence. General Edward Pine Coffin, of Devon, was appointed Deputy Commissary of the Limerick depot for the supply and distribution of food. He estimated that four million people would have to be fed during May, June and July of 1846 before the new crop of potatoes would be fit to eat. At that stage no one anticipated Black '47 or even dreamed that the dreaded potato blight would re-appear by July 1846. In June of that year government supplies of Indian corn at less than 1/2 pence a pound were exhausted, and the British Treasury refused to supply any more as their depots closed down. By the time supplies were resumed in February 1847 it was too late. Despite the desperate situation in which the people found themselves, the Limerick docks were kept busy as cereals, livestock and agricultural products were shipped out of the famine-stricken country. It was no wonder the Irish people refer to this episode in history as the Great Hunger rather than the Famine. Food was never as plentiful but it usually went to pay the rent. On 5 August 1846 a group of labourers tore up a road they had just laid when they were told their employment had come to an end. On another occasion the military officer commanding the city complained that his troops were "harassed off their legs by daily calls" on their services to

protect stores and depots.

THE LONG CAN owes its name to Joseph Lancaster, a London-born Quaker, who established a non-sectarian school here about 1806. In 1827 forty children of both sexes were educated in the Lancastrian School which was located behind what is now the chapel of the Good Shepherd Convent in Clare Street. Mary Anne Walshe sold pigs' toes, *crubeens*, at one end of the Long Can for fifty years. She announced her retirement by closing the door of her premises and putting a note, "No more toes" on her window.

THE CHRISTIAN BROTHERS were asked to establish schools in Limerick by the Catholic Bishop, Dr. Charles Touhy (1814-1828). Three brothers, Austin Dunphy, Francis Grace and Aloysius Kelly arrived in Limerick on 26 June 1816. They lived in Hill's Lane, north of Curry Lane at first; moved to Denmark Street in 1817 until 1824; and then settled into the Diocesan College in Corbally where they opened a school in 1824.

THE ASSEMBLY ROOMS in Charlotte's Quay were hired by the Christian Brothers at an annual rent of £75. On 11 September 1816 they opened their first school in the city and within six months had enrolled 648 pupils.

THE GOOD SHEPHERD CONVENT is built on the site of the old Lancastrian School. As school attendance figures dropped in Joseph Lancaster's school the building gradually fell into disrepair. In November 1821 the Christian Brothers purchased the building for £200, subject to a yearly rent of £20.371/2. They let part of their garden to Madame De Beligond, superioress of the Good Shepherd Convent, in 1858 at an annual rent of £10. When they left the building in 1888 they sold it to the nuns for £200.

THE THOMOND BREWERY, off Old Clare Street, was owned by the Stein family in 1865 and was one of three breweries still operative in the city in that year. It was sold in 1879 and demolished soon afterwards. The Good Shepherd nuns established a girls' reformatory on the site where young women who had become pregnant out of wedlock sometimes endured a harsh existence.

THE GOOD SHEPHERD LAUNDRY is built on the Farrancroghy execution site on which public executions took place during the sixteenth and seventeenth centuries.

SEXTON STREET was named after Edmond Sexton Pery in 1797. On 1 September 1825 the Christian Brothers leased a half-acre site behind the Artillery Barracks, on Sexton Street, from Samuel Dixon at an annual rent of £15.75.

THE SEXTON STREET CHRISTIAN BROTHERS SCHOOL had the foundation-stone of its monastery laid on 21 September 1825. On 13 June the Brothers left the Diocesan College in Corbally and moved into their own, new, quarters. On 2 July 1828 the foundation-stone of their school was laid and on 20 May 1829 the school opened. The erection of the monastery cost £859.81, and the school was built for £562.29. Between August 1852 and April 1853 the monastery was extended. The directors of the Waterford and Limerick Railway gave the Brothers a site next to their monastery which they enclosed with a boundary wall between 22 September 1862 and March 1863. Over the next few years two new wings were added to the school. In 1871 Br. Welsh bought an adjoining house, John Russell's, for £700 where he later built St. Joseph's Male Orphanage.

ASIATIC CHOLERA swept through Asia and Europe before it reached Ireland, and Limerick, in 1832. It was transmitted through poor sanitation, inefficient sewerage disposal, an unsafe water supply, contaminated food and a lack of personal hygiene. The city hospitals were unable to cope with all the casualties and the Christian Brothers allowed their schools to be used as cholera hospitals from May to October 1832.

LAUREL HILL CONVENT was founded by Mother D'Hover, superioress of the Faithful Companions of Jesus in 1854, with the help of Br. J.P. Welsh of the Christian Brothers who procured the site for her. One of this convent's most famous students, Kate O'Brien, was born nearby, in Mulgrave Street.

KATE O'BRIEN (1897-1974), novelist, playwright, journalist, critic, and travel-writer was educated in Laurel Hill before completing her education at University College, Dublin, in 1916. Kate belonged to the rich, educated, Limerick middle class but left Ireland, to seek her fortune, as Ireland offered few opportunities for qualified women. Spain influenced her most. She worked there as a governess in 1922-1923 but lived, for most of her life, in England. "Kate found employment successively as a teacher, a journalist, a writer, and, during the war years, with the Ministry of Information. She contracted a short-lived marriage and thereafter remained single. In these ways she was atypical of many women of her time, who still saw no role for themselves apart from the traditional ones of wife and mother". Her exile was voluntary as Kate "belonged to the world of writers and artists who traditionally are at home any place where they may live in peace and practise their art". She died in Faversham, Kent, on 13 August 1974.

LIMERICK RAILWAY STATION may have been designed by Sancton Wood (1814-1886), the English architect who designed Heuston Station and all the other railway stations stretching from Monasterevan to Limerick Junction. The Waterford and Limerick railway was the first Irish railway to receive parliamentary approval, although it was not the first line to open as the Dublin and Kingston line opened in 1834. The first train to run between Limerick and Tipperary, connecting the cities of Dublin and Limerick, did so on 9 May 1848. The Limerick Railway Station opened in 1858. This is a spacious stone building close to the city with plenty of space for freight, buses and parking. Lavatories were provided on trains in 1872. This was a luxury third-class passengers were unable to avail of, but there were frequent and lengthy stops at almost every station. On 1 June 1898 dining-cars were available on the Cork mail train. Michael Quin, a retired merchant who took a prominent part in civic affairs, was elected Mayor in 1848. His mayoral medallion states; "Got possession of the Island Bank for the citizens. Railway communications opened 9th May between Dublin and Limerick." Robert E. Mitchell was the first superintendent of the Great Southern and Western Railway, which employed up to 600 men at a locomotive repair yards in Roxboro, by the turn of the century.

SEAN HEUSTON took first place in Ireland at the Great Southern and Western Railway Company's examination of 1908. He worked as a railway clerk in Limerick until he was recalled to Dublin in 1913. Where there he worked in Kingsbridge Station in the traffic manager's office while his spare time was devoted to organising for Fianna Eireann. He was a captain in D Company, First Battalion Dublin Brigade. During Easter Week he commanded the occupation and defence of the Mendicity Institute on Dublin's South Quays. On 8 May 1916 he was executed by firing squad in Kilmainham Jail. Kingsbridge Station later had its name changed to Heuston Station in his honour.

THE ENGLISH MAIL reached the city between 12.00 noon and 1.00 p.m. instead of in the evening during William Monsell's tenure as Postmaster General. During his term of office he extended the telegraph system throughout Ireland. William got into trouble in the House of Commons for exceeding the Irish Postal estimates by spending money in Ireland out of the General Post Office (England) fund. He was selected for Grand Jury service by Caleb Powell in 1858. Caleb, himself, was unlucky in politics. Although he served his constituents fairly, the Catholics disliked him because of his religion and the Protestants because of his policy.

ROBERT BYRNES was one of Limerick's earliest casualties during the War of Independence. He was jailed on an arms

charge, and instigated a riot in Limerick Prison when his campaign to get political status for himself and his fellow-prisoners failed. This riot was followed by a hunger strike in which several prisoners participated. Bobby, as he was called by his friends, was removed to the Limerick Union Hospital when he became ill. A rescue attempt by the I.R.A. succeeded, but Bobby was wounded in the process and died after escaping on the evening of 16 April, 1919.

CLARE STREET was the scene of an abortive ambush in April, 1920. An informer leaked details of I.R.A. plans to the authorities. As the men of C Company of the I.R.A. took up their positions the British Army encircled them. The commandant of the I.R.A. unit ordered his men to retreat across the canal, by boat, as lorry loads of soldiers had cordoned off the bridges.

THE WELSH FUSILIERS went on a rampage through the city in April 1920. Armed with bayonets, revolvers and entrenching tools they ran amok in the streets and raided houses, bars and cinemas. They attacked and beat up the citizens who retaliated with a barrage of bottles, stones and anything else they could lay their hands on. Other troops came to their rescue by firing indiscriminately on the people. A publican named Dwyer was shot dead behind his own counter in Roches Street, while a cinema usherette, Miss Johnson, was killed as she was returning home from the Coliseum Cinema where she worked.

WHITE'S LANE, near the junction of John Street, Broad Street and Mungret Street was the scene of a shoot-out on Friday 8 April 1921 when a group of I.R.A. men were almost surprised by six R.I.C. men who emerged suddenly from a public-house. Two R.I.C. men and two civilians were wounded; another civilian killed; and the I.R.A. commandant, Dundon, was wounded slightly. A few minutes before this incident a Black and Tan constable, Wiggins, was shot dead when his patrol stumbled across an I.R.A. unit as they were about to disband in the vicinity of Church Street and Palmerstown. Three of the I.R.A. men, Dundon, Downey and McGrath found shelter in an unoccupied house located between the homes of two R.I.C. sergeants on Lelia Street while Jack Madigan's home, on the same street, was wrecked by the police who spent most of that night raiding Sinn Fein, and suspected Sinn Fein, homes. A proclamation ordered everyone to remain indoors by 2.00 p.m. on the following day, Saturday 9 April, 1921 when General Cameron led a motorised convoy on official reprisals within the city. He supervised the bombing of Tommy McInerney's public-house, Nos. 9 and 10 Lock Quay, and the

shop and residence of a Mrs. Nealon in John Street. Mrs. Nealon was the aunt of Henry Meany, an I.R.A. activist. Tommy McInerney was the transport officer of the Mid Limerick Brigade of the I.R.A. On 21 April 1916 Tommy had driven off Ballykissane Pier, Kerry, while conveying people to meet Roger Casement. His three passengers drowned. Tommy survived.

THE BLACK AND TANS were the masters of Limerick by April 1921. They operated a curfew; banned the holding of fairs, markets or auctions within an eight-mile radius of the General Post Office; cordoned off the streets whenever they wished; searched, arrested and brutalised the population; ransacked, looted and wrecked the homes and business premises of suspected I.R.A. or Sinn Fein sympathisers; and indulged in orgies of destruction whenever they were attacked, frustrated, drunk or annoyed. They were considered "the sweepings of the English jails", discharged ex-servicemen fit for little else but the terrorising of a civilian population.

HENRY CLANCY was one of three I.R.A. men captured in Ballysimon on Sunday, 1 May, 1921.On their way into the city he jumped from the Crossley tender in which he was being transported only to be riddled with bullets as he regained his footing. Ironically he had survived the worst days of World War I with the Warwickshire Regiment only to die fighting the army he had once served in. The Black and Tans refused to allow all but five mourners to accompany his funeral procession. They attacked the cortege and drove the sympathisers away. Michael Downey, one of the mourners, was shot as he crossed the Fair Green, and the priest officiating at the Clancy funeral had to leave it hurriedly to administer the last rites. Thomas Keane, who was captured with Henry Clancy, was executed in the New Barrack on 4 June 1921.

EAMON DE VALERA was in Limerick on Monday night 5 December 1921. At 2.15 a.m. on Tuesday, 6 December, 1921, the Anglo-Irish Treaty was signed in London and was later approved in Dail Eireann by a vote of 64 to 57 on 7 January, 1922. On that Monday night Eamon De Valera said; "This is a separate nation and never till the end of time will they [the English] get from this nation alle-

P. 65. *The River Shannon near Thomond Bridge.*
P. 66. *Distinctive architecture on O'Connell Avenue.*
P. 67. *Saturday morning market scene.*
P. 68. *The Abbey River.*

giance to their rulers". He cautioned his listeners against optimism. The following day he returned to Dublin. Early in 1922 the Black and Tans and the Auxiliaries left Limerick, and the new Free State. The Royal Irish Constabulary force was disbanded and the new *Garda Sìòchana* was established. The uncrowned harp was now the new national emblem.

CIVIL WAR soon broke out. The Mid Limerick Brigade should have moved in to occupy the posts evacuated by the British but the general headquarters of the Free State suspected that Liam Forde, the Mid Limerick Brigade commandant, might not recognise their authority. Michael Brennan, Commandant of the 1st Western Division, was asked to move into Limerick with his own men to occupy barracks buildings vacated by the departing British military and police. Soon, three entirely different forces occupied the city which, as in former times, commanded the Shannon and the entry to the south and west of Ireland. These groups consisted of Brennan's Clare men who favoured the Treaty; the men of the Mid Limerick Brigade who disagreed with Forde's views but resented the presence of the Clare men as a slur upon their loyalty to the Free State; and anti-Treaty forces who had moved into the city and set up posts of their own on 6 March 1922. Shortly afterwards both Free State forces withdrew from Limerick in an acceptable compromise drafted by Liam Lynch and Oscar Traynor and confirmed by General Eoin O'Duffy. A small occupying garrison, responsible to Liam Lynch, was left to hold the city. War erupted on 28 June, 1922. General Michael Brennan believed that "the Civil War turned on Limerick". Liam Lynch controlled most of the south and west with the exception of parts of Limerick, Clare and South Galway. He reinforced Limerick in the belief that the opposing Free State forces were stronger, or as strong, as his own, and was afraid to move men to Dublin in case Limerick would fall. He tried to neutralise his opponents, Brennan and O'Hannigan, by drafting agreements to prevent either side attacking the other, and actually persuaded Donncada O'Hannigan to sign such an agreement on 4 July 1922. General Dermot MacManus revoked this agreement, personally, the following day. He had travelled from Dublin to Limerick, posing as a tramp, to tell Liam Lynch that neither Brennan nor O'Hannigan had authority to enter into negotiations. But on 7 July MacManus, though "absolutely disapproving" of any such agreement, wrote that he would allow one signed by Lynch and Brennan to stand, leaving the city in an uneasy state of truce. Brennan observed these terms until he sent Lynch a polite note ending the truce on 11 July. By 5.00 p.m. that day the Free State troops had taken up new positions. Brennan had entered into negotiations while he was waiting for arms to arrive. The bluffing was over. The Civil War had started in earnest. As the Free State troops took up their positions one of their number was shot.

WILLIAM STREET became a battle zone by 7.00 p.m., on 11 July 1922 when the Free State forces opened fire on the Republican garrison holding the Ordnance Barracks. On Sunday, 16 July, Seamus Hogan, the man who had delivered the necessary arms to Brennan, reported that his men were running short of ammunition during an attack they were making on the Strand Barracks which was held by the Republicans. There was heavy street fighting in the city on 18 July when the Republicans tried to take full control before Free State reinforcements arrived. On Wednesday, 19 July the Free State army set up an 18-pounder gun on Arthur's Quay to bombard the Strand Barrack. This eventually fell but some of its defenders managed to escape. The Castle Barrack was captured by the Free State Army on Thursday 20 July. On Friday 21 July 1922 the Republican forces abandoned the city to the victorious Free State army. By then the area around what is now Sarsfield Barrack, Little Jerusalem, Wolfe Tone Street, Lord Edward Street, St. Joseph Street and Bowman Street, had become a no-man's land. Limerick prison had been designed to hold 120 prisoners a century before. By 6 November 1922 it contained 800, with up to 12 prisoners each in cells meant to contain only one person. While the Republican men were in prison or on the run with the various guerilla units, many of the day-to-day details were managed by their womenfolk in the *Cumann na mBan*. Two of the most active of these women, in the city, were Madge Daly and Nurse Guthrie who

Matthew Bridge over the Abbey River.

were involved in numerous escape plots. The Civil War ended in May 1923. De Valera and Fianna Fail remained outside the Dail until 1927. In March 1932 Fianna Fail secured 70 seats in a general election, thus putting the men who had opposed the Treaty effectively in government.

ROCHES STORES was looted during the Troubles. One man, a prominent citizen in later life, was seen wheeling a rack of men's clothes towards his own premises, a drapery. In another incident, between the time the Republicans left a certain barracks and the Free State Army moved in, a motor car abandoned in the barracks' yard was moved into a nearby premises. Soon after the end of the Civil War this "liberated" vehicle appeared on the streets of the city as a taxi.

GARRYOWEN, *Garraí* or *Gardín Eoghain,* Owen's Garden was a favourite resort of the citizens from the mid-eighteenth century until well into the nineteenth century. The original Garryowen was located outside the city walls east of the Citadel.

THE GARRYOWEN BOYS were the sons of Limerick's wealthy merchants who formed a gang of that name. They specialised in smashing street lamps, rattling door knockers and baiting the night watchmen. Their exploits were celebrated in the Bard of Thomond's *Drunken Thady and the Bishop's Lady* and *Garryowen in Glory* another epic work written by an unknown poet. Harry O'Brien and Johnny O'Connell were the ringleaders of this wild bunch.

"For Johnny Connell, the dreaded man,
With his wild-raking Garryowen clan,
Cleared the streets and smashed each lamp,
And made the watchmen all decamp!"

Johnny later became a prominent member of the city's business community and donated a site at Baker Place to the Dominicans who erected their church on it. Johnny's father, John O'Connell, founded a brewery in 1780 on a site between Green Hill Road and Mulgrave Street. This was closed down in 1881. The inscribed foundation-stone from the old brewery is in the Limerick Museum but the site itself was built over, in succeeding years, with rows of houses; Grattan Villas, 1899; Garryowen Villas, 1897; Geraldine Villas, 1899; and Fairview Terrace in 1905. Soldiers from the Strand and Artillery barracks occupied these houses. The nearby Sarsfield Avenue was the first local housing venture carried out by the Irish Free State. Johnny O'Connell was buried in Donoghmore graveyard.

GARRYOWEN IN GLORY was set to music, with a rousing martial air. During the

Limerick Railway Station.

American Revolution three volunteer corps were formed under the names of the Limerick Union, the Loyal Limerick Volunteers, and the Limerick Volunteers. After the termination of the war in America the improvement and extension of the city were renewed with unexampled spirit: and although contested elections and alarms of insurrection in the neighbouring districts at times disturbed its tranquility, they never retarded its improvement. *Garryowen in Glory* was "exported" during these years. It was played by the 1st New York Regiment on the march to Quebec in 1775; became the original regimental march of the 1st Battalion (83rd. Foot) Royal Ulster Rifles; and was played by the 28th Gloucestershire Regiment on the field of Waterloo. The 18th Royal Irish Rifles and the 18th Foot also adopted *Garryowen in Glory* as their regimental march, as did the 69th New York Regiment, the Fighting 69th, during the 1860s. The Sioux indians called it *Devil's Music* because it was played by the 7th U.S. Cavalry who also had the words *Garry Owen* inscribed on their regimental shield. Several Limerick men were killed at the Battle of the Little Big Horn in 1876 when General Custer was defeated by Chief Sitting Bull.

THE GARRYOWEN KICK was described by Des Harty as a ploy, also known as *The Up and Under,* which originated with Limerick's famous Garryowen Rugby Football Club. He also referred to their friendly city rivals, the Shannon Rugby Football Club, and said that both clubs had celebrated their centenaries only a few years ago. The Garryowen R.F.C. has played in Australia, New Zealand and South Africa as well as in interprovincial championship games, Munster Senior Cup, Musgrave Cup, Munster Shield

and Charity Cup matches. They lost their grounds, *Under the Tower* after the liquidation of the Limerick Markets and they played the last game on their home ground, a Munster Final, against University College Cork in 1937.

THE MARKETS' FIELD was the cradle of the Gaelic Athletic Association long before they moved to their main grounds on the Ennis Road. In September 1888 the first great Gaelic sports were held here under the rules of the G.A.A. and I.C.A.

GREYHOUND RACING is also held in the Markets' Field on Monday, Friday and Saturday nights. The greyhound was originally bred as a hunting dog and was known as a *mílchu* to the ancient Irish. This was a term applied to all hunting hounds whether they were greyhounds, wolfhounds, or any other breed used for that purpose. A ninth-century book, *Cormac's Glossary,* mentioned how greyhounds, and coursing contests, could be found at every *aonach,* or fair. Although the ninth-century record is the earliest written account of greyhounds tradition, folklore and legend associate them with the *Fianna* and other mythical and legendary figures of an earlier time.

ST. LAURENCE'S CHURCH was located near the old County Hospital on what is now Mulgrave Street. By 1827 Fitzgerald could find no vestige of it.

GARRYOWEN PORTER had to compete for business with the Guinness Brewery in the 1870's. On 15 October 1872 John Cronin proposed at a meeting of the Guardians of the Limerick Union that "the resolution ordering that Guinness's porter be supplied to the house be rescinded" as Garryowen porter could be supplied instead. His proposal was seconded by the Mayor, John Watson

Mahony, who stated that the "Garryowen porter was supplied to the lunatic asylum for a long time past and not a single complaint was made against it," Alderman Myles supported the motion and quoted a Dr. Cameron who had certified that the local product was unadulterated and good. Lord Clarina objected to this motion on the grounds that they, the guardians, "were not there to protect local trade, but to protect the poor and the rate-payers. They were aware that Guinness's was the best porter in the world and he believed that the medical officers were in favour of continuing it in the hospital". The original motion was carried at the meeting, but it is doubtful if it was ever implemented. Porter, or stout, was first brewed in 1722, by Ralph Harwood in London. Roasted barley gave it its distinctive dark colouring, and its name was derived from the London porters with whom it had soon become a popular beverage. On 1 December, 1759, Arthur Guinness entered his name on the minute book of the Brewers and Maltsters Corporation of Dublin and took out a 9,000-year-lease on a premises at St. James Gate, Dublin, at an annual rent of £45. In 1799 he brewed the last traditional Dublin ale there before switching over to the newer drink, porter.

PARNELL STREET is named after Charles Stewart Parnell (1846-1891) who, it was alleged, made some very uncomplimentary remarks about his parliamentary colleagues on the platform of Limerick Railway Station according to a report in the *Freeman's Journal* of 1 August 1879. These remarks were investigated by the *Limerick Reporter* and discovered to be fabrications which reflected Whig chagrin at the results of an Ennis by-election in which Parnell had ousted Lysaght Finegan. Charles Stewart Parnell wrote to Maurice Lenihan, editor of the *Limerick Reporter* on 5 August 1879 to thank him for his "manly and common sense appreciation" of the situation. When Parnell died in 1891 his last words were; "Kiss me, sweet wifie, and I will try to sleep a little"; not; "Let my love be given to my colleagues and to the Irish people".

LIMERICK CORPORATION came into existence by prescription and charter, its authority was confirmed and regulated by statute, and its first documentary grant of municipal privileges was made in 1197 — ten years before London achieved the same recognition. The Corporation's governing charter dating from 1609 was granted by James I. This constituted the city a county of itself with the exception of the king's castle, the county court-house and the jail. It conferred an exclusive admiralty jurisdiction, both civil and criminal, over so much of the Shannon as extended three miles north-east of the city to the main sea, with all its creeks, banks and rivulets within those limits; constituted the mayor, recorder and four of the aldermen annually elected, justices of the peace for the county of the city; and incorporated a society of merchants of the staple with the privileges of the merchants of the Staple of Dublin. The Corporation according to this charter, other charters had been issued in 1292, 1399, 1413, 1429, 1486, 1552, 1574 and 1582, consisted of a mayor, two sheriffs, and an indefinite number of aldermen, burgesses, and freemen, aided by a recorder, four charter justices, a town-clerk (who was also clerk of the crown and of the peace for the county of the city), chamberlain, common speaker, water-bailiff (an office abolished in 1823), sword-bearer, high constable, petty constables, sergeants-at-mace, weigh-master, crane-master, and "other inferior" officers. James II granted a new charter which was later set aside and the constitution continued unaltered until 1823. The Limerick Regulation Act of that year remodelled the powers of the Corporation. Numerous incorporated trading companies or guilds were established under various charters but by 1837, although these companies still existed, they were not recognised as component parts of the Corporation, nor did they appear to have exercised any corporate rights. The guild of merchants, incorporated by James I, became extinct but was revived in 1823. Its members never met, nor was any attempt made to enforce its charter as its objects were effectually accomplished by the Chamber of Commerce. In 1837 the Corporation revenues were derived from rents of houses and lands in the city and Liberties, the fishery of the salmon weir, tolls, customs (the most profitable source of income that year), and the cleansing of the streets in the old city. This produced a gross income of between £4,000 and £5,000 per annum in the 1830s. Between 1890 to 1931 the Corporation built a total of 297 houses. Their public housing development schemes between 1931 and 1940 led to the erection of 822 dwellings, starting with 454 houses in St. Mary's Park and the others in Janesboro, O'Dwyer Villas and Killalee. During the 1940s 1,137 houses were provided in Kileely and Prospect but even this figure was surpassed by the completion of 1,751 dwellings in Ballynanty Beg, Ballinacurra-Weston, Garryowen, Assumpta Park, Rathbane and the inner-city scheme at Carey's Road. Most of the public housing develop-

ment between 1961 and 1971 concentrated on the south side of the city, Green Hill, Tankfield, St. John's, the upper section of Carey's Road and the beginning of the Kennedy Park - Keyes Park complex at Galvone. Carew Park, Glasgow Park, O'Malley Park, other parts of South Hill, and the inner-city developments at De Valera Park, Watergate and Vizes Court have all taken place since 1971. After 1973 there was a major change as most of the development took place on the north side of the city, starting with Moyross and continuing through Ballygrennan and Thomondgate, back into the city with Island Road, Lelia Place and Fitzgerald Place. The Corporation is also responsible for the fire-fighting service, water supply, drainage, public lighting, maintenance of the existing roads, construction of new roads, provision of car-parking facilities at Arthur's Quay, Bank Place, Charlotte Quay, Dominick Street, Denmark Street, Francis Street, Michael Street, Pike's Bow and St. John's Square, and the introduction of disc-parking in 1984.

THE MAYOR OF LIMERICK was an office first held by Adam Sarvant in 1197-1198. This office and hose of the sheriffs, recorder and town-clerk were elected annually by the common council on the second Monday after 24 June, and the four charter justices by the same body on the second Monday after 29 September. The chamberlain was elected from among the burgesses for life, or during pleasure, by the mayor, sheriffs and recorder. The aldermen were elected for life among the burgesses by the common council: the title, however, was an honorary distinction, usually conferred on the person who has served the office of mayor. The common speaker was elected every two years, under the provisions of the 1823 Act, by the body of freemen assembled on the first Tuesday after 24 June, in the court of D'Oyer Hundred, and had to be approved of by the common council before he could be sworn into office: the other officers were appointed respectively by the common council, the mayor, and the sheriffs. The mayor was a justice of the peace within the county of the city, and ex officio a magistrate for the county at large according to Samuel Lewis in 1837. He was also admiral of the Shannon, and, with the recorder and aldermen, had very extensive magisterial and judicial powers connected with the exclusive admiralty jurisdiction given by the charter of 1609, and was empowered to appoint all the officers of a court of admiralty, a court which had fallen into disuse by them. The mayor was also a judge in local courts and was named first in the commission with the judges at the assizes

for the county of the city; and was a coroner within the county of the city and the parts of the Shannon comprised within the admiralty jurisdiction, and clerk of the markets. The other magistrates were the recorder, four charter justices and six additional justices appointed by the Lord-Lieutenant under the Act of 1823. There have been many changes since the foundation of the Republic of Ireland but the mayoral office has continued although many of its functions have altered and other offices associated with it have been abolished. The biggest change of all was between 1962 and 1964 when Frances Condell held the mayoral office for two terms, the first woman to do so since the office was inaugurated 765 years before.

THE FREEDOM OF LIMERICK was obtained by birth, for the eldest son, or marriage with any daughter, of a freeman, also by apprenticeship to a freeman within the city, and by gift of the Corporation: the admissions of freemen were made by the common council, subject to the approbation of the Court of D'Oyer Hundred. This court was comprised of the entire body of freemen, and a certified minute of all proceedings at the meetings of the common council had to be transmitted by the town-clerk to the common speaker who presided over the court, for its approval. The word *oyer* means an assize or a hearing in a law-court. The Court of D'Oyer Hundred had ceased to function by the 1750s but was revived in 1823. Isaac Butt was made an honorary freeman on 1 January, 1877. On 14 July, 1880, Charles Stewart Parnell received the same honour. Amongst those who received the freedom of the city were Cardinal Logue in 1894, Thomas J.Clarke in 1889, Maude Gonne in 1900, Andrew Carnegie in 1903, Douglas Hyde in 1909, Mrs. Thomas Clarke, Eoin MacNeill and Eamon De Valera in 1918, Sean T. O Ceallaigh in 1948, John Fitzgerald Kennedy in 1963, Dr. Kenneth David Kaunda in 1964, Rev. Robert Wyse-Jackson in 1970 and Pope John Paul II in 1979.

LIMERICK CITY returned two representatives to the Irish Parliament from its earliest convocations until the Union, after which it sent one member to the Imperial Parliament. In 1831 the city again sent two representatives to Parliament, under an Act passed by William IV. In that year there were about 2,000 Freeholders of the county of the city, making up a total of 2,413 electors. Under William's Act the voting franchise was extended to £10 householders, and to £20 and £10 leaseholders for the respective terms of 14 and 20 years; the non-resident freeman, except within seven miles, was disenfranchised; and the £2 freeholders retained the privilege only for life. The number of electors

on 14 February, 1837, was 3,186. Of these 912 were freeholders, 14 rent-chargers, 34 leaseholders, 1946 £10 householders and 280 freemen: with the sheriffs acting as the returning officers. Until 1899 the right to vote was restricted to ratepaying occupiers or owners of property. Married women, of thirty years or over, received the vote in 1918 but it was not until 1935 that every citizen, of twenty-one years or over, became entitled to vote, and this age was reduced to eighteen years in recent times.

THE SOUTH LIBERTIES extended from four to five statute miles about the city and comprised 14,754 Irish acres in the 1830s. In 1831 Limerick city contained 4,862 houses. The principal residences, six years later, were Mount Shannon, Hermitage, Clarina, Doonass and the mansions of the Earl of Limerick and the Church of Ireland Bishop within the city. In the vicinity of Limerick there were several good houses and neat villas, but by no means so numerous as its wealth would lead strangers to suspect. The rich merchants chiefly resided in Newtownpery, the spacious streets of which still intersect each other at right angles, and were occupied by elegant houses, splendid and well-stocked shops, and merchants' stores. Patrick Street, George's Street (now O'Connell Street), and the Crescent formed, and still do, a continuous line of elegant houses, extending about a mile from Mathew Bridge. The environs of the city were described as flat but beautiful in 1837. The soil was extremely rich and the sinuous course of the Shannon presented the appearance of a succession of lakes although the landscape was deficient in wood. The city was then the headquarters of the south-western region, which comprised the counties of Clare, Limerick, Tipperary (including Nenagh but excluding the barony of Lower Ormond) and that part of county Kerry north of the Flesk, and contained four military barracks.

SINGLAND, or St. Patrick's Parish, is on the southern banks of the Shannon, close to the city, where the river sweeps round the eastern, northern and western sides of the parish. During the various sieges of the city the military camps of Cromwell, Ireton, William III and Ginkel were located here. Traces of their camps and entrenchments have been discovered over the centuries, military weapons were frequently found, and the remains of the ancient military roads from Dublin and from Cork could still be traced by Samuel Lewis in 1837.

ST. PATRICK'S PARISH CHURCH AND ROUND TOWER were destroyed during the war of 1641. Most of the remaining buildings were taken down by an English army to build batteries during one of the sieges, and the por-

tions that were left standing were demolished in 1766. In 1837 the graveyard remained and Samuel Lewis claimed that only Catholics were interred here. St. Patrick is believed to have baptised Cairthenn, a Dalcassian king, here in ancient times. St. Patrick's Well was still the scene of an annual pilgrimage on 17 March, into the 1960s. In 1750 another St. Patrick's Catholic Church was built in Pennywell, mainly at the expense of a Mr. Harrold. This appears to have been replaced by a newer church built in 1816, in the form of a letter T, which was small but "neatly fitted up". This was improved in 1835.

THE GROODY RIVER passes through St. Patrick's Parish and enters the Shannon east of the canal. Most of the land through which it flows was under tillage in the 1830s, "and supplies the city with large quantities of vegetables; along the banks of the Groody is a tract of rich meadow, liable, however, to casualties from floods. On the river are a bleach-green, a paper-mill, and a flour-mill: at the salmon weir near the Shannon, is a very extensive flour-mill which commands the whole water of that river: in the city suburbs is a large brewery ... The city water-works and the county infirmary are in the parish. There are several very elegant seats, with small but highly ornamented demesnes: the principal are Park House, the residence of the Rt. Rev. Dr. Ryan, R.C. Bishop of Limerick; Corbally House, of Poole Gabbett, Esq.; and Corbally Park, of Pierce Shannon, Esq." Over 150 years later this is one of the two large tributaries, the other is the Ballinacurra Creek south-west of the city, into which surface water is discharged. A short canal from the Abbey River to the Shannon intersects the parish from east to west. The Lock Quay, at the city end, is one of the few cobbled quays left in the city. The canal walks, like the quay and adjoining works are now disused, derelict, and deteriorating, a far cry from the busy work-place envisaged in 1758. Over forty individual sewer outfalls discharge directly into the Shannon as it passes through the city. Seven pumping stations within the city and two in the environs regulate the flow of the untreated effluent.

THE SEWERS OF NEWTOWNPERY are in all probability the city's least mentioned Georgian architectural features. As the new town developed a vast network of sewers was built on the original ground level to cater for the population envisaged by the city planners. These sewers are quite literally streets beneath the streets of Limerick. A deep central channel, or gutter, carried raw sewage and water from the overhead drains to the Shannon. As internal plumbing was only in its infancy during the late eighteenth and early nineteenth century each house, on either side of a street had its own access to the sewer. This was located off the basement area where a door opened directly on to the sewer, allowing house staff to walk onto the service pavement which ran parallel to the channel on either side. Slops were then emptied into this rather unsavoury stream from the safety of the pavement. Several of these access doors can still be seen off the basement areas of Limerick's Georgian buildings although the majority of them have long since been sealed off by the Corporation. Like the streets the sewers too were named. In fact many of Britain's monarchs are commemorated in the sewer's place-names.

TROY'S LOCK is a short distance upstream from Lock Quay. The nearby hump-backed canal bridge had its pronounced shape flattened in recent times to allow modern vehicles to use it but the old walls were retained. Paddy's Hedge, a popular boreen used by courting couples, has almost vanished, but its route can still be discerned west of the ruined keeper's house.

THE CANAL BREWERY was built on the north bank of the canal by Messrs. Walker and Company of Cork, at a cost of £25,000. Despite its location it never prospered and closed after a brief period.

SOUTH HILL possesses the largest corporation estate in the city, a total of 1,201 houses containing 6,500 inhabitants, built between 1966 and 1972. In October 1986, one shop, one public-house, a church which doubled as a community centre, two small playgrounds, a swimming pool, a junior school, a park and two playing pitches catered for the growing population, over half of whom were unemployed. Many city employers seemed to be biased when interviewing applicants with a South Hill address, for employment, although the nearby Krups factory are quite happy to recruit locally. An industrial project centre set up in 1982 encouraged fifteen small industries to open in Galvone. A neighbourhood youth project set up in 1975 initially catered for about 35 children aged between ten to sixteen years of age but in 1987 it was looking after 80 to 100 children.

SOURCE REFERENCE NUMBERS

1 9 14 28 30 31 33 37 39 40 59
61 63 64 71 75 80 81 82 84 85 90
94 96 97 98 101 103 108 110 117 118 120 123
127 128 129 130 131 132 133 137 138 142 143
144 146 150 156 160 161 169 173 175 176 189
195 205 206 225 226 227 238 240 244 246 255
260 261 263 264 267 280 282 284

One of the tunnels discovered near the site of the new Civic Offices.

The new bridge over the Shannon in Limerick City.

Limerick Corporation (Bardas Luimni)

RECREATION & LEISURE

SWIMMING: Roxboro Pool Telephone: 40303
Ennis Road Pool Open June, July & August

SPORTS CENTRES: Indoor Football, Table Tennis, Basketball, Gymnastics, Badminton
Moylish Sports Centre Telephone: 55802
Corbally Sports Centre Telephone 41299

LIBRARY SERVICE: City Library, The Granary, Michael St., Limerick. Telephone: 061-314668
Adult & Children's Lending Library. Hours of opening: 10.00 a.m. - 1.00 p.m. Monday-Saturday
2.30 p.m. - 8.00 p.m. Monday - Friday

LIMERICK MUNICIPAL ART GALLERY Pery Square, Limerick. Telephone 061-310633
Hours of Opening: 10.00 a.m. - 1.00 p.m. Monday Saturday   2.00 p.m. - 6.00 p.m. Monday, Wednesday & Friday

LIMERICK MUSEUM John's Square, Limerick. Telephone: 061-47826
Hours of Opening: 10.00 a.m. - 1.00 p.m. Tuesday to Saturday
2.15 p.m. - 5.00 p.m. Tuesday to Saturday

Thomondgate

and the North Liberties

THOMONDGATE takes its name from what was only the only entrance to the city from the Clare side. The name is now applied to what had become a suburb of considerable extent some centuries ago. In 1760 the population of Limerick was 32,196. The two main inns in 1790 were Taylor's New Inn in Irishtown and the Black Swan at Thomondgate. When a new line of road was under construction in the 1830s heaps of skeletons were found laid out in rows about fifteen yards in length and six feet in depth. They were supposed to have been the remains of those who died in the great plague.

THE TREATY STONE is the name given to a roughly hewn rock which is located near the northern end of Thomond Bridge until it was moved to its present position, and mounted on a pedestal, in 1865. It is now located to the south of the bridge, on the western wide of the river. The Treaty of Limerick is supposed to have been signed on this stone in 1691 but it is most unlikely that either of the opposing forces was unable to provide a writing-table for such a momentous occasion. In all probability it marked the site on which the actual signing took place, some distance away.

MICHAEL HOGAN (1832-1899) is better known under his more popular name, the Bard of Thomond. The critics and literati of his day, and latter, considered his verse abominable but it found great appeal amongst the ordinary people. His mixture of patriotism, satire and humour was appreciated in the pages of *The Nation* and other periodicals to which he contributed articles. His *Lays and Legends of Thomond* could easily be listed as a tribute in verse dedicated to the more famous people and events in the history and folklore of North Munster. Within its pages can be found some extremely fascinating

The Treaty Stone.

footnotes, some of which are more interesting than the lays and legends themselves. Over the years he produced small editions of many poetry pamphlets, most of which are now quite scarce. *Drunken Thady and the Bishop's Lady* is reputedly his masterpiece;

"This true she lived - tis true she died.
Tis true she was a Bishop's bride:
But for herself tis little matter
To whom she had been wife or daughter".

Michael "The Bard" Hogan, a nominal employee of the Limerick Corporation, was buried in Mount St. Lawrence Cemetery. His memorial was destroyed by vandals in 1986.

FR. JOHN McENERY (1796-1841) was educated in St. Munchin's Seminary at Park House. Ordained in 1819 he was appointed chaplain to the Cary family, Torquay, England in 1822. He spent the remainder of his life there, near the underground chambers known as Kent's Cavern, devoting his spare time to palaeontology, the study of fossils. Rev. John McEnery was the first to discover the remains of the prehistoric sabre-toothed tiger in Britain. Many museums were enriched with his finds and his own collection was acquired by the British Museum after his death. His epitaph summed up his career; "Mr. McEnery was the pioneer of systematic observation in Kent's Hole and other Caverns in this neighbourhood, the sagacious and reverent observer of the works in nature of Him whose is the earth and the fullness thereof". He was buried in Torre churchyard.

ST. MUNCHIN'S CATHOLIC CHURCH, on the North Strand (now Clancy's Strand) was built in 1744. In 1827 it was described as "a commodious place of worship, but destitute of any particular object of interest". In 1837 the parishes of St. Munchin and St. Nicholas with the North Liberties formed the composite parish of St. Lelia's, the original parish church of which was replaced with the present edifice in 1922. Samuel Lewis claimed that the "chapel, situated at Thomond-gate, is a large cruciform structure ... the first R.C. place of worship publicly erected in Limerick since the revolution".

GEORGE CLANCY was a native of Grange. Better known as Seoirse he was a teacher, an Irish speaker, an organiser of both the Irish Volunteers and the Gaelic League, a leader of the anti-conscription campaign and a collector of the Dial Eireann Loan. In January 1921 he was elected Mayor of Limerick. At 1.30 a.m. on Monday morning, 7 March, 1921, he went downstairs to answer a loud hammering on the door of his home. "It's all right Moll", he reassured his wife, "it's only a raid". Moll Clancy glimpsed three men at the door. They were tall, wore goggles, had caps pulled low over their foreheads and their coat-collars were turned up, concealing their faces. She overheard the ensuing conversation. "Are you Clancy?" "Yes! I am". "Come out here then. We want you." "What for?" "Come out-side". "No I won't", said George as he stepped back into the hallway opening the front door wider. "Then take that!", one of the men shouted and he started shooting at George. Moll rushed forward and threw herself between her husband and his assassins. She was too late. George was fatally wounded and she was shot in the hand. This shooting was one of several such killings on that night, later known as the night of the Curfew Murders.

THE CURFEW MURDERS on the night of 6-7 March 1921 were believed to have been perpetrated by a group of British intelligence officers variously known as the Cairo Gang or the Murder Gang. This group had first come together in Cairo, hence the former name, but they had been reassembled in Ireland to carry out a series of raids, searches and assassinations at the behest of Sir Henry Wilson. Michael Collins suspected that the British were "shooting by roster" when seventeen Irishmen were murdered in October 1920. On the morning of Sunday 21 November 1920 his special counter-intelligence unit shot fourteen of these special agents dead. Despite the Collins' coup on Bloody Sunday the under-cover war was continued by the English. A notorious ex-convict, and rapist, Captain Nathan, was the ringleader of Wilson's Murder Gang in Limerick. He is generally believed to have been responsible for the Curfew Murders, and was definitely involved in the murder of Denis O'Donovan in Castleconnell. During the Spanish Civil War (1936-1939) he was killed fighting on the Communist side with Bela Kun.

MICHAEL O'CALLAGHAN was Mayor of Limerick in 1920. His grandfather, Eugene O'Callaghan, once proposed a motion urging the repeal of the Union at a Corporation meeting in 1843. Michael had continued in the family's nationalist tradition. He was a member of Sinn Fein, a volunteer officer, and a member of the Gaelic League. He was shot at 1.00 a.m. on the morning of 7 March, 1921, by two men whose descriptions matched those of two of George Clancy's killers. Like George, he was murdered in the presence of his wife. She later refused to attend the inquiry into his, Michael's, death and was elected in the "Partition Election" of May 1921. During this general election 124 Sinn Fein and 4 Independent candidates were returned for the Southern Ireland Parliament while the Northern Ireland Parliament returned 40 Unionist, 6 Nationalist and 6 Sinn Fein candidates. Clancy's Strand and O'Callaghan's Strand are named after the two murdered mayors.

JOSEPH O'DONOGHUE of Ballinacargy, County Westmeath, was also slain on the night of the Curfew Murders. At 11.40 p. m. on the night of 6 March 1921 he was taken from the Lyddy home at *Tig na Fáinne*, Janesboro, by twelve R.I.C. men under the command of a Detective Leech. His body was discovered on Janesboro Avenue the following morning.

THE THOMONDGATE DISTILLERY of Stein, Browne and Company produced 455,000 gallons of whiskey annually in 1837. In the same year the city possessed seven breweries which brewed a total of 5,000 barrels of porter, ale and beer annually, mainly for local consumption. Several cooperages, iron-foundries and comb-manufacturers also existed locally.

THE HOUSE OF INDUSTRY on Clancy's Strand had its foundations laid on 10 March 1774, by Joseph Johns, Mayor of Limerick, after legislation was introduced in 1772 to establish poorhouses and workhouses in every county. Bishop Gore granted the land at an annual rent of one pepper corn for ever and the Grand Juries of both city and county donated £500 towards the erection of house of industry. Launcelott Hill supervised the building of this "respectable edifice, forming a large square, built in courses, with a handsome front of cut stone", designed by Rev. Deane Hoare. Doctor Edward Smyth of Dublin gave £200 towards the provision of a number of cells for lunatics in the infirmary which was behind the main building, in the garden. By 1827 the building was considered inadequate as 450 inmates were confined in s space meant for 200. In 1838 the Irish Poor Relief Act led to the establishment of workhouses in the unions of Limerick, Croom, Kilmallock, Rathkeale and Newcastle West. The Corporation now use the building for storage and as offices.

THE CHRISTIAN BROTHERS opened a school in Thomondgate in September 1844. By 1852 they had four schools in the city, in Sexton Street, Clare, Street, St. Mary's Parish and St. Munchin's Parish. On 12 September 1888 they laid the foundation-stone of the Brother Welsh Memorial School, in John Street, on a site purchased from Crehan McMahon for £100. This last was built and furnished for £1,700.

THOMAS HENRY CLEEVE (1844-1908) was a son of Edward Elms Cleeve, Plumstead, Woolwich, England. He was reared and educated in Quebec, Canada, and first came to Limerick, on holiday, in 1864. The Irish agricultural scene offered him opportunities he was quick to avail of. His career commenced with the purchase of hay from Limerick farmers, which he baled and sold to the cavalry stationed within the city and county. He persuaded his brothers to join him. They established a chain of creameries, opened factories in Limerick and Tipperary to process the cream and skim milk, and then branched out into the manufacture of butter, sweets, and tinned condensed milk and cream. Golden Vale have now taken over the old Cleeves factory which contains the tallest remaining chimney stack in the city. This is built out of red bricks and was originally 150 feet high — but it is believed that the height was lowered by 30 feet some years ago. Thomas Henry Cleeve and his brothers dominated the milk trade of the region into the opening decades of the twentieth century. Thomas became a Justice of the Peace, High Sheriff (1899-1900), Deputy Lieutenant, and was created a Knight in 1900. The business was at its most prosperous during World War I when they possessed a condensed milk factory on the north bank of the Shannon, a cooperage, a box factory, a toffee factory at Charlotte Quay and several creameries. Many of the latter were burned out by the British Forces in 1920. Cleeves were amongst the largest employers in the city and, in their heydey, had a staff of almost one thousand.

KILRUSH, *Cill Rois,* may mean the Church of the Wood or Peninsula although it is also supposed to derive its name, Rose's Church, from a sister of St. Munchin's. The location of the old church suggests that in former times it was located on an island or a promontory of some kind and up to a few years ago some traces of a causeway were evident. The area was zoned for development in 1837 as it was "in contemplation ... in consequence of the facilities of communication recently afforded by the erection of Wellesley Bridge". Despite much development in the area since 1837 it was not until 1979 that the old church from which the area took its name stood in danger of demolition.

KILRUSH CHURCH, Old Church, St. Munchin's or St. Mainchin's Church is possibly the oldest building with its walls still standing in the city. Bulldozers damaged all but a small portion of the surrounding site before it could be excavated in 1979. Even so, the area almost directly beneath the Quinlivan window contained either 36 or 41 bodies. These burials were post-Medieval and dated from the sixteenth or seventeenth centuries. Some had been buried in coffins, others in shrouds, as both coffin nails and shroud pins were discovered during excavations. These

burials lay quite close close to the surface, no more than 16 inches (40cm) below the modern surface, with only a shallow covering of soil over bedrock. The burials were mainly of infants, there was evidence of late weaning, which would suggest that the site had been used as a *cillìn* or children's burial ground. 23 of the bodies were of infants under five years of age and one of them had been buried, face-downwards, in a prone position. The adults were all buried in "the modest man" position, one of them had worn a copper bracelet on the left wrist. Kilrush Church was first mentioned in 1201 but it is generally believed to be much older, possibly dating from the tenth century. It is now located in an attractive *cul-de-sac* off the North Circular Road, off Barrington's Pier, and is the chief focal point in the centre of a new housing complex. A modern brick-buttress and frame supports the west wall with its flat-headed doorway. The church is a small rectangular structure and contains a round-headed east window. The window in the south wall dates from the fifteenth century but, despite its age, it was only inserted here in 1900 by Robert Vere O'Brien. This window is believed to have belonged to the old Franciscan church in St. Mary's Lane, the eastern portion of it is inscribed with the name of the Quinlivan family.

THE QUINLIVAN NAME is derived from *O Caoindealbháin,* the descendant of *Caoindealbhán,* the Gracefully-Shaped, who died in 925. Variants of the name include O Guindelane, O Kennellan, O Kenolan, O Quinelane, Kindellan, Kennellan, Connellan, Kinlan, Kinlen, Kenlan, Conlon, Quinlan, *O Caoinliobháin, O Caoinleáin* and Quinlivan. Originating in *Cinel Laoghaire* in Meath, the name can be found in Leinster and all the counties of Munster.

THE NORTH CIRCULAR ROAD contains the residences of both Bishops of Limerick. The Church of Ireland Bishop, Dr. Edward Darling, resides in Portland House while Dr. Jeremiah Newman lives in Kilmoyle House. The latter building is an early-nineteenth century one built in classical style.

ARDHU HOUSE on the Ennis Road was the residence of Robert De Ross Rose who married the daughter of Benjamin Frend of Boskell.

THE ENNIS ROAD became the main road into Clare from the city with the erection of Sarsfield Bridge. In the latter half of the nineteenth century it became an exclusive residential area in much the same way as Newtownpery did in the previous century. The new Shannon Bridge with its auxiliary road and traffic roundabouts has already altered the traffic flow but it is still too early to gauge the long term effects this will have

on the area. In 1859 the Corporation built a reservoir here which gave the population of the time, 44,500 people, an average supply of 20 gallons each. In more recent times the reservoir was converted into a swimming-pool.

THE LIMERICK COUNTY BOROUGH is a separate and quite distinct entity from County Limerick. The easiest way to describe it would be as a county within the county encompassing the city and its immediate environs.

THE POPULATION OF THE COUNTY BOROUGH varied considerably over the years as the following chart illustrates:

Year	Total	Males	Females
1831	44,100		
1841	48,391		
1851	53,448		
1861	44,476		
1891	37,153		
1911	38,518		
1936	41,061		
1951	50,820	24,103	26,717
1956	50,886	24,047	26,839
1961	50,786	24,134	26,652
1966	55,912	26,747	29,165
1971	57,161	27,626	29,535
1979	60,665	29,593	31,072
1981	60,736	29,723	31,013
1986	56,276	27,537	28,742
1981	60,736	29,723	31,013
1986	56,276	27,537	28,742

THE CHURCH OF OUR LADY OF THE ROSARY was designed as a temporary wooden church by W.H.D. McCormick and F.M. Corr. Erected in 1949-1950 it serves a dual purpose as both a church and a show-place for modern Irish ecclesiastical art. Oisin Kelly designed the teak statue, *Our Lady of Fatima,* on the tower; the *Annunciation* is by Imogen Stuart; the *Deposition from the Cross* by Andrew O'Connor is a plaster model for the bronze now in London's Tate Gallery; the sanctuary figures of the *Sacred Heart* and *Our Lady* are by Yvonne Jammett; the *St. Anne* is by Eamon Costello; the font is by T. Quinn; and the single-light window, *The Baptism of Christ,* in the bapistry, is by Evie Hone.

COMMANDANT EDWARD 'NED' DALY was the youngest child and the only boy in a family of ten children. He was born in Frederick Street and was educated in the Presentation Convent, Sexton Street, the Christian Brothers' School in Roxboro Road and Leamy's School, an academy for commercial training. His father, an old Fenian, died in 1896. His sister, Kathleen, was married to Tom Clarke, the first signatory of the Proclamation. In 1907 Ned emigrated to

Glasgow but returned because of ill-health, and took up a clerical post with Francis Spaight and Sons Ltd.. In 1912 he left Limerick for Dublin where he worked for Brooks Thomas and Company Ltd. At the time of the 1916 Rising he was on the staff of a wholesale chemist's on Westmoreland Street, May Roberts and Company Ltd.. On Easter Monday, 1916, he commanded the First Battalion of the Dublin Brigade and was in charge of the Four Courts Garrison. He was court-martialled; sentenced to death; and executed in the big yard of Kilmainham Jail, on the morning of 4 May, 1916. He was buried in Arbour Hill with the executed leaders of the Easter Rebellion. His sisters continued to support the Nationalist struggle. Their home, Ardeevin, on the Ennis Road, was wrecked by the British forces on the night of 9 April, 1921.

JOHN DALY (1846-1916), Ned Daly's uncle, was an old Fenian and Irish Republican Brotherhood leader. On 11 April, 1884, he was arrested in Birkenhead and charged with carrying explosives. While on remand in Windsor Green Prison, Birmingham, he corresponded with his old friend Michael Hogan, the Bard of Thomond. He was sentenced to life imprisonment but was released after serving twelve and a half years in jail, where he had become the first political prisoner to use the hunger strike weapon against the British. In 1899 he was elected Mayor of Limerick and retained Mayoral office for three consecutive terms, 1899, 1900 and 1901. He died on 30 June, 1916, almost two months after the death of his nephew, Ned.

ST. CAMILLUS'S HOSPITAL was originally built by Sir Thomas Deane and Company as the Limerick Workhouse to replace the House of Industry on Clancy's Strand. Opened in May 1841 it has undergone many changes over the years but is still in operation as a hospital. The oldest part is a large Tudor-Gothic-style edifice with pointed arches over the upper windows, and pointed gables.

THE NORTH LIBERTIES varied from one to four statute miles, comprising 1714 Irish

acres in 1837. St. Munchin's Parish was situated partly in the Barony of Bunratty, County Clare, but chiefly in the North Liberties of the city of Limerick, on the River Shannon, and immediately adjoining the city. The main residences in the late 1830s were Castle Park; Ballygrennan, the home of Richard Smyth; and Clonmacken.

CASTLE PARK may have been designed by Francis Bindon (c. 1698-1765) about 1750 for Edward Ormsby. It was then leased to a Limerick solicitor, Nicholas Smith and, apparently, sold to Christopher Delmege (1785-1863) who occupied it in 1837. The building contains the stump of an old tower-house which was used as a pavilion and joined to the main structure by a screen wall. This wall, the castle remains and the single-storey wing at one end of the house were crenellated with Irish battlements of a type in vogue during the early years of the nineteenth century. The house was sold in 1969.

CLONMACKEN HOUSE is mentioned in Hugh Weir's *Houses of Clare* as a two-and-a-half storey gable-ended house with chimney stacks on each gable. Thomas Dineley wrote of it in 1680 as "a small house belonging to Mr. John Clenett, a Fleming (Dutchman), a gentleman of extraordinary civility towards strangers". He continued to relate that the house "is situated very pleasantly and commodiously upon the river Shannon, where the shipping passes by daily". In 1827 it was occupied by a Mr. D'Esterre. It was unoccupied in 1837 but listed as the property of the

Marquess of Lansdowne. Some time later John Browne Finch of Clonmacken married Maria Singleton of Quinville. The house later came into the possession of the Dixon and O'Brien-Kelly families. Hugh described the building as standing but uninhabited in 1985, and published a photograph of it as it was then.

COONAGH AIRFIELD is situated northwest of the city. Dr. Robert Wyse Jackson described Coonagh as "that ancient fishing village of Viking origin". The flying club started the aerodrome here in 1945 under the tutelage of Arthur Toppin who before his death was the oldest practising pilot in Ireland. This is still the only airfield within the county boundaries. The next nearest one is Shannon Airport, twelve miles west of here, in County Clare.

THE FIRST AERIAL FLIGHT from Limerick took place on Thursday 27 April 1786, when Richard Crosbie (1755-c.1800) made an ascent, by balloon, from the House of Industry, on a south-east by east wind, which brought him down near Ballygirreen, outside Newmarket-on-Fergus, County Clare. In 1849 John Hampton ascended from Marshall's Yard, Cecil Street, in a balloon named the *Erin-go-Bragh* which had been inflated by the Limerick Gas Consumers Company. Two Limerick men, Hampden William Russell and a Mr. Townsend accompanied him. The three landed safely at Rathlahine, near Shannon, but were thrown from their light two-wheeled carriage as they

Kilrush Church

returned to Limerick, by road. James Leslie Allen of Limerick set out from Wales on 17 April, 1912, in a fifty-horse-power Bleriot monoplane. His companion, Denys Corbett-Wilson of Kilkenny, reached County Wexford safely in a similar machine, they had taken off together, but James Leslie Allen was never seen again.

CECIL O DONOVAN, seventeen-years-old, and his fourteen-year-old brother, Aidan, were shot dead by Black and Tans as they walked through the fields at Blackwater on 20 February, 1921. They had been accompanied by their cousins, Thomas and Benjamin O'Donovan, who had managed to escape when the Black and Tans had opened fire. None of the four youths had any paramilitary connections, nor were they associated with Sinn Fein or Fianna Eireann.

KILLEELY OR MEELICK PARISH was known under both names in 1837. It was located "partly within the North Liberties of the city of Limerick, but chiefly in the Barony of Bunratty". There were then 5,141 inhabitants living on 5,135 statute acres which were nearly equally divided between tillage and pasture. The old entry into Limerick is still guarded by the castles of Cratloemoyle and Cratloekeel nearby, in County Clare, on the road to Bunratty, Shannon, Ennis and Galway.

SOURCE REFERENCE NUMBERS
1 11 27 28 33 39 42 63 70 71
86 96 97 98 103 110 120 129 131 146
150 161 173 176 178 181 188 193 195 227
228 238 246 255 266 282

Opposite page: *A view of Pery Square, from St. Michael's Church.*
Limerick Market scene.

THE
COUNTY

Abbeyfeale

Athea · Carrigkerry · Ardagh · Cahermoyle

ABBEYFEALE, the third largest town in the county, derives its name *Mainister na Fáile,* the Monastery or Abbey of the Feale, from an old Cistercian foundation established here by Brian O'Brien in 1188. This abbey had been annexed to Monasteranenagh in 1209 and was later affiliated to Margam in Glamorganshire. By 1837 a new Catholic church had been built on the site, which incorporated part of the older structure within its framework. No trace of the original building is now visible nor is much known of its history. It may have been leased to laymen about 1350, but Carmelite friars came into possession of it at a later date.

THE FEALE RIVER is named after the Lady Fial according to the *Leabhar Gabhala* - a most uncertain source, as it was mainly a collection of mythology, folklore, history and religion concocted from pre-Christian and early Christian sources in order to provide Ireland with a respectable history. Fial was bathing in the river when she saw someone approaching along the river bank and died of shame, *Féile ogos Náire,* without realising that it was her own husband who had seen her in the nude. The river rises in Rockhill East on the southern slopes of Mullaghareirk, *Mullach an Radhairc,* the Peak of the View, in the heart of the *Sliabh Luachra,* Rushy Mountain, range, in the north-western corner of Cork. An unusual feature of this river is that it passes through no lakes along its entire length.

BANDIT TERRITORY is the most fitting description of the Abbeyfeale region of the late eighteenth and early nineteenth century. The town was situated in a wild mountainous district that was virtually inaccessible until Richard Griffith was sent to south-western Ireland to build roads and bridges in 1822. Between 1823 and 1829 he built 142 miles of road which opened up communications in an area which had, until then, been a safe haven for cattle rustlers, smugglers, potheen-makers, political agitators and outlaws. Until then the only roads to traverse this hilly western corner of the county had been the hard-packed mud roads and passes dating from the sixteenth century, which were unsuitable for

wheeled vehicles, and a road from Newcastle West to Kerry which was built through Abbeyfeale in 1787. There are two bridges in the town, the Allaghaun Bridge to the south and the Kerry Bridge, a concrete one, to the west. The railway line closed in 1977 but the town is on the main Limerick-Killarney bus route.

CAPTAIN ROCK was the self-styled title of the "invisible" chief who waged a guerrilla war against the authorities during the agrarian revolts of the eighteenth and nineteenth centuries. Captain Rock was an anonymous title that embodied, and concealed, a collective identity, and was not the *nom de guerre* of any particular person. In fact the Provisional I.R.A. used a similar device in the 1970s when their notices and pronouncements were signed in the name of P. O'Neill. In 1822 Captain Rock issued proclamations "from our camp at Abbeyfeale", which was then the headquarters of the Rockites. The end of the Napoleonic wars led to a fall in agricultural prices. In 1817 famine and disease devastated the countryside, and in 1820 most of the Munster banks collapsed. The people were in a desperate plight by 1821. Recession, high taxes, tithes, rents, absentee landlords, unscrupulous farmers, greedy merchants, subdivided holdings, and a class system in which the rich got richer and the poor poorer fuelled the resentments of the landless labourers and the other poor. During the spring and summer of 1821 the weather was bad, crops rotted in the fields, the turf was unsaved, and the people were left to starve without food or fuel. Alexander Hoskins, the land agent for the Courtenay Estate, was an Englishman, new to Ireland, whose inflexible attitude towards his employer's tenants contributed towards, and probably fomented, the Rockite uprising. In 1821 he sought the army's aid in evicting tenants who had fallen into arrears and were refusing to sign new leases. This supported the Rockite contention that the establishment was basically anti-peasant, deepened the sectarian divide between Catholic and Protestant, and left the area in a state of armed unrest from 1821 to 1824. Between 1822 and 1823 the Rifle Brigade and several English and Scottish regiments were stationed in West

Limerick to quell disturbances and hunt down the Rockites. It "was only under the application of the insurrection act, and the most vigorous exertions of the magistracy, that the spirit of violence was at length suppressed" and the Rockites disbanded.

THE WHITEBOYS were the forerunners of the Rockites. Their name derived from the custom of wearing white shirts over their clothes, when they assembled to dig up cornfields, level enclosures, knock walls, hough or kill cattle, and injure or kill anyone engaged in the collection of tithes or taxes. They rebelled in 1762 and 1786, objecting to the payment of tithes and taxes for the upkeep of a religion and a government alien to them. The Whiteboys were eventually suppressed, but martial law, the gallows and transportation left the basic problems unresolved. Agrarian disturbances continued into the days of the *Great Hunger* until starvation and emigration settled the issue by wiping out the class who had protested most, the landless labourers.

THE RIGHTBOYS originated in Mallow between 1785 and 1788 but soon spread to North Kerry and West Limerick. Newcastle West became one of their centres. At one stage the Catholic Bishop of Limerick, Dr. Conway, denounced the Rightboy movement, after proclamations warning people not to pay tithes had been followed by attacks on both people and property. His wishes were ignored, and the Rightboys angered him even more by asking him to sign a resolution in their favour. Because of its past associations with agrarian revolt Newcastle West also became a Rockite stronghold in the 1820s, second only to Abbeyfeale.

THE DEFENDERS came into existence in 1793 to continue the struggle begun by the Whiteboys. On one occasion they captured Bruff but were unable to hold it, and were driven out soon afterwards. They dispersed in 1803 after a plot to capture Limerick with Robert Emmet's Dublin insurgents was revealed. They rebelled again in 1809 and in 1815. When the Rockites were formed the Whiteboys, Defenders and Rightboys were welded into a loosely-bound alliance in defiance of the gentry, military and clergy.

POTHEEN-MAKING was a recognised, if

An aerial view of Abbeyfeale.

illicit, trade during the eighteenth and nineteenth centuries — and even today, as the advent of bottled gas in the 1960s made the illegal distillation sites harder to detect. Rev. John Begley blamed the consumption of raw spirits for the sheer savagery of some of the incidents that occurred during the Rockite disturbances. Many people made potheen in order to pay their rents. In the 1820s it sold for 12½ pence to 15 pence a gallon, and people indulged in heavy drinking in order to alleviate the drudgery of a harsh existence.

POVERTY was prevalent in the early 1800s. In 1823 more than half of the congregation attending Mass in Abbeyfeale wore ragged clothing and went with bare feet. By 1829 there were eleven handsome slated houses, two storeys high, and eleven licensed public houses in the town, and the people were as well-dressed and good-looking as could be found anywhere. By 1837 many of the farms had large dairies, and a considerable quantity of butter was sent to Cork and Limerick. Fairs were held on 29 June and 24 September, and people were able to market their produce and deal in pigs, cattle and sheep.

THE GREAT HUNGER led one inspector with the Board of Works to report that Limerick was "regularly riddled with roads". Stephen Spring Rice wrote that "our roads were nearly perfect. We had already the roads we wanted and they were as good as we wanted". The network of roads in Ireland were legacies of the various famine relief schemes. The winter of 1846-1847 was the most severe in living memory. Europe was gripped in a cold so bitter that the Thames was a mass of floating ice. Money became completely useless; even if people had it, there was nothing to buy. Before the *Great Hunger* Ireland had a population of 8,175,125, in 1841. Ten years later this figure had been reduced to 6,552,385. In that ten-year period 360,000 mud huts disappeared. No death records were kept and many were buried, their identities unknown, in now forgotten graves. The figures quoted in the censuses of 1841 and 1851 were approximates only. Many census forms were never filled in or returned. The true death toll or emigration figures will never be known.

THE POPULATION of Limerick County including the County Borough (Limerick City) is illustrated in the following chart.

Year of Census	Total	Males	Females
1841	330,029	161,997	168,032
1851	262,132	127,387	134,745
1861	217,277	105,712	111,565
1871	191,936	93,112	98,824
1881	180,632	88,311	92,321
1891	158,912	78,607	80,305
1901	146,098	72,456	73,642
1911	143,069	72,229	70,840
1926	140,343	71,172	69,171
1936	141,153	72,407	68,746
1946	142,559	72,039	70,520
1951	141,239	71,691	69,548
1956	137,881	69,622	68,259
1961	133,339	67,173	66,166
1966	137,357	69,135	68,222
1971	140,459	70,786	69,673
1979	157,407	79,302	78,105
1981	161,661	81,595	80,066
1986	164,569	82,686	81,883

THE POPULATION OF ABBEYFEALE in 1986 was 1,935 persons.

FATHER WILLIAM CASEY (1844-1907), the Catholic parish priest supported, and guided, the farmers of the region in their fight for the "Three F's", fair rent, fixity of tenure, and freedom for the tenant to sell his interest in his holding, during the land wars of the late nineteenth century. His memory is commemorated with a statue in the market place.

PURT CASTLE, Port or Portrinard Castle is located 1½ miles north-west of the town, on the northern bank of the Feale River. Its name is derived from a corruption of *Port na d Trí nArd*, the Fort of the Three Heights. This tower house was built by a branch of the Fitzgeralds of Desmond to command the ford of the Feale, not far from where it is joined by the Oolagh river. The castle is believed to date from the fourteenth century. It was in existence in 1418 when Thomas Fitzgerald, Sixth Earl of Desmond, was deprived of his lands and title for contravening one of the articles of the Statutes of Kilkenny, by marrying Catherine MacCormick. He had been forbidden, as a Norman, to marry anyone of Gaelic stock but had ignored this law when he fell in love with his tenant's daughter. The couple moved to Normandy in 1418. Thomas died in 1420. Pelham, the Lord Justice,

Memorial statue of Fr. William Casey.

camped at the castle in 1580. On 28 April, 1583, Garret, the Rebel Earl of Desmond, wrote a letter to St. Leger, from here, offering to come to terms with Queen Elizabeth, only a few months before he was killed in the valley of Glenageenty, five miles east of Tralee.

MAJOR RICHARD ELLIS married Mary Hilliard of Kerry and purchased his Abbeyfeale estate from a Mr. Meredith in 1791. His son Thomas was born in 1774, married Dymphna Monsell of Tervoe in 1804, became a member of Parliament for Dublin, and was the "idol of the Orange Party in Ireland" because of his opposition to Catholic Emancipation. Thomas bought 1700 acres of land, adjoining Abbeyfeale, from Sir Robert Shaw soon after he married Dymphna and spent a lot of money on reclaiming the land and improving the town. Protestantism was the religion of the ruling class, yet in 1840 the parish of Abbeyfeale contained only 40 Protestants and 5,000 Catholics. Richard Ellis of Glenasrone inherited the estate from his father, Thomas. Richard became one of Caleb Powell's Grand Jurors in 1858. The "very ugly mansion" erected by his father was burned during the Troubles.

THE WAR OF INDEPENDENCE is still remembered in the town. A notorious Black and Tan named Huckerberry was transferred to the R.I.C. barracks in Abbeyfeale, from Shanagolden, because he had killed an old man, named Reidy, in the latter place. His presence in this barracks caused an abortive I.R.A. raid which resulted in the death of a Constable Mahony. Shortly afterwards Huckerberry shot, and killed, two young men as they strolled past the barracks, Patrick Hartnett, a postman, and Jeremiah Healy, a blacksmith. Sean Treacy and Dan Breen received medical attention here from Dr. Edward Hartnett after they had been wounded at Knocklong.

THE ABBEYFEALE OR KNOCKABOUL COIN HOARD may have been the proceeds of a raid on the planted lands to the east or, possibly, the savings of one of the dispossessed who had been driven into this mountainous region by the plantation. No one will ever know! The original owner never returned to collect his hoard which was discovered in 1943. 117 coins from this collection, one of them an English sixpence from 1585, were lodged in the National Museum.

GOULBURN BRIDGE, near Templeglantine, was erected by Richard Griffith, and still bears a commemorative plaque testifying to that fact. This bridge over the Allaghaun River has been replaced by a larger one built north of it but has not been allowed to fall into decay. Mrs. Murphy, who lives at its eastern end, has maintained the older structure.

TEMPLEGLANTINE won the *Glór na nGael*, (Voice of the Irish) award in 1962 and 1963 for its efforts in promoting the Irish language and retaining traditional music and dance.

Athea.

ATHEA derives its name from *'Ath an tSleibhe,* the Ford of the Hill, or from *Teampull a' tSléibhe,* the Church of the Mountain, which was later Anglicised to Teampleatlea or Templeatea. By 1840 little of this church remained but its name and a large burial ground which was still in use. In 1986 the village had a population of 406 persons, 206 males and 200 females.

TEMPLEATEA, or Temple Athea, was the name under which Athea was known in 1837 when, with Ardagh, it formed part of the 'R.C. Division' of Rathronan. Despite this tenuous connection the two places are separated by more than distance as the inhabitants of Athea, to a certain extent, consider themselves to be Kerry people.

RATHRONAN derived its name from *Ráth Ronáin,* the Rath, or Earthen Fort, of Ronan. No record remains as to who or what Ronan was, but in later times a church was erected here of which no trace remained by 1840. A Church of Ireland parish church on this same site was virtually rebuilt after renovations were completed in 1820, and in 1827 a glebe house was constructed. In 1837 Athea contained a constabulary station, and the only houses of note in the parish were Glenville, the residence of J. Massey, and Cahermoyle, the home of William Smith O'Brien, near

Ardagh. In 1840 Rathronan parish contained two ruined castles in almost identical states of preservation. The arch over the ground floor of each still remained and both were approximately 25 feet high. One was located in the townland of Ballyegan, the other in Ballyvoughaun, *Baile Ui Bhuadhacháin,* possibly the Townland of the Victorious, from which this second castle took its name. The old townland of Rathronan was co-extensive with today's townlands of Kerrykyle and Glenville and has no modern counterpart, while the church of Rathronan was situated in what is now the townland of Glenville.

BALLYVOGHAN CASTLE, the townlands of Ballyvoghan and Carrowblogh (possibly Knockaunagun and Glendiheen), a mine and a wood were held by Garrett McMorris Hubert, a tenant of the Earl of Desmond, prior to 1580. After the Desmond Rebellion, Oliver Stephenson came into possession of the Hubert holdings, which later passed to Sir Daniel O'Brien after the Cromwellian confiscations. O'Brien affirmed that he held the same lands in trust for Richard Stephenson in 1678. In 1840 Standish Stephenson was the landlord for the townlands of Ballyvoghan, Knockaunagun, and Glendiheen, which he let to Christopher Delmege at a head rent of £10 per year. Delmege, in turn, sub-let the lands at

£30. His son, John Christopher Delmege, bought out the Stephenson interest and, between 1887 and 1889, earned himself a notorious reputation as an evicting landlord. The Delmege family were unable to hold these lands at the start of the present century, and sold out their fee simple interests between 1902 and 1923.

CARRIGKERRY VILLAGE derives its name from *Carraig Chiarraí,* the Rock of the *Ciarraí,* the people from whom the neighbouring county of Kerry takes its name. In the 1830s the road to Athea which runs past the Catholic church and the old schoolhouse had not been constructed, and the road to Ardagh followed the line of the "Bucks Hill" road. All of the other public roads followed much the same routes as they do today. In 1831 the village contained 93 persons in 16 houses and was little more than a townland. By 1891, 37 people lived here in 7 houses. By 1911 Carrigkerry contained 50 people in 10 houses.

GLENSHARROLD was the birth-place of Eithne Strong, poetess and novelist.

THE MOUNTAIN RANGE extends from the village of Ardagh, in the east, to the confines of the county west of Athea, where it joins the County of Kerry. In 1837 Samuel Lewis reported that coal had been found here but was never properly exploited, although

Carrigkerry.

"no district in Ireland seems better adapted for the establishment of iron-works" as nodules of ironstone had been discovered in the rivulets and limestone was abundant. The land in the eastern portion is of good quality ... and produces excellent crops under a good system of cultivation; the meadows and pastures are extremely rich; great numbers of sheep are fed on them annually, and the mountain districts afford good pasturage for numerous herds of cattle; there are not more than 300 acres of waste land ..."

THE CON COLBERT COMMUNITY HALL, in Athea, is named in honour of one of the executed leaders of the Easter Rebellion who, although born at Monalena, Castlemahon, was reared in Galeview House, Athea, from the age of three. In the War of Independence another local man, Paddy Dalton, was one of three men killed in an encounter in the valley of Knockanure, Gort na Glanna, County Kerry. The other two were Paddy Walshe and Jerry Lyons. A fourth member of this unlucky quartet, Con Deed, escaped on that fateful day, 12 May 1921.

CON COLBERT was a member of the Irish Republican Brotherhood, a pioneer of *Fianna Éireann* and a captain of F Company, Fourth Dublin Battalion. He was opposed to John Redmond's attempt to place the Irish Volunteers at the disposal of the Irish Parliamentary Party, who would have sacrificed them as "cannon fodder" in World War I. During Easter Week he served under Eamonn Ceannt and commanded the garrison at Watkin's Brewery, Ardee Street, and Jameson's Distillery, Bow Street. He also took part in the fighting at Marrowbone Lane. On 8 May 1916 he was executed for his role in the Rising.

ATHEA BRIDGE was originally a wooden structure over the Gale, or Galey River. A man fell through a hole in the bridge while taking part in a faction fight, and was impaled on one of its wooden piles. During the Great Hunger a woman starved to death underneath one of its arches. In 1860 the old bridge was replaced with the present structure.

THE SHANNON FAMILY give their name to Ballyguiltenane, *Baile Giltenane* or Giltenane's townland. Giltenane is a variant of *Mac Giolla Seanáin* or *Mac Giolla tSeánáin*, the Son of the Servant of St. Senan — Senan being the saint associated with Scattery Island in the Shannon Estuary. Variants of this surname can be found in Cavan, Meath and Tyrone where it has often been Anglicised as Nugent or Leonard, and in Clare where it has been Anglicised as Shannon.

ARDAGH derives its name from Ard-ach, the High Field. In 1837 it contained 65 houses, some of which were in a ruinous condition, and the ruins of an old parish church which had been destroyed in the Insurrection of 1641 and never repaired. In 1867 about 250 Fenians managed to break into the ground floor of the barracks but failed to capture it. In 1986 there were 324 inhabitants here, 171 males and 153 females.

ST. PATRICK may have visited Ardagh when he toured through the southern half of Ireland. Tradition relates that the saint visited Knockpatrick and journeyed to Ardagh where he decided not to cross the Sliabh Luachra mountains, and turned back eastwards instead. St. Molua was commemorated in a well to the southwest of the church ruin which was still resorted to in 1840, for the cure of various illnesses on 3 August. The neighbouring townlands of Kilrodaun, Killard and Killréish were probably named after long-vanished churches, but all traces of these buildings had disappeared 150 years ago.

REERASTA RING FORT, in the townland of Reerasta South, is a large, damaged fort at the western end of the village. This ring fort, with its high bank and deep ditch to the north and south, was also called locally the Rath of Reerasta, the Fort of Arrears, and may trace its name back to the days when Ardagh first became a Bishop's manor. In 1868 Reerasta ring-fort was part of the local Church of Ireland archdeacon's property which was apparently leased to the nuns of St. Mary's Convent who had, in turn, sub-let it to the Widow Quinn. This fort is also known as the Ardagh Ring Fort, and is one of many such monuments in this region.

THE ARDAGH CHALICE was discovered in September 1868 by a member of the Quinn family when he was digging out a crop of potatoes planted within Reerasta Fort. He first struck some metallic substance which turned out to be the long pin of a penannular brooch, and decided to dig a little deeper in the hope of uncovering something else. At a depth of three feet he discovered four more brooches, a wooden cross, a bronze cup which he had broken with a careless spade-thrust and a chalice now known as the Ardagh Chalice. He presented the wooden cross to his local parish priest and sold the rest of his find to Dr. Hanlon of Rathkeale for £50. Dr. Hanlon purchased these objects on behalf of the nuns of St. Mary's Convent who notified Dr. George Butler, (coadjutor Bishop of Limerick from 1861 to 1864, and later Bishop from 1864 to 1886), of the find.

LORD DUNRAVEN was consulted by the Bishop of Limerick and the unearthed cache was sent to the Royal Irish Academy for examination. The various items were cleaned and repaired. Edmond Johnson, warden of the Goldsmith's Company, wrote a detailed account of the workmanship and materials of the seven-inch-high two-handled cup known as the Ardagh Chalice. This chalice dates from the eighth century; is made of gold, silver, and bronze, with a rich decoration of enamel, amber, glass and crystal; and can be seen today, in the National Museum, Dublin. One of the brooches is also on display.

THE ANTIQUITIES COMMITTEE of the Royal Irish Academy tried to purchase the Ardagh Chalice and other items from the Catholic Bishop of Limerick in 1871. He refused to sell. On 3 June 1872 the Ardagh Church of Ireland archdeacon wrote to the Academy saying that the cache was found on his property but that he would forego all

Con Colbert Memorial Hall.

rights to it and present it to the Academy if the widow Quinn was "liberally compensated". In January 1873 Dublin Castle stated that treasure trove procedures would be initiated and demanded an accurate description of the items. In 1874 Dr. George Butler returned the objects to the museum on the understanding that the government would purchase them for £500 and deposit them on loan in the museum. The dispute concerning ownership continued. In November 1874 Mrs. Quinn laid claim to the goods. She renewed her claim in 1875. In 1877 the Treasury demanded a second assay of the objects in order to avoid "a long and angry lawsuit touching the right ownership of the articles". The matter was resolved in 1878 when the

The beautifully embellished Ardagh Chalice, probably the finest piece of eighth-century metalwork existing.

Treasury asked the Academy to make an *ex gratia* payment of £100 to Dr. Butler who retained £50 to cover his own expenses and gave £50 to Mrs. Quinn.

THE ARDAGH CROSS which was presented to the local parish priest was "about eight inches in length and well carved, having on the reverse side the figures 727 which are intended for 1727", according to Archdeacon Begley. He wrote that the "cross could not have been buried earlier than this date with the other articles. They were ecclesiastical vessels, and may have been heirlooms that came down in the parish from one priest to another".

FR. CHRISTOPHER BERMINGHAM is usually credited with having hidden the Ardagh Chalice, cross and brooches in 1736 when Oliver Stephenson, the local landlord, swore information against him and accused him of assault and using scandalous words against him. Fr. Bermingham, who had been parish priest of Ardagh for some years prior to 1736, had interceded when Stephenson tried to seduce a newly-wed bride as the couple were leaving the place where they had been married. Even though the Penal Laws were being eased somewhat, at that time, Fr. Bermingham was forced to flee from here. He found a temporary refuge in Limerick City until he fell foul of another Protestant worthy, Thomas Odell, in 1739. Odell had Fr. Bermingham arrested to prevent his appoint-

ment as parish priest of Ballingarry, as he wanted this particular appointment for a Catholic friend. Soon afterwards Thomas Odell repented of his conduct and had Fr. Bermingham released. Fr. Bermingham remained on as parish priest of Ballingarry until he died in 1848, apparently while holidaying in Bath.

CAHERMOYLE HOUSE was built in 1870 or 1871 for William Smith O'Brien's son, Edward, to a design by J.J. McCarthy. It replaces an earlier house of the same name, on the same site, which was the home of William Smith O'Brien.

WILLIAM SMITH O'BRIEN (1803-1864) was the second of Sir Edward O'Brien of Dromoland's five sons. He was educated in Harrow and Trinity College, Cambridge. Although the son of a Protestant landowning family he espoused the cause of Catholic Emancipation and, in 1828, was elected a member of Parliament for Ennis, County Clare. In 1843 he joined O'Connell's Repeal Association and became that movement's leader during O'Connell's imprisonment in 1844. William Smith O'Brien was sentenced to death for his role in the 1848 Rebellion. Family influence had this sentence commuted to penal servitude for life, and so this particular Young Irelander was transported to Hobart in Van Dieman's Land. Transportation to Tasmania ceased in 1853. In May 1854 William received a pardon on condition he

stayed away from the British Isles. He lived in Brussels until May 1856 when he received an unconditional pardon which allowed him to return to Ireland. Caleb Powell selected him for Grand Jury Service in 1858 although he was, technically, a landless man, and therefore did not qualify as a Grand Juror. Before the '48 rebellion William had transferred all of his property to trustees to secure it from confiscation by the state, a device to protect his heirs. Powell's posthumous memoirs mention William Smith O'Brien as "a vain, silly, mischievously inclin'd man and exceedingly egotistical and headstrong". William died while visiting his sister at Bangor in North Wales. His last words were, "Well, the night is so long and dreary, I think I will wait up a little longer". He was buried at Rathronan. William was the father of Charlotte Grace O'Brien of Foynes, and his third son, Lucius Henry O'Brien (1842-1913) was elected Dean and Rector of St. Mary's Cathedral, Limerick, in 1905.

SIR EDWARD O'BRIEN (1773-1837) was an opponent of the Act of Union and had married the heiress of Cahermoyle, the descendant of a Cromwellian grantee, Smith.

THE BIVALLATE RING FORT, near Dunganville Bridge, is located at the edge of a gorge cut by the Daar River. It contains souterrains and a wet fosse, and is in an excellent state of preservation.

THE BALLYLIN HILLTOP FORT may date from the late bronze age and it is characterised by the presence of two widely spaced ramparts. This is an extremely large hilltop fort in the townland of Ballylin the outer wall of which encloses over fifty acres of ground. This fort is 797 feet above sea level and is believed to be the largest of fifty, or so, such monuments in Ireland. Despite being called forts there is now some doubt as to whether these served a ritual purpose rather than a military one.

ELM HILL is a two-storey eighteenth-century house erected over a basement. This was the property of I. Studdert in 1837, while Kiscannell House was the residence of R.L. Condon. It is now in ruins.

THE PARISH OF KILSCANNELL, to the east of Ardagh, contained a neat Church of Ireland church which was erected on the ruins of an older church in 1822. In 1837 the Wesleyan Methodists had their own place of worship and Catholics were catered for in Ardagh and Rathkeale. There were "also sev-eral substantial and well-built farm-houses, occupied by highly respectable farmers" within the parish, which was noted for its "rich meadow and grazing land, affording plentiful pasture to great numbers of milch cows". There were several large dairy farms, and great quantities of butter were exported through Cork and Limerick.

THE FEALE RIVER, flowing by Abbeyfeale, forms the south-western bound-ary of the county; while the Funcheon river forms three miles, or so, of the south-eastern boundary.

SOURCES
9 11 13 17 18 26 27
39 47 48 58 66 75 76
86 87 109 112 113 120 129
145 150 172 173 192 195 203
233 238 246 255 260 280 282

The River Feale flowing by Abbeyfeale.

Adare

The Palatinate · Clonshire

ADARE derives its name from the Irish for the Ford of the Oaks, *Ath Dara*. The earliest written record concerning Adare dates from 1226 but in 1839 a Viking coin hoard was discovered nearby that may have been concealed early in the second half of the eleventh century. This contained Hiberno-Norse coins of a type circulated only in Ireland and the Isle of Man because they were inferior in weight to the English coins. Medieval coin hoards have been found in Limerick, Mungret and Adare that were hidden between 900 to 1200. Others concealed from about 1350 to 1600 were discovered in Athea, Askeaton, Knockaboul, Kilmallock, Limerick and Rathkeale.

ADARE BRIDGE was built by Gerald, the Fifth Earl of Kildare, sometime between 1390 and 1410, to replace an earlier wooden bridge on the same site. The chevron-style openings, or v's, on the southern side were used by pedestrians to avoid being crushed by horses or carts. During the nineteenth century the bridge was widened on the northern side but the other side was preserved as it was by the Earl of Dunraven. The river derives its name from the *Maigh,* or Plain, over which it passes and is known as the Maigue. It is tidal to this point, over eight miles inland from the Shannon, but is very hard to negotiate southwards because of the large number of steep and rapid weirs.

THE DESMOND CASTLE lies on the east bank of the Maigue River. When Henry II ignored the terms of the Treaty of Windsor (1175) and granted the O'Brien "Kingdom of Limerick" to Philip de Braose, it did not take the Anglo-Normans very long to turn this part of Munster into one of the most French of countries outside of France. Geoffrey de Marisco was in possession of the castle in 1227 and is often credited as its founder. The Fitzgeralds became the owners in 1228. They rebuilt and strengthened it in 1326, and over the years it was enlarged and fortified by other members of the Fitzgerald family. In 1329 it was described as a ruin. It was in use by 1331 because a description of Adare in that year mentions the castle, and observes that it contained a hall, a thatched chapel, a slated kitchen, a thatched chamber and a tower covered with planks. Some time before 1376 the castle was reported as damaged yet again. During Elizabeth's reign it was attacked, unsuccessfully, on several occasions, by the English who eventually succeeded in capturing it after an eleven-day siege in 1578. It was garrisoned by a "powerful body" of English troops under the command of Captain Carew in 1579. Sir John Fitzgerald, brother to the Earl of Desmond, attacked but failed to capture the castle although the garrison suffered heavy losses in its defence. It fell to the combined forces of the Earls of Desmond and Kerry in 1581. They slaughtered all within it. In 1582 they abandoned it without a fight and the English — under the command of Captain Zouche, reoccupied it. The Desmond Castle took its name from the Earls of Desmond who occupied it for close on fifty years. In 1583 it reverted to its original owners, the Fitzgeralds of Kildare, who had long since become the Earls of Kildare. On 8 June 1599 the English and the Geraldines fought an indecisive battle near the town, in the bog of Rower. Early in 1600 the Sugan Earl of Desmond was in possession but he had abandoned it to the English by July 1600.

A BESIEGED ENGLISH GARRISON excavated an underground tunnel to the bed of the river in order to acquire water, late in the year 1600. In 1641 the Confederate Irish captured the castle but they were soon driven out by the Earl of Crosshaven's forces. In 1657 the Desmond Castle was dismantled on Cromwell's orders. The second Earl of Dunraven carried out some repairs in 1825. Twelve years later the old stronghold was described as being of considerable extent. The most important part was the large tower or keep in its north-western corner which is situated within the ruins of a contemporary ringwork, surrounded by a strong battlemented rampart with semi-circular bastions. The

The Desmond Castle.

entire section was encircled by a fosse or moat to create a secure inner ward. There was a gate, with a draw-bridge to the south, while on the other side of the fosse there is another wall which had two gates, the southern one of which was flanked by two towers. The outer ward contains a large courtyard, the ruins of two old buildings and traces of several others, all enclosed by the main outer wall. The building south-east of the keep dates from the late thirteenth century and may have replaced an older structure on the same site. There are remains of a fifteenth century bakery and kitchen nearby. The gateway to the east leads to an enclosed, but unwalled space, inside the outer ditch which was once part of the outer ward or bailey. The two-storey building near the main gateway, close to the river, contains pairs of round-headed windows, with sandstone mouldings, which date from the thirteenth century. This last building is known as the Great Hall, and is the older of the two buildings.

THE GREAT EARL, Garret Mór Fitzgerald, succeeded to the Chief Governorship of Ireland in 1478. During the early 1490s he was implicated in the plot to place Perkin Warbeck, the Yorkist pretender, on the English throne. He lost his estates to the Crown but was restored to power by Henry VII in 1496. Until his death, in 1513, he remained loyal to the English King and was considered "all-but-King of Ireland". Garret Og succeeded his father but unfortunately entrusted the government to his oldest son,

The Franciscan Friary.

Silken Thomas, when he was summoned to England in 1534. Thomas led an abortive revolt, possibly with his father's connivance, which was probably intended to prove to Henry VIII that he could not rule Ireland without the Geraldines (Fitzgeralds). Henry proved that he could. He quelled the rebellion and smashed the Geraldine power forever.

THE CHURCH OF ST. MICHAEL ARCHANGEL OF THE FRIARS MINOR, or the Franciscan Friary, is located in the grounds of the Adare Golf Club, east of the Maigue River. It was also known as the Poor Abbey, because the Franciscans were an order of mendicant friars. It was founded by Thomas Fitzgerald, the 7th Earl of Kildare, and his wife Johanna, the daughter of James, Earl of Desmond. It was dedicated in 1464 and consecrated for Observants in 1466. Suppressed in 1539, the Franciscans were driven out for a while as the buildings were unoccupied in 1559. By 1573 the friars had returned, as Justice Walshe reported to London that the "Abbaye of Adare is stoared againe with Friers". They were still there in 1579 but were expelled from it again about 1581, during the Desmond Rebellion. The Franciscans returned to Adare in 1633 and were re-established for a time. In 1595 the friary was granted to Sir Henry Wallop, as were the other monastic buildings of Adare. The Franciscan possessions amounted to 16 acres of land. These consisted of a church, cloister, hall, dormitory, library, three chambers, kitchen, bakery, three parks including a great park or close on the west side, water-mill, salmon weir and eel weir. The transept, with

The Friary cloister.

side chapels, was added before 1484 and the tower before 1492. There is a cloister on the northern side which is also flanked by a refectory and a dormitory that was added some time before 1502. The infirmary, which is within the group of buildings separated from the main structure, was donated by the Knight of Glin and his wife before 1503. Other main features include the fine mullioned windows, the recessed tombs in the side chapels, a carved piscina, the finely-wrought sedilia, the ornamented western side of the cloister, and the low-relief carving of a Franciscan friar. In 1875 the friary was repaired by the Earl of Dunraven.

JOHN WESLEY preached to the people of Adare, in 1765, from the shade of an ash tree close to the east wall of the Franciscan friary. This tree was still there until about 1860. By 1976 a stone marked the spot.

THE KILMALLOCK GATE is located to the west of the friary but the Geraldine Arms which once adorned it have disappeared.

THE PARISH CHURCH OF ST. NICHOLAS OF MYRA was named in honour of a fourth century archbishop in Asia Minor who is regarded as the patron saint of children. Santa Claus is a corruption of his name. The church is located between the castle and the friary, and was built and rebuilt several times between the thirteenth and sixteenth centuries. This is a nave and chancel church, with a gabled division west of the nave which contains a low pointed arch. Church of Ireland services were held in this old parish church until the Augustinian friary was restored to use, as a Protestant church, in 1807.

THE EARL OF DESMOND'S CHAPEL OF EASE is located to the north of the old parish church. Its title describes its function, as it was customary in this part of the county for the castle owners to erect chapels of ease close to their castles, especially if the latter were not near the parish churches. This small chantry chapel dates from the fifteenth century and contained chaplain's quarters which were located over its eastern end.

THE VILLAGE OF ADARE was situated east of the Maigue River in ancient times. Over 150 years ago Adare had the appearance of an old village whose growth had been gradual. It contained 114 houses, many of which were old and badly built, but as the leases fell due Lord Dunraven, the proprietor, demolished many of these unsightly dwellings. The village owes its present appearance mainly to Edwin, the Third Earl of Dunraven (1812-1871) who was an Oxford Movement convert to Catholicism and an improving landlord best commemorated in the architecture of his village. Today Adare's

wide main street lined with thatched cottages is more typical of an English setting than an Irish one. Most of the present village is located to the west of the river.

HENRY III (1216-1272) gave Geoffrey de Marisco permission to hold a fair here in 1226. In 1310 it became an incorporated walled town, and Edward II levied tolls on merchandise to enclose it with a wall. The "Irish enemy" destroyed and burned it in 1376, but Edward II exempted the provost or commonalty of Adare from any services or customs until the town was fully rebuilt and inhabited. Throughout the fourteenth and fifteenth centuries Adare remained a small market town, its fortunes inextricably bound to those of the Geraldines and the Desmond Castle. In 1537 the Earl of Desmond seized Adare town which the Geraldines had forfeited because of Silken Thomas's rebellion. The Lord Deputy was unhappy with Desmond's claim in 1541, but finally accepted the situation although he would have preferred to see the earl living nearer to Dublin where he could keep an eye on his activities. Desmond became a loyal subject and later achieved the rank of Lord Treasurer of Ireland. When he died in 1558 he was succeeded by his son, Gerald, who instigated the Desmond Wars. Adare was destroyed on several occasions during this period but it was always rebuilt. It reverted to Geraldine ownership in 1583 and remained so, except for some exceptions, until 1683. In 1586 Camden, the historian, mentioned only three towns in the county, Limerick, Kilmallock and Adare. Early in 1600 English soldiers commanded by Maurice Stack burned the town, and after that last great disaster it seems to have enjoyed a rather placid rural existence. After the Cromwellian occupation it remained a quiet market town until the agrarian troubles of the time intruded, towards the end of the eighteenth and early nineteenth centuries.

THE PALATINATE derives its name from the Palatines who settled in the south-western region between Adare and Rathkeale. During the second half of the eighteenth century the Palatines were introduced onto the Adare estate, where they rented land near the river for £1.50 to £1.80 an acre annually and £1 an acre elsewhere. They occupied small farmhouses, developed gardens and orchards, grew flax for spinning, specialised in mixed farming, and augmented the Protestant congregation in the parish church of St. Nicholas. They continued to live here even when "this was the scene of much confusion and many atrocities during the prevalence of Whiteboyism in 1786, and of Defenderism in 1793; and also under the system of the Rockites many persons were destroyed near

the place, on the chapel of which were posted notices, signed, 'John Rock, R.C.B., Commander-in-Chief of the army in Ireland'". The Palatines remained here and in Rathkeale, Cappagh, Ballingarrane, Askeaton, Kilfinnane, Pallaskenry and elsewhere in the county.

LORD DUNRAVEN saved the people of Adare from the worst ravages of the *Great Hunger,* particularly by providing much needed employment on his estate. In 1683 Thady Quin leased part of the Earl of Kildare's estate. Thady's wife was the Mrs. Quin satirised in Seán O Tuama's poem, *Bean na cleithe caoile.* She had once employed the poet as her "keeper of hens". Valentine Quin, Thady's son, purchased the leased land in 1721 and bought other large parcels of land from the Kildare estate in 1724 and 1726. The Dunravens descended from the Quins.

THE CHURCH OF IRELAND PARISH CHURCH is located at the eastern side of the bridge. This was originally the Augustinian Priory, but it was also known as the Black Abbey because the Augustinian monks wore a black habit. It was founded by John Fitzgerald, Baron of Offaly (created Earl of Kildare in 1316), possibly before 1315 although dates of 1315 and 1325 are also given for its foundation. In 1319 the Augustinians accused the Trinitarians of seizing their goods here. The rents and farms of this friary were valued at £5.22 in 1541. The Augustinians possessed nearly 80 acres of land, several cottages and gardens in the village, and a fishing weir in the river. John Gold leased the property in 1583 but by 1595 it belonged to Sir Henry Wallop. Although the monastery was suppressed in 1539-1540, and the Augustinians were driven out about 1581, they were still in occupation in 1599. They had moved to Limerick City by 1633 where they established a church in Fish Lane.

There is a nave, chancel and a south aisle with a cornice moulding, both internally and externally, which is of a later date than the nave. The outer moulding dates from the fourteenth century, and contains ornamental carvings of foliage, animals and human heads. The tower and some of the domestic buildings date from the fifteenth century. This tower is partly attached to the old wall and, as a later addition, blocked up the most westerly of the south windows beneath which three sedilia are positioned. The west doorway of the nave is plain, but the corbels above it may have been used to support a wooden porch in earlier times. This is a fine example of what a medieval Irish church must have looked like. In 1814 the refectory, or dormitory was roofed over and converted into a school, and between 1807 and 1814 this former ruin was

The Church of Ireland Church, formerly the Augustinian Priory.

restored by the Ecclesiastical Commissioners to replace the old parish church which was falling into decay. From 1852 to 1854 further renovations were carried out at the behest of Caroline, the dowager Countess of Dunraven, who was responsible for installing most of the stained glass in the windows. The cloisters contain the Quin family mausoleum which was erected in 1826, and carries the Kildare and Desmond arms alternately displayed on several carved shields, while the remains of the old friary gate-house are located in the north-eastern corner.

THE CATHOLIC CHURCH was originally known as the Monastery of the Holy Trinity, the Trinitarian Priory or the White Abbey. The Trinitarian Order was founded on the Continent in 1198 to ransom and liberate Christians captured by the Mohammedans during the Crusades. St. James was the patron saint of this church, and despite its foundation date being given as 1230 it is quite possible

that it was in existence by 1226. It was rebuilt in 1272 and it was the only monastery in Adare in 1292. The story of the prior being beheaded for refusing to take the oath of supremacy in 1539 has been disproved; no other monks were killed or imprisoned on that occasion, and they were still in occupancy, twenty years later, in 1559. It was leased to James Goold before 1583 and was later granted to Sir Henry Wallop in 1595. The remains of the tower, nave, and part of the choir were restored in 1811, for use as a church, by the Earl of Dunraven. In 1852 his son, the Third Earl, had the nave lengthened, and rebuilt the chancel. He also added the Lady Chapel, sacristy and south porch. With P.C. Hardwick as his architect, he had the tower battlemented, and later added a newer nave and north aisle. Amongst the church's more noteworthy features are the corbels on the tower, the cornice along the south wall, the set of twelve sixteenth-century carvings in the vestry and the

low turret which once housed a bell.

THE COLUMBARIUM is situated at the north-western corner of the Convent of Mercy gardens. This is a circular building in which doves were housed. It is over 4 metres in external diameter, with walls nearly one metre thick. There are no windows but there is an opening almost one-half-metre in diameter, in the dome-shaped roof through which the birds could come or go as they wished. This opening, through which the interior is lit, is framed with a ring of carved stonework. The internal walls were lined with niches on which the doves nested, and a doorway at ground level admitted the monks.

THE CONVENT OF MERCY and the school which incorporates the remnants of the western cloister range was designed for the nuns by P.C. Hardwick. He was employed by Edwin, 3rd Earl of Dunraven, an authority on early Irish architecture. Edwin also invited the Christian Brothers to Adare. They moved into a house and school he had built and furnished for them on 24 April 1854. He charged them a nominal rent of 5 pence a year and contributed £60 annually to their upkeep. In 1857 he increased his contribution to £80 when the brothers extended the school.

THE WASHING POOL was restored by Limerick County Council and Adare's Tidy Town Committee. Located alongside the village park, it is quite close to the main street, and serves as a reminder of another era when horses were watered here and housewives gathered to wash the family clothes in convivial but hard-working groups. Such occasions are now a thing of the past, but a small tributary stream of the Maigue is contained with gently-curved stone side walls as it feeds the triangular washing pool, before it makes its exit under the small two-arched bridge, *The Drehideen.*

THE COURT-HOUSE is a Gothic-style two-storey limestone building erected in 1840.

THE FOUNTAIN was erected by Caroline, Countess of Dunraven in 1844.

ADARE MANOR is a Gothic-style mansion with a turreted entrance tower at one corner rather than in the centre of its facade. The lettered text carved into the front of the south parapet reads: "Except the Lord build the house, then Labour is but lost that built it". Most of the present building dates from 1832, but it incorporates part of an eighteenth century house of which a painting still existed in 1976. This Georgian house had been renovated by 1812 but it had, apparently, been erected on the site chosen by Thady Quin for his original dwelling, which had been constructed some time after 1683. Adare Manor was designed by the Pain brothers for the second

The Catholic Church, formerly the Trinitarian Priory.

Earl of Dunraven and his wife, Caroline, although some accounts, mainly folklore, claim that he did not employ an architect. Work commenced in 1832. By 1837 the centre and north wing were completed. The Pains have been credited with the planning of the long gallery and twin towers. Most of the actual construction was carried out by an Adare man, James Connolly, a mason, who was employed on this project for over twenty years. Local labour and materials were utilised whenever it was possible to do so. The black marble used in some of the fireplaces was procured from Craggleith, near Ennis, County Clare, and other materials had to be brought from elsewhere. All of the carving, in wood and stone, was done by local craftsmen. A.W. Pugin designed the carved grey stone chimney piece in the Great Hall, the carved oak staircase, the minstrels' gallery, the panelled walls and ceilings of the dining-

room, and several of the marble chimney pieces. The building was eventually completed in 1876 and is located on the western bank of the Maigue.

THE LANTERN LODGE, on the Limerick Road, is a Gothic-style gate lodge, which marks one of the entrances to Adare Manor. It allowed access to the manor over one of several bridges which the Dunravens had built over the Maigue as it flowed through their estate. Many of the older bridges have been replaced by modern concrete ones between the manor and Castleroberts bridge.

THE ESTATE GARDENS were laid out in geometrical box patterns below the south terrace by P.C. Hardwick in the 1850s. The present one-way traffic system around the estate utilises an old drive which passes between two high walled ha-has (sunken walls or retaining banks) which allow an unimpeded vista from the manor.

An old-world village scene.

THE ANCESTRAL HOME of the Earls of Dunravan has recently entered a new era. Today the tradition of elegance is retained in the gracious transition from family home to Ireland's most renowned country house hotel for the discerning traveller. The Manor's new owners, Tom and Judy Kane are based in New Jersey, where Tom is a founding partner of Printon Kane and Company, an Investment Banking firm. They have spared no expense in the refurbishment of Adare Manor and the celebrated interior designer Carleton Varney was given responsibility for planning the luxurious furnishings and glowing colour schemes which now enhance the buildings original architecture. Mr and Mrs Kane take a great interest and pride in their new Irish home and are frequent visitors here, often accompanied by family members or personal friends. The Manor in all its preserved glory reads like an intricate novel in wood and stone. The panels of the beautiful oak stairway are dominated by finely carved ravens which are reminders of the Second Earl's wife, heiress to Dunraven Castle of Wales. The magnificent Gallery, resplendent with intricately carved wooden panelling and choir stalls, stained glass windows and vaulted ceiling is reputed to be the second longest in all of Europe. Formerly the chapel, it now provides a regal setting for business conferences and gala entertainments of all kinds: Banquets, Balls, Weddings, Receptions and Fashion Shows. More than fifty individually carved fireplaces embellish the design of gracious bedroom-suites and bathrooms, each a meticulous re-inspiration of the original design. The dining room at Adare Manor under the superb cuisiniers' daily guidance provides a feast of French and Irish haute cuisine prepared from Ireland's finest fresh produce, whilst a traditional and more casual dimension to the splendid facilities of the Manor is captured in the spirit of the Tack Room Bar. Formerly an unused dungeon the Tack Room is resonant with the sound of music, conversation and Irish 'Crack'. The careful development of an additional wing will provide a further 36 luxury bedrooms, a magnificent indoor swimming pool and a

The elegant sittingroom.

One of the luxurious bedrooms.

health area. This new wing of river facing rooms which, incidentally, will be faced with stone identical to the original Manor, will have two Conference/Diningrooms which will be fitted with telephone/fax lines and up-to-date conference equipment. The new wing and sports facilities will be ready for June 1989. The magnificent wide ranging vistas over the River Maigue and rolling parkland of this 840 acre estate are breathtaking in their beauty and the expansive landscape provides an ideal setting for all country pursuits. Hunting, horse-back riding, shooting, fishing and golf are all easily arranged on the estate which is surrounded by Ireland's leading golf courses and home to the prestigious Limerick Hunt. Future amenities will include Championship Standard 18 hole golf course designed by Robert Trent Jones, a fully equipped equestrian centre and an 1800 seat amphitheatre-styled Performing Arts Centre which will serve as a leading cultural venue for Ireland for classical and contemporary events. Once again the glamorous life has returned to Adare Manor, its ambience enlivened with the activities of guests partaking of afternoon tea in the drawing room, a quiet browse in the cosy library, or enjoying a meal in the elegant dining room with its views over the river and Par-Terre gardens. Now transformed into an elegant world-class home away from home, Adare Manor is truly a haven for those who appreciate the fine lifestyle of a bygone age enhanced by all the comforts of the present day.

The famous Long Gallery

THE OGHAM STONES south-west of the manor, amongst the trees, were "imported" from Kerry by Edwin, the Third Earl. Three of them came from the townland of Kilbonane, near Killarney, where two had been found inserted in a farm-house wall. A group of five are close together. The tallest one is over two metres high and another one, split into two parts, is lying on the ground. Ogham stones date from the early fifth century to the middle of the seventh century. They are mainly Christian in context and are usually associated with old churches or early Christian burial sites. Ogham inscriptions are in an early form of Irish, which is frequently followed by Latin inscriptions, written in Roman characters. These inscriptions are mainly commemorative; the name of the person commemorated is often succeeded by that of a father and ancestor, and many are inscribed with crosses. Letters are represented by lines and notches, from one to five in number, and are marked across, or on either side, of a stem line. There are five main groups of letters and one, or more, of a standing stone's corners can be used as a stem line. More often than not the inscription reads from the bottom upwards. Ogham stones can also be found on the Isle of Man, Wales, Cornwall and southern Britain. An animal cemetery is located close to the Ogham stones with carved memorials to Dunraven pets like *Kudo 1937-1950* and *Jock. Died Dec. 1939*.

THE REASK STONES were taken to Adare from Reask, County Kerry, about 1855. These were two cross-inscribed stones. One is a small narrow sandstone pillar, 114 cm. long, with a simple Latin cross on both sides. The letters *DNS*, an abbreviation of *Dominus*, are on one face. The other is a purple sandstone slab, 87cm. by 59cm., decorated on one face only with a simple Greek cross with widely expanded head and arms of the larger cross. It could date from the late Medieval period, whereas the first stone may be a late sixth, or early seventh century one. Thomas Fanning wrote of both stones, after seeing them here, in 1971. On 20 February 1989 he told me that the Dunravens had given him permission to take these stones back to Reask, where they are now on display.

NINETEENTH-CENTURY DEVELOPMENT commenced with "the erection of an hotel, post-office, and several other substantial houses" in 1837. The mail coach from Limerick to Tralee passed through Adare on a daily basis in those days, and the village possessed a constabulary station. The long stucco

The Desmond Chapel of Ease.

building of the hotel has long since expanded. By 1900 it occupied the sites of the old post office and two other separate houses. Like the inns of a bygone era it proclaims its presence with an old-fashioned sign showing the Dunraven coat-of-arms.

DREHIDTARSNA derives its name from the Irish for cross-bridge or bridge across. Variations of the name still in use are Drehedharsnie and Droghetarsney. Early in the nineteenth century a Church of Ireland church was built here to replace an older parish church which was located in the church-yard.

CLONSHIRE HOUSE is located mid-way between Drehidtarsna and Adare. This is a one-storey late Georgian structure built over a basement. It was erected by the Greenall family but is now the property of Hugh Robards. In 1837 it was the residence of J. Dickson, who built and supported the parochial schools in which 60 boys and 30 girls were enrolled as pupils in that year. There were two flour-mills nearby which were "worked by excellent machinery" during the early 1800s. Their produce was chiefly sent to Limerick.

CLONSHIRE, Cloonsheer, Clounshire or Clonshere, takes its name from *Cluain Siar*, the Western meadow.

CLONSHIRE CHURCH has been better known as Templenakilla since the early 1800s. Lewis reported on "the shafts of two very ancient crosses" that were visible in the church-yard in 1837. This early church ruin derives its name from *Teampall na Cille*, the Church of the Burial-ground, and contains an interesting east window and west doorway.

CLONSHIRE CASTLE is less than half a mile west of the church ruins. This is a ruined three-storey castle which has a square tower at its northern end containing the staircase. The tower was enlarged twice and reaches a height of five storeys.

GARRAUNBOY CASTLE or Garranboy Castle is half a mile west of Clonshire Castle. This dates from the fifteenth century and derives its name from *Garrán Buidhe,* in all probability, the Yellow Shrubbery. This conspicuous castle contains a small tower within a rectangular bawn with d-shaped angle-turrets.

TRINITY CHURCH is located in the townland of Dunnaman. This ruined church, *Teampall na Trionóide*, is north-east of Dunnaman tower-house.

DUNNAMAN TOWER HOUSE is south-west of Castleroberts Bridge. Only the stump of this six-teenth-century castle now remain. It contains a *Síle-na-Gig*, that carved fertility symbol of former times so often inappropriately found in Christian churches and castles.

CASTLEROBERTS BRIDGE took its name from the castle of that name which was dismantled in order to build this bridge with its stones, according to Jim Mackessy who lives nearby.

BALLYNACOURTY HOUSE, a small Georgian house in Ballysteen, is the residence of George Stacpoole, a descendant of the Stacpooles of Edenvale, County Clare.

FR. WILLIAM DOWNES may have died after falling from his horse near Castleroberts on 14 December 1840, but the suspicion that he was killed by the Whiteboys, with whom he had many disagreements, still lingers.

THE CLORHANE WEDGE-SHAPED GALLERY GRAVE is located about two miles north of Adare, in the Maigue basin. In 1980 this was heavily overgrown, the roofstone was tilted and it was in a ruinous condition.

THE POPULATION OF ADARE, north and south, in 1986 was 1,953 people. This was composed of 998 males and 955 females. Dunnaman then had a population of 463 persons, 237 males and 226 females.

SOURCES
1 4 5 9 10 11 12 13 18
26 28 35 42 44 45 47 48 50
57 76 86 107 120 123 129 173 183
184 192 229 246 253 283

Annacotty

Plassey · Castletroy · Derrygalvin

ANNACOTTY derives its name from *Àth na Coite,* the Ford of the Cott or River-boat. In ancient times this was an important crossing-point over the Mulkear River.

THE PARISH OF KILMURRY is located on the southern bank of the Shannon east of Limerick City. It derives its name from *Cill Mhuire,* Mary's Church, a place-name which could link it with the Normans who had a great devotion to the Blessed Virgin and erected churches in her honour wherever they settled. In 1837 the parish contained 1,803 inhabitants on its 3277 statute acres; the land was mostly meadow or pasture, and well planted near the Shannon. Limestone was quarried at Newcastle, and elsewhere in the parish. There was a paper and an oil mill at Ballyclough, a paper-mill at Annacotty, and flour-mills at Ballysimon. The big houses of the period were Newcastle, the residence of M. O'Brien; Milford, of T. Fitzgerald; Shannon View, of T. Kelly; Willow Bank, of Captain Hickey; Shannon Cottage, of G. McKern; Killonan Cottage, of H. Rose; Ballyclough of P. Cudmore; and Plassey of R. Harvey. In 1812 a Church of Ireland church was built on the site of the original parish church which had long since been converted to Protestant use, while the nearby glebe house had been erected in 1790. In 1840 Killonan grave-yard was used for the burials of children and strangers and was then known as Killeen, the Little Church.

ST. MARY MAGDALENE'S WELL is still the scene of an annual pilgrimage on 22 July, her feast day, when local people make their traditional "rounds", and leave flowers and candles at the well. A century and a half ago it was "resorted to by pilgrims for the cure of sore eyes and other complaints".

NEW CASTLE is located north of the well, on a rocky promontory close to the Limerick-Dublin road. About 1800 its west side, and a square tower on its south-western corner, collapsed. It has changed but little since John O'Donovan and Eugene O'Curry described it in 1840. No tradition then existed concerning the period in which it had been erected, and no one appeared to know who its founder

was. In 1902 the Jewish community of Limerick purchased land nearby for use as a cemetery.

ROBERT CLIVE, Clive of India, was born in Market Drayton, Shropshire, in 1725. He was a wild youth, and his parents were quite glad to ship him off to India at the age of eighteen. While there he distinguished himself in war, fighting against the French and the Indians. His victory at the decisive battle of Plassey on 27 July 1757 resulted in the British domination of India which lasted for almost two centuries. In this battle he defeated Surajah Dowlah and an Indian force of 60,000 men with a small force of 3,000 men, 2,000 of whom were Indians. This epic action enabled Clive to promote one of Surajah Dowlah's former officers as Nabob of Bengal in Dowlah's place. The new Nabob, Mir Jaffir, enriched Clive, who was also rewarded with an Irish title by the grateful British. To qualify for this honour he had to buy an estate in Ireland, so he purchased a disjointed patch-work of several thousand acres stretching from Bunratty to the Fergus, including Rineanna (now Shannon Airport), Tullyglass and Drumgeely, on the Clare side of the Shannon; while nearer to the city of Limerick he acquired Cappantymore in the Clare Hills, other holdings in Gortatogher, Corbally, Rosmadda, three houses in St. Mary's parish, and Ballykilty Manor and lands in Kilmurry. From these assorted lands he took his title, Baron Clive of Plassey, County Clare, Ireland. On his return to India he practically became the governor of that sub-continent through his own connivance, and that of the English East India Company, until he eventually retired to England.

PLASSEY HOUSE, in the townland of Srelane, was re-named by Robert Clive soon after he purchased it from Thomas MacMahon. The present structure is a Victorian Italiante building which was built for the Russell family and completed in 1863. It is believed to incorporate part of the late-eighteenth-century house built by the Maunsell family and, quite possibly, may retain some features of the original house known as Ballykilty Manor. The house and

grounds have taken on a new role since the National Institute for Higher Education was established here in the 1970s and it is now an integral part of the college complex linked by corridors, at first-floor level. N.I.H.E. is in the process of becoming the University of Limerick at the time of writing. The campus also hosts a separate institution, Thomond College of Education, and a technological park linked to the proposed university.

THE HUNT MUSEUM is located within the main structure. This was offically opened by Desmond O'Malley, Fianna Fail Minister for Industry, Commerce and Energy, on 17 April, 1978. It contains a selection of items from the Bronze Age, early Christian period, Medieval times and later. These include cauldrons, stone axe-heads, early Christian brooches, a damaged *Síle-na-gig,* medieval crucifix figures and pottery, the ninth-century Cashel Bell, Irish silver-work, and two glass chamber-pots, one with a lid, which survive from the end of the eighteenth century. These chamber-pots, a nineteenth-century decanter inscribed "Cannock and Tait", and an incomplete drinking glass engraved with a crown and inscribed"Lord/Arch/Bishop/of/ Dublin/ 1715" are the only four items of Irish glassware in the museum. The drinking glass may have been made to celebrate the Jacobite defeat in 1715, while the engraved crown may have been a punning symbol based on the Archbishop of Dublin's name, William King. A pre-1611 map of Limerick is also on display here and is probably the most fascinating exhibit of all.

JOHN HUNT was a noted art historian, archaeologist, and collector. The Craggaunowen Project in County Clare was his brainchild, and is now an important tourist asset. It is located on the shores of a small lake close to a large state forest, outside Kilkishen, and contains a restored tower house-cum-museum, Craggaunowen Castle; replicas of a *crannog,* ring-fort and a *fulacht fiadha* or cooking-place; an authentic bronze age trackway; and the reconstructed model of St. Brendan's boat in which Tim Severin sailed across the Atlantic. There is also an authentic megalithic tomb, discovered by Bill

Plassey House.

McInerney, in the woods to the west of Craggaunowen. John Hunt donated his collection of artifacts to the Irish Nation. He did not live long enough to see the museum opened but he had seen and approved the general outline of the plans prepared by Arthur Gibney, of Dublin, who had designed the lay-out on his recommendation.

THE GROUNDS OF PLASSEY form an attractive campus today. The wooded demesne was established by Robert Clive but was retained and developed by the Campbell, Maunsell, Harvey, Baily and Keating families, owners of the estate over two centuries, until the Rehabilitation Institute of Ireland cut down most of the trees in 1961. The old stables have been expanded into a complex that includes a private bar and other services.

THE PLASSEY MILL was built by Major Hodges Maunsell shortly before 1827, as Fitzgerald referred to it as "lately erected" in that year. Major Maunsell took advantage of a ten-foot drop in the river level between Bohogue and Drominveg. After the Harvey family purchased Plassey, Rueben Harvey leased the mill to the Russells who improved it, installed a turbine, and later became one of Europe's largest flour-millers.

THE GARRISON WALL pre-dates the mill. This was erected to dissipate the force of the river current along the southern shore of the Shannon and protect the horse-ferry which operated here until the Shannon Navigation Company built the Black Bridge about 1830. In 1949 this bridge was reconstructed. Mrs. Sheehy owned the ferry-keeper's house on this side of the river in 1979. By then the ferry-keeper's house on Peg's Height, on the Clare side, had vanished.

THE AMERICAN GROUND was the name applied to the low-lying field to the west during the middle years of the nineteenth century when the ballast from the returning coffin ships was dumped here to fill the area.

THE MILFORD HOSPICE is located east of the entrance to Plassey.

CASTLETROY may have been built by Dermot O'Brien during the reign of Henry III (1216-1272). O'Donovan and O'Curry were unable to ascertain when it was built, or by whom, but they doubted that it had been erected by a family of the O'Treos or Troys. Thirteen years earlier, in 1827, Fitzgerald mentioned the "ruins of Castle Troy ... and the rich plantations of Mr. Arthur of Glanomera on the opposite side of the river". In 1837 Lewis wrote of a modern gazebo near the castle "and not far distant are the ruins of the ancient church of Killonan or Killowen". By 1840 only the eastern and northern sides were in a state of "tolerable preservation" and the other two sides were "nearly destroyed".

MOUNTSHANNON HOUSE was a two-story eighteenth-century structure with a seven-bay entrance, erected by the White family in 1750. They later sold it to the Fitzgibbon family of Ballysheedy. Black Jack Fitzgibbon (born 1748) may have renovated the house at a later stage. He was notorious as an opponent of Catholic Emancipation, the architect of the Act of Union and Lord Chancellor of Ireland. In 1795 he was created Lord Clare. He suppressed the Rebellion of 1798. At his funeral a dead cat was thrown at his coffin in memory of his boastful taunt that he "would make Ireland as tame as a mutilated cat". Lewis Wyatt remodelled Mountshannon for Black Jack's son, John, after 1813, while James Pain is also believed to have contributed to the overall design. John, the Second Earl of Clare, was a close friend of Lord Byron. The pair of them invaded a Turkish harem on one memorable occasion. Byron escaped but John Fitzgibbon was captured and received the unkindest cut of all in punishment. After his death in 1851 he was succeeded by his brother, Richard, the Third, and last, Earl of Clare. Richard lacked the government pension of his two predecessors; his personal fortune had been diminished dur-

ing the *Great Hunger* by contibutions to famine relief; his only son was listed as missing, presumed dead, after the Charge of the Light Brigade; and he left an impoverished estate to his daughter, Lady Louisa Fitzgibbon. She was the last of the Fitzgibbon family to reside in Mountshannon. Her first husband assumed her name on marrying her. After he died she married a Sicilian nobleman in the hope of repairing the family fortunes, only to discover he had married her for a similar reason. She left Ireland in 1887. In 1888 she sold the contents of the house, and in 1893 the house was purchased by Thomas Nevins, a wealthy Irish-American. Louisa was buried in a convent on the Isle of Wight. Mountshannon House was burned down in 1920 during the War of Independence and the Land Commission divided the 900-acre estate after Thomas Nevins died. Even today the gaunt ruins of Mountshannon House form an impressive monument.

THE ANNACOTTY FOUNTAIN MEMORIAL commemorates Charles Richard George Fitzgibbon, the eldest son of Lady Louisa and her first husband Gerald N. Fitzgibbon, who died on 30 April 1870 at the age of twenty-one. Louisa's uncle, John, had erected the pump here, near Finnegan's public house, at an earlier stage, and Louisa renovated it and erected the memorial in 1875.

ANNACOTTY was the site of the now-closed Ferenka factory. The area achieved prominence in 1975 when Dr. Tiede Herrema was kidnapped here. As Limerick City extended south-eastwards from the 1950s onwards it covered a lot of intervening region with residential estates. The population of the village of Annacotty was 523 in 1986 while that of Kilmurry was 760 persons.

KILLEENAGARRIFF derives its name from *Cillín na nGarbh*, the Little Church of the Rough People. This may also be a corruption of *Cillín Aith Gairbh*, the Church of the Rough Place. The ruin of this old parish church still stands in the graveyard to which it gives its name on the northern bank of the Annacotty River, which is here called the Killeenagarriff river. Tradition maintains that Mass was last celebrated here in 1648, but this is at variance with the Lewis account which refers to it as a Church of Ireland church which was destroyed in the war of 1641. It was rebuilt and re-used as the Protestant parish church but had lapsed into ruin by 1837.

ST. PATRICK'S CHURCH at Ahane was described as a large new chapel in 1837. This replaced a mud-and-wattle "Mass house" which had been erected near Biddiford in 1758. During Penal times the people of the locality had resorted to a Mass rock near

Aerial view of Annacotty.

Ardvarna, and the hill on which they placed look-outs is still known as *Cnoc an Aifrinn*, Mass Hill. St. Patrick's church was partially destroyed on the Night of the Big Wind, 6-7 January 1839, but was repaired soon afterwards. It was last renovated in 1977-1978 and is still in use. The arch around the door is believed to have been taken from Quin Abbey in County Clare.

THE EARL OF CLARE'S DEMESNE was located near the western boundaries of Killeenagarriff parish. In 1837 the principal seats were Thornfield, the residence of Major-General Sir R. Bourke; Woodstown, of Major Gough; Mulcaher, of the Rev. J. Crampton; and Rich Hill, of W. Howley.

WOODSTOWN HOUSE is now a convent. William Gough Gubbins succeeded his relation, Major Gough, in 1853. He moved from Woodstown House to Castletroy in the 1860s and eventually sold Woodstown for £3,000 in 1875.

WILLIAM HOWLEY, the son of John Howley of Charlotte's Quay, Limerick, was one of Caleb Powell's Grand Jurors in 1858. He lived in Rich Hill and played a prominent part in the Limerick celebrations that preceded the proclamation of Queen Victoria in 1837.

DERRYGALVAN PARISH was located within the Liberties of Limerick City in 1840 when the only trace of antiquity was a small burial-ground east of the Limerick-Tipperary road, in the townland of Ballysimon. Some small fragments of a ruined church were "visible among the luxuriant weeds" but little else remained to indicate how large it had been, or to reveal anything else about it. The land was considered remarkably good, with about half of it under tillage and the remainder attached to the large dairy farms which supplied the city with milk and butter. The principal houses were Coolanave, Ballyclough House and Killonan House.

SCART TOWNLAND is unique insofar as the dioceses of Limerick, Cashel and Killaloe meet here.

DERRYGALVAN derived its name from *Doire Uì Ghealbhàin*, the Derry or Oak Grove of O'Galvan, a family name still found within the city and Liberties. It was in Derrygalvan townland that the orignal parish church was built.

GALVAN, Galvin, Galven, Gallivan, *O Gealwaine, O Gallivain* and *O'Galvane* are all derivatives of *O Gealbhàin*, the descendants of *Gealbhán*, the Bright-white. This is a Dalcassian name once prevalent in Derrygalvan, found throughout Munster, and most numerous in Kerry. It is also found in County Rosommon.

SOURCES
11 25 26 39 51 61 63
68 82 120 129 135 192 238
246 264 282

Askeaton

Greenish Island · Tomdeely · Lismakeery

ASKEATON derived its name from a water-fall south of the town which was known as *Eas Geitine, Eas Gebhtene* or *Eas Gheiphtine,* the Water-fall of the Geiphtine, a tribe who settled here in pre-Christian times. Maurice Lenihan believed that the water-fall may have been known as *As-ceád-tinne,* the Cascade of the Hundred Fires. The town has been known throughout the centuries as *Inis Eeibhtine,* the Island of Eeibhtine, Inikkefty, Iniskesty, Inisketti, Hiniskefty, Hinksty, Innkefty, Asketon, Askeyton, Asketton, Askeating, Rockbarkley, Rock Barkley, Rock Berkeley and Inysgebryny.

A BRONZE AGE SETTLEMENT may have been one of the earliest towns on this site. In 1834 two fibulae, or collars, of gold were found near the town. Later in the nineteenth century Maurice Lenihan was shown two gold ornaments for the hair which came from a find which included a gold penannular bracelet with expanded ends. The find also included a hammered gold ingot which had been worked by a convex hammer (possibly of stone) on a stone anvil. The date and location of this discovery has been forgotten, but even though these four items were said to have been found together, they may have belonged to different periods in the Bronze Age. In 1835 workmen found several gold coins while sinking a wall foundation on the west side of the river. Two years later, in 1837, silver chalices, croziers, and more gold coins were discovered near the friary and the castle.

ASKEATON CASTLE was built on a rocky limestone islet in the Deel River some time around 1199, possibly by William de Burgo although Hamo de Valognes who was appointed Justiciar by Prince John in 1195, is also credited with its foundation. Thomas de Clare was in possession of the castle in 1287. King Edward II (1298-1328) awarded it to Robert de Welle in 1318. The Earls of Desmond made Askeaton Castle their principal residence from 1348 although they have been in possession before that date. Most of the surviving structure dates from the fif-

teenth century. The ruined tower belongs to this period. It contains some fine windows, and a fire-place on the third floor. The entire island was encircled with a strong wall which the tower protected at its most vulnerable point, the southern end of the bailey. The keep, located on the northern end of an eminence, and the tower were further defended by a battlemented curtain wall which enclosed the bailey. The ruined tower replaced an earlier structure on the same site.

THE DESMOND HALL is on a lower level, the lower ward or bailey, to the west. At one stage it may have been connected to a tower on the upper bailey by either a bridge or a wall. It was known as the *Halla Mór,* the Great Hall, the Desmond Hall., or the Banquet Hall. This building was erected by the Seventh Earl of Desmond, between 1440 and 1459, on the site of an earlier hall. The kitchen, chambers and cellar on the ground floor belonged to the older hall which was superseded by the Desmond Hall. This fifteenth-century hall, 72 feet long by 30 feet wide was probably built by some of the craftsmen who were employed by the Franciscans as the carved windows here resemble those of the Friary.

THE FITZGERALDS OF DESMOND had connections in the city of Florence where another branch of their family, the Di Gherardini, lived. In 1440 Giovanni Di Gherardini "gloried and drank deep" here with his Irish cousins. Leonardo Bruni, the humanist, wrote his letter of introduction on behalf of the Republic of Florence while staying as a guest in Askeaton Castle. The castle resisted the English commander Malby successfully in 1579. On 3 April 1580 the garrison abandoned it to Pelham's forces when they appeared before it with artillery. The Earl's followers destroyed some of the castle's out-buildings before they abandoned it. Captain Edward Berkeley took command of Askeaton Castle on behalf of the Crown, and remained on as constable for nine years. He retired in 1589, the victim of a recession, and died later that year. Edward's brother, Francis, defended the castle in his stead. The Earl of Essex came to his rescue on 10 June, 1599,

after Francis had resisted a siege of 247 days by the followers of the Sugán Earl of Desmond. Francis was knighted on 2 June 1599 "for his brave maintenance of the siege". Afterwards Essex and Berkeley departed to "haunt and hunt" Sir Garret FitzNicholas and his troops around the Killmallock area. The Sugán Earl made a second attempt to capture the castle, and failed again. The 300-strong garrison held out until government troops arrived to relieve them and re-victual the castle after Christmas 1599. Sir Anthony St. Leger received a grant at Dublin, on 17 October, 1599 of a "castle or chief house called the castle of Askeatinge, with all edifices, buildings, towers, gardens, courts and bawns" and forty acres which had been demised to Sir Francis Berkeley. Sir George Carew passed Askeaton in the summer of 1600 and installed a garrison of 700 foot-soldiers and 75 horsemen, while Berkeley served the Crown in other disturbed areas. Sir Francis Berkeley skirmished successfully against O'Donnell's forces at Elphin and, later, took an active part in the siege of Kinsale. In 1602-1603 he repaired Limerick Castle and maintained a garrison of 150 men in Askeaton Castle. When the St. Leger grant was revoked in 1610 Askeaton Castle reverted to Sir Francis Berkeley.

THE CASTLE was garrisoned by 200 soldiers, sent there by Lord Broghill, in 1641. On 14 August, 1642, Askeaton Castle was surrendered to Colonel Purcell and "the council of His Majesty's Catholiques for the Province of Munster". The articles of capitulation mentioned that the arms, munitions, garrison horses and goods belonging to Catholics were to be surrendered. The English and Irish warders were allowed to live and offered safe conduct to "Downarayle or Corcke" with their goods, and half the books in the castle. They also had to swear not to bear arms against the King, and a guarantee was given that any Protestants amongst the garrison or inhabitants would be unmolested. In 1652 the castle was taken without any record of a struggle. It was dismantled on the orders of Captain Axtell, Governor of Kilkenny. According to tradition the castle

Aerial view of Askeaton, the Friary in the foreground.

was undermined by "Cromwell" who propped it up with beams as he worked: when he burned these wooden supports, half the massive keep fell by its own weight. This story was in circulation as late as 1875. Cromwell's presence on the scene is extremely doubtful, but the method of demolition described was one in use during the Cromwellian period and may have been employed by Axtell's men.

ST. MARY'S CHURCH OF IRELAND CHURCH may have been founded as a commandery of the Knights Templars in 1298. It was dedicated to Mary, which may be an indication of its Anglo-Norman origin, as the Normans had a special veneration for the Blessed Virgin. Hubert de Burgo, the Bishop of Limerick, granted this church to the Abbey of Keynsham, Somerset, during the thirteenth century. After the dissolution the original building became the parish church of the Established Church. This was later replaced with the present structure but "the remains of an ancient tower, square at the base and octangular above" can still be seen, as well as a portion of the old chancel. Aubrey de Vere, the poet, was buried in the church-yard. His

grave lies, just inside the gate.

ASKEATON FRIARY was probably founded by Gerald, the Fourth Earl of Desmond, the legendary *Gearóid Iarla,* who left his camp one night in 1398 and was never seen again. A convent definitely existed on this site in 1400 despite another date of 1420 being given for its foundation. This was built for the Conventual Franciscans. In 1497 the friars changed to the Observant rule. The friary was reformed under the provincialship of Patrick Hely in 1513, which may indicate that the earlier reform was not successful. James, the Fourteenth Earl of Desmond, was buried here in 1558. In 1564 a provincial chapter of the Franciscan Order was held in the friary. English forces under Sir Nicholas Malby plundered the building in 1579, killed some of the friars and expelled others. Malby wrecked the ancestral tomb of the Desmonds. According to folklore, he took the body or bones of the rebellious Earl's wife out of the grave to taunt her widower who was defending Askeaton Castle with a garrison of 160 gallowglass mercenaries, 300 Irish *kernes* or foot-soldiers and 30 horsemen. In 1617 Fr.

Donat Mooney wrote of this incident, and reported that the friary had "not been inhabited by the friars for many years. In the wars against the Geraldines of Munster the inmates were treated in the most barbarous manner by the English under Sir Nicholas Malbi. Some were put to death for the faith; amongst these martyrs of Christ was Father John Conor whose remains are buried in the Chapter Room. I have been unable to ascertain the names of the others".

THE FRIARS returned in 1627. They "began to dwell among the ruins of the convent and repaired it, so far as the persecution would allow them". Records of the time fail to note the various guardians of the friary from 1629 to 1645. In all probability the Franciscans did not organise themselves until the Confederate Irish took the town in 1642. This enabled the friars to repair and openly re-establish their friary in 1643. No actual re-building took place; the *debris* of the fallen tower was cleared from the church; and the buildings, or a portion of them, were re-roofed and re-furnished. Jerome Herbert was guardian of Askeaton Friary from 1645 until 1650, when

Owen O'Caghan was elected in his stead. In 1647 the bodies of two Franciscans who had been tortured and hanged in Kilmallock in 1587, were buried "with great pomp" within the friary. These were Patrick O'Hely, the Bishop of Mayo, and Conn O'Rourke. After this sombre ceremony, little else is heard of Askeaton Friary. By then the Cromwellians were overlords of Ireland and the friars had to flee abroad or go into hiding. William Hurley was elected guardian from 1661 to 1670. He was succeeded by Francis Wall and several others elected between that date and 1714, when Francis Hickey became the last guardian. T.J. Westropp wrote that "the guardianship must have been a mere shadow after 1690, though we may suppose that a few monks long dwelt in the neighbourhood and haunted the ruins of their 'holy and beautiful' house; we find no such traces of the survival of the convent as are found at Quin, Clare-Galway, Ennis — where one of the monks assisted the parish priest, and was always as such chosen guardian — and elsewhere". Part of the ruined friary was used as a Catholic Church until 1851 when a new church opened in the town.

ROCK ABBEY is another name often applied to this ruined Franciscan Friary. Most Franciscan friaries had their cloisters located to the north of the church. Askeaton is unique insofar as its cloister was built to the south, but this may have been because of the slope to the south and the rocky ground to the north. The cloister contains traces of work from the nineteenth century. In its north-eastern corner there is a crude depiction of St. Francis, with stigmata, the face of which has been worn away by people kissing it, in the belief that this would cure toothache. The nave, chancel and northern transept are in a good state of preservation. The buildings above, and around, the cloister, including the dormitory, are laid out in the usual way. In 1837 the other portions were "much decayed, and large masses of the walls lie scattered around, as if detached by the force of gunpowder". The ruin has altered only a little since then. The refectory dates from the mid-fifteenth century, and was in all probability a later addition, as was the enormous aisled wing north of the church. The delicately carved windows resembling those of the castle's banquet hall, the triple tomb niches, the sedilia or wall seats, the reader's niche in the old refectory south of the cloister, the small prison in the south range, and the Stephenson tomb are the friary's more notable architectural features.

THE STEPHENSON TOMB is located to the right of the main altar. This commemorated Oliver Stephenson, a prominent member of the Confederate Irish Forces, whose family are reputed to have expelled the friars for "the second time"; whether this was in 1651 or 1691 is now impossible to verify.

ASKEATON was attacked by Sir Nicholas Malby in 1579. He had no artillery to batter down the castle walls, so he vented his fury on the friary and burned the town. After the Desmond Wars Francis Berkeley was given a grant of Askeaton, with the exception of the castle which was reserved to the Crown. This grant was later revoked in favour of Sir Anthony St. Leger. Sir Francis Berkeley regained possession of Askeaton in 1610 after a letter of King James I directed Sir Arthur Chichester to pass Askeaton Castle and forty acres of land to him, in fee-farm, as he had

Friary cloister.

offered to wall Askeaton Town and make the castle a refuge for the English in those parts. James I also constituted the Constable's lands to be the Manor of Rock Barkeley, and established a fair and weekly markets. In a second letter, dated 25 April 1611, the King promised the Constableship of Limerick to Maurice Berkeley after his father's death, a tribute to the family's loyalty to the Crown.

THE WALLED TOWN was incorporated as a borough on 20 October 1612. Edmund Drew was the first provost and the burgesses were Sir Francis Berkeley, Edmond Ley, Roger Rue, Gilbert Rue, William Rastell, Henry Widnam, John Eaton, Anthony Cooper, John Green, John Atkinson, John Stokes and Andrew Davys. Sir Francis Berkeley received his Askeaton holding at an annual rent of £87.50 under various terms, one of which was an obligation to erect houses for over fifty English families. Many of these early English Protestant settlers later established some of the "county" families of Limerick, Tipperary and Clare. Berkeley looked after the interests of his Irish neighbours as well as those of the new settlers. On one occasion he was accused, and found guilty, of harbouring Irish husbandmen on his lands, but the charges were dropped by the authorities, who had few friends to spare in the West Limerick of the early seventeenth century.

THE ROCK BARKELEY HOLDINGS, or *seignory,* including the town, contained 1200 acres of demesne, 900 in fee-farm, 1200 evicted, 1100 leased and 36 in other tenures. Francis Berkeley could muster 21 foot-soldiers and 7 horsemen, and he "succeeded in undoing much of the ravage of two civil wars, before his death, which took place at Askeaton Castle on December 20th 1615". His sons Maurice and Henry succeeded him but died young. By 1626 the estate had passed to two of Francis's daughters, Elizabeth, the wife of George Crofton, and Gertrude, the wife of John Taylor. None of his other daughters appear to have inherited. One of them, Frances, was married to Thomas Blayney of Tregonan, Denbighshire. Frances was an ancestress of the Crofton, Blayney, Ormsby and Browne families, while her sister, Gertrude, was an ancestress of the Barons Massy, the Taylors of Hollypark, and through her daughter, the Gores, the Gore-Hickmans, and the Westropps.

THE 1655 CIVIL SURVEY described the mid-seventeenth century town. "Asketton town and lands, beinge a mannor with the Priviledge of a Courte Leete and Court Barron, five plowlands and a halfe with a Castle and a great stone buildinge, an Abbie and church; a corporate Town; two mills, whereof one belongs to Mrs. Crofton, with a

greate Bridge, a fishing Leape, Three Eele wears, Three Salmon weares, Two ffaires in the yeer and a markett once in the weeke." In 1690 unrest in the area prompted Richard Taylor of Ballinort to correspond with King William's officers. He complained of the dangerous state of his district and asked for a garrison to be stationed in Askeaton although the castle was ruined but still worth repairing.

THE EARL OF ORRERY tried to persuade Queen Anne to refit Askeaton Castle in 1712. He wrote: "This castle was built and fortified as a stronge hold by the Earl of Desmond, and was of great and singular service to him in his Rebellion in the Reign of Queen Elizabeth: the town was made a Burrow and corporation by letters patent from King James the First ... It is scituated [sic] in an Island made by a Division of the River about one hundred yeards above the Castle, and united again at a less distance below to which the tyde flowes and makes it a navigable river to the Shannon where it empties itself after a course of Three mile and is one of the best passes for crossing that river into the County of Clare. The want of wch conveniency was of great detriment and delay to the speedy reducing of Limerick in both the late rebellions of '41 and '88 ... it will alsoe be of great security to the Protestants already settled there, as well as being an encouragement to others to settle, there being at present no barracks near to protect them from the insults of Irish Rapparees". Orrery described Askeaton's proximity to the "Confines of Kerry" which made it a key to that county and commanded the best passes from there "for carriages, etc., which may be annoyed or sustained by this garrison ... it will also greatly secure the navigation of the Shannon, there being noe fortress now Thereon from the mouth of the River to the citty of Limerick, the sixty mile distant". The Earl related how ruinous the fortress was by 1712, but suggested that if the government provided him with £500 for its repair he would maintain it at his own expense from then onwards, on condition that he was appointed governor "at the usual allowance and with the accustomed profitts made to the other Governors of Corke and Limerick". Queen Anne paid little attention to his request. The castle remained a ruin.

THE HELL-FIRE CLUB PREMISES is located alongside the ruins of Askeaton Castle. This ruined building may date from the late seventeenth century, although other accounts date it from the 1740s. The original Hell-Fire Clubs were established by Lord Wharton, later the Duke of Wharton, in 1720, but were abolished by a Royal proclamation on 28 April 1721. Another such club, founded by Sir Francis Dashwood, may have evolved

from the meeting of a coterie of literary men at some unspecified date between 1748 and 1755. Dashwood claimed it was an offspring of the Dillettanti Society which he helped to found in 1732. His more notorious society — The Amorous Knights of Wycombe, The Monks of Medmenham, The Medmenham Monks, The Order of St. Francis, The Franciscans, Dashwood's Disciples, or The Brotherhood of Saint Francis of Wycombe — became better known as the Hell-Fire Club, a name which its members did not use until towards the end of the eighteenth and early nineteenth centuries. Rumour, gossip and hearsay abounded about the clubs' activities; membership flourished; and clubs were formed in places as far apart as Dublin, Edinburgh and Paris. The membership included at least one Prime Minister, the Earl of Bute; a Chancellor of the Exchequer, Sir Francis Dashwood, Baron Le Despencer; a First Lord of the Admiralty, John Montagu, the Earl of Sandwich; Thomas Potter, Paymaster-General, Treasurer for Ireland, and son of the Archbishop of Canterbury; John Wilkes, Lord Mayor of London; various cabinet ministers; several members of Parliament; distinguished wits; aspiring politicians; and the cream of Georgian society. The society also possessed a female membership, The Nuns of Medmenham, which included Frances, Viscountess Vane, authoress of *The Memoirs of a Lady of Quality* and many other rather dubious "ladies". Chevalier D'Eon de Beaumont, a French diplomat, is believed to have been a member of both the nuns' and the friar's orders. The members masqueraded as Satanists. Some of them may have been interested in the occult but the club-houses and grounds of the various Hell-Fire Clubs were devoted to more earthy pleasures. Young and not-so-young bucks indulged in drinking bouts, heavy gambling sessions, and frequent orgies. The Hell-Fire Clubs are also thought to have had a more serious aspect. Sir Francis Dashwood's passion for black magic is believed to have been a reaction against Catholicism and organised religion generally, and to have been as much a political force as a social one. A portrait depicting the only known female member of the Askeaton Hell-Fire Club hangs in Glin Castle. The club-house contains a curved bow on one side of each of its two main fronts, one of which may be the earliest example of a Venetian window on the curve, anywhere. During the nineteenth century this building was used as a barracks.

THE TOWN was disenfranchised by the Act of Union. £15,000 was paid in compensation to the Earl of Carrick, Lord Massy, Sir Vere Hunt and Sir Joseph Hoare. The Corporation became extinct. Richard Taylor, Vice-Provost of Askeaton, complained in 1811 that he "had never heard of there being any public record, roll, instrument, manuscript book, or paper belonging to the borough" so there was little chance of a history being compiled on its days as a "pocket borough". In 1834 the manorial court was replaced by the petty sessions court. There were 260 houses in the town in 1837. The main trade was in grain and flour which were exported directly to foreign markets. There were then two flour-mills here, the larger one, Hewson's, being near the castle. The river was "capable of admitting vessels of 60 tons' burden, and ... might be deepened at a trifling expense, so as to admit vessels drawing 15 feet of water to" the ancient five-arched bridge connecting the opposite portions of the town.

CASTLE HEWSON derives its name from an old tower-house which is still standing at one end of the present structure. This mansion was built in the early 1700s, probably before 1750. Because of a depression in the ground, one section of the house, near the old castle, is two-stories high, and the other part rises to three stories. In 1837 it was the home of the Hewson family. The other big houses of the period were Inchirourk-More of R. Hunt; Shannon View, of J. Browne; Mantle Hill of J. Hunt; and the Abbey of the Rev. M. Fitzgerald. Castle Hewson is located east of the town, near Curragh Chase.

BALLYCULLEN HOUSE, southwest of Askeaton, dates from the eighteenth century. In 1978, Mark Bence Jones noted that it had been recently restored.

GREENISH ISLAND is situated on the southern bank of the Shannon, near the mouth of the River Deel. This is the principal island of a group in the bay of Tramore and covers an area of approximately forty-five acres. The present name is derived from an older one, *Inis Grein*, the Island of the Sun. Samuel Lewis believed that the name originated "from a very large heathen temple erected on its highest point, probably appropriated to the worship of that pagan divinity, and of which there are are still some slight vestiges".

TOMDEELY derives its name from *To m Dhaoile*, the Bush of the River Deel or from *Tuaim Daoile*, the Tumulus at, or near, the River Deel. In 1840 John O'Donovan favoured the latter explanation.

TOMDEELY CASTLE was described in 1840 as the ruin of a castlelike house of a rectangular form. No tradition of its original founder or occupier remained. It did not appear to be old. Three years before, Samuel Lewis described it as a small, square, tower built by the Mahon family, which had fallen into decay soon after the expulsion of the Geraldines.

TOMDEELY CHURCH, a small nave and chancel church, had most of its features destroyed by 1840. John O'Donovan believed it dated from the fifteenth century but conceded that it may be a century older than that. This ruin is north-east of the castle.

LISMAKEERY RING FORT is located in the parish to which it gives its name, west of the Deel River, and two miles south-west of Askeaton. This fort contains the remains of a stone revetment. Lismakeery was also known as Lismacdiry.

LISMAKEERY CHURCH is located near the ring fort. This church dates from the late fifteenth century, and may be the one referred to by Samuel Lewis in his description of the ruins of an old church on an eminence near Altavilla.

ALTAVILLA, the residence of T.G. Batemen in 1837 was situated close to the River Deel, at the south-eastern extremity of the parish of Lismakeery.

DR. PAT WALLACE of Askeaton was appointed director of the National Museum of Ireland in 1989. He is the youngest man ever to assume this position. He served as a director of the Woodquay excavations; was involved with Irish Life in building *The Viking Adventure;* and has contributed to popularising the history of the Vikings in Ireland.

SOURCES
9 11 13 29 35
43 44 47 50 76
77 86 120 122 123
129 152 173 184 192
231 238 264 272 275

Athlacca

Kilbroney · Rathcannon · Dromin

ATHLACCA derives its name from *An t-Ath Leacach,* the Flaggy Ford, an ancient crossing of the Morningstar River. This was once the seat of the Lacy family who ruled the surrounding territory from the days of the great Anglo-Norman thrust into Limerick. They had two strongholds here, one near the village and a second one at Tullerbuoy which was later known as Castle Ievers. Prior to that Juliana Fitzgerald, the widow of John de Cogan, had owned the Manor of Athlacca. It passed from her to John FitzThomas Fitzgerald but reverted to the ownership of her son, John de Cogan, for a while in 1304. John FitzThomas Fitzgerald fought a legal battle to reclaim the manors of Adare, Athlacca, Castleroberts, Croom, Dromin and Wregedy, which Juliana had originally signed over to him, and won possession on a technicality. In 1310 the sitting tenant of Athlacca Manor, Agnes de Valence, died without an heir. John FitzThomas Fitzgerald had his retainers occupy the manor and lands. They were soon ejected by John de Cogan and his men. The de Cogan retainers were unable to hold Athlacca for more than a day and a night as John FitzRobert, the King's representative, took possession in the King's name and returned Athlacca to John FitzThomas Fitzgerald's ownership.

JOHN FITZTHOMAS FITZGERALD

became the First Earl of Kildare in 1316. In 1318 the occupancy of Athlacca was held by J. Gower, or Goer, from whom *Oileán an Ghabhair* or Illaneagour may have taken its name. This townland in the parish of Dromin may have been mistranslated as Goat Island because of some confusion between the surname Gower and the Irish name for a goat, *gabhar.* In 1328 David Chaumpeny appears to have occupied Athlacca, and soon afterward the Lacy family came into possession.

ATHLACCA CHURCH OF IRELAND

CHURCH was built for £560 in 1813. It was burned by the Rockites in 1822, but was replaced by another new church on the same site in 1823. A new glebe house was also built, in the same year, on a glebe of fourteen acres. Today only the spire of the church remains. The church was closed in 1942 and demolished in 1957. The churchyard is still used for burials.

ATHLACCA OLD CHURCH

ATHLACCA OLD CHURCH was dedicated to St. John the Baptist in 1410. After the Reformation it was converted to Protestant worship, and appears to have remained in constant use until 1813, when it was demolished in order to build a new Church of Ireland parish church on the same site.

ATHLACCA CASTLE

ATHLACCA CASTLE was described as a manor of Maurice Fitzgerald in 1285. From the fourteenth to the seventeenth centuries it was a seat of the De Lacy family, until David Lacy lost it to Charles Ormsby during the Cromwellian plantation. By 1700 only a part of this old castle remained.

OLD COURT

OLD COURT, the *Cúirt,* or Ormsby's Court, is an early eighteenth-century mansion which may have been built by Charles Ormsby's son, John. It was abandoned towards the end of the eighteenth century, and some parts of the ruin were demolished by the Land Commission during the 1930s. Old Court was located on the bank of the Morningstar, or *Samair,* River.

JOHN ORMSBY

JOHN ORMSBY was a man whose "character was noised abroad as a man of tyrannical disposition, and as it appears Government gave him great authority to suppress the rebellious peasantry, it was said by tradition he often put, on his own judgement, persons to death, previously imprisoning them in his castle cellars before execution". The foregoing description was written by Rev. George Gough Gubbins in his *Memoirs of the Gubbins Family,* who were neighbours of the Ormsbys and occupants of another Ormsby residence, Maidstown Castle.

AGRARIAN UNREST

AGRARIAN UNREST was rife in the region during the eighteenth and nineteenth centuries. In 1798 Lord Edward Fitzgerald visited the Greene home in Ballybeg, Dromin, where he received a deputation of three United Irishmen from Kilmallock, Fleming, Gaffney and Hawthorne. Whiteboys, Rockites, anti-tithe campaigners, evicting landlords, tithe-proctors, high rents, land clearances, high food prices, lack of tillage, a surplus of pasturage, unemployment, hunger, and desperation kept the area in a constant state of turmoil. On Tuesday 25 February 1800 over 200 armed men dragged a tithe-proctor from his home, whipped him, wrecked his furniture, and burned his tithe-books and notes. Landowners, farmers, gentlemen and magistrates banded together for mutual protection, and 10 constables were appointed to the Athlacca district, ranging from Tullovin and Dohora as far as the Cork border. By 1822 the entire region was in revolt, and the Rockites were in virtual control until the Rifle Brigade was called in to quell the disturbances.

JEREMIAH ROURKE

JEREMIAH ROURKE was charged with firing two shots at Robert Ievers of Tullerboy during the Rockite campaign. He missed, but was captured and sent for trial. He was sentenced to death, and hanged in Limerick on 10 August 1822. Local tradition maintains he was innocent, but was executed in order to set an example which would cow the Rockites.

THE LAND

THE LAND is very fertile, but by 1837 half of it was under tillage and the other half was rich meadow and pasture land, on which a great number of cattle were fed. There was not an acre of waste land or turbary but "a great want" of timber prevailed throughout the district, and scarcely a tree, shrub or even a hedge-row was to be seen, except around the houses of the principal inhabitants.

KILBRONEY CHURCH

KILBRONEY CHURCH, *Cill Bruaine* or *Brónach,* the Church of St. Brónach, Broney or Bromana may have been an early Christian foundation on which the Knights Templars probably erected another church about 1289. The present ruin may date from the fifteenth century. Its east wall, complete with "a remarkably rude window", fell, during a storm in 1982. Cornelius and Oliver Irwin, on whose land it lies, have left the remains undisturbed. Their parents would not allow a stick or a stone to be removed from this ancient ecclesiastical site and adjoining holy well in the south-western corner of Tullerboy townland, and their sons feel the same way today. During the 1940s Mrs. Irwin had refused to demolish the old church when a Department of Agriculture official had urged her to do so, and utilise its stones as the foundations of a farm-building.

ST. BRONEY or Bronach may be the saint known as the Virgin of *Glen-Seichis* who is registered in the martyrologies of Tallaght and Donegal. No dates or other particulars are now remembered, save that her feast day was observed on 2 April. This saint was also known as St. Bromana. Kilbrony or *Kilbrónach* in County Down was originally known as Glen-Seichis.

ST. BRONEY'S WELL, *Tobar Brónaí,* is located north of the church, on the north-eastern section of the enclosure on which the church was built. This deep stone-lined well is in excellent condition and is cleaned regularly by the Irwins. In former times pilgrims made their rounds at this well from 7-11 February and a pattern day was observed on 15 August, according to local tradition. In 1840 O'Donovan recorded that rounds were made on Sunday mornings and Good Fridays. A second enclosure can still be identified to the north and east, encircling that on which the church and well are situated.

ROSS-TEMPLE MANOR was located on a gentle eminence, from which the Knights Templars could view Kilbroney Church. The name was commemorated in Ross Temple Railway Station, which is now a private residence.

CASTLE IEVERS is also known as Tullerboy Castle and incorporates part of the original castle within its walls. The present house dates from 1740 when it was erected by the Ievers family. It was later owned by the Haines family, and is now occupied by the O'Regans.

TULLERBOY CASTLE was held by John de Kerredy in 1319-1320. The Bishop of Ossory received a grant of the castle at a later stage. In 1583 Edmond Leo occupied it, and it was later held by a W. Riordan, or Ryurdane, who was killed during the Geraldine Rebellion. The Civil Survey of 1655 refers to the castle of "Tullervoy", its bawn, a thatched stone house, and another house located on one plowland which were let by the Earl of Kildare for 50 pence a year. The tenants in that year were Morcas and Walter Lee (or Leo). Part of this castle still survives and appears to have been incorporated into the south-eastern corner of Castle Ievers. An external staircase leading to the upper floor may have belonged to it.

RATHCANNON CASTLE is the most impressive-looking ruin in the area — from a distance. The ruin consists of two walls, one to the east and another to the west. A square tower, and a bawn, were once located to the north-west, with a later residence built to the west. Part of the bawn wall to the east is still visible, and to the west and south of the bawn

and castle ruin the remains of some long-vanished enclosure, or enclosures, can be discerned. If these buried foundations formed an outer bailey this would have quadrupled the size of the castle. Because of its strategic position on top of the hill, it is most unlikely that this ruined castle was the first defensive structure erected on the site. A family named O'Casey are reputed to be the original founders of Rathcannon Castle but John O'Donovan was unable to verify this in 1840. Mainchín Seoighe mentions Rathcannon as a manor of the Earls of Kildare which came into the possession of William Casey, a man who was alternately Catholic and Protestant Bishop of Limerick between 1551 and 1591. In 1637 Thomas Casey made a will leaving his castle and lands in trust for his wife Bridget and his two daughters, Anne and Juane. He died shortly afterwards, and Sir Philip Perceval applied political pressure to become the girls' guardian. Juane died, and Perceval failed to persuade fourteen-year-old Anne to marry his son in 1650. Her uncle, Sir Hardress Waller, encouraged her to marry an Englishman, Captain Drury Wray, who settled on Rathcannon Hill and built a mansion alongside the castle. Part of the ruined mansion was thatched and occupied, by a poor family, in 1840.

SIR DRURY WRAY fought on the Jacobite side and lost his lands to the Hollow Blade Sword Company of London when he was attainted. He managed to retain some of his holdings, however, but this may have been due to his son Christopher having fought on the Williamite side. Sir Drury died in 1710. In 1851 Archdeacon W. Wray Maunsell owned more than 1700 acres of land around Rathcannon.

THE CORCASSE, north of Rathcannon Hill, was once considered as a prospective airport site before Shannon Airport was constructed.

MAIDSTOWN CASTLE is situated in *Baile Uí Bhenóg* the townland of the young woman or maid. Lewis claims it was built by the O'Hanlons during the fifteenth century, while O'Donovan wrote that it did not appear to be very old. It was dismantled in 1654 and its owner, John Fox, was dispossessed by the Cromwellians in favour of Captain Arthur Ormsby. John Ormsby is believed to have built the adjoining Maidstown House during the early eighteenth century, before he moved to Old Court. In 1840 part of the castle was occupied by a farmer, identified as a Mr. Coll. It then possessed three storeys while the portion containing the staircase had five. Daniel Webb (c. 1719-1798), author of the *Harmonies of Poetry and Music* was born here as this was the home of the "Napper"

Webbs who settled in Maidstown after leaving Gloucester. Napier Webb was on Caleb Powell's Grand Jury in 1858. His father was the son of Daniel James Webb and his mother Ann Wilhelmina was descended from Charles Monck, King Charles I's Surveyor of the Customs in Ireland. Robert Coll sold the structure in 1972. In 1986 the castle was in a good state of preservation and the house was habitable but unoccupied.

DROMIN derives its name from Dromain *O Cleireachain,* the hill or ridge of O *Cléirceacháin.*

CLERIHAN, Clerkan, Clerkin, Clarkins, Clarke, *O Clercan, O Clearkane, O Cléireacháin* and *O Cléirchín,* are descendants of *Cléireacháin* or *Cleirchìn,* the Clerk or Cleric. The *O Cléireacháin* family were chiefs of *Ui Cairbre Aodhbha* in East Limerick in ancient times, a territory which extended from Bruree to the Shannon.

DROMIN RING FORT, on Dromin Hill, in the townland of Dromin South, is also known as the Caher or *Cahirnadrumin.* Its name is derived from *Cathair na Dromain,* the Fort of the Ridge. This ancient stone, or stone-faced, fort is 400 feet in diameter, and is the largest fort in the area. This region is noted for its concentration of such monuments in the townlands of Ballinstona North (3 forts), Clogher East (7 forts), Cloonbrien (3 forts), Dromin South (3 forts), Drombeg (3 forts), Knockuregare (3 forts) and Rathcannon (7 forts). In 1088 the men of Tyrone and Tyrconnel raided this area under the leadership of Donall Mac Lochlainn; penetrated as far as Emly, in County Tipperary; demolished Limerick City; and brought away the head of Art Uallach O Ruairc from the hills of Fearann-Saingill.

HOLY TRINITY CHURCH was dedicated in 1410. The ruins of this old church, with a priest's residence at its west side, still stands in Dromin graveyard. It appears to have been used for Protestant worship from Reformation times until 1700. It was finally abandoned in 1784. A crypt within the ruins was known as Ormsby's Hole, and is believed to have been the burial place of John Ormsby. The Holy Trinity is still commemorated in the dedication of the Catholic Church in Dromin which dates from 1828. The Catholic Church in Athlacca dates from 1840, and was built to replace one damaged on the *Night of the Big Wind,* 6 January 1839.

THE CHURCH OF ST. MARGARET was dedicated in 1410 but was demolished between 1826 and 1840. The stones were used to enclose its old churchyard of Uregare, which continued in use as a burial place.

ST. MARGARET'S WELL, *Tobar Sam Mairghéd,* was located to the east of Uregare graveyard, but the pattern or "stations" had ceased there by the early 1800s.

UIRGEDI CHURCH was often confused with Uregare Church. Today only a few stones are left, a short distance away, near the Uregare Cross to Goat Island road.

TRINITY WELL, *Tobar na Tr;ónóide,* was the scene of a regular pattern within living memory, on Trinity Sundays. In 1976 the custom was revived by the Athlacca *Glór na nGael* committee, who managed to attract a large crowd to this well in the townland of Ballynamuddagh, not far from Dromin Church.

ADMIRAL SIR EDMOND NAGLE (1757-1830) was a native of Uregare Parish. He was generally regarded as a Corkman — "the only naval celebrity of Cork origin" during the eighteenth century.

ST. PATRICK'S WELL, on the Lane Farm in Ballincurra, is north of Knocktwo Hill. A pattern once held here on St. Patrick's Day was continued almost into modern times by local pilgrims. A stone beside the well is believed to contain imprints of St. Patrick's knees and elbows, and another large stone nearby is said to have been used as a Mass rock during Penal times.

THE ASSEMBLY OF CLOGHER, *Aonach Chlochair,* the Fair of Clogher, may have been located in the parish of Dromin rather than in Raheennamadra, near Knocklong, in ancient times.

THE DROMIN FAIR was notorious for its faction fights during the early nineteenth century. The Three Year Olds and Four Year Olds were two of the best-known faction fighting groups. These were originally known as the Shanavests and Caravats until 1818, when members of the latter group assembled n Guerin's public-house in Kilteely and swore to stay together for another three years for mutual protection. The Shanavests, on hearing of this, swore that they would band together for four years. The groups thus earned new names, the Three Year Olds and Four Year Olds, although other explanations for the origin of the names may be equally valid, such as an argument over the age of a heifer sold at the Fair of the Well in Ballyagran. The Baron of Dromin Fair was Matthew Duhig of Knockuregare. Tom Duhig, a descendant of his, stated that six men were killed in faction fights here. Three men were shot dead on 23 September 1825 during one such fight. Many others were "desperately wounded" in the *melee* in which scythes were used as weapons. After this incident the military kept the fair under observation to avoid a repetition.

TRAGEDIUS LYONS, Trag Lion, or Trog Lion, was a steward of John Ormsby's, and as unpopular as his master. He lived in Maidstown Castle. His quarters were in the old tower-house, while Ormsby lived in the newer addition adjoining it. According to local tradition the Devil suddenly appeared in Trag Lion's room, seized him by both legs, dashed his brains out against the wall over the fireplace, and carried him off. One chamber in the old castle is still pointed out as Trag Lion's room, and stains over the fire-place are reputed to be blood stains. The truth is more prosaic. The Devil was "framed". Lyons was so hated by the locals that a group of them conspired against him. They broke into his quarters, killed him, and got rid of his body by throwing it into a bog hole.

SOURCES

9 12 39 120 129 190
191 192 235 270 282

The spire of the Church of Ireland Church.

Ballingarry

Knockfierna Hill · Kilmacow

BALLINGARRY derives its name from *Baile an Gharrdha*, Gardenstown, a not uncommon placename in Ireland. *Baile an Gharrdha*, or *Baile an Gharraidh*, is also translated as the Town of the Enclosed Garden. It was known as *Garthbiboys* in 1228 when it was the seat of the Biboys family who appear to have been Anglo-Norman settlers here. Ballingarry was Latinised as *Villi Horti* in the Papal registers, and appears as *Garthocconnyll* in other accounts because of its location in the barony of Upper Connello. The place-name was also abbreviated to Garth or Le Garthe and it was recorded as *Ville de Garth* before 1300. In 1452 the boundaries of the old parish of Garth were co-extensive with those of the tribal division of Gortcolgyn or Cortculligon. The parish was referred to as Gare, Garre, Gorth, Garry, Garrystown and Ballingarrie in 1492.

THE DIOCESE OF LIMERICK was divided into six deaneries early in the thirteenth century. These were Limerick, Adare, Rathkeale, Ardagh, Kilmallock and Garth. The Deanery of Garth comprised twelve parishes at that date. By 1930 the Church of Ireland Union contained only seven of these parishes, Kilfinny, Cloncagh, Cloncrew, Kilmeedy, Corcomohide, Mahoonagh and the original parish of Garth or Ballingarry. In 1295 John le Blond was the parson of Garth. In 1302 the parish paid a tax of £2.65 which was imposed, nominally, "for the relief of the Holy Land". A similar imposition, in 1306, yielded only £1.00, as some of the churches had been destroyed in a war.

THE LACY CASTLE, Ballingarry Castle, or Garrystown Castle, in the townland of Knight Street, is believed to have been erected by the Knights Templars. The present structure dates from the early fifteenth century, as both Ballingarry and the castle had been destroyed, in earlier times, "by Irish foes and English rebels". In 1408 Henry IV (1399-1413) granted certain taxes or customs to the bailiffs and commons of the village of Garth in order to repair their defences and wall the town. The castle was a Geraldine stronghold held for the Fitzgeralds by their allies and

kinsmen, the Lacys. Captain John Ward slaughtered the garrison of 40 men when he captured the castle for Elizabeth I in 1569, during the Desmond Rebellion. John Lacy forfeited both his castle and estates in 1583 but later regained possession only to lose them again in 1607. Richard Boyle, the Earl of Cork, acquired the Lacy holdings, but the former owners, the Lacy family, remained as Boyle's tenants. In the *Civil Survey* William "Lacie of Ballingarry" was listed as an Irish papist and the proprietor of the castle in 1654. Major John Odell was awarded the castle in

1667. The government refused to help him renovate and fortify the building so he eventually built a mansion nearby in 1685. The castle may have been further damaged during a Jacobite attack on the town in 1691. The 42nd Regiment were stationed here in 1822 as the castle served as a barracks during the Rockite disturbances. In 1837 it was known as Parson's Castle because the Church of Ireland minister had lived there until the Glebe House was built. It was used as a temporary hospital during a cholera epidemic, and when Mr. O'Keefe of the Ordnance

The Lacy Castle.

Survey Office inspected this structure, before 1840, some glass still remained in the windows. Prior to his visit a Mr. Gibbons had resided here as the following account shows: the "castle consists of three stories, the ceiling over the second floor being arched and plastered. On the third floor there is fixed a large old chimney-piece brought from Kilmallock by Mr. Gibbons, who at one period fitted up this castle as a dwelling place. On the centre of the upper part of this chimney piece there is a slab" with the date 1638 inscribed on it. Dr. Robert Odell, his wife, and children lived here during the mid-nineteenth century. When Brian de Breffney wrote of this elegant tower-house in *Castles of Ireland* (1977) it was still occupied, this time by cows. It still was in 1989.

THE LACY FAMILY derived their name from *De Laci,* that is of Lacy or Lassy in France. This surname appears as *De Lacy, De Lesse, De Lease,* De Lacy, Lacey, Lacie and, in Irish, *de Leís.* The Lacys arrived in England with William the Conqueror and were mentioned as tenants-in-chief in the *Domesday Book.* Hugh de Lacy was granted the province of Meath at the time of the Anglo-Norman invasion, but as he had no male heirs when he died, about 1242, it passed into other hands. By 1275 Richard Lacy of Ballingarry had established his branch of the family here. These Lacys established a network of castles in this area, the main ones being in Ballingarry, Bruff and Bruree. They supported the Geraldines, but even though they were listed among the attainted in 1598, they were still numbered among "the chief men" of the county. The Lacy family were amongst those dispossessed by the Cromwellian and Jacobite wars. They ranked amongst the Wild Geese, and distinguished themselves in military service. Count Peter de Lacy (1678-1751) served as a field-marshal in the Russian army; his son, Maurice F. de Lacy (1725-1801) was a marshal in the Austrian army; and another Maurice De Lacy (1740-1820) became a Russian general. Other Lacys served in Spain where Count de Lacy became a famous general and diplomat during the eighteenth century. Mary Lacy (c. 1743-1827) was the last of the Lacy family to live in Ballingarry. She was the wife of Thomas Hoare, a Catholic.

SIR GEORGE CAREW wrote to the Privy Council in 1600 stating that the "County of Limerick is a marvellous fine country, excellent good land, and very profitable, where most of the undertakers (settlers) were, and came very well forward till that late revolt ... The occasion whereof was, the too many weeds that grew amongst them, I mean the Irish freeholders ... Therefore pluck out these

weeds, and let the children of Israel dwell together, for in placing all English in that county there will be a good commonwealth for ever, especially good sound Desmond being placed in the back side. I will tell you what the weeds be that are there ... Piers Lacy, of the Bruff, the beginner of the rebellion; Lacy of Ballingerry, chief of the name; McIneyrie, chief of his name ..."

THE CIVIL SURVEY OF 1655 listed the landowners of the parish in 1641. Edward Standish owned Frankfort; Lieut. Col. William Piggott owned Kilshane; Philip Cullom, Ballyknockane; W. Cullom, Lisamote and Woodstock Castles; W. Lacy, Cloontemple and Ballyneale; Edward Sheehy, Ballynaroogabeg, Ballynoe and Ballykevin; Miles Jackson, Lisduane and Granagh; while Ballingarry itself with castle, mill and patent of fair belonged to John Massy. Edward Sheehy, W. Cullom and W. Lacy were deprived of their property by the Cromwellians. Their places were taken by new planter families with names like Odell, Cox, Monckton, Scanlan and Peppard.

THE ODELL FAMILY replaced the Lacys as the premier family in these parts. The name Odell signifies Woadhill, or the Hill where Woad Grows. Woad was a plant from which a blue dye was obtained in ancient times. The Odells are descended from Lieutenant John Odell who was a tax commissioner in the county in 1660. Another John Odell was posted at Athlacca in 1691 with a detachment of militia and dragoons.

COLONEL WILLIAM ODELL used his first wife's dowry and his childrens' legacies to build a new mansion, The Grove. His children sued him for spending what had been left in trust for them, and after years of litigation he spent his latter years in the Debtors' Prison, Dublin. In 1798 he took an active part in suppressing the rebellion and engaged the rebels between Ballingarry and Rathkeale. He was a member of Grattan's Parliament and, later, voted in favour of the Union. He married, for the second time, at the age of 66, the heiress and niece of the parish priest of Kilfarboy. He died in 1831. The Grove was looted during the days of the *Great Hunger*. It later fell into decay and its stone was quarried by local builders.

JAMES BAGGOTT (1770-1805) kept a school in Ballingarry in the late eighteenth century. He was active in the United Irishmen; was visited by Lord Edward Fitzgerald during that worthy's tour of Ireland in 1798; and was the architect of a plan to capture Limerick City during the Emmet Rising of 1803. There is no conclusive proof that he was ever arrested, and the government was kept aware of all of his activities by a spy

who signed himself (or herself) "J.D.". General Payne wrote of him: "That rascal Baggott can neither be frightened nor bribed, and when Mr. Odell returns I think we had better take him up". James Baggott was a friend and correspondent of La Place, the French scientist and tutor to Napoleon. This worried the authorities but James died, suddenly, at Charleville on 31 August, 1805.

THE VILLAGE owes its existence to the fact that it occupied a strategic pass through the hills. In 1837 it consisted of one long irregular street and several smaller ones, and contained 276 houses. The Fort-William flour-mills were near the town and the Kilmore flour-mills were three miles to the east, near Kilmore House which was adjacent to a good bridge. The market days were Tuesdays and Fridays, chiefly for the sale of vegetables, and there were public scales in the open street. Petty sessions were held every Saturday and there was also a station for the constabulary police. The Church of Ireland church was a small neat edifice, and there was also a Catholic church in the village and two more outside it, one near *Cnoc na Fírinne,* and the other at the south-eastern extremity of the parish. The principal houses over 150 years ago were Ballynoe, of W. Cox; Glenwilliam Castle, of William Hamo Massy; Ballyknockane, of W. Scanlan; The Grove, of Major Thomas Odell; Odell Ville, of T.A. Odell; Fortwilliam, of T.H. Odell; Woodstock, or Woodstock Cottage, of Richard D. Graves; Ashborough, of D. Dickson Power; Kilbeg, of Hugh Wheeler Scanlan; Frankfort, of Richard Standish; Ballyneale, of John Cox; Ballinamona, of John Cox, Junior; Springmount, of E. Fitzgerald; Liskennett, of R.K. Sheehy; Ballykevin, of Crone Odell; and The Glebe of Rev. T. Gibbings.

THE TURRET is believed to have been built originally by the Knights Hospitallers. In 1683 it was repaired by the Odells, who incorporated part of the original structure into their seventeenth-century residence. In 1725, Captain John Lacy who fought in the Jacobite army, was residing here, although it was then an Odell property. His eldest son, John, is said to have been the last priest to celebrate Mass at the old Boreena-Thrownta church, and the first to do so in the, then new, church at Ardaglish. In later years it was the home of Charles Townley until his death in 1887. At the end of the nineteenth century it became a presbytery; a wing was added to the back; and a porch was built to enclose the front. It is now known as the Presbytery.

ODELL VILLE was built by John FitzCharles Odell during the period 1777 to 1780. Thomas Henry Odell was born here in 1807, and in 1860 Edmund Morony married

Aerial view of Ballingarry.

Helena, the only child of John Odell of Odell Ville. In 1917 Edward Locke Lloyd, of Heathfield, married Helen Mary Matilda, the only daughter of Henry Vereker Lloyd Morony. In 1975 the Gothic-style gate-lodge was still occupied, even though the avenue to the house had been changed to follow a different route. In 1978 it was the home of a Lloyd desdendant, Mrs. Allott.

BALLYNOE was erected by William Cox between 1654 and 1659. It was rebuilt during the early eighteenth century, and Hugh Cox incorporated the remains of the two earlier houses into a new mansion he erected in 1770. It was derelict in 1978.

BALLINAHA was the home of Conor Scanlan in 1703. This remained the seat of the Scanlan family until Conor's grandson, Michael Junior, purchased the Ballyknockane estate in 1793. The large, partly-cobbled, sta-ble -yard at the back dates from this period.

BALLYKNOCKANE HOUSE was built by Michael Scanlan, Junior, between 1793 and 1794. Michael was High Sheriff of the county, twice, and he was married to Frances Odell of The Grove. When his grandson, another Michael (1835-1895), died, the property passed to William Scanlan in Canada. E.H. Sheehy of Ballingarry bought Ballyknockane from John Scanlan, William's brother, in 1920. The building is best described as a box-style villa. This type of house was popular during the late eighteenth-century and cost about £1000 to build. In 1978 it was the residence of the Murray family.

BALLYNEALE HOUSE was built by John Cox, Junior, in 1858, to replace an earlier house of the same name. It was the residence of Daniel Hederman in 1914.

GLENWILLIAM CASTLE is believed to have been erected by Rev. William Massy, the second son of Rev. Godfrey Massy, in 1797. However Rev. G.F. Hamilton in his *Records of Ballingarry, Limerick Diocese* (1930) states that William enlarged Glenwilliam Castle in 1796. The Massys must have lived here prior to 1792 as William's son George, was old enough to be a churchwarden in that year. One of the Massys is believed to have shot a gambling opponent in the little card-room here during the early 1800s, but the only account of a duel I came across was that in which William Lloyd (1801-1829) was killed by Thomas S. Odell on 11 July 1829. The Massys were notorious gamblers, and another member of the family is believed to have gambled, and lost, Glenwilliam Castle in a card game. Dr. Edward Atkinson (1801-1876) purchased Glenwilliam Castle about 1853. He built the castellated tower which was designed by James and George Richard Pain. The last of the Atkinson family to live here was Edward Atkinson's great grand-daughter, Sybil Worlledge. It is now the home of the Rawson family.

BEALDUROGY TOWER HOUSE was the home of William Odell until he built The Grove. He made several additions to this medieval structure, but eventually abandoned it and moved to his new neo-Classical man-sion. This was more in keeping with his status as a Member of Parliament in the Irish and Imperial Parliaments, and, later, a Lord of the Treasury. He let this building to the rector of Ballingarry.

FORT WILLIAM was erected outside the bawn of the modified tower house of Bealdurogy. This "gentleman's residence with

The fine courtyard of Glenwilliam.

a small demesne" was of a type popular during the 1840s and was never classed as, or considered, a cottage.

THE SPARR, or Sparr Street, derives its name from the spur of the hill. This is the highest part of Ballingarry, and it is located above the Square or Village Green. Over the years the old Odell house on the square had fallen into decay; served as a pawn-shop for a while; but had become derelict by 1930 when Rev. G.F. Hamilton wrote: "The principal thoroughfare is known as Main Street. The side of this street on which the [Church of Ireland] Parish Church stands, belongs to the townland of Cloontemple or Church Meadow; while the houses across the way, with the Castle and Glebe House, are in the townland called Knightstreet ... Behind this [the Odell house] is the ancient fair field, last used as such in 1866. In the Square are also the old Courthouse and Bridewell (now Dineen's Hall), with the resuscitated Police Barracks. The ruin occupying the middle of the green is all that remains of the new Sessions House, built in 1883 ... the other streets are Pound Street, with boreen running down by the old 'twig yard' (sally beds or osiery) to the unfailing spring behind the Parish Church, Pound Well, so named from its proximity to the village pound; Castle Lane, once the fashionable, residential quarter where Dr. Robert Odell lived for thirty years (1835-1865); Turret Street, starting from the bridge; The

Mall, strictly the row of houses, along the left side of the river; and Boithrín-an-Treannta, the old road to Rathkeale. This last was named Echo Lane after a thatched cottage which stood where the convent stands today, Echo Lodge ... the town is divided into two sections by the Grinoch (greanach, gravelly) stream. This flows between two hills or ridges, up the lower slope of which the streets climb, Main Street towards Knockfierna, Turret Street passing up over a shoulder of the ridge opposite. On the slopes of this latter, Ballingarry Hill, are the Convent and Girls' School, the Presbytery (formerly The Turret), the handsome R.C. church (completed in 1879), with spire conspicuous for miles around; and, near the bridge, just where the ground begins to rise, the Boys' School (built in 1841). Then, on the Knockfierna side of the stream are the parish church, Glebe House, Hotel, Post Office, and principal places of business ... and people still speak of the "glen road", which is today [1930] the chief entrance into the village".

PADRAIG O FIONNGHALAIGH, a poet, taught here in 1771.

THE CHURCH OF IRELAND PARISH CHURCH stands near to, and parallel with, the foundations of the older parish church which it replaced in 1812. The older building had all but disappeared by 1930, except for a portion of the eastern gable and a section of the north wall, which had been incorporated

into the boundary wall between the old disused graveyard which had been closed around 1900 and the newer one opened about the same time. The original parish church was founded before 1292, and was converted to Protestant worship after the Dissolution. In 1800 the parishioners decided to rebuild this church, and work had actually commenced by 1810 when it suddenly collapsed. The new church is closed since the 1970s and many of its windows were broken by 1989. Rev. Brian Snow was the last rector here.

SUNDAY'S WELL, or *Tobar Rí an Domhnaigh,* the Well of the King of Sunday, is still remembered in the locality. The well's name is inscribed on the E.S.B. sub-station which was built over its site.

SCHWETZER'S FLOUR-MILL, in Ballingarry, retained its name after it was purchased by a man named O'Grady. The surname Schweitzer, however, in this case, appears to be of different origin to the more familiar Schweitzer, Schwetzer, or Switzer introduced by the Palatines.

JEWISH HISTORY within Limerick appears to be confined to the city rather than the county. When the Cork synagogue closed in 1788 the marriage of a Cork Jewess, Fanney Levy (1765-1829), took place in the Church of Ireland parish church here. She married Jacob Schwetzer (1759-1829) who was described as "a German Jew".

THE FENIANS assembled by the bank of

the Grinoch in 1867.

KILNAMONA HILL, to the south-west, was described by Lewis in 1837 as rising to a lake "supposed to have been formed by the excavation of a coal mine, and called Lough-na-Gual, or 'the Lake of Coal'."

KILSHANE ABBEY, on the outskirts of the village, was recorded as the Monastery of St. John in 1410. This may have been founded for the Franciscans by either Donnchadh Cairbreach O Brien or the Geraldine Lord of Clenlis, during the early thirteenth century. From before 1300, until the Dissolution, the Abbot of Keynsham, Somersetshire, appointed the vicar of Kilshane. In 1295 this mandate was called in question by the Papal authorities, who did not always approve of the abbot's appointees, or his right of presentation. This proved to be an ongoing dispute, as the matter was still unresolved in 1450 when another appointee, Gillacious O'Keyt, was absolved "from all sentences of excommunication ... incurred on account of simony, perjury or immorality", and was granted the vicarage of Limerick. By 1930 the walls of this old church were levelled to the ground, but Kitty Conway told me that the remains behind the Turret were part of Kilshane Abbey.

RYLAANS TOWNLAND was originally known as *Ard Eaglais,* the High Church. Colonel William Odell's house, The Grove, was built here near a site known as the Priory, or the Friary, during the early nineteenth century. This religious edifice had long since disappeared, by then, but the field in which it had been situated was known as the Friary Garden, and it was believed that Ballingarry derived its name from this.

THE KNIGHTS BANNERETS were knights who had knighthood conferred on them for their valour in battle. Such a knight was also allowed to have vassals in the field under his own banner. In 1840 *The Ordnance Survey Letters* mention that *Ard Eaglais* may have been established by Knights Bannerets; that the Odells sheltered here; and that both the Odells and the Knights deposited valuable possessions in the Friary for safe-keeping.

ST. JOHN'S WELL was once the scene of a pattern or pilgrimage. The well is located near the eastern boundary of Rylaans townland.

SHANAVOHA CHURCH, in the townland of Grenagh, derived its name from *Seana Bhoithe* or *Sean Bhothán,* the old hut. By 1840 only a part of the eastern gable remained, but its churchyard was still in use for burials.

LISSAMOTA CASTLE, in the townland of the same name, derived its own name from the fact that the original stronghold here was surrounded by a *lios* or earthen rampart. This

is located on the Grinoch, the stream that flows through Ballingarry. The castle was surrendered to Sir George Carew's forces in 1599. By 1840 not a trace of the *lios* remained.

BONISTOE CASTLE, or Woodstock Castle, derived its name from *Bun a Stóigh,* possibly *Bun a Stuaigh,* the Bottom of the Hillock (?). W. Cullom owned both Lissamota and Bonistoe Castles in 1641.

KNOCKFIERNA HILL is believed to be the home of a fairy chief, Donn Firinne, a notable character in both local and national folklore. P.W. Joyce described Donn as a Milesian chief, and son of Milesius, who was drowned in a magic storm raised by the spells of the De Dananns, when the eight brothers came to invade Ireland. Donn changed his earthly existence for a more pleasant one as King of the Fairies, ruling from his palace on Knockfierna Hill. In several accounts this place is rendered into Irish as *Cnoc Fírinne,* the Hill of Truth but, personally, I believe it should be written as *Cnoc Féaruaine,* the Grass-Green hill, a more fitting description. In Clare, Donn is remembered as Donn Dumhach, Donn of the Sandhills, so in Limerick he may have been known as Donn Fèaruaine, Donn of the Grass-Green (Hill). He is more closely identified as a Pagan Irish god of death and fertility, an ancestor deity. Until the 1960s the local people regarded it as a duty to visit the hill at least once a year and place a stone on the Lying Boy. This is one of the most famous fairy hills in Munster and is remembered as a site on which the festival of *Lughnasa* was celebrated.

THE LYING BOY, *An Buachaill Breágach,* is a *carn* or cairn on the summit of Knockfierna, 948 feet above sea-level. This cairn, according to the local explanation, varied in size from time to time as stones were added or slipped off. In *The Festival of Lughnasa* Dr. Màire Mac Neill thought that the words *breagach,* false or lying, and *firinne,* meaning truth, may have had something to do with weather observations drawn from the hill. Stories of Donn and the weather were recorded in *Fairy Legends and Traditions of the South of Ireland* which was published by T. Crofton Croker in 1828, and Dr. Mac Neill probably based her observations on this body of folklore. The Irish Folklore Commission collected various anecdotes on Donn Firinne in 1944, and Kate Muller-Lisowski published these in *Béaloideas.* Patrick Kennedy and David Fitzgerald have also written on Donn and his hill. Ordnance Survey sappers demolished the cairn on one occasion, but by 1905 the local people had rebuilt it. It was in ruin again by 1910 but repaired soon afterwards. A deep

hole in the side of the hill is called *Poll na Bruidhne,* the Hole, or Cave, of the Royal Residence. According to tradition, this hole led to Donn's residence, a great hall, within Knockfierna, from which tunnels radiated to the Shannon, Tory Hill, and other places Donn liked to visit.

FIONN'S FORT is recorded in the Ordnance Survey Map as Lissnaberne but is known locally as *Lios an bhFian.* This is a large earth-fort with a rampart, on the northern slope of Knockfierna Hill, and located 775 feet above sea-level. In 1904 an old man who owned the land here showed Dr. Henry Molony a depression, near the centre of the lios, where he had found a well and "drains made of hammered stone-work". It was this old man who stated that the fort had been built by Fionn. He also said that the glen beneath the fort was known as *Glownanérh a ,* the Glen of Broth, because of "the broth that flowed plentifully down from the great house of the giants". In his talks with Dr. Moloney, the old man never used the word fairy, possibly, because of his proximity to Donn Firinne's dwelling-place.

THE KILMACOW WEDGE-SHAPED GALLERY GRAVE on the northern slope of Knockfierna is also known as the Giant's Grave or Fawha's Tomb. This damaged chamber-tomb is fairly well-preserved, although it had been dug into in 1911. Its roof-stones are missing.

THE KILMACOW FLINT JAVELIN-HEAD, in the Limerick City Museum was found in either the Lying Boy or the Giant's Grave. If it came from the latter it is, at present, the only javelin-head known to have been found in such a tomb.

KILMACOW CHURCH was built within a ring-enclosure. By 1840 its western gable had been destroyed; only a breach in the southern wall marked the location of the doorway; and there was a small round-headed window in the northern wall. O'Donovan noted that this building was "evidently old", and recorded "a castlelike house in ruins" in Kilmacow townland. This church was once known as the "Abbey", and may derive its name from *Cill Mo-Chua* from which the townland is also named. This church may also have been the medieval religious house known as Kilmacanearla, *Cill Mac An Iarla,* the Church of the Son of the Earl.

SOURCES
9 11 28 34 42 44
45 47 76 79 92 101 120
123 129 157 164 184 191
192 252 262 264 282

Bruff

Ballygrennan

BRUFF derives its name from *Brúgh na Déise*, the Chief Seat, Fort or Palace of the Deisy or Desii, a people who occupied east Limerick in ancient times.

THE LITTLE FORT OF BRUFF, *Lisín a Bhrogha*, or *Lisín Aerach a 'Bhrogha*, the Airy Little Fort of Bruff, is located on the south-western bank of the Morningstar, Samair or Dawn River, west of Bruff. In 1840 it consisted of a double mound with two moats, the upper moat of which was damaged. It has now been developed as an amenity area, with trees growing on it, and seating provided for visitors. During the eighteenth century Brian O Flatharta wrote a song in which he referred to the Sweet Little Airy Fort of Bruff, *Binnlisín Aerach an Bhrogha*.

BRUFF appears to have been an important place in early times. During the reign of Henry III (1216 - 1272) the Lacy family built a castle here and another one at no great distance from it. They subsequently became tributaries of the Fitzgeralds and "held the castle under the princes of Desmond, in all whose misfortunes they largely participated, especially during the reign of Elizabeth". On 4 April 1600 Piers Lacy, Governor of Bruff Castle, was defeated in battle by troops of the Kilmallock garrison, under the command of Captain Slingsby, and lost 300 of his men. On 18 April 1600 the Lord-President seized Bruff Castle and installed a garrison of 140 men. Piers Lacy was later killed during a minor skirmish on the banks of the northern Black Water on 28 July 1601. During his life-time he had been a noted horseman, an ally of the northern princes, O' Neill and O'Donnell, and had been dubbed the "arch-rebel of Munster" by his enemies. In 1641 Bruff was the scene of a bloody battle "between the English forces and the insurgents, in which the latter were victorious, and committed acts of great cruelty".

BRUFF CASTLE was located on the north bank of the river, west of the bridge. In 1790 Sir Henry Hartstonge owned most of Bruff while Lord Carbury (Evans) owned the land on the other side of "a stream called Cavouri or Morning Star". Bruff then contained two

excellent inns, a Catholic church and a Protestant one. Sir Henry Hartstonge once lived in the castle, but by 1840 it was badly ruined, and the ground floor of the remaining structure was inhabited by a poor family from the town. Another old building known as the Court was hard to identify in 1840 because it was thatched with straw and its features were closed up with stonework. This had been situated north-east of the castle.

THE WHITEBOYS assembled here in great numbers in 1762 and committed various outrages. On 15 July 1786 they returned to the town, burned several houses and destroyed a lot of valuable property.

THE DEFENDERS made a desperate effort to seize the town in 1793 but were repulsed by the 34th. Regiment of Foot, with heavy casualties on both sides.

THE ROCKITES came here in strength and made an attempt to burn the Church of Ireland church and several houses, but were frustrated "by the active and judicious exertions of the neighbouring gentry, aided by a large body of the military stationed in the town".

BRUFF formed part of the Earl of Limerick's estate in 1837. It then consisted of one principal street and several smaller streets and lanes, and contained 314 houses, a large commodious court-house, a small well-regulated bridewell, the ruins of an old castle, and the remains of an ancient friary "not far distant". This last structure was known as Templebodeen, or Templeen, and was believed to have been erected by the Knights Templars in 1284. John O'Donovan listed it as *Teampuillín* in 1840, but wrote that there was no trace of a church foundation on the site which was north-west of the town.

PENALTY CLAUSES were introduced in the early 1800s to prevent more than one acre in twenty, and in some cases more than one acre in fifty, being broken up or cultivated. A farmer who tried to bring his land into tillage was regarded as someone who was approaching poverty. The landowners about Bruff, Dromin, Bulgadine, Kilpeacon, Crecora and Lough Gur were extremely wealthy around this time, and later. Most of them had stocks of 400 or 600 head of cattle, which were

crosses between the Leicester, Devon, Durham, Teeswater, Kerry and older native breeds.

THE LIMERICK HEIFER of the early nineteenth century was so-called by the Cork and Kerry farmers who considered it admirably suited to the soil. The horses were mainly light crosses between the Suffolk and Ayrshire. Sheep had been domesticated in Ireland long before the Anglo-Norman invasion, but it was the Normans who really developed sheep farming and the woollen trade in the county and country. They were also responsible for introducing the rabbit into Ireland. By the 1800s sheep had been improved by crossing them with English stock, principally the Leicester breed. Pigs were developed from a mixture of the Berkshire and the Irish, which seemed to fatten with very little trouble and appeared to be the most profitable.

A NEW CATHOLIC CHURCH was erected in 1833 as part of the new wave of church building heralded by the passing of the Catholic Emancipation Act of 1829. This was a handsome building in the early English style, the interior was well-arranged and the altar of Scagliola marble was embellished by a local artist, J. Haverty.

DEAN PATRICK MACNAMARA (1792-1838) was a native of this parish and lived in Crawford's Lane, Bruff. He later became parish priest of Shanagolden and Dean of the Diocese. In August 1838 he died while visiting the Bishop of Limerick and was buried in Bruff. Rev. Godfrey Massey became the Church of Ireland vicar here in 1831. He wrote scathingly of Dean MacNamara: "It is enough, that of the gentry residing around the town the Romish priest was hailed as a familiar friend by nearly all, and that in some houses there was an apartment called in honour of his repeated visits 'the priest's room'. As the natural result of this intimacy one very respectable family had already lapsed into popery ... the priest was exactly adapted to the place. His smooth, oily manners and insinuating address, his electioneering power and ready wit secured his welcome at the tables of the rich. While his singular skill in ruling and

Aerial view of Bruff.

pleasing the mob made him a perfect dictator among the poor. It would be hard to meet a priest who had such a complete command of countenance and as thoroughly knew his own strength. His fine intellectual forehead, the bland smile which ever played over his handsome face, and his plausible address would make you set him down as particularly mild and peaceable, but to a close observer he occasionally exhibited a keen, sly, fox-like aspect ..."

REV. GODFREY MASSEY (1803-1852) was known as "The Orphans' Friend". He founded the Limerick Protestant Orphan Society soon after six young children had lost their parents during a cholera epidemic, and also built the Adelaide School. He was buried in St. Mary's Cathedral, Limerick. The Church of Ireland church here, to which he was appointed in 1831, was a large edifice in the early English-style, with a tower surmounted by an octagonal spire. This church replaced an older one which had been demolished by Lady Hartstonge in the 1780s because it was "going into decay". This was the burial-place of the Hartstonge family.

THE CHRISTIAN BROTHERS opened a school here on 30 April 1860 with 300 pupils and three brothers. In November 1897 the school was closed and the Christian Brothers

left the town because of "the petty persecution" to which they had been subjected. The Brothers had built a residence and school on land donated by the Earl of Limerick and had taught there without any trouble, until the local clergy established a seminary with one of the parish curates on its teaching staff. The "Scandal at Bruff" appears to have erupted after Bishop Edward Thomas O'Dwyer visited the convent in Bruff and found "a nun and a Christian Brother" arranging the altar in preparation for a Mass. He made inquiries and discovered "that the Brothers heard Mass daily, and frequently answered Mass in the nuns' chapel, which was situated in the centre of the house, and there was no separation whatever between them and the nuns and the young-lady boarders". O Dwyer was scandalised as he considered this most improper, and he decreed that the Brothers could not continue to hear Mass in the convent. They were not allowed to hear Mass in their own oratory either, as the Bishop had earlier invoked an old ecclesiastical ruling which forbade religious communities of fewer than four people from reserving the "Blessed Sacrament". Mass times in the parish church clashed with school-opening times, and the local clergy failed to provide earlier Masses which would enable the Brothers to function

adequately in their religious and educational roles. The Brothers left. O'Dwyer was quite indignant when they departed without even saying "good-bye", but this did not prevent him from trying to take over their school. He appointed Thomas Bowman, a national teacher, to run the school. The people of Bruff showed their sympathy and support for the Christian Brothers. No pupils turned up. The R.I.C. had to be called to line the streets, surround the school and protect the unfortunate Bowman, who was forced to flee for "his life" from Bruff despite the R.I.C. protection. The R.I.C. barracks in Bruff is similar to the one in Pallas Greane. Both were built about 1870.

SEAN WALL (1888-1921) is one of several local men who died during the War of Independence. They are commemorated with a monument in the village. Sean was born nearby and educated in St. Munchin's College, Limerick. He left school in 1904 after the early deaths of his parents, and went into business. His contracting firm, Wall and Forde, erected many new creameries throughout the county. With Nicholas O'Dwyer he invented new cheese-making machinery; manufactured milk-powder; and advocated the use of the newly-designed milking apparatus which he demonstrated and introduced to the county. He was appointed to the East Limerick Brigade, when it was formed in 1918, and organised five self-sufficient battalions. He also formed an active service guerrilla unit which operated effectively, independent of his local commanders, and was known as *The Circus*. Sean participated in the attack on Kilmallock Barracks on 28 May 1920. On 25 June 1920 he was elected chairman of Limerick's first Republican County Council. He was killed on 6 May 1921 when he and his staff, were attacked by the R.I.C. near Annacarty, County Tipperary. He was interred in the Republican plot, Mount St. Lawrence Cemetery, Limerick City.

BALLYGRENNAN CASTLE is located one mile south of Bruff. This four-storey fifteenth-century tower-house is in a good state of preservation. It is enclosed within its original bawn which is divided into two courtyards. The tower contains some fine mullioned windows and its second floor is vaulted. This castle was built by the Lacy family who held it on behalf of their Geraldine overlords. After the Desmond rebellion the ffoxe family came into possession of Ballygrennan Castle and were listed as its occupants in 1583. Between 1621 and 1657 it was granted to a Dr. Metcalfe and a man named Jones, but reverted to ffoxe ownership some time after 1657. The high-gabled house remains within the bawn are of a later date than the castle, and may date from the seventeenth century. The ffoxes sold the castle to the Evans family in the latter half of the seventeenth century.

GEORGE EVANS came to Ireland with King William's forces and established his family here. By 1826 the Evans or Carbury family were the largest landowners in the area.

BALLYGRENNAN CHURCH RUINS had a somewhat modern appearance in 1840. Local tradition maintained that it had been built as a Protestant church by George Evans. Its eastern end was enclosed by then and used as a burial place for members of the Evans family.

UREGARE or Owregare Parish derived its name from *An Iubhar Ghearra*, the Short Yew. In 1837 the big houses of this parish were Green Park, the Cottage, Miltown, Ballincolloe and Owregare House of the Evans family. Two unusually large skeletons were found within ten yards of Owregare House in the early 1800s.

KILBALLYOWEN HOUSE was located north-east of Bruff. This was the residence of the O'Gradys, who claimed descent from the ancient kings of Ireland. They had settled in Killballyowen in 1309 after Hugh O'Grady had acquired land here on marrying the daughter, and heiress, of O Kerwick, chief of the *Anlan Cliah*. During the Georgian era they incorporated the remains of their medieval tower house within the framework of their new mansion. Between 1967 and 1978 the ruins of Killballyowen House were demolished and a new house built on the site.

CAMAS HOUSE is located south of the Morningstar River. It has a small battlemented tower near its entrance gate.

SOURCES
1 9 11 39 47 50 86 120 123 129 150 155 178 195 207 223 238 255 264

Ballygrennan Castle.

Bruree

Castletown Conyers · Tankardstown

BRUREE derives its name from *Brugh Ríogh,* the Fort, or House, of Kings. In *A Smaller Social History of Ancient Ireland* (1908) P.W. Joyce claims that Bruree was one of the seats of the kings of South Munster, and was occupied by Munster royalty from remote times until after the Anglo-Norman invasion. Minor Dalcassian kings had their seats in the vicinity from the seventh to the ninth century until they were displaced by *Eoghanacht* Kings of the *Uí Fidgeinte* line, one of whom, Donnabhán, was responsible for the treacherous killing of Brian Boru's brother, Mahon, in 976. Domhnall Mór O Brien drove the Uí *Fidgeinte* out of the county in 1178, creating a vacuum filled by the Anglo-Normans, after his death in 1194. John de Marisco and his wife, Mabel, were in possession of Bruree in 1242. Mabel was a grandchild of Richard de Burgo and was given the Manor of Bruree as her marriage portion. In 1289 Maurice and Eva de Lesse, or Lacy, held the manor as tenants of Robert de Marisco.

THE HOUSE OF KINGS, or *Brúgh Ríogh,* from which the village took its name, is located to the west of the mills below the fine six-arch bridge. In 1826 this was "a very strong and lofty rath surrounded with a deep fosse, outside of which are three others of smaller dimensions". Two of these smaller forts, the *Ratheens,* can be found beside the roadway where the ground dips down to the river. The *Brúgh Ríogh* can be best described as a platform-type ring-fort. Seán P. O Ríordáin classed this flat-topped mound as such a monument, and wrote that its concentric defences and lack of a bailey distinguished it from the Anglo-Norman earthworks. A similar mound excavated at Ballingarry Down dated from the eighth century.

THE KNOCKDUHA TUMULUS is located on a high ridge of ground west of the river. A chambered, or unchambered, burial mound is generally referred to as a *cairn,* or carn, if it is built of stone, and a *tumulus,* if it is built of earth. Surface indications can be misleading, as carns can be covered with vegetation, so the term tumulus is applied to both classes of mound. An earthen mound is called a barrow in Britain, but it is impossible to determine if such a mound covers a megalithic tomb, or not, without excavation.

LISSOLEEM RING FORT is situated on the western bank of the Maigue River, a mile below the village, in the townland of Lower Lotteragh. It derives its name from *Lios Oluim,* the Lios or Residence of Olom. King Ailill Olom is believed to have lived here in the second century. His full name means Ailill Bare-Ear, as he lost one of his ears in a struggle. This fort has altered considerably since P.W. Joyce described it over eighty years ago. He then wrote that it was located "in the angle formed by the Maigue and a little stream joining it from the west. It is a circular fort with three ramparts, having the reputation — like most other raths — of being haunted by fairies; and, as it is very lonely and much

View over the river towards the castle and Church of Ireland church.

Aerial view of Bruree.

overgrown with bushes, it is as fit a home for fairies as could well be imagined".

THE CASTLE OF UPPER BRUREE is located in the churchyard of the now-closed and rather neglected-looking Church of Ireland church. The castle was badly overgrown with ivy and a large section of its eastern wall was missing when I examined it during the summer of 1988. This was a square tower, five storeys high. Samuel Lewis claimed that it was erected by the Knights Templars during the twelfth century, but there is no record of a preceptory here so this account is most unlikely.

THE CASTLE OF LOWER BRUREE, or Callaghans' Castle, may date from the twelfth

century according to John O'Donovan. He was also of the opinion that Amhlaoigh O'Donovan may have built the circular wall of this strong triple fortress, as it resembled another twelfth-century stronghold, *Caisleán na Cailly,* in Lough Mask. This O'Donovan was one of the *Uí Fidgeinte* driven south of Mangartan. He appears to have resumed the possession of his former territory until he was killed by William de Burgo's forces in 1200. This was a triple fortress "consisting of a strong and high circular wall, on which originally stood three towers of great height and strength". In 1840 the wall was 150 feet in length; the tower on the east side of the circle was in a good state of preservation; the one

on the north-west was badly damaged; and the one to the south had been totally destroyed. By 1988 only the eastern tower and some of the wall remained; the south-western tower had to be demolished as it was in a dangerous state; and a new house was built on the site of the southern tower. The Lacy family came into possession of this castle after the O'Donovans, and held large estates in the neighbourhood until they were driven out by the Cromwellians. In more recent times it was known as Callaghans' Castle, after Jim and Bat Callaghan who lived here. It is now the property of the O'Regan family.

THE VILLAGE contained 81 houses over

150 years ago. It had a constabulary police station; several good houses; a boulting-mill; a grist-mill, mainly for oatmeal; a factory for combing, carding, and spinning wool; and a new road had been constructed through the western part of the parish, from Croom to Charleville. In 1812 a Protestant church was built on the site of an older foundation while, in 1837, there were three Catholic churches in the parish, at Bruree, at Rockhill, and at Colemanswell. The village also contained a dispensary in 1837, as well as a fever hospital which was housed in a building constructed during the cholera epidemic of 1832.

THE MAIGUE flows through Bruree, separating the modern village on the east bank from the older settlement, containing the royal forts, on the western side. The river was harnessed in the not-so-distant past to operate the massive water-wheel of the old corn-mill, below the bridge, weir and falls.

ARAS DE VALERA is located in the old national school which was erected in 1862. In May 1888 Eamon de Valera first attended this school as a pupil. On Sunday 8 October 1972 he returned here, as President of Ireland, to re-open it as a museum and community centre.

EAMON DE VALERA (1882-1975) once told Dàil Eireann, "My father and mother were married in a Catholic church on September 19, 1881. I was born in October 1882. I was baptized in a Catholic church. I was brought up here in a Catholic home. I have lived amongst the Irish people and loved them and loved every blade of grass that grew in this land". His father, Vivion de Valera, was a Spanish artist. His mother, Catherine Coll, came from Bruree. His birth certificate lists him as George de Valera, but he was baptized, and called Edward or Eamon. He was born on October 14, 1882, in the Nursery and Child's Hospital, Lexington Avenue, 51st Street, New York, U.S.A. His uncle Edward, after whom he was named, returned to Ireland, for health reasons, taking his young nephew, and namesake, with him. The Colls lived at Knockmore, about a mile from the centre of Bruree. Eamon de Valera said, years afterwards, "I was brought up in a labourer's cottage". He was educated locally until he was fourteen years of age. Another uncle, Patrick Coll, sent him to the Christian Brothers school in Charleville where he won a scholarship which took him to Blackrock College, Dublin. In the meantime his mother had remarried. His stepfather was an Englishman, a non-Catholic, Charles E. Wheelwright. Catherine and he had two children, Thomas and Annie. Annie died in infancy. Thomas became a Catholic priest.

THE YOUNG EDDIE COLL, as he was sometimes called locally, took up a part-time position as a junior master at Blackrock College. In 1901 he enrolled in what was then the Royal University of Dublin. Between 1904 and 1905 he taught in Rockwell College, County Tipperary. After a year there he returned to Dublin City.

EAMON DE VALERA was one of the leaders of the 1916 Rising, "The Hero of Boland's Mill". At one stage he was sentenced to death but this was later commuted to life imprisonment. Freed in a general amnesty, he became a Sinn Feìn Member of Parliament after the historic Clare by-election of 1917. He retained his seat in the General Election of 1918. Sinn Feìn were returned with 73 seats, the Irish Party 6, and the Unionists 26. Eamon de Valera, or Dev, became President of the new Irish parliament, Dáil Eireann, on April 1, 1919. The career of Eamon de Valera is well documented. So many books have been written on this famous statesman and scholar, over the years, that there is little need to record much more in this account. The plain people of Ireland loved him or hated him, idolised or despised him. Few were indifferent. He founded the Fianna Fail party, in Dublin, on May 16, 1926; withheld land annuities to Britain in 1932; fought an "economic war" with England from 1932 to 1938; outlawed the I.R.A. in 1936; gave Ireland a new Constitution in 1937; recovered "Treaty Ports" under an Anglo-Irish agreement in 1938; and kept Ireland neutral through World War Two. On the other hand he has been blamed by his enemies, and others, for sheltering behind his United States' citizenship during the War of Independence. He has also been accused of fomenting the Civil War, betraying his old comrades within the I.R.A.; interning and executing many leading republicans; handing his country over to the Catholic Church or British institutions; and retarding Ireland's growth as a developing nation. Depending on one's viewpoint, nothing was too good, or too bad, if it was said about de Valera. Dev died, at the age of ninety-two, on August 29, 1975. As Taoiseach and President of Ireland it is a strange coincidence that such a man should come from Bruree, the residence of kings, because, during his life-time,

The massive mill-wheel

Eamon de Valera was virtually the uncrowned King of Ireland.

A REBEL SONG, probably composed around 1917, was to prove almost prophetic in later years.
"Up de Valera, the leader of the fight,
We'll follow him to battle for the Orange,
Green and White;
And when we meet the English, we'll show
them how to fight,
And we'll crown de Valera King of Ireland".

THE IRISH BARDS met here, twice a year, from ancient times until 1746. In October 1982 *Feíle na Máighe,* the county's annual bilingual Festival of literature and the arts, was held in Bruree. The theme for the *feile,* or celebration, that year was *Oidhrecht de Valera,* the Heritage of de Valera. Despite his long political career the people of Bruree did not get a chance to vote for Dev until the presidential election of 1959, 42 years after he had entered the political arena.

EAGLE MOUNT RING FORT, Mounteagle ring fort, or *Lios a'deocha* is a platform-type ring fort with a low pillarstone. This steep high mound is in Ballynoe, half a mile west of Bruree.

THE O'DONOVAN SURNAME is derived from *O Donnabháin,* the descendant of *Donndubhán,* from *dubhán* brown, or a compound of *donn ,* brown and *dubh,* black, finishing with a diminutive termination, *-áin .*

The Donovans or O'Donovans were originally kings of Bruree and chiefs of the district lying along the banks of the Maigue, *Ui Cairbre Aedhbha,* until they were forced to take refuge in south-west Cork. Allied with the O Mahonys they settled in the O Driscoll territory of *Corca Laoighdhe,* to which they gave their clan-name of *Ui Cairbre.* They maintained their power and possessions until the close of the Jacobite wars.

HOWARDSTOWN was also known as Temple Coleman or Cooleen in 1837. The Knights Templars are believed to have erected a small church here in 1287. By then the Anglo-Normans were firmly established in the region, as Maurice and Eva Lacy paid rent on Howardstown in 1281. Later, in 1284, Alexander de Anno granted Culbalisward, now Cooleen, to the Archbishop of Dublin, John de Saunford — and it remained with that see after the Reformation. The Fitzroger and Moyll families were recorded as free tenants, in Howardstown, during the thirteenth century.

THE SHEEHY FAMILY, or MacSheehys, a Gallowglass family who had settled in West Limerick played a familiar role in the Confederate wars around Newcastle West. Edmund of Ballyallinan, Grange; Brian of Glenquin; and another Sheehy of Garryduff led bands who "continually infested the town of Newcastle" and "did many outrageous acts of hostility", but, up to Whitsuntide, there seems to have been little loss of life, only five of the warders having been killed on the cas-

tle during the actual assaults". The garrison sallied forth on 3 May, 1642, to punish the rebellious Irish. Five of the soldiers were captured by the Sheehys who promptly "hanged them in a most lamentable manner ... afterwards their corps, boulting or standing upright, were thrusted with stakes through and then left standing till their bodies rotted by the end of May"..

GRANAGH is the home of Kay Sheehy who was the first arts officer appointed to the staff of any local authority in Ireland. She joined the Clare County Council in September 1985 and successfully launched the Ennis Arts Festival. She left Ennis to take up a new position with the Ringsend Road Music Group, as artistic Development officer, in February 1989.

CASTLETOWN, Castletown-MacEniry, or *Kilmoodan,* was the site of a castle erected by the MacEniry family in 1349. They are also believed to have established a "magnificent abbey" here. Aubrey Gwynn and R. Neville Hadcock doubt that there was ever a monastic settlement in Castletown.

CORCOMOHIDE CHURCH, or Castletown Conyers Church was destroyed in 1302 but repaired by 1410. By 1837 it was "long in ruins". The remains of this fine sandstone church can be seen today, beside the roadway to Castletown Conyers House.

CASTLETOWN CONYERS became the name of the parish after William III (1689-1702) granted it to Captain George Conyers, according to Lewis. Brian de Breffny wrote

that it was first granted to the Odells who resold it to the Conyers's family a few years later, in 1697. Fairs were held on 11 February, 17 April, 3 November and 1 December during the nineteenth century.

CASTLETOWN CONYERS HOUSE dates from the early eighteenth century although there is a possibility that some parts of the original house on this site were incorporated into the present structure. The bow-fronted wing was removed before 1978 but the house and its two-storey stable block are still intact. The house was occupied in 1989 although it did not appear to be so. There is a small artificial lake, containing a large statue in its centre, in front of the house. Other big houses of the parish in 1837 were Rossmore, of J.W. Shelton Capanishane, of R. Mason; Glenbrook, of M. Mason; Fort Elizabeth, of E. Nash; Ballyegran Cottage, of A. Odell; Gortroe Cottage, of H. Hart; and Drew's Court, the property of the Drew family, which was then unoccupied.

DOROTHEA CONYERS (1871-1947), the daughter of Colonel J. Blood Smyth, married into the Conyers family. (See Cappagh).

MacENIRY is derived from *Mac an Inneirghe,* Son of the Rising, or Son of the Early Riser. This is the surname of an ancient Limerick family who were chiefs of *Corca Muicheat,* now Corcomohide, who managed to retain control of their territory until 1688 despite the encroachment of Anglo-Norman, and later settlers. Variants of the name include *M'Ineirie, M'Enerie, M'Keneyry,*

The Coll cottage, where Eamon de Valera spent his early years.

MacKeniry, MacNeiry, MacKennery, MacKenery, MacEnery, MacEnry and Kiniry. The ruins of their chief seat, a brown sandstone castle, can still be seen a short distance from Castletown Conyers.

McINERNEY is another Thomond surname which is often confused with MacEniry. The McInerneys were numerous in Clare and Limerick, and held considerable property in the parish of Ballysally until they lost it during the Cromwellian confiscations. The name is derived from *Mac an Airchinnigh,* the Son of the *Airchinneach* or Erenagh. The erenaghs were stewards of church lands, and variants of the McInerney surname include *Mac an Oirchinnigh, Mac an Oirchinn,* MacAnerney, MacEnerney, MacNerhenny, MacNerney, MacNirney, MacNertney, Connerney, Kenerney, Kinerney, Nerhenny, Nerney, Nertney, and Nirney.

BALLYAGRAN was a small village containing only a few thatched cottages and two churches, one Protestant, the other Catholic, in 1837.

ST. GOBINET'S WELL is located in the townland of Kilgobnet. *Cill Ghobhait,* the Church of Gobinet, may have been located in the nearby "Boys Fort" which was demolished by a road contractor about a century ago. In the process, a large quantity of human bones was uncovered, proving that there had been a burial-ground, and, in all probability, a church, on this site. A cattle fair was held at the well on 11 February, the feast of this saint, until the turn of the century. Rounds are still made here and at another holy well, Lady's Well, which is located in the same field as Castletown Conyers Castle.

COLMANSWELL takes its name from *Tobar Cholmain,* Colman's Well, which was the scene of a regular pattern into the nineteenth century. As St. Colman's Day was observed on 29 October, the St. Colman commemorated here may be St. Colman of Kilmacduagh whose feast falls on that day. John O'Donovan wrote that the pattern was held on 28, 29 and 30 October, and it may have originated as a *Samhain* festival.

ST. COLMAN of Kilmacduagh died about 630. The St. Colman associated with this well was not a saint to trifle with. According to folklore he cured a cripple of lameness, but when the latter returned here to collect the crutches he had left behind, meaning to sell them, Colman cursed him and withdrew the cure, leaving the man lame. Another story tells of how a man who worked on the saint's day had his payment vanish from his pocket as he passed the well.

COLMANSWELL CHURCH, or Clouncoragh Church, may have been converted to Protestant worship after the Dissolution.

It remained in use until the beginning of the nineteenth century, but by 1837 it had "long since fallen into decay", and the Protestant parishioners attended Divine Service in the parish church of Bruree. Three years later John O Donovan reported that the church was ruined, but it had a well-chiselled limestone doorway; and the graveyard was still in use.

THE SAMHAIN FESTIVAL was observed on 1 November in ancient times. This was the first day of winter and it was coupled with the previous night, *Samhain Eve,* by the Pagan Irish who counted time by nights rather than by days. *Samhain Eve* was the night on which all of the fairy hills opened and the *Sidhe,* or Fairy Folk, ventured abroad, to roam where they wished as mortals stayed indoors.

TANKARDSTOWN, or Ballytankard, derives its name from the town of Tankard or Tancard, a personal name rather than a family surname. It was first recorded as a placename in 1280 when Anne De Cogan claimed it as dowry from John le Penrys.

THE TANKARD FAMILY may have been Flemings who joined William the Conqueror's invasion forces when the Normans overran England in 1066. Some of these families settled in Wales and probably moved to Ireland from there. Tancred, Thanchard, Tankward, Tanquard, Dankard and Tanquardus appear to be variations of the name. John, the son of Tankard, held a freehold in Tankardstown in 1307.

ST. DAVID'S CHURCH, the parish church of the pre-Reformation parish of Tankardstown, was founded in 1410 but no trace of it now remains, other than the graveyard which is still in use. The dedication to St. David is unusual insofar as it links the church with a Welsh saint. The oldest monumental inscription discovered here dates from 1760.

TANKARDSTOWN CASTLE was originally known as *Caisleán Bhaile an Airighthe.* This may be a corruption of *Caisleán Bhaile an Inneirghe,* the Castle of the Town of MacEniry. This was located in the townland of Tankardstown North.

EFFIN probably derived its name from *Cill* or *Teampall Effin,* the Temple or Church of St. Effin.

COSHLEA derives its name from *Cois tSléibhe,* near the mountains.

ST. EFFIN'S CHURCH was a nave and chancel structure which served as a Protestant parish church until it fell into ruin and its congregation moved to Kilmallock. In 1840 John O'Donovan reported that its choir appeared to have been in use for a longer period than the nave, but by then it was completely ruined although its graveyard was still in use. Two holy wells, Lady's Well and Toberacran, had

ceased to be pilgrimage sites by 1840. Lady's Well was north-west of the church and Toberacran derived its name from *Tobar a Chrann,* the Well of the Tree.

KILBIGLY CHURCH had disappeared by 1840 although the ruins of an old castle still survived within the same townland, Brickfield. In Ballymacshaneboy townland only part of a castle arch remained, in that year.

TOBERNEA CASTLE was only "a heap of rubbish" in 1840. This was located in the northern part of Leagaun townland, and was also known as Leagaun, Leagauns and *Liagán* Castle. A *liagán* is a standing stone. In 1207 King John granted a large holding between Inishannon and Kinsale to Philip de Prendergast. Philip was succeeded by his son Gerard who married twice. Gerard's second wife was a daughter of Richard de Burgo and she had been given the manor of Tobernea as a dowry. By 1240 Gerard de Prendergast was in possession of his wife's dowry. When he died in 1251 the lands were sublet to Gerald Fitzmilo, Henry de Prendergast, and Henry Barat; while the *ville* was set to Richard Gar, Thomas the Chaplin, Richard Kartere, William Hantlan, John Goss and Konewore O'Lougan.

PRENDERGAST, de Prendergast, *de Priondargás, de Priondragás,* Prindergast, Pendergast, Pendergrass, Pender and Pinder is a Norman surname, meaning of Prendergast, a parish in Pembrokeshire, England. Maurice de Prendergast was one of the knights who accompanied Strongbow to Ireland, and the surname has been associated with Tobernea from at least 1240, if not earlier.

BARRETT or Barat appears to be an Anglo-Saxon name, as variants of that name *Bare d, Baret,* Boret, Borrett, and Borred occur in the *Domesday Book* as the names of persons holding land in England during the reign of Edward the Confessor (1042-1066). Henry Barat leased land in Tobernea in 1251.

MYLES JACKSON held a grant of 800 acres in Lisdwane and Granagh in 1622, and was responsible for the settlement of eight English families in the area.

SOURCES
8 9 11 12 13 16
17 32 42 47 76 79
108 120 123 129 135 173
192 207 233 237 238 246
257 264 275 282

Caherconlish

Ballyneety · Caherelly · Ballybrood · Ballyclough
Knockea · Friarstown · Lickadoon

CAHERCONLISH derives its name from *Cathair Chinnlis*, the Caher at the Head of the Liss. The terms *cathair* and *caiseal* usually apply to stone-built forts; *lios* and *rath* are generally used to describe earth forts, and the word *dún* seems to be reserved for large forts and promontory forts. Ring forts such as those excavated at Cush may date from the end of the Bronze Age (circa. 1200 B.C.) up to early Christian times, while the Carraig Aille forts were occupied from the eighth to the eleventh centuries. *Cathair Chinnlis* can therefore be translated as the Stone Fort or Castle at the Head of the Earth Fort. This stone building may have been an early Anglo-Norman foundation, as those invaders had firmly established themselves in Limerick City by 1197, Knockainey by 1200, Castleconnell by 1201 and Hospital by 1215. By 1250 the Anglo-Normans occupied most of Ireland, with the exception of Connaught, West Ulster, and West Munster, where the Irish kings and chieftains still held power, possibly because they had resisted or never been attacked.

ANGLO-NORMAN WARFARE was superior to that of their Irish opponents. The Irish rushed into battle without an organised plan, armed with axes and short swords, and clad only in linen tunics. The Anglo-Normans planned their battles; used lances and long swords; and wore iron helmets and long coats of chain-mail to protect their bodies, thighs and arms. The main battle tactic used by the invaders was to stay out of the range of Irish spears, javelins, and sling-stones, and return fire by utilising Welsh archers who were experts in using long-bows, a weapon with a far greater range than any others then in use. When their opponents were suitably demoralised and in disarray after being subjected to attack from the far-flying arrows, the Anglo-Norman knights usually charged on horseback, supported by Flemish foot-soldiers. Once they conquered an area, the Anglo-Normans colonised and controlled it by erecting defensive structures on its borders or other strategic points, and divided the land out among their own supporters. Most of these early strongholds were motes of earth and timber, and as a general rule the Anglo-Normans did not build stone castles until the thirteenth century. Their settlements in Ormond, or East Munster, had become stabilised by the middle of that century and enjoyed comparative peace until 1285 or 1304.

TURLOUGH O'BRIEN was King of Thomond from 1277 to 1306. He came to power after the previous incumbent was torn apart by horses at Bunratty, at the behest of a de Clare widow. Turlough's reign was one of almost continual strife, war, robbery and plunder which was later documented in *Caithreim Thoirdhealbhaigh,* the Wars of Turlough. In 1285 or 1304 he crossed the Shannon; forced the clans of Ormond, or East Thomond, to submit and acknowledge him as king over all of Thomond, both by right and descent; and compelled Richard de Clare, who was then in possession of Caherconlish, *Aesa Gréine,* and Coonagh, to acknowledge his authority. Caherconlish was an Anglo-Norman stronghold in 1304 when Turlough and his army attacked it, slaughtered the garrison, destroyed the castle and burned Caherconlish from "the bawn or bulwark to the other end of the city". The town and castle were reduced to a "hideous blackened heap". Robert Bruce and his Scottish army had penetrated as far as the neighbourhood of Limerick by April 1317, where they intended to "effect a junction" with Irish forces under Donough O'Brien. Edmond Le Botiller was then Justiciar, and he and his magnates set up head-quarters here while Bruce and his men were at Castleconnell. The Justiciar's army and their allies, Richard de Clare's and Murrough O'Brien's forces, lived off Caherconlish and the surrounding countryside for two weeks. Robert Bagod later petitioned the Justiciar for £266.67 for grain, cattle, sheep and pigs requisitioned by his forces during this period. By 1338 the Manor of Caherconlish had fallen to about one third of its value in 1300.

BAGGOT, *BAGOD, BAGOTE,* Bagot, Bagott and Baggott, meaning the son of Bagot, was a diminutive of a common Anglo-Saxon personal name. The Baggotts settled in Limerick, Carlow, Dublin, Kildare and Meath soon after the Anglo-Norman invasion. Robert Bagod was Chief Justiciar of Ireland in 1280. He received a grant of the Manor of Rath, near Dublin, and of Bonevilstone and Brownstown in County Limerick, since known as Baggottstown. In 1651 Maurice Baggott of Baggotstown was one of the twenty men Ireton exempted from pardon.

CAHERCONLISH was an incorporated walled town with four castles and an extensive and celebrated college. In 1358 Edward III conferred certain privileges on the provost, bailiff and common people of *Catherkenlyshe.* No trace of the college remains except for an area behind the present national school called the "College Field".

KING WILLIAM III encamped here on 7 August, 1690. He returned in 1691 and stayed with the Frend family who had a house in the town. His army encamped nearby, in the townland of Boskill, south-east of Caherconlish. The Prince's Field, *Páirc a Phrions,* and the track of King William's Road, were still pointed out to visitors as late as 1927. The Frend family were descendants of John Frend, a Cromwellian captain, who had acquired a considerable amount of confiscated land in the county. In 1858 Caleb Powell described one of the family, Ben Frend of Boskill, as having an iron leg which was "the softest part of him!"

CAHERCONLISH CHURCH was used for Protestant worship until 1871 when the vicar, Rev. James Carson, had another church constructed almost half a mile away. This church was located within the old diocese of Emly until it was united to Cashel in 1718 in the Catholic hierarchy, and in 1791 by the Church of Ireland. In 1837 the church was "a spacious edifice, in the early English style, with a lofty square tower surmounted by an octagonal spire of hewn stone". It is now in ruin but appears to have been a parish church from an

Aerial view of Caherconlish.

early date. A plaque in the ruined porch states that: "The family vault beneath the chancel of this church was erected ABı A.D. 1670 by William Gabbett Esq. of Cahirline Co. Limerick. Great grand son of Robert Gabott of Acton Burnell Salop exon. of the Yeoman Guard Ao2 Henry VII 1486". The fish-shaped weather-vane on the churchspire is a symbol almost as old as Christianity, and the grave yard is still in use.

THE WAR OF INDEPENDENCE MEMO-RIAL, facing the street, commemorates the officers and men who died in action; Patrick Casey, Grange (28 February, 1921); Timothy Hennessy (1 May, 1921); James Horan (1 May, 1921); Richard Leonard, Pallas Greane, (31 December, 1920); Edward Donnelly, Croom (June, 1920); James Hogan, Fanningstown (June 1920); and John Moloney, Croom (June 1920). The monument is in the form of a Celtic cross, mounted on a cut-stone base.

THE ORIGINAL CAHERCONLISH HOUSE, a tower house, one of the town's four castles, was located on a rocky emi-nence. Lewis recorded how this old mansion "which stood on a rock ... though previously exhibiting no extraordinary marks of decay, suddenly split from top to bottom, one half falling into a heap of ruins, and the other half left standing; the gateway, on which are the arms of the Wilson family yet remains". By 1837 Major William Wilson was living in a handsome modern residence, named Caherconlish House, which he had erected near the site of the old one. He was descended from another Wilson who had been both chancellor and chaplain to William the Conqueror. The family had settled in Elton, Yorkshire, until Sir Ralph Wilson came to Ireland as civil war erupted between Charles I and Parliament. Ralph settled in Caherconlish after the Confederate Wars. His descendant, Charles Monck Wilson, borrowed money from Attorney Tim O'Brien of Limerick City to purchase a farm at Kilmore, near Broadford, but was unable to repay the loan on his mortgage of Cahirconlish House. In 1864 he sold out and left the country. Daniel Fitzgerald Gabbett (1841-1898) of Caherconlish House served as a Member of Parliament for Limerick from 1879 to 1885.

Local tradition maintains that the Gabbetts purchased Caherconlish House from "Knockroe" Wilson who was unable to main-tain it; changed the name to Oakley Park; and later sold it to the Cleeve's creamery chain, who demolished it and built a creamery (burned during the *Troubles* of the 1920s) on the site.

THE GABBETTS OF CAHERLINE are descended from William Gabbett of Caherline and Rathjordan whose will was proved in 1691. William was married to Alicia England, of Lifford, Ennis.

THE 1871 CHURCH OF IRELAND CHURCH contains two inscribed stone tablets in its porch. The smaller one looks like a family crest, but is actually the 1st Verse of the 23rd Psalm in hieroglyphic form. The larger one, located underneath the former, is a commemorative slab dedicated to various members of the Gabbett family; William (1659-1713) and Marcy (1766-1718); Thomas Spire (1683-1717) of Rathcanna; and Mary (1686-1717).

CARRIGOREELY CASTLE derives its name from *Carraig Fhear Gaile*, Fergal's

Rock, Farrel's Rock or, maybe, the Rock of the Foreign Man. The name has been anglicised to Farrell's Rock, which John O Donovan believed was a Christian name rather than a surname. The castle is now an ivy-covered ruin, located on a high rock, and was built by the Bourke family, who, like the de Clares, were associated with this region from the earliest days of the Anglo-Norman settlement.

THE HILL OF THE OLD CASTLE, or the Old Hill of the Castle, derives its name from *Cnoc a tSeanchuisleann.* By 1866 only the outer wall of this fortress remained.

EYONE TOWNLAND contained *Poll Eidhin,* the Ivy Hole Cave, which was only partially explored by 1840. Pot-holers of the period reported that they had found no end to the cavern as they descended. This was located on the centre of a high limestone hill and had an entrance twenty feet in diameter.

INCH ST. LAWRENCE is a corruption of *Díseart Labhrán,* Lauran's Hermitage. By 1363 it was known as Dysirt Lauran. The Anglo-Normans may have been familiar with *Díseart Labhrás,* a version that later became Disert Louras. The dropping of the initial D changed the name to Isert Lawrence, and the Isert was supplanted by Inch thus altering it to Inch Lauran or Inch Lawrence. Inch was corrupted to *Inis* and Insin Lawrence was recorded as the name in 1583. Insin Lauran and Insin Lawrence then came into use. When O' Donovan carried out his survey the name had been altered to Inch St. Lawrence which he believed to be *Inis San Labhrás,* St. Lawrence's Riverside Meadow. Other variations on the name were Tristel laueran in 1242 and Esterlawran in 1405.

ST. LAWRENCE'S CHURCH was located on the southern side of the old grave yard, which is still in use today. No trace of the old parish church remains.

ST. LAWRENCE'S WELL is located on the western side of Inch St. Lawrence grave yard. A regular pattern was held here on St. Lawrence's Day, 10 August, until about 1810. Thirty years later the well, "with a stone flag over it, and a large ash tree growing near it", was still frequented on Saturdays. The water was quite deep and believed "to be a specific for disorders of the bowels". There is a Mass Rock north-east of the grave yard. Another well to the south of the grave yard is still visited by people seeking a cure for warts.

BRITTAS may derive its name from the old French *bretesche,* meaning a wooden tower, according to Goddard H. Orpen who expressed the opinion that this word had given the name to the thirty-seven townlands in Ireland in the *English Historical Review,* 1906. In June, 1908, he wrote in *The Journal of the Royal Society of Antiquaries of Ireland* that he had found an entry of £10 for a *britagium,* or *bretesche,* at Carkenlys (Caherconlish) in the *Irish Pipe Roll.* This referred to an early thirteenth-century castle of the de Burgos or Bourkes. G.H. Orpen identified "a low, rectangular platform, surrounded by a wet ditch; near Brittas Castle, as the site of the *bretesche,* a wooden tower which was enclosed by a palisade.

BRITTAS CASTLE, on the west bank of the Mulkear River, was established by the Bourke family, Lords of Brittas and Clanwilliam. This consisted of a massive keep with an enclosed court-yard, and was surrounded by a moat. John Bourke (c.1550-1607) of Brittas Castle refused to take the Oath of Supremacy and conform outwardly to the state religion. As a result he fell foul of the Lord President of Munster, Sir Henry Brouncker, when his kinsmen and neighbours, Theobald Bourke of Castleconnell and Sir Edmund Walsh of Abington, laid information against him, accusing him of harbouring "popish priests ... and that he openly had Mass said at Brittas for the surrounding country". Sir John Bourke refused to admit Captain Miller to his castle when the government acted on information received. Captain Miller was forced into besieging the castle. After a siege of 15 days he captured the castle, but Sir John and his chaplain, Fr. John Clancy, escaped. Sir John was later taken prisoner at Waterford and sent back to Limerick City where he was tried, and executed for treason. He had ignored an edict of James I, issued in 1605, which forbade "all our subjects of Ireland to shelter or countenance any Jesuit, Seminarist or other priest who will dare to remain in Ireland"; and had converted his vaulted banquet hall into a chapel. Sir John Bourke was sentenced to death by Dominick Sarsfield, later Chief Justice of the Common Pleas and Viscount Kilmallock. John O'Donovan remarked on two round towers on the south-western and north-western corners of the castle in 1840.

TEMPLEMICHAEL TOWNLAND derives its name from *Teampall Mhicíl,* St. Michael's Church, which was located in the western part of this townland. Both church and graveyard had virtually disappeared by 1819, when human bones and old coffins were discovered here as ground was being dug up to prepare it for cultivation. This grave yard was still used by the older families of the locality in 1989.

GINKEL'S GRAVE, in Templemichael, is named after several Williamite soldiers who died of some illness while encamped nearby.

SKAHARD TOWNLAND contained a *cillin* or children's burial-ground, in its north-western corner. This was called *Cill a Bhothair,* the graveyard of the Road, and remained in use until about 1800. The word *cill* is sometimes used to denote a burial-ground rather than a church.

KILLANURE TOWNLAND derived its name from *Cill an Iubhair,* the Church of the Yew Tree. No church or graveyard remained by the early nineteenth century, when human bones were found, buried, on the small hill of Killanure.

KILMURRY, *Cill Mhuire,* Mary's Church, may have been an Anglo-Norman foundation. In 1840 John O'Donovan wrote, "There are no old church ruins found here at present. The ruins of a Roman Catholic old chapel and a graveyard enclosed by a wall, are situated in the west end of the townland".

MOLAGA TOWNLAND derives its name from *Tobar Molaga,* St. Molaga's Well. By 1840 the well had dried up. St. Molaga or St. Molua is believed, locally, to have been a disciple of St. Columbkill. In 1989 no trace of the well remained.

KNOCKEEN HILL derives its name from *Cnoc Caoin,* the Delightful Hill. John O' Donovan wrote in 1840 of a cavern here "whose entrance is about five feet in diameter. It branches inwards into several apartments overhung with massive cliffs".

GREENAN CASTLE derives its name from Grenane or *Grianán* and was once owned by the Nunan family. Samuel Lewis described it as a ruin in 1837 while, three years later, O' Donovan wrote of it as a site.

THE SPA WELL is located in the north-western corner of Pust South townland. In 1840 John O'Donovan wrote of it as Spaw Well, and mentioned that it was covered by "a small house about five feet high". It can be found by the entrance gate to Jerry Mulcaire's land although few locals now avail of its waters which were "esteemed good ... proceeds from iron ... equally available for liver or scorbutic affections".

SHANCOURT was the name used in 1840 to describe the entire summit of a hill in Knockroe townland. It was called after a mansion, or some other edifice, named *Sean Chúirt,* the Old Court, which stood here until the early 1800s.

BALLYBRICKEN COURT, or Ballybricken Castle, is located on low-lying ground in the northern section of Ballybricken South townland. This was the home of James Goold, the father-in-law of Colonel Sir George Ingoldsby, who died here in 1600. During his life-time he acquired the famous Dominican Convent of Limerick; the castle, town and lands of Corbally; and used his family connections to further his career and acquire wealth. The original structure on this site may have been founded by the Clanchy family, possibly a branch of the Clare or Leitrim MacClancys or Clancys. It is now a ruin. During the 1830s Ballybricken Catholic church was erected on the site of an earlier church.

CAHERELLY OLD CASTLE, situated on an eminence, was badly damaged but still standing in 1988. Another castle, the Black Castle, had disappeared by 1840; only its site was remembered.

CAHERELLY GRANGE is an old tower house which was occupied by the Croker family into the middle of the nineteenth century.

BALLYBROOD derives its name from *Baile Bhrúid,* which O'Donovan translated as the Bally or Town of Brood. He thought that the name was probably of Anglo-Norman origin. Local tradition maintains that the name means the Place of Feasting, or the House of Entertainment, and is derived from *Baile Brua.* This house of entertainment is believed to have been located on top of Ballybrood Hill, a chieftain's house which was used to offer hospitality to strangers. During the nineteenth century a local farmer uncovered the foundations of a building on the summit of the hill, a discovery that reinforced local beliefs.

BALLYBROOD CHURCH was a Franciscan friary. According to tradition, all but one of the Franciscan friars here were slain by Cromwell. The survivor managed to get as far as a small ford near Dromkeen before Cromwell managed to overtake, and kill him. A bridge was later built over this ford, which was known as Friar's Bridge. The original church was used for Protestant worship until it was replaced by a more modern building in 1807. In 1822 the Rockites burned Ballybrood Church and attacked its rector, Rev. Madden, by forcing him to his knees and firing pistols above his head. In 1823 a third church was built on the site. This, like many other of the period, was "in the early English style, with a tower surmounted with an octagonal spire". This is now a ruin but the grave yard is still in use.

BALLYBROOD, pronounced Ballabrood, was located on the old road from Limerick to Cashel. In former times it contained a castle, friary, church, glebe-lands, burial-grounds and a two-acre fair green at the cross-roads where it was joined by the old road from Kilmallock. The Ballybrood Fair was one of the county's most important fairs and was held annually on 12 June into the 1940s. Another fair was held on 11 October into the nineteenth century and, according to tradition, a charter for two other annual fairs was not taken up.

BALLYBROOD CASTLE was located on the summit of the hill under the junction. This old tower house was a military station during the 1800s but was later converted into a public-house. The constabulary police force was stationed in a small castellated tower just over the brow of the hill from the tower house which was, and still is, known as the Tower.

BALLYNEETY derives its name from *Baile an Fhaoitigh,* White's Town or Townland. It was of little importance until a new line of road leading from Limerick to Charleville opened in the 1830s. The late nineteenth-century court-house is the most distinctive building in today's village.

CAHERNARRY derives its name from *Carn Fhearadhaigh,* the Burial-cairn or Mound of Fearadhach, an ancient warrior, not the Stone Fort of Maraidh as related in O'Donovan's notes. By 1840 little remained of the old church of Cahernarry except for a portion of the small square tower which had been joined to it. Three years earlier Lewis had described the parish. He wrote of the Church of Ireland church "... a small plain building, with a tower and spire of hewn stone, erected ... in 1810. The Glebe House was erected ... in 1813 ... in the R.C. divisions this parish forms part of the union or district of Donoughmore or Knockea ... on the summit of the hill east of the church, is a small turret, erected by the late John Howley, Esq., in 1821 to commemorate the election of Thomas Spring Rice, Esq., the present Chancellor of the Exchequer, as a member of parliament for the city of Limerick. In the church-yard is a very splendid monument covering a large vault, also erected by Mr. Howley, and in which his remains are interred. From the summit of the hills are some very extensive views; and not far distant from it are the ruined castles of Rathsiward, Drombanny, and Liccadoen". The big houses of the period were Ballyneguard of J. Croker, Cahirnarry House of J. Cripps and Ballyneedy of J. Fitzgerald.

THE SPRING RICE MEMORIAL a small circular tower of masonry, nine feet in diameter and fifteen feet high, was erected by John Howley and the Catholic merchants of Limerick. John lived near Annacotty and had a business in Charlotte's Quay, Limerick.

ST. SENAN'S WELL, *Tobar Seanain,* is located in the townland of Cahernarry Kane. This was a recognised pilgrimage site in 1840. The small church and graveyard on top of the hill in Cahernarry Cripps were still in use at that date.

KNOCKEA HILL-TOP is only 150 feet above the surrounding countryside yet it gives an almost all-encompassing view of the counties of Limerick, Clare, Cork, Kerry and Tipperary. In bygone days this was a strategic site, commanding the plain beneath, and it eventually became an important habitation site. A complex of earthworks and enclosures cover the southern side of Knockea Hill. Michael J. O'Kelly excavated one small enclosure here in 1960. He uncovered the remains of at least 66 individuals, laid on their backs, with their hands mainly placed by their sides, although some few exceptions had their hands crossed over the pelvis in the "modest man" position. Because of the western orientation of the bodies, the absence of grave-goods, and the western entry to the enclosure, he concluded that this enclosure had been built as a cemetery for the hill's community during the early Christian period. He was unable to be more specific on the date.

KNOCKEA RING FORT was badly ruined by 1960. The western half had virtually disappeared, and although the rest of it had been ploughed over it was still discernible. This ruined fort contained a surprising number of hut and house sites, built over a long period of time. Michael J. O'Kelly was unable to provide a date for the erection of the original fort, but he did mention how St. Patrick had come to *Mullach Cae* to meet Lonan, King of the *Ui Fidgeinte,* in the fifth century. Although he equated *Mullach Cae* with Knockea he did not like to connect named persons or people with particular material remains.

BALLYNEGUARD HOUSE may have been built on the site of an earlier Bourke castle. When John Croker, its owner, lay dying, his son, a rector, assured him that he would enjoy Paradise. "I doubt it", said Croker and his last words passed into the history and folklore of the county. His memorial slab was transferred from Fedamore church to St. Mary's Cathedral, where it was relaid on the western side of the pillar at the west end of Limerick's finest ecclesiastical structure. Ballyneguard House is a ruin since earlier this century. Plans to remove a statue of Hercules from the front of the house to the city were abandoned when a committee of inspection decided that "he would never do for the confraternities". Richard Wellstead "Boss" Croker, the grandson of a younger Croker son, returned to Ireland after spending some time in Tammany Hall. He purchased Glencairn House in Sandyford, Dublin, in 1904. In 1907 one of his horses, *Orby,* won both the Irish and English Derby. His house, Glencairn, later became the British Embassy. The name Ballyneguard is traditionally believed to have been derived from *Baile na gCeard,* meaning in this case, the House of the Tradesmen.

CAHERVALLY derives its name from *Cathair Uí Bhachalla,* the Stone Fort of O'Boughil, an old circular stone fort in the townland of Raheen. This was covered with

Friarstown friary.

grass in 1840 but the foundations of what may have been a castle were still visible. One hundred yards downhill, to the east, the graveyard of Cahervally was still in use 150 years ago, although the old church was then completely ruined.

FRIARSTOWN FRIARY, *Baile na mBrathar,* the Town or Townland of the Brothers, was a Franciscan foundation. It is still in a fair state of preservation and has changed little over the last century and a half. O'Donovan then wrote that it was still known as "the abbey"; there were no marks of graves about it and the walls were perfect; it contained a fine mullioned window in the eastern gable, and another window from which the mullion had been removed on the southern wall. The lateral building attached to the main structure, on the southern side, was probably a dwelling-house as it contained two fireplaces and two chimneys. One of the chimneys is raised on the wall of the friary, and the other is in the middle of the gable to the south. The windows on this building resemble those of the friary, the walls are almost as thick, yet it does not appear to be as old. The original foundation dates back to the thirteenth century when it was erected by the Clan-Gibbons family. The Franciscan Third Order Regular may have occupied this friary but there is some doubt about it, as friars of the Third Order were generally referred to as *na sagairt ,* the priests, while those of the First Order were usually called *na mbráithre ,* the brothers. This friary, with three acres of ground, was granted to Robert Browne at an annual rent of 5 pence on 4 February 1544. An inquisition of 1589-1590 mentions that it was in the possession of a rebel, Gerald Baluff F. Philip.

LICKADOON CASTLE derived its name from *Lic á Duín,* the Stone Flag of the Fort. Dermot O'Hurley (1519-1584), the Catholic Archbishop of Cashel, was born here. By the middle of the nineteenth century only two floors of the castle remained. There was a square tower, containing the stairs, at the eastern end which was indistinguishable from the rest of the building.

A HOLY WELL in the townland of Lickadoon was reputed to be efficacious in curing sore eyes during the 1830s. Known as Tobar-Stroke, this may be the one referred to by Lewis as "a very good spa, the water of which is strongly impregnated with iron and sulphur, but is much neglected, and other waters are allowed to mingle with it".

CARRIGPARSON derived its name from *Carraig A'Phearsùn,* the Rock of the Parson or Parish Priest. Carrigparson church gave its name to the townland in which it was located. By 1840 only a small part of its eastern gable and north wall remained.

TOOREEN CASTLE was in poor condition by 1840. Its northern wall reached a height of 25 feet while the eastern and western walls were only eight feet high. Nothing was then known about its founder, owners or history.

DONAGHMORE CHURCH derives its name from *Domhnach Mór,* The Big Church. The word *Domhnach* is a word for church which is reserved for those visited or founded by St. Patrick. According to tradition, Patrick stayed here when this territory was known as *Ard-Chliach.* He was entertained by a chief-

129

tain named Lonan, and made the acquaintance of a young man, Nessan, whom he would later put in charge of his Mungret foundation. From the top of Mount Fintine he blessed the country of Thomond and foretold the birth of St. Senan of Scattery. This prophecy, and several others he made while here, is also associated with other Patrician sites. The ruins of this early church are quite extensive. It contains the tombs and monuments of many of Limerick's most famous families, the Roches, Kellys, Fitzgeralds and the Connells of Garryowen.

DRUMBANNY HILL gives its name to the townland in which it is located. Drumbanny Castle was located on top of this ridge, but it had all but disappeared by 1840.

RATHURDE CASTLE was described by John O'Donovan, in 1840, as a remarkable building, "being round on the outside, and square inside ... the first floor over the ground floor is newly boarded, and the third floor is arched (underneath) ... it appears to have had another storey above the three that now remain". He also mentioned an old fort about thirty yards north-west of the castle which was nearly level with the ground. This castle appears to have been a Bourke stronghold. It later passed to the Frend family.

DONAGHMORE contained several big houses in the 1830s. These included Ballyseeda, Clonlong and South Hill. By then the city had begun to encroach on what had previously been farmland, and Limerick merchants had started to build substantial houses within this ancient parish while others were busy acquiring farms.

ROXBOROUGH HOUSE stood in the townland of the same name. It was erected by Connell Vereker of Cork, who bought the lands of Roxborough from the Hollow-Blade-Sword Company during the reign of Queen Anne (1702-1714). He built his mansion "in a park laid out with canals, terraces and hedges, in the stiff Dutch fashion". Charles Vereker was created Viscount Gort in 1817. Roxborough House changed hands several times after the Verekers left. In 1879 its contents were auctioned, and it eventually became the property of Alexander W. Shaw, of Shaw's Bacon Factory, Limerick.

THE LIMERICK GOLF CLUB at Ballyclough owes its existence to Alexander W. Shaw, a wealthy Limerick industrialist, an equally keen sportsman and one of the first people to promote golf-playing within the city and county. He was also instrumental in establishing the Lahinch Golf Club with officers of the Black Watch Regiment. The club's present location is entirely coincidental, as it had been established elsewhere before winding up in Ballyclough, close to its founder's home.

Golf became a popular pastime during the 1880s. It was played in an informal way, usually by landowners who laid out six or nine holes on their own land. Limrick was among the first places to establish a formal club and this was done as a result of a meeting held on 12th December 1891 in the library of the Athenaeum chaired by Mr.A.W. Shaw. It was proposed that a course be laid out on ground at Greenpark with the permission of the Race Committee and that it should be ready for play within two weeks. A large attendance was well pleased with the new ground when the first game of golf, under the auspices of Limerick Golf Club, was played on Christmas Day 1891. The first competition was played on 5th February, 1892 for the Captains Medal and was won by Lt. Harvey, 2nd Batt., Black Watch Regt. with a score of 107 gross. Between 1891 and 1908 the club moved eight times before arriving in the general area of Ballyclough. Some minor movements took place between 1908 and the early 1920s but only a matter of a few hundred yards. In 1919 the club bought the bulk of the land that is now Limerick Golf Club from Mrs. Crawford for the sum of £2,000. Further purchases were made in the 1950s and 1960s to complete the present course. A British Army hut was bought and erected in 1920 and served as the clubhouse until 1966 when the present building was opened. It now caters for almost 1,100 members. Limerick Golf Club, though one of the leading clubs in Ireland had a low profile in the first seventy years of its existence. This profile changed radically from the early 1960s with the election of Tommy O'Donnell to the Presidency of the G.U.I. and the election in the early 1970s of Paddy McPolin to the same office. Up to 1945 the Club had only won one Munster title but since then has annexed 29 Munster titles. In 1967 the Barton Shield Team won the Club's first Irish crown. The unique distinction of winning the Big Three, Irish Junior Cup, Senior Cup and Barton Shield, in the one year fell to the club in 1976 and over the next twelve years fifteen Munster and six Irish titles came its way. In 1980, as Irish Senior Cup holders, the club was invited to compete in the European Club Championship held at Santa Ponza G.C. Majorca. The team members were Vincent Nevin, Jackie Harrington, Ivan Morris and Pat Cotter (captain). They created Irish sporting history in winning the European crown, the first club in Ireland to win a senior European title.

BALLYCLOUGH HOUSE dates from the late eighteenth century. It was the residence of Michael Furnell who killed his neighbour, Henry Vereker, in the last duel fought in the county. The house was sold in 1973.

DOMINICK ROCHE was created Viscount Cahervally by James II. Like his ancestor, in Cromwell's day, he had fought on the wrong side in the hope of reclaiming the Roche lands that his family had lost under the Cromwellian Settlement.

LUDDENBEG PARISH CHURCH has been referred to as "an old abbey" but Aubrey Gwynn and R. Neville Hadcock suggest in their definitive *Medieval Religious Houses Ireland* that Fitzgerald may have confused it with Louth Park, Lincolnshire, England. Tradition mentions that it was founded by a knight called Owin who had served King Stephen in his wars, and decided to lead a solitary life after a visit to St. Patrick's Purgatory. In 1826 Rev. P. Fitzgerald noted "a rude figure of our Saviour on a cross" in *bas relief* on the south and north walls. Lewis mentioned in 1837 that there was hardly a trace of Luddenmore Castle left to the south of the church. The ruins of Luddenbeg Church can still be seen at the foot of a gentle eminence. Its name evolved from the Irish word *Luidín* for which there are several meanings.

KILCOOLIN TOWNLAND contained a *cillín*, killeen, kyle or burial place, which was used as a place of interment for children until 1780 or 1790.

SOURCES

5 9 11 18 21 28 39 47 63 65
69 76 86 95 107 120 123 129 156 164
167 168 173 174 184 192 194 195 201 202
207 213 221 233 246 255 258 259 264 279
282

Cappagh

Nantenan · Ballinagarrane · Croagh

CAPPAGH derives its name from *An Ceapach*, the Tillage Plot. In 1837 Samuel Lewis wrote that the parish contained 694 inhabitants on 1,124 statute acres. Cappagh was not a prosperous place as the land was stony containing large limestone outcrops and the bogs near Rathkeale had been exhausted. The Church of Ireland church was then in ruin and the Catholic church was a large plain thatched edifice on top of Cappagh Hill. This latter building was blown down on the *Night of the Big Wind*, 6 January 1839. Cappagh was part of the old *tuath* of Nantenan, in the territory of *Uí Fidgeinte*, from the fourth century onwards.

KILMACLUANA CHURCH, a small plain Gothic building, was first recorded in 1201. It was destroyed by war in 1302, and in 1541 the Knight of Glin granted it to the friars of Askeaton. It contains a large east window with two pointed lights and a round-headed splay. The doorway is in the south wall, and Frank Whelan wrote that it was the oldest church in Cappagh, in his book, *Cappagh — A Sense of History*.

CAPPAGH CASTLE was built by the Knights of Glin during the late fifteenth century, although the first castle on this site may have been founded by Dermot MacEniry during the reign of King John (1199-1216). The windows of the five-storey tower house have been dated to 1460-1480. It stands within the ruins of its double bawn, which still contains the remains of the gate-house and an angle-turret. Its banquet hall was used as a handball court during the nineteenth century, and a cement floor was laid there in 1917. It remained in use for that purpose until 1969 when the handball club moved to new quarters. Edmond FitzThomas Fitzgerald, the Knight of Glin, assigned his interest in the Manor of Cappagh to Arthur Carter in 1578. Carter was allowed to export corn, grain and victuals to England and Wales, free of duty, on condition that he would build houses for twenty families. In the same year the Knight of Glin was accused of treason, and his manor of Cappagh was granted to Sir William Drury,

the Lord-President of Munster. Walter Bourke, who held the castle for the Fitzgeralds, was displaced by Ulick Browne who was in possession in 1583. In 1587 the "lands long wasted and unpeopled" had been granted to Gilbert Gerrard, and then to J. Stroude. In 1591 W. Carter was granted the castle, which still had a barbican on its south side, and 320 acres of ground. The Bishop of Limerick claimed it in 1615; Edmund Southwell conveyed it to Richard, Earl of Cork, in 1629; and F. Morton surrendered it to Confederate Irish forces in 1642. Sir Hardress Waller may have ordered its destruction after it had been recaptured by the Cromwellians as it was described as a ruined castle, held by N. Dowdall, in 1655. According to folklore, one of the Fitzgeralds of Ballygleaghan Castle blew it up to prevent his sister-in-law from occupying it. It is now owned by the Barry family who live nearby.

CALLOW CASTLE was mentioned in a rent roll of 1452. In 1588 it was granted to H. Billingsley after its previous occupant, Richard London, was accused of treason. Part of the castle still remains.

ARDGOWLE CASTLE may have been near the present bridge and mill. No trace of it remains although it is mentioned in various accounts from 1289 to 1655.

CAPPAGH HOUSE is believed to be one of the oldest residences in Ireland. The flagstone at the front door had the date 1607 inscribed on it but the style of the building is more reminiscent of the 1500s. The Peppard family were recorded as the owners of Cappagh House in 1660, and they continued to occupy it into the late 1800s. The Cooke family succeeded the Peppards as owners until Alice Cooke, the last of that family to live here, died in 1938. Her ghost is believed to have appeared to her brother, on the day of her funeral, and told him to leave Cappagh House. The Land Commission took over the estate when it was declared bankrupt; divided the land among the neighbouring farmers; and sold the house and a small portion of land to Arthur Pearse Pollock who took up residence there on 7 May, 1940. Hugh B. Brassey

bought the house on 10 March 1945, and sold it to Doreen Wordsworth on 7 May 1954. She, in turn, resold it to Captain Edward H. Pearse in 1960. The house was badly damaged by fire on 27 December 1983, and its magnificent staircase, with a carved bog oak balustrade, was totally destroyed. When his mother died in 1985 Roderick Pearse completed the renovations she had begun. In December 1986 he sold the house to its present owner, Michael Morrissey.

THE PEPPARD FAMILY came to Limerick from County Louth about 1650. This is an old Anglo-Norman surname, and variants on it include *Piobaire, Piobar, Piobart, Pippart, Pipard, Pippard,* Piper, Pipper, and Pepper. The family appear to have settled in Kilmacow before moving to Cappagh.

CAPPAGH CATHOLIC CHURCH evolved from a small church established in Ballymorrisheen which remained in use from Penal times until a new church was erected on Cappagh Hill in the early 1800s. When this was destroyed in a storm, Fr. Jeremiah Halpin acquired the present site on which he built this church, by the end of 1839. This building was reconstructed in 1986 and officially re-opened on 15 February 1987.

CANON JOHN BEGLEY, the noted Limerick historian, was parish priest of Cappagh from 1915 to 1917. He is buried here. His works are still used extensively today.

FR. PATRICK WOULFE, the genealogist, is also buried here. He was parish priest of Cappagh from 1926 to 1934. His work on the surnames of Ireland is an extremely valuable source of genealogical information.

CAPPAGH contained twenty houses in 1831, including two public-houses, a carpenter's shop, four shoemakers' shops, a forge and a constabulary police station.

LEE HOUSE, or Law Hill, Cappagh, are two of the names applied to the former R.I.C. barracks in the village. This housed a sergeant and seven constables, members of the old constabulary police force, which became the Royal Irish Constabulary on 20 May 1867. The house was renovated and restored by

William McGuire who now lives here.

BALLINVIRICK HOUSE was erected for the Royce family in the middle of the eighteenth century. The name is derived from *Baile Mheidhreach*, the Townland of the Merry or Cheerful. The Royces remained here until 1919. Before Brian Cusack purchased it in 1986 it had passed through the hands of the Hewson, Hunt, Tellender and MacMahon families. Brian Cusack restored Ballinvirick House and resides there with his family.

GORTEENNAMROCK RING FORT is located 2 1/2 miles west-north-west of Cappagh. The fort and townland derive their names from *Goirtín na mBroc*, the Little Field of the Badger.

NANTENAN takes its name from *Neantanán*, the Land Abounding in Nettles.

NANTENAN CHURCH the Church of Ireland church is believed to be the third church on this site. The first church may have been a small structure with a thatched roof. The second building was levelled to the ground about 1810 or 1817 to make way for the present edifice. This appears to have been completed by 1821, according to a tablet on its porch wall. The congregation dwindled over the years and the church was closed in 1972. Brian de Breffny described this church as having the appearance of an English country parish church of the Norman period.

ST. JAMES'S WELL is much as it was 150 years ago when it was "enclosed by ancient massive stone walls, the water of which issues from a limestone rock; it is much resorted to on festivals by the peasantry of the neighbourhood". Its waters were believed to be efficacious in curing sores of every description. The patterns have long since ceased but St. James's Day, 25 July, is still observed as a holiday. A stone plaque on the side of the well carries an inscribed date of 1750, but the well was in use long before this.

NANTENAN FAIR GREEN, the Fair Field, is located alongside the well. This was a spacious green on which fairs were held on 10 July, 5 August and 12 November, "for cattle, sheep, pigs and pedlery". Faction fighters such as the Three Year Olds and the Four Year Olds also assembled here on occasion.

NANTENAN HOUSE was originally built by the Royce family who received a grant of Nantenan in 1707. In 1849 John White purchased the house and over 145 acres of land under the Encumbered Estates Act of that year. He demolished the old house and erected the present structure, on the same site, some time before 1858. He retained the impressive eighteenth-century gateway at the entrance. Dorothea Conyers, a widow and authoress of hunting novels, including *Peter's Pedigree* (1904) and *The Boy, Some*

Horses and a Girl (1908), married Captain John Joseph White who succeeded to Nantenan in 1892. Dorothea (1871-1949) claimed that the local countryside was too thorny for riding side-saddle and became the first woman in the county to wear britches and ride astride. Lieutenant-Colonel Martin William "Bill" Helenas White inherited Nantenan House and his nephew, Simon, lives there today.

JOHN WHITE had gone to Jamaica as a young man. He made a considerable fortune there as a sugar planter before returning to Ireland. In the early 1830s he married Eleanor Mary Irwin and resided in Belmont, Castleconnell, the old home of Tom "Spectacles" O'Grady. He died in 1858.

NANTENAN GLEBE HOUSE was built in 1819. The glebe, consisting of a house and eight acres of land, was the property of the Church of Ireland until 1954, and housed the various rectors of Nantenan over that period. Rev. John Armour Haydn (1881-1957) was the rector here for 25 years. He ministered to many of the Palatine families, and is perhaps the last priest to have buried a German bible with its Palatine owner. He was also the first secretary of the Friends of St Mary's. Cecile Isabel Caroline Smythe purchased the house for £1,174 in 1954. William Peter Fitzgerald bought it on 26 September, 1973. Since then he has repaired and renovated the building and was still living there in 1989.

STONEVILLE HOUSE was erected as a hunting lodge by Henry Southwell during the early eighteenth century. After his death in 1758 the Massy family purchased the house, the back of which is reputed to be much older than the rest of it. J.F. Massy enclosed a court-yard in 1802 to make a stable range, and in 1837 it was occupied by H. Massy. Stoneville House, pronounced Stony-Ville by the locals, is now the property of Pat O'Riordan, Blossomhill. Three of the house's more striking features are the *Stony Man*; a bog-oak fireplace and an unusual glass-case that may have come from Mountbrown House.

THE STONY MAN is a life-size statue set into the gable of a building at Stoneville, beside the roadway. In some of the old maps of the area this figure was known as the Vulcan, and as it depicted a lame man working on an anvil it is more than likely a representation of Vulcan, the Roman god of fire, sometimes confounded with the Greek Hephaistos, a skilled worker in metals. The statue was carved by Martin Scanlon, Blossomhill, Rathkeale, during the late eighteenth century, and may have been placed here to decorate a workshop associated with the silver-mines across the roadway, possibly

a silver-smith's.

ALTAVILLA may have been designed by Francis Bindon for John Bateman about 1745 or 1746. In 1837 it was the residence of T.G. Bateman, but was allowed to lapse into ruin earlier this century. In 1978 it was restored by Lord Daresbury.

BALLINAGARRANE derives its name from *Baile an Gharráin*, the Townland of the Shrubbery, or the Garden. The land here was of poor quality, stony and overgrown with vegetation, but this did not prevent the Palatines, pronounced Palantines, from establishing a settlement here in the early eighteenth century. One old Palatine described Ballinagarrane as "grand land but cursed with stones and bushes", a description with which local people concur today.

THE PALATINES OF COUNTY LIMERICK came from the German Palatinate, *Die Pfalz am Rhein*, on the banks of the Rhine River. When Louis XIV annexed the region, for France, Queen Anne of England sent a fleet to Rotterdam to transport about 10,000 displaced persons to England. Anne returned 2,000 of these refugees to the Palatine when she discovered they were Catholics, mainly because, as a Protestant champion, she had no intention of sheltering members of the Catholic faith within her kingdom. The people of England had no welcome for "a crowd of blackguards who could have lived happily in their own land were it not for their inherent laziness and the knowledge of English generosity which motivated their coming". 821 Palatine families, 3073 people, were sent to Ireland, while the rest were shipped off to North America. These people were fifth-and-sixth-generation Protestants, a mixture of German, Dutch, French and Swiss. The reception they received in Dublin was equally hostile, and the Mayor of Dublin had to order the citizens of that city to treat the Palatines fairly.

IN 1709 the Irish Parliament passed an Act, "That it is the opinion of this House that Her Majesty by sending over a proportion of Protestant Palatines into this Kingdom has very much consulted the strengthening and securing [of] the Protestant interest in Ireland. That it will very much contribute to the security of this Kingdom that the said Protestant Palatines be encouraged." The Irish Government of the day provided £25,000 to help the Palatines settle within the country. Each Palatine family received a lease on eight acres of land at a nominal rent of 25 pence per acre. These leases were issued for a period of three life-times, or 50 years. The men were enrolled in the local yeomanry militia, the True Blues or the German Fusiliers, and issued with muskets which they never used

The Embury and Heck Memorial Church.

against their Catholic neighbours. In fact the Palatine settlement never became the Protestant colonisation force envisaged by the Queen or others. Half of the refugees who settled in County Limerick became dissatisfied with conditions in the colony and emigrated to America. In 1712 the Government subsidised the others by paying each household £2 annually for a period of seven years. By 1730 many of the Palatines had assumed responsibility for their own lives, and many of them had become free-holders by 1747. By the middle of the nineteenth century they had been assimilated into the life of the county.

SIR THOMAS SOUTHWELL was one of the prime movers behind the Palatine settlement in Limerick. His estate, outside Rathkeale, was the base from which they spread throughout the county. In 1716 he sent a petition to the Lord Lieutenant, requesting the reimbursement of what it cost him to start the colony and its upkeep since the colonists got into difficulty.

"The humble petition of Sir Thomas Southwell showeth:- that the said Sir Thomas Southwell having sent down 130 German Protestant families on his Estate in or about Michaelmas 1712 and for their encouragement to settle and be a security to the Protestant interest in the county he (the said Sir Thomas Southwell) set them his land at almost one half of what it was worth, and

gave them timber also to build their houses to a very great value, and for their further encouragement did from time to time supply them with cash and other necessities.

That all these families are since well settled and follow the raising of hemp and flax and have a good stock which the said Sir Thomas Southwell (though very unwillingly) must seize upon to reimburse him for his great expense, unless His Majesty will be graciously pleased to repay Sir Thomas".

SIR RICHARD QUIN, Earl of Dunraven, gave land to the Palatines in the district between Rathkeale and Adare in 1766.

JOHN WESLEY found his staunchest followers amongst the Palatines. The following extracts from his journal cover a series of visits which he made between 1756 and 1765.

"June 10, 1756. In the afternoon I rode to Ballygarrane, a town (townland) of Palatines which came over in Queen Anne's time. They retain much of the temper and manner of their own country, having a resemblance of those among whom they live. I found much life among this plain, artless serious people".

He travelled between the various settlements. "June 18, 1756. I rode back through Adare, once a strong and flourishing town, well walled, and full of people, now without walls and almost without inhabitants, only a few poor huts remain".

He found plenty of support, however, wherever he went.

"June 23, 1756. I rode over to Court Matress, a colony of Germans whose parents came from out of Palatinate about fifty years ago. Twenty families of these settled here, twenty more at Killiheen, a mile off, fifty at Ballygarrane, about two miles eastward, and twenty at Pallas, four miles further. Each family had a few acres of ground on which they built as many little houses. They are considerably increased in number of souls, though decreased in numbers of families. Having no minister they became eminent for drunkenness, cursing, swearing and other neglect of religion. But they are washed since they heard and received the truth, which is able to save their souls. An oath is now rarely heard among them, or a drunkard seen in their borders. Court Matress is built in the form of a square, in the middle of which they have placed a pretty large meeting-place ..."

When the Palatines came to Glenisheen they wore clothes made out of canvas, with shoes also made of the same material, except for the soles and heels. They were "a quiet inoffensive people", according to Patrick Weston Joyce (1827-1914) author of *The Origin and History of Irish Names of Places*. He described them as a temperate and industrious people "with a great flair for horticulture and bee-keeping".

JOHN WESLEY was impressed with the

Palatine people of Limerick, and failed to understand why the ruling class of the day did not make better use of their abilities.

"July 9, 1760. I rode over to Killiheen, a German settlement near twenty miles west of Limerick. It rained all the way, but the earnestness of the poor people made us forget it. In the evening I preached to another colony of Germans at Ballygarrane. The third is at Court Matress, a mile from Killiheen. I suppose three such townlands are scarce to be found again in England or Ireland. There is no cursing or swearing, no Sabbath-breaking, no drunkenness, no ale-house in any of them. How will these poor foreigners rise up in the judgement against those who are round about them".

"July 19, 1765. About noon I preached at Ballygarrane to the small remains of the poor Palatines. As they could not get food and raiment here with all their diligence and frugality, part are scattered up and down the kingdom and part are gone to America! Have landlords no common sense (whether they have common humanity or no) that they will suffer such tenants as these to be starved away from them".

THE PALATINES introduced many new farming methods to the native Irish. According to Niall Behan, they were the first to sow potatoes in drills, and brought in new harvesting methods. They cultivated vegetable gardens and orchards, and it is thought that they introduced the brewing of cider to Adare and Pallaskenry. The Palatine custom of keeping flocks of geese in the orchards to manure the soil also led to the perpetration of a joke on a visiting travel writer which resulted in the name Cackagay being given to the cider. The quality of the goose-flesh was improved by the fallen fruit they ate, and so the geese served the Palatines in a practical and economical manner. In 1786, 300 Whiteboys raided the Palatines of Ballinagarrane, took their arms, but left them unharmed.

GERMAN was still their spoken language as late as 1786, according to Ferrar, although its use was then diminishing. They slept in the German fashion, between a mattress and a feather-bolster — or as Begley so quaintly phrased it, "they slept between two beds". They appointed a burgomaster to whom they appealed for the settlement of disputes. In 1840, two English travellers, Mr. & Mrs. Samuel Hall, mentioned that "the elders of the family preserve in great degree the language, customs and religion of their old country; but the younger members mingle and marry with their Irish neighbours. In their dealings they are considered upright and honourable. Like the Quakers of old, they do not interfere with

either politics or religion, are cautious as to land taking and in troublous times, when the generality of persons were afraid to walk forth, the quiet Palatine pursued his avocations, without let or hindrance, being rarely if ever molested".

THE EMBURY AND HECK MEMORIAL CHURCH is the name of the small Methodist church here in Ballinagarrane. The Embury, Heck and Ruttle families were instrumental in the foundation of the Methodist Episcopal Church in America, which has over fourteen million adherents today. The bullock's horn which was used to call the faithful to prayer here in John Wesley's time is on display in the church. Barbara Ruttle was born here in 1734. She married Paul Heck, whose home was on the site now occupied by the church. In June 1760 they emigrated from Limerick on the *Pery* , with Barbara's cousin, Philip Embury, and his wife Margaret (ne Switzer). The two cousins were a formidable team, and their joint efforts and religious fervour were major factors in the propagation of American Methodism. The house in which Philip Embury was born in 1728 has long since disappeared, but a stone plaque marks its site opposite Walter Ruttle's House, Fortview.

THE RUTTLE FAMILY are descended from Casper Ruckell, or Roogall, who was listed as "John" Roogall when he arrived in Ireland in 1715. He was a tenant on the Southwell Estate in 1720, and died in 1751. His son, Sebastian Ruttle was a free-holder in Ballinagarrane in 1747, and the father of Barbara and Paul Ruttle. Paul was a registered free-holder in Ballycahane in 1753. He emigrated to America and married Mary Bowman in New York in 1764. Paul and Barbara Ruttle had two other brothers, Henry (1742-1799) and Daniel (1729-1808). Sebastian Ruttle and his wife, Margaret Embury, Barbara's parents, called their home Ruckle Hill. This building has undergone many changes over the years, is still occupied today, and is now known as Fortview.

BALLINAGARRANE RAILWAY STATION came into existence when the railway line from Limerick to Foynes was built in 1858. The Rathkeale and Newcastle West Junction Railway Company was formed in 1861, and in January 1867 the ten-mile line between Ballinagarrane and Newcastle West opened. After World War II the operations on the line were scaled down and, after 1963, passenger services were discontinued except for special excursions. The line to Rathkeale closed in 1977 but the Ballinagarrane-Foynes line is still in operation.

CROAGH derives its name from *Cruach,* a Rick or Stacked-up Hill. It "appears to have been anciently of considerable importance; so

early as the year 1109, it had a very rich abbey, a corporation and two castles". By 1831 it consisted of one irregular street containing 46 small houses.

CROAGH CHURCH dates from medieval times. This ruined cruciform structure and tower is all that remains of what is believed to have been a collegiate church. It was converted to Protestant worship some time after the Dissolution, and appears to have been in use as late as the 1830s, although by then it was "nearly in ruins; the eastern portion, or chancel, is the only part now roofed". A glebe house was erected for £1,000 in 1831, about half a mile from the village. The other principal houses then in the vicinity were Ballylin, Hollywood, Smithfield, Ballinvira and Newpark.

CROAGH HOUSE was the residence of John Walcott in the early nineteenth century. Originally from Clifton, near Bristol., he built the three Ballylin alms-houses for six poor widows, endowed each of the houses with half an acre of land for a garden, and gave a weekly allowance of five pence to each inmate. He also granted each widow a payment of fifty pence at Easter and Christmas, which was "payable for ever out of his estate at Croagh".

AMIGAN CASTLE was one of several Geraldine castles erected in this region. It was ruined by 1837, but was then remembered as a place where James II slept for one night, after his defeat at the Battle of the Boyne. Samuel Lewis cautiously amended his description of this by adding, "but it is not certain that he came farther south than Waterford. Near it [Amigan Castle] is a small stream, supposed to be efficacious in cutaneous disorders".

SOURCES

9 10 11 13 22 28 32 39 43 47 64 76
105 107 120 123 129 173 184 192 224 233
264 278 282

Cappamore

Abington · Annagh · Murroe · Glenstal · Barrington's Bridge

CAPPAMORE derives its name from *Ceapach Mór,* the Large Plot of Land Laid Down for Tillage. Breandán O'Cíobháin of the Irish Placenames Commission defines *ceapach* as an area cleared of trees in order to accommodate tillage. This is the largest town in the north-eastern part of the county even though it contained only a population of 765 inhabitants in 1986. In 1837 the district of Cappamore included the parish of Tuoragh and part of the parishes of Doon and Abington.

CASTLE GARDE, almost two miles southeast of Cappamore, is a nineteenth-century house which incorporates a medieval tower house within its framework. This latter structure was enlarged and restored in the baronial style by Waller O'Grady in the 1820s. James Pain may have been the architect as the castellated two-storey Gothic-style house attached to one side of the tower-house resembles his, and his brother's, work elsewhere in the counties of Limerick and Clare. The work is typical of the baronial trend of house building popular at the time and has the appearance of a lofty keep and ramparts. The original castle, known as *Kass Lanengard , Castle ne Gaurde,* or Castle Guard, was a Geraldine stronghold but little appears to be known of its earlier history. During the *Civil Survey of 1654* the Earl of Bath was in possession. Henry Baylee and his son, John, were listed as its *tituladoes* in 1659. The castle changed hands several times before it became an O'Grady property. The present owner, Hugh Thompson, inherited Castle Garde from the O'Gradys.

THE PARISH OF DOON was the haunt of a famous *rapparee,* Eamon an Chnoic O Riain, Edmund of the Hills O'Ryan, during the early eighteenth century. Towards the end of that century more than 100 acres of bog moved from one townlanán into two others; destroyed thirteen cabins, and killed the inmates of five of them.

THE RYANS OF MUNSTER derive their name from *O Maoilriaghain,* the descendant of *Maolriain,* the Follower of *Rian* or *Riaghan.* The family originated in Leinster but settled in *Uaithne-Tire* and *Uaithne-Cliach,* now respectively the barony of Owney in County Tipperary and the barony of Owney Beg in County Limerick, in the thirteenth or fourteenth century. The Ryans became a numerous and powerful family in this region, along the Limerick-Cork border. In 1610 William Ryan surrendered his holdings in the barony of Owney O'Mulrian to James I and received them back by letters patent. During the confiscations of the seventeenth century the family lost their property. By 1890 the Ryan surname had become the eighth most common surname in Ireland. It is now the most numerous name in County Tipperary and has been listed as one of the 200 commonest names in the United States of America. Variants of the Munster surname include *O Maoilriain, O'Mulrigan, O'Mulryan, O'Mulrean,* Mulryan, Mulroyan, Mulryne, Mulrine, Mulrain and O'Ryan. The original Ryan surname originated in *U i Dròna,* the Barony of Idrone, County Carlow, as *O Riaghain* or *O Riain,* meaning the descendant of *Riaghan* or *Rian.* The surname is confused with *O Ruaidhin,* the descendant of *Ruaidhin* (the diminutive of red) a Connaught family name.

DOON, like Cappamore, was located in the old parish of Doon, the patron saint of which was St. Fintan of *Dunbleschiae,* the brother of St. Findlugan of *Tamlaght Finlagen.* St. Fintan's feast-day was observed on 3 January and his holy well was the scene of devotions into modern times according to *The Book of Saints* (1921) compiled by the Benedictine monks of St. Augustine's Abbey, Ramsgate. Like many other early Irish ecclesiastical sites St. Fintan's sixth-century foundation ceased to exist some time before the eleventh century.

LORD STANLEY donated a two-acre site, rent-free, to the Catholic population of Doon village in the 1830s. By 1837 a Catholic church had been erected on a small hill which, like Doon, nestled into the south-western slopes of Gortnageragh. A Church of Ireland church had been built in 1800, quite possibly on the site of an earlier foundation as Eamon an Chnoic O Riain was buried in its small church-yard. Samuel Lewis described

the land of the parish as remarkably rich in some areas but poorly developed and prone to flooding by the Dead and Mulkear rivers. Another nearby river is called after the townland through which it flows, *Beàl-Àth-Bò,* the Mouth of the Ford of the Cow. Over 150 years ago fine quality freestone was quarried here for use in public buildings under construction in Limerick City, and elsewhere, and large quantities were shipped abroad, mainly to England.

TUOGH derives its name from the word *Tuath,* a District. In the 1820s Rev. R. Fitzgerald wrote: "The parish of Tuogh Island, in the union of Abington is in the diocese of Emly, and contains 1067 acres of land. In this parish situated on the river Mulchair, was the ancient mansion of the Hayes family, and also Tower-Hill, a fine house and demesne belonging to the Rev. Rickard Lloyd". John O'Donovan explained in 1840 how Tower Hill got its name when he wrote; "This hill is called Tower Hill, which name is also extended to the townland of Tuogh, and which the hill obtained, it is said from three towers that formerly stood on it, whose site is occupied by Towerhill House, the seat of Wm. Lloyd, Esq., built in 1800 at the expense of £1,500. These towers probably, were the yokes or follies erected either as ornaments, or as objects of no consequent utility, but for the purpose of employing, during the building of them, such persons as were in a state of extreme want, and had no daily engagements in work, which might afford them a means of obtaining the necessaries of life". O'Donovan also recorded a *cillín,* or children's burial-ground, known as *Cill Mhuire,* Mary's Church, in the western extremity of Pallisbeg townland; St. Brigid's Well, *Tobar Brìghde,* or Toberbreeda, in the eastern part of Tuogh townland" within a short distance to the north of the road running through this townland"; and the remains of a church in Tuogh of which only the eastern gable remained in 1840. By then the "foundation of the rest of the building is not traceable ... there is a small building attached to the south side of this ruin which is on a line with the east gable and runs southward ... this appears to be coeval with

Street scene, Cappamore.

the church".

TOOMALINE HOUSE is believed to have been a priory of the Canons Regular before it was converted to private use after the Dissolution of the Monasteries. Queen Elizabeth I granted it to Miler Magrath, the famous Archbishop of Cashel, who like Murrough the Burner O'Brien, was all things to all men. Like Murrough, Miler is believed to have died a Catholic. Both men had a talent for survival. Miler served as a Catholic or Protestant bishop whenever the occasion warranted it and, more often than not, served both churches in a dual role. In 1837 Lewis noted that both Templebuie and Castletown churches were in ruin and that Castletown derived its name from a fourteenth-century O'Hurley castle, to the north of Castletown Church.

ABINGTON may be a corruption of Abbeyowny, a derivation of *Mainistir Uaithne,* the Monastery of *Uaithne,* Woney, Wotheney, or Wodney. This was the name of the territory in which it was located, a name still remembered in the baronies of *Owney-Beg* and *Owney-Arra.* The name may have been anglicised to Abington by somebody, now long dead, who was familiar with the English village of Avington, near Winchester, in Hampshire.

WOTHENEY ABBEY, or Abbeyowny, was founded by Theobald Walter, Butler of Ireland, Lord of Carrick, and the ancestor of the Butlers, Earls of Ormond. Some time before 1204 he transferred a colony of monks from Wyresdale, Lancashire, an abbey he had endowed in 1196, to Ireland. In 1205 he granted land to these Cistercians, in Abington, and the original church of St. Mary de Wodeney dates from then. Theobald was

buried here in 1206. The monks recognised the Abbey of Savignac in France as their mother-house and the Wyresdale colony, transferred to Abington, were augmented by others from France. King John favoured Wotheney with extensive land grants, and its abbot sat as a spiritual peer in the Irish House of Lords. In 1290 one Abbot was fined for sheltering the King's enemies while another, Hugh, mortgaged Thurles Church to the Company of the Ricardi of Lucca in 1292.

JOHN WOGAN, Lord Justice of Ireland, accepted the Abbot's oath of fealty in 1295. This Abbot may have been Thomas who was deposed from the abbacy in 1297. A licence for the election of a new abbot was granted on 25 April of the same year. Theobald Butler, the fifth of that family, was interred here on 27 May, 1299. In 1307 the abbot was recorded as having paid an annual pension of £5 to the prior of Kells. The abbot of St. Thomas, Dublin, recovered the right of patronage (advowson) to the church of Loghmoy, Tipperary, from Wotheney Abbey in 1341. This business of dealing in advowsons occupied the abbot's affairs in 1342 and 1363. Thomas, the abbot in 1365, was jailed but later released on payment of a £2 fine for annoying Thomas de Kildare. William Odwirti, archdeacon of Emly, was appointed abbot in 1428. He resigned in 1437 but retained the abbey unlawfully for another three years. On 25 June, 1537, the O Mulrian, lord of this region, Ulick Bourke of Clanrickard, and Thybot Bourk McWilliam, submitted to the Lord Deputy here, and swore an oath of allegiance to the Crown. Lord Deputy Grey was later accused, in 1540, of forcing the abbot of Wotheney to pay him £40

in order to preserve his abbey from destruction. According to the *Annals of the Four Masters,* the abbey was burned by O'Carroll in 1550. Queen Mary confirmed a grant of the abbey, made by Edward VI, to Walter Aphoell in 1553. By 1540 the abbey had become a secular establishment. The last abbot, John O'Mulrian, in 1553 held eight rectories, had an interest in eight others, owned at least 1,680 acres of land and "the site of the abbey, a church and two chambers of no value". The abbey still existed early in the seventeenth century, and the title of abbot was apparently revived as it was recorded in 1684. In 1562 the lease on the Abbey lands had passed to Captain Piers (Peter) Walshe. He erected a mansion nearby. In 1641 the Walshe family estates were forfeited to the Crown. Six years later Murrough the Burner O'Brien destroyed the buildings of this old Cistercian foundation at the head of a Parliamentarian force. Two centuries later only fragments of the house and abbey remained near the old Church of Ireland church, which was a small neat edifice without tower or spire. Today only the graveyard remains. By 1967 vandals had destroyed the remains of a Renaissance monument erected by Patrick Kerin in 1618 to commemorate Sir Edward Walshe.

THE POPULATION of Abington was 591 persons in 1981. By 1986 the figure had risen to 613.

ECUMENISM was practised in 1821 when Dr. John Jebb, the Church of Ireland Rector of Abington, joined Fr. Costello, a Catholic priest, at the altar of the Catholic church in Murroe. They addressed the congregation together and succeeded in quelling agrarian revolt in the area. Abington remained "like Gideon's fleece, the only inviolate spot", throughout this troubled period. Rev. John Jebb was rector for thirteen years, had great influence amongst the Catholic population, and later became the Church of Ireland Bishop of Limerick.

CASTLE COMFORT was built for £800 in 1824 and occupied the site of an old castle of the same name. In 1837 it was the home of Fr. T. O'Brien, the Catholic parish priest of Costelloe. His Protestant counterpart, Rev. Thomas P. Le Fanu, Dean of Emly, occupied the Glebe House. He was father of Sheridan Le Fanu, the Victorian novelist, and had brought his family to live in Abington in 1826. Other large houses of the period were Borroe Ville, occupied by Doctor Wilkins; Maddebuoy House, of Captain Wickham; Balovarane, of T. Holland; Ash Row, of T. Evans; Farnane, of Mrs. Costello; Lillypot, of Mrs. Bradshaw; and Lord Carberry's Deer Park.

ANNAGH derives its name from *Eanach,*

Glenstal Abbey.

Marsh. In 1840 Annagh Old Church, in the northern part of the townland, was described as a ruin about 60 feet by 20 feet, with walls reaching to a height of 10 feet. Fred Bourke of Clonlara told me that Annagh was a favourite meeting-place, or battle-ground, for those early nineteenth-century faction-fighters, the Ryans and the Coffeys.

MURROE is located quite close to the Tipperary border, below the foothills of the Slievefelim Mountains which still form the north-eastern boundary of Abington parish. Murroe derives its name, the Russet Plain, from the red sandstone area on which it was built, and owes its past prosperity to the Barrington family with whom it had a long association. In 1811 a Catholic church was built in the village. During the 1880s Lord Cloncurry had a series of evictions carried out on his holdings in the area. The Land League came to the aid of the dispossessed tenant farmers and erected huts to house the homeless people. Canon John Hayes, the founder of *Muintir na Tìre*, a rural community-based co-operative orgaisation was born in one of these huts, in Murroe, in 1887.

THE CLARE GLENS is the name of the region through which the Clare River flows, along the length of a magnificent red sandstone gorge, creating many attractive cascades, waterfalls and pools en route. The Barrington family owned the Glens until 1927

when they donated them to the Limerick and North Tipperary county councils.

GLENSTAL CASTLE was built for Sir Matthew Barrington (1788-1861) who left the city in 1818 to reside at Clonkeen House near Barrington's Bridge. He purchased the Carbery estate for £30,193.74 and commissioned the Pain brothers to design a house for him in the townland of Glenstal. He subsequently rejected their plans and employed William Bardwell, a London architect, who produced an alternative design and suggested changing the location of the house to the townland of Garranbane, White Nag. The original name, Glenstal Castle, was retained. Work on it commenced in 1837 and the first part, the Windsor-style round-tower, gatehouse and long facade, were completed by 1839. Work on the house stopped until 1846. It continued under the direction of a Dublin architect, named Dargan, who implemented Bardwell's design, and John Kelly, who supervised the work from 1847 to 1849. In 1853 Joshua Hargraves, a Cork architect, was employed to continue the work. He modified the Bardwell plans and completed the house. Work continued on parts of this massive sandstone structure as late as 1880 and, under the Barringtons, the estate and gardens were a constant hive of activity. The main building is a large Windsor-style square keep, or tower, three storeys high, joined by a lower range of

buildings to a round tower. Its entrance door is flanked by stone figures of Henry II and Eleanor of Aquitaine while another stone figure, that of a soldier, mans the look-out tower. A local man, named White, carved the main drawing-room doorway which is a copy of the Romanesque doorway in Killaloe Cathedral. Another local, Sheil, may have done the carving in the octagonal-shaped library with its central pier containing a stone fire-place and a stone-ribbed vault springing from carved capitals.

THE BARRINGTON FAMILY lived in Glenstal Castle until the 1920s. Their relationship with the locals deteriorated during the War of Independence. The castle was raided for arms in 1920 and the Tricolour put on its flag-pole. On 14 May 1921, Winifred Barrington, Sir Charles Barrington's only daughter, was mortally wounded in an I.R.A. ambush. She died later that day in her own home. Her boyfriend, Captain Biggs, was a Black and Tan officer. The attack was an attempt to assassinate Biggs as Winifred and he returned, by car, from Killaloe to Glenstal. Winifred was wearing a Black and Tan cap, as she travelled, and was mistaken for a Black and Tan. Biggs ran for cover and was killed before he could return fire.

GLENSTAL ABBEY is now the name of Glenstal Castle. The Barringtons offered the house to the new Free State Government as an official residence for the President in 1925. The offer was declined. In 1926 Monsignor James J. Ryan purchased the house and grounds for £2,000 in the belief that it would make an ideal site for a Benedictine monastery. The Barringtons moved to Hampshire, England. In 1957 Glenstal Castle was given abbey status. It is now both a boys' boarding-school and an abbey. On 25 June 1964 Glenstal was the venue for one of the first ecumenical meetings between members of the different churches in Ireland.

THE ABBEY CHURCH has four three-light windows installed by Patrick Pye in 1960, 1961 and 1964, and another one installed by Patrick Pollen. Its foundation-stone was laid on 27 June, 1930 and the completed building was blessed on 13 April, 1932. A pre-fabricated building, nearby, is one of several huts bought by the Benedictines after the completion of the Shannon Hydroelectric Scheme.

PETER HARBISON was educated at Glenstal Abbey. In 1965 he became the first person outside the German-speaking world to be awarded the German Archaeological Institute's Travelling Scholarship since its institution in 1859. In 1966 he joined the Irish Tourist Board, *Bord Fáilte,* as their archaeological officer. He produced his *Guide to the National Monuments in the Republic of Ireland including a selection of other monuments not in State care* in 1970. This is an invaluable guide book to the archaeological and historical monuments of his native country, and a very interesting and readable book. It has not been out of print since it first appeared.

RUGBY may have been introduced into Ireland by Sir Charles Barrington who was educated in Rugby.

CAPPANAHANNAGH, north of Murroe, contains a roofless prehistoric chamber tomb known as *Tuaim an Fhir Mhóir,* the Big Man's Tomb.

THE TOWNLAND OF GLENSTAL is north-east of Glenstal Castle. Its name is derived from *Gleann Stail,* the Valley of the Stallion.

THE CAPPERCULLEN MASS ROCK is located in the ravine of the same name within the grounds of Glenstal Castle. Mass was heard here in Penal times between 1650 and 1700. A William III penny was found in this secluded glen, which would suggest it was in use at the time of the Williamite siege of Limerick. Folklore referred to this deep valley as *An Séipéal,* the Chapel. W.T. Le Fanu designed a stone bridge to link the townlands of Cappercullen and Garranbane for the Barringtons, about the time they laid out several artificial lakes and extended the terraced garden, originally built between 1679 and 1781, to include an orchard.

CAPPERCULLEN HOUSE, was the residence of Standish O'Grady in 1772 and part of the Fourth Lord Carbery's estate, at the time of his death in 1804. It was located on the site of the Glenstal Abbey tennis-courts.

THE GLENSTAL HOARD is a collection of Bronze Age tools discovered on the estate of Sir Charles Barrington in the 1890s and now in the National Museum.

BARRINGTON'S BRIDGE derived its name from an elegant one-arched cast-iron bridge built over the Mulkear river by Sir Matthew Barrington in 1818.

CLONKEEN CHURCH is an extremely old building. Lewis believed that it was of Saxon or early Norman architecture. The antae, projections of the north and south walls beyond the gables, an architectural hangover from the wooden churches, lend credence to this suggestion. Peter Harbison wrote that the round-headed window in the north wall dated from the twelfth century, mentioned that the eastern two-thirds of the church dated from the fifteenth century, and described the doorway as

Barrington's Bridge.

"well-preserved Romanesque ... with bulbous capitals, a decorative pillar and a head at the top". This small ancient structure is located in the middle of a graveyard. It was founded in the sixth or seventh century by a St. Modimoc or St. Mó-Diómóg. In 1089, it was plundered by Ruaidhri Ua Conchobhair and Domhnall Ua Maeleachlainn who "scarcely left a single head of cattle" in Munster and carried off many captives. In 1111 it was incorporated into the diocese of Emly, and in 1200 its revenue was used to support the Bishop of Emly's table. Some time after that it was handed over to the Cistercians of Wotheney Abbey. This church was in ruin by 1657 but it must have been repaired some time afterwards as it was used as a Church of Ireland church until 1762, when it was damaged by the Whiteboys. A vandal carved his initials on the Romanesque doorway in 1779.

CALEB POWELL (1793-1881) lived at Clonshavoy, near Murroe until William Hartigan Barrington purchased it some time after 1858. William's descendants were still living there a century later. When Robert Cussen bought a book over thirty years ago, in a Limerick bookshop, he found lists of presentments, made by the Grand Jury of the County of Limerick. Some additional pages had been bound between two lists, and on examination he found memoranda written by Caleb Powell. There were posthumous memoirs composed by Caleb who having "derived some instruction and much amusement in the perusal of posthumous memoirs, I have resolv'd to record in the interest of those who shall become entitled to my papers and manuscripts after my decease, some facts within my knowledge connected with those gentlemen of the County Limerick who plac'd by me on the Grand Jury during my occupation of the Office of Sheriff (a barren eminence upon which I was fixed quite unsolicited by me) ... ". Caleb then provided a series of short pithy, witty biographies of each man he had selected for his Grand Jury of 1858. His thumbnail sketches throw an interesting — one wonders how true! — light on well-known names; Davy Roche was an expert in procuring young peasant girls for the 4th Lord Carbery; Hugh Massy O'Grady committed suicide when he discovered his sister Nina had been seduced by her brother-in-law; Colonel John Vandeleur's parents' first marriage was invalid; John White of Belmont was very much under the control of the priest; Samuel Frederick Dicksen was an honourable eccentric of a penurious disposition; Henry Lyons of Croom was a self sufficient coxcomb; and several other Grand Jurors mentioned, by Caleb, are referred to elsewhere. Robert Cussen wrote an enlightening article

Romanesque doorway of Clonkeen Church.

based on the Powell Papers in *North Munster Studies* which was produced by the Thomond Archaeological Society, and edited by Etienne Rynne, in 1967. Caleb Powell was descended from Robert Powell, a Cromwellian officer, who received extensive land grants around the City of Limerick. He was married to Georgina Waller, Prior Park, County Tipperary and had one son and four daughters. He was a liberal, witty, humourous, enlightened, broadminded, and, in his writings, somewhat mischieviously malicious man.

THE GREAT HUNGER did not affect this area as seriously as it did others. Work on Barrington's Glenstal Castle and on roadworks instigated by Caleb Powell offset the worst effects of the famine. On 25 March, 1847, in *The Times*, Lord Monteagle spoke deploringly and earnestly of the idleness of the Irish people, and their reliance on others and their mendicant propensities. Unproductive works were the hallmark of the Great Hunger. Bridges and piers for which there was no purpose or necessity, and roads that began where there was no need for them, and led to nowhere in particular, were constructed.

THE IRISH REPUBLICAN ARMY, previously known as the Irish Volunteers, organ-ised companies in 1913-1914 from which they later developed a battalion organisation which was then further divided into brigades. The county had four battalions in 1916; a Limerick City battalion, a Doon-Castleconnell battalion, a West Limerick battalion and a Galtee battalion. All of which, including four Clare battalions, formed the Limerick Command under Michael Colivet. The threat of conscription led to an increase in membership for a while in 1918, but few of these new members became active once the threat had passed. After the War of Independence many of them qualified for I.R.A. pensions, claiming that they had worked in intelligence, and undercover, during the Troubles. They were known as the "piss-pot" volunteers because they had, presumably, spent the war years hiding under their beds, clutching chamber-pots. Between 1919 and 1921 the county had three active I.R.A. brigades, the West Limerick, Mid Limerick and East Limerick Brigades.

SOURCES
9 11 12 13 26 34 39 44 47 66 76 86
107 120 123 129 150 151 159 192 195 233
238 255 258 282

Castleconnell

Worrall's End · The Falls of Doonass · Montpelier

CASTLECONNELL was originally known as *Mur Mic an Duinn,* the Fortress of Donn's Son. Donn was a common name in Celtic mythology, but the son of Donn commemorated here may have been Eogabal, the father of Fer Fi and Aíne of Knockainy, Gods of the *Eoghanacht* who were venerated in this region before the coming of St. Patrick. Castleconnell derives its name from *Caisleán Uí Chonaill,* O'Connells' Castle, which is a corruption of *Caisleán Ui gConaing,* O'Gunnings' Castle.

THE O'GUNNING, or *O Conaing,* family held sway over that length of countryside which stretched along the Shannon from Castleconnell to Carrigogunnell, *Carraig O' gConaing.* Before the Anglo-Norman invasion, they were Lords of *Aos Greine,* which was conterminous with the later barony of Clanwilliam. *O Conaing* or *O gConaing* was later Anglicised to O'Gunnng, Gunning or Cunning. The Gunnings were *Eoghanacht* chieftains, kinsmen of the O'Briens, and they ruled here until they were ousted by the O'Briens and Bourkes. By 1923 the surname had virtually disappeared from the county.

CASTLECONNELL CASTLE was located on the summit of a steep flat-topped rock plateau close to the town, within a short distance of the River Shannon. The ruin is so badly damaged that it is virtually impossible to describe it as anything other than a mound, with the remains of the south-western and north-western towers protruding. The original structure had four corner towers and a large court-yard, the dimensions of which can still be traced, 160 feet by 100 feet. In the seventeenth-century Down Survey, the castle is depicted as a fortified house rather than a military stronghold. Ginkel ordered its destruction in September 1691. Eighty-four barrels of gunpowder were used to demolish both of the former Gunning castles of Castleconnell and Carrigogunnell. The large blocks of masonry scattered around the mound and plateau date from this period.

THE O'BRIENS took over from the Gunnings who had erected the first defensive structure here. No date has been given for the

foundation of the first stronghold on this site, nor is there one available for when the O'Briens came into possession. In 1174 Dermot O'Brien was in residence here. He entertained his nephew, Domhnall Mór O'Brien, when Domhnall Mór was returning from his victory at Thurles. Domhnall repaid his hospitality by blinding both Dermot and Mahon O'Brien in order to prevent them from succeeding to the Kingdom of Thomond. Dermot died a few days later. In 1200 Cathal Crobhderg O'Connor attacked and burned the bawn of Castleconnell.

THE DE BURGO FAMILY came into possession of Castleconnell through William de Burgo's marriage to Domhnall Mor O'Brien's daughter, and a grant from King John in 1201. William erected a castle which he fortified on the King's orders, after John had assured him that if the Crown required the castle, he (William) would receive another in exchange for it. The de Burgos retained their royal grant. The King of Thomond, Conor na Siudaine O'Brien, was involved in a war with the *Ui Bloid* of eastern Thomond in 1261. He entrusted the command of his army to Brian Roe O'Brien, his son. Brian attacked Castleconnell Castle, destroyed it and killed the garrison. Walter de Burgo repaired, enlarged and strengthened the castle. The de Burgo surname has been anglicised to Bourke, Burke or de Burgh, and is generally rendered in Irish as *de Búrca* or *de Búrc.* The Bourkes of Limerick became Lords of Clanwilliam and allied themselves with the O'Briens of Thomond during the fourteenth century. Clanwilliam derived its name from William Bourke, the son of Edmond Mac An Iarla Bourke, and Slainy O'Brien, the daughter of Turlough O'Brien. Sir William Bourke was married to a daughter of the Great Earl of Desmond, and sided with him in the wars of 1569 and 1575. When Sir Philip Sidney visited Limerick in 1575, William Bourke and his kinsmen submitted to Queen Elizabeth and were confirmed in their estates. James Fitzmaurice Fitzgerald failed in his attempts to persuade the Bourkes into rebellion. In frustration, he ordered his followers to requisition horses, forcibly, from the Bourkes.

Theobald Bourke, William's eldest son and heir, refused to hand over his mounts to the rebels, when they encountered him with a party of gallowglasses he had borrowed from the O'Briens, in a wood near what is now Barrington's Bridge. Theobald Bourke, his brother Ulick, and James Fitzmaurice Fitzgerald were killed in the ensuing skirmish which took place one month after the Spaniards landed in Smerwick in 1579. On 16 May 1580 William was created a peer with the title of Lord Baron Bourke of Castleconnell. He died in 1584 and was succeeded by Theobald's son, John. In 1592 John Bourke, who had been living in London, was about to participate in a duel on Hounslow Heath when his opponent, Captain Arnold Cosby, stabbed him in the back as he was dismounting from his horse. John Bourke died, and Cosby was hanged for murder.

RICHARD BOURKE, John's brother, succeeded him as Lord Castleconnell. During the Sugán Earl of Desmond's revolt, Richard sided with the Crown. While patrolling his territory, he became suspicious of what appeared to be an enemy force approaching him. Richard initiated hostilities, killed the leader of the other group and routed his escort, only to discover that he had attacked his own allies and killed Sir Thomas Norris, the Lord President of Munster. Norris was succeeded by Sir George Carew, but no action seems to have been taken against Richard by the Crown. Soon afterwards, Richard tried to claim the lands of Portcrusha from the widow of the Fourth Baron Inchiquin. His followers attacked harvesters on the disputed holding and drove them back into Clare. Several of the Bourke men, including Richard's uncle, another Ulick, were killed in the conflict. When the O'Connors travelled south to help the Sugán Earl, they were harassed by the Bourkes and the O'Ryans. The Connaughtmen made a stand at Bunbristy Bridge, now Grange, where, reinforced by the Fitzgeralds of Lough Gur, they defeated the Castleconnell forces, killing Richard Bourke and his younger brother, Thomas, in battle.

EDMUND BOURKE, the son of Thomas, succeeded to the title as Richard had been

Aerial view of Castleconnell.

killed before Thomas. Despite this Edmund's uncle, Theobald, assumed the title of Lord Castleconnell during Edmund's minority and sat as a peer in the Parliament of 1613. When his nephew came of age, Theobald questioned his legitimacy and refused to surrender the castle and lands of Castleconnell. Theobald spent seven months, as a prisoner, in Dublin Castle until he renounced all claim on his English-educated nephew's estate in December 1619. He had to give a security for £3000 not to interfere with his nephew before he was freed. Edmund died in 1638 and was succeeded by his son William.

WILLIAM BOURKE reverted to Catholicism, and sat amongst the peers in the General Assembly which took place in Kilkenny in 1642. His support of the Confederate Irish, with whom he played a prominent role, led to the loss of his estates and forced him to flee to France. In 1651 Ireton garrisoned Castleconnell Castle with Cromwellian troops, but after the Restoration the Bourkes returned to Castleconnell. Another William, the Eighth Lord Castleconnell, became Lord Lieutenant of the county and city, took his seat in the Irish Parliament of 1687-1689, sided with James II, became a Lieutenant-Colonel in Colonel Hugh Sutherland's Regiment of Horse, and fought in the Battle of Aughrim. He went to France after the fall of Limerick and died there, unmarried. The title passed to his relation John Bourke, the Fourth Lord Brittas. The Brittas Bourkes had also fought on the Stuart side, and both titles became extinct with the death of John's great-grandson, a captain in Rothe's Irish Regiment and a Knight of St. Louis, who died unmarried. The last member of this family in Ireland died in 1762. This was Rickard de Burgh of Dromkeene, a Member of Parliament for Naas. He bequeathed his estates to Chief Baron Walter Hussey, who took the name of De Burgh.

CASTLECONNELL CASTLE was manned by a Jacobite garrison of 126 men under the command of Captain Barnwell in August, 1690. They surrendered to a Williamite force led by Brigadier Stuart, who had threatened the castle with four field pieces. The Williamites held Castleconnell Castle until their first siege of Limerick City was raised. They blew up the castle after abandoning it, but it must not have been too badly damaged on this occasion, as 250 Jacobite Irish were in occupation again on 27 August 1691. Two days later this garrison also surrendered to the Prince of Hesse, who had marched on it "with his own regiment, Colonel Tiffin's and Colonel St. John's, five pieces of cannon, and about 700 horse and dragoons". One month later the castle was demolished, with gunpowder, to prevent the Jacobites from occupying it again.

ALL SAINTS' CHURCH OF IRELAND CHURCH is a comparatively modern building, insofar as the present structure was erected in 1809 to replace an older parish church, the remains of which can still be seen within the church-yard. This earlier foundation was established as a monastery about 1300. It was called *Idumyn* in 1302; Donald O'Mullryn was listed as the vicar of *Castra Conayng* in 1412; and in 1615 the village was known as Stradbally alias *Capella de I'dum*. In 1633 this church was a rectory, impropriate to the Earl of Ormond. The present structure was enlarged in 1830, into "a beautiful cruciform edifice with a lofty octagonal spire". The walls of All Saints' Church are lined with memorials dedicated to the various members of once-prominent families who resided in the area. The pulpit was built in 1910 to commemorate John Ulick Bourke of Thornfields; the brass lectern was donated in memory of the Sixth Baron Massey who died in 1915; and the panelling around the chancel came from St. John's Church, in Newport, which was demolished in 1963. The Lords' Gallery is still visible, although it is no longer in use and has been boarded-up. Beside the church is a Tudor-style house built for the sexton of All Saints' Church.

ST. JOSEPH'S CATHOLIC CHURCH was erected between 1863 and 1867, to replace an older building at the bottom of Chapel Hill which dated from 1797. The present structure was designed by W.E. Corbett, and was built in the Gothic-style architecture so popular at the time. John White of Belmont is commemorated with a stained-glass window, while the altar was presented by Helenus White in 1865.

CLOON CHURCH is a small early medieval church which may date from the eleventh century. There are two cross-slabs set into its western wall which may date from this period. Little else is now known about the building, which is also believed to have been a Franciscan friary founded by Renald de Burgo in 1291. In 1837 this church was located on an island which was then connected to the mainland by a causeway 23 feet wide. The level of the river has since dropped, and in the intervening years the island has become an integral part of the mainland. The ruin was converted into an out-house for Island House during the early 1800s but over the intervening years the owners of Island House have preserved this ancient ecclesiastical structure, which is now the chief architectural feature of the attractive garden. A short distance from the west door of Cloon Church there is a large stone which contains a peculiar hollowed-out section.

ISLAND HOUSE derives its name from the island on which it was built, *Inis-cluan,* the Island of the meadow, or Cloon Island. The house was originally built, as a fishing-lodge, for a wealthy Welsh coal-mine owner. In 1837 the island contained four acres of ground and the only access to it, other than by boat, was the causeway. In 1866 Island House was the residence of Sir Richard Donnellan de Burgo. This house is very like Annaly Lodge, Broadford, County Clare.

SIR RICHARD DE BURGO, Baronet, owned most of the land around Castleconnell, which was also known as Stradbally, during the eighteenth century. He had inherited the estates of Lord Castleconnell through his grandfather, Richard Bourke of Dromsally, who died in 1734. Robert Herbert was unable to determine what connection existed between the Castleconnells and this branch of the Bourkes, nor did he know why they had inherited the Castleconnell holdings, nor could he discover where the Bourkes of Dromsally had lived before 1734. Richard was created a baronet in 1785 and assumed the name de Burgo. The family continued to hold lands in the area into modern times. When Robert Herbert was writing of Castleconnell in 1948, the family was then represented by the Bourkes of Thornfields.

STRADBALLY, another name for Castleconnell, is a derivative of *Stradbhaile* or *Sraíd Bhaile,* meaning Street-Town or Town of One Street, a name which may have been applied to the village which developed about the castle. In 1837 the village contained 178 houses, many of which were large villas and cottages which can still be seen about the neighbourhood. There were "two good hotels and a number of commodious lodging-houses in the town; a coach runs daily to Limerick, and there is a daily post ... the bulk of the inhabitants are agriculturists, or dependent on the visitors to the spa; but many obtain employment in cutting turf and conveying it to Limerick, particularly for its large distillery; River Lawn, a mile below the town", had an extensive bleach-green, a cloth mill and Taylor's Sawmill in which spools and bobbins for the cloth mill, next door, were produced, as well as household furniture.

THE CASTLECONNELL SPA made the village a popular resort during the late eighteenth and early nineteenth centuries. Treatises were written on the nature of the spa waters, and many people claimed they had been cured by these waters which "resemble those of Spa in Germany, and are considered efficacious in scorbutic affections, liver complaint, jaundice and worms. They are a strong chalybeate, having a mixture of earth and marine salt". This was a famous and well-patronised spa resort to which the Ascendancy class flocked from all over Ireland. In its heyday it rivalled Mallow; assembly rooms were built in which balls were held twice weekly; and the Castleconnell Club was founded for the entertainment of the young bucks and dandies who wished to drink and gamble for high stakes. In 1834 Henry D. Inglis remarked that houses are scarce and dear, and that even a small house cost £10 a month to rent. Three years later Samuel Lewis wrote that the waters of the well were "enclosed in a mean yard".

THE SPA ASSEMBLY ROOMS were erected in 1738 to cater for the gentry who assembled here for dancing and other entertainments. As business declined the rooms fell into disuse, and, eventually disrepair. In more recent times it was renovated and converted into an attractive house, and the old medicinal well and pump-house were restored. It is now known as Spa House.

FISHING replaced the spa waters as the area's main attraction towards the end of the nineteenth and early twentieth centuries. The Enright family owned a rod and tackle factory, and specialised in the production of a long heavy durable fishing rod which became known as the Castleconnell Rod. This was the ideal rod for catching salmon, which usually ran to over 30lbs in weight in those days. In 1879 a 53lb salmon was caught here, and in 1896 and 1904 John Enright successfully competed in World tournaments with his own rod and tackle gear. The rods were manufactured for the Enrights by the Hogg family, who were of Scottish origin. Fly-tying was also developed by the Enrights, who kept an aviary of tropical birds in their back garden in order to ensure a constant supply of exotic feathers. The Shannon Hydroelectric Scheme put an end to salmon fishing in Castleconnell, although eel and coarse fishing still continue. John Enright died in 1908. His factory closed in the 1930s. A small river-boat designed for, and used in, these waters was known as the Castleconnell Cott. There is a small memorial tablet on the river bank downstream from River Lawn, which states that "Benny fished here. None better."

THE TONTINES are a block of four three-storey Georgian houses built opposite Cloon Island in 1812. Tontines were usually formed by public subscription, particularly during the eighteenth and early nineteenth centuries. A limited number of people usually agreed to invest a certain sum of money, each, in a particular enterprise over a specified period. At the end of that designated time, the company, or tontine, would wind up its affairs and distribute all of its assets and monies amongst its surviving members, as only those who were still alive at that stage could participate. Relatives, or next of kin, of those who had died before the tontine redistributed its assets had no claim; only the survivors could benefit. The tontine was called after its inventor, Lorenzo Tonti. Tontines eventually became illegal in some countries, as their members tried to "assist" nature with the "odd accident", or two, in the hope of furthering their own claims. These houses here were erected by W. Gabbett. They did not come up to their subscribers' expectations and were sold off. Bulmer Hobson, a founder member of the Irish Republican Brotherhood, lived in No. 1

Street scene at Castleconnell.

from 1964 until he died there in 1969. The Church of Ireland rectory, or glebe house, was located in No. 4, the largest house, until recent times. During World War II the four houses were occupied by the Irish Army. They are now privately owned, modernised, and have been restored in keeping with the Georgian architecture.

THE HERMITAGE was built for George Evans Bruce of Cork, who arrived here from London, in 1789, purchased the Hermitage estate, and tried to establish himself as a country gentleman. Bruce was a notorious character with a most unsavoury reputation. He married for wealth; was caught cheating at play in Miles's Club in London; fled to France where he made £90,000 by gambling; was ostracised by his fellow Grand Jurors who refused to sit in the jury box with him in Limerick; incited the poor to revolt in order to prove his worth as a magistrate; ill-treated his wife; had a son by his sister-in-law; derided religion; professed to be an atheist; corrupted the youth of the area; betrayed the secrets of the jury room; changed his mistress as often as his clothes; acted as a pimp to Lord Headford in the seduction of Mrs. Massy; and when Furnell's Bank, in Limerick, collapsed in 1806, he opened a bank there in order to place his enemies within his power by first giving them loans and then forcing his company, which they would otherwise have avoided, on them. He founded the Limerick County Club in 1813, and was on the verge of social success until he ran foul of Tom O'Grady. His house was purchased by the Massy family in 1802. It was burned during the War of Independence in 1920, and the ruin

was demolished in 1970. A modern bungalow was built on the site, and only the gates of the original estate remain.

BELMONT HOUSE was the home of Thomas "Spectacles" O'Grady, a member of the Irish Bar, an accomplished scholar and a brilliant satirist. He spoke in favour of the Union:- "The Irish are only the rump of an aristocracy. Shall I visit posterity with a system of war, pestilence and famine? No. Give me a Union. United with that country where all is peace, order and prosperity. Without a union we shall see embryo chief justices, attorney-generals in perspective and animacula sergeants". The failure of his marriage soured his outlook on life. He retired from the Bar — Lord Clare had made him a county judge after hearing his speech in favour of the Union — and from society. He became a bitter misanthropic recluse, and his merciless wit was reflected in his writing. The victims of his satirical poems were usually corrupt or dishonest, and he spared no one. Lady Clare, his next-door neighbour, was the target of *The Flesh-Brush,* and his former colleagues featured in *The Barrister.* In 1810 he borrowed £1,300 from George Evans Bruce. Bruce demanded the money back in 1812. O'Grady immediately repaid the loan but the two men quarrelled. Bruce circulated anonymous letters besmirching O'Grady's character, and printed a lampoon accusing "Spectacles" of murdering his nephew and robbing the Post Office during his appointment as Post-master of Limerick. Thomas O'Grady was unable to prove Bruce had libelled him, so he responded by publishing a satirical poem, *The Nosegay,* which in venom, violence and sheer

savagery exceeded anything written by Dryden or Swift. The first edition, dedicated to Thomas Moore, sold out within a week. Grady issued a second edition to which he added an unmistakable caricature of Bruce and a frontpiece portrait of himself, complete with the spectacles which gave him his nickname. Bruce tried to claim damages of £20,000 from O'Grady. The trial took place in Limerick; not one single County Limerick gentleman came forward to vouch for Bruce's character; and the jury returned a verdict for one fortieth part of the sum involved. The remains of the second edition of *The Nosegay* were destroyed, and Bruce bought up two reports of the trial to try to prevent the details becoming public knowledge. Thomas "Spectacles" O'Grady left the country rather than pay the £500 in damages and 2 1/2 pence in costs awarded to Bruce. He settled in Bordeaux where he lived, and died, in obscurity. Bruce never achieved the social status he desired. Belmont House is now a nursing-home, but for a time it was a girls' boarding school, Rosary Hill Secondary School, run by the Presentation Sisters who lived in the former Woodlands House, nearby.

CHARLES MASSY, the Marquis of Headford, eloped with the wife of his namesake, the Reverend Charles Massy, while her husband was officiating at church one Sunday morning in 1803. The Marquis was charged with having criminal conversation with Mrs. Massy. Her husband took an action against the Marquis and sought damages of £40,000. The case was tried at the Ennis Summer Assizes on 27 July 1804. After twelve hours the jury decided in favour of the Reverend

Charles Massy, and damages of £10,000 were awarded against the Marquis of Headford who was described in court, as "a hoary veteran, in whom, like Etna, the snows above did not quench the flames below".

WORRALL'S END is the name of a small quay at the end of the narrow half-mile-long road which extends along the river bank from the modern pump-house. The name is derived from that of a family who once lived here, but variants on this name include Worrall's Inn and, more often, World's End. During, and after, the *Great Hunger*, this quay was an embarkation point for countless emigrants fleeing from Ireland to the New World. Regattas were held here in later times, and, more recently, the custom has been revived. Worrall's End is now a popular swimming area, complete with two diving-boards.

THE FALLS OF DOONASS derived their name from either *Eas Danainne*, Danaan's Cataract or *Dún Easa*, the Fort of the Cataract or Rapids. The earliest mention of *Eas Danainne* was dated to 1124 by the *Four Masters*. Samuel Lewis was impressed by this region in 1837 when he wrote that "the parish is connected with the county of Clare by an ancient structure called O'Brien's Bridge, originally built by one of the royal line of Thomond, and in later times often strongly contested by the various parties who strove to obtain possession either of the important fortress of Castle-Connel, or the wealthy city of Limerick. It was partially destroyed by the Earl of Ormond, in 1556, but was soon afterwards restored. The Shannon is not navigable here until within about a mile of the bridge, where the canal from the Clare side joins the river, there being many shoals, rocks and cascades in its channel. It abounds with trout and salmon, of which latter there is a valuable fishery at the waterfall called the leap. The falls here are numerous, there being a descent of 50 feet in less than three miles, and add greatly to the scenery, which is embellished with the mansions and parks of the neighbouring gentry, and the ruins of three ancient castles, that of Castle-Connel being in the parish, and those of Newcastle and Castle-Troy being distinctly visible from its higher parts, while the Keeper Mountains form a noble background on the north-east". The Falls of Doonass no longer merit the Lewis description of over 150 years ago, when they had "a striking and picturesque effect; the river, which above the falls is 300 yards wide and forty feet deep, here pours its vast volume of water over large masses of rock extending upwards of a quarter of a mile along its course, and producing a succession of falls forming a grand and interesting spectacle". The river is still an impressive sight as it pours over a series of limestone shelves, but it is no longer the spectacular sight it once was.

THE SHANNON HYDROELECTRIC SCHEME reduced the volume of water considerably in 1929, when the Shannon was diverted by a massive weir at O'Brien's Bridge and its waters forced down a newer canal, the eight-mile-long Headrace, to operate turbines at Ardnacrusha. This hydroelectric scheme was initiated in 1925, and eventually led to the rural electrification of the West of Ireland. Some of the salmon pools were restored in 1936, but the Shannon Hydroelectric Scheme put an end to traffic on the canal.

THE LIMERICK TO KILLALOE CANAL was referred to in the Irish House of Commons in 1697. It was then proposed to make the Shannon navigable from County Leitrim to County Limerick. Committees were established in 1703 and 1705, but work on the construction of the canal did not start until 1755. In 1799 the canal came into operation; steam-boats were introduced in 1815; and the canal remained in use until 1929.

A FERRY SERVICE operated across the Shannon from an area beside the car park, near Castleconnell Castle, which was once known as the Lough. The old road to the village once passed through here to the western side of the castle before branching eastwards near Cloon Island.

MONTPELIER and O'Brien's Bridge are linked by a bridge, the last of several built across the Shannon at this point. According to the *Four Masters*, Turlough and Donald O'Brien and the Bishops of Killaloe and Kilfenora built the first bridge here in 1506. The stretch of water from here to Castleconnell is considered one of the best lengths of the Shannon for fishing and for water sports. International rowing and waterskiing competitions have been, and still are, held here. Montpelier, like Castleconnell, had a spa, but by 1837 this "sulphureous spa of great virtue in ulcerous and cutaneous diseases" had deteriorated, because other waters had been allowed to mingle with it and its "efficacy had been diminished".

THE SHANNON VIEW HOTEL was patronised by three R.I.C. men on the evening of 17 April, 1921. they had cycled from Newport and decided to have a few drinks before continuing back to their barracks. As they relaxed at the bar, two men rushed in with revolvers in their hands, shouting, "Put 'em up". Believing they were under attack by an I.R.A. unit, the three men responded by grabbing their own pistols and returning fire. One of their attackers was killed, the other rushed out of the bar. The hotelier, Denis O'Donovan, remained in the bar with his three customers, Sergeant Hughes, Constable Morrison, and a third man whose name was not released at the later inquiry. A group of twelve auxiliaries, Black and Tans, had surrounded the hotel, believing that it was being used by the I.R.A.. When two of their number failed to capture what they thought were three I.R.A. men disguised as policemen, the raiding party pumped hundreds of rounds of ammunition through the bar door, with a Lewis machine-gun. Sergeant Hughes was killed, Constable Morrison was wounded, Denis O'Donovan was unharmed, and so was the third policeman who shouted out, "Cease fire. We're member of the R.I.C.. There are no shinners here". The shooting stopped. The three men walked out into the yard with their hands up. Denis O'Donovan and Constable Morrison were ordered to face the wall and keep their hands up. They were shot as they did so. Denis O'Donovan died ten minutes later. The unnamed R.I.C. man was never identified, for "security reasons", while the Black and Tan who died was named as Pringle. Only for the presence of William Harrison Cripps, President of the British Royal College of Surgeons, in the Shannon View Hotel, that night, the affair might have been completely hushed up. He later wrote that Denis O'Donovan was "an innocent, respectable and much beloved man ... killed before our eyes". His brother, Lord Parmoor, called for a public inquiry, but his demands were ignored.

CAHERLINE was the Limerick seat of the Gabbett family. Originally from Acton Burnell, Shropshire, the family established themselves at Shepperton House, Newmarket-on-Fergus and at Strand House, Limerick City. This was the residence of W.H. Gabbett in 1837.

THE FIRST RAILWAY TRAIN passed through the village in 1856. During the *Great Hunger* the people of Castleconnell survived by working on the local estates; on the Castleconnell Bog, between Nelson's Cross and O'Brien's Bridge; and on the railway line from Birdhill to Limerick. The Castleconnell railway station closed in 1963 but wasre-opened on 15 May 1989.

WOODLANDS was the residence of J. Tuthill in 1837. It was later purchased by the Presentation Sisters before it was resold and became a luxury hotel, The Castle Oaks.

SOURCES
9 11 13 25 28 39 47 64 65 68 76 91 92 107 120 123 129 177 192 195 238 246 255 273 282

Clarina

Carrigogunnell · Pubblebrien · Kilkeedy

CLARINA derives its name from *Clár Aidhne*, Aidhne's Plain. The village is a comparatively modern one which developed along the new mail road which was built between Limerick and Tralee in the early nineteenth century. Samuel Lewis noted that the Church of Ireland parochial school erected in 1826 had 130 pupils in 1837. There were then five other schools located within the parish of Kilkeedy, one of which was founded by the Monsell family to educate their tenants' children, while the four remaining schools catered for 220 students.

JOHN MONSELL purchased lands at Court Browne, near Askeaton, when he arrived in Ireland, from London, in 1612. His grandson, Thomas, acquired the lands of Tervoe.

WILLIAM MONSELL was the most distinguished member of the Monsell family. Born in 1812, he was married twice. His first wife, Anna Maria, was a daughter of the Earl of Dunraven, while his second wife, to whom he was married in 1857, was a daughter of the Comte de Montegny, Berthe. William and Berthe had two children, Gaston William Thomas who was born in 1858, and Mary, who was born in 1860. In the election of 1847 William defeated Caleb Powell, the sitting Member of Parliament. Eleven years later, Caleb, as High Sheriff, selected William as one of his Grand Jurors. William Monsell enjoyed a successful political career as a Member of Parliament, President of the Board of Trade, Postmaster-General, and a Privy Councillor. In 1874 he was created Baron Emly of Tervoe.

THE MONSELL ALMS CROSS was erected by William Monsell to commemorate his first wife, who died at Hastings. She had borne William two children who predeceased her. The carved inscription explains its purpose. "On the seventh of January in each year at the foot of this cross an alms will be given to twenty poor widows in memory of Anna Maria Monsell. January 7th. 1855". A terrace of six alms cottages was located at the Tervoe crossroads, behind the alms cross. The four middle houses are still occupied and one of them contains a shop.

Monsell Alms Cross.

TERVOE HOUSE was built by Colonel W.T. Monsell, M.P., in 1776 or 1785 on the site of an older house erected by Thomas Monsell in 1690. The house contained a lot of Adams-style decoration. About 1830, single-storey wings were added to the three-storey main block. The Monsell family lived here until 1951. Tervoe House was demolished in 1953.

ST. MARGARET'S CHURCH in Newtown, or Churchfield, may have been Esclon Church as Thomas J. Westropp could find no evidence to support the theory that Esclon Church was located within Kilkeedy parish. By 1419 the combined parishes of Kilkeedy and Esclon had made the two names interchangeable. Early in 1988, young Brendan O'Brien, a twelve-year-old historian, showed me around the ruins of this church, which is located on his father's land. It was in use as a *cillín* or childrens' burial-ground until 1840, and possibly later. The walls are in fairly good condition, although badly breached in two places, and covered in ivy. A massive ivy stem probably helps to preserve the damaged window in the east gable by retaining it in position. There is a high earthen bank southeast of the church, and the foundations of a large enclosure, with traces of several others within it, can also be discerned. Some cut stones from the church were used in the construction of a stile at its north-eastern corner.

THE MASS WALK was an ancient pathway which connected St. Margaret's Church to Carrigogunnell Castle. Parts of it are still visible, and the entire route can be traced by some of the area's older inhabitants.

CARRIGOGUNNELL CASTLE derives its name from *Carraig O gConaing,* the Rock of the O'Conaings or O'Gunnings. The Knights Templars' castle of *Carrig-a-Quincy,* the Rock of the Quince Tree or Arbutus Producing Land, may have been established on this "volcanic rock", long before their order was suppressed but apart from a brief reference in the Lewis account, there is little else to support this statement. The Carew manuscript of 1537 refers to

Aerial view of Carrigogunnell Castle.

"*Carekogunyel,* in English, candell rock", an explanation of the castle's name which has been perpetuated in folklore as the Rock of the Candle, while other accounts tried to connect the derivation of the name with the *Uí Chonaill Gabhra,* a tribe of the *Uí Fidgeinte,* who controlled nearly all of the county to the west of the Maigue river.

WILLIAM DE BURGO is generally recognised as the founder of the first castle on this site about 1201. He was a son-in-law of Domhnall Mór O'Brien. *The Annals of Innisfallen* record how William's brother-in-law, Donnchadh Cairbreach O'Brien, was confirmed in the ownership of the lands of *Carraig Ui gConaing* about 1209 and received his patents from King John in 1211. This did not interfere with the de Burgo possession of the castle and lands of Carrigogunnell. The O'Briens and MacNamaras destroyed Bunratty Castle in 1332, and may have crossed the Shannon to raid the former O'Brien holdings in this area, as the O'Briens appear to have held Carrigogunnell Castle in 1336 or 1339. This was, however, only a temporary occupancy, as the Earls of Desmond were by then the overlords of most of the former O'Brien holdings south of the Shannon. Earlier in the fourteenth century the Crown claimed Carrigogunnell on the unfounded statement that the O'Briens held it from "Lord Clere", possibly Richard de Clare, whose lands had

returned to the Crown.

CONOR O'BRIEN was inaugurated Prince of Thomond in 1406. He abdicated in 1414 and apparently lived in Carrigogunnell until the time of his death in 1426. Conor was possibly installed here by "James MacGarrott Earle of Desmonde, Lorde of Poblebryan and Corkemore" (1422-1457), as the Earls of Desmond had a policy of supporting O'Brien factions in order to check the power of the O'Briens of Thomond and to protect this dangerous and deserted stretch of country opposite Bunratty and the MacNamara seat at Cratloe. Brian Dubh O'Brien, Conor's son, married Mary MacMahon of Corca Bhaiscinn (West Clare). Brian is credited with strengthening this multi-sided keep and enclosing it with a strong wall during the fifteenth century.

MAHON O'BRIEN surrendered the castle to the Lord Deputy, Leonard Grey, after a siege in 1536. Grey hanged the garrison, and the castle was later granted to Donoth O'Brien. Two of the ruined towers that survive today were probably erected in the second half of the sixteenth century; one was a large four-storey structure to the north while the other was a later three-storey building with a gabled roof and a fire-place on the first-floor. There were two entrances; the main gateway was to the south, guarded by a porter's recess with a wooden porch to the right, while the other entrance was a small sallyport to the west,

leading to a narrow pass down the crags. The castle commands a spectacular view of the Shannon River, the Bunratty Roads, the Fergus Estuary, the Plains of Limerick, the borders of Clare, Cork and Tipperary and, on a clear day, the mountains of Kerry to the south-west. Thomas J. Westropp wrote that for "so large a building, on so commanding a situation, little knowledge of defensive science is shown in its plan; this probably implies its purely Dalcassian origin, for the O'Briens built few strongholds, and even of the peel-towers scarcely half a dozen seem to have been built by them in the fifteenth century. No towers and few salient angles defend the very vulnerable gateway, with its easy ascent and (for a fortress) flimsy walls barely 5 feet thick. The gateway is in the face of the wall, while it could easily have been set back between towers, and the gate itself is of less protective design than that of many a little peel-tower or bawn in the same county. The walls of the upper ward ran into the outer rampart, with not even a turret to defend the weak point of juncture; and the buildings there are confused in design, rude in execution, huddled together in any way, and adjoining, embedding, and thereby weakening the keep. Contrasted with Adare, Askeaton, or even Castleconnell, the whole is an absurdity as a military work, and must be regarded merely as a strong residence, for active assault and siege operations were evidently

146

unfeared by the builders". The ruins still dominate the skyline and can be seen quite easily from the opposite shore of the Shannon, from as far away as Bunratty Castle.

THE O'BRIENS OF CARRIGOGUN-NELL refused to take part in the Desmond Rebellion. Brian Duff O'Brien remained in his castle when the Sugàn Earl swept all before him. Queen Elizabeth I rewarded him for his loyalty by regranting him practically all of Pubblebrian after he had made a formal surrender to her. Brian was responsible for erecting the wing to the south-east of the keep and many of the castle's later features. He died in 1615 and was succeeded by his only son, Donough, who died without issue. Brian Duff O'Brien's grand-daughter, Margaret Stephenson of Dunmoylin, married her cousin Donough O'Brien of Dooneen who succeeded to Carrigogunnell after his namesake's death. Donough supported the Confederate Irish in 1642 but he may have died before the fall of of Limerick in 1651. Carrigogunnell Castle does not appear to have put up any resistance against the Cromwellian forces. Captain Wilson held the castle in 1651, and paid £7 to have a stable built here by Morris King. Sir Hardress Waller became the next owner, in 1655, when the tenancy was held by Michael Boyle, the Bishop of Cork. On 7 March, 1660, Michael Boyle renewed his tenancy for a period of sixty-one years and sub-let the castle, in which he did not reside, to John Caper. During the sieges of Limerick in 1690 and 1691 the castle was garrisoned by a Jacobite force of 150 men who surrendered it to General S'Gravenmore without a fight. One month later, in September 1691, Ginkel ordered its destruction as it held no road or passage, was useless for defence; not worth maintaining a garrison in, but still quite capable of harbouring enemies who could hamper the Williamite efforts to capture the city of Limerick. Eighty-four barrels of gunpowder were set aside for the demolition of two castles, Carrigogunnell and Castleconnell. Mines were placed under the great round bastion, the strong tower to the south of the inner ward, the wall of the western postern, the reaches of the ramparts, the corners of the houses and the southern turret. Carrigogunnell Castle was then blown up. Parts of the foundation walls were repaired by William Monsell in the 1830s but the castle was damaged again during the War of Independence when the Black and Tans blew up "some steps" to prevent I.R.A. snipers from using them to gain access to, and from, the remaining staircase.

PUBBLEBRIEN derived its name from *Pobal Uí Bhriain*, the Congregation or People of O'Brien during the fifteenth century.

DANIEL O'BRIEN managed to retain some of the lands lost by his father, Donough, after the Restoration. His son, another Daniel, fought on the Stuart side during the Jacobite war, and lost the family lands which were forfeited to the Crown. This younger Daniel married Helen O'Shaughnessy of Glin and went to live there. Their son, Donall O'Brien (1747-1833), was the head of the O'Briens of Carrigogunnell in the early nineteenth century. He was known as Dònall an Roinnteoir, Donall the Dispenser or the Generous. He was married twice; first to Margaret Burke, by whom he had no issue; and secondly to Mary Culhane, by whom he had two sons and a daughter. He resided in Glin, where his descendants can still be found today.

KILKEEDY PARISH derives its name from *Cill Chaoidhe*, which can be translated as the Church of St. Keedy, Kedda, Ketta or Cedda, whose feast-day was celebrated on 3 March. The Catholic parish was co-extensive with that of the Church of Ireland one, and contained two Catholic churches. One of these, Ballybrown Church, was a large plain edifice of hewn limestone on which work had commenced in 1831, and it was still incomplete when Samuel Lewis described it six years later. This church was renovated in the 1980s.

KILKEEDY CHURCH appears to have been of less importance than St. Margaret's Church from the fifteenth century onwards, as the O'Briens apparently favoured the latter church for their devotions. This building was later converted to Protestant use. In 1813 the church was rebuilt. Lewis described it as a neat building, with a square tower and octagonal spire, in 1837. Three years later O'Donovan wrote that it appeared "to have been a lateral building formerly attached to a larger one, as it lies contrary to the direction of almost all old churches". Its greatest length stretched from north to south, and the north wall of the more modern building was attached to the southern end of the older ruin, leading O'Donovan to conclude that this building, with its east to west orientation was, in all probability, erected on the site of the original church. The grave-yard is still in use, and a new section has been added in recent years. To the east the Smith tomb can be seen, while to the west lies a third Kilkeedy church which was built towards the end of the nineteenth century. The Monsell family were buried in a tomb which is located within the remains of the medieval church.

THE THIRD KILKEEDY CHURCH, standing in its own grounds, with a neglected lodge to the north, is no longer used for Protestant worship. Jim Reid, a local farmer, told me how Richard Lee purchased it from the Church of Ireland authorities in 1980 and had it extensively renovated. Dwarf walls were built within the interior to raise the floors to window level, and an upstairs section was added without altering the roof-line. The stained-glass windows, brass plaques and other church fittings were sent to St. Michael's Church, Pery Square, Limerick. When I visited Kilkeedy church in 1988, Jim Reid told me that the building was for sale.

THE PRINCIPAL SEATS in 1837 were "Elm Park, the residence of Lord Clarina; Tervoe, of W. Monsell Esq., commanding some fine views; Cooper's Hill, of Mrs Cooper; Faha, of G. Tuthill Esq.; Cragbeg, of G. Vandeleur, Esq.; and Vermont, of the Rev. R. Dickson".

VERMONT is now a roofless ruin west of Kilkeedy church. This was erected as a glebe house in 1792, and was burned, accidentally, in 1987. It had not been lived in for some years prior to the fire.

FAHA was the residence of the Moss family until quite recently. In 1815 a meteoric stone, consisting of iron pyrites strongly impregnated with sulphur, fell on the estate. It weighed 56lbs. and was in the possession of G. Tuthill over twenty years later.

CRAGBEG is now the home of the Kennedy family.

ELM PARK, or Clarina Castle, a large irregularly castellated house, was built in the impressive Gothic-style architecture of the early nineteenth century. This was the seat of the Massy family whose head, Lord Clarina, took his title of Baron from the village. The house was demolished in the 1960s.

CLARINA LODGE is the former gate arch which guarded the main entrance to the Elm Park demesne. In 1985 the Quinn family closed in the archway to connect the lodges on either side, and transformed this late-Georgian structure into an attractive castellated residence.

COOPER'S HILL was built in 1741 and renovated in 1791. The building was demolished in recent times. This had been a two-storey structure to the front and a three-storey at the back.

SOURCES

9 11 39 67 86 107 120 129 183 184 192 238 246 271 273

Croom

Monasteranenagh · Tory Hill · Ballycahane · Dysert

CROOM, or Crom, may derive its name from *Cromadh*, the Sloping Place; the Stooping, Bending, or Reaching Position; some now-forgotten association with the old Celtic god Crom or Crom Dubh; or a reference to Croom's location.

THE WAR-CRY, barran-glay or *barrán-glaed,* of the Fitzgeralds of Kildare, was, *Crom Abù,* Crom Forever. Each clan or tribe had its own characteristic war-cry, call or warrior-shout which was uttered by Irish warriors as they rushed into battle. The Anglo-Normans adopted the custom which continued almost into modern times.

CROOM CASTLE may have been founded, originally, by Dermot O'Donovan to protect both a ford over the Maigue River and the territory he had taken from the MacEnirys during the reign of King John (1199-1216). Between 1197 and 1200, Hamo de Valognes granted the manor of Croom to Gerald Fitzmaurice Fitzgerald, the ancestor of the Fitzgeralds of Kildare. The O'Donovans were driven into West Cork, and the Fitzgeralds secured their new possessions by erecting a strong castle, flanked by four circular towers, on this site, some time before 1216. This became the chief seat of the Kildare Geraldines, the bastion immortalised in their war-cry. John Darcy repaired Croom Castle in 1334. It was attacked many times in successive wars. During the reign of Elizabeth I (1558-1603) the castle was besieged on three occasions. In 1600 "Lord-President Carew, at the head of 1500 men, attacked the castle, which had a powerful garrison under its constable, the celebrated Pierce Lacy, who made his escape in the night, and in the morning the fortress was surrendered. In 1610, the castle and manor of Croom were restored by James I to the Fitzgeralds, who, however, again forfeited it by joining in the insurrection of 1641; in 1678, Charles II granted both to the Duke of Richmond, who resided in the castle for several years. In 1691, it was garrisoned by the adherents of James II, but on the approach of the forces of William III they abandoned the fortress, and took refuge in Limerick". The castle remained unoccupied until it was partially repaired by John Croker, in the early part of the nineteenth century, but he had sold it to Colonel Dickson, by 1866. The castle is still occupied today. All that remains of its circular bawn is a fragment of a fifteenth or sixteenth-century tower.

CROOM is located north of a juncture in the river system, where the Camoge River joins the Maigue, after forming a loop to the south, west of Monasteranenagh Abbey. Croom was a place of considerable importance from an early date, but it did not develop as a town until the castle was built. The town was walled in 1310, and over the intervening years both town and castle often shared the same fate. In 1837 Samuel Lewis wrote that the "town is situated on the eastern bank of the river Maigue over which is a handsome bridge of six arches, and on the new road from Limerick to Charleville, which, when completed, will be the most advantageous line from Limerick to Cork; it comprises two principal streets with smaller ones branching from them, and contains 213 houses ... At Carass, on the river Maigue, is a very powerful flour-mill, fitted up in a superior style, with machinery of the most improved construction, the property of D. Roche, Esq.; and close adjoining the bridge of Croom is another large mill, belonging to H. Lyons, Esq.. In addition to the interesting castle, the residences of the gentry in the parish are Carass ... Toureen ... Croom House ... Carass Court ... Glen-Bevan ... Cherry Grove ... Bellevue ... Clorane ... Newborough ... the glebe-house ... and Tory Hill ... the [Church of Ireland] church stands on the western bank of the River Maigue, and is a small neat edifice, in the early English style of architecture, with a square tower; it appears to have been erected on the site of a larger building ... in the R.C. divisions the parish is the head of a union or district, comprising the parishes of Croom, Anhid, Dunaman, Carrigran and Dysart; and containing two chapels, one at Croom, the other at Ballynabannogue ... There is a small place of worship for Wesleyan Methodists; also a dispensary". By then Croom contained 1268 inhabitants within the town and a total of 6978 within the parish. In 1986 the town population stood at 1024 persons, and the Croom Rural District electoral division contained a total of 10,846 people. The large mills are a noteworthy feature. The Church of Ireland church is in use and the churchyard contains several vaults. The Dickson vault, dating from 1806, has been recently re-roofed while the roof of the Lyons vault is in need of repair.

CROOM HOUSE is now the residence of Denis Brosnan. Glenbevan House, a late-Georgian structure, dating from the early nineteenth century, overlooks the Maigue. So, too, does the impressive white-painted Islandmore House, a square two-storey nineteenth-century house. The old Glebe House is also occupied but is better-known today as Croom Rectory.

CROOM'S HISTORY dates back to pre-Christian or early Christian times. In 1972-1973 two single-banked ring forts were demolished in the townland of Croom in order to build new houses on the site. Elizabeth Shee-Twohig excavated these sites in March 1974. She discovered human and animal remains, an iron knife, a bronze penannular ring and a bone comb side-plate. A preservation order was placed on a third ring fort nearby. These forts were located north of the Croom-Rathkeale road, one mile from Croom, and over 65 ring forts are shown on survey sheet No. 30 of the 6-inch Ordnance Survey Maps, mainly two to three miles south-west of these excavated sites.

DOMESTIC CATS were introduced into Ireland during the first centuries AD. Wild cats were plentiful here in ancient times, and folklore speaks of a monstrous enchanted wild cat which dwelt in a cave and was a match for the bravest champion. Stories of demon cats also abound. Cats became more numerous during the early Christian era, and the remains of several diminutive cats were discovered when medieval sites were excavated in Cork. The radius and humerus of a larger cat were found in one of the Croom forts.

THE MAIGUE POETS are associated with Croom rather than Limerick City in the history of Irish literature. Seán O Tuama invited the *filí* to form a Court of Poetry, *Filí na Máighe,* the Maigue Poets, on the death of

Aerial view of Croom.

Seàn Clàrach MacDomhnaill (1681-1754). This body continued to meet, at intervals, over the succeeding years. These poets enjoyed life, wine, women and song. They were savage satirists; wrote Jacobite songs; mourned lost wars, loves and possessions; composed verses on every subject under the sun; and, according to folklore and the most popular theorising, they coined the Limerick.

THE LIMERICK is described as a nonsense verse in a five-line stanza, said to have originated from an eighteenth-century ale-house chorus or refrain, *Will You Come Up to Limerick.* Limericks are characterised by the most outrageous puns and simple but fantastic rhyming;

"The Limerick packs laughs anatomical
In to space that's quite economical.
But the best ones I've seen
So seldom are clean
And the clean ones so seldom are comical".

The humour can vary from subtle wit to the coarsest of crude earthiness. No subject seems to have escaped the Limerick composer's attention, and the verse has been handled, and mishandled, by various poets, would-be-poets, entertainers and satirists, over the centuries.

THE IRISH BRIGADE are also supposed to have been adept in the composition of Limericks. This form of poetry is as popular today as it may have been during the seventeenth century when, according to tradition, Jacobite soldiers amused themselves with nonsense verses as the city of Limerick lay under siege. After the Treaty of Limerick these men of the Irish Brigade were dispersed throughout Europe, and further afield, as mercenary soldiers, the Wild Geese. They took their verse-form with them;

"The Limerick form is complex
Its contents run chiefly to sex.
It burgeons with vergeons
And masculine urgeons
And swarms with erotic effects".

SEAN O TUAMA AN GHRINN (1706 or 1708-1775) was a hospitable publican in Croom and Limerick City, as well as a poet who earned himself the soubriquet of *a n Ghrinn,* the Wit or Humourous. In his heyday he presided over many assemblies of his fellow-poets in Limerick and Croom. He kept a tavern at Mungret Gate, near the Fair Green, in Croom, and another, in Mungret Street, Limerick. His open-handed hospitality eventually ruined him, as he kept open house and entertained many penniless *filí.* James Clarence Mangan (1803-1849) translated some of the work of the Maigue poets into English, including Sean O Tuama's lament as an inn-keeper, and Aindrias MacCraith's reply;

"I sell the best brandy and sherry
to make my good customers merry,
But at times their finances
Run short as it chances
And then I feel very sad, very".

MacCraith thought that this Limerick was aimed at himself and rejoined with;

"O Tuomy! you boast yourself handy

At selling good ale and bright brandy,
But the fact is your liquor
Makes everyone sicker,
I tell you that, I your friend, Andy".

Seán O Tuama died in 1775 and was buried in the old churchyard of Croom.

DAVID ROCHE rented the Evan's Mill, at Carass, from Lord Carbery towards the end of the eighteenth century. When Bulgaden Hall was burned, Carbery transferred his residence to Carass Court and appointed David as his agent. David lost one of his feet in an accident, as a young man, and wore an artificial iron leg from which he derived the name "Roche of the Iron Foot". David acquired a lease on the lands around the mill and, later, purchased Carass Court from Carbery. When his daughter Frances married Geoffrey Browning, an army officer, David presented her with Carass Court. His son, David, born in 1791, was created a baronet in 1833. This David was married twice; first to Frances Vandeleur who died in 1841; and, secondly, to Celia Caroline O'Grady. Celia's father,

Thomas O'Grady, was accused of selling his vote at the time of the Act of Union. "Thank God I have a country to sell!", he replied.

THE CROKER FAMILY originally came from Devon. This surname may have been a derivative of Crawcour, *Crevecoeur* or the more prosaic Crocker, meaning a potter or crockery-maker. Edmund Croker was the first of the family to settle here. He was killed at Raleighstown in 1641. His grandson was an agent for the Earls of Kildare and received "a lease forever" on Croom castle and lands under an act of parliament passed at the end of the eighteenth century. This lease also included the advowsons of Adare and Athlacca.

JOHN CROKER acquired Ballinagarde in the 1730s. His great-grandson, and namesake, succeeded to the extensive Croker estates in 1830. This John farmed on a large scale; amassed a fortune; and left everything to his extravagant son, Captain Edward Croker, who sold what he inherited and died a comparatively poor man. Caleb Powell selected Edward for Grand Jury service in 1858

although he thought him "a very worthless spendthrift having run thro' a fine estate and brought up an arrogant race of uneducated blockheads of both sexes".

JAMES O LYNE settled in Croom in the 1740s. His surname may have been a derivative of *O'Floinn* or *O'Fhloinn,* meaning the descendant of Flann, the name of several distinct families in different parts of Ireland. His son, Denis, changed the family name to Lyons, the 80th in a list of commonest surnames in the Ireland of 1890.

THOMAS BLAKE (1894-1921) worked in Laird's Pharmacy, O'Connell Street, Limerick. His knowledge of chemistry helped him to direct, and assist, in the manufacture of munitions and explosives. He lived at No. 1, St. Alphonsus Avenue, Limerick, with his two brothers. All three were members of the Irish Volunteers. On Friday 28 January 1921 his bullet-riddled body was found on the city's Clyde Road. His funeral took place the following Sunday, at Shanavoher, Croom. The burial was marred by disturbances. The Crown forces attacked the mourners during

Monasteranenagh Abbey.

the interment, and another Volunteer, Paddy O'Halloran, died a few days later from injuries received on this occasion.

MONASTERANENAGH CISTERCIAN ABBEY

derives its name from *Mainistir an Aonaigh*, the Monastery of the Fair, after an *aonach or* fair which was held here in ancient times. The abbey was founded by Turlough O'Brien, King of Thomond, in 1148, as a daughter house of Mellifont. In 1154 Monasteranenagh Abbey established its own daughter house in Abbeydorney. Domhnall Mór O'Brien became the patron after Turlough's death. In 1174 he witnessed a grant to Gill Abbey in Cork. Six years later Monasteranenagh Abbey established two more daughter houses in Midleton and Holy Cross. The abbey was confirmed in its possessions by King John and, in 1209, Abbeyfeale was united to it as a cell or grange. The monks supported their O'Brien patrons during the Anglo-Norman wars. In 1228 the Irish monks drove out the Abbot and the non-Irish monks; they fortified the abbey; built a defensive tower above the altar; provisioned the place against a siege; and were, themselves, excommunicated for revolting against their ecclesiastial superiors. Hubert de Burgo, the Bishop of Limerick, recaptured the abbey by armed force; reinstalled the monks who had been driven out and those who had not taken part in the rebellion; and absolved the fugitive monks who asked for mercy. By the end of the thirteenth century the abbey had fallen heavily into debt. It owed Ricardi of Lucca £209.33 in 1302. The abbots of Monasteranenagh sat in parliament as spiritual peers. In 1370 Gearóid Iarla, the Earl of Desmond, his sons and several nobles were captured by O'Brien of Thomond while they were visiting the abbey. The Geraldine retainers were slaughtered and a considerable portion of Monasteranenagh was destroyed. In the same year, 1370, Brian O'Brien and the MacNamaras met, and beat, the King of Thomond in battle, outside the walls of the abbey. The defeated O'Brien forces sought sanctuary within the abbey but were pursued and captured by their victorious enemies who demanded a large ransom. In 1540 the Monastery of the Fair was dissolved. Although the abbey was granted to Sir Osborne Echingham in 1543, the monks appear to have been left in possession until 1579.

THE SECOND BATTLE OF AONACH

also took place around the abbey in 1579. Some of the defeated Irish and Spanish soldiers sheltered within the walls, which were badly damaged by the English cannon. The refectory and cloisters were destroyed and the surrounding walls were razed to the ground.

Roger Stalley wrote in *The Cistercian Monasteries of Ireland* (1987) that there was no evidence to support the story of Sir Nicholas Malby executing 40 monks here after the battle. The ruins consist principally of the church, dating from about 1170 to 1220, and an early Gothic chapter house. The church was divided near the centre by a stone screen separating the choir from the nave, possibly built during the fifteenth century. The choir was lit by a triple-lancet east window "of lofty dimensions" most of which was destroyed when the chancel vault collapsed in 1874. The nave is separated from the aisles by ranges of square pillars, which appear to have been encased, and there are some small remains of the south transept, and a small chapel of "very elegant design". Originally the church had been built with "three chapels opening off each transept, but these have been almost completely destroyed". The belfry [sic], "a noble square structure of great height", fell in 1807, and shortly afterwards a Mr. White of Manister demolished the outbuildings and used the material to build stables and yards. The belfry that collapsed may have been a sixteenth-century house constructed over the south transept.

SIR HENRY WALLOP

received a grant of Monasteranenagh from Elizabeth I, according to Samuel Lewis. Sir Henry renovated the choir and had it "fitted up" as a Protestant parish church. Elizabeth Norreys came into possession in 1603 after the abbey had been through several changes in ownership, including that of George Moore.

MONASTERANENAGH ABBEY MILL AND BRIDGE RUINS

have disappeared since they were last recorded in the *Shell Guide* over twenty years ago. P.W. Joyce wrote that there "is no evidence to show that the Irish built stone bridges before the Anglo-Norman invasion", and I was unable to determine where the bridge and mill had been located.

STEPHEN OF LEXINGTON

was appointed to visit every Christian abbey in Ireland, in 1228, to purge the undisciplined Irish abbeys and to banish, and excommunicate, monks who were antagonistic to Anglo-Norman dominance. He introduced a rule that men should not be admitted to the Cistercian order unless they could confess in French or Latin. Monasteranenagh, like many Anglo-Norman foundations, was dedicated to the Blessed Virgin, or St. Mary.

THE FAIR SITE,

which gave Monasteranenagh its name, was located on the north side of the river. The overgrown damaged monument (two conjoined cairns) known as the Fort marks the site of the ancient fair which was known as *Aonach*, or

Aonach Cairbre, the Fair of Carbery. Monasteranenagh was also known as the Abbey of Mage, Maigue, De Magio, Maio, Nenagh, Eanach, Nenay, Mainistir an Aonagh and Mainistir na Maighe, the Monastery of the Maigue.

RATHMORE RING FORT

took its name from *an Rath Mór*, the Great Fort or Rath, which pre-dated the castle and gave its name to both the castle and the townland. The fort is believed to have been a Viking fortification, or occupied by Vikings, in 1148, when Turlough O'Brien is said to have taken an oath to build Monasteranenagh Abbey "previous to the battle in which he defeated the Danes, who, in 1148, had encamped round their strong fortress of Rathmore; and which took place on the plains of Kilmargy, the site of the present ruins [of Monasteranenagh]". The Earl of Desmond built a castle here in 1306. The present ruined square tower house probably dates from the fifteenth century. This was garrisoned by Spanish and Irish soldiers who abandoned it to Sir Nicholas Malby after the battle of Monasteranenagh in 1579. The Desmond forces later re-occupied the castle until they were expelled by Sir George Carew. Some time after this episode Rathmore lapsed into ruin.

TORY HILL

was originally called *Cnoc Droma Asal* or *Druim Assail*, the Hill of the Ridge of Asal or the Ridge of Assail. It became a haunt of "numbers of freebooters and haters of English power" who "frequented its sheltered sides during the seventeenth and eighteenth centuries". These outlaws were known as raparees or tories. The word tory was derived from *Tóraidhe* for which Dinneen's *Fóclòir Gaedhilge agus Beárla* (1927) gives the following explanations: a tory, a robber, a highwayman or a persecuted person. As a result, the refuge of *Cnoc Droma Asal* became better-known as *Cnoc Tòraidhe*, Tory Hill. Gerald, the Earl of Desmond, observed the second battle of Monasteranenagh from this high vantage spot while his brother, John of Desmond, was locked in combat with Malby's forces. The Irish and Spanish soldiers led by the Geraldines were defeated and any of them who were taken prisoner were executed. Amongst the dead was a medical doctor, Dr. Allen, who was mistaken for a Papal legate. The Earl of Desmond refused to commit his own forces to battle and retreated to Askeaton, leaving his brother's men to their fate.

BALLYCAHANE

derives its name from *Baile Uì Chathàin*, the town of O'Cahan, or Cathan. In 1212 the Knights Hospitallers were confirmed in their ownership of Ballycahane church, although there is no record of a preceptory here.

THE CAHANE FAMILY from whom Ballycahane takes its name may have been a branch of the Derry family of the same name who settled in Thomond at an early period. Variants of the name include *O Catháin, O'Caghane, O'Cahaine, O'Cahane, O'Kahane, O'Kaane,* O'Cahan, O'Caughan, O'Kane, O'Keane, Cahan, Cane, Cain, Kane and Keane.

BALLYCAHANE CASTLE was built by the O'Grady family in 1496. During the early 1800s numerous ancient silver and copper coins were found near this ruined castle.

JOHN SCANLAN OF BALLYCAHANE earned himself an unenviable reputation, on both sides of the Shannon, as the murderer of Ellen Hanley of Manister, the *Colleen Bawn*. This beautiful sixteen-year-old girl vanished from her home on 28 June, 1819. On 6 September, 1819, her body was washed ashore at Money Point, County Clare. John Scanlan, a Lieutenant in the Royal Marines, was accused of her murder. He was tried in Limerick. Daniel O'Connell defended Scanlan who was found guilty of the crime, sentenced to death, and publicly executed at Gallows Green, Singland, Limerick City, on 20 March, 1820. His accomplice, and servant, Stephen Sullivan was later apprehended, tried, convicted, and hanged on the same gallows on 27 July, 1820. Gerald Griffin based *The Collegians* on this incident. The *Colleen Bawn* was buried in Burrane Cemetery, east of Money Point.

FANNINGSTOWN CASTLE, is a battlemented nineteenth-century house designed by P. Nagle of Cork. It is located in the corner of the bawn of an authentic medieval castle, and was erected as a two-storey structure with square towers, of different sizes, at either end. This is located 3 miles north-north-west of Croom.

DYSERT derives its name from *Disert Aonghusa,* the Hermitage or Wilderness of Oengus. There are two places called *Disertaengusa* in Irish: this Dysert, and *Dysartenos* in County Laois. Both attribute their foundation to St. Oengus the Culdee. This Oengus was a reformer who achieved fame through the writing of a celebrated martyrology. He died in 815.

THE CULDEES or *Cèile De* were a band of ascetic celibate hermits.

DYSERT CHURCH may have been established in the late eighth or early ninth century. The present building dates from the fifteenth or sixteenth century but it incorporates parts of an older church within its framework. Donn, the Erenagh of Dysert, and of Mungret, died in 1033. In 1083 the death of one of its abbots was recorded, and the building was in

River scene at Croom.

use as a parish church until at least 1418. The eastern gable was constructed at a later stage, and the western gable was rebuilt before 1869. In May 1832 William Morrison wrote to George Petrie: "There is no appearance of more than the one church in the immediate vicinity; about half a mile off there is another, but it is of a much later period". This latter building may be the one Samuel Lewis referred to in 1837 as long since fallen into ruin, with its parishioners having to attend divine service at Croom.

GEORGE PETRIE (1789-1866) was employed to superintend the topographical department connected with the *Ordnance Survey of Ireland* , in 1833. He worked with men like John O'Donovan and Eugene Curry. In 1845 he published *The Ecclesiastical Architecture of Ireland: An Essay on the Origins and Uses of the Round Towers of Ireland,* for which he gained a prize of £50 and a gold medal from the Royal Irish Academy.

DYSERT ROUND TOWER is located near the church, in the townland of Carrigeen. It dates from the twelfth century. In 1837 Samuel Lewis wrote that it was "about 70 feet in height, standing on a rock of limestone: 14 feet from the foundation a circular-headed door opens to the north-east; on the opposite side is a pointed window, over which are three stories with square-headed lights, and at the top are four small slip windows. The mouldings around the door are in relief, and of superior workmanship in freestone, of which the window-frames are also composed; the remainder of the tower is constructed of limestone". When the tower was excavated, human bones and a solid clay floor were uncovered.

KILFINNY CHURCH and townland derives its name from *Cill Finche,* the Church of St. Finneach, a virgin saint. The ruined church is also known as Ballinakill, and an early record describes it as Kellnafidnaigi in 1201. John O'Donovan noted it as a nave and chancel church in 1840, but he was unable to describe the chancel as John Pigott had placed an iron gate on the chancel arch, segregating that part of the ruined church in order to use it as a burial-place for his family. This church was used as a Protestant parish church after the Dissolution. It was repaired in 1615 but was "long in ruins by 1800".

KILFINNY CASTLE may have been founded by Cormac MacEniry during the reign of King John (1199-1216). The present structure was a Geraldine stronghold which was forfeited during the reign of Elizabeth I (1558-1603). The widow of Sir John Dowdall defended it against the Confederate Irish led by Colonel Purcell, in 1641. She was forced "to surrender. The Irish having got possession of the hill in the rere, and two windmills, which commanded the castle". Kilfinny Castle consisted of two quadrangular towers, with a court to the north of the southern one.

BALLYNAKILL HOUSE was converted into a soldiers' barrack during the agrarian unrest of the early 1820s. It was burned by the Rockites in 1822.

FINNITERSTOWN CASTLE was held by the Fitzgeralds until 1598.

ANHID PARISH, or Athnett, contained 475 inhabitants in 1837, when a new line of road was constructed between Croom and Charleville to intersect the direct mail coach road from Cork to Limerick. The parish land, on the western bank of the Maigue river, was considered, then and now, very fertile.

SOURCES

9 11 13 26 32 34 39 43 47 64 65 76 79 86 97 107 108 120 123 129 150 164 184 192 213 214 220 233 238 242 246 248 264 282

Dromcolliher

Broadford · Killaliathan · Springfield

DROMCOLLIHER derives its name from *Drom Collachair*, which may be a corruption of *Drom-coll-Choille*, Hazelmount, according to John O'Donovan. P.W. Joyce agreed with this rendition, but translated *Druim-Coll-Choille* as the Ridge of the Hazel Wood. The hills to the south of the village form a natural boundary between the counties of Cork and Limerick.

ST. BARTHOLOMEW'S CHURCH, the old parish church of Dromcolliher, was located near the village, in the townland of Carhooard West. In 1410 and 1418 it was recorded as *Capella Dromcolkylle.* By 1840 the western gable had disappeared but the large graveyard was still in use. T.J. Westropp examined the site in 1901 but had little to say about it.

KILLALIATHAN CHURCH derives its name from *Cill Acadh Ui Liathain,* the Church of the Field of O'Leehane. According to tradition, one of the *Ui Liathain* women wished to establish a church but was unsure as to where she should locate it. An unseasonal snow-storm at the start of the summer blanketed all but one field in the area with snow. This was construed as an omen indicating where the church should stand and when Killaliathan Church was built it was dedicated to *Muire na Sneachta,* Mary of the Snows. Killaliathan was the parish church for the area incorporating Dromcolliher and Broadford, and it is not surprising to find that the nearby Catholic church, in Broadford, is dedicated to Our Lady of the Snows, today. The earliest records of Killaliathan Church date back to 1201 and 1209. In 1302 the original church on this site was destroyed by war but it was soon rebuilt. It may have served as a monastery, possibly of the Augustinian Canons, but, if so, it is not listed in *Medieval Religious Houses Ireland* (1988). The division of its east window is one of the church's more notable features. The window niche,

Aerial view of Dromcolliher.

behind the altar, contains a fine baptismal font; the tomb in the north wall dates from the fifteenth century; a gallery was once positioned above the doorway; parts of the sacristy still remain; and the graveyard is still in use for burials.

IN 1837 Samuel Lewis wrote that the parish of Killaliathan contained 1,590 inhabitants. "The lower part of the parish is tolerably fertile, and about 2,000 acres are under tillage, about 800 in meadow and pasture, and the remainder is bog and mountain land. The mountains contain coal, which is worked by Francis Sullivan, Esq., at Banmore; and limestone, of which an excellent quarry is worked near Broadford; iron stone is also abundant". The population of Dromcolliher was 658 in 1831. In 1837 there was a constabulary police station in the village and "a daily penny post to Charleville. Fairs are held on 15 March, 2 May, 17 June, 24 August, 5 November, and 3 December; they are in general large and well-attended".

THE DROMCOLLIHER CINEMA FIRE occurred on the evening of Sunday, 5 September 1926. William "Baby" Forde hired an upstairs room in Patrick Brennan's two-storey shed at Church Street in order to use it as a make-shift cinema. An estimated crowd of 150 men, women and children had arrived to watch two films, *The White Outlaw* and *Baby be Good,* by about 9.15 p.m. A lorry engine generated electricity to power the projector, but lighting within the building was provided by candles. About 9.40 p.m. one of the reels of celluloid film was ignited by a candle. Within minutes a fire had started which rapidly got out of control. Most of the people sitting near, or behind, the projector managed to escape but those nearest the screen were trapped. Forty-six people perished in the blazing inferno, and another two died shortly afterwards in hospital. The victims of this tragedy were buried in a communal grave in the grounds of the Catholic parish church. A large Celtic cross was erected over their grave.

SPRINGFIELD CASTLE "with the surrounding manor, formerly belonged to the Fitzgeralds, Lords of Glenlis, and, on its forfeiture in the Desmond Rebellion, was, in 1591, granted to Sir W. Courtney". The Fitzgeralds of Claonghlais recovered possession of Springfield which was then known as *Gort na Tiobrad,* the Field of the Spring. During the Jacobite war Springfield held out for James II. It became forfeit to the Crown, and the last Lord of Claonghlais, Sir John Fitzgerald, left to serve with the Irish Brigade, in France, where he ended his days in the *Hotel des Invalides,* Paris. The sixteenth-century four-storey-high tower house

was later bought by the Fitzmaurice family, an heiress of whom married Sir Robert Deane who was created Lord Muskerry in 1781. During the eighteenth century a mansion was built adjoining the older castle and, in the following century, a new wing was added, in the then-prevailing Gothic-style. In 1923, during the Civil War, the eighteenth-century house was burned, but the nineteenth-century wing within the sixteenth-century bawn, was converted, and extended, to form the present building. The same Gothic style was used in the renovations, and Springfield Castle is still owned by a Lord Muskerry.

DAIBHI O BRUADAIR (c. 1625-1698) was born in Barrymore, County Cork. Seán O Tuama wrote in *An Duanaire 1600-1900: Poems of the Dispossessed* that Dáibhí was "the first of the well-known seventeenth century poets to try to live completely out of verse, in the manner of the medieval professional poets". He spent most of his life in County Limerick. The Fitzgeralds were his chief patrons, and his association with Sir John Fitzgerald led Dáibhí to describe Springfield as a Mansion Abounding in Poetry, Rewards and Crowds of People, *Dúnadh Duanach Duasach Dreamach.* By "1674 he appears to have been reduced to labouring in the fields ... He ended his life in misery". The inscribed plaque set in the wall, at the entrance to Springfield, commemorates Dáibhí and his patrons, the *Gort na Tiobrad* Fitzgeralds, Lords of Claonghlais. Seamus Murphy, the Cork sculptor, carved the inscription on the plaque.

DROMCOLLIHER, or Drumcollogher, was one of the places in which the Sheehys, or MacSheehys, settled. They came to Ireland, originally, as Scottish gallowglasses, to serve the de Burgos of Galway. When James, the Seventh Earl of Desmond, married Mary de Burgo, early in the fifteenth century, she brought a guard of Sheehy gallowglasses to County Limerick as part of her dowry. The Sheehys prospered under the Earls of Desmond but lost all their lands, and holdings, after the Desmond Rebellion. The Dromcolliher Sheehys maintained a low profile in this area until one of them purchased a considerable amount of land from Lord Muskerry, towards the end of the eighteenth century.

SIR MATTHEW DEANE (1626-1710) acquired vast estates around Dromore, County Cork, and was created a Baronet of Ireland on 10 March 1709. He was married three times: firstly, to Mary Wallis of Somersetshire, from whom Lord Muskerry's family have descended; secondly, to Martha, daughter of Richard Boyle, Archbishop of Tuam, and widow of Lieut.-Col. John Nelson; and thirdly, to

Dorothy, daughter of John Ferrar of Dromore, County Down, and widow of Richard, Second Earl of Barrymore.

SIR ROBERT TILSON DEANE (1747-1818), the Sixth Baronet, married Anne Fitzmaurice, the daughter of John Fitzmaurice, and sole heir of her grandfather, John Fitzmaurice of Springfield Castle, in 1775. Anne's great-grandfather, Thomas Fitzmaurice, was the First Earl of Kerry. On 5 January 1781 Robert was elevated to the peerage of Ireland, as Baron Muskerry. He, and Anne, had four sons: Robert (1776-1796); John Thomas (1777-1824) who succeeded to the title but died without issue; William (1792-1811); and Matthew (1795-1868), the Third Baron Muskerry. Matthew's son, Robert (1826-1857), married Elizabeth Geraldine, the daughter and co-heir of H.K. Grogan Morgan, of Johnstown Castle, County Wexford, in 1847. Robert assumed the additional surname and arms of Morgan in 1855, and his son, Hamilton Matthew Tilson Fitzmaurice Deane-Morgan, became the Fourth Baron Muskerry.

GORTNATUBRID CHURCH, or Springfield Church, was a ruin by 1840. Today only the east gable remains. This may have been erected as a chapel-of-ease by the Fitzgeralds, who are said to have been established as Lords of Claonghlais by the Black Knight, Sir John FitzJohn Fitzgerald, Seán Mór na Sursainge, and his wife, a member of the Collins family.

THE COLLINS FAMILY were Lords of Claonghlais until the end of the thirteenth century when they were dispossessed by the Fitzgeralds. Their name is derived from *O Coileán,* the Descendant of the Whelp. Variants on the name include *O Cuileáin, O'Collaine, O'Collan,* and Collin. Originally they were of the same stock as the O'Donovans, and were Lords of *Ui Conaill Gabhra,* now the baronies of Upper and Lower Connello, until they were expelled in 1178 and settled in Claonghlais and West Cork.

DR. NICHOLAS SANDERS, an English Jesuit and papal diplomat, arrived in Ireland with James Fitzmaurice Fitzgerald in 1579. They landed in Smerwick, County Kerry, with arms and money. Fitzgerald was killed in a skirmish with the Bourkes but Sanders remained with the rebel forces. He was present at the battles of Gortnatubrid and Monasteranenagh but spent his last months, as a fugitive, hiding in the wooded hills to the south of Broadford. He died of dysentery towards the end of 1581, but is said to have received the last rites from Bishop O'Maoilrian of Killaloe. Tradition relates that he "was borne by four Irish Knights to" *Gort na Tiobrad,* but the site of his burial is not

Springfield House.

remembered.

THE BATTLE OF GORTNATUBRID was fought between the Geraldines and a superior English force, in the area around *Pairc na Staille,* the Field of the Stallion, in the last days of September, 1579. The English were defeated; three hundred of them were slain, including three captains, Eustace, Herbert and Price; and their military stores, and standards were captured.

THE LEHANE SURNAME is associated with Sligo and Cork, the home-places of two distinct but separate families. The Lehanes of Cork are descended from the *Ui Liatháin* of south-west Limerick, who later settled in the baronies of Barrymore and Kinnataloon, County Cork. The name is often anglicised to Lyons, from *O Liatháin,* the descendant of *Liathán,* the diminutive of the Grey. Other variants of the name are *O Lyhane, O Leaghan, 'O Lehane, 'O Liathàin,* Leehan, Lyhane, Leehane, O'Leehane Leyhane, Lihane, Leeane, and O'Lyons.

THE SULLIVAN SURNAME is the most numerous one in Munster and the third most numerous one in Ireland. This family's principal seat was at Knockgrafton, about two miles north of Cahir, County Tipperary. In 1192 they were driven westwards by the advance of the Anglo-Norman invaders and settled mainly in the mountains of Cork and Kerry. The name is derived from *O Súileabhán,* which

Rev. Patrick Woulfe defined as the descendant of the Black-eyed, *Sìul-dubhàn,* although Edward MacLysaght was in some doubt about this translation. *O'Sullivan,* Sullevan, Soolivan and *O Súilleabháin* are variants on the name, and this family were of the same stock as the MacCarthys and O'Callaghans. They were divided into several branches, the major heads of which were the O'Sullivan More (Dunkerron, Kenmare), the O'Sullivan Beare (Beare, Bantry), and the O'Sullivan Maol. Another minor branch of the family appear to have settled in this part of south-west Limerick. Many of the Sullivans lost their estates during the confiscations of the seventeenth century and went abroad where they distinguished themselves in Spain, Belgium, France, Germany, Italy, and the Americas.

RATHURDE RING FORT derives its name from an *Rath Ard,* the High Fort. This is located on a rise of ground overlooking the Springfield demesne.

THE ANKETELL FAMILY are descended from Robert Anthessel of Compton, Wiltshire, who was given a grant of the lands of Killaliathan, 2600 acres, in Elizabethan times. Variants of this surname include Annesley, Ansloe, Anthezell, Antikle, Ankettle, Antle, *Ankettil,* Anketell, Ankethill, and *Ancoitil.* The original version of the name, Anthessel, may be English; the name

Anketell, is derived from a Teutonic personal name, the son of Ancytel, and can be found in the *Domesday Book* and early Dublin rolls, although it has also been found as an Anglo-Norman name; and the Ansloe-Aynnesley name was introduced into Munster, from Nottinghamshire in 1606. In 1611 the Anketell family held the castle and lands of Rathurde. This castle was, apparently, located between Rathurde Ring Fort and *Pairc na Staille,* 200 yards south-west of the entrance to Springfield castle. An area south of this was still known as Farrihy Anketell in 1842. Robert Anketell was the last member of the family to live here. He died in 1771, and was buried at night "by the light of torches according to the aristocratic custom of bygone days". The name is still found in Boherbue, County Cork.

CLONCREW CHURCH derived its name from *Cluain Creamh,* the Insulated Meadow, or the Bog Island of the Wild Garlic. It was mentioned as Cluoncrema in 1201 but was destroyed in the war of 1641. By 1840 only the two gables remained standing. Rev. G.F. Hamilton wrote that the pre-Norman east window was still preserved in 1930.

MUSKERY NOWNAN, the north-eastern portion of Dromcolliher, was investigated, by English Undertakers, soon after the survey of the confiscated Desmond lands in 1585. By 1593 a jury had concluded, in an inquisition,

Broadford village.

that Sir Henry Oughtred had no claim to the demesne lands here, and that most of the tenants "were mere Irish and especially the persons whose names ensue: Conagher O'Begley, Teige McDermody, O'Brien, Geoffry O'Conyll, Teige O'Connell and others". This latter point was a direct violation of the deed of grant which Sir Henry Oughtred had obtained from Robert Stroud, the first grantee. The Undertakers generally let their estates to free tenants, farmers and copy-holders, who in turn left them in convenient farms to the native Irish who, in all probability, were already in actual possession. By the time of the Cromwellian confiscations the Irish practically formed the entire population of the parish, as the Elizabethan grantees set their lands in much the same way as the Fitzgeralds of Desmond. Even the Williamite confiscations, which were comparatively few, made little difference to this system. The Catholics of the old Anglo-Norman and English families who lost their estates were admitted as tenants, but the "mere Irish" were excluded by the terms of these deeds of grant. Muskery Nownan belonged to the Nunan family, supporters of the Geraldines, until Donough Nunan was slain in the Desmond rebellion, and his lands and castle, Gardenfield West

Castle, or Muskery Nownan, were granted to Robert Stroud. By 1840 the castle had been levelled and a barn built on its site.

BROADFORD, rather than Killaliathan or Killagholehane, is better known today. The history of the village is more recent than that of the ancient parish in which it lies, and is closely associated with the premier landlord family of this area, the Plummers of Mount Plummer.

CONNIE NEENAN, of Cork, was one of the men interviewed by Uinseann MacEoin in his book *Survivors* (1987). Connie recalled how, on hearing of the attack on the Four Courts, in Dublin, the Republican forces decided to reinforce Limerick. "My party was stopped at Buttevant but we reached Broadford in Limerick the first night. We were caught between two Free State posts. With me were a number that I recall, Corney Sullivan and a lad called Spillane. Next thing the shooting started and Spillane fell. We all lay prone. I could see his rifle had dropped away from him. He died in five minutes. That was the start of it for us. We went from there to Rathkeale where we met Liam Lynch. We moved on to Adare; we captured a post there. Then we arrived in Limerick. We lost a couple of great lads there. One fellow that I recall

now, Paddy Naughton, he was very good in the Tan war. We were crossing Georges Street separately when he was hit ... Dear Christ, but he was a terrific man at a time when we needed men".

RICHARD PLUMMER, of Bodwyn, Wiltshire was the progenitor of the Plummers of Mount Plummer. His son, another Richard, was the first member of the family to settle in Ireland, first in Cork, and, later, in Donoman, County Limerick. Robert's son, Daniel, lived in Castle Quin, and married Mary Williams of Mundill. Daniel's will was dated 24 August 1728, and proved on 17 January 1729. Brudenell Plummer, Daniel's grandson, married Frances Fitzgerald, daughter of Thomas, the Knight of Glin, and was High Sheriff of Limerick in 1808. Brudenell's second son, also named Brudenell, later became a county inspector of the Royal Irish Constabulary. The family are still remembered in Broadford. Their surname, Plummer, may be derived from Plumber, a worker in lead, or Plumer, a dealer in plumes or feathers.

KILCOORA CHURCH no longer exists but the site, on the northern bank of the Darrery River, about half a mile above its meeting with the Camuisce, was identified by T.J. Westropp at the turn of the century. This is located mid-way between Gortnatubrid Church and Killeedy Church. The name was derived from *Ceill Curtha*, the Sweet-smelling Church.

KILLILA CHURCH derived its name from *Cill Adhladh*, possibly Adhladh's church, but I was unable to discover any translation of *Adhladh*. This site is located about twelve yards west of Killila Bridge and consists of an oblong, raised mound with a double rampart, or wall, on the western side, and the river to the east. It was used as a *cillín*, or children's burial ground, in 1842 but was re-opened as a graveyard during the *Great Hunger*, 1845-1847. It is still remembered locally as the Kyleen; was fenced off, and planted with trees, in the 1960s; and in ancient times gave its name to the townland now known as Mount Plummer.

TULLYLEASE is about three miles southeast of Broadford but is actually located in County Cork. The original foundation on this site is said to have been founded by St. Berechert, an Anglo-Saxon saint, who is believed to have come to Ireland with St. Gerald of Mayo, during the seventh century. Berechert is also known as St. Benjamin. An inscribed stone, with an incised cross and other patterns, was once used to mark his grave, rather than that of a later namesake who died in 839. The inscription on the stone reads, *Quicumquae hunc titulum legerit orat pro berechtuine.* Dunadach Ua hInmaineìn was recorded as the Erenagh of Tullylease, *Tulcha Leis, Tulach-Leis, Tollelyche, Tullales, Tulachles,* or *Tolleleyleyse.* He died in 1059, but his family, the Nunans, remained as hereditary coarbs of Tullylease into the sixteenth century, and were considered the custodians of the site of Kilcoora church into modern times.

TULLYLEASE CHURCH, a nave and chancel church, with work dating from the twelfth, fifteenth and sixteenth centuries, was built by Mathew son of Grifin, as an Augustinian priory, some time before 1170. Soon after 1193 it became a cell of Kells. Tullylease Church is mentioned in the taxation of 1302-1306, but it may have ceased to be conventual by then. In 1541 the *ville* of Tullylease contained 480 acres. The inscribed stone, mentioned earlier, is an eighth-century early Christian cross-slab. It is now fastened to the interior of the eastern gable and implores its readers to pray for Berechert. Berechert's House and Berechert's Well can be seen nearby, as well as a bullaun stone known as *Cloch na hEilte,* named after a doe who was milked here. The south end of the east wall is probably the oldest part of the church; the window and door in the south wall date from the thirteenth-century; and the present chancel was built in the fifteenth century.

THE NUNAN FAMILY derive their name from O'hIonmhaineàin, the descendant of Ionmhaineàn, the diminutive of *Ionmhain,* the Beloved. This name was later shortened to `O Nuanaìn, and the family were erenaghs of St. Berechert's Church, in Tullylease. This surname is now numerous in Cork, Limerick, Tipperary and Clare. Variants of it include *O'Hununane, O'Hinownan,* and Noonan. Anlane Nunan was Bailiff of Limerick in 1279, 1280 and 1295, and the family gave their name to Muskery Nownan.

GLENDUFF CASTLE, west of Broadford, is now a roofless ruin although some of its out-offices and yards are still in use. This castellated house, with a tower at one corner, dates from the early nineteenth century. In 1837 Glenduff, or Glanduff, Castle was the property of Eyre Massy, and was apparently leased by R.J. Stevelly.

THE BEGLEY SURNAME originated in County Donegal. During the fifteenth century some of the Begleys travelled southwards, with the MacSweenys, to serve as gallowglasses, in Kerry. During the sixteenth century this surname was almost peculiar to the counties of Cork and Donegal, although some Begleys had apparently settled in Muskery Nownan. The name *O'Beaglaoich* may be derived from *O'Beaglaoch,* descendant of the Little Hero, or from *O'Beigfhile,* descendant of the little poet. Other variants of the name are O'Beagly, O'Begely, O'Begley, Bagley, and Bigly.

CONNELLAN, is a surname found throughout all of Ireland in the sixteenth century. In Irish *O'Conallaìn* means the descendant of Conallàn, the *diminutive* of Conall. Variants include Conlan, Conlon, *O'Connellane* and *O'Conlan.*

THE O'CONNELL FAMILY in this region may be descendants of the *O'Conaill* of East Kerry, who were chiefs of *Magh O'gCoinchin* until they were dispossessed by the O'Donoghues towards the middle of the eleventh century. They became followers of the MacCarthy More, and were hereditary castellans of Ballycarbery, near Caherciveen, from the time of the Anglo-Norman invasion until the seventeenth century. Maurice O'Connell, the head of the family at the time of the Cromwellian confiscations, was transplanted to the *Brentir,* or Foul Land, the Kilnamona-Inagh region, in Clare. The name is derived from *O'Conaill,* the descendant of *Conall,* the High-powerful. O'Connell and Connell are the more commonly used versions of the surname.

O'GORMAN was described by Rev. Patrick Woulfe as a rare and scattered name. It is derived from *O'Gormaìn,* the descendant of *Gormàn,* the diminutive of *Gorm, Blue.* Variants of the name include Gorman and *O'Gormane.* It should be distinguished from *MacGormaìn* which is often anglicised to O'Gorman and Gorman.

SOURCES
9 11 20 21 34 39 42 47 76 79 86 107 111 120 129 154
159 192 208 212 233 246 269 282

Killaliathan Church.

Fedamore

Cahir Guillamore · Grange · Knocknagranshy

FEDAMORE derives its name from *Fiadamair, Fiadh Damair,* the Wood of Damar. A century and a half ago the village contained 26 house. Fairs were held on 5 May and 9 September chiefly for cattle and pigs, and occasionally for horses. In 1986 the population of this attractive hill-top village was 989 persons.

FEDAMORE GLEBE HOUSE is now a nursing home. The Church of Ireland church (built in 1740), for which the glebe house was erected, was demolished in 1956. The old national school built in 1891 was recently renovated by the community, and there is a new school opposite the Catholic church, St. John the Baptist National School.

ST. JOHN'S WELL was a place of pilgrimage in the early 1800s. This was located in the grave-yard of the old Protestant church.

FANNINGSTOWN was known as Fanning's Town as early as 1597. By 1840 only a remnant of its castle remained, standing to a height of six feet.

A DUEL was fought near the site of Fanningstown Castle, in 1792. When Michael "the Banker" Furnell was walking past Roxborough House, his dog entered the grounds which Henry Vereker had preserved. The infuriated Vereker shot Furnell's dog, and in the ensuing argument Furnell challenged Vereker to a duel. Vereker accepted. The two met here. Shots were exchanged and Vereker fell, fatally wounded, with a bullet in the thigh. "Pistols for two, coffee for one" was a popular saying when duelling was in vogue.

THE KNIGHTS TEMPLARS may have erected a church in 1288 in what later became Fanningstown. By 1840 only the foundations of this ancient structure, *Temple Roe,* were visible within its graveyard, according to John O'Donovan. He wrote in the same year that only small portions of the side walls of Rockstown Church remained, but both graveyards were still in use. There were then five forts within the parish of Fedamore. The two most important were *Rath na Gréine,* the Fort of the Sun, and its well, *Tobar Raith na Grèine,* in the townland of Ballyea, and Cashelmangan Fort, *Caisiol Mangain,* in the

Williamstown castle.

townland of Cloghadaloorty. Kilcaskin townland derives its name from an old burial-ground, *Cill Chaiscin,* which had almost passed out of use in 1840.

THE WHITE HORSE in Ballyea townland was the name applied to a large stone, *a n Gearán Bán,* which was seven feet high, five feet broad, and one foot thick. At some unspecified date, before 1840, human bones of an extraordinary size were discovered underneath it.

FRIARSTOWN HOUSE was occupied by the Vere Hunts in the 1820s when Rev. P. Fitzgerald explored the area. He referred to the ruins of Skule Castle as "being observable on the north side from Knockfennel" and explored "the fine remains of an ancient abbey embosemed high in tufted trees", Little Friarstown. He also mentioned some ancient buildings in the townland of *Cloch na*

Monach, the Monks' Stone, but was unable to discover who built them or when. By 1840 John O'Donovan wrote that they had disappeared completely. Pat Mulcaire of Ballyclough owns Friarstown House today.

WILLIAMSTOWN CASTLE was strategically placed on the top of a hill from which it could command the surrounding area, and may have been erected by the Bourke family. In 1826 it was described as a plain square building destitute of outworks or fortifications of any kind. One of the Crokers, of the adjoining Ballyneguard, repaired its walls and enlarged the windows, but Williamstown Castle lost many of its ancient features in the process which made it part of the adjoining farmhouse. Lewis maintained in 1837 that even though it retained a plain exterior it was curiously fitted up internally (in the Gothic-style), and had been renovated and restored by the Pain brothers.

GLENOGRA CASTLE is a Desmond stronghold dating from about 1400 to 1420, although it is also quite probable that the Fitzharris or Lacy families had erected an earlier structure on the same site during the thirteenth century. In 1536 the Earl of Desmond was unsuccessfully besieged here by Lord Thurles. Glenogra Castle was an octagonal keep set in a rectangular bawn. The ruins became quite dilapidated in recent years. Michael Quaine mentioned that one of the castle's towers, complete with roof, section of staircase, and windows, was blown into the field north of the castle during a storm about twenty years ago. This fragmented tower was still lying there in 1988, its mortared stonework intact. The main entry to the castle appears to have been on the south side, and there are some remains of another tower on the north-eastern corner. Some of its walls, cellars and underground stairs were "moderately perfect" 150 years ago, but now look as if they have been quarried for stone, particularly the western and eastern walls.

ST. NICHOLAS'S CHURCH, on the opposite side of the road to Glenogra Castle, may be "the abbey church founded here by the De Lacys, which at the Reformation contained nine amply endowed chantries, and was governed by a prior. Four of these chantries", or chapels, could still be located within this cruciform church ruin 150 years ago. The entrance appears to have been in the north wall. The gable of the south transept was still standing in 1988, and the three-light east window was intact although one of its lights, to the south, had been filled in. This church is also known as Glenogra Church. Tombs of the Lacy, Roche, Bourke, O'Grady and Fitzgerald families were the most prevalent in the last century, but today most of the monuments seem to be inscribed with the Quaine surname.

QUAINE, O'Cuayn, *O'Cuain,* O'Quane, Quan, Quann, Quane, Coyne and Quaid, the descendants of Cuan or Donnchaun, Lord of Harbours; this was the name of a branch of the *Ui Fiachrach* of Dooncoy, in the parish of Templeboy, County Sligo. The family were scattered by the end of the sixteenth century, and the name is now found mainly in Limerick and Cork, where it has been anglicised to Quaine and Quaid. A tradition in the Quaine family mentions that their ancestors had served with Hugh O'Donnell, and remained in Limerick after one of his raids on the south.

GLENOGRA BRIDGE spans the Camoge river north of the church and castle. Note the attractive stone-terraced garden in front of the modern red-brick house, at the western side of the old bridge.

MEANUS CATHOLIC CHURCH looks remarkably like the Church of Ireland churches described by Samuel Lewis in his *Topographical Dictionary of Ireland* (1837), in its layout and design, internally and externally.

CAHIR GUILLAMORE DEER PARK and the surrounding area, which comprises this unique and exclusive square mile of a long-lost ancient Ireland, is best viewed from the air. Only aerial photographs of the region can do justice to the various prehistoric and medieval sites by revealing the shapes and contours of hidden building, and other, foundations. Fort, field, road, house, and hut sites make Cahir Guillamore as important archaeologically , as the nearby Lough Gur. Sean P. O Riordáin excavated some rectangular building sites here, which dated from the fourteenth to the sixteenth centuries.

THE CAHIR GUILLAMORE BURIAL SITE has been tentatively dated to 2000 B.C., because of the coarse beaker pottery and other associated articles discovered with the burials it contained when it was excavated. The bodies of at least fourteen people were interred within the remains of this prehistoric chamber-tomb, which was formed from a large boulder leaning against the rock face, at an angle. One body, the only one buried in a crouched position, near the entrance, may have been the last burial.

CAHIR GUILLAMORE, the original *cathair* or fort after which the area was named, may have been demolished to build a stone circle, according to John O'Donovan's letters (1840).

CAHIR GUILLAMORE HOUSE dates from the late-seventeenth century. In 1837 it was the residence of Lieutenant-Colonel O'Grady, the son of Viscount Guillamore. During the War of Independence, the then Viscount Guillamore left a caretaker, Tom O'Donoghue, in charge of his house. On St. Stephen's night, 1920, the Sinn Fein *cumanns* decided to raise funds by holding a dance in Cahir Guillamore House. A mixed force of military, R.I.C. and Black and Tans, surrounded the old mansion. Just before midnight they fired indiscriminately through the walls and windows on the young Sinn Fein dancers and their friends, as over 90 women and 150 men had gathered for the occasion. Five volunteers were killed in this onslaught: Daniel Sheehan of Cahir Guillamore, Ned Moloney of Grange, John Quinlan of Grange Lower, Harry Wade of Cahernorrey, Ballyneety, and Martin Conway of Bruff. A Black and Tan constable, Alfred C. Hogsden or Hodgkinson, was shot and killed by the Sinn Fein sentries who had failed to spot the encircling cordon until the firing commenced. Over 100 Sinn Fein prisoners were savagely beaten before they were taken to Limerick the following day. This old house was totally derelict in 1978. By 1988 most of it had disappeared.

ROCKBARTON was a late eighteenth-century house, the seat of Viscount Guillamore, who had been raised to the peerage in 1831, by the titles of Baron O'Grady of Rockbarton, and Viscount Guillamore of Cahir Guillamore. The house was modified during the nineteenth century, and came into the possession of the Baring family. In 1856 it appears to have passed from the possession of the Barings into that of the Roche family, yet, during the War of Independence it was occupied by Colonel Baring and his wife, Lord Fermoy's daughter. Only the shell of Rockbarton now remains.

ROCKBARTON CASTLE had disappeared by 1840. John O'Donovan found a description of "an old castle in ruins", but it may have related to another such structure in the adjoining townland of Caher rather than the townland of Rockbarton, in the parish of Tullabracky. The other big houses of Tullabracky three years before that were Ballynanty of Mrs. Creed; the glebe house of Rev. John Fitzgerald, which was erected for £800 in 1813; and Cahir Guillamore House.

THE CAHIR GUILLAMORE STANDING STONE is located about half a mile west of Rockbarton House. In 1840 this was described as "7 feet high, 3 feet 4 inches wide at the top and middle, and 5 1/2 feet in width at the lower part. The original flag seems to have been split ..."

TULLABRACKY derived its name from *Tula Braice,* but although *Tula* signifies a Gentle Hill the original meaning of *Braice* has been lost. *Brac* is the Irish for an arm or bracket; *bràca* signifies a rake, a harrow or an apparatus for combing flax; *brach* means the hop plant or hops; and *braich* can be translated as malt.

TULLABRACKY CHURCH may have been founded originally by St. Blunny. Although the ruin was in poor condition in 1840, it was still remembered as a church or friary. At a later stage it appears to have served the Protestant community as their parish church until a new Church of Ireland church was built for £2,500 in 1819, about a quarter of a mile from here, mid-way between the glebe house and Rockbarton on a different site.

TULLABRACKY CASTLE, in the townland of Tullabracky Bishopland, was levelled by a local farmer, John Molony, about 1810. His son occupied a house on, or near the castle site thirty years later. Part of an old castle

The stone circle at Grange.

wall was said to enter a stable building belonging to the house.

BLUNNY'S WELL, Mullany's Well or Lunny's Well derived its name from *Tobar Mhullana,* the well of a saint now remembered as St. Blunny. He is not listed in the *Irish Calendar of Saints,* and by 1840 his feast day had been forgotten and patterns in his honour had ceased, in Tullybracky. Despite this, a few people still visited the well seeking cures for various diseases. Two incisions on a rocky stone over the well were believed to be the impressions of the saint's knees, and the portion of a wall running north to south, immediately over the well, may have been part of the outworks of Tullabracky Castle. The feast of St. Mlubhnáin Liaigh, the nearest name equivalent to that of Mullana, was celebrated on 29 March.

ROCHESTOWN, or Ballywilliam Parish, derived its name from *Baile an Roistigh,* the Townland or Town of Roche. In 1826 there was no Church of Ireland church or glebe house here.

ROCHESTOWN CASTLE was erected by the Roche family during the reign of Henry VII. This was described as a conspicuous ruin on top of "a bald rock", over 150 years ago.

BALLYWILLIAM FRIARY was a Dominican foundation, in all probability a cell or vicarage of Limerick or Kilmallock. It was also known as Rochestown Abbey and *Baile na mBratharbeg,* the Town or Townland of the Little Brothers. This last name was used in order to differentiate between the two Friarstowns; this one, of which only the site can be traced and the other one in Cahervally. In 1544 this house of the Dominican friars and 16 acres of land was granted to Robert Browne. It was then called Ballyniwillin. In 1826 Fitzgerald referred to "the burying place and walls of the old church" which was located north of the Camoge River near Sixmilebridge. The church had been razed to the ground by 1840 but the graveyard remained, enclosed with a wall, in a small valley, in the northern corner of Rochestown townland.

FRIARSTOWN TOWNLAND contained a standing stone, *Cloch á Liagàin,* which was located almost in its centre in 1840. This was five feet in height and three feet in diameter.

THE SPRING WELL, *Tobar an Fhuaráin,* was frequented as a holy well until early into the nineteenth century, as its waters were believed to be effective in curing several diseases. John Croker prohibited visitors from using it about 1830, and within ten years it was "very much injured by cattle".

GRANGE, or Manister Grange, is a corruption of *Mainstir na Gráinseach,* the Monastery of the Granary. In Elizabethan times, Grange belonged to Monasteranenagh. Like County Clare, this district contains a village named Sixmilebridge but its main claim to fame in the 1830s was its proximity to "three druidical circles" and the earth forts above Knockfennell. On 10 July, 1837, Dr. Ryan, the Catholic Bishop of Limerick, laid the foundation stone of a new Catholic church on a site provided by the Count de Salis, adjacent to the graveyard of the old eighteenth-century church. This older building was later demolished on the orders of Dean MacNamara.

THE GRANGE STONE CIRCLE, or the Great Stone Circle at Grange, is situated east of the Limerick-Bruff road. This is the most impressive such monument in Ireland and consists of an accurately laid out ring of contiguous standing stones. The largest stone to the north-east, north of the entrance, is known as *Rannach* or *Ronadh Crom Dubh* which may mean the Staff, or something more basic, of Crom Dubh — the original meaning has been lost. The entire circle is ringed by a large earthen bank with an entrance to the east. It was excavated in 1939. Late Stone Age and early Bronze Age pottery was found, and it was also discovered that the bases of the larger stones had been packed about with boulders when they were set into sockets in the old ground surface. This was in all probability a ritual monument, dating from about 2000 B.C. to 1500 B.C..

BLACK CROM, Crom Dubh, or Crom, is an old Celtic god whose feast was celebrated at the end of July or the beginning of August. Observed originally as part of the Festival of *Lughnasa* this marked the end of summer and the start of the harvest season. Irish country people now know it as Garland Sunday, but its older Pagan name was *Domhnach Chro m Dubh*, Black Crom's Sunday. The people of Grange, Lough Gur and the surrounding countryside, traditionally brought their harvest offerings into the great circle to lay before *Rannach Chrom Dubh*. Crom Dubh is still commemorated in parts of the county, and the Festival of *Lughnasa* has not been forgotten, although it may have been Christianised as a harvest festival by the Catholic and Protestant churches. Lough Gur has long been a *Lughnasa* site, and so is Knockainy or *Cnoc Áine*, the Hill of Aine. Crom is also remembered in the mis-named Cromwell's Hill, which is called after him and not England's Lord Protector of the Commonwealth, Oliver. Crom has lingered in the folk memory as "the little black man who first brought wheat into Ireland".

THE PILLAR STONE is the larger of two standing stones nearby. This is located northeast of the Great Circle while the smaller one, Cloughavilla, is south of it. There are also two other stone circles about 100 meters north of the Great Circle. One of them consists of a ring of fifteen free-standing stones, whereas the other, more damaged one, contains only nine such stones.

THE STONE HEAD kept in the farm-house across the road from the Grange Stone Circle is known as Gearóid Iarla's Head. This is believed to date from the fourteenth or fifteenth century. There is also an old, and interesting-looking, sundial in the garden of the farmhouse.

THE MASSIVE IRON POT lying inside the wall of the field in which the stone circle is located is said to be a cooking-pot used during the *Great Hunger*.

GRANGE MOTE is a small ring fort containing hut sites, located two miles north-north-east of Holycross crossroads. In the adjoining field to the south there is a rectangular platform with ring-barrows. More ring-barrows, and house-mounds with ring-ditches, can be found in the townland of Ballingoola. These may date from the Iron Age.

CAHERCON ROCK was known as *Carrig a' Mheára* in 1840. The ruined castle on top was so damaged, by then, that it was impossible to measure its dimensions.

THE GRANGE, a fine three-storey mansion, is now a ruin. This is the older of two houses of the same name in the neighbourhood, and was the seat of Standish Grady, who had a life-interest in it. After his death, ownership reverted to the Count de Salis. The Grange once housed a collection of rare books. It was built in the eighteenth century and refaced during the nineteenth century. Thomas, the son of Standish Grady, built a new house in Skule, which he also called the Grange during the nineteenth century. When he died, his estate passed on to his sister's family, the Crokers.

THOMAS O'GRADY (1789-1861) was a member of Caleb Powell's Grand Jury. In 1858 Caleb wrote of Thomas: "In his youth he profess'd the Roman Catholic creed and frequented the chappel [sic] of Bruff, with his father, but his mother, who 'was in t'other interest' prevailed upon her husband to transfer the children to Church or as his cousin Tom Grady the poet declared that his cousin Standish of Grange 'sent his children to church thro' fear of his wife and went to Mass himself for fear of the Devil' ... the greater portion [of Standish Grady's estate] fell eventually into the possession of Thomas his son who in modern times prefixed the O' to his paternal name and he has now I suppose two thousand pounds a year in land and money and a very ugly comfortable mansion on the land of Skule now called the Grange which was purchased by Standish from Ingoldsby Massy between 60 and 70 years ago after which he erected the present mansion house having resided in a house (now dilapidated) built on the De Salis estate on the opposite side of the river. This gentleman who resembles his cousin the poet in one respect, namely being an indefatigable quality hunter, I made Foreman for which he thank'd me in very warm and insincere terms as I have since ascertained".

THE GRANGE AMBUSH took place near Sixmilebridge and the townland of Friarstown South on the morning of 8 November 1920. No casualty figures were released concerning the number of British soldiers wounded, after the I.R.A. ambushed two lorry-loads of military personnel, but two of the I.R.A. were injured in the attack. Armed rebellion was not new to this region. The murdered Mayor of Limerick, George Clancy, had an uncle who had led 600 Grange men across the snow to take part in the abortive rising of 1867.

KNOCKNAGRANSHY is a corruption of *Cnoc na Gráinsighe*, the Hill of the Granary. The remains of an old horizontal mill were discovered by Geoffrey Lane when he was clearing land here in 1942. David Cantwell of Croom notified the National Museum of the mill's existence on 8 December 1954. A.T. Lucas later excavated the site between 16-20 August 1955.

THE KNOCKNAGRANSHY HORIZONTAL MILL was probably, like other such mills, a small two-storied structure erected over a race or channel which may have been fed by a stream of water from the nearby well of *Tobarlaghteen,* over 60 yards away. A small pond was possibly located above the mill to ensure a steady supply of water, which found its way through a large wooden chute to the wheel which was placed in a horizontal position. Jets of water playing on the paddle scoops of the wheel caused it to revolve in a clockwise direction, turning the millstone in the upper storey. Mills like this were used throughout Ireland from the seventh century until well into the nineteenth century. The chute, and its supporting beam, of the Knocknagranshy Mill is now in the National Museum.

THE HOLY WELL OF KNOCKNAGRANSHY, or *Tobarlaghteen,* had a small stone cupola built over it by James Keating of Knockhill in 1791. There was a St. Laichtin regarded as the patron saint of West Clare's fighting men, who used to stay immersed in cold water praying for their success in battle, but whether he had any connection with this part of Limerick is now only a matter of supposition, as a different Laichtin may have been commemorated in the well or *tobar* of Laghteen. The well dried up in 1955, but appears to have been the only source of water from which the mill could have been operated.

SOURCES
9 11 26 39 47 63 76
86 93 114 120 123 125 129
139 150 164 184 192 195 202
207 238 246 255 264 282

Foynes

Aughinish · Shanagolden · Shanid · Knockpatrick · Loghill

FOYNES derives its name from *Inis Faing* or Foynes Island in the parish of Robertstown. *Faing* may signify a Raven but it could also mean the Western Boundary. The *Annals of the Four Masters* record how Traolach O'Conchúir plundered the surrounding countryside from here in 1124. Sir John Norris recommended, in 1597, that the island should be fortified for the protection of the City of Limerick.

IN 1836 Limerick was promoted by railway entrepreneurs as having no shortage of "good houses for the billetting of troops before and after sea voyages" but when this scheme failed Foynes was selected as the packet station for all trans-Atlantic voyages. By then a battery of 24 guns, which had been erected on the island to protect shipping on the Shannon and prevent invaders from sailing up to Limerick, was no longer in operation. Samuel Lewis was able to write in 1837 that this "place has been recommended by Captain Mudge, the government engineer, as affording extensive and secure anchorage for shipping, and consequently as a proper situation for the construction of docks and quays; at present it is seldom resorted to by mariners, but the steamers plying between Limerick and Kilrush call off the island to take up passengers. On the south side is a handsome marine villa, the summer residence of the Earl of Dunraven; and there are several neat cottage residences in different parts of the island". During the early nineteenth century the new sport of yachting was introduced by the landed families who kept their cutters, rather than yachts, here. These boats included the Knight of Glin's *Rienvella* (30 tons), Crofton More Vandeleur's *Caroline* (49 tons) and Captain John Hamilton's *Adelaide* (23 tons).

THE COMMISSIONERS FOR THE IMPROVEMENT OF THE RIVER SHANNON presented a report to both Houses of Parliament in 1837. They stated that the "harbour of Foynes, on the south side of the river, is situated ten miles to the eastward of Tarbert. This place affords excellent shelter from all winds, being protected from the south and west by high lands adjoining the river banks, and from the north and north-east by Foynes Island. The harbour, in fact, consists of the channel that separates Foynes Island and the mainland, in which there is an ample depth of water at all times of tide". The report related how Foynes was "well situated as a converging point for the traffic of the north-western portion of the county ... a facility of export for the constantly increasing agricultural products of the country is much required; this can be effected most advantageously by the erection of a shipping wharf at Foynes, in a situation affording peculiar facilities for that purpose, where there is an ample depth of water, a sheltered anchorage, an extensive platform in the rear of it, close to the high road between Limerick and Tarbert, and within 1,100 yards of one of the finest limestone quarries in the south of Ireland". The commissioners then submitted plans and estimates of £8,500 to complete the necessary work.

THE WEST PIER was erected as part of a famine relief scheme in 1847. This was a joint undertaking by the Spring Rice family and the Commissioners of Public Works each of whom shared the cost of its construction, £10,000.

THE WATERFORD AND LIMERICK RAILWAY reached Foynes in 1858. The main street was moved from the edge of the Shannon to accommodate the railway line. During the American Civil War (12 april 1861 - 26 April 1865) Foynes, and Limerick, prospered. William Dargan, a shareholder in the Waterford and Limerick railway, operated a steamship, *Kelpie,* between Kilrush and Tarbert in the hope of benefiting when Foynes would eventually become the American packet station. When the Civil War started Dargan became a blockade runner. The *Kelpie* ran the blockade imposed by the Federal Navy and was eventually sunk at the height of the war. Sir Peter Tait, three times Mayor of Limerick, and a merchant price, was also a blockade runner; he owned the Limerick Clothing Company which manufactured uniforms for the Confederate forces; and the steamship *Evelyn* which ran the blockade to deliver uniforms and other supplies.

WILLIAM TRENCHARD, with £1000 to his name, was given a grant of 14,000 acres of land in West Limerick, in 1587. He was a native of Wiltshire, England, and his family surname can be best described as an occupational name signifying a cutter of some kind, with cleaver, sword, carving-knife, or trenching-spade. William retained 1,500 acres for himself and allotted the rest of his holdings, at Clounagh, Kilmoylan, Knockpatrick, Robertstown, and Shanagolden, to other Englishmen.

CORGRIG CASTLE, about two miles south-east of Foynes, was described in Elizabethan times as "belonging to Master Trenchard the Undertaker, and of strength sufficient to hold out against any force except the cannon. But the example of Glynne was so fearful unto the rebels that upon the first summons they yielded the same, with safety of their lives". The Trenchard family continued to live here until they built a mansion, in Cappa, now Mount Trenchard, in Georgian times. Corgrig House, the ancestral home of Gerald Griffin, derived its name from Corgrig Castle. A large part of this massive structure and its wall-faced moat still survive. In 1837 it was known as Congreiff and was one of the principal seats of Robertstown Parish, the other ones being Fort Anne, of S.E. Johnson, and Old Abbey.

MOUNT TRENCHARD has reversed its original facade. Early in the nineteenth century the rock of Lehy's Point, the point nearest to Foynes Island, was excavated to form a new line of road, the coast road, and this resulted in the approach road to the big house being altered. Mount Trenchard is a late Georgian three-storey house built over a basement some time before 1777. In that year the Trenchard estate, then reduced to 4,000 acres, was divided between the husbands of the two daughters of the last Trenchard male heir. Late in the eighteenth century Andrew Rice of Kerry purchased the Trenchard estate. His son, Stephen Edward Rice, was employed as a tutor to Catherine Spring, the only child and

Aerial view of Foynes town and harbour, with Foynes Island in the foreground.

heiress of Thomas Spring of Castlemaine. The young couple married and returned to Mount Trenchard where they established the Spring Rice family. In Victorian times a wing which was almost as high as the original main block was added to one side of the house. At that stage a porch was added onto one bow but this was later replaced by a more conventional front entrance between the two bows. The Spring Rice family remained in occupation until Lady Holland purchased Mount Trenchard in 1952. It was the home of Lieutenant-Commander C.E. Hall until 1957 when it was bought by the Sisters of Mercy. They replaced the west wing with modern extensions in order to accommodate a girls' boarding school. Lennox Robinson (1886-1958) wrote a play, *The Big House,* which was based on the home and lives of the Spring Rices.

STEPHEN EDMOND SPRING RICE (1814-1865) is commemorated with a large cross which was erected on the hill overlooking the village. Although he was the eldest son of Thomas Spring Rice (1780-1866), Lord Monteagle, he never succeeded to the estate and title as he died at sea, a year before Thomas died. Stephen managed the Mount Trenchard estate while his father pursued a political career. Stephen is now remembered as a liberal Protestant landlord who favoured Catholic Emancipation. Both father and son did their utmost to combat the privations of the *Great Hunger*, Thomas nationally, and Stephen locally. While his father was busy in Parliament Stephen applied himself almost totally to the management of the estate. In 1846 incompetent Board of Works officials left Mount Trenchard tenants, who had worked on relief schemes, without wages. Thomas paid "out of his own pocket". Thomas later helped to send tenants who were in poor circumstances to Australia since he came to the conclusion that emigration was the solution to Ireland's population problem.

SIR STEPHEN EDWARD DE VERE (1812-1904) was a nephew of the first Lord Monteagle. He was a notable writer and poet although his poetical reputation was overshadowed by that of his brother, Aubrey, during his lifetime. He was a Member of Parliament for Limerick City from 1854 to 1859 but is best remembered for his account of a voyage on one of the infamous coffin ships used to carry Irish emigrants to America. He travelled as a steerage passenger in order to observe conditions at first-hand. Lord Grey read Stephen's description of this harrowing journey to the British House of Lords and legislation was enacted which resulted in the elimination of the coffin ships.

THE MONTEAGLE MILLS purchased timber from Russia and Scandinavia during the nineteenth century. Huge ships from these countries used Foynes regularly as did many other ships engaged in the trans-Atlantic trade. The Monteagle or Spring Rice involvement with the development of the village continued. The second Lord Monteagle, another Thomas, was responsible for having the Harbour Order passed in 1890 to keep Foynes harbour independent of the Limerick Harbour Board. Thomas also founded a co-operative creamery in the main street and his daughter, Mary Spring Rice, was involved in gun-running in 1914. Thomas arranged for the erection of two jetties, during his 36-year chairmanship of the Foynes Harbour Trustees.

The Royal Navy used Foynes as a naval base into the early twentieth century and warships came frequently to the port.

CONOR O'BRIEN of Foynes Island, played an exciting role during the early summer of 1914 - that of a gun runner. The Irish Volunteers had been formed as a defence against Carson's armed rebels and Conor found himself, and his yacht *Kelpie* pressed into service "being in this age of steam and oil, the most improbable outfit for a gun running expedition". Conor recruited "two good seamen" in Foynes, and in addition "I had my sister as mate and, in emergency, cook; and a barrister who was no doubt an excellent authority on prize-court procedure; a big crew, but we did not know in what difficult conditions we might not [sic] have to tranship or land our cargo".

DARRELL FIGGIS posed as a Mexican revolutionary to purchase a consignment of arms in Germany. This deception was necessary as an embargo had been laid on the shipment of "warlike stores" to any European power. The guns had to be smuggled past the Hamburg customs. The tug *Gladiator* took the arms aboard and sailed to the rendezvous point near the Ruytingen Bank lightship where the *Kelpie* and Erskine Childers's *Asgard* had arranged to meet it on 12 July, 1914. The *Kelpie* was first on the scene having left the *Asgard* in Cowes. Conor O'Brien had his share of the cargo transhipped to the *Kelpie* while he waited for Erskine Childers to arrive. The *Asgard* sailed into history at Howth while the role of the *Kelpie* has been largely ignored. Conor O'Brien transferred his cargo to the 40-ton *Chotah,* which was owned by the Surgeon-General of the British Army in Ireland, at another rendezvous point southwest of Bardsey Island, before "we drifted into Kingstown to hear of the very sensational landing of *Asgard's* share at Howth ... my sister and I had, of course, to assist at the landing of our share. With some difficulty,

because we were now marked characters, I persuaded the authorities that we were the only people that could manage boats on a beach — God forgive me the lie! I don't think our notoriety mattered; every one who saw us sail out of Kingstown on a dirty-looking evening in an open whale-boat knew what we were going to do, but they did not know where we were going to do it. We stood away past Howth and out to sea till we were swallowed up in the night, and then reached in for Kilcool in Wicklow, where the lamps of the railway station were to light the landing ... We had only just time to lower our masts and clear away the gear when *Chotah* arrived; we were rushed up on the beach among a crowd of other small boats, and many willing hands unloaded us; and as we pushed off again I heard the distant rumble of lorries taking the goods away to a destination of which I am still ignorant". The *Chotah* was selected to run the arms ashore because of its engine which made it a more predictable vessel for meeting tight schedules.

CONOR O'BRIEN ostentatiously polished his rifle aboard the empty *Kelpie* before leading the authorities on a wild-goose chase northwards with his whaler, an open boat, which he later used to run the arms consignment, from the *Chotah,* ashore in, under cover of darkness. He wrote; "I doubt if half of us were contemplating war with England; the rest were merely protesting against the apparent collusion of the government with the Carsonite gun runners". The Howth gun running took place on 26 July 1914 and the Kilcoole gun running took place on the night of 1-2 August 1914. Britain declared war on Germany on 4 August 1914. Roger Casement landed at Banna Strand on 3 August 1916. His last words, in a letter to his sister, were; "It is a hard thing to die with all men misunderstanding".

NED DALY, of Limerick City, enrolled in the Irish Volunteers in 1913. He was appointed Captain of B. Company, First Battalion of the Dublin Brigade, early in 1914, and was in charge of this Company at the time the arms consignment was landed at Howth. Foynes and Glin were used as ports for ferrying I.R.A. volunteers across the Shannon during the War of Independence. On 14 July 1920 the Black and Tans burned the co-operative creamery in Foynes as a reprisal for the I.R.A. killing Constable Fahey, of the R.I.C., in an ambush, near Loghill.

TRANS-ATLANTIC TRAVELLERS had been using Foynes harbour from the early nineteenth century onwards but this phrase took on a new meaning in the late 1930s. On 19 October 1936 the Limerick Harbour Commissioners announced their decision to

locate an airport at Rineanna, now Shannon Airport, County Clare. Work commenced immediately on the construction of an airfield., and the dredging of a lagoon for seaplanes as an experimental trans-Atlantic flight had been scheduled for 1937. It soon became obvious that difficulties in Shannon would delay completion of the base and that the lagoon would not be usable in time for the first experimental flight. Foynes was selected as an alternative place for use by seaplanes. It already possessed extensive oil-storage facilities and Seán Lemass, the Minister for Industry and Commerce, had opened a new pier capable of accommodating large vessels, in March 1936.

THE FOYNES SEAPLANE TERMINUS was quickly set up as very little work was required to make this a suitable base for seaplanes, or flying boats. C.F. Peters of Croydon established the necessary communications and meteorological services in the Monteagle Arms Hotel, and direction-finding equipment was located on Foynes Island. On 25 February 1937 a flying boat arrived from Southampton to carry out test flights. The new terminus was considered satisfactory and in July 1937 a number of experimental trans-Atlantic flights took place. The Taoiseach, Eamon de Valera, witnessed the departure of the first west-bound trans-Atlantic flight from Foynes on 5 July 1937 and the arrival of the first east-bound flight on 6 July 1937. In that same year a Pan-American Yankee Clipper flew from Botswood, Newfoundland, to Foynes, in 12 hours 31 minutes. The first scheduled flying boat to alight here was a Pan-American Boeing 314 on 28 June 1939. Foynes became Ireland's first commercial trans-Atlantic air base and was used as an air terminus throughout the duration of World War II by Pan-American, the British Overseas Airway Corporation and the American Export airlines. The port handled up to ten flights a week and many of the passengers who passed through it were associated with the Allied war effort but strict press and radio censorship ensured that these facts were never revealed to the general public. The development of aircraft, accelerated by wartime requirements, shifted the emphasis from aeroplanes that alighted on water to those that could land on the ground. These latter planes proved to be more practical as flights were no longer hindered by weather conditions that could delay flying boats from taking off for days at a time, or forced their pilots into taking more circuitous routes on trans-Atlantic flights. Scheduled flying boat services to Foynes were phased out towards the end of 1945 and Shannon Airport began to replace Foynes as Ireland's international airport.

FOYNE'S HARBOUR has large oil-storage installations, a pier for ocean-going ships, and is still used by shipping commercially. Vessels of up to 22,000 tonnes can be accommodated in its deep-water anchorage.

CONOR O'BRIEN (1880-1952), was an architect, voyager, author, and gun-runner. He was educated in Winchester and Trinity College, Oxford. He was the first son of Edward William O'Brien by his second wife, Julia Garth Marshall of Monk Coniston, Westmoreland. Conor designed his own yacht, *Saoirse;* sailed her around the world; and became the first man to display the Irish tricolour in many foreign ports. After this he was commissioned to build a boat which he personally delivered to the Falkland Islands. He married Katherine, the daughter of Sir George Clausen, and wrote several books about sailing. His wife died in 1936. Conor returned to Foynes Island after World War II, and continued to live there until his death.

AUGHINISH ISLAND derives its name from *Each Inis,* Horse Island. It is now the scene of a large-scale industrial development. The massive aluminia plant complex which was established here in recent years is the largest single employer in the region and its buildings dominate the southern shore of the

Aughinish Island, now the site of the giant alumina plant.

Shannon. In 1837 Samuel Lewis wrote that this part of the parish of Robertstown "called Ahenish, and improperly considered as an island, is flat and is frequently inundated by the River Shannon".

ROBERTSTOWN CHURCH had many of

its features broken and disfigured by 1840 although its walls were still perfect. Only the eastern end of Robertstown castle then remained standing on the edge of an inlet from the Shannon.

ROBERTSTOWN PARISH, including

Foynes Island, had 1,794 inhabitants in 1831. The system of agriculture was considered backward by Samuel Lewis who wrote that large portions of land were cultivated with the spade while manure was carried to the fields on the shoulders of the women.

DYSERT CASTLE was originally four storeys high but only the arches of two remained in 1840. The walls were then about 50 feet high.

MORGANS PARISH CHURCH, *Templemuireguiededan,* may have been founded by the Knights Templars, and later rebuilt by the Franciscans of Askeaton in 1496, according to Samuel Lewis. In 1837 he described the extensive ruins of the old church and wrote that the land of the parish, four miles west of Askeaton, was fertile but badly cultivated. Most of it was subdivided into small holdings, yet it produced good corn and potato crops.

MORGANS is an irregularly built house dating from the seventeenth century. It was built by Thomas Rose of Morgans, Aghabeg and Ballyclough. He became Sheriff of Limerick City in 1674, was attainted by the Parliament of James II in 1689, and became Mayor of Limerick in 1695. In 1696 he erected at his own expense the first lamps to light the city and was the first man in the county to drive his own coach. His son, Henry, was a member of Parliament for Ardfert from 1703 to 1713 and another descendant, Captain Thomas Rose, occupied Aghabeg, or Little River, in 1827. Brian de Breffny and Rosemary ffolliott wrote that Morgans was occupied in 1975 and that the building to which it was joined, a single-storey erection with a panelled chimney-stack, seemed to be much older. The upper floor has many of the features of "a long house" as there are no corridors and the drawing-room, dining-room and bedrooms open off of one another. The windows of this upper storey are much larger than those of the ground floor, which contains the kitchen and offices. The building is believed to be haunted by the ghost of Madam Rose. The ruins of an old castle can be seen in the garden. During the nineteenth century the Odell family came into possession of Morgans.

SHANAGOLDEN derives its name from *Sean Ghualainn,* the Old Shoulder or Hill according to the more usual sources. Tony Fitzsimmons of Shanagolden and Kilkishen, County Clare, believes that *Seanaghualainn* means the Rolling Lowland. In 1831 the parish of Shanagolden contained 3,213 inhabitants, of which number, 847 were in the town. In 1837 Samuel Lewis wrote that the town consisted of one long irregular street containing 150 houses "of which three only are slated, the remainder being thatched, and all are small and ill built. It has a constabulary police station ... fairs take place on the Wednesday after Trinity Sunday, and on 4 September, chiefly for cattle and pigs. A new line of road from the town joins the mail road on the banks of the Shannon, at Robertstown, opening a ready communication with the county of Kerry. The substratum in and around the town is limestone, of which blocks of a very large size are procured for cutting into gate-posts, pillars slabs, etc., but all are sent away, as no attempt has been made to cut or work them on the spot ... The town and the surrounding lands are principally the property of the Rt. Hon. T. Spring Rice, Chancellor of the Exchequer, whose seat is about three miles distant. Close adjoining the town is Shanagolden House, the elegant residence of the Rev. G. Vincent; and the glebe house, more than a mile distant from the church is at present occupied by J. Fitzgerald, Esq." The Church of Ireland parish church was "a large and handsome building, apparently very old; the chancel being in ruins, the nave was fitted up for divine service, having been roofed and a lofty square tower built in 1815, by aid of a loan of £450 from "the late Board of First Fruits. Samuel Lewis related how the original

Aerial view of Shanagolden.

structure dated from the early thirteenth century; there was a fine east window in the ruined chancel; the east window of the more recent structure was inserted into the choir of the older; and the church contained an unusual medieval font and a tombstone dating from 1585. The 11 1/2 -acre glebe was in three portions; one near the glebe house which was built in 1813; another in Barrigone; and the third near the church.

BARRIGONE derived its name from *Barraig Eoin*. In the 1830s there was a holy well located in the townland of Craggs, whose waters were believed to be efficacious in curing diseases. Samuel Lewis referred to "the little village called Barracks" in his topographical dictionary.

OLD ABBEY was a name applied to the site of Manisternagalliaghduff Abbey until the house known as Old Abbey was built. This house was one of the principal seats of Robertstown parish in 1837 and was the residence of W. Morgan. Old Abbey House was demolished early in 1989.

MANISTERNAGALLIAGHDUFF ABBEY derives its name from *Mainistir na*

gCailleach Dubh which is generally translated as the Monastery of the Black Hag, possibly in reference to the last prioress of this convent who is commonly believed to have been a witch. Another rendering of *Mainistir na gCailleach Dubh* as the Monastery of the Black Nuns may be a likelier translation as this is one of the few medieval nunneries known to exist in Ireland.

THE MONASTERY OF ST. CATHERINE DE O'CONYL, the religious house of St. Catherine in O'Conyl, Monasternecallowduffe, *Negaylagh, Kaylaghe, Negillah,* or *Monasternicalliagh* are other names under which this monastery is known. An inquisition of 1298 proved that a nunnery was founded here some time before the battle of Callan was fought in 1261. This nunnery was established for Augustinian canonesses during the thirteenth century and most of the church and cloister seems to date from this period, while the east window and north door were inserted during the fifteenth century. The church opens off the eastern side of the cloister court which was the centre of this monastery as the refectory and kitchen were

located on its southern side and the domestic buildings, with undercrofts, were situated to the west. The church contains a piscina, a finely-decorated double-sided west doorway, and a room to the south which is known as the Black Hag's Cell. The monastery was valued at £2.01 1/2 in the taxation of 1302-1306. The revenue was not sufficient to support the prioress and nuns, in 1306. The Earl of Desmond complained that the prioress and nuns, or several of them, were leading lewd, loose, and dissolute lives and had converted the goods of the monastery to unlawful uses. The only nun who remained had married a layman, by whom she had offspring, and had to be removed from Manisternagalliaghduff by order of Bishop Cornelius O'Dea (1400-1426) of Limerick. The monastery church was a parochial one whose priest was appointed by the prioress and nuns. The Earl's complaint was lodged in Rome as Pope Martin V was aware of the situation in December 1432. The Pope ordered the suppression of the monastery, and appointed Awly Olongsygh as rector, but there is no evidence that the convent was suppressed. It seems to have continued into the sixteenth century and was dissolved some time before 1567 when the priory was granted to Sir Warham St. Leger. In 1583 it was leased to James Goold and in 1594 it was granted to Sir Henry Wallop.

A COLUMBARIUM is located to the southwest of the monastery. This is one of two surviving medieval pigeon-houses in the county, the other one is in Adare. The remains of the gate-houses and fish ponds can also be found nearby.

KILCOSGRAVE CASTLE had disappeared by 1840 although its site, on which a ruined house then stood, had not been forgotten. St. Senan's Well was located close to Shanagolden and was frequented as a pilgrimage site into the early nineteenth century.

KILCOSGRIF, or Kilcosgrave House, is a two-storey structure with one-storey sections on either side of the entrance door. This was named after an earlier castle and house.

BALLYSTEEN HOUSE was the home of Michael Dore during the War of Independence. The house was used as an I.R.A. headquarters from 1916 onwards. It was raided, by the British, on several occasions but no arms were ever found, or arrests made here. The *Big Four* sheltered in Ballysteen after the raid at Soloheadbeg on 21 January 1919 and General Lucas was held captive here in July 1920.

KILBRADRAN CHURCH, or Kilbraydron Church, derives its name from *Cill Bradhrán*, the Church, or Cell, of St. Bradran. John O'Donovan was unable to find a saint of this name in *The Calendar of Irish Saints.* The church is located at the foot of Kilbradran Hill. This was a nave and chancel structure originally although all but a portion of the southern wall of the chancel had disappeared by 1840. The walls of the nave were then described as perfect, and constructed out of large unquarried stones, irregularly laid, with lime and mortar. The large graveyard around the ruins is still in use. Kilbradran church gave its name to the nearby hill and the old parish.

LISBANE RING FORT gives its name to the townland in which it is located. This large hill-top fort is situated close to the ruins of Kilbradran church. It possessed stone-faced ramparts and had large annexes to the north and east.

NEWBRIDGE derived its name from "a good bridge" over the River Deel which was built in 1747.

LISNACULLIN CASTLE, or Lisnacille Castle, is said to have been built by the MacSheehys about 1445. This is located two miles south of Newbridge.

COOLCAPPAGH contained a Catholic church, a large plain building, in 1837 when

Samuel Lewis wrote of it and mentioned the remains of the old church of Clounagh, the ruins of Rathgonin Castle and "a good old mansion", Waterfield, which was then the residence of J. Creagh.

SHANID CASTLE was the oldest, most important stronghold of the Earls of Desmond. Their warcry of *Shanid Abú* originated here and was used on the battlefields of Ireland until Henry VII abolished such cries in 1495. From then onwards *Shanid Abu* appeared on the Fitzgerald family crest as they, like other chieftains, could cry only on St. George, England, or their English sovereign when going into battle. A *motte and bailey* fortification was built here, possibly in 1190, by Thomas Fitzmaurice Fitzgerald. Early in the thirteenth century a polygonal, or multi-sided, tower was erected on the same site, before the fashion for circular towers, like that at Nenagh, was established. Peter Harbison dated the earliest mention of Shanid Castle to 1230. T.B. Barry reported in *The Archaeology of Medieval Ireland* (1987) that half "of the keep is still at its full height ... Although the castle is not mentioned before 1230 in the sources its design is earlier in date, and this is another site where an excavation might give us a more precise date for its construction". The tower was erected on the outer bank of the ditch surrounding the 35 foot high *motte* which is topped with the remains of a battlemented curtain wall. The remains of the D-shaped *bailey* are on a lower level, to the east of the tower. In 1569 the castle was surrendered during the first Desmond Rebellion (1568-1572). Red Hugh O'Donnell captured it in 1600 and, after that, little was heard of the castle until it came into the possession of F. Trenchard in 1611. It was pillaged in 1641, lapsed into ruin, and little else is recorded about its subsequent history. According to locals, in the early 1800s, the site of a much larger castle was located half a furlong north of Shanid Castle. The road from the castle to Loghill is believed to be the oldest road in West Limerick.

SHANID RING FORT is located south-east of Shanid Castle. This is a large bivallate ring fort and contains the remains of several structures within its interior. This was described in 1837 as an extensive, spacious circular fort surrounded by embankments and fosses, and "divided by earthworks into four compartments: but these subdivisions appear to be of later date than the original formation". The earliest reference to the area recounts how the Vikings were defeated in battle here, in 839.

KNOCKPATRICK, derives its name from *Cnoc Phadraig,* Patrick's Hill, a mile to the north of Shanagolden. The summit of this hill

is 572 feet above sea level. Maurice Lenihan wrote that this is "said to be the highest land in the county, whence the surrounding country is seen stretching in extensive perspective, with the majestic course of the Shannon through its numerous windings to the sea ... From this hill are extensive and interesting views, embracing the high grounds of the counties of Tipperary, Galway, Cork, and Kerry, with the rich lands of Clare and Limerick in the foreground, and the towns of Limerick and Ennis rising beyond the expanded waters of the Shannon".

KNOCKPATRICK CHURCH on the summit of Knockpatrick Hill, is said to have been consecrated by St. Patrick. Only some fragments of an old medieval church remain. By 1837 the gables of the church had disappeared and the space on the western wall was "occupied by a large curious tomb belonging to the families of Bourke and Griffin".

PATRICK'S SEAT, *Suidheachán Phadraig,* consisted of "five rude unhewn stones" in 1837, the remains of a small cist.

ST. PATRICK'S WELL is believed to be the place in which a druid tried to poison St. Patrick. According to folklore, Patrick left a golden cup at the well. A cup or chalice was kept here until 1785 when a member of the O'Niadh family pledged it to "Mr. Roche of Limerick who brought it to Paris" where it was last heard of in 1840.

NEVILLE is a surname derived from *O'Niadh,* the descendant of *Nia* or the Champion. This was the name of an ancient Kerry family who were originally seated in the neighbourhood of Tralee. In a later period they became coarbs, or erenaghs of Knockpatrick. Variants of the name include *O'Nee, O'Nea, O'Ney,* O'Knee, Nee and Knee. This surname was fairly rare in Kerry and Limerick by 1923 but was quite common in West Galway where it was sometimes Anglicised to Needham.

CHARLOTTE O'BRIEN (1845-1909) is buried in the old graveyard of Knockpatrick. She was a daughter of William Smith O'Brien and collaborated with Sir Stephen de Vere in a joint campaign against the coffin ships.

CROAGHANE FORT, a large oval ring fort, was the more complete of the two ring forts in the townland of Knockpatrick in 1967.

BALLYHAHILL was located in the parish of Kilmoylan in 1837. The parish then contained 3,326 inhabitants, possessed a Catholic church in Ballyhahill, and the ruins of Kilmoylan church about a mile south of Shanagolden.

KILMOYLAN CHURCH derived its name from *Cill Maolain,* the Church of St. Moelan. John O'Donovan was unable to ascertain which saint of that name the church was called after. The building was in a fairly good state of preservation until the western gable collapsed about 1838.

DUNMOYLAN derives its name from *Dún Maoilín,* the Fort of Maoilin, a man's name possibly a saint's.

DUNMOYLAN CHURCH took its name from the nearby earth fort which was still visible in 1837. By the time John O'Donovan wrote of this church, in 1840, only its south wall remained. Locals pointed out a court or castle site 300 yards south of this church but no one then living, in 1840, remembered any of its walls standing.

THE WELL OF THE KING OF SUNDAY, *Tobar Rí an Domhnaigh,* was located in Gortadrumna townland but there was no observance of a pattern, patron or feast-day here 150 years ago. Gortadrumna Castle was then in ruin and only a portion of its walls remained.

DUNMOYLAN CASTLE was the seat of the Wall family from the thirteenth century until 1580 or 1583. Oliver Stephenson killed Ulick Wall, an old man, blind from birth, and confiscated his castle and lands on Pelham's orders. Stephenson was described by Rev. J. Begley as a greedy, ruthless man who served as constable of Glin Castle and custodian of Corgrig Castle during the Desmond Rebellion. In 1654 Thomas Chamberlain was given a grant of Dunmoylan Manor and lands.

WALL is a Norman surname derived from *du Val,* of the Vale, or Valley. The name dates back to the thirteenth century and is found in various parts of the country. In 1335 John and Walter de Vale joined Sir John D'Arcy's expedition to Scotland. Stephen de Wale was made Bishop of Limerick in 1360; Bishop of Meath at a later stage; and became Lord High Treasurer of Ireland. Variants on this name include *de Val, de Vaal, de Vale, de Wale* and *de Bál.* During the sixteenth century the Walls were found in Limerick, Galway, Tipperary, Cork, Kilkenny, Carlow and Kildare. They were quite numerous and formed a distinct clan of their own, under a Wall chieftain, in County Galway.

KILCOLMAN PARISH contained 510 inhabitants in 1837. It derived its name from *Cill Cholman,* the Church of St. Colman. John O'Donovan was unsure which St. Colman was the patron here. He thought St. Colman of Temple Shanbo, or Shanbotha, at the foot of Mount Leinster, was the saint in question as his festival was observed on 27 October and a regular pattern was held at St. Colman's Well, Kilcolman, on 29 October. This well, about one furlong to the north of Kilcolman Church, may have been the site of a *Samhain* festival in the more distant past. The church was destroyed during the war of 1641 and was

Spring Rice Memorial Cross, Shanagolden.

never rebuilt. There were several ruined castles in the parish in 1837. Castle-Egney was then the most prominent of these ruins although only one slender square tower remained.

LOGHILL, or Loughill, derives its name from *Leamhchoill,* the Elm Wood. The village, on the mail road from Limerick to Tarbert, contained a population of 277 inhabitants in 53 houses in 1837. Fairs were generally held at Mount Trenchard in March, June, September and December. The parish of 150 years ago, situated on the southern bank of the Shannon, was described as having rocky land and light soil, except for some better ground near the village. The principal manure was of sea-sand and sea-weed which was "either collected on the slab or brought from the opposite coast of Clare". Despite "extensive beds of coal lying above each other in five different strata" in the northern part of the parish only the thinnest uppermost section was worked as it was cheaper to import coal from England or Wales.

OUVANE QUAY was used by sloops to deliver cargoes in the early nineteenth century. It took its name from Ouvane Cottage, the seat of Lieutenant Hewson of the Royal Navy

in 1837. Some time before that date Hewson's father, or uncle, had demolished a very strong castle near the shore, and used the material to build a garden wall. More than 100 skeletons were found in the nearby demesne of Woodcliffe, the Taylor residence, on a piece of ground called the Field of Sculls [sic]. Numerous brass coins dating from the reign of James I were found on Rev. D. O'Sullivan's estate, Curragh. In the townland of Knockabooley the Protestant Bishop of Limerick was enabled to grant leases for three lives whereas elsewhere in Loghill Parish he could only grant 21-year leases, a singular tenure which still prevailed in 1837. The other big houses of the parish, excluding Mount Trenchard, were Fairy Lawn of the Griffin family and Rock Lodge of the Hardings.

SOURCE REFERENCE NUMBERS
2 3 5 9 11 28 32 34 42 44
53 63 64 67 75 76 86 107 108 120
129 135 150 173 175 182 192 195 196 215 230
233 238 241 243 246 255 275 282

Galbally

Duntryleague · Ballylanders · Anglesborough · Kilbeheny

GALBALLY derives its name from *Gall-Bhaile Eatharlach,* the Foreign Town of Aharlagh, or Aherlow. In 1837 Samuel Lewis wrote that it "was situated at the head of the Glen of Aherlow, which being the only pass into Tipperary from the northern and eastern parts of Cork and the western parts of Limerick, was frequently contested by rival chieftains, but remained for more than 300 years in the possession of the O'Briens and Fitzgeralds ... This place, in which are the ruins of several religious establishments, appears to have been formerly of considerable importance; an abbey for Franciscan friars was founded near the town ... which flourished till the dissolution, when it was granted to John of Desmond. In 1601, the Lord-President Carew summoned the chiefs of every county in this province to meet him at this place, where he appointed Lord Barry general of the whole force of Munster. The abbey being included in the forfeiture of Sir John Fitzgerald's estates, the rectory, parsonage and vicarage of Galbally, the parsonage and prebend of Killenellig with all the glebe and tithes, except those belonging to the vicar, and other lands belonging to the abbey were, in 1611, granted to Thomas Cantwell". A Cromwellian garrison was later established in Galbally to expedite the transplantation of many of the original inhabitants to "Hell or Connaught".

LOWESTOWN is the name which should actually be applied to the town, as the original townland of Galbally is located east of the

Aerial view of Galbally .

town. The bridge near Hedigan's farm-yard marks the boundaries of Lowestown and Galbally. In 1837 Samuel Lewis wrote that Galbally had 560 inhabitants and "is situated near the foot of the Galtee mountains, and contains 110 houses, of which some are well built and roofed with slate, but the greater number are mean thatched cabins. Fairs for black cattle and pigs are held on 12 May and 15 October, and petty sessions every alternate Wednesday. A penny-post and a constabulary police force have been established in the town. The parish is mountainous ... The scenery is boldly diversified, and there are several handsome seats, of which the principal are Massy Lodge, the elegant residence of Lord Massy; Riversdale, of Hugh Massy, Esq.; Castlereagh, of G. Bennett, Esq.; Janeville, of the Rev. R. Lloyd; the Cottage, of W. Lewis, Esq.; Annagurra, of T.T. Adams, Esq.; and Stagdale, of W. Massy, Esq.". Riversdale, Annagurra and Castlereagh had disappeared completely by 1989, although the last-named house is still commemorated in the name of a townland. Stagdale is in ruin. A Catholic church was erected in the village in 1834. This was renovated over the intervening years, but was eventually demolished in 1972. The new Catholic church opened in 1974. Only a two-foot high wall remains of the old Church of Ireland church.

THE MASSY FAMILY amassed more land in the county than any other Cromwellian settlers. They claimed descent from Hamo de Massy, a companion-in-arms of William the Conqueror. General Hugh Massy arrived in 1641, and later settled in Duntryleague. He married five times, and was succeeded by his son, and namesake, who was married to Amy Benson, the daughter of another Cromwellian planter. This Hugh and Amy had four sons: Hugh of Duntryleague; John of Knockaneevan, progenitor of the Ingoldsby Massys; Will of Stoneville, Rathkeale, whose descendants are still living there today; and Charles, who became Dean of Limerick and ancestor of the baronets of Doonass. The third Hugh married Elizabeth Evans, the sister of Lord Carbery, and they had six sons, the eldest of whom was created Baron Massy in 1776. In 1858 Caleb Powell selected John Massy, for Grand Jury service. Powell wrote in his posthumous memoirs that John's maternal grandfather, Luke White of Woodlands, a famous Dublin bookseller, had "commenced life hawking books in a green apron and died worth a million acquired by stock jobbing and hoarding". Massy Lodge was built as a summer residence, about 1800. Part of it was demolished by 1978, but the remaining portion is still habitable. It is now the property of the Hanley family.

GALBALLY ABBEY, or Moor Abbey, is actually located within County Tipperary, half a mile east of what is now the village of Galbally. The original church on this site was founded by Donnchadh Cairbreach O'Brien during the thirteenth century. Aunfurn (?) M'Bryon of Aherlow re-founded the friary here in 1471. This was reformed for Franciscan Observant friars in either 1536 or 1567. Moor Abbey was plundered in 1472 and officially suppressed in 1540. In 1543-1544 it was granted to John Fitzgerald of Desmond, along with its three gardens, six acres of land, and six dwellings and offices with the adjoining lands set apart for each household's use. The Franciscans were allowed to remain on, but abandoned their friary during Sir Henry Sidney's campaign in the region, in 1570. They returned to Galbally shortly afterwards. About 1588 the English arrived and surrounded the church. Three of the friars fled into the tower when their escape was cut off. Fr. Dermot O'Mulrooney came downstairs to put out a fire, started by the soldiers, and was captured, wounded,

Moor Abbey.

decapitated and dismembered. His two companions also perished. During the War of Independence, the Royal Irish Constabulary attempted to blow up the ruins to prevent the I.R.A. using them as a strong point. Tradition credits the Cromwellians with blowing up part of the building from similar motives. The Office of Public Works excavated Moor Abbey in 1984, but "no medieval features were found inside the fifteenth-century church because of widespread disturbance caused by post-dissolution burials and modern drains". This is a nave and chancel church, with a tall slender tower, a sedilia, and some fine windows. There is another church ruin in the village. This is located on the hill north of the bridge separating Lowestown from Galbally. Its graveyard is still in use.

THE I.R.A. MEMORIAL

in the square commemorates the officers and men of Galbally who died "on scaffold, field and from hardships endured in the struggle for Irish independence": Thomas Whelan, hanged in Mountjoy, 14 March 1921; Edmund Foley and Patrick Maher, hanged in Mountjoy, 7 June 1921; Michael Scanlan, killed in action, 27 October, 1920; James Scanlan; Sean Lynch; William P. O'Brien; Michael Quish; Liam Fraher; John J. O'Brien; and Eamonn O'Brien, one of those who took part in the Knocklong Rescue.

THE I.R.A. were active in this region during the War of Independence. On 23 September, 1919, Ned Foley, Patrick Maher, Michael Murphy and Michael Shanahan, were arrested and charged with the murders of two R.I.C. men during the Knocklong Rescue. They were held on remand for three months. In the interim Thomas Shanahan (Michael's brother), and Michael O'Connell of Thurles were also arrested, while two other local men, Sean Lynch and John Joe O'Brien went "on the run". An R.I.C. man, Sergeant Reilly of Roskeen, County Tipperary, was a witness for the prosecution. He was kidnapped in Armagh on the eve of the trial, which had been set for a hearing on 7 July, 1920. He was released unharmed on 8 July, 1920. The grand jury returned "true bills" against Ned Foley, Patrick Maher and Michael Murphy; the Shanahan brothers were acquitted; and Michael O'Connell had been released, after a Mountjoy hunger strike, before the trial commenced. Court-martial, rather than trial by jury, came into effect before the five-day trial began on 15 March, 1921. Patrick Maher and Ned Foley were sentenced to death, and Michael Murphy was acquitted. Patrick and Ned were the last men executed in Mountjoy jail before the Truce came into effect on 9 July 1921.

MICHAEL SCANLAN, commandant of the First Battalion, East Limerick Brigade, was arrested on 27 October, 1920. He was conveyed, under escort, to Limerick City. He jumped off the lorry in which he was being transported, outside the gates of the R.I.C. station in William Street, Limerick, and escaped through Little Catherine Street. The Auxiliaries found him hiding in a basement in Thomas Street, shot him in the stomach and neck, and dragged him back to the lorry. He died, later that evening, in the New Barrack. The military removed the tricolour from his coffin as his funeral cortege passed through William Street the following day, but the mourners replaced it with another, some distance away.

BALLYWIRE HOUSE is actually in County Tipperary but the estate straddles the boundary between both counties. This was the home of Roseanne Wheeler, a famous eighteenth-century landlady still remembered in the folklore of the region. The present owners, Helen and Richard Bourke, have sealed off the round tower, from which Roseanne once surveyed the countryside, as they consider it too dangerous for their children to play in. Helen also told me that they intend to retain the old ballroom, which is in poor condition at present. Ballywire was originally known as Ballydwyer, and over the centuries has been owned by Trinity College and the Damer, Delmege, Wheeler, Bolton and Massy families. It is located on what was once the toll road to Emly.

CHIEF BARON BOLTON settled in Ballywire about the middle of the seventeenth century. One of his descendants, John Bolton, changed his name to John Bolton Massy on succeeding to a large competence on the death of his grand-uncle, John Massy.

DUNTRYLEAGUE derives its name from *Dún Trí Liag,* the Fort of the Three Pillar Stones. The old Church of Ireland church is now a ruin, and the lead has been stolen from the coffins (formerly lead-lined) within its large wrecked vault.

THE DUNTRYLEAGUE PASSAGE GRAVE

is located in a depression between two hill-tops on the summit of Duntryleague Hill, 822 feet above sea-level. This ruined megalithic tomb is still known locally as Darby's Bed. This almost inaccessible tomb has a long entrance passage leading in to a chamber which expands inwards. The tiered roof-stone system resembles that used in other such chamber tombs in Brittany. Some ring-barrows were excavated nearby but only a piece of iron was found, insufficient material on which to establish a date. There was also a stone circle which I was unable to find; this may be the stone kerb of a vanished cairn.

The tomb, ring-barrows, and circle are now very difficult to locate because of the surrounding forestry.

BALLYLANDERS derives its name from *Baile an Londraigh* which seems to signify the Town of *De Loundres,* or the Town of the Londoner.

DE LOUNDRES, meaning of London, was a family name introduced soon after the Anglo-Norman invasion. William de London witnessed a grant of land by the Dean and Chapter of Limerick Cathedral in the early thirteenth century. His surname, *de Londún, de Londra* or *de Londras,* is peculiar to the counties of Limerick and Waterford, and, like Landers, is derived from the same base, de Loundres. In 1234 Maurice de Loundres brought a law suit against Monasteranenagh, in which reference was made to *Aonach Cúile,* near Ballylanders.

THE ROOFLESS CHURCH OF IRELAND CHURCH,

on the hill, is the most prominent landmark in the village. Local folklore claims that work on the church commenced in the 1880s but the building was never completed. A stone tablet in its facade announces, in English and Irish, "Glory to God in the highest and on earth, peace goodwill to man". Evidence of plaster-work on the interior suggests that the church was probably roofed at some stage.

THE ORIGINAL PARISH CHURCH may have been a foundation of the Knights Hospitallers as it was also known as Spittle Church. This is located near the village and its graveyard is still in use

LADY'S WELL was still the scene of an annual pattern, or *pátrún,* on 15 August 1988. This well is located about thirty paces north of the old church, and its waters are "reputed to be efficacious in curing sore eyes". In 1840 there were four white-thorn trees growing over this well, their branches filled with old rags deposited by persons visiting the well. The devotional exercises, parades, games and dances are still practised to a certain extent, but the pattern's importance has diminished over the last 150 years.

IN 1837 Samuel Lewis wrote that Ballinlondry, or Ballinlanders, had a population of 281 inhabitants living in the village "which is large and of modern erection, consisting of good houses built of stone and roofed with slate; it is a constabulary station. The parish is the property of the Earl of Kingston. The land is generally good ... producing good crops" there is a considerable tract of bog in the centre of which rises a very copious spring supplying two streams, one flowing to the north and the other to the south, and both forming a boundary between this parish and that of Ballingarry".

THE PARISH OF BALLINGARRY was described by Lewis in 1837: "The land is generally good ... the surface is varied, and there are some hills of considerable elevation, of which the Black Mountain and Sliagh-Reagh are the principal, stretching westward towards Kilfinnane ... Near Grierston, on the border of the parish, is a very extensive and valuable bog; in the midst of it rises a copious stream flowing southwards towards Mitchelstown, and also another flowing northward and forming part of the Daun ... There are several large and handsome houses, the principal of which are Annagurra, the residence of Thomas T. Adams, Esq., and Grierston, the fine old fami-

Aerial view of Ballylanders.

ly mansion of the Masseys [sic] ... The church is a ruin situated on a gentle elevation, and forming a conspicuous object".

BALLINGARRY DOWN RING FORT has been described by T.B. Barry in *The Archaeology of Medieval Ireland* as a platform *rath,* an earthwork deliberately heightened by human labour. The remains of a rectangular medieval house were found on the summit, from which there is a spectacular view of Slievereagh and the Galtees. This house may have dated from the twelfth century, and the foundations of several older buildings were found beneath it.

THE GLENBROHANE MOTE, over two miles west-north-west of Ballylanders, is an oval ring fort with two ramparts. This is located on the northern slope of Slievereagh and is also known as *Dún gCláire* or Doonglaura Mote.

GLENBROHANE VILLAGE contained 233 inhabitants in 44 houses in 1831. In 1837 it possessed a constabulary police station and a Catholic church, erected for £600 in 1819.

THE BALLYFROOTA CROMLECH is over two miles north-west of Ballylanders. This is a ruined chamber tomb which people still resort to when seeking a cure for backache. The cure can be obtained by creeping under the cap-stone.

ST. MOLUA'S WELL is still the scene of an occasional pilgrimage. The "rounds" are made here between 3-15 August, the date on which the original pattern was held. St. Molua, a seventh-century abbot, was a disciple of St. Comgall, and founded 120 monasteries in Ireland and Scotland. He died on 4 August 622; this date is observed as his feast-day in Ireland while 25 August is observed in Scotland. St. Molua may be remembered in this area as St. Molaga, although there were twelve Irish saints named Molaga so the patron saint of this well is more likely to be one of these. St. Molaga was buried here, but, according to tradition, his skull kept returning to the surface until a stone niche, covered with a slab, was constructed for it, in the graveyard. The graveyard also contains a ruined church known as Temple Molaga, or the *Teampaillín,* Little Temple, *Leaba Molaga,* Molaga's Bed, and four large rocks believed to be men who were turned to stone because they stole a chalice from Molaga's Church. Pilgrims doing the "rounds" pause at two ancient slabs which are said to mark the site of Emlygrennan Church, and tradition also claims that an eel and trout can be found in the well.

DARRA, Daragh or Glenroe is located about five miles south-south-west of Ballylanders. In the early nineteenth century the parish was known as Daragh-Glenroe, *Darach Gleann Rua,* the Red Valley abounding in Oaks. It was named after an extensive forest in the valley of Glenroe, which extended from the hills of Glenosheen to the river at Tooraleagan.Darra Catholic church was erected for £750 in 1834, and a new line of road from Limerick to Mitchelstown was under construction in the 1830s which "when completed, would become the principal road from Limerick to Cork".

SPITTLE CHURCH, in Darra, may have been a foundation of the Knights Hospitallers, like the Spittle church just outside Ballylanders. This ruin, north of Darragh Hill, was a later nave and chancel structure, of which little remained by 1840. The graveyard is still in use.

ST. MACDUAGH'S WELL, *Tobar Mac Duach,* was south of the church, at the foot of Darragh Hill. No trace of it remained by 1989. A pattern was held here on 31 August until about 1820.

BALLYNACOURTY CASTLE "was reduced to a heap of rubbish" by 1840. It was then so ruined that its dimensions could not be measured. Ballynacourty House was the residence of M. Bourke in 1837, while Darragh House was occupied by F. Bevan. Both houses were burned during the War of Independence.

ANGLESBOROUGH has a rebel tradition which is commemorated on a stone plaque embedded in the wall of the community centre. The central inscription reads: "1867-1923. Erected to the memory of the men and women of *Gleann-na-gCreabhar* who fought for Irish independence. *Ná dean dearmad orthu ná ar an éacht a rinneadar. Éire go deo.* [Do not forget them or the deeds they did. Ireland forever]." The inscriptions on either side are "Ye live but once. Hold fast your lands, and if you can, your lives. Fanny Parnell "and" We have kept faith with the past. And handed on a tradition to the future. P.H. Pearse." The Anglesborough Pipe Band was one of the region's best known institutions until it died out in the 1950s.

GLANEGREWRE is an Anglicised version of *Gleann na gCreabhar,* the Glen of the Woodcocks, the old name for Anglesborough.

COMMANDANT-GENERAL LIAM LYNCH (1893-1923) was born in Anglesborough. He was a member of the Irish Republican Brotherhood's Supreme Council for the province of Munster; an organiser of volunteers in Cork; an opponent of conscription; and second-in-command of the North Cork Brigade of the I.R.A.. His most notable exploit was the capture of Brigadier-General Lucas while the latter was fishing the Blackwater on 27 July, 1920. Lucas was held as a hostage in East Limerick; he escaped, but was later wounded in an ambush, near Oola. Liam Lynch is commemorated with a roadside monument, in the form of a Celtic cross, on the summit of a hill outside the village.

COMBAUN WOOD is located in the valley pass between Anglesborough and Kilbeheny. The remains of Combaun House were levelled during the forestry plantation work.

THE GLENACURRANE AMBUSH took place in December 1920. This was a joint operation carried out by the East Limerick and Cork Flying Columns under the command of Tomás Malone and Tom Barry. Guests on their way to a party in General Frank's house, near Knocklong, were detained as prisoners, in a nearby house, until after the ambush took place. Four soldiers of the Lincolnshire Regiment were killed in the encounter.

KILBEHENY derives its name from *Coill Beithne,* the Birch Wood. In 1837 the parish comprised "much light land and a well-planted glen extending among the hills to the Galtee mountains, on the highest of which, called Galtee More, which separates this parish from Galbally, is a lake. The Earl of Kingston's beautiful seat, the Mountain Lodge, with its extensive demesne, is in this parish; as is also Lord Massy's lodge, with its fine woods and grounds". The Mountain Lodge is now a ruin. A ruined tower house can be seen to the north of the road in the townland to which it gives its name, Castlequarter.

KILBEHENY CHURCH is located on the northern bank of the Funshion River close to the county boundaries of Tipperary and Cork. This ruined red-sandstone church was fenced off with barbed-wire when I visited the site on 22 January 1989, and several notices were posted on the fencing, warning visitors that the building was in dangerous condition. A large Celtic cross in the graveyard marked the burial-place of John Mandeville (1849-1888), Clonkilla, the nephew of Colonel John O' Mahony.

JOHN O'MAHONY was born in Kilbeheny. In 1858 he was one of a group who established a new revolutionary society, the Irish Republican Brotherhood, almost simultaneously in New York and Dublin. The others were James Stephens, Charles Kickham, John O'Leary, Michael Doheny and Thomas Clarke. John O'Mahony died in 1877.

SOURCE REFERENCE NUMBERS
5 9 11 12 28 39 47 64
76 86 107 120 129 150 166 173
192 195 238 246 265 282

Glin

Glencorbry · Kilfergus

GLIN derives its name from *Gleann Corbraigh,* the Glen of the Corbry, a vassal people whose territory was usurped by John Fitz John. John had established his authority over many parts of West Limerick by 1262, and by 1299 he controlled half a *tuath* of Glencorbry which corresponded to the present parish of Kilfergus or Glin.

GLIN CASTLE, the original stronghold, was known as *Cloch Ghleanna,* the Rock of Glin. The first castle on this site was built by John Fitz John over a rocky base in the bed of the Glencorbry River. This later consisted of a tower or keep at one angle of a rectangular bawn, with turrets at each corner, and a detached banquet hall. This was the seat of the Knights of Glin from about 1260 until some time after 1642, when they abandoned it to build an unfortified house near the site of the present Georgian structure of the same name. While I was looking for the entrance to this ruined tower, I met Denis Mulcahy who told me that the only way to gain access was through a hole in the eastern wall, which was about nine feet above ground level. This led onto the remaining portion of the spiral staircase. On the north-eastern corner of the north wall is a plaque commemorating the garrison who fell defending the castle in 1600. The castle may have been erected to protect a ford over the river.

THE GLENCORBRY RIVER is also known as the Glencorbry Stream or the Glin River. It rises on the Kerry border and almost describes a complete circle before pouring into the Shannon at Glin. This river is only a tiny stream until it crosses the Athea road between the townlands of Ballyguiltenane and Kinard, but by the time it reaches Killeany Wood it has become the Glin River proper. Beyond the wood it flows through a rocky gorge before pouring over *Poll an Eas,* the Hole of the Waterfall. The river passes under the bridge of the Ballyhahill road before it flows past Ballybeg and Killacolla Barker, a tract of land which never reverted to the Knight of Glin's ownership because of a clause in the will of a previous owner, William Barker, an English Undertaker who

hated the Knights. Before the river reaches Glin it travels past the ruins of Kilfergus church and the valley from which *Gleann Corbraighe* took its name.

THE VILLAGE OF GLIN was listed amongst the principal towns of the county in 1598. From the thirteenth century onwards it had developed around Glin Castle, and the Elizabethan English acknowledged its strategic value by using it as a base from which they could launch their attacks on the Geraldines. Despite the castle being encircled by water, in 1600, the garrison destroyed a number of thatched houses in Mill Street to improve their own defences before Sir George Carew approached the town. The town was owned by the Knights of Glin until 1654, when most of the Knight's lands passed to William Barker, a London alderman, described as "a crass, unmannerly, but an artful and indefatigable man". Barker lost all but 55 acres of his Glin lands to Sir Edward FitzHarris who was the husband of the Knight of Glin's only daughter and heir, Ellin or Olive, in 1661. Barker retained possession of the "Castle of Glinn with the bawne, all the outhouses, yards, orchards, gardens and the lands ... lying most contiguously to the castle". In 1662 William Barker received a grant for a market and two fairs. In 1782 Glin was described as a market-town with a harbour and "every convenience to render it a most desirable seat wherein to establish any branch of the woollen, linen or cotton manufacturers". In 1837 Samuel Lewis wrote that this town "owes much of its improvement to its present proprietor, is beautifully situated on the southern bank of the River Shannon ... and contains about 280 houses, several of which are well built and of handsome appearance. Among the more recent improvements is a handsome terrace, built by John Hamilton ... a new line of road from Askeaton to Tarbert ... and a road through the mountains to Abbeyfeale, a distance of 12 miles, which was opened in 1836. In the summer the town is much resorted to for the benefit of pure air and the advantages of sea-bathing, and is admirably situated for carrying on a very extensive trade, the river affording great facil-

ities for intercourse and secure anchorage for vessels of any burden ... This place is the great depot of the salmon fishery of the Shannon and its tributary rivers, of which large quantities are annually shipped for England; oysters of very superior flavour and other fish are also taken in abundance. The manufacture of linen and cotton checks is carried on to some extent, and there is a considerable trade in corn and butter, which are shipped to Cork and Limerick". The market was held on Saturdays, and fairs took place on 8 June, the first Wednesday in September, and 3 December, for cattle and pigs. There was a constabulary force stationed here and a substantial bridewell which contained six cells, two day-rooms and two spacious airing-yards. Lewis also wrote that there "are numerous ancient forts in the various parts of the parish, five of which are within the demesne of the Castle Glin; and at Flean, in the mountains, are the remains of a very ancient church" The big houses of the area, in those days, were Glin Castle, Westwood, Shannon View, Shannon Lawn, Fort Shannon, Ballydonohoe, Eastwood, Cahara Lodge, Villa, Glin Lodge, Clare View, Gardenville and Cahara House.

THE KNIGHTS OF GLIN were a minor branch of the once powerful Fitzgeralds. There is some doubt as to how the title originated but two explanations are generally accepted, although it is also quite possible that a title like this may have been the result of an Anglo-Norman "becoming as Irish as the Irish themselves".

JOHN FITZ THOMAS FITZGERALD, Lord of Connello, the grandson of Maurice Fitzgerald of Windor, the ancestor of all the Geraldines, had four, or five, illegitimate sons and the royal authority to confer knighthoods. He knighted three of his sons. Gibbon was created White Knight; Maurice was made the Knight of Kerry, or the Green Knight; and John Fitz John became the First Knight of the Valley, the Black Knight, or the Knight of Glin.

KING EDWARD III 1327-1377 has also been credited with the creation of these three titles, and is believed to have conferred

Aerial view of Glin.

knighthood on the three Fitzgerald half-brothers after the Battle of Halidon Hill in 1333, or later on in 1335.

THE TITLE, Knight of Glin, was first documented in 1425 when Andrew Daundon conveyed lands in Drumloghan, Kenry, to Philip, Knight of Glen. Up to the end of the seventeenth century, the Knight was often referred to as the Knight of the Valley in official documents. The Knights of Glin are familiar figures in the history, legends, poetry, song and folklore of West Limerick.

JOHN FITZ JOHN FITZGERALD, the First Knight of Glin, was the son of John FitzThomas Fitzgerald and the wife of an Irish chieftain, O Coileáin of *Claonghlas*. By 1307 he controlled an area sixteen miles long by nine miles wide, which was later subdivided into the baronies of Upper Connello, Lower Connello, Shanid and Glenquin. In the Irish genealogies he is listed as Seán Mór na Sursaigne, Big John of the Girdle. He was succeeded by his son Thomas FitzJohn Fitzgerald.

COLLINS *O Coileáin, O Cuileáin, O'Collaine, OCollan,* or Collen is derived from the descendants of *Coileán,* the Whelp.

This family were Lords of *Ui Conaill Gabhra* (later the baronies of Upper and Lower Connello) until they were expelled in 1178. Most of the clan moved to West Cork but some of them remanied in south-west Limerick, as Lords of *Claonghlas,* until they were dispossessed by the Fitzgerald's towards the end of the thirteenth century.

THE KNIGHTS OF GLIN are so interlinked with the history of West Limerick that it is virtually impossible to separate the two. Thomas FitzJohn Fitzgerald escaped execution for treason in 1567, but his son and heir was hanged, drawn and quartered at Limerick Docks. Edmund Fitzthomas Fitzgerald retained possession of the castle and manor of Glin, together with his lands at Cappagh and Castletown, even though they had been granted to Sir William Drury in 1578. Despite a brief skirmish with some English planters in 1579, Edmund did not become involved in the second Desmond Rebellion, and in June 1588 his castle, manor, and 6,800 acres of land were restored to him. He failed in his attempts to recover the Lordship of Kenry and the Manor of Cappagh. In 1595 he lost an additional 1100 acres to English settlers and some

of the old English families who used government pressure to expand their holdings. Despite his losses, the Knight was considered amongst the chief men of the county in 1598, when he sided with the Sugán Earl of Desmond to drive the English out of Munster. When Sir George Carew laid siege to Glin Castle in 1600, he threatened to kill the Knight's six-year-old son who had been held as a hostage to ensure Edmund's loyalty. The Knight's aide replied; "*Gread leat. Tá an ridire go meidhreach fós agus a bhean go bríomhar. Tá an pit oscailte fós agus an bod bríomhar. Is fuiriste leanbh eile do gheiniúint*". This reply stated, somewhat graphically, that the Knight and his lady were both willing and able to have more children if their son was killed.

THE SIEGE OF GLIN CASTLE was a short but bloody affair. Turlough Roe MacMahon and Captain Flower led two abortive assaults before they succeeded in capturing the building with a third assault, on the morning of 9 July, 1600. The Knight escaped, and despite a £100 reward offered for his capture, he remained at large to join O'Donnell on the march to Kinsale, and share

£12,000 of Spanish coin brought over to finance the campaign. His garrison was slaughtered, and only three men got away with their lives out of a total of eighty. Amongst the dead were the Knight's two commanders, Tadhg Dore and Dónall na Searrach, Donal of the Colts, Culhane Captain Flower, An Captaen Riabach, the Swarthy Captain had conceived "an extraordinary lust" for the Knight's wife, Honora, and became the most diligent of Edmund's pursuers. Edmund earned himself the sobriquet of Eamon na gCath, Edmund of the Battles, over the next three years. He was wounded at Kinsale, excluded from amnesty, and forced to go "on the run" in North Kerry and Sliabh Luachra. When the Treaty of Mellifont brought the nine-year war to an end in March 1603, all of Edmund's estates were restored to him with the exceptions of the manors of Beagh and Castletown. In 1615 he repaired Glin Castle and inserted a stone inscribed with: "Edmund Gerrald Night of the Valley. Onner arti feare God allways and remember the poore. IHS. Anno Domini. 1615", over the fireplace of the castle's main room. This stone was later re-set in the courtyard of the Georgian Glin Castle. Edmund was succeeded by his son Tomás Spaínneach, Thomas the Spaniard, in 1623.

THE DORE FAMILY derive their name from *O'Doghair*, the descendants of *Doghar*, the Sorrowful. Variants of the surname include *O'Dowar, O'Dower, O'Dore,* and Dower. In 1574 "the Earl of Desmond put his man, James Dore, at the head of all the carpenters and masons", in order to demolish the strongholds of Castletown and Glin. In 1600 Tadhg Dore and his brother perished in the siege of the castle. The Dore name is mainly found in County Limerick.

COLMANSTOWN CASTLE is badly ruined and can be seen on the opposite shore of the Shannon from Glin. In 1600 it was the seat of Turlough Roe MacMahon (1563-1629), a "bloodthirsty savage", who fought on the English side.

THE UNDERTAKERS, a group of English speculators who financed the Parliamentary campaign in Ireland, hired a flotilla of ships to participate in a private expedition of their own. Under the leadership of Lord Forbes, "that lovely and useful castle of the knight of the valley" was attacked and captured on 23 September 1642. The defenders were slain; Eamon Og the Knight's brother was taken prisoner and hanged on board one of the ships; and the castle stores were ransacked. Massive quantities of wheat, barley, malt, salted-beef, and butter were seized by the raiders, but the Knight's silver-plate had been sent to Limerick City, for safe-keeping, some time before. Tomás Spaínneach was educated

in Spain; had his father's lands re-granted to him in 1635 but lost them to William Barker in 1654; took no part in the Confederate Wars because of ill-health although his brother, John, was a captain in the Confederate Army; and was ordered to transfer to Gort, County Galway, on 1 May 1654. Tomás Spaínneach did not transplant to Connaught. He remained near Glin, and tradition maintains that Liosaritter, *Lios an Ridire,* the Knight's Fort, in Ballyculhane may have been his home until he died in 1659.

AFTER THE CROMWELLIAN WARS Thomas Cunningham and Lewis Dike came into possession of 15,555 acres of land which included the Glin estate. They sold out their interest in Glin to William Barker. In the *Civil Survey* of 1654, the parish of Kilfergus contained "a manor house with court leet and baron, an old castle and bawn ruined, with two mill seats, a brook running by the castle side". In 1655 John Widenham leased the castle but never lived in it because, by then, it was uninhabitable. The people of the parish were listed in 1659. Of 210 mentioned only 9 were English, and William Barker and Richard Hunt were listed as the *tutuladoes* of the district.

GERALD FITZ JOHN FITZGERALD, son of the Confederate captain, petitioned Charles II in 1669 and reminded him of how he, Gerald, and his brothers, had served the Stuarts abroad, in the Royalist regiments of Colonel John Fitzgerald and the Duke of Ormond. Charles granted the 4,000 acres Gerald had requested in 1672, despite a counter-petition lodged by Sir Edward Fitzharris. On 10 May 1689 Gerald was fatally wounded, fighting on the Stuart side, at the battle of Windmill Hill, during the siege of Derry. His estate was not forfeited to the Crown because Gerald was only a tenant for life of the Glin Estate, according to a deed of settlement dated 5 December 1672. His widow was left in clear possession. On 12 March 1701 his sons, Thomas Geanncach, The Snub-Nosed, and Seán na gComhrac, John of the Duels, obtained a certificate stating that neither of them had taken part in the war in which their father had died.

JOHN FITZGERALD (1711-1737) became the first member of the Glin family to conform to the Protestant religion in 1730. In 1732 he succeeded Thomas, but died five years later. The next Knight, Edmund, conformed in 1741 in order to prevent Richard, a younger brother who had conformed in 1740, from claiming the estate. Edmund died, intestate and bankrupt, in1765.

THE KNIGHTS OF GLIN blended more easily with the new Protestant Ascendancy from the mid-eighteenth century onwards.

Richard the Duellist was married twice; first to Mary Fitzgibbon, a cousin of the First Earl of Clare; and secondly to a daughter of Dominick Roche, First Viscount Cahiravahilla and Baron Tarbert, a Limerick merchant and landowner. Richard, who was equally adept with either sword or pistol, died in 1775. His heir, Tomás Og, also converted to Protestanism. He married Mary "Molly" Bateman, "a charming young lady with a fortune of £3,000". In 1781 Tomás Og was succeeded by John Bateman Fitzgerald who had been tutored in his youth by Seán Bán Aerach O Flanagáin, the Airy Blonde John Flanagan, a noted poet and musician. Seán Bán instilled a love of Irish music and culture in the young Knight who let his estate in 1782 in order to enjoy an annual income of £4,000. Six years earlier, in 1776, John had been instrumental in the formation of two volunteer corps, the Royal Glin Hussars and the Royal Glin Artillery, when Irish Protestants banded together in order to prevent the French and Spanish from taking advantage of Britain's involvement with the American War of Independence.

THE 1798 REBELLION in Glin was fomented by Tom Langan and "Long" Murty McElligot. Tom Langan, alias Captain Steel, was the local leader of the region's United Irishmen. He was captured and sentenced to death by hanging but the sentence was later commuted to seven years' transportation, to Botany Bay.

THE CATHOLIC CHURCH was renovated in 1814 by Fr. William MacEnery, one in a long line of Catholic clergymen who had served the parish of Kilfergus since Fr. Maurice Gallagher was registered as the priest for Kilfergus and Loughill in 1704, with the help of John FrFauncis Fitzgerald. In 1858 the old "large plain building" was replaced with the present building, the Church of the Immaculate Conception. In 1924 David Canon Keane, the former parish priest of Kilfergus, was consecrated Bishop of the Diocese of Limerick.

THE CHURCH OF IRELAND CHURCH was built either in 1815 or 1816, on an eminence close to the town, with a gift of £600 from the Board of First Fruits. In 1867 it was rebuilt, and in 1871 the tower-porch and baptistry were added. One Sunday morning a visitor was told that this church "only opens for the (K)night". Desmond John Edmund Fitzgerald was the first Knight of Glin to be buried here, within the church grounds.

KILFERGUS PARISH derives its name from the old church and town of *Cill Fhearghasa,* the Cell or Church of Fergus, which is located one mile south-east of Glin. The name is pronounced locally as *Keel*

Fareesa, but little remains of the old church. The graveyard is still in use, and all but six of the thirty Knights of Glin were buried here from 1400 to 1866, as well as members of the Costelloe family of Killeany, who fostered all of the Knights from 1500 to 1850.

TIMOTHY COSTELLOE is buried in the graveyard of Kilfergus. He was a foster brother of the Knight and one of his loyal supporters. His epitaph was composed by his son and namesake who was a poet, sculptor and engraver. Timothy Junior carved and erected a tombstone for his father which can still be seen. Its inscription reads as follows:

"This is the grave of Tim Costelloe,
Who lived and died a right good fellow;
From his boyhood to his life's end,
He was the poor man's faithful friend.
He fawned before no purse-proud clod,
He feared none but the living God;
And never did he do to others,
But was right to do to brothers.
He loved green Ireland's mountains bold
Her verdant vales and abbeys old;
He loved her music, song and story,
He wept for her departed glory.
And often did I hear him pray,
That God would end her spoiler's sway;
To men like him may be peace be given,
In this world and in heaven.
Amen."

HAMILTON'S TOWER is a large stone structure, resembling a castle, on an eminence overlooking the pier. This was built as a curiosity or folly by Captain John Hamilton in 1838, and originally had four cannon mounted on its battlements. A field piece was also housed within it. The cannon were used to signal the start, or finish, of yacht and boat races on the Shannon.

JOHN FRAUNCEIS FITZGERALD, the Protestant Knight of Glin, was a supporter of Catholic Emancipation, a generous benefactor to Catholic and Protestant alike, an Irish scholar, historian, antiquarian, and a noted sexual athlete. He fell foul of Fr. MacEnery's successor, Fr. Daniel O'Sullivan, when that priest condemned his (the Knight's) mistress, Mary Wright, from the pulpit of his church. Mary converted to Protestanism, and the Knight financed her action for slander against the priest. The jury brought in a verdict in Mary's favour for £2 and costs of £25. John Fraunceis was known as *Ridire na mBan,* the Knight of the Women, and his amorous exploits were recounted in a ballad of 1830:

"His vices have made, and still make him so poor,
That bailiff or creditor is ne'er from his door,
And deep tho' in debt, yet he's deeper in sin,
That lecherous, treacherous Knight of the Glin".

Like many of his contemporaries, he was a supporter of the establishment, but, unlike other landlords, he was also closer to the people. He served as Lieutenant-Colonel of the Royal Limerick County Militia, and became High Sheriff of the county in 1830. During the *Great Hunger* he protected his tenants, and personally supervised the soup kitchen in Glin Poorhouse. The ballad in which he featured so notably also contained the following lines:

"No, no, he spends his wealth among the poor,
Dispensing happiness from door to door".

John Fraunceis laid the foundation stone of the new workhouse he had procured for the town in 1851. He died in 1851. *The Limerick Chronicle* noted ... "the influence of his position and his personal exertions were ever directed to relieve the wants of the poor".

JOHN FRAUNCEIS EYRE FITZGER-ALD (1813-1866) was kept under some restraint during his father's lifetime. He became known as the "Cracked Knight", probably because he never bothered to conceal his feelings, was an inveterate practical joker, and despised the pretensions of his neighbours. He was popular amongst the locals, had friends within the Fenians, associated with Joseph O Longáin, and actively discouraged gombeenism. On one memorable occasion, in Tralee, he publicly whipped Colonel Henry H. Kitchener, father of the future field-marshal, because of his mistreatment of the Kitchener tenants. John Fraunceis Eyre insisted on being consulted in regard to the shape and design of the chamber-pots which were supplied to Glin Workhouse and was even known to shoot chamber-pots off peoples' heads.

THE LAND LEAGUE was discredited locally in 1886 when the Knight made political capital out of outrages committed on the farms of two men who had taken the places of evicted tenants. This did not suit the *Munster News* of 13 March 1886 which commented: "It does not read well to find ... the representative of an old Irish family, who having lived at peace with priests and people, adopting a style and language more becoming some of the Cromwellian gang".

THE FITZGERALDS OF GLIN survived the Land League, the Great War, the War of Independence and the Civil War. An attempt to burn their home, in February 1923, was resisted by Desmond Fitz John Lloyd Fitzgerald, an invalid, who refused to leave the endangered building. His successor died of tuberculosis in 1949. The Knight's widow married Horatio Ray Milner, and the two of them spent £60,000 to restore Glin Castle between 1957 and 1959.

GLIN CASTLE or Glin House, the seat of the Knights of Glin since the 1790s, is located about a mile to the west of the original Glin Castle. John Bateman commenced building in 1780. Tradition states that a contractor named Sheehy brought all of the stone used in the house from a quarry near Athea by horse-drawn sledge. Ten years appeared to elapse before John's wife, Margaretta Maria, encouraged him to continue the work in 1790. By 1798 the house interior was as near to completion as it is today, as some of the rooms on the top floor were never completed due to the Fitzgerald's impending bankruptcy. The craftsmen simply downed tools and departed, leaving the walls scored for plaster and the ceilings unfinished. The carpenters and masons who worked on Glin Castle were the same craftsmen who worked on two adjoining houses in Henry Street, Limerick, for the Bishop of Limerick (later Lord Glentworth) and his older brother, Viscount Pery. Michael Stapleton, a famous plasterer of the period, did most of the decorative plaster-work, which consisted of dolphins, harps, spidery vines, sprays and castellations of flowers. Around 1815 John Fraunceis added the west wing, Gothic-style battlements and the castellated "pepper-pot" gate lodges. The original Glin Castle was uninhabitable in the late seventeenth century and the Knights apparently abandoned it to build an unfortified house, Glin Hall, near the site of the present mansion, Glin Castle. This is supposed to have been a long low-roofed thatched house which was burned down in 1740. No description of the house which replaced Glin Hall survives, possibly because the "Cracked Knight" burned a lot of the family papers in the 1860s. The rooms however must have been fairly substantial, as several of the paintings owned by Richard the Duellist would not have been accommodated in small rooms.

DESMOND JOHN VILLIERS FITZGER-ALD is the present holder of that ancient title, Knight of Glin. Born in 1937, he is an authority on Irish architecture and the decorative arts. Between 1965 and 1975 he worked in London's Victoria and Albert Museum, but has since made Glin Castle his sole residence. He is an active writer and publisher, and in recent years has established a restaurant and craft-shop in the western gate-lodge, facing the Tarbert Road.

DURING THE WAR OF INDEPEN-DENCE the *Big Four* found a safe shelter, in James E. Dore's, a week after the Knocklong Rescue. As the British military combed the countryside looking for them in July 1919 they stayed around West Limerick in the Long, Sheehan, Keane, Kennedy and Duffy homes. Michael Geoghegan, Church Street,

Glin Castle and grounds.

survived both the War of Independence and the Civil War. At the age of seventeen he had joined the British Army; trained as a marksman; and deserted to fight for Ireland. During the war years he had several narrow escapes, and in peace-time had earned a reputation as a sportsman and athlete. He often swan across the Shannon, where his successful negotiation of the river was usually marked by a signal-fire to announce his safe arrival. His death was reported in 1930, supposedly, by drowning. He left Glin, married in Dublin; worked in England, and lived to a ripe old age.

CLOONLAHARD WOOD, three miles south of Glin, was the scene of a massacre on 12 March, 1580, when a man named Sheahan, or MacShane, led Pelham's troops to where 400 fugitives were hiding from the English forces. A few young people managed to escape but the rest were killed. In 1927 Archdeacon John Begley was shown a large mound which was "still pointed out as an enduring monument to this great crime".

THE FLEAN BEG CROMLECH is three miles south-east of Glin, in the townland of Tinnakilla. This is a prehistoric chamber tomb. *Cloch Liosliagáin,* the Stone of the Fort of the Standing Stone, is a pillarstone about 300 yards south of the cromlech.

SOURCE REFERENCE NUMBERS
9 11 28 44 47 60
64 67 73 120 129 150
192 203 238 251 264 282

Herbertstown

Raleighstown · Ballynamona · Cromhill · Kilteely

HERBERTSTOWN derives its name, Herbert's Town, or *Baile Hiobáird,* from the Herbert family who would have been amongst the earliest Anglo-Norman settlers in the region. Variants of the surname Herbert would include *Hoireabard, Hoireabárd , Hubberd, Herbard,* Harbert, Harberd, Herebeorht, *Hiobárd, Hobárd,* and *Hoibeárd .* The family settled in Kildare, Meath, and Limerick. They were freehold tenants of the Earls of Desmond, but the name seems to have almost disappeared after the eighteenth century, with the death of Maurice Herbert of Templeglantine. The village is located on the summit of a hill overlooking flat, low-lying marshy ground which is, in turn, encircled by a series of individual hills. In 1837 Herbertstown contained a constabulary police station, a Catholic church, erected for £800 in 1836, and formed part of the parish of Cahercorney. Pig fairs were then held four times a year, on 15 January, 17 March, 28 June, and 7 November.

CAHERCORNEY CHURCH was granted to Monasteranenagh Abbey in 1185 by a charter of Prince John. This was later confirmed by Turlough O'Brien in 1200, and little else was recorded about *Cahercornii* after that date. After the Dissolution, it remained in use as a Protestant church, but is now ruined, without any architectural features which would indicate its age. In 1943 the oldest tombstone in the graveyard was a low slab bearing the date 1717. Cahercorney Church was the burial-place of the Croker family, who erected a tomb here in 1723.

REV. PATRICK FITZGERALD, co-author of *The History, Topography and Antiquities, of the County and City of Limerick with a preliminary view of the History and Antiquities of Ireland* with J.J. M'Gregor, was vicar of Cahercorney and lived in the glebe house, at Ballingoola.

THE BALLINGOOLA PAPER-MILL was

Aerial view of Herbertstown.

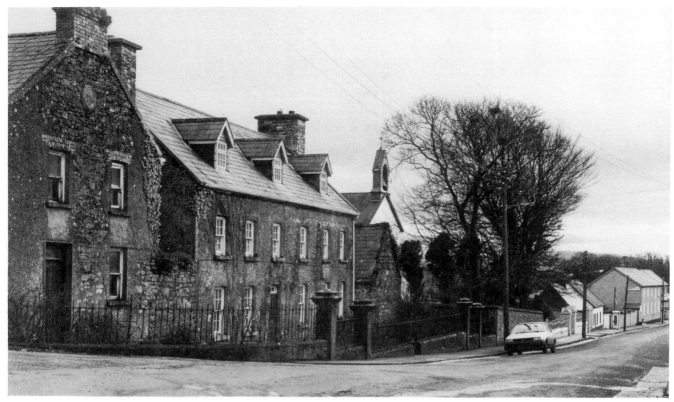

Street scene, Herbertstown.

in existence in 1840, employed 20 people, and closed in 1861.

CAHERCORNEY derives its name from *Cathair Coírne,* the Caher or Stone Fort of Coirne, a man's name in Pagan times. This entire region was occupied from about 2000 B.C., and nearly every surrounding hill-top bears some remains of old field systems and other monuments. Brian Boru fortified and held garrisons in the forts of *Aíne, Dún Gair,* and *Loch Ceann,* between 1002 and 1012, chiefly to subdue the Vikings who had settled here. In the early 1940s Michael J. O'Kelly carried out a survey of the barony of Small County, and published a record of his findings in two articles in the *North Munster Antiquarian Journal,* in Autumn 1942 and Spring 1943.

THE CAMOGE RIVER has its source near the ancient cathedral of Emly, and taking a westerly course passes through the parish of Cahercorney, near the ruins of Glenogra Castle and church, the castle of Rathmore, and the splendid remains of Monasteranenagh, and falls into the River Maigue at Croom. It may even have formed the northern boundary of *Deisbeg,* later the barony of Small County, while the Saimer or Morning Star River constituted the southern border.

RALEIGHSTOWN, or Rawleystown Court, was located south of the Camoge and north of Cahercorney. This fortified dwelling was enclosed with a bawn, defended by four small square turrets at the corners. Lewis claimed that it was built by Thomas Raleigh, an uncle of Sir Walter Raleigh, while T.J. Westropp claimed it was built by another member of that family during the reign of James I (1603-1625). Only one gable wall and fragments of an enclosing court-yard wall remained in 1943.

RAWLEYSTOWN STONE FORT, "on the summit of a hill above Releighstown is an extraordinary circular building of huge blocks of stone, curiously fitted into each other without mortar". This fort was noted by Michael J. O'Kelly, who stated that it was surrounded by a fosse, and was the centre of an extensive system of ancient field fences which ran in many directions over the hill. In1986 it was covered in vegetation. On the edge of the nearby marsh there was a low flat-topped circular platform earthwork surrounded by a slight fosse, in 1943.

CAHERELLY ABBEY, or Caherelly Church, may have been founded by St. Ailbe, a fifth century contemporary of St. Patrick. Ailbe, Ailbhe or Albeus was venerated as a patron saint of Munster, and was the first bishop of the see of Emly, which was later united to Cashel. *The Annals of Innisfallen* recorded his death in 528. His feast-day was celebrated on 12 September. The church may

have taken its name from *Cathair Eillidhe* or *Cathair Ailleach,* the Fort of the Stone House. The church ruins did not appear to be very old in the 1830s, and the graveyard is still in use over a century and a half later.

LONGFORD BRIDGE, *Ath Fada,* was a major crossing point and meeting place from ancient times. Standing stones, some distance north and south of this bridge over the Camoge River probably marked the route of an older road known as Boherlegaun, *Bóthar Liagaín,* the Road of the *Liagáns* or Standing Stones.

RATHJORDAN derived its name from an old earth fort, *Ráth Siurdáin,* Jordan's Fort, which had been destroyed by 1840. Jordan was a name which became popular throughout Western Europe during the Crusades. Variants on this surname include Jurdane, Jurdan, Jordane, *Siúrdán* and *Siúrtán.* The name was associated with that of the River Jordan in the Holy Land, and the Jordans were an Anglo-Norman family who settled in Dublin, Meath and Limerick.

ST. JOHN THE BAPTIST'S WELL, west of Rathjordan townland, was still visited by pilgrims in 1840, although no pattern was then held on the saint's feast-day. There was a Church of Ireland church east of the well.

RATHJORDAN CHURCH was located on level ground in the glebe. By 1840 only a few stones remained and the graveyard had nearly passed out of use.

KILCULLANE CHURCH, a nave and chancel church, was located in the townland of the same name, 300 yards west of the Camoge River. It derived its name of Kilcullane, Kilkellane, or Kilkilaun, from *Cill Chathláin,* the Church of Cathlan, in all probability a local chieftain rather than a saint. By 1840 this old building was in poor condition.

KILCULLANE CASTLE was erected by the Hurley family during the fifteenth century. After the Desmond Rebellion Robert Bourchier received a grant of Kilcullane. He built Kilcullane House which later became the property of the Viscounts Guillamore. By 1840 only the first arch of the castle remained.

BALLYNAMONA CHURCH may be the *Chapel Mora* or Moortown Church first recorded in 1302. It was the property of Walter de Bonneville in 1327, and was mentioned as Morestown or Ballymoneyny in 1607. This church still stood in 1827, but by 1942 only part of its walls were still standing, without any architectural features which would indicate the date of erection to Michael J. O'Kelly.

BALLYNAMONA CASTLE, which may have been built by the Raleighs in the days of Queen Elizabeth I, had disappeared by 1942, except for one small angle of masonry which may have fallen from an upper portion of the building.

THE BALLYNAMONA STONE CIRCLE was no longer complete by the 1940s. Only the stones in the north-eastern arc remained in their original positions and many were missing on the north-western and southern sides. In the remaining arc the stones are almost contiguous, but where stones were taken from the north-western arc of the circle there was a "step-down" to the level of the outside field which was not apparent elsewhere. The large stones were held in position by a packing of smaller stones. When the field was tilled in 1941 the packing that had been around the missing stones was disturbed, but no finds were made.

THE BALLYNAMONA EARTHWORKS were mainly located on low marshy ground or near the bank of the Camoge River. In the late 1930s Seán P. O Ríordáin excavated two conjoined rectangular platform forts here. He located one sherd of green-glazed fourteenth century pottery, along with other glazed pottery sherds and animal bones of pig, young calf and ox. Similar forts have been dated to the late thirteenth or fourteenth centuries.

CROMWELL is a name which was well-known in Limerick long before the advent of Oliver Cromwell, the Lord Protector. Isolde

Streetscape at Herbertstown.

Cromwell had a dower on Ballygodan in 1325; James Cromwell had a lease of Corcomohead in 1597; and there was even a Cromwellstown, *Baile Chromail* or *Ghromail,* in the county which was distinct from Cromhil or *Cnoc Gromail.* In 1578 there was a reference to the surname Cromal, and in 1583 to that of Gromwall. *Gromail* and *Cromail* were Irish variants on this surname which was introduced into the county by an old English family, the Cromwells. In 1598 James Cromwell was Mayor of Limerick.

BALLINLOUGH, Ballinloghyy or Ballinlough Parish was the joint property of the Earls of Sandwich and Aldborough in 1837. The land was good, but subdivided into a great number of small farms. In the Catholic divisions it was part of the union or district of Hospital and Herbertstown. Lewis wrote of "two eminences, one called Cromwell's Hill and the other Cromwell's Moat, both have traces of works on them, but apparently of much greater antiquity than the time of Cromwell".

THE HILL OF CROMHILL, Cromaill Hill, Cromwell's Hill, or Cromhill may derive its name from the old Celtic god, Crom, Cromm, Crom Dubh or Cenn Cruaich, who is also associated with Lough Gur and other parts of the county. Crom was venerated until the advent of Christianity led to the abandonment of the older religion. The great idol of Cromm Cruach was overthrown in *Magh Slecht,* the

Plain of Prostrations, near Ballymagauran, County Cavan, by St. Patrick. This was surrounded by twelve other idols dedicated to Crom's twelve sub-gods which were also overthrown, and remained "buried up to their heads in the earth, as St. Patrick had left them" into the eighth, ninth and tenth centuries. Cromhill is 586 feet above sea-level and contains Dermot and Grainne's Bed, Fionn's Seat, Crom Dubh's Castle, two ring forts, the Seat of the Fianna, and other remains.

CROMHILL may also be a derivative of *Cromchoill,* the Sloping Wood or *Cro m Ghleann,* the Sloping Glen. It was known as *Cnoc Gromail* during the early sixteenth century. The Desmond Roll refers to it as Knockgromell in 1583, and it is mentioned as Cnockegromwille in 1637.

DERMOT AND GRAINNE'S BED is a ruined wedge-shaped gallery grave west of the highest point of the hill. It was apparently divided into two chambers, with the smaller chamber at the north-eastern end.

FIONN'S SEAT is a tumulus or mound of earth that had a stone kerb about its base, outside of which there is a fosse. In 1943 only five of the kerb stones remained; the top of the mound may have been flattened by surveyors using it as a trigonometrical station while conducting an ordnance survey; and it was known locally as *Suidhe Finn,* Fionn's Seat.

THE SEAT OF THE FIANNA, *Suidheachán na Feínne,* is a large oval mound of earth surrounded by a fosse. There is a causeway across the fosse and a ramp leading to the mound on the south side. There is a smaller mound east of the centre.

CROMWELL'S FORT is the local name for this small earthen ring fort encircled by a fosse. The bank has collapsed, filling the fosse to a certain extent, and giving the earthwork a bowl shape.

THE CROMHILL STONE FORT is built on a limestone outcrop on the southern slope of the hill. By 1943 it consisted of a platform of stone, earth and scree, and the stone rampart was "very collapsed".

CROM DUBH'S CASTLE, *Caisleán Chruim Dhuibh,* is the name applied to the southern spur of Cromhill. Tradition refers to a castle on this site, possibly the one referred to as Knockgromell in 1583. No trace of a castle or peel tower now exists. In the valley below Cromhill there are two caves known as Dermot and Grainne's Bed, and the Fairy Piper's Cave.

BALLINLOUGH CHURCH had virtually disappeared by 1942. Only fragments of the south wall and west gable remained. This was located on low ground which may have contained a lake in ancient times. In 1289 the Bishop of Emly stayed here when the sheriff seized all his horses and twenty plough oxen in settlement of a debt. In 1290 William Le Deveneis claimed the right of sanctuary in this church when he was pursued after killing William FitzHugo. He later escaped. The graveyard is still in use.

ST. BRIGID'S WELL, in Ballinlough Parish, was still the scene of an occasional pilgrimage on St. Bridget's Day and on May Eve during the 1940s. Rounds were made for the curing of sore eyes; and rags, or ribbons were tied, or hung, on the tree near it. There were two stone forts and two large earthworks in the parish in 1943, while the oval mound on top of Knocknastaigue may have been a long barrow.

ST. JAMES'S WELL was still remembered as a holy well in 1943 although all devotion to it had ceased by then. Its waters were believed to be effective in curing stomach complaints.

MILLTOWN ABBEY or Ballywilliam Abbey was established by Donald Ygormellay and William de Burgo, two Carmelite Friars in 1459-1460. They founded their friary at a place called *Villa Molendi,* in the townland of *Baile Mhuilinn* or Milltown, in the parish of Aglishcormick. As Milltown and Ballinegaul were adjoining townlands, the friary usually took its name from one or the other. It was dissolved about 1544. The prior, Donough O'Dangane, was found to be in possession of a two-acre site containing the friary and church in 1556-1557, as well as a water-mill and ten acres of land on which he paid a yearly valuation of 51 1/2 pence. It was still in existence as a convent, *Vallae Mollindeni,* as late as 1737. The abbey was located on the north side of the road from Kilteely to Limerick. Its walls collapsed about 1800, and were used to build a nearby wall and several houses. By 1840 no vestige of the abbey remained, the graveyard was no longer used, and its site was merely "a spot of untilled ground".

AGLISHCORMICK probably derived its name from *Eaglais Chormaic,* the Church of Cormac, in much the same way as Liscormuck took its name from the Fort of Cormac. Who Cormac was will hardly now be known. By 1840 the old church of Aglishcormick was remembered only as *A n Eagluis,* but nothing of it remained except for an old overgrown graveyard surrounded by a cultivated field.

BALLINARD CHURCH gave its name to the parish. This church was recorded as Caherhussoc in 1251. By 1837 some ruins were still visible, but these had disappeared by 1942 although the graveyard was still in use. Cahirfossorge was another name for this parish.

BALLINARD CASTLE was founded as early as 1287. The last structure on this site was erected by the Fitzgeralds during the fifteenth century. By 1943 no trace of this castle remained.

EAGLESTOWN MANSION, the former home of the Powel family, was a ruin by 1837.

CLOUGHAVILLIER CASTLE or Clogh Ivillin, the decayed castle of W. Marshall, had disappeared by 1943, and its site could not be located.

KILTEELY CATHOLIC CHURCH was a large cruciform structure erected on the site of an older foundation in 1803. This served the local community until it was dismantled and replaced with another church on a new site. This last building opened as a church on 13 November 1960. The original church is believed to have been built for Muin and Lommchu, who were buried here, by St. Patrick, although O'Donovan assumed that this Kilteely had nothing to do with the national apostle. He based this assumption on the translation of *Kill Teidhill,* the Foot of the Mountain, as being a reference to another Kilteely in the north-western part of Tipperary county. Limerick's Kilteely has no mountain nearer to it than the Galtee Mountains, so it may not be the *Kill Teidhill* mentioned in the *Tripartite Life of St. Patrick.* No trace remains of another foundation, Kildromin Church, which the Knights Templars are said to have built in Kilteely in 1291.

KILTEELY VILLAGE contained a constabulary police station in 1837. Fairs for horned cattle and pigs were held on 1 February, 1 June and 25 October. The local Church of Ireland church was in ruin by then. The *Great Hunger* decimated Kilteely, Dromkeen, Aglishcormick and Ballinlough, where the total population of 4512 inhabitants in 1841 dropped to a figure of 2796 by 1851.

THE FENIANS had an active membership. The men drilled at *Cuínne Dorcha,* the Dark Corner, which was easily accessible and could be overlooked, by their sentries, from the top of Kilteely Hill. They raided the constabulary station for arms on the night of 4-5 March, 1867, and assembled on the Mall the following morning, under the direction of Seán O'Carroll, Cromhill, and Michael Grogan, Kilteely. The old Ballyvistea creamery was later located on the site of the Mall.

SINN FEIN COURTS, were held in the Parochial Hall here soon after Austin Stack became Minister for Home Affairs in 1919. The Sinn Fein judge was Tom Murphy, Barnacoolea, who was assisted by Liam Hayes and David Guerin. Ernie O'Malley spent some time in the Kilteely area during the Troubles, and had a new holster made to his own design by Ned Cooney, a local shoemaker. The Kilteely R.I.C. barracks was abandoned by the R.I.C.. It was demolished by the I.R.A. on the evening, and night, of Easter Saturday 1920, in order to prevent the British forces from occupying it.

CARRIGKETTLE CASTLE, *Caisleán Carraig Chiotaíl,* was first mentioned in September 1199 when it was granted to William de Naas, along with five knights' fees in the neighbourhood of *Karakytell* and *Kildruman.* This building, and another built by the Earl of Kildare as Lord Chief Justice of Ireland in 1510 on the same site, has long since vanished, mainly because of quarrying which has long since removed the limestone outcrop on which it stood.

SOURCE REFERENCE NUMBERS
5 9 11 12 45 47 76 95 108 120 129 140 164
167 173 174
192 200 201 207 223 264 282

Hospital

Knockainy

HOSPITAL, or Hospital of Anye, derives its name from a preceptory of St. John the Baptist which was founded here, in the Glen of Anye, by Geoffrey de Marisco. The Glen of Anye, like the nearby Hill of Anye, pre-dates the arrival of the Anglo-Normans.

ANYE OR AINE is remembered as the daughter of a *Tuatha de Danann* chieftain; a Celtic sun-goddess; and the banshee whose appearance, and keening heralded the imminent death of a Fitzgerald of Desmond.She is still commemorated in the place-names of this part of the county; *Ospideál, Aíne*, Hospital of Anye; *Rath Aíne*, the Fort of Anye; *Cnoc Aíne*, the Hill of Anye; *Clochán Aíne*, the Valley of Anye; and *Aíne Cliach*, which is generally translated as the Territory of Anye.

KNOCKAINY derives its name from *Cnoc Aíne*. Anye is believed to have had her fairy palace on the summit of this hill, which was named after her. Michael Mitchell, whose new house is located on what was originally Knockainy Fair Green, showed me Aine's Throne, a rock formation located on the upper section of a field north-west of his house. *Carn Aíne*, Anye's Cairn, on the highest summit of Knockainy Hill has an ordnance survey marker placed on it. There is a large rath, or earth-fort, on the western summit which is simply known as the Fort. Mid-way between these two summits, on a lower level north of Aíne's Throne, is an area known as *Mullach an Triúir*, the Summit of the Three, but I was able to find only two of the three ring-barrows from which it took its name. A circular enclosure with a small cairn in its centre, north of *Mullach an Triúir*, and last noted in 1967, also seems to have disappeared.

THE FAIR OF ANYE, *Aonach Aíne*, was held here in ancient times, at the beginning of the harvest, probably to coincide with the feast of *Lughnasa* on 1 August. This fair was probably a religious occasion as well as a public assembly, because the custom of bringing burning bundles of hay or straw to the summit of Knockainy Hill, on poles, was continued into the nineteenth century, until 1879. The men who carried these flaming burdens to the top of the hill made a circuit of

Aerial view of Hospital.

Mullach an Triúir before returning downhill to visit the village, fields and animal herds in order to wish them good luck.

THE HOSPITAL OF ST. JOHN OF JERUSALEM was founded in the early twelfth century to care for pilgrims visiting the Holy Land. This establishment later extended its activities to care for the sick and provide armed escorts for visitors on pilgrimage. The Knights Hospitallers, an army of mounted knights, evolved from this function almost as an early form of security service. This new order, like that of the Knights

Templars, was divided into three sections: the armed and mounted knights formed a highly-trained military wing; the chaplains catered for the spiritual welfare of the order and all those associated with it; and the infirmarians tended to the sick. The order was international, and funded by the Christian kingdoms of Europe who donated grants of land to it. These estates were farmed and managed by communities of Knights Hospitallers which were generally called preceptories in Ireland, and commanderies elsewhere. Each community was run by a preceptor, or commander, usually a knight seasoned in warfare, who ruled the community with the aid of one, or more, of his military companions and chaplains. The preceptories were used as recruiting and training centres; were built as fortified manor houses or castles rather than as monasteries; and were grouped together under the care of a priory. The Knights Hospitallers established a preceptory in Wexford in 1172, and one in Kilmainham was founded as the Priory of the Hospital in Ireland in 1174. When the Knights Templars were suppressed in 1312 a portion of their possessions passed to the Knights Hospitallers. After the Black Death ravaged the country, from August 1348, several preceptories were leased to lay farmers, and their holdings were diverted by some of the Kilmainham priors.

THE PRECEPTORY OF ST. JOHN THE BAPTIST

was founded by Geoffrey de Marisco. After Kilmainham, this was the most important house of the Knights Hospitallers in Ireland. The knights of *Gleann Aíne,* the Vale of Anye, obtained royal privileges in 1215, so the preceptory had obviously been established before this date. A preceptory could be defined as an estate or a community of the Knights Hospitallers, containing all the appurtenances necessary to the smooth functioning of such an enterprise, including castles, churches, hospitals, farms, houses, villages, mills, weirs and fisheries. The foundation here must have been quite an extensive one because of its importance.

A LEPER HOSPITAL

was also founded here in 1467. This was dedicated to St. Brigid, and was probably administered by the Knights Hospitallers.

GEOFFREY DE MARISCO (c. 1171-1248),

the son of Robert de Marisco of Huntspill, Somerset, and the Island of Lundy, England, received a grant of the castle and lands of St. Nemus, Hollywood, County Wicklow, in 1192 from his uncle, John Comyn, Archbishop of Dublin. He later received half of the barony of *Coillacht,* in Dublin, a forest region stretching from the Dodder to Tallagh, which he exchanged for the lands of Anye in 1200. In 1208 he led an uprising against Hugues de Lasci, Earl of Ulster and Justiciar, or Viceroy, of Ireland, defeating his forces at Thurles. By 1210 Geoffrey was pardoned and fighting his king's enemies in Mayo. In 1213 he headed the administration while the Justiciar, de Grey, went to England. He ruled the country until Henry of London arrived as Justiciar. Geoffrey served as Justiciar himself from 1215 to 1221. Geoffrey de Marisco was the most powerful magnate in Ireland at this time. "He was a tenant-in-chief in Limerick and in

Kerry ... he held part of Offaly in right of his wife, Eva de Bermingham ... and had ... a special interest in the great Butler property in Munster, which was still in wardship, and therefore under the justiciar's control". During the wars of the rival MacCarthys in 1214, the Anglo-Normans "overran the whole of Munster in every direction, from the Shannon to the sea". Geoffrey's reign as Justiciar appears to have been a peaceful one except for "a hosting" into Desmond, which seems to have been confined to West Cork, in 1220 or 1221. Geoffrey used his influence to have his nephew, Robert Travers, consecrated Bishop of Killaloe in January 1217. Geoffrey was then in receipt of two mandates from the king, instructing him not to permit any Irishman to be elected or appointed to any cathedral church in Ireland, or allow one to be elected or promoted to any Irish see. Robert Travers was deposed as bishop when Geoffrey's reign as justiciar ended. In 1220 an attempt to unravel Geoffrey's financial management of the state revealed that peculation rather than incompetence was the reason for such confusion.

GEOFFREY DE MARISCO

was married three times, and had a large family by his first two wives. In 1223 he paid homage to Hubert de Burgo, Bishop of Limerick, for lands at Kilmallock, Drehidtarsna, Killonehan, Kilmecrail, Kylcoban, Kilairly, and Kilkelbeg. Soon afterwards the pair of them quarrelled, for some reason now unknown, and Geoffrey laid waste the bishop's lands; inflicted serious injury on the bishop's tenants; violated the sanctuary of the church; imprisoned both clergy and laity; and circulated rumours that Hubert was unfit to hold his ecclesiastical office. Hubert de Burgo retaliated by excommunicating Geoffrey, his son, William, and their accomplices. Griffin, the Bishop of Lismore, confirmed the excommunications imposed by Hubert; and upheld his fellow-bishop's complaints about the de Mariscos. Geoffrey became justiciar again in 1226, at an annual salary of £580. On assuming power he discovered many of the Anglo-Norman barons, including his son-in-law, Theobald Fitz-Gaultier, engaged in a conspiracy against Henry III (1216-1272). Geoffrey denounced these enemies to the king, promised to subdue them, but experienced great difficulty in so doing. He was replaced as justiciar, by Richard de Burg in 1228. In the same year Aedh O'Connor was murdered by an English carpenter while staying in Geoffrey's house. Geoffrey was not implicated in the killing, and the carpenter was hanged. From 1230 to 1232 Geoffrey assumed the governorship of Ireland until he was succeeded by Hubert de Burgo. In 1234

Earl Richard Marshal arrived in Ireland, after quarreling with the king, to claim his Irish estates. The Irish barons conspired against the Earl; Geoffrey abandoned him on the field of battle; and the Earl was killed by Geoffrey's fellow-conspirators. In 1242 Geoffrey de Marisco was expelled from Ireland. His relatives in Scotland, the Comyns, refused to shelter him, and he was forced to flee to France where he died six years later.

WILLIAM DE MARISCO

was outlawed for killing a priest who had been sent to England, with complaints against William, by Maurice Fitzgerald. The killing took place at the King's Gate, Westminster. William de Marisco later employed an assassin to attempt to kill the king. The would-be killer was discovered hiding under Henry III's bed and William was forced to flee to the Island of Lundy. He maintained a crew of pirates on this island, until he was captured, with 16 of his men, and hanged.

THE HOUSE OF ANYE

continued as a preceptory until 1541 when Sir John Rawson, the Prior of Kilmainham, pensioned off its preceptor, Aeneas O'Hernan, who was then living in Kilmainham. John le Mareschal was preceptor of Anye from at least 1326 until he was replaced by John de la Battail in 1338 or 1339. In 1335 a man named Richard was hired as a cook. Under the terms of his employment he was granted, "during his life, his entertainment in this house at the table of the free servants; with clothes the same as theirs", and an allowance of $33\frac{1}{2}$ new pence for shoes. In the event of illness confining him to his chamber, he "was then to have a daily allowance of a white loaf, and one of the second kind, a flaggon of the best ale and one of an inferior kind, and a dish of meat from the kitchen". In 1348 Richard was still employed on the same terms, but was given the choice of wearing clothes the same as the other servants or having an allowance of 50 pence a year to purchase his own. In 1349 Meyler, the son of Hubert de Burgo, was allowed "entertainment for himself during life, and for a chamberlain, a servant, and two horses, in this house; and if should be confined to his chamber, then to have the daily allowance of three white loaves and one of the coarser kind, three flaggons of the best ale, and one of the second kind, with a sufficiency from the kitchen". In 1541 all the buildings of the preceptory were standing, as well as a water-mill, twelve cottages, seventeen rectories, and 280 acres of land leased to various tenants, the total valued at £41.89 annually. This low valuation was partly because of recent wars, and did not include all of the preceptory holdings. The last preceptor, Aeneas O'Hernan, was created Bishop of

Emly in 1543, after the Dissolution. The Crown leased the preceptory of Anye for £53.331/2 to Sir John Browne who, later, became known as the Master of Awney. Browne's eldest daughter and co-heir, Annabella, married Captain William Apsley of Pullborough, Sussex. They had three children, Edward, Mary and Joan.

SIR VALENTINE BROWNE of Totteridge, Herts., Crofts in Lincoln and Hoggsden, Middlesex, was constable-warden, victualler, and treasurer of Berwick. His experiences as a revenue officer helped him when he was appointed Auditor-General of Ireland during the reign of Queen Elizabeth (1558-1603). In 1583 he surveyed several escheated lands, jointly, with Sir Henry Wallop, and was subsequently sworn onto the privy council. In 1588 he represented County Sligo in Parliament and, later that year, obtained a grant from his Queen, which gave him all of the estates of the MacCarthy More Donald, Earl of Glenclare. When Edward Apsley committed suicide, it would have been Sir Valentine's duty as surveyor of escheated lands, lands forfeited to the Crown for lack of an heir, to investigate the matter. He probably saw this as an opportunity to establish his youngest son, Thomas, in a comfortable estate. Thomas married Mary Apsley, and her sister, Joan, married John Boyle, the Bishop of Cork and Ross.

THOMAS BROWNE received a grant of: "The entire manor, Lordship and Preceptory or Hospital of Anye, with all its appurtenances and all its castles, forts, lands and hereditaments in Anye, Ballinelough, Limerick, Kilmallocke, Adare, Crogh, Burgage, Asketton, Rathkeeyle, Ardagh, Cashell, Carrick, Ardartry, Ratow, Dingle, Bullen, Carrintubber, and Knockgrafton, being the temporal estate of the said hospital, the church, the rectory and chapel of the said hospital with the tithes thereof and the glebes", on 16 May 1604. His son, and heir, Sir John Browne of Hospital was killed in a duel, but John's only daughter and heiress, Elizabeth, married her kinsman, Captain Thomas Browne. This second Thomas served in the Duke of York's regiment and attended Charles II in exile. After the Restoration he was rewarded, in 1670, by having his quitrent reduced from £212.60 a year to £16.67. In 1684 the marriage of Helen Browne, the daughter of Thomas Browne of Hospital, to

Doorway of Kenmare Castle.

Nicholas Browne, later Second Viscount Kenmare, united the Hospital and Kerry estates, making this one of the largest estates in Ireland, over 130,000 acres. The title Viscount Kenmare was bestowed on Nicholas's father, another Sir Valentine, by James II in 1689. This first Viscount Kenmare was taken prisoner at Aughrim; his family were driven into exile; and his estates forfeited to the Crown. Sir Valentine died in 1690 but the estates were still forfeited to the Crown during his son's lifetime.

SIR VALENTINE BROWNE (1694-1736), claimed the estate from the Chichester House Trustees, who dealt in forfeited estates, when he came of age in 1716. His brother-in-law, John Asgill (1658-1738), had so mismanaged the property that it took Sir Valentine almost thirteen years to make it profitable. By 1729 he was in receipt of an income of £1,200 a year. By the time he died it was bringing in £3,000 annually. His grandson, Valentine, was created Baron of Castlecrosse and Viscount Kenmare on 12 February 1798, as the honours bestowed by James II, over a century earlier, were never recognised in law. On 3 January 1801, Valentine (1754-1812) was also created Viscount Castlerosse and First Earl of Kenmare. Thomas, the Third Earl of Kenmare (1789-1871), was created Baron of the United Kingdom on 12 March 1856. Samuel Lewis wrote that the Brownes derived their title

from Kenmare in Kerry, although local folklore claims the title was derived from the Browne seat in Hospital.

KENMARE CASTLE may have derived its name from the time of Sir Valentine Browne's (1637-1694) elevation to the peerage as 1st Viscount Kenmare, by James II. His ancestor, Sir Valentine Browne, had acquired vast tracts of land in the counties of Cork and Kerry in 1588. As joint-surveyor of escheated lands, with Sir Henry Wallop, Sir Valentine may have come into control of the Anye estate while acting as a guardian to the Apsley sisters. His eldest son, Valentine, remained in England and was the ancestor of the Brownes of Crofts; his second son, Nicholas, succeeded to the Irish estates; his third son, by his second wife, also named Valentine, died at an early age; and his fourth son, Thomas, through his marriage to Mary Apsley, came into possession of the lands of Anye. The first Sir Valentine is generally credited with the erection of Kenmare Castle on the site of the original house, or hospital, of Anye. Whichever of the Sir Valentine Brownes was responsible for the erection of Kenmare Castle, he must have incorporated part of the original building of the Knights Hospitallers within his later building. In 1837 Samuel Lewis stated that "a very pretty cottage" had been erected on the site by J. Gubbins, and in 1840 John O'Donovan commented on the ruins of the formerly magnificent castle behind it. Both buildings constitute the present Kenmare Castle, part of which, to the south-east, resembles Old Court, near Ferry Bridge. The house is now owned, and occupied, by Roy and Patricia Shireby.

HOSPITAL CHURCH, or the Abbey, contains three effigy tombs, one of which "is a rudely shaped statue of a knight ... with sword and buckler, which is supposed to be that of the founder", Geoffrey de Marisco. This de Marisco tomb with its high-relief effigies of a mailed knight dates from about 1260; the effigies of a knight and his lady on another de Marisco tomb date from later in the same century; while a third slab, with a low-relief effigy, dates from the fourteenth century. The living-quarters of the clergy were located in the square two-storey tower, the east wall of which formed the western gable of the church. This may have been built initially as a

The Abbey and the Catholic Church at Hospital.

belfry-tower but the top part of it now houses a grotto. The ruin of the original church still stands, and contains lancet windows and a door in the south wall. After the Dissolution the church was leased to John Cockerhan in 1566. By 1578 William Apsley was in possession.

THE TOWN OF HOSPITAL was about half a mile long and contained 179 houses in 1831. Most of these houses were demolished shortly afterwards because, six years later, the sites on which they stood had become a large cultivated field. In 1837 it contained a population of 1121; possessed a constabulary police station; and the Catholic population were in the process of rebuilding their church, "a large plain structure". Cattle fairs were held on 10 May, 9 July, 8 September and 30 October. Sir Thomas Browne was given a licence on 24 September, 1608, to hold a Saturday market and a fair on the feast of St. Peter the Apostle, 29 June, and the day after "at the Hospital". The Mahore River flows to the north of Kenmare Castle and Hospital Church, from east to west.

THE STEPPING-STONES OF ANYE, *Clochán Aíne,* spanned the Camoge River near Knockainy. These were large blocks of stone, placed across the ford at regular intervals, with flagstones laid from one block to another to provide a continuous pathway. According to folklore Aíne brought the stones here in her silken apron. Brian Boru is also credited with its construction, as he built many bridges, roads, and causeways during his reign. A modern bridge was built over the ford in 1929, but the stepping-stones were left intact until 1932 when they were destroyed during the implementation of a minor drainage scheme.

KNOCKAINY CHURCH or the Church of Anye, is supposed to have been an Augustinian foundation, established in 1349, according to Lewis. John FitzRobert Fitzgerald may have been one of its founders. In a fourteenth-century record Walter Wogan accounted for 19 pence in rent and issues from this church, which he claimed the Augustinians took from John FitzRobert Fitzgerald without licence. During the seventeenth century the Austin friars may have acquired possession, but nothing now remains of this particular building which later became a Protestant parish church. The present Church of Ireland church on this site was erected in 1861 and enlarged in 1867. The tower standing beside it contains a 1592 O'Grady slab, fixed to its base, in its interior. This octagonal spire belonged to an older church described in 1837 as a neat edifice on which the Ecclesiastical Commissioners had sanctioned payment of £183 to carry out some repairs. In 1941 there was another slab stored in the base of the tower. This depicted a Crucifixion scene, and may have dated from the seventeenth century. There is a modern Catholic church to the south.

KNOCKAINY CASTLE may have been erected by John Fitzgerald, John of Callan, in 1248. This was believed to have been an important, spacious and "very strong fortress" of which only some "very inconsiderable fragments" remained, on the western bank of the Camoge River, in 1837. The present tower house seems to be of a later date, but I did not enter it as it appeared to be in use as a store.

THE KNOCKAINY STUD was established by John Gubbins of Bruree House who reared a Derby winner, *Galtymore,* here. Two other horses, *Ardpatrick* and *Linwell,* were later associated with the stud which is now owned by a man who rode a Grand National winner to victory.

ST. AILBE, Ailbhe or Albeus, was a fifth century Irish saint, a contemporary of St. Patrick, and the first Bishop of Emly. He is believed to have been born in Knockainy. Another Ailbe, Fr. Ailbe Hanley, was born here in 1738. He composed a song called *A n Chúileann* which was written in praise of Nellie O'Grady, a local girl. This song is also known as the *Coolin* or *Coulin* and is considered to be an unofficial national anthem. Fr. Hanley died in 1805 or 1806 and was buried here in Knockainy.

SOURCE REFERENCE NUMBERS
9 12 20 28 39 47 76 86 108 120 158 162 163 184
192 209 210 213 218 233 234 264

192

Kildimo

Ferry Bridge · Ballyculhane · Ardcanny · Dromore

KILDIMO derives its name from *Cill Diomo,* St. Dioma's Church. Dioma was a son of Cas, King of Munster, an uncle of St. Munchin, and the instructor of St. Declan. He founded his church here, before St. Patrick arrived into Munster, on a site occupied thirteen centuries later by the Church of Ireland church. During Penal times Fr. Cornelius Shenane was registered as the Catholic parish priest for Kildimo and Ardcanny. He was succeeded by Fr. Nicholas Molony who, after his departure from Kildimo to Rathkeale, was forced to flee to France for a while before returning to die as parish priest of Kilkeedy and Adare. Fr. Daniel O'Brien (1694-1771), Fr. Darby Enright (1742-1806), and Fr. Michael Copps (1737-1817) were succeeded by Fr. Edmund Connery who was the parish priest here when Catholic Emancipation was granted. Kildimo Catholic church was a large plain building in 1837, when the Catholic union consisted of the parishes of Kildimo, Ardcanny and Chapel-Russell. Fr. Connery's church was located in old Kildimo but there was also another Catholic church at Whiteforge.

KILDIMO was divided into two villages during the early nineteenth century, when a new mail road was built between Limerick and Tralee. This was superceded by a more direct mail route through Newcastle West in the 1830s. Kildimo was prosperous, according to Samuel Lewis, who wrote that it was located in fertile and picturesque countryside. The principal seats were Kildimo Court of the Hartstonge family; Court Cottage of T. Rose; Bollane Cottage of Arundel Hill; and Ballynolane House of H. Potter. New Kildimo developed alongside the mail road, which is now better known as the Coast Road, or the main Askeaton-Limerick road, while old Kildimo is located south of this highway.

KILDIMO SEMINARY was founded by Rev. Samuel Jones, soon after he was appointed Rector of Ardcanny, to train parish clerks and school-masters. It was financed by the Commissioners of Education and an anti-Catholic group called the Association for Discountenancing Vice and Promoting the Knowledge and Practice of the Christian Religion, which had been established in 1792 and was incorporated in 1800 "to stem the baseful torrent of infidelity and immorality which was making progress through Ireland" (Catholicism). Rev. Jones was in charge of the seminary from 1808 until 1817, but was rather careless in keeping accounts. William Walker, secretary for the Commissioners of Education, accused him of fraud, and conducted an inquiry into the financial affairs of the seminary. His fellow-clergymen rallied around Samuel Jones, who was held in high repute, and Walkers's charges were discovered to be without any foundation. Walker died in 1825. In 1829 the Commissioners of Education published a report stating that "the late secretary had for a considerable time past carried on a system of fraud ..."

FERRY BRIDGE derives its name from a ferry which serviced the Maigue River at this point, until a bridge was built here. During the sixteenth century Sir George Carew had a castle erected east of the river to guard the crossing. This building was known as Ferry Castle or Court Tower, and local tradition maintains it was knocked to provide the stone for the three-arch Ferry Bridge which was erected in 1792. In 1837 the river was "navigable here for lighters of 40 tons burden which pass by means of a canal, over which is a swing bridge, and near it a small wharf".

KILDACOLAM TOWNLAND was shown as an 86-acre site on the *Down Survey* of 1657. The old church ruins have long since disappeared but part of the castle still remains. Kilodacolam derived its name from Colm's Church, *Cill Da Cholaim,* but it now forms part of the townland of Court.

COLAM'S CASTLE, or Kildacolam Castle, was built by the Fitzgeralds in 1514. Sir Hardress Waller captured it in 1651, but by 1655 the building was in ruin. Despite its condition the Jacobite army may have camped in the vicinity of this castle, as I have heard of a metal-detector user who located the latrine trenches dug by the soldiers. He found several items here, but refused to elaborate on his discoveries other than to state he had got quite a few coins. The ruins of this castle, mainly one wall, can be seen quite clearly from the Ferry Bridge. Colam's Castle can be approached from a track leading off a secondary road behind it, which is concealed by the high ground. Garrett's Castle is a name applied to this ruin by today's shooting fraternity.

COURT CASTLE was, and still is, a Geraldine castle, as the present owner of the land on which the small but unusually-shaped edifice stands is also a Geraldine, Denis Fitzgerald. On three sides, Court Castle resembles a conventional tower house, but its fourth side, to the south, is rounded. The entrance faces north, there is no trace of a murder-hole above the doorway, and the stairs is to the left. Basket-weave plaster work can still be seen on the roof arch and there is a small chamber off the staircase in the rounded section. The name is derived from *An Chúirt* , the Big House or Castle, or the Court. In 1583 it was listed as *Cúirt Mhic Raghnóid,* a possession of the Knights of Glin, according to the *Desmond Rolls.* In 1655 Gearóid Mac Tiobóid MacGearailt of Court was a Juror of Inquisition for Kerry.

BALLYCULHANE CASTLE, *Caisleán Baile Uí Chathaláin,* the Castle of the O'Culhane Townland, was a Geraldine castle which was held by the Purcell family from the thirteenth to the seventeenth century. The ruins cover about one half acre of ground and consist of the remains of a large high-walled bawn with angle-turrets on three of its corners, and the rubble of another such tower on its north-eastern corner. The separate portion to the north-east is believed to have been a detached bawn. This small ivy-covered structure could just as easily have been a chapel-of-ease. The long low earthen bank north of both structures, but curving eastwards up to the north gable of the smaller ruin, may have been part of the fortifications at some stage. Ballyculhane Castle was attacked several times during the Desmond and Cromwellian wars. Sir George Carew ordered the massacre of 150 women and children here in 1581. In 1651 Major-General Patrick Purcell of Ballyculhane was among those whom Ireton excluded from amnesty, and hanged, in Limerick. Sir Charles Barnadiston came into possession of Ballyculhane under the Cromwellian settlement, and the castle was in good condition as late as 1703. I.R.A. volunteers were trained here during the War of Independence.

CULHANE is a surname derived from *O'Cathaláin*, the Descendant of *Cathalán* — a diminutive of *Cathal*, the Battle-Mighty. The name was found in Roscommon, Monaghan, Louth, Offaly, Leix, Kildare, Cork and Kerry during the sixteenth century, but the surname has been associated with Limerick since the Culhane's were chiefs of *Uaitne Cliach* in what later became the barony of Owneybeg. They were dispossessed by the O'Mulryans. Variants of the name include *O'Cahallane, O'Cohallan, Cahallane, Cahillane, Cahalane, Cohalan, Callan, Clahane* and *Clehane*.

PURCELL has been recorded as a Norman surname, in Ireland, since the middle of the thirteenth century. It is derived from *Porcel*, a diminutive of the old French *porc*, which was based on the Latin *porcus*, meaning the Little Pig (a nick-name). The Purcells were an Anglo-Norman family of great influence in Ormond, and the name was quite common in Munster by the beginning of the fourteenth century. Kilkenny, Tipperary, Limerick, and Dublin are the main counties associated with this surname, variants of which include Purcill, Pursell, *Porcell, Purshell, Puirséil* and *Pruiséil*.

BALLINACARRIGA NATIONAL SCHOOL was established in1877 and closed down in 1968. Some alterations were carried out before Brian Penn purchased the building and moved in during December 1972. Further renovations were carried out in 1981 and by 1988 it was an attractive, and eye-catching private house.

FROST HILL, now the property of Seamus Moore, was once used as a barracks. An old gun-turret can be seen on its south gable.

ARDCANNY derived its name from either *Ard Chana*, the Hill or Height of Cana, or from *Ard Chaithne*, the Height of the Arbutus Tree. In 1837 Ardcanny parish was a prosperous area bounded by the River Shannon to the north, and the River Maigue to the east. The big houses of the period were Cartown, the residence of J.E. Langford; Mellon of M. Westropp; Ballincarriga of the Dawson family; Rockfield of E. Fitzgerald; Mount Pleasant of Mrs. Hill; Ballystool , of the Hewson family; Ballincarreg of the Hurst family; Ardcanny Rectory; and Shannongrove House which was then the residence of Bolton Waller and the ancestral home of Charles William Bury, Earl of Charleville. Samuel Lewis mentioned that the Rockfield demesne contained "a very capacious and ancient

fortress, constructed of large blocks of stone very ingeniously put together without mortar, and forming walls of great thickness". Part of this fortress is believed to have survived into modern times and boatmen used it as a point at which to tie up their boats out of reach of the Maigue's tidal waters. Other forts can still be found in the vicinity; there are three in Kilmareen, one of which contains a souterrain.

BOLLANE CASTLE may derive its name from *Beolán* or *Bealán* meaning a Little Mouth but no explanation of this name was available by 1988. This was a Geraldine castle, the ruins of which are located on a low rock overlooking County Clare and the Maigue Valley. Tradition maintains it was originally built by the O'Donovans.

ARDCANNY RECTORY, Ardcanny Glebe House, or Mellon Glebe House has been replaced by an attractive modern traditional-style building which now occupies the same site. The original glebe house was erected with the aid of a £100 grant from the Board of First Fruits in 1791. By 1837 it had been "greatly improved" by the rector, whose school-house had been converted into a courthouse. The old structure was demolished in 1976, but part of the out-buildings still survive.

TEMPLE MELLON, or Ardcanny Church, derived its name from *Teampull a'Mhulláin*, which may mean the Church of the Hillock, although *mullán* can also signify a stack of corn, a rick of hay, the paten of a chalice or a type of milking vessel. Denis Aherne was appointed to this church in 1400, but was deprived of his position, as vicar, because he practised medicine, publicly, for reward. Ardcanny was noted as part of the Archdeacon's prebend by the Protestant church commission in 1615. In 1738 the old church was demolished and a new one was erected on the same site. By 1837 this "spacious edifice" was in "a very dilapidated condition". The roof was removed shortly afterwards but the building was left open to the elements, as John O'Donovan reported that it had not been re-roofed by 1840. Temple Mellon was covered with ivy on the exterior, while its interior was overgrown with small trees, bushes and more ivy in 1988. There is a ruined porch on the western gable of this edifice, which is located in the centre of a graveyard. In December 1987 Steve Wooley, the producer of Neil Jordan's film, *High Spirits,* was not allowed to film scenes in this cemetery because it was feared that this would "do some damage to the souls of the dead".

ST. BRIGID'S WELL is located half a mile south of Temple Mellon. This is still the scene

of some devotions, but the annual pilgrimage which was usually held on 1 February seems to have ceased. The well is located behind the gate-lodge quite close to the road. Statues and candles are still left here, and it appeared to have been recently cleaned in 1988.

MELLON HOUSE is a two-storey Georgian mansion erected over a basement. The Mellon estate had been a Fitzgerald property prior to the Cromwellian settlement, after which it became the property of Phineas Bury. Phineas rented the estate to Thomas Westropp of Ballysteen, and in 1780 John Westropp erected Mellon House. Montiford Westropp purchased the Mellon estate from Charles William Bury, the Earl of Charleville, in 1844. His descendants, Rose and Grace Westropp, still lived in the house in 1975. R.J. Barry was in possession of Mellon House in 1988.

THE THIRD EARL OF LIMERICK decided to build a country seat in County Limerick soon after he succeeded to the title. Despite owning the ground rents of a large portion of Limerick City and over 5,700 acres of land in the counties of Cork and Limerick, the Earl's family home was in Tewin Water, Hertfordshire, England. His former Irish seat was at Limerick House, Limerick City, his family's eighteenth century town house. Edward William Godwin was commissioned to design an imposing baronial-style mansion for the Earl on the *Drom Mór*, the Big Ridge, from which Dromore Castle took its name.

DROMORE CASTLE dominates the wooded sky-line against which it is silhouetted. Even though it was built in the latter half of the nineteenth century, it resembles a massive medieval fortress and contains many of the features of such a structure including the fortifications which were incorporated into the overall design. The castle walls are six feet thick, rising from a battered base; all the main rooms were designed to face into the courtyard; there was a separate banquet hall; a round tower from which to survey the surrounding countryside; and wall-walks, machicolations, and battlements from which any besiegers could be repelled. By 1867 the building was so secure that it could have withstood a Fenian attack. Tradition claims that Godwin played on the Earl's fears of a Fenian rising in order to complete his "Walt Disney style" architectural fantasy. The Earl of Limerick lived here for a while, but as problems with dampness and other inconveniences arose, he gradually spent less time in Dromore and eventually returned to England. The castle was occupied on an on-and-off basis until 1896. The Fourth Earl sold it to Morgan MacMahon of Limerick, along with 130 acres of land, in 1939. The MacMahon

Dromore Castle and lake.

family lived here until about 1950. The contents of Dromore Castle were auctioned some time around 1956. Soon afterwards the roof was removed, and the interior "stripped". Neil Jordan's film, *High Spirits*, was filmed on location here in 1987.

DOG'S ISLAND is the name of a stretch of ground located between Dromore Lake and a smaller lake to the east of it. This may have been a *crannog* or lake-dwelling as the water levels were once much higher, according to local tradition. Folklore relates that the waters of the Maigue extended as far as Dromore Ridge until that river was banked. During the 1950s a bone crucifix was discovered on Dog's Island.

BLEACH LAKE contains a *crannog* but I was unable to discover anything else about either the lake or lake-dwelling.

KILCURLEY CHURCH was located east of Kilcurley House on the 1841 ordnance survey map, but by then only the foundations remained although the site was still in use as a *cillín* or childrens burial ground. This church was located west of the Maigue River, more than midway between Ferry Bridge and Adare.

SOURCE REFERENCE NUMBERS
9 11 13 42 44 47 64
76 86 107 120 123 129 157
184 188 192 217 238 273 282

Kilfinnane

Ardpatrick · Glenosheen · Castle Oliver · Cush

KILFINNANE derives its name from *Cill Fhionáin*, the Church of St. Finan, Fionán Lobhar, or Finan the Leper who founded his church here during the seventh century.

THE RUINED CHURCH, opposite the imposing red sandstone Catholic church and parochial house, once served as a Church of Ireland church. This was rebuilt in 1760, probably on the site of St. Finan's foundation, while a glebe house was erected nearby in 1813. The present Church of Ireland church is located on the west side of the town.

THE CATHOLIC CHURCH is dedicated to St. Andrew rather than to St. Finan. Church dedications in the county are divided between local and foreign saints: Athlacca is dedicated to John the Baptist, Bruff to St. Peter and Ballingarry to St. Evanjanus, while others are dedicated to native saints such as St. Patrick, St. Munchin or St. Ita. Throughout the Penal times Kilfinnane was rarely without either a Catholic church or priest. Father John Rahilly (1654 - c. 1719) appears to have resided here in 1704. Fr. Timothy "Thaddeus" O'Hea (or Hayes) was present in 1737. The latter priest may have been succeeded by his nephew, Fr. Matthew O'Hea, (1737-1775) who worked in this parish with Fr. Paul Slattery (1706-1787), a Domincan priest. Dr. James Conners appears to have been present in 1774. In 1787 Fr. Edmund O'Donnell may have been appointed to Kilfinnane. Fr. John Gleeson registered himself as parish priest under the Act of Parliament in 1782, and on his death in 1789 he was succeeded by Fr. Edmund O'Donnell who may have been parish priest until 1798. Fr. John Sheehy (1749-1844) was

Aerial view of Kilfinnane.

The Kilfinnane moat.

appointed to Kilfinnane in 1789. Nine years later he became its parish priest, and retained that position until his death on 24 October 1844. In 1835, after the Catholic Emanicapation Act was passed, Fr. Sheehy erected a new Catholic church in Kilfinnane. One of his successors, Fr. Patrick Lee, was responsible for building the present church before his death on 23 July 1892. The parochial house was built during Fr. John Carrick's term as parish priest. He died on 19 April 1915.

KILFINNANE is situated in the middle of a group of mountains, by which it is surrounded on all sides but the north. The Vikings raided in this region before they settled in Munster. Brian Boru's brother, Mahon, was killed by the King of Desmond's son, Molloy, at the Gap of the Red Chair, six miles to the south, in 976. Mahon's death was later avenged by his nephew, Murrough, who killed Molloy and 1200 of his men near the same place. In 1291 the Anglo-Normans were established here, and King Edward I (1272-1307) granted Kilfinnane a charter for the holding of fairs.

THE KILFINNANE MOAT, *Tréada an Rí,* or the Dane's Fort, was described by Seán P. O'Ríordáin as a splendid example of a platform-type ring fort, which may have been used for a ritual purpose, such as an inauguration. Platform-type ring forts can be found in many parts of the country, and one excavated at Ballingarry Down dated from the eighth century. According to Seán P. O'Ríordáin, their "concentric defences and lack of a bailey distinguish them from the normal Norman earthwork". In 1837 Samuel Lewis described the Kilfinnane Moat as "a mound about 130 feet high, 50 feet in diameter at the base; and 20 at the summit, encircled by seven earthen ramparts about 20 feet apart, gradually diminishing in height from the innermost to the outermost, which is about 10 feet high and 2000 feet in circuit". By 1908 only three ramparts remained. In 1988 about 66% of the inner rampart, approximately 30% of the middle rampart, and less than 10% of the outer rampart, were visible from the ground. The view from the summit of the moat is quite extensive overlooking the county's central plain and the town of Kilmallock to the north-west. Aerial photographs of this ancient earthen mound reveal a lot of details not apparent from ground level.

KILFINNANE CASTLE was founded by the Roche family. In 1602 O'Sullivan Beara encamped in the vicinity of the moat and according to tradition, as recounted by Terry Lynch, a sword of the O'Sullivan Beara's was found in the nearby mountains during the last century. The castle was attacked and captured by the Cromwellians, who killed all the defenders and then blew it up. Part of this old building still stands and was in use as a rubbish-tip-cum-incinerator in 1988.

PALATINE FAMILIES were brought here, from Rathkeale, by Silver Oliver, the area's biggest landowner. When the Defenders attacked the town twice in 1793, it was defended by the Palatines and other inhabitants under the leadership of Charles Silver Oliver. Palatines' Rock, to the east of the town, was used as an assembly point by the Palatines, who are also commemorated in the name of a small wooded hill visible from the moat, Palatine Hill.

IN 1837 1,752 people lived in the town which consisted "of two principal and several smaller streets, containing 314 houses, many of which are large and well built, and is the property of R. Oliver Gascoigne ... The inhabitants are mostly engaged in agricultural occupations; a few are employed in the weaving of linen and cotton goods; and nor far from the town are oatmeal-mills, and others at Sunville about two miles distant. The market is on Tuesday, and is well attended; and fairs for farming stock and implements, are held on 19 May, 9 August and 25 October. The market-house is a large and commodious building, and was substantially repaired in 1836. Here is a constabulary station, and petty sessions are held on alternate Saturdays ... a small bridewell has recently been built; and the sessions-house, which is large and convenient, is about to be repaired. A spacious and handsome fever hospital was erected in 1836, at an expense of £700, to which an accident ward and a dispensary are attached ... The mountains consist principally of coarse conglomerate and red sandstone; silver and iron ores are found, and coal is supposed to exist; limestone gravel is abundant, and is much used for manure. The land is generally good and there are large dairy farms, and a considerable tract of bog and mountain pasture; much of the mountain land, however, has been brought into cultivation, and in a great measure provides for many poor families. The principle seats [of town and parish] are Spa Hill, the residence of W. Oliver, Esq.; Bossonstown, of G.W. Bennett, Esq.; Kilfinane House, of C. Bennett, Esq.; and Brookeville Cottage, of T. Massey, Esq. ... Near the town are a rath and three strong forts; also a large artificial cave".

THE POPULATION

of Kilfinnane was 1,099 in 1986, consisting of 527 males and 572 females. In 1988 Spring Lodge was still occupied, the residence of the Connery family. Parts of the old mill on the southern side of the bridge over the Loobagh river showed signs of recent demolition, and the old holding-pond had disappeared under the tracks of a bulldozer. On the western side of the Tipperary road there is a nine-house Rent An Irish Cottage complex which has brought a lot of business to the town in recent years. Some ring forts are visible on the surrounding mountains, from the moat, and Seán P. O'Ríordáin found a pair of standing stones which marked the entrance to a destroyed ring fort. Kilfinnane is noted today as a sports centre. It still contains a ball-alley, and despite several neglected and dilapidated-looking structures scattered throughout the town there was no evident sign of wanton vandalism visible in 1988. A lot of iron-work can also be seen around the place. Plans are now being made to restore the old market house which is roofless and derelict, and bring it into line with the surrounding architecture. When Patrick "Staker" Wallis (1733-1798) was hanged, his head was cut off and placed on a spike above this eighteenth century building as a warning to his fellow rebels — the United Irishmen of 1798.

CHARITY SCHOOLS were set up about 1710 to feed, clothe, and educate poor children, and wean them from the Catholic religion, as Catholic schools were forbidden under Penal Laws, and Catholic teachers were outlawed. The Established Church hoped that children taught, clothed and fed by Protestants, would in time take instruction in the Protestant religion, and become English in faith, language and outlook. By 1719 such schools were operating in Kilfinnane, Kilmallock and Limerick City. By 1752 it was obvious that the results of this enterprise did not match Protestant expectations. In 1733 George II (1714-1760) granted a charter to "rescue the souls of thousands of poor children from the dangers of Popish superstition and idolatry, and their bodies from the miseries of idleness and beggary". The Kilfinnane Education Centre, a recently constructed adult education centre with accommodation, illustrates how education has advanced since then. Next to this modern building is a girls' national school which was erected in 1909.

DURING THE WAR OF INDEPENDENCE,

Kilfinnane had the unique distinction of being subjected to an air raid. A two-seater Bristol fighter plane got into difficulty above Ballinanima. The pilot made a forced landing, was taken prisoner by the I.R.A. under the command of J.M. McCarthy, and his aircraft was destroyed on the ground. The local Black and Tan contingent threatened to bomb Kilfinnane from the air unless the pilot was released. The I.R.A. ignored this ultimatum, and soon after the deadline had expired two smoke-bombs were dropped on the town. Some days later the pilot was released. He requested an explanatory note for his commanding officer in Fermoy, and reciprocated with a written statement saying he had been well treated and made comfortable by people "who were forced to house me by the I.R.A. ... I do not consider that they could be held responsible — (Sgd.) G.O. Mackay, F.O., R.A.F.". The Fermoy Black and Tans later took him on a tour of the locality to see if he could identify any of the houses in which he had been held captive. In one particular farmhouse he admired racing trophies which he had earlier noticed as a prisoner but he refused to identify the family as his captors, and left, taking the Tans with him.

DR. MAURICE FITZGERALD, of Mortalstown, tended an I.R.A. man, wounded during the Ballylanders raid, at Mrs. Burke's home in Laurencetown. In 1919 he treated Sean Treacy, after the Knocklong Rescue of Sean Hogan, and remarked: "The coolest man there, far cooler than I was. That was Sean Treacy!"

CUSH is a townland on the western slopes of Slievereagh, about 700 to 800 feet high, and two miles north of Kilfinnane. It contains an extensive complex of ancient fields and enclosures, and was excavated in 1932-1934. Excavations revealed that the site was continuously occupied by an agricultural community from around 1000 BC to 400 AD, according to Seán P. O'Ríordáin. In 1987 T.B. Barry wrote that "there is some dispute as to the date of these features, ranging from the Early Iron Age to the Early Christian period". To the south, six ring forts were joined together with a large rectangular enclosure located to the west. Seventy rotary querns, glass beads, a Bronze Age urn, an abundance of iron slag and several burials were found. One fort was apparently set aside as a burial ground, while other cremated burials in decorated urns were discovered under Bronze Age tumuli or mounds. A field system, marked out by earth banks and ditches of the early Iron Age or early Christian era, surrounds the site.

CAHER MORTLE may have been known as Chapel Martel in 1837, when a "circular enclosure, having the appearance of a military station, within which it is said that a converted Dane founded a chapel" was located on its summit. This chapel and lands may have been given to the Abbey of Buttevant, later.

SLIEVEREAGH derives its name from *Sliabh Riabhach*, the Grey, Brindled, Striped, Varied or Reddish Mountain, in all probability the last, because of its red sandstone. The summit is 1531 feet high, and affords a spectacular view of the region.

ARDPATRICK St. Patrick's Hill or Height, owes more than its name to that legendary saint. According to tradition, the first monastery on this hill was founded by St. Patrick himself. From the graveyard on its summit one can see Kilfinnane, Kilmallock, the chimney-stacks of the cement factory on the shore of the Shannon, the Cratloe Hills and Bunratty Castle, in Clare.

ARDPATRICK CHURCH, at least the first church on this site, may have been founded as early as the fifth century. The present ruin is of a much later period and probably dates from about 1200. Its northern and southern walls project beyond the gables to the east and west, forming antae, those curious reminders of an earlier period when walls such as these were made out of wooden logs. Pagans, Christians, Vikings, Anglo-Normans and English have known this ancient settlement. Bishop OSuairlig died here in 1079. The O Longáin family were the traditional *coarbs* (overseers or keepers of the church lands, more often than not laymen rather than priests) of Ardpatrick until they were dispersed throughout Limerick, Kerry and Cork at the end of the sixteenth century. The earliest written record of this family's involvement with the church was in 1113 when Diarmait OLongáin the *coarb* of Ardpatrick, died here. In its heyday contributions from all over Munster poured into Ardpatrick from where they were forwarded to Armagh. It was burned in 1114. Torlogh O'Connor plundered it in 1127, drove off numerous herds of cattle and killed many people in the process. Ceallach, the coarb, "successor of St. Patrick ... the only head obeyed by the Danes and the Irish", died here in 1129. He was buried at Lismore, in accordance with his own wishes. The O Longáins are mentioned as the Langanes, coarbs of the monastic lands of Ardpatrick, in 1590 and 1597. The O'Sullivan Beara sheltered here for a night in 1602. By then his followers were beginning to desert him and he "was not a day or a night during this period without receiving fierce assaults and battles, all which he sustained and responded to with manliness and vigour". After this date little else was recorded about Ardpatrick.

ST. PATRICKS WELL was once resorted to by people seeking cures for lameness, rickets and rheumatism. Tradition claimed that any pilgrim who was unable to see his reflection in its water would die within the year. This well was enclosed by stonework "20 yards south-west of the church" in 1840. Seán O Murchadha pointed out the remains of the well and traces of *Leaba Rian Bó Phadraig* to members of the Shannon Archaeological and Historical Society during a visit here on 21 August 1988. On the same day David Meskill told me that the graveyard is now the scene of an annual pilgrimage each August, weather permitting. A Fr. Greene initiated Mass-gatherings on one fine August Sunday about five or six years previously and the custom has been continued by his successor, Fr. Kennedy, who hopes to establish it as a tradition. David also mentioned that a special hearse-type trailer, drawn by a tractor, is used to carry coffins up this steep hill for funerals.

THE ROUND TOWER is now only a stump. This is probably older than the ruined church but the greater part of it collapsed in the early 1800s, so only a portion of it now remains outside the graveyard wall.

THE SLUG OF ST. PATRICK'S COW'S HORN, *Leaba Rian Bó Phadraig*, is an ancient entrenched roadway near the church. There are also some remains of an ancient

Ardpatrick graveyard.

field system nearby. These small fields, smaller than their modern counterparts, can be traced by looking for the small low banks which enclose them. They are often found in the vicinity of early Christian monasteries.

ARDPATRICK CASTLE was supposedly built by the Anglo-Normans in 1198. O'Donovan was unable to determine whether this castle was erected north-west of Millmount, where a castle-site was located in 1840, or in another Ardpatrick elsewhere. In 1837 the big houses of the locality were Bettyville of J. Austin and the former Godsall seat, Sunville, which was occupied by E. Sayers. Sayer's extensive mill produced 3,000 barrels of flour annually and gave a lot of employment locally.

BALLINGADDY PARISH was the more usual name for Ardpatrick parish over the last few centuries but in more modern times this trend has been reversed. Ardpatrick is now better known than Ballingaddy, *Baile an Ghadaihe*, the Town of the Thief, the thief in this case was an Gadaihe Dubh Ua Dubháin, the Black Thief of O Duane.

DOWNES or O *Dubháin* was a common surname throughout the southern half of Ireland at the end of the sixteenth century. In Limerick the name was generally Anglicised to Downes, but there are several other variants: *O Dovayne, O Dwane, O Duan, O Dowane, O Doane, O Downe,* Dewane, Devane, Divane, Divan, Dwane, Duan, Dune, Doane, Dooan, Doon, Down, Devine and Devany. The name is derived from the descendants of *Dubhán*, which is a diminutive for *dubh* or black, but it can also be translated as the Irish for kidney.

KILQUAN CHURCH was a brown sand-

stone church erected by the Knights Templars at the foot of Cahir Hill. By 1840 little remained of this ancient structure, but its graveyard was still in use.

CAHIR HILL derived its name from a small earth fort built on its summit. A great carn, or cairn, of stones to the west of the fort was believed to be much older than the legend it inspired amongst the country people of the 1800s and earlier. Tradition claimed that *Sean Buidhe* gathered a heap of stones here with which he intended to build a castle. This was never erected but the townland of Ballymacshaneboy owes its name to *Baile Mac Seán Buidhe,* the Town of Yellow John's Son.

BALLYSHONBOY derives its name from *Baile Seán Bhuidhe,* the Town of Yellow John, and the parish of Kilquan was also known under this appellation. In 1579 the outlawed Earl of Desmond found shelter among the surrounding mountain range of Jamestown, Ballyhough, Ballyshondebuie and Ballylopin. In those days, the mountains were covered with extensive woods and forests in which he found a safe refuge. His followers were not so lucky, as great numbers of their bones were found by the early-nineteenth century "interred in the grounds of Mount Coote", and elsewhere, in the region.

LADY'S WELL, in Ballyshanedehey, and *Tobar Rígh an Domhnaigh,* or Sunday's Well, to the south of Ballyshonboy townland, were still frequented as holy wells during the nineteenth century. *Tobar Rígh an Domhnaigh* can also be translated as the Well of the King of the World.

GLENOSHEEN derives its name from *Gleann Oisin,* Oisin's Valley. This was named

Castle Oliver.

after Fionn Mac Cumhail's son, the equally legendary Oisín, who returned from *Tír na nOg* on a white steed, several hundred years after leaving Fionn and the Fianna. His saddle-girth broke as he lifted a heavy weight and he fell to the ground, where he was immediately transformed into a very old and feeble man. Legend also maintains that he met St. Patrick here and converted to Christianity before he died. This area was originally situated within the Castle Oliver demesne but became a village when a colony of Palatines settled here in 1761 at the invitation of Silver Oliver.

OSCAR'S BED, *Leaba Iscur,* is named after Oisín's son, and is located on the head of a broad valley, on the northern side of the Ballyhoura mountains. This is also known as the Mountrussell wedge-shaped gallery grave, and is an unusually constructed tomb, consisting of a "narrow gallery with sidestones overlapped by corbels in several irregular tiers, which narrow the gap to be spanned by the roofstones".

SEEFIN MOUNTAIN towers over Glenosheen village. This is the highest peak in the Ballyhoura mountains and derives its name from *Suí Finn,* Fionn's Seat, another link with the Fianna of old. The cairn on its summit, easily visible from the village, is known as Ossian's Tomb. The view from the top embraces every county in Munster.

GLENOSHEEN contained a constabulary station in 1837. As there was no Church of Ireland church in the village divine service was regularly performed in a building attached to the constabulary station. In 1988 the home of Patrick and Robert Joyce was still occupied, and is regularly pointed out to visitors.

PATRICK WESTON JOYCE (1827-1914) was born in Ballyorgan but soon afterwards the family moved to Glenosheen. In1845 he started work with the Board of National Education, and soon afterwards was appointed principal of the Marlborough Street

Training Centre, a position from which he retired in 1893. In 1861 he graduated from Trinity College with a B.A., received his M.A. in 1864, and an honorary degree of LL.D. in 1870. In 1863 he became a member of the Royal Irish Academy and in 1865 he joined the Royal Society of the Antiquaries of Ireland. The history, folklore, lays, legends, music and song of his native place inspired the many books he produced. *The Origin and History of Irish Names of Places* is as valuable a source book today as it was when P.W. Joyce first produced it in 1870 under the title of *Irish Local Names Explained. The Social History of Ancient Ireland* (1903) and *English as We Speak it in Ireland* (1910) are equally valuable. He was a prolific writer, and his material can never really be outdated. He became President of the Royal Society of Antiquaries of Ireland, 1906-1908, and died at his residence, Lyre-na-Grena, Dublin, on 7 January 1914.

DOCTOR ROBERT DWYER JOYCE

(1830-1883) was born in Glenosheen. He knew George Petrie (1789 -1866) and contributed many airs which were included in *The Petrie Collection of the Native Music of Ireland* which was published in 1855. Robert produced a volume of poems but his main interest was in the field of old Irish music. *The Wind that Shakes the Barley* was one of his better-known compositions.

THE PARISH OF PARTICLES derived its name from the detached particles or portions of other parishes which were combined to form it. The townlands of Down Gadmond, Down Innish, Chapel Martel and Ineycahel belonged respectively to the abbeys of Butte, Kilmallock, Monasteranenagh and Adare before the Reformation. These townlands were given to the churches by the O'Kelly, or O'Hely, family at a very early period. There were three churches here in medieval times, Castleotway, Clough-a-Nutfoy, or *Dún Ghadamoinn* Church, Sithcathil or *Sióth Chathail* Church and Chapel Martel or Mortelstown Church. By 1840 there was neither an ancient nor a modern church in Particles parish.

CASTLE OLIVER derived its original name of Otway's Rock or castle from the Irish *Cloch an Otbhaidhigh* after an Anglo-Norman family who settled there soon after the Invasion. This was later Anglicised to Cloghnotefoy, Cloghanodfoy, Clonodfoy or Cloghnodfoy and a house of that name, Clonodfoy House, was erected here before the present Gothic-style structure was built. Castle-na-Doon, the seat of the Roches until they were ousted by the Fitz-Harris family was the oldest edifice on this site. Sir Edward Fitz-Harris was the owner of an old ruined house, bawn, stable, orchard and garden here in 1654. This was described in 1655 as a bawn with a crenellated wall and four turrets with conical roofs at the angle. In 1666 Robert Oliver, a Cromwellian captain, was confirmed in his ownership of the estate. Richard Oliver changed his name to Gascoigne on inheriting the estates of Sir Thomas Gascoigne of Parlington, Yorkshire, in 1812. In 1837 the estate consisted of 20,000 acres. Robert Gascoigne neglected his Irish holdings and allowed his bailiff to live in the old mansion which had become very dilapidated. G. Fowler Jones, a York architect, was employed to design a new house which may have been built as a famine relief scheme. The stable block of the older house was retained but the rest of it was demolished to make way for the present house with its massive keep-like tower, steeped gables and battlemented turret. Work commenced in 1846 according to Tony Browne, although other sources claim a date of 1850. Tony commented on the iron framework of the high-pitched roofs, which is a modern feature. He took members of the Shannon Archaeological and Historical Society on a tour of the house, which has been closed for a number of years and is now in a dangerous and dilapidated condition. Castle Oliver had been badly vandalised by then, August 1988, and "stripped" of many of its fittings, but even so it was still an impressive building. A French company purchased Castle Oliver some time before August 1988, and intend to restore it.

OLIVER'S FOLLY, located on one of a series of small hills north of Castle Oliver, is older than the present Castle Oliver. This is a small gateway tower which was erected by Silver Oliver during the eighteenth century.

MARIA DOLORES ELIZA GILBERT (1818-1861), alias Rosa Anna Gilbert, alias Elizabeth Rosanna Gilbert, alias Lola Montez, was "everything by turns and nothing long". Her mother was an Oliver of Castle Oliver and her father, Edward Gilbert, was an English ensign who died in India when Lola was seven years old. Lola was educated in Scotland and Paris. She lived for a while in Bath but eloped with, and married, Captain Thomas James in 1837 to avoid another marriage her mother had planned for her. She travelled to Ireland with her husband and then accompanied him to India where he rejoined his regiment. By 1842 she was back in England, supposedly divorced and preparing for a theatrical career. She studied under a Miss Fanny Kelly, perfected her dancing in Spain, and made her debut in London where she was hissed off the stage of Her Majesty's Theatre. She was successful in Dresden and Berlin; was expelled for her political associations from Warsaw; received many presents from Czar Nicholas in Russia; and caused the death of an editor in a duel in Paris. She was a woman whose beauty allied to "a certain power of fascination" enabled her to do as she liked with men. In Munich she completely captivated Ludwig I of Bavaria and became his mistress. She was created Baronne de Rosenthal and Comtesse de Lansfeld, received a state pension, and possibly provoked the Revolution of 1848 which resulted in Ludwig's dethronement. She returned to the stage, in England, after fleeing from Munich. Lola was sued for bigamy after marrying George Trafford Heald in 1849, and was forced to flee to Spain with her new husband. Heald was drowned in Lisbon in 1853. Lola went to America where she appeared on Broadway, and later married P.P. Hull, the owner of the *San Francisco Whig*. She left him within a short space of time. In 1855 she went on a tour of Australia, where she horse-whipped the editor of the *Ballarat Times* for casting aspersions on her character, but had returned to America by 1857. In 1858 she became a public lecturer, lecturing on her own career, that of other beautiful women, heroines in history, and similar subjects. She met a former school-mate, Mrs. Buchanan, a New York florist, in 1859, and spent the rest of her life visiting outcasts of the Magdalen Asylum outside New York. She died in an asylum at Asteria, New York, on 17 January 1861. Her last words were, "I am very tired". Lola Montez, the most famous member of the Oliver family, was buried in the Greenwood Cemetery, New York. She had been born in the old Castle Oliver within sight of a woodland area known as the Greenwood which has long since been incorporated into a State forest complete with walks and picnic areas.

BALLYORGAN can be translated as Organ's or Horgan's Town. In 1837 it had a population of 369 persons, and contained the Church of Ireland and Roman Catholic churches for the parish of Kilflyn. The former building was a neat edifice with a square tower, built in 1812, while the latter was a small thatched building.

HORGAN, Organ, Hargan, *O'hArgaín, O'Horgaine, O'Horgane, O'Hargan,* is a contracted variant of *O hArragáin,* which in itself is a corruption of *hAnradhaín,* the descendant of the Warrior or Champion. The *O hArragáin* name can be found in North Munster but the *O'hArgáin* is more common in Cork or Kerry.

KILFLYN CHURCH is situated in the townland of Abbey and is believed to have been founded by St. Finian or St. Flann about 547. Kilflyn is generally translated as the Church of Flann. However, St. Finian may be another name for St. Finan the founder of Kilfinnane four miles north of here on the map, about seven by road. This ruined church is believed to have been a Trinitarian monastery which was rebuilt by the Geraldines in 1296. A considerable portion of the building collapsed in 1835, undermined by people digging for a treasure supposed to have been deposited here. The parish of Kilflyn was located in the middle of a group of mountains separating the counties of Cork and Limerick, and was considered a wasteland until 1761 when a considerable number of Palatines settled around here at the invitation of the Oliver family. Within three-quarters of a century they had brought the former wilderness into cultivation. The principal mountains in this grouping are Kilcruig and Coolfrie, or Houndscourt.

SOURCE REFERENCE NUMBERS
5 9 11 18 26 32 44 45 47 64 75 76 86 92 96 105 107
108 109 120 123 129 135 143 150 167
187 188 191 192 195 207 233 238 264 282

Killeedy

Glenquin · Tournafulla · Monagay · Templeglantine

KILLEEDY was originally known as *Cluain Chreadháil,* the Meadow or Pasture Land with a Good Depth of Soil. In 1840 John O'Donovan referred to *Cluain Chreadháil* as the Religious Retirement but mentioned that in later ages it had taken the name of *Cill Ide,* the Church of St. Ita, from a nunnery which was founded here in the sixth century.

ST. ITA, Ide, Míde, Idy or Deirdre, was known as the St. Brigid of Munster. She was born before 484 the daughter of a chieftain and features in the legends, history and folk- lore of West Limerick. She is mentioned as a noble virgin of royal blood "who from the font of baptism was filled with the Holy Ghost; for all admired the continence and morals of her infancy and her abstinence on days on which the servant of God ought to fast". St. Ita "succoured many grievous dis- eases". On one occasion Ita allowed a *daol darbh,* an insect which the people believed to feed on human flesh in the churchyards, to suck her blood until "it grew to a size greater than that of a suckling pig". This account prompted John O'Donovan to note, in brack- ets, "Poor Idy was an idiot". Further on in his letters he mentions that "St. Ita should have been put under the care of such a person as Mr. Jackson at Limerick". When her sister Nessa's husband was slain in battle Ita is said to have restored him to life. She is also believed to have suckled Jesus when he came to her in the form of an infant and to have trained St. Brendan the Navigator and St. Mochoemog in her school for boys. She was venerated as the "Fostermother of the Saints" and the "White Sun of the Women of Munster". She died some time between 570 and 577. After noting many details of her life, in his *Ordnance Survey Letters* John

Ashford.

Killeedy Church.

O'Donovan added another postscript "This is all fudge!" St. Ita's hagiography did not impress him.

KILLEEDY CHURCH was established by 546 as a monastery for monks and nuns. St. Ita is generally acknowledged as the founder of this religious settlement at the foot of the mountain in the territory of *Uí-Chonaill-Gabhra*. St. Ita's nunnery gradually evolved into a monastery for men. The names of two of its abbots are recorded: Cathasach, who died in 810 or 815; and Finnachta, who died in 833. The monastery was raided by the Vikings on several occasions. A Romanesque nave and chancel church developed from the original foundation but this has been badly damaged over the centuries, particularly the nave. After the Dissolution it became a Church of Ireland church. During the early eighteenth century the chancel was modernised and the building remained in use as a place of Protestant worship until about 1800. In 1822 the Rockites destroyed both the church and the glebe house. Neither was rebuilt. O'Donovan maintained that it had contained a doorway similar to that in the west gable of Clonfert Cathedral but by 1840 no trace of the doorway remained. The nave was dismantled "by the unenlightened venerators of St. Ida, who are in the habit of pulling out the cut stones of this building to place them at the heads of the graves of their departed friends". The middle gable was surmounted with a small belfry which was placed directly over the chancel arch. Both the belfry and arch were erected when the church was remodelled. A large statue of St. Ita, is located on the western side of the arch, obstructing the view of the chancel behind it.

ST. ITA'S GRAVE is located at the junction of the nave and chancel, on the southern side. The custom of strewing it with flowers has continued into modern times.

ST. ITAS'S WELL is located opposite Margaret Anglim's tombstone which is about ten paces north of the stile leading into Killeedy Church. The well is a small circular opening in the ground lined with large stones cut in semi-circular sections. St. Ita's feast-day was observed on 15 January into the nineteenth century and the well was "celebrated for curing the small pox in children and other diseases". The well was dry on the occasion of John O'Donovan's visit, prior to 1840, but it contained water on 2 January 1989. St. Ita so impressed the chieftain of *Uí-Chonail-Gabhra* that he offered her a large tract of land around her foundation but all she would accept was a small spot sufficient for a garden. She fasted so much that, it was said, an angel cautioned her to be less abstemious.

ANGLIM is derived from *O hAngluinn* or *O hAngluim*, the Descendant of *Anglonn*, the Champion or Hero. Variants of the name are *O'Hanglin* and Anglin. This is really a Cork surname rarely found outside that county, or this part of south-west Limerick.

THE MULLAGHAREIRK MOUNTAINS form a boundary between Limerick and the neighbouring counties of Cork and Kerry. The three boundaries converge south of Mountcollins where the Feale river forms a border between Limerick and Kerry.

LUACHRA was the name of the district in which Killeedy was located rather than the name of the mountain itself. This part of *Uí-Chonaill Gabhra* was so called, apparently from its abounding in rushes.

KILLEEDY CASTLE north-west of Killeedy Church, may have been built on a *motte*. Tradition ascribes its foundation to either King John or the Knights Templars. Only a fragment of the south wall remained in 1840. This portion was further reduced in 1988 when it was struck by lightning. The tall narrow ruin, resembling a chimney-stack, can be seen from a distance.

GLENQUIN takes its name from *Gleann-a-Chuim*, the Glen of the *Cúm* or Hollow. The Anglicised version of this name should be Glenquim rather than Glenquin.

GLENQUIN CASTLE may have been built by the O'Hallinans in 1462. According to tradition it was captured by the O'Briens who put all of the O'Hallinans to death, with the exception of a boy who survived to avenge

Glenquin Castle is a battlemented tower house containing features comparable to those in Castle Matrix.

Glór na nGael, Drom Collachair, 1966.

THE WEST LIMERICK VOLUNTEERS

assembled here on Easter Sunday morning, 1916. Glenquin Castle was the rallying point for the men of Monagay, Templeglantine, Killoughteen, Broadford, Rahenagh, Athea, Newcastle West, Abbeyfeale and the other districts of West Limerick. They waited with their chaplains, Fr. Michael Hayes, the curate at Newcastle West, and Fr. Thomas Wall, who later became parish priest of Ballingarry, until conflicting orders they had received from Dublin were resolved. Michael Colivet, commandant of the Limerick Volunteers, led his own unit to Killonan that morning before sending Major McInerney to Glenquin Castle to notify the assembly of Eoin MacNeill's countermanding order. The volunteers returned to their homes.

INGHEAN BHAOITH'S CHURCH was mentioned by Samuel Lewis in 1837 as the church ruin of *Teampul-na-Hinghine-Bugdhe,* the Church of the Devout Daughter. This was a reference to Inghean Bhaoith, Inghean Bhuidhe, or Baoth's daughter, the seventh-century patron saint of Kilnaboy in County Clare. Her name may have been Findclu and her feast-day was generally celebrated on 1 March or 29 December. She is often mentioned as a contemporary of St. Flannan. John O'Donovan believed that a fourteenth-century church was erected on the site of the original foundation. When he visited this site, a short distance from Glenquin Castle, he discovered it was in a poor state of preservation with no notable features.

TEMPLE STRAN was erected by the Knights Templars near Strand in 1291 according to Samuel Lewis.

CASTLE ENGLISH, or the Castle of Cleanlis, was described in 1837 as "a strong fortress, of which the owner enjoyed peculiar privileges". I was unable to locate this in 1989 and wondered whether it had been situated within the district of Cleanglass or *Claonghlais.*

THE WOODY FASTNESS OF THE GERALDINES, the Commons of

Claonghlais, was located in the south western part of Killeedy parish. By 1840 the name had been Anglicised to Cleanglass. Cuilen of *Claonglais,* lord of *Uí Chonaill Gabhra* was felled by the O'Kinnealy, who was immediately killed, in revenge, by Cuilen's people, in 1155. In the following century the Lord of *U í Chonailol Gabhra,* Mahon O'Cuilcin was stabbed to death by his jealous wife in 1266. Another Lord of *Claonghlais,* this one a Geraldine, died in battle in 1535. In 1579 the Desmond forces passed through here on their way through the county. During the cold spring weather of 1580 the Lord Chief Justice

his family. The O'Briens lost Glenquin to the Geraldines who may have been the founders of the present structure. The castle contains two barrel-vaulted rooms and is six-storeys high with a seventh-storey section located above the top of the spiral staircase. The catwalk around the battlements is in excellent condition and part of it which has four narrow windows, is still roofed over. There are double-lighted windows on each side of the top-floor chamber, and a fireplace in the north-west wall. The castle possesses two garderobes; the outlines of basket-weave plaster work are still visible on the vaulted ceilings; the murder hole is intact; and the access to the spiral staircase is to the left of the entrance door which faces north-eastwards. The ground-floor is peculiar insofar as it contains five windows at ground level and one above that level. The northern corner contains an unusual feature which looks rather like a well or the entrance to a small chamber. The building is in an excellent state of preservation; was recently restored; and is undoubtedly the finest of Limerick's unoccupied tower houses. Walter Raleigh captured and dismantled Glenquin Castle after the Desmond Rebellion. In 1587 it was granted to Hungerford, and in 1591 it passed into the possession of Sir William Courtenay. In 1595 Captain Collum of *Glengoune* occupied the castle. The Earl of Devon's agent, Furlong, restored the building, before 1840, and lived there for a while. A plaque near the southern corner of the castle commemorates a more recent contribution to its history; *I gCuimhne Oglach Iarthair Luimní a Dhein Sluaghadh ar an Láthair seo Domhnach Cásca, 1916.*

ordered English marauders into *Coill-Mór*, the Woods of Cleanglass, and the wilds of Delge, where they slaughtered young and old, men women and children alike as they passed and plundered. Sir John of Desmond made a successful foray across the Suir in May 1581. He destroyed over 300 of his pursuers, both by drowning and slaying, before he retired with his plunder, into his haunts in the woods of *Claonghlais* and *Coill Mór.* Woodland covered most of this region into the seventeenth century, and later.

ASHFORD contained a large plain Catholic church in 1837 when the only other building of note was "the very neat residence of M. Aherin". Killeedy parish was the head of the Catholic union or district, called Ashford, which also included a small part of Monagay. About 270 children were then being educated within the parish, (in two public and two private schools) which contained 5,420 inhabitants on its 26,005 statute acres.

BOOLAVEEDA is located on Seeconglass Hill four miles south-west of Killeedy. This oval enclosure was once surrounded by a stone rampart and is believed to have been the site of St. Ita's dairy.

TOURNAFULLA may derive its name from *Tuar na Fola*, the Bleach-Green of the Blood, the Blood Dung, or the Pasture Enriched with Blood. This name may have come into use after a long-forgotten battle or from the once prevalent habit of taking blood for human consumption from living cattle, a practice which was once quite common in the poorer districts of Ireland. Tournafulla was part of Killeedy parish until 1838, when it became a separate parish. The Catholic church here was built in 1867. The original village was abandoned because of flooding and a new village of the same name was built on higher ground.

THE ALLAGHAUN RIVER may be a corruption of *Abha na Locan*, the River of the Little Lakes. It rises at Tooreennagreana, *Tuairín na Greíne*, the Little Bleach-Green of the Sun, on the north-eastern slope of the Mullaghareirk Mountain about 1,000 feet above sea-level. It crosses the Abbeyfeale-Newcastle West road at Goulburn Bridge. The old bridge was abandoned after the new bridge was built in 1979. In 1841 a tuck mill was located west of this bridge to stretch, dress and finish cloth supplied by local weavers. Two inscribed stones on the old bridge detail its history. One states the bridge was built in 1827 and the other notes who built it, "Goulburn Bridge, Richard Griffith, Engineer".

TOMMY LEAHY of Tournafulla was one of the first I.R.A. men in West Limerick to go "on the run". Early in 1919 two R.I.C. men, Lyons and Hearst, tried to arrest him. He evaded capture, wounding Lyons in the encounter. In 1921 he was taken prisoner at Mountcollins creamery. He was sentenced to death for being in possession of arms but the Truce was signed before sentence could be carried out.

MONAGAY, Monagea, or Monegay may derive its name from *Moín a Ghédh*, the Bog of the Goose, possibly because the nearby bog was frequented by geese or maybe because the place was called after a man who was surnamed Goose. The Protestant and Catholic parishes of Monagay were coterminous in 1837 and were also known as Mulchronriah or *Temple-na-Mona* Parish. The Church of Ireland parish church was located in Newcastle West and the Catholic church was in Monagay. This latter building was replaced by a new church in 1839. In 1870 Fr. James Clifford, the Catholic parish priest, built the national schools in Monagay.

TEMPLE NA MONA CHURCH takes its name from *Teampull na Móna*, the Church of the Bog. In 1840 the walls were in good condition and the graveyard was in use.

THE BIG HOUSES of Monagay in 1837 were Glanduff Castle, Woodlawn, Tulliline, and Mount Plummer.

LADY'S WELL, *Tobar Muire* or Mary's Well, was located in the townland of Rathcahill. Mary's feast-day was observed on 15 August but by 1840 the patterns had almost ceased. The original parish church, to which Fr. Philip Reidy was appointed in 1643, was dedicated to the Blessed Virgin Mary. Fr. Thomas Quinlan (born in 1634) succeeded as parish priest. In 1833 the townlands of Knockane, Cullina, Shanagarry, Rathina, Ballinvallig, Killelan, Ballymackessy and Gurtynaveen were placed outside the jurisidiction of Monagay Parish and put under that of the Catholic parish of Newcastle West. In 1845 the townlands of Ardnacrehy and Tiermena were incorporated into the Catholic parish of Newcastle West.

ST. BRIGID'S WELL, *Tobar Bríghde,* was located in the townland of Shangarry. In 1840 the inhabitants of Ballyshane told John O'Donovan that *Tobar Banbháin* was called after a man they remembered as a saint, but they had forgotten everything else about him, including his feast-day.

TEMPLEGLANTINE CHURCH derives its name from *Teampull a Ghleantáin*, the Church of the Little Glen. This is supposed to have been erected by the Knights Templars. A tomb of the Lacy family which both Lewis and Fitzgerald referred to was not visible in 1840 so it was either covered with ivy or totally destroyed by then. The gables of the church had vanished and only parts of the side walls were left standing 149 years ago. The graveyard was still in use in 1989.

TEMPLAGLANTINE CATHOLIC CHURCH was built by Fr. James Cleary in 1829 but Templeglantine did not become a separate parish until 1864.

SOURCE REFERENCE NUMBERS
9 12 47 76 86 107 120
122 129 145 150 192 195 220 238 246 282

Kilmallock

Bulgaden · Kilbreedy

KILMALLOCK derives its name from *Cill Mocheallóg,* the Church of St. Mo-Cheallóg or Mochelloc. The original monastery was founded by Mochelloc in 749, on a site one mile northwest of the town. The ruins of a later church can still be seen on its hillside location. The town was also known in former times as *Killocia* and "appears to have been inhabited at a very early period by several of the chief nobility and gentry, and to have been a corporate town either by prescription or by charter, granted at a very early date, as its privileges as a borough are recited in a charter of Edward III (1327-1377), by which that monarch granted to the provost and commonalty certain tolls and customs towards the repair of its fortifications. It was surrounded with a stone wall of great strength, fortified with mounds of earth, and having four gateway towers of lofty and imposing character, called respectively St. John's Gate, Water Gate, Ivy Gate and Blossom's Gate ..."

BLOSSOM GATE, the *Bla Porte* or *Blae Port* derived its name from the Irish, *Bláth Port* or Flower Gate. This is now the last remaining gate-tower of the old walled town and is located in Emmet Street, overlooking the Charleville road. This road was known as the Turn Pike Road in the eighteenth century.

THE ANGLO-NORMANS built the present town. Soon after their arrival the parish was placed under the patronage of Saints Peter and Paul. St. Mochelloc was laid aside but his feast day was observed on 26 March and his name is still perpetuated in *Cill Mocheallóg,* Kilmallock. In the early nineteenth century some historians were reluctant to identify this place at St. Mochelloc's foundation and believed the name should be reserved for the original site on Kilmallock Hill rather than the present town in the valley of the River Lúbach. Kilmallock became the chief stronghold and town of the Earls of Desmond, the seat of the White Knights, and the capital of a Geraldine territory encompassing 577,000 acres of Munster land. Records of its fortifications extend as far back as 1375. In 1482 the inhabitants obtained a grant of tolls for murage. Because of losses sustained in

defending the town against the Irish enemy Kilmallock was again incorporated by Edward IV (1461-1483) who established a royal mint here. In 1483 it was enumerated among the principal towns in which a coin of Richard III, then recently struck, was made current.

THE FIFTEENTH EARL OF DESMOND, Gerald, succeeded to the Desmond territories in 1558. In 1567 he, and his brother, John, were arrested. The earl's cousin James Fitzmaurice Fitzgerald administered the earl's estates in his absence. James revolted in the summer of 1569, partly because of the imprisonment of his cousins, the earl and his brother, but mainly because of the insecurity of land tenure during this period. Two years later Elizabeth I wrote that she "found it strange" that Thomas, the Tenth Earl of Ormond (1532-1614), was unable to quell the Munster Rebellion. Shortly afterwards she restored the Earl of Desmond and his brother, John Fitzgerald, to their possessions. Sir William Drury became President of Munster in 1578. Drury was determined to force Gerald into submitting to English authority and eventually drove him into reluctant rebellion. Gerald was declared an outlaw by Pelham, the Lord Justice of Ireland who was then performing the duties of the Lord Deputy. On 13 May 1580 Gerald was granted temporal jurisdiction over the city of Limerick and its surrounds by Pope Gregory XIII. In September 1580 Colonel San Joseph landed at Smerwick harbour and occupied an old fort, *Dunanoir,* which was besieged by the English. After it was surrendered 500 of San Joseph's soldiers were slaughtered on the orders of Lord Deputy Grey. The presence of Spanish soldiers in Smerwick and Kilmallock was an issue neither questioned nor repudiated by the Spanish ambassador. The Fitzgerald castles began to surrender after Fiach Mac Hugh received favourable terms in Leinster and Lord Baltinglass fled to Spain. James, the Earl of Desmond's younger brother was captured and hanged in Cork. Sir John of Desmond was killed by a former servant, Fleming, who had deserted to Zouch. Within a short time, Gerald, the Fifteenth Earl stood

alone against his foes. In November 1583 he was assassinated. His lands were forfeited to the crown. With his death confiscation of property was now seen, for the first time, to involve the territory of a major Anglo-Irish family. The Crown lawyers set the legal machinery in motion to annex the lands of the Geraldines. *The First Desmond Survey* was undertaken by commissioners in 1584. *The Second Desmond Survey,* or *Peyton Survey,* was made in 1598. The Nine Years War (1595-1603) disrupted the Munster Plantation. Between 1602 and 1622 the planters were restored to the lands they had settled on after the Desmond Rebellion. English law was finally established in Munster.

KILMALLOCK was at its most prosperous during Queen Elizabeth's reign (1558-1603). It was important, well-populated, substantially built, a centre of commerce in time of peace and a safe refuge in time of war. By the time of the Desmond Rebellion Kilmallock had become an English military station. In 1571 Sir James Fitzmaurice Fitzgerald took the town by surprise, sacked it, killed several of its more important citizens, demolished their houses, set fire to the town and turned it into "a receptacle and abode of wolves". Sir Henry Sidney, the Lord Deputy, restored Kilmallock shortly afterwards and installed a garrison for its defence.

SIR JAMES FITZMAURICE FITZGERALD, a cousin of the Earl of Desmond, became the leader of the Geraldines, in his cousin's absence. James was a noted fighter with a reputation as "a scorner of ease". Allied to the Sheehys and Sweeneys he kept the English at bay until 1572 when he surrendered to Sir John Perrot in the Collegiate Church of Kilmallock. The Earl and Sir John of Desmond were released but James was unhappy with the help from Pope Gregory XIII who offered him a small Papal force under the command of an English adventurer, Stukely. Stukely simply accepted the money but never came to Ireland. He went off to fight the Moors instead. John of Desmond landed in Dingle in 1579 with an expedition of 300 Spanish and Italian soldiers and a Papal commissary, Dr. Nicholas Sanders, an

English scholar. One month later James Fitzmaurice Fitzgerald was killed in a minor skirmish near Castleconnell. His body was quartered and hung above the gates of Kilmallock.

SIR WILLIAM DRURY arrived in Kilmallock with a force of 900 men in 1579. From here he issued a proclamation summoning all the nobility and gentry of Munster to his standard to aid him against Sir John of Desmond. He died soon after his defeat at *Gort na Tobrid* and was succeeded by Sir W. Pelham.

THE SUGAN EARL OF DESMOND, James, was nominated earl by Hugh O'Neill. He besieged Kilmallock in 1590 but was repulsed by the English garrison commanded by Norris and the Earl of Ormond. He was betrayed by Edmund Fitzgibbon (1552-1608) the last White Knight, in 1600, and submitted to the English in the Collegiate Church of Kilmallock. He died in the Tower of London in 1608.

THE SIXTEENTH EARL OF DESMOND, James, was educated in England, where he had been detained as a hostage after his father's, Gerald's, release in 1572. He was sent over to Ireland to destroy the popularity of the Sugán Earl. James was warmly welcomed by the Irish who acclaimed him as their chieftain, until he outraged them by attending a Protestant service in the Collegiate Church. His renounciation of the Catholic faith angered his followers who quickly abandoned him. The English had no further use for him. He was returned to England where he died in the Tower of London.

QUEEN ELIZABETH granted Kilmallock a new charter in 1585 which included "extensive tracts of land and various tolls and customs; empowering the inhabitants to elect a sovereign, to hold courts of record ... to levy assessments for the repair of the fortifications, to grant licenses for making spirituous liquors, and various other privileges, as ample as those of Kilkenny and Clonmel with exemptions from all taxes except those assessed by parliament".

THE CORPORATION OF KILMALLOCK under Elizabeth's charter consisted of a sovereign or ruler and an unlimited number of burgesses, of whom twelve formed the council. These twelve were assisted by a town-clerk, a sergeant-at-mace, and other officers. The sovereign was elected annually from the burgesses, was empowered to appoint a deputy, and selected the twelve burgesses who formed the council. This council decided who qualified as burgesses. There was no separate class of freemen distinct from the burgesses. The sovereign served as a jus-

Blossom Gate.

tice of the peace within the borough and as a county magistrate. The Corporation continued to return members to the Irish Parliament until the act of union in 1800, when the borough was disenfranchised. By 1837 the Corporation existed only nominally and was "to all available purposes extinct".

KING'S CASTLE dates from the fifteenth century even though it is named after King John. This is a four-storey building with pointed mullioned windows. Cyclists and pedestrians still pass through the open ground-floor section but motor traffic has been stopped for several years from doing so. H. Billingsley received a grant of the castle in 1588. In 1604 it was granted to T. Browne of Anye. Lord Castlehaven's Irish forces used it as an arsenal in 1645. After the Parliamentarians occupied Kilmallock they utilised King's Castle as a hospital and depot, in 1651. Early in the nineteenth century the Corporation leased it to the Church of Ireland authorities who established male and female parochial schools here. By the end of the nineteenth century the castle was partly blocked up and the lower portion was in use as a forge. Because of the way in which the tower was constructed it is possible to believe it was designed originally as a gate-tower

which became obsolete when the town expanded along what is now Sheares Street.

THE CONFEDERATE IRISH occupied the town under the leadership of Lord Mountgarret, Lord Purcell and Garret Barry in 1642. Throughout the 1640s and early 1650s rival armies passed through and around Kilmallock which was often selected as either a military base, or a military target. The Earl of Castlehaven, commander-in-chief of the Confederate forces deposited military stores in the town in 1645. In 1646 Murrough the Burner O'Brien, Lord Inchiquin, Ireland's ablest general, failed in an effort to capture Kilmallock. At that stage he was a leader of the Parliamentarian forces. Murrough accepted £1,000 from the citizens of the town after burning the surrounding countryside "to induce them to purchase what I must have done for my own safety, they sent me an offer of a composition to be gone out of their confines".

THE CROMWELLIANS eventually occupied the town. They retained King's Castle as a hospital, military depot, and stables. Some of their records for this period indicate that W. Evers was paid £1 for cleaning the church; Edmond Burke received £1.50 for cleaning the streets; Colonel H. Ingoldsby paid £100 for horses given up "by the Irish party" for the use of the State; and the Governor of Kilmallock, Lieutenant-Colonel Nelson spent £200 "in giving entertainment to all parties marching to and fro" from June 1650 to June 1652. The Cromwellians dismantled the town's fortifications but used the town as one of a series of garrisons which stretched across the territory through "Kilmalocke, Athdare, Ballingary, (Connelo); Rathlahane (Clare); Gortnatobrett, Castlebanke, Castletown (Kenry); Ballyvorneene, Greenane, Doonemylen, Galbally, Loughgur (Gur); Brittas and Tuogh". By the end of the Cromwellian War Kilmallock was almost totally destroyed. The fortifications were rebuilt, most probably under the direction of the Cromwellian garrison, and the town regained some of its former prosperity. In 1654 surnames such as Benson, Bentham, Bound, Cooke, Harris, Hill, Holmes, Glour, Jubbs and Tilly were introduced by planters established in the region by the Cromwellian settlement.

THE TOWN WALLS "enclosed a spacious quadrilateral area, in which were several castellated mansions inhabited by noble and wealthy families. They were all built of hewn stone, and communicated by noble castellated gateways with the streets of the city, inhabited by the trading and commercial classes, of which only the foundations" could be traced by 1837. In that year only two of the ancient mansions and castles were still preserved, one belonging to the Earl of Buckinghamshire, and the other to the family of Godsall. A large portion of the old town walls and the remains of these other buildings can still be seen today.

THE WILLIAMITE WAR saw the town destroyed again in 1690 by Jacobite forces under the command of the Duke of Berwick. This time the town took longer to recover from the ravages of war. From 1692 to 1745 the Corporation was dominated by new English Protestant planter surnames such as Batwell, Blakeney, Bowerman, Conyers, Coote, Emmot, Franks, Gough, Gubbins, Gwand, Hill, Holmes, Langton, Oliver, Ormsby, Owen, Plinor, Ponsonby, Rogers, Ryves, Touchstone, and Webb.

THE BALBEC OF IRELAND was the romantic appellation applied to Kilmallock in the following centuries, an allusion to the "ghost town" it had become after the Williamite War. Kilmallock was virtually abandoned by those of its former inhabitants who had survived the war. It remained in a state of decay throughout the eighteenth century, its status, like its appearance, was that of a rural village, the prosperous medieval town was, by then, an all but forgotten memory. In 1837 Samuel Lewis wrote that "since 1816, several good houses of stone have been erected in the principal street, which is now a handsome thoroughfare, inhabited by

Aerial view of Kilmallock.

The Collegiate Church.

respectable tradesmen. The streets are neither paved nor lighted, and the inhabitants are supplied with water chiefly from the River Lubach. The property is much divided, probably from its great eligibility as a place of residence at an early period; the principal proprietors are the Earls of Buckinghamshire, Sandwich, Kenmare, Ranfurley, and Cork, Lord Lisle, Sir Leonard Holmes, and the Maunsell family". The Glenfield oat-mills were built by a Mr. Ivers in 1825, on the site of the old manor mills, but there were more extensive flour-mills, owned by a Mr. Creed closer to the town, on the same river, in 1837. The Kilmallock market had been discontinued for many years but, by 1837, fairs were still held, mainly for pigs, and sometimes for cattle and sheep on 21 February, 25 March and Whit Tuesday. Attendance at these fairs was generally poor until much later into the nineteenth and early twentieth century because Kilmallock was still regarded as a "ghost town".

ST. SAVIOUR'S PRIORY, the Dominican Priory, was established by friars of that order on land purchased from a burgess of the town,

John Bluet, in 1291. William de Vesci, Justiciar of Ireland, held an inquiry at Cashel on 31 December 1291 in which he discovered that the Bishop of Limerick's clerks and servants had, on the bishop's orders, ejected the friars and levelled their house, seven weeks after they had taken possession of the site. A general chapter of the order was held here in 1340 and the monastery flourished under the Dominicans until the Dissolution. The Fitzgeralds were the patrons of this priory which had no lay founder. In 1541 the church, cemetery, cloister, dormitory and other buildings covered a two-acre site and the priory also possessed 12 acres of land a water-mill and 6 cottages with a total value of £4.10 of of which they paid an annual rent of 30 pence to the Bishop of Limerick. The priory was leased to James FitzJohn Fitzgerald, Earl of Desmond, who owed over £21 in arrears in 1548. In 1569-1570 it passed to the sovereign and commonalty of the town and the friars were probably driven out when the town was sacked and burned in 1571. It may have been known as the abbey or religious house of *Flacispaghe* in 1587. In 1594 it was granted

to Nicholas Miagh, sovereign of Kilmallock, and to the brethren and commonalty of the town at an annual rent of £2.68 1/2 . The Cromwellians killed Fr. Gerald Fitzgerald and a lay brother, David Fox, here in 1648. The choir of the church may date from 1291. This has a five-light east window and six windows which have lost most of their tracery. The central tower probably dates from the late thirteenth or early fourteenth century but its height was added to during the fifteenth century. The south aisle of the nave and the transept date from the first half of the fourteenth century and the domestic buildings were altered and reconstructed during the fourteenth and fifteenth centuries. In the early 1800s Sir Richard Hoare described the architecture, "as surpassing in decoration and good sculpture any he had seen in Ireland" while Peter Harbison (1970) remarked on the decorative stone-carving executed by the skilled craftsmen of the thirteenth and fourteenth centuries.

THE LAST WHITE KNIGHT was buried in the centre of the choir. His tomb was broken open by Limerick soldiers, stationed with the Kilmallock garrison, who thought they might find some treasure within it. Lenihan referred to a small hollow in this tomb which was formed by a continuous dripping of water, the *braon shinsior* or hereditary drop, which was regarded as a mark of divine displeasure at the cruelty of the knight to his Catholic countrymen. Only a fragment of the tomb remains. Other features of note are the sedilia, piscina and the Easter tomb.

THE WOODEN FOOTBRIDGE over the Lubach or Loobagh River is an attractive and useful modern feature. After the Fifteenth Earl of Desmond had been declared an outlaw he, and his countess, are believed to have hidden in the Dominican priory. They were almost surprised by the English garrison but concealed themselves from their enemies by plunging into the river. The couple spent an entire winter's night standing in the cold water, submerged to their necks, in order to escape.

THE COLLEGIATE CHURCH, the Church of SS Peter and Paul, was a collegiate church by the thirteenth century. This Anglo-Norman foundation replaced the earlier eighth-century one established by St. Mochelloc and was probably founded during the thirteenth century. The door in the south wall dates from that period but the belfry at the western end of the northern aisle may be the truncated remains of a much earlier round tower, "pierced with numerous windows, and differing greatly from others of that class". Unlike the Dominican priory the Collegiate church was enclosed within the walled town. The nave and transept were extensively altered during the fifteenth century. A porch, with a richly carved door, was added to the south side of the nave, which "is separated from the aisles by a series of massive square pillars, supporting lofty pointed arches. In the aisles and transepts are altar-tombs to the Fitzgeralds, Verdons, Healys, Blakeneys, and Coppingers. They are generally of the seventeenth century, and rudely sculptured; the figures are sunk, and the inscriptions in relief. The exterior of the church is embattled".

THE CHURCH OF IRELAND CHURCH was located in the chancel of the Collegiate Church as the nave, aisle and south transept "have been roofless since 1657, when it was partly destroyed". The chancel contains a fine east window, combining five lancet-shaped lights, and the remains of the Coote family tomb. This part of SS Peter and Paul's was used as a Protestant church into the 1940s or 1950s.

ANDREW MacGRATH was one of the Maigue poets better known as *An Mangaire Sugach*, the Jolly Pedlar, Aindrias MacCraith. In 1795 he was buried in the Hawthorne family grave. This is located at the west side of the fifteenth-century southern doorway, the porch of which has long since disappeared. Seamus O Cinneíde, another well-known eighteenth-century poet also lived in Kilmallock. Members of the Emmet family were buried in the grounds.

THE CATHOLIC CHURCH of SS. Peter and Paul was built between 1879 and 1889. This large neo-Gothic structure is dedicated to the two saints commemorated in the Collegiate Church. The Dominican priory is also remembered in this comparatively modern building as two of its windows in its sanctuary are copied from windows in the older church.

THE UNKNOWN FENIAN is the name of a monument in Sheares Street. This memorial is dedicated to a mysterious stranger who was killed taking part in a raid on Kilmallock R.I.C. barracks during the Rising of 1867. His identity was never discovered, or, more likely, never disclosed.

KILMALLOCK R.I.C. BARRACKS was attacked on the night of 27-28 May, 1920, by the East Limerick Brigade of the I.R.A. under the command of Tomás Malone (alias Seán Forde) and Sean Wall. An early forerunner of the Molotov Cocktail was used to set the barracks ablaze. Sergeant Keane and Constable Martin (or Morton) of the R.I.C. were killed in this attack.

LIAM SCULLY of Glencar, County Kerry, an I.R.A. captain and a member of the East Limerick Brigade was killed in action on the night of the attack on Kilmallock barracks. He had moved to Kilmallock only a short time before to take up a post with the Gaelic League, as a teacher. His body was removed to Tournafulla and interred in Templeglantine with full military honours. Later on, during the War of Independence, there were several shootings in the Kilmallock area. Amongst the casualties, on the Irish side were J. Lynch, 22 September 1920, and M. Scanlon, 5 November 1920. R.I.C. casualties included a Constable Kinsella and Sergeant Maguire, both of whom were killed in March 1921.

THE TOWN'S PAST is commemorated in the name of the Water Gate Bridge which spans the Lubach River; Patrick Sarsfield, Robert Emmett, the Sheares brothers and Lord Edward Fitzgerald are remembered in the street names; and the county council offices are located in part of an old workhouse, erected in famine times.

ASH HILL TOWERS was erected by the Coote family on the site of Chidley Coote's "New Stables" in 1781. It took its name from two slender battlemented towers which were removed sometime between 1950 and 1967. James and George Richard Pain rebuilt the back of the house in Gothic-style in 1833. In 1837 it was a large castellated mansion "now in progress of erection in the ancient baronial style, consisting of a centre flanked by lofty circular towers, and two extensive wings, of which one on the west is connected with a noble gateway leading to the offices which occupy the sides of a quadrangular area". It was then the seat of Eyre Evans. The other big houses of the locality over 150 years ago were Abbey View, the residence of Rev. J. Gabbett, which was located close to the town; Mill View of E. Moore Creed; and Riversfield of T. Weldon. John Henry Weldon came into possession of Ash Hill Towers later in the nineteenth century. Only one Georgian wing and some of the Adam-style stucco remained by 1967. In 1978 Major Stephen Johnson owned Ash Hill Towers.

THE ASH HILL DEMESNE of Chidley Coote consisted of 159 acres, according to the *Civil Survey* of 1654. This adjoined 516 acres of land he held in the liberties of Kilmallock. The demesne also contains a *cromlech,* described by P. Lynch in *Cromlechs in County Limerick* (1904). But even though three stones are *in situ* it is debatable as to whether this is a megalithic tomb or not as it was not listed in the *Survey of Megalithic Tombs of Ireland* (1982).

MOUNT COOTE, the seat of the Coote family, was described as a spacious and handsome modern mansion in 1837. It was "finely situated in the centre of an ample and picturesque demesne, highly improved by the proprietor with ornamental plantations, in which, and in the general improvement of his large estate, many of the labouring classes have found employment". This was demolished about 1960 and the present Georgian-style house was erected in its place. The present structure, now the residence of Alan and Lady Vivienne Lillingston, is often mistaken for the original Mount Coote. Martinstown House, east of Kilmallock, is also a modern house built in 1972 but looks older because it was built in a Classical style, reminiscent of the big houses of the past.

Opposite Page: clockwise from top left.
St. Saviour's Dominican Priory.
One of the many finely carved stone heads in the priory.
A view from the priory to King's Castle.
The impressive five-light east window.

GENERAL SIR EYRE COOTE (1726-1783) was born in Ash Hill. In July 1781 he defeated Haidar Ali, the Rajah of Mysore, in the Battle of Porto Novo or Cuddalore. Both died shortly afterwards, Haidar Ali in 1782, and Eyre Coote in the following year.

GENERAL SIR EYRE COOTE (1762-1823) was a nephew of his namesake. He was the second son of the Dean of Kilfenora, Rev. Charles Coote, was educated in Eton and received his first commission at the age of 14. He was promoted to captain at 16. During the American War of Independence he was captured at Yorktown and later released. In 1793 he took part in the West Indies campaign under Sir Charles Grey and was promoted to Colonel. In 1795 he became aide-de-camp to the King. He rose to the rank of Brigadier-General in 1796 when he commanded the camp at Bandon. As Major-General he was placed in command of Dover port. Some time after that he was captured by the French, after cutting the sluices at Ostend, and flooding the Netherlands. He was exchanged for a French officer and later distinguished himself at the Battle of Bergan. He helped Sir Ralph Abercromby to disembark in Egypt, took part in the Egyptian campaign, was made a Knight of the Bath, given command of an expedition to South America, and became Commander-in-Chief of Jamaica in 1805. His health suffered in the West Indies and he resigned after a few years. By then he had become noted for his eccentricity and the West Indian climate was believed to have affected his brain. In 1815 an inquiry into his behaviour reported that he was eccentric rather than mad but that his conduct was unworthy of an officer and a gentleman. He was dismissed from the army, and degraded from the Order of the Bath. General Sir Eyre Coote was married twice, and left children by both wives. At various times he was a Member of Parliament for Ballynakill (1790-1797), Maryborough (1796-1800), and, after the Act of Union, Queen's County (1802) and Barnstable (1812-1818). He died on 10 December, 1823.

BULGADEN contained only a few thatched cottages in 1837. The meadows and pastures were very extensive because occupiers of land in the neighbourhood were subject to a penalty of £10 per acre if more than two acres out of every twenty were tilled. By the early 1800s the population of the county had expanded considerably as the ordinary people were supplanted by middlemen or tenants. Labourers and their large families had to subsist on small potato crops grown on half-acre or one-acre plots. Work was scarce as the agricultural boom engendered by the Napoleonic War came to an end in 1815. By 1817 farmers were unable to pay landlords £7 an acre for land, prices had risen from £5 to £7 an acre during the war, and surrendered their holdings. This meant they were unable to supply their dependant cottiers with free corn or work. The Whiteboys came into existence mainly because this rather loosely-knit organisation was the only way in which the poorer class could express their resentment.

BULGADEN HALL was once "the superb seat of John Evans, Esq., who was brother to the First Lord Carbery". Fitzgerald commented on "the ruins of a castle, a little to the north of which is Bulgadeen (sic) Hall" in 1826. Eleven years later Lewis commented that Lord Carbery had allowed what was formerly one of the most magnificent residences in the province to deteriorate into a state of miserable dilapidation.

BULGADEN CASTLE in the townland of the same name contained two doorways on the south wall in 1840. The spiral staircase was on the left and the stones in the arched floor were not lime.

KILBREEDY derives its name from *Cill Bhrighde,* the Church of St.Brigid. In 1837 the parish of Kilbreedy Major was in the barony of Coshlea while Kilbreedy Minor was in the barony of Coshma.

KILBREEDY MAJOR CHURCH was in such poor condition by 1840 that the *Ordnance Survey Letters* were unable to state its original dimensions. It was located to the left of the old road leading from Kilmallock to Knocklong. In 1837 the parish of Kilbreedy Major contained several fine raths, "some of which were perfect" and Kilbreedy House, the residence of J. O'Donnell was the principal house of both parishes, Kilbreedy Major and Kilbreedy Minor.

FANTSTOWN CASTLE was built on a "gentle eminence" by the Faunt family during the reign of James I (1603-1625). Three of its four stories were intact in 1840 and comparatively fresh plastering was then visible on some of the apartment walls. Fantstown also contained the remains of an old church, on low ground, with an oddly-named well, *Tobar na Doili Muirí,* located in its north-eastern corner, in 1840.

A PATTERN was observed at *Tobar na Doili Muirí* on 3 August according to the O'Donovan letters of 1840. This well was enclosed "with a stone building, covered with green sod on a level with the surface of the ground. A chiselled stone spanning the entrance to it, which looks (or) faces to the south, forms a semi-circular arch over the water" and a small stream issued southwards from the well, past the eastern gable of the old church.

KILBREEDY MINOR CHURCH was badly ruined by the late 1830s. Only the middle gable and side walls of the choir remained. This nave and chancel church was located in the centre of Kilbreedy townland, on the south bank of the Subtach.

ST. BRIGID'S WELL, in Kilbreedy townland, was no longer a pattern site in 1840, although her feast-day, St. Brigid's Day, was still observed as a holy day.

FATHER JOHN MULQUEEN, the parish priest of Bulgaden and Ballinvana, was shot dead by the Whiteboys, on the road leading from Fantstown to Kilbreedy, in 1819. He had intervened in a dispute between the Whiteboys and a farmer, named Clifford, whom they had refused to allow to pass along the route. In the heated exchange that followed the clergyman was killed. His attackers were never charged. They may have perished on the mountains into which they fled. The Protestants and Catholics of the area united in offering a £500 reward for their capture. Fr. Mulqueen was buried in Kildimo, his native place.

EMLYGRENAN PARISH, or St. Malo, was part of the Catholic union of Ballinvana in 1837. The parish contained a large modern Catholic church at the Red Bog and the Protestant population worshipped in Kilmallock, over four miles away, to the west. The old parish church of St. Malo was destroyed in the war of 1641 and never repaired. Samuel Lewis believed this church to have been a collegiate one.

SOURCE REFERENCE NUMBERS

5 9 11 28 47 76 86 92 102 120 123 129 150 153
173 185 187 191 192 195 230 233 238 252 264 274

Knocklong

Clogher · Scarteen · Kilfrush

KNOCKLONG was originally known as *Druim Damhghaire,* the Ridge of the Oxen, but takes its present title from *Cnoc Luinge,* the Hill of the Encampment. According to tradition, King Cormac Mac Airt set up his camp on this hill when he invaded Munster during the third century. The King of Munster consulted a druid, Mogh Ruith. The druid used his magical powers to help the Munstermen who then defeated Cormac's forces in a legendary battle said to have taken place about 250. Four centuries later, about 650, a more significant fight took place here when Dioma, King of Thomond, defeated the Connaughtmen, who were endeavouring to recover County Clare from North Munster. This historic battle secured Clare for the Dalcassians so *Cnoc Luinge* may derive its present name from an encampment of the seventh century rather than the third century. *Cnoc Luinge* has also been translated as the Hill of the Ships as the tents on the hill resembled ships under sail.

KNOCKLONG CASTLE may have been founded in the fourteenth century but the present ruin dates from the sixteenth century. The building resembles a strongly-built three-storey mansion rather than a tower house. This was the chief seat of the Hurley family in Limerick. In 1570 T. Hurley of Knocklong received a pardon. The castle was held by Garret MacThomas in 1583 but was re-occupied by the Hurleys in 1606 and 1635. By 1655 the castle was in ruin, according to a report of the time which listed Sir M. Hurley as its owner. In 1669 Cornet E. Cooper was confirmed in the ownership of Knocklong Castle. T.J. Westropp wrote in 1906-1907 that there were "two large defaced windows in each of the south and west walls. There were four gables; one still has a plain chimney. The

Aerial view of Knocklong.

under vault has collapsed; and the stairs and cut stones are removed". Tradition tells of a cave beneath the castle. In 1840 John O'Donovan wrote of the two wells, St. Patrick's and St. Paul's, which were located on the eastern side of Knocklong hill. These had disappeared by 1989 but John Carroll, Church Road, Knocklong, told me about Curraheen Well, north of the hill, which "never went dry" and was still used by some of the local people. There is a greyhound-track situated on the low ground to the east of the hill.

KNOCKLONG CHURCH was located south-west of the castle. John O'Donovan described the ruined church that stood here, in 1840, as "a very rude one", with most of its architectural features missing. In 1989 only the foundations of the church remained, within the graveyard that developed around it. There is a large depression in the ground, west of the cemetery wall, with a reservoir situated south of the depression. A smaller depression, or crater, lies between the castle and the graveyard. The parish contained 2,842 inhabitants in 1831 and, six years later, Lewis noted two Catholic churches, one in Knocklong, and the other in Glenbrohane. The Morningstar River formed the southern boundary of the parish and was noted for its trout.

THE VILLAGE developed near the castle and church initially. An excavation of some of the interesting-looking mounds on either side of the track leading from the public road to the graveyard, would probably bear this out. In 1655 the Hurleys had mills, and two fairs in Knocklong. In 1837 fairs were held on 23 May and 1 October for cattle, sheep and pigs. The October fair usually had "a large show of good horses" and fairs were also held at Knocktoran, on 3 March, 6 April, 29 July, 1 November, and 20 December. A butter market was held in Knocklong on Tuesdays.

THE FAIR OF CLOGHER, *Aonach Chlochair,* may have been held in the townland of Raheennamadra, about a mile south of the village. The *aonach,* or fair was an assembly "of the people of every grade without distinction: it was the most common kind of large public meeting; and its main object was the celebration of games, athletic exercises, sports, and pastimes of all kinds ... In all the fairs there were markets for the sale and purchase of commodities, whether produced at home or imported ... Some meetings were established and convened chiefly for the transaction of serious business: but even at these there were sports in abundance ... Important affairs of various kinds, national or local, were transacted ... Laws were publicly promulgated ... the ancient Irish were very careful that there should be no quarrelling or

fighting, or unseemly disturbance of any kind that might 'spoil sport' at the formal *dals* or *aonachs*". Each territory, or *tuath,* had its own *aonach.* Begley and Westropp agree that an *aonach* was held here in the townland of Raheennamadra but disagree about the details. T.J.Westropp maintains that this Clogher was the site of *Aonach Chlochair,* although there is another Clogher ten miles east of Knocklong. Rev. John Begley maintains that this, and not Monasteranenagh was the site of *Aonach Chairbre,* the Fair of Carbery. Begley bolsters his argument by stating that it was unlikely anyone would erect a monastery on an *aonach* site, a spot sacred to the people, during the twelfth century.

THE RAILWAY STATION, or rather Knocklong's position on the Limerick Junction-Charleville railway line, meant that the village developed to the north of Knocklong Hill, from the 1850s onwards.

SEAN HOGAN was arrested at Meaghers' of Annefield, near Thurles, on 12 May, 1919. He was one of a group known as the Big Four for whom the British authorities had offered a reward of £10,000. The other three men were Dan Breen, Seamus Robinson and Sean Treacy. When Sean Treacy heard of Hogan's arrest he realised that the British would probably send their prisoner to Cork, by rail, and decided to mount a rescue operation. An R.I.C. escort of three constables and one sergeant accompanied Sean Hogan on to the Cork-bound train. When the train stopped at Knocklong Railway station the other members of the *Big Four* swung into action. Sean Hogan was freed between 8.13 and 8.27a.m. Sergeant Wallace and Constable Enright were killed; and Sean Treacy was wounded in the throat. Sean Hogan later served in Dublin and Tipperary; ambushed Lord French on 19 December, 1919; took part in the raid on Drangan Barracks, Tipperary, on 3 June 1920; and commanded the flying column of the Third Tipperary Brigade. Patrick and David Clancy of Ballylanders sheltered Sean Treacy and Sean Hogan in their home on the night following the Knocklong Rescue. Patrick was vice-commandant of the Third Tipperary Brigade and was killed three months later in Kanturk on 17 August 1920.

LACKELLY near Knocklong was the scene of an engagement between the Sherwood Foresters and the Limerick Flying Column, in May 1921. Four of the I.R.A. volunteers were killed. The British were beaten off when reinforcements arrived in time to save the other members of the Flying Column who had been surrounded and were in imminent danger of death or capture. The volunteers who died in this ambush were Tom Howard, Willie Riordan, Jim Frahill and Pat Ryan.

SCARTEEN, the home of the Ryan family since the early eighteenth century, has undergone many changes over the centuries. Parts of this older house were incorporated into the present two-storey structure which dates from 1798. Scarteen remained unoccupied in 1837 and it was not until 1893 that the Ryan family secured full possession of both house and estate.

THE SCARTEEN FOXHOUNDS are better-known as the Black and Tans. Hunting-dogs, or greyhounds were known as *mílchu* to the ancient Irish; watch-dogs were called *archu,* from *ar* or *air,* to watch; and any fierce dog was generally called a *cú,* or hound. The more general name, *madra,* is also an old word and is commemorated in the name of the townland of Raheennamadra. This townland is named after its fort, *Ráithín na Madra,* the Little Fort of the Dogs. In 391 a Roman citizen named Flavianus presented seven Irish wolfhounds to his brother Symmachus, a Roman consul. Greyhound coursing was recorded as one of the more popular sports at *aonachs* and is mentioned in the ninth-century work called *Cormac's Glossary,* or *Sanas Cormaic,* which may have been written by Cormac Mac Cuilleanáin, King-Bishop of Cashel. The Normans introduced hunting from horseback with hounds into England. They were also responsible for the introduction of the St. Hubert hound and the preservation of special hunting sites or areas which they reserved for their own use. The Anglo-Normans probably inaugurated this style of hunting in Ireland. Today, the Scarteen Pack, the Black and Tans, is recognised as the oldest and best pack of foxhounds in the country.

THE RYAN FAMILY originally lived in Ballyvistea, Emly. Their ancestors were huntsmen and family tradition relates how they came into possession of hounds that had been brought ashore from an armada ship, wrecked off the Kerry coast, in 1588. The first authentic record of the Ryan association with hunting hounds dates back to a receipt which was issued in 1642. The Ryans have been associated with the present mode of hunting since its inception in England towards the end of the seventeenth century. Jack Ryan started the now internationally famous pack with Irish hounds and another strain he introduced from south-western France in 1735. These dogs interbred to produce the black-and-tan coloured foxhound known as the Kerry Beagle, a breed which has been refined and improved over the last two centuries.

BALLYSCADANE CASTLE probably derived its name from the Scadan or Hareng family of Tipperary, *Baile Atha na Sgadadan,* the Town of the Ford of Scadan. In

1229 Richard de Burgo gave seisin of Baliscadan to William de Marisco. Under the Act of Settlement it was granted to Joseph Reeves in 1657 and was confirmed in 1667.

RYVES CASTLE became the new name of Ballyscadane Castle. It was later known as Castle Jane. Ballyscadane House was the last name applied to the latest structure on this site. When this building was being levelled some years ago the spiral staircase of the original Ryves Castle was found, a name now remembered only in the townland. Before its demolition locals claimed Ballyscadane was haunted. Two youths who broke into it claimed that they heard unearthly sounds, "a type of mad music", before they fled.

THE FRANKS FAMILY were established in Ballyscadane by Captain J. Franks of Campsall, Yorkshire, in 1650, according to T.J. Westropp.

BALLYSCADANE CHURCH OF IRELAND CHURCH no longer exists but its graveyard is still used for burials. By 1837 the church had fallen into decay but it contained a "monumental obelisk" commemorating the Ryans and a large vault belonging to the Lowe family who had owned Ryves Castle before the Ryans.

BALLINAHINCH CASTLE, or the Castle of Dunmoon, or Cloheen, derives its name from *Baile na hInse*, the Town of the Island. In 1300 an Anglo-Norman family, the de Moltons were listed as free tenants of Dunmoon. This later passed into the custodial care of the MacSheehys who acknowledged the White Knights as their overlords. In 1576 Edmund Fitzgibbon, the White Knight, received head-rent from J. MacSheehy for Dunmoon. In 1590 the regrant of the same was acknowledged. Maurice Fitzgibbon was listed as the owner of Ballinahinch Castle in 1625 and in 1655 Gibbon Fitzgibbon sold it to Robert Oliver. In 1666 the grant of *Doonmoon* alias Ballinahinch was confirmed. In 1840 John O'Donovan noted that the northern and southern gables of the castle with a chimney on each, had been built with bricks inside, and with stones outside. There was no sign of a church in the townland of Ballinahinch in 1840 but John O'Donovan recorded the presence of a small burial ground called Cloheen, a derivative of *Cloichín*, a Little Stone; and made a brief reference to *Tobar Gobnait*, or St. Deborah's Well.

THE FITZGIBBON FAMILY of Limerick are said to be a branch of the Geraldines although Rev. Patrick Woulfe believes they are descended from Gilbert de Clare, the owner of Castlemahon Manor and many other valuable estates in the county, at the beginning of the fourteenth century. The surname means the Son of Gibbon, which is a diminutive of Gilbert. The head of the Limerick family was known as the White Knight but there is another, entirely unconnected, family of the same name descended from a branch of the Burkes of Mayo. Variants on the name include *MacGiobúin, M'Gibbone, M'Gibowne,* MacGibbon, MacGibben, MacKibbon, O'Kibbon, Gibbonson, FitzGibbon, Gibbons, Gibbins, Gibbings and Gibbon.

KILFRUSH was a de Clare holding in 1287, when it was held by the de Carren family. Two years later, in 1289, Matilda Anevil claimed a dowry from the manor here. The original castle of Kilfrush probably dated from this period but a later building may have been erected on the same site. The Earl of Desmond owned Kilfrush Castle in 1583. In 1587 W. Nugent occupied Kilfrush and his head-rent was granted to Sir E. Fyton. Maurice Hurley of Knocklong was confirmed in the occupancy of the castle in 1604 and it was held by another Hurley, Sir Maurice, in 1655. In 1657 Kilfrush Castle was sold to J. Bullingbroke.

THE GUBBINS FAMILY of Kilfrush are believed to be old Gaelic stock who settled along the southern part of the Limerick-Tipperary border. This surname is, more usually, found in Derry and Donegal where it has been Anglicised to Gubbins or Gobban from the original *O Goibín* or O Gobaín, the descendant of *Goibín*, the diminutive of *Gob*, Mouth, or Snout. The Kilfrush family claimed they had come from England during the seventeenth century; if so their name may have been derived from the old French *Giboin*, or old German *Gebawin*. Joseph Gubbins of Kilfrush died in 1693. He was the progenitor of the Gubbins family of Kilfrush and his descendants occupied Kilfrush House into the latter half of the twentieth century. Another member of this family, James, occupied Kenmare Castle in Hospital; married Annie Henn of Paradise, County Clare; and served as High Sheriff of Limerick in 1806. In 1855 Mary Franks of Ballyscacane married into the Gubbins family. John Gubbins of Bruree House was the owner of the Knockainy Stud where he bred a Derby winner, *Galtymore.* President Nixon was entertained here in 1970 by John A. Mulcahy, a Waterford man, who had amassed a fortune in the United States and purchased this early nineteenth century house. There is a pillared gate-lodge opposite the main entrance on the Knocklong-Hospital roadway.

KILFRUSH CHURCH had disappeared by 1840 but its burial-ground remained in use. St. Colman's Well, 300 yards to the west of the burial ground was still resorted to in the nineteenth century by people seeking cures for eye diseases. Both sites were located within the Kilfrush demesne.

ATHNASSEY, Atheneasy, or Athanasy, derives its name from *Atha na n-Déisigh*, the Ford of the Desii, an ancient river crossing over the Morningstar River. This river has its source in the Bog of Grierston and it was once known as *Abhainnandeiseag*, the River of the Desii. Near Elton bridge is a graveyard which developed around a church known as *Teampall Bheul Atha na nDeisig*, the Church of the Mouth of the Ford of the Desii. In 1837 Lewis claimed there were some fragments of a seventh-century church here as well as "several traces of ancient military works within the parish, and several military weapons of rude workmanship have been found; also the ruins of a small religious house called Adam's Church, and fragments of castles or buildings at Fauntstown, Gormanstown, and Stephenson, near the first of which are a ruined chapel and a celebrated holy well". Three years later O'Donovan was unable to locate *Teampall Bheul Atha na nDeisig* although he looked for it to the left of the road leading from Kilmallock, via Kilbreedy Major, to Elton Cross. He located the Fort of the Mouth of the Ford of the Desii, *Dún Bheul Atha na n-Deisig*, "to the north-west of the burying ground and very close to it stands a moat or doon". This moat was encircled by the remains of a destroyed fosse in 1840.

THE FORD OF THE FORT, half a mile east of the graveyard was spanned by "13 stones placed as stepping stones *(clochán)* across the river here". In 1840 John O'Donovan wrote of this place as *Ath na n-Deisig*, from which the name Athnassey was derived. In 1579 the Lord Chief Justice of Ireland, Sir William Drury, had contracted a disease here which subsequently brought on his death. He had camped here after his defeat at the battle of *Gortnatubrid*, outside Dromcolliher.

BALLINVANA was part of the Catholic union of Athnassey in 1837. There was a holy well here which was resorted to on 25 March, the patron day. In the early nineteenth century there was an ash tree close to it on which votive gifts were hung and the branches were often weighed down with the numerous offerings.

SOURCE REFERENCE NUMBERS
9 11 19 39 100 107 108 120 129 140 150 154 159 192
195 233 235 268 269 270 282

Lough Gur

Knockadoon · St Patrick's Well

LOUGH GUR is better known today than the ancient parish of Aney or Knockainy in which it is located. The lake runs into four townlands, Grange, Knockfenne Ballyna-gallagh, and Lough Gur and its name may be derived from *Loch Cuar*, the Circular Lake. The lake is now crescent-shaped but this is mainly because of drainage work carried out during the middle of the nineteenth century which reduced the level of the water by about three metres.

KNOCKADOON is now a peninsula jetting into the lake from the east. This was once an island totally surrounded by water. It derives its name from *Cnoc a' Dúin*, the Hill of the Forts, and has been occupied for almost 5000 years. A stone mound on top of Knockadoon Hill may be a natural feature rather than a man-made one although its site was marked as *Dun Gair* on the Ordnance Survey maps. The rock face south-east of the mound has a stone enclosure attached to its base which seems to have been used as a temporary shelter for a brief period and may date from Neolithic times. A stone circle formed by two concentric stone rings, with the space between filled with rubble, lies near a natural rock outcrop which forms its north-western sector. Of two house sites superimposed on the interior of this circle one was given a radiocarbon dating of 2600 B.C. and the second was dated to 2000 B.C. because of its

Knockadoon.

association with Beaker pottery found on the site. Two other stone circles can be found between the Black Castle and the shore opposite Garret Island. Professor Harkness of University College Cork, excavated one of these in 1869 and Seán P. O Ríordáin continued his work almost a century later. Both men discovered that the stone circle had been used as a burial place since many human skeletons, particularly skeletons of children, were found there. The remains of several other structures were also uncovered, one of which surrounds the base of a small standing stone in the south-eastern quadrant of the circle. The third Knockadoon circle was the largest of the three. Excavation showed that the gap to the east was the entrance and revealed that the rock-cut post holes had once contained the jambs of wooden gates. The presence of gates, combined with the outline of a rectangular building within the enclosure, may signify that this circle was one of the earliest of the Irish ring forts. A mixture of pottery found on this site dated from the late Neolithic into the early Bronze Age (c. 2,000 B.C. - 1200 B.C.). The bodies of seven children, all under eight years of age, and an adult female were found buried within the circle. Two more burials, also of young children, were found on the floor of an older hut site outside, but partly under, the north-eastern arc of the circle.

THE KNOCKADOON HOUSE SITES are famous for the quality and quantity of pottery found here although the first site was not excavated until 1936. The people who occupied these huts, or houses, had no closed insular society but one which was open to traffic and trade from the outside world. Stone axes manufactured as far away as County Antrim were discovered here while the varied styles of pottery showed that the early inhabitants of Lough Gur were receptive to change from external influences. Stones were used as foundation courses for the walls which would have been composed of mud; while post holes seemed to indicate that the roofs were in all probability thatched and supported on timbers. Most of these sites are no longer visible but some of the most impressive finds were made in the south-western sector of the Knockadoon Peninsula. A group of circular hut sites was discovered with hearths in the centre of each, as well as refuse pits which contained items dating from the Bronze Age into Early Christian times. East of this group of huts, on top of the rock above the cliff, was an oval house with stone foundations, dating from the Middle Bronze Age, in which two infant burials and some round-bottomed Neolithic pottery were found. A rectangular area south of this, with the long axis running

north to south, on the slope of the hill contained a three-aisled structure with a doorway at its south-western corner. The remains of four other sites were nearby. Elsewhere on the peninsula three irregularly-shaped enclosures, a Bronze Age hut site, and the site of a seventeenth-century farmhouse, were excavated.

THE PEOPLE who settled here about 3000 B.C. were Ireland's earliest farmers. They lived by growing crops; kept cows, pigs and sheep; and hunted with flint-tipped spears or arrows. They used stone axes to cut trees and hoe the ground; antler horn was utilised in agricultural picks; and implements such as needles, borers and awls were manufactured out of bone. Heavy flat-bottomed pots were used for cooking; food was stored in round-bottomed pottery; and grain was ground by rubbing it across blocks of stone. Michael J. O'Kelly suggested in 1942 that "Lough Gur was a sacred lake and that as a result of this sanctity, people were attracted to it and settled down in its neighbourhood. This suggestion is quite reasonable, and in part at any rate gives a rationale for the concentrations of ritualistic monuments on Knockadoon (the stone circles), and similar structures (stone circles and megaliths) around the lake on all sides ... the many antiquities found in and around the lake are additional testimony to the sacredness of the water, and they suggest that such an object as the gold-chased bronze spearhead, now in the British Museum, was 'most likely a votive offering cast into the waters of the lake, as the Continental Gauls cast gold and other precious objects into the ponds of Tolosse' ... the god of the lake would have required propitiation from time to time ... It may have been in this way that the circular bronze shield now in the National Museum, Dublin, came to be in the water. Maurice Lenihan states that 'the shield was found in a bog between Ballynamona and Herbertstown' ... the descendants of the original owner, who live near the lake, are quite certain that the shield came from the marsh on the east side of Knockadoon and that it was found after the partial drainage of the area".

GARRET ISLAND was occupied from Neolithic times. This low wooded island is a natural one, not a *crannóg*. A large platform of stones found here is believed to be the remains of a Desmond castle mentioned in *Pacata Hibernia* in 1600. A stone head was discovered here in the late nineteenth century. This is still kept in the farmhouse across the road from the Grange stone circle. The wooden box in which it was found was lost when the family allowed both box and head to be put on display in Limerick. This is called Gearóid Iarla's Head.

GEAROID IARLA, Garret the Earl, the

Fourth Earl of Desmond, has been associated with the legends, myths, history and folklore of Lough Gur for almost six hundred years. Gearóid, quite literally, vanished from history in 1398. He left his camp one night and was never seen again. He may have been slain by a personal enemy or by an agent of the O'Brien of Thomond. Other accounts claim that he disappeared at the Island of Kerry but it is probable that he died at his home in Newcastle West. His followers always expected him to return and tradition relates how his ghost, and that of his horse, will not rest in peace until the silver horse-shoes of his milk-white steed are worn out by cantering across the waters of Lough Gur once every seven years. Gearóid Iarla must have been an impressive man to linger so long in the hearts and minds of the people. In life he was a warrior and a poet. In death he became a fairy king who has been confused with, "become one with", the Old Druid of Lough Gur.

IRISH DRUIDS did not believe in the immortality of the soul but they thought that some few individuals lived on after death often reappearing as men or animals, or occasionally living on in fairyland, without the intervention of death.

ST. PATRICK is also associated with Lough Gur. He is said to have cast a large serpent, which was terrorising the Bruff district, into the lake where it must remain until the Easter Monday before the Day of Judgement.

LOUGH GUR CASTLE was erected on the site of an older fortification which guarded the only natural passage onto the Island of Knockadoon. T.J. Westropp claimed that this was the only access to the island until the Earl of Desmond built his great causeway to the south of the lake. This linked the Black Castle to the mainland at the lake's narrowest and most easily-forded point before the water drainage scheme of the mid 1800s. The present fifteenth century tower house is an oblong structure built in two sections, but on the same foundations. A Dineley sketch of 1681 shows other buildings in front of this castle as well as a bridge which may have been built by the Countess of Bath. It is also quite probable that part of the lake was deepened and narrowed when the castle was being erected so that a moat could be constructed for its defence. Such a moat and draw-bridge had become obsolete before 1681. The stairs wind from right to left in order to allow the sword arms of defenders full play; the castle is five storeys high with vaulted ceilings on the ground and top floors; and the spiral staircase gives access to all floors. The original roof was pitched and gabled but the present one is flat. Lough Gur Castle was a Geraldine fortress that was attacked and besieged on

Lough Gur Castle.

several occasions. After the Desmond Rebellion it passed to Sir George Bourchier, the son of the Second Earl of Bath. It is since known as Bourchier's Castle and is now owned by Count de Salis.

THE BLACK CASTLE is in very poor condition. This was also a Geraldine possession and dated back to the thirteenth century. The scant remains of two square towers, connected by a tall curtain wall, stand at the southern corners of this rectangular enclosure. Most of the stone causeway which linked it to the mainland has been removed except for a portion contained within an oblong walled area which acts as a boundary between two farms.

THE LOUGH GUR INTERPRETATIVE CENTRE was officially opened on 2 May 1981 by Desmond O'Malley, T.D., the Minister for Industry, Commerce and Tourism. The centre is located on the north-eastern point of Lough Gur in two conjoined buildings which were modelled on some of the huts or houses excavated during the 1930s and 1940s. The rectangular house is based on one erected during the late Neolithic Age and the circular hut resembles one built during the late Neolithic or early Bronze Age. The modern interior houses an information centre; a small museum; and an audio-visual presentation describing the history of the area. The building also contains a display of scale models and photographs of the various sites scattered around the lake which is also a wildlife sanctuary. The entire amenity area was excavated by members of the Department of Archaeology, University College, Cork, before any development commenced. Anyone wishing to explore the area around the lake should consult *The Illustrated Guide to Lough Gur, Co. Limerick,* which was published by M.J. and C. O'Kelly in 1978.

PROFESSOR SEAN P. O RIORDAIN began excavations around the lake in 1936 and continued until 1941. He resumed work in 1947 and was still exploring Lough Gur's past when he died in 1957. Glyn Daniel wrote "Professor O Riordáin found a western Neolithic culture with round-bottomed, undecorated pottery, leaf and lozenge arrowheads, and polished stone axes, which gradually is replaced by coarse flat-bottomed ware, and overlain by beaker. The Lough Gur peo-

ple, or some of them, were buried in a gallery grave nearby, and also built a circular ritual monument". The professor, familiarly known as Seán P., proved that the region was extensively populated from about 3000 B.C. His best known book, *Antiquities of the Irish Countryside,* has rarely been out of print since it was first published in 1942.

CROCK ISLAND is a man-made island or *crannóg.* Islands such as this were made by dropping large boulders into the water. As these boulders formed a solid, usually circular, outline the inner area was gradually filled in. When this new structure neared the surface the enclosed space was filled with smaller rocks, stones, earth, brushwood, and the *cranns,* trees, from which the *crannóg* derived its name. When the lake was drained this onetime island on the western shore of the lake, north of the drainage outflow channel, became part of the dry land now surrounding it.

BOLIN ISLAND, the island nearest to the Interpretative Centre is a *crannóg.* This was excavated in 1938.

THE SPECTACLES is the name given to two adjoining circular stone structures north of the centre. One of these is a natural rock formation but the other one contains the manmade foundation of a large house with two hearths within it. A paved path led from the doorway to a series of rough steps on the edge of the plateau giving access to the lake. Seán P. O Riordáin unearthed the remains of two huts, one oval, the other oblong; found fragmentary remains of other structures; and discovered an adjoining field system. This site was occupied from the eighth to the tenth century and, maybe, even in the eleventh century. Fragments of bronze ring-pins, iron knives, bone combs, spindle whorls, whetstones, jet bracelets, glass beads, and querns were also found here.

THE CARRAIG AILLE AREA contains two stone forts and a number of associated sites excavated in 1937-1938. The more northerly dating from the tenth century was built to an oval design. This gave Seán P. O Ríordáin the impression that its occupants were slovenly. The second fort was built in the form of an irregular circle and was occupied from about the eighth to the eleventh century. Part of a tenth-century Viking silver hoard was found between two stones on the inner face of the northern rampart. Iron-smelting was also practised here. The remains of a series of rectangular houses and yards were discovered between the two forts, apparently some of the more adventurous people felt less need for defensive buildings in time of peace. The silver hoard is believed to have belonged to a Viking who lived here and who may have been killed in Kilmallock in 927.

A STONE CIRCLE is located south of the Herbertstown road. Peter Harbison describes this as "a fine stone circle with an inner row of stones surrounded by an outer ditch with interior and exterior facing". Professor O Riordáin made no finds here during excavation so no date was given for its erection. Because of the existence of the ditch this may have been a ritual monument.

THE FLAT-TOPPED CAIRN south of the stone circle was crowned with a circle of standing stones. This burial mound contained two Middle, or Late, Bronze Age burial vessels dating from about 1500 B.C.

THE WEDGE-SHAPED GALLERY GRAVE was fully excavated in 1938 but only some human bones, fragments of pottery and poor quality flints were found. A century earlier Mrs. Samuel Hall had visited this megalithic tomb and written that it was "a complete oblong chamber formed by great stones and covered with vast flags. An old woman resided in it for many years, and on her death the covering stones were thrown off and it was left in its present state by 'money diggers, who found only some buried bones in a ould jug that surely was not worth a brass farthing!' Some stones almost opposite this tomb on the other side of the road may have formed one or more stone circles in the distant past.

THE BALLYNAGALLAGH MONUMENT is unclassified but may have been a wedge-shaped gallery grave. Only four stones survive, on a low ridge overlooking the lake. This is also known as *Leaba na Muice,* the Pig's Bed.

THE NEW CHURCH, *An Teampall Nua,* was originally built as a Geraldine chapel of ease and is at least as old, if not older, than Lough Gur Castle. This church was in a state of ruin in 1642 but was restored by Rachel, Countess of Bath, soon after Charles II ascended the English throne in 1660. Rachel added a belfry to the western gable, renovated the existing structure, and converted the church to Protestant worship. Its name, the New Church, dates from the seventeenth century. In 1840 Mrs. Samuel Hall wrote of the roofless and deserted walls of this ruined church "which stands on an eminence that descends to the southern shore of the lake", and referred to a chalice and paten which were found here and were preserved in the neighbouring Church of Ireland church in Knockainy. This chalice is still in use but is stored in a bank, in Hospital for safe keeping. Count de Salis carried out repairs here at the turn of the century and had a glazed plaque of the *Madonna and Child* inserted in the southern wall of the church.

THOMAS O'CONNELLAN, the minstrel bard, may have been buried in the graveyard of the New Church since he died in Lough Gur Castle in 1700.

A MASS ROCK, Carriganaffrin, *Carraig an Aifrinn,* the Rock of the Mass, is located three hundred yards south-east of the New Church.

BALLYNAGALLAGH CONVENT, *Mainister na gCailleach,* the Monastery of the Nuns, or Monaster-ni-Cailleach Juxta Aney, is believed to have been founded as a monastery by St. Patrick. This early foundation was destroyed in a Viking raid but was re-established as a convent for nuns in 1283 by a branch of the Fitzgibbon family. Llanthony Priory had land here in 1360 and after the Dissolution the house of *Ballenegallaghe by Loghguyre* was granted to

219

Edmund Sexton. This ruined convent was located on a hill, 400 yards south of the Ballynagallagh megalithic tomb, and was locally known as the Abbey. To the north-west there is a cairn called the Hero's Grave. There are several other monuments in the townland which was known as Hagstown in the 1841 Ordnance Survey map. The ruined house, near the abbey, was the residence of the Brown family of Camas, Germany and Russia.

ST. PATRICK'S WELL is located at the foot of the northern face of Knockderk. This is still visited by local people who continue the rounds here although the week-long pattern ceased during the last century. The well is surmounted by a small rectangular stone building; there are two small ponds nearby; and a natural mound known as St. Patrick's Bed on which that saint is supposed to have slept. A pilgrim making the rounds must first collect nine stones from the roadway near the well. He uses these to keep a tally of his rounds as he must make nine circuits of the well, stopping in front of it each time to pray. When his nine circuits are completed he collects five stones and makes five circuits of St. Patrick's Bed repeating the same prayers as before. When his rounds are completed he half-fills a bottle with water from the well and visits the two ponds taking some water from each in order to fill the bottle. His devotions are not complete until he returns home and takes three sips of the water from his bottle. This is probably a Pagan Celtic tradition that continued into the twentieth century. The worship of water, as represented in wells, was quite common in pre-Christian Ireland as it prevailed all over Europe. Wells have been venerated by both Pagans and Christians and many of the Pagan Irish worshipped wells as gods. In later times the Christian saints blessed and consecrated the wells. The water of St. Patrick's Well is believed to cure all kinds of disease and is regularly given to sick people, even today. Tradition maintains that there was a church in Patrickswell graveyard in which Mass was heard during Penal times.

Lough Gur Interpretative Centre.

THE FARM BY LOUGH GUR stands on a green ridge above the lake where the southern slopes of Knockfennel fall steeply into the water. In 1937 Mary Carbery published the memoirs of Sissy (Mary) O'Brien under the title of *The Farm by Lough Gur.* Mary Carbery, formerly Mary Toulmin, an Englishwoman married to Lord Carbery of Castlefreke, Cork, was fascinated with her husband's Irish background and later became an expert on the history, folklore, customs and traditions of her adopted country. She met Sissy O'Brien in 1904 but it was not until 1935 that she managed to persuade Sissy to write her recollections of the life she and her family had led before she met, and married, Richard Fogarty and went to live in Bruff. Sissy's father was born in 1816 and the family lived and farmed under the Counts de Salis, benevolent landlords who owned most of the surrounding region. Sissy was born in 1858 and her biography presents a picture of nine-teenth century farming life, customs, and manners which has never been equalled. The world she described has now almost vanished but a little of it still lingers. Mary Carbery edited Sissy's memoirs and wove them into a continuous, and very readable, narrative.

ANCIENT REMAINS can be found all over this region. Some are highly visible, others are covered by overgrowth of some kind of other; some have been damaged, lost of destroyed; and some still await discovery.

KNOCKFENNEL HILL has a small cairn on its summit, 531 feet above sea-level. There are also traces of ancient cultivation here some of which have been excavated. Red Cellar Cave is located in the valley to the east.

THE MacELLIGOT FAMILY ran a "safe house" here during the War of Independence. After the massacre at Cahir Guillamore they sheltered the wounded John Gerard O'Dwyer. This youth, a noted horseman, later led Irish Army equitation teams to victory in some of the world's capitals. Joseph and Bob Rryan also survived the same event but were savagely beaten. Bob Ryan became a T.D. for East Limerick.

SOURCE REFERENCE NUMBERS
4 9 13 23 28 41 44 45 47 50 64 76 77 86 93 108
114 120 123 124 129 150 157 163
164 173 184 200 207 219 236 238 265 272 275 282

Mungret

Temple Mungret · Dooradoyle

MUNGRET may derive its name from *Muine Gairid,* the Short Hill, but this is "a mere etymological guess" on the part of John O Donovan in 1840. In earlier times it was known as *Imungram* and *Moungairid.* John O'Connor, the author of *Mungret History and Antiquities* (1971), accepts Mungairit as an acceptable form because it has the sanction of antiquity and believes it is derived from *Mong Ghairid,* the Short Swamp or Morass, an apt description of the land between Mungret and Limerick.

MUNGRET MONASTERY was one of Ireland's earliest and greatest foundations. John O'Donovan claimed that an abbey was erected here in the fourth century long before the coming of St. Patrick and his appointment of St. Nessan as prior here. According to the long lost *Psalter of Cashel* this monastery had

six churches within its walls and, exclusive of numerous scholars, 1500 monks, of whom 500 were learned preachers, 500 psalmists, and 500 wholly employed in spiritual exercises. The *Psalter of Cashel* disappeared from Cashel in 1647 after Murrough the Burner O'Brien attacked Cashel and killed 3,000 of its inhabitants. Mungret Monastery was raided and plundered by Viking marauders in 820, 834, 840 and 843. In 908 the king-bishop of Cashel, Cormac MacCuilleanáin, bestowed three ounces of gold and a satin chausible on this foundation. In 1080 the abbey was damaged by fire. Donal MacLoughlin and a raiding party of Ulstermen destroyed Mungret in 1088. The Augustinian rule may have prevailed here during the twelfth century although this has never been proved, nor is there any evidence to support a link with the Dominicans. In 1152 Mungret claimed dioce-

san status as it would have been the obvious centre of what later became the Diocese of Limerick. The Synod of Rathbreasail, however, failed to recognise the claim of Mungret since the city had been established as the O'Brien capital in 1106. No bishops were recorded here during the twelfth century and Brictius, the Bishop of Limerick, received the monastic lands of Mungret from Domhnall Mór O'Brien between 1192 and 1194.

ST. NESSAN, St. Nessan the Deacon, or St. Neasan the Leper, was a disciple of St. Patrick, according to the folklore of the region, but as Nessan did not die until 551 or 561 this is extremely unlikely. He is also believed to have been a disciple of St. Ailbe of Emly.

BAUNACLOKA TOWNLAND may derive its name from *Bán a Chloiche,* the Bawn of the Stones or Stone Huts, as the earliest

Mungret Abbey.

The Oldest Church.

monastery probably consisted of a series of *clochans,* huts made of stone, wood or mud and wattle, in which the monks lived, clustered around a small church and other communal buildings located within an enclosure.

ST. NESSAN'S CHURCH, or the Monastery Church, is located on the edge of the road. It contains a monumental east window dating from the twelfth century but the building is much older, possibly dating from the tenth century, and may have been erected before 1100. This tall building with its high walls also contains two blocked-up windows in its south wall and a lintelled doorway in the west wall.

THE OLDEST CHURCH on this site is also the smallest. This is located a short distance south of St. Nessan's Church and is a narrow rectangular building containing two small windows in the south wall and a similar window in the eastern gable. The western gable and original doorway have disappeared, replaced by a modern wall. John O'Connor in *Mungret History and Antiquities* believes it was constructed between 800-1100.

MUNGRET ABBEY was built between 1251 and 1272. This is the largest and most important of the three ruined churches, and is divided into three parts. The eastern section, or chancel, dates from the thirteenth century; the nave is of doubtful date as no details by which it could be dated are *in situ;* and the

western portion probably dates from the fifteenth century as the workmanship is in the style of that period. A Gwynn and R.N. Hadcock described this medieval parish church as partly-fortified in *Medieval Religious Houses Ireland* (1988). The residential quarters, and the unusual square tower at the western end of the church, date from the fifteenth century. The tower, on the northern side of the priests' residence, contains a staircase and belfry, although its topmost storey is more modern than the rest of the building. This church, known as the Abbey, was later used for Protestant worship and remained in use as a parish church until 1822. In 1880 the three ruined churches were vested in the Board of Works and repairs were carried out on them in 1932. The graveyard is still in use. A few yards from the north-eastern end of the church is an old tombstone erected in memory of James Daly (1750-1810), the Loughmore poet, better known as Seamus O Dálaigh, a tailor of Croom. The inscription on this stone is in Irish. Another tombstone about fifteen yards east of the eastern gable of the church was possibly erected in 1811 in memory of Robert MacNamara. This, too, carries an Irish inscription, as well as a crucifixion scene showing the instruments of the Passion. The most interesting inscription in the graveyard, however, is that on the Holohan Stone. This unique memorial

is twelve yards south-west of the south-western corner of the abbey. It depicts a Crucifixion scene on the front, with the legend I.N.R.I. above it, and carries an inscription in both Roman and Ogham lettering beneath. The dedication on the back of the tombstone is in English and commemorates John Holohan (1752-1809), his mother and his brother. I was unable to verify if these monuments still existed. The Holohan and MacNamara tombstones may have been placed in Mungret Abbey which is under the care of the Office of Public Works. The keys of two of these churches, however, are kept in Killarney. A modern *cillín* can be seen in the graveyard of the Abbey

HOLOHAN, *O hUallacháin,* the descendant of *Uallachán,* the diminutive of *Uallach* or the Proud, the name of several distinct families in Offaly and Thomond. Variants of this surname include *O Holohan, O Houlihan, O Huolighane, O Holeghane,* Hoolihan, Houlihan, Holland, in West Cork, and Nolan, in Mayo and Roscommon.

THE MONKS' MILL, or Shannillian Mill, was located about halfway between Mungret and Limerick. By 1971 only one wall remained.

MUNGRET CASTLE, or Castle Mungret, was mentioned as early as 1201. Part of its basement still survives beneath a farmhouse south of the modern corcass road to Limerick Docks. Bishop de Rupefort mentioned the castle in 1336 and it contained two towers in 1583, when it was mentioned in another account. Bishop Adams was in possession before 1621 and in 1655 David Roche and H. Bindon held Castle Mungret and Temple Mungret respectively. The castle remained in a good state of preservation until the early nineteenth century when part of it was demolished. By 1840 only an arch over the ground floor and one wall remained.

THE MANOR OF MUNGRET comprised the lands granted to Brictius by Domhnall Mór O'Brien. In 1201 Donoh O'Brien, as Bishop of Limerick, set up a commission, consisting of twelve Irishmen, twelve Vikings, and twelve Anglo-Normans, to inquire into Church possessions. Colm O'Regan was given the church and district of Mungret by Donoh O'Brien, before 1207. About 1216 Edmund, the Bishop of Limerick, received a royal grant of *Omayl,* possibly the lands of the O'Malleys, near Mungret. When Hubert de Burgo was Bishop of Limerick (1223-1250) he got permission from King Henry III (1223-1272) to have a weekly market, on Tuesdays, here. By the time Hubert died in 1250 the main ecclesiastical positions in the Diocese of Limerick were held by Anglo-Norman clergymen.

THE BRETEUIL LAWS were privileges bestowed on the town of Breteuil, in Normandy, by William the son of Osbuir, later the Earl of Hereford. These rights, the *Consaietudines de Breteuil,* were conferred on the burgesses of Mungret by Robert of Emly when he became Bishop of Limerick (1251-1272). This gave them the right to choose their own rulers; hold their own courts; fix their annual rents at a set rate of five pence for each tenure of land in the town; gave them freedom to transfer ownership of tenancies within the town; and the right to levy fines or establish punishments for all but the more serious offences. The burgesses were also allowed a certain independence from the lord of the manor as they could limit the period for which he could have credit, deny him any rights or wardship or marriage, and restrict him from imprisoning burgesses. These inducements attracted a lot of Anglo-Norman settlers into the area, particularly from the Welsh boroughs.

THE PEOPLE OF MUNGRET were divided into three classes by the fourteenth century; the native *Betagi, Betaghs* or *Biadhtaigh,* tenants who were classed as serfs until Bishop Rochefort recognised them as free tenants in 1336; the free Anglo-Norman tenants; and the burgesses of the *vill* of Mungret.

THE LOFTUS FAMILY were associated with the area from an early date. Folklore relates that, at one stage 100 of the monks in the monastery were named John Loftus and the road from the monastery to Raheen Cross was known as Loftus Road, and was marked as such in the 1844 *Ordnance Survey Map.* The surname Loftus, *de Lochtús,* de Lofthouse or Loftis is found mainly in Wexford and may have been of Danish or Viking origin as it was derived from *Lofft* or *Lloft.* The surname is also found in England and Normandy but there is a possibility that the family, in Limerick, may have been of Irish origin. In 1434 the *Papal Letters* mention the excommunication of John Loftus who was later appointed Bailiff of Limerick. Piers Loftus served as mayor in the same century. Another Piers Loftus of Mungret sought a pardon from Queen Elizabeth after the Desmond Rebellion. The Loftus family appear to have held the lands of Dooradoyle, Ballykeefe, Sluggary and Gouldavoher for which they paid an annual rent of £80, in the early seventeenth century. The name does not appear in the *Civil Survey* list of proprietors in 1641.

TEMPLE MUNGRET contained one plowland with a thatched house, fifteen cabins, four ruined churches and other stone walls in 1654 when its lands stretched from Mungret to Dooradoyle and from the Shannon to Ballycummin. Some time before 1865 a coin hoard was discovered in a quarry near the churches. It was hidden around the middle of the tenth century and is the earliest Viking hoard found in Thomond. It contained eight Anglo-Saxon pennies dating from about 905 to around 950; a rare Viking coin struck at York for one of the Hiberno-Norse kings about 942; and seven small ingots of silver. A bell of "very rude workmanship" was found at Loughmore about 1837 and twelve years later a bronze bell was discovered near Mungret Abbey.

MUNGRET MANOR was profitable for the Protestant Bishop of Limerick. On 1 January 1871 an Act of Parliament disestablished and disendowed the Church of Ireland. At that time the bishop owned 3,700 acres of land here from which he derived an annual income of £2,100 in rents and fines. Colonel Gough of Fethard held the former Loftus estate, of 1,570 acres, from the Bishop for an annual rent of £447. He held 100 acres for his own use and sublet the rest at £2 to £4 an acre. Sir David Roche leased 700 acres at Ballycummin from the Bishop, as well as the lands of Ballyhourigan, which he held in perpetuity from the diocese. The Compton family leased 185 acres for £144 and sublet it for £2 to £3 an acre and in 1868 Edward L. Griffin leased the lands of Ballymacashel and Castle Mungret which had been leased to Robert Wogan Studdert in 1850. Tenants at will occupied farms in the townlands of Rathmale and Loughanleigh. These holdings varied from 6 to 84 acres and were let at an average rent of £1 an acre.

MUNGRET COLLEGE evolved from a college and model farm established by the trustees of the Bindon estates after they had purchased 70 acres of land at Drumdarrig in 1852. This model farm closed in 1878 but the college re-opened as a non-denominational school on 23 September 1880. Lord Emly, First Baron Maunsell, and Postmaster-General, became a Catholic through the efforts of a French Jesuit refugee, M. L'Abbe l'Heritier. He used his influence to acquire the model farm for the Jesuits. In 1882 Fr. W. Ronan became the first rector of Mungret College. Lord Emly later lost his fortune, his mortgaged property, and his home, Tervoe House. The college closed over a century later but its front entrance is still adorned by the pillaried portico from Tervoe House.

THE KNIGHTS TEMPLARS were an international military order established to protect pilgrims after the recapture of Jerusalem in 1099. They operated under the Augustinian rule until 1128 when they adopted a rule similar to that of the Cistercians. The order was introduced into Ireland before 1180 and their chief house, or preceptory, was located in Clontarf. They were similar to the Knights Hospitallers in many respects but the rivalry between both orders was largely the reason for the fall of Jerusalem in 1187 and the capture of Acre in 1291. After 1312 all of the Irish possessions of the Knights Templars should have become the property of the Knights Hospitallers but this matter was still unresolved in 1329. The Knights Templars are believed to have had a preceptory in Temple Mungret which later became the mansion house of the prior. Samuel Lewis claims that their establishment here was granted to the Augustinians. A hospital for lepers was located on the ruins of a hermitage opposite Ballincurra, near the eastern boundary of the parish in ancient times but no record remains of the founder.

MOUNT MUNGRET was built as the Church of Ireland glebe house in 1832. This is a neat three-storey structure.

THE CHURCH OF IRELAND CHURCH was a small handsome cruciform structure with an octagonal tower. This was built in 1822. It was closed down in 1877 and the roof was removed in 1900.

CONIGAR HOUSE was originally built as a county residence for the Protestant Bishop of Limerick, in 1774. In 1827 a new two-storey farmhouse was built near the old mansion which had fallen into ruin by then. By 1837 Conigar House had been sold to Charles Wilson. *The Griffith Valuation* states that a Mrs. Wilson leased 200 acres at Conigar Farm from the Bishop in 1855. In 1837 Lewis reported that the constabulary police had converted the entrance lodge into a barracks. Conigar is an Anglicised form of *Coinicear,* the Place of Rabbits.

BALLYCUMMIN derives its name from Baile Uí Chomáin, the Townland of Commons, Comane or Hurley.

BALLYCUMMIN HOUSE is a fairly modern castellated house. It is now the property of Joe O'Brien.

DOORADOYLE derives its name probably from *Tuar an Daíl,* the Tribe's Bleach Green. Other explanations given are *Túr an Daill,* the Blind One's Tower, or *Turradh an Daill,* the Blind One's Crypt or Souterrain. The Limerick Regional Hospital is located in Dooradoyle.

THE MORMON CHURCH, in Dooradoyle, was erected in 1982-1983. The building may be new but the Church of the Latter Day Saints, in Limerick, can trace its history back to the dissenting Protestant Palatines of Rathkeale. These Palatines contributed to the establishment of the Mormon faith after they left Ireland to start new lives in England and America during the 1830s and 1840s. A few

Mormon missionaries arrived into Limerick in the late 1960s. They left but returned to open a meeting-place in Thomas Street, Limerick City, in 1972-1973. The Church of the Latter Day Saints in Limerick had 130 members in March 1989. Robert Kearney was its branch president, or church leader, in that year.

GENEALOGICAL RECORDS play a major role in the Mormon faith. Records are compiled and kept but not for the usual bureaucratic reasons. Special ceremonies are held in their temples in order to baptise the dead and to "seal families for time and eternity". Temples should not, however, be confused with churches. The nearest Mormon temple, to Limerick, is in London, and the nearest collection of records is in Cork. One of the earliest Mormon churches established outside of America was founded in Rathkeale in the early nineteenth century, by Palatine converts.

SLUGGERY RING FORT is located almost directly behnd the Limerick Regional Hospital. This fort, about an acre in size, was polygonal in plan and consisted of two concentric sets of banks and ditches with a third dry-stone built bank on the outside. Dr. Elizabeth Shee, University College Cork, and Liam Irwin, Thomond Archaelogical Society, excavated here in 1973 and 1974. They found an ornamented bone comb, a bronze ring-headed pin, nails, pins, iron knives, a central cist-like heart, and numerous post holes and pits. The fort has been preserved and landscaped. *Slogaire* has been translated as a swallower, a glutton, a gulf, a quagmire or as a common river-name.

LOUGHMORE derives its name from *A n Loch Mór*, the Big Lake. This is supposed to be an enchanted lake which disappears every few years. Grattan's Volunteers trained here and it was used for military tattoos or musterings into the early twentieth century. Loughmore Catholic church was a small thatched building in 1837 and the parish was known as Loughmore rather than as Mungret because both the church and the priests' residence were located here.

RAHEEN CATHOLIC CHURCH was partly built and roofed by Fr. Jeremiah Halpin, who was parish priest here for only one year, before he died on 5 October 1845. The church was later completed by Fr. Michael Casey and his parishioners in 1862. Between Raheen Cross and Willow Park the remains of another earth fort can be seen in the centre of a built-up area.

SOURCE REFERENCE NUMBERS
18 47 48 76 86 120 129
173 186 192 213 227 238 242 252 264 282

P. 225. *The stark landscape on the road to Athea.*
P. 226. *Lough Gur.*
P. 227. *Adare Village.*
P. 228. *Tranquil scene near Dromcolliher.*

Regional Hospital, Dooradoyle.

Newcastle West

Grange Bridge · Mahoonagh · Kilmeedy · Knockaderry · Feenagh

NEWCASTLE WEST derives its name from *An Caisleán Nua Thiar*, the New Castle to the West. Newcastle is the name under which it is described in Samuel Lewis's *Topographical Dictionary of Ireland* (1837) and Maurice Lenihan's *History of Limerick* (1866), although it was also known as *Castle Roe, Castle Nua*, and the New Castle of Oconyll.

THE KNIGHTS TEMPLARS have been credited with the erection of the original castle of Newcastle West in 1184 although the Anglo-Normans had no secure footing west of the Maigue until after the death of Domhnall Mór O'Brien in 1194. The Geraldine occupation of Connello has been dated to 1180, a date T.J. Westropp disagrees with. He also questions the presence of the Knights Templars here and in Limerick, Temple-Mungret, Carrickaquincy, Carrigogunnell, Askeaton, Newcastle, Strand, Temple-Glantan, Teampullin and Rosstemple, which "were all reputed to be preceptories of the Order. We can understand that the ignorant-learned men of the day took the common Irish prefix "teampul" as evidence; other errors may have arisen from confusing the Templars with the Hospitallers, or supposing that the latter in all cases took over the lands of the former ... A few Templars may have helped the Geraldines in some crisis, and impressed themselves unfavourably on local tradition, but, at least, the story of the Geraldine acquisition being subsequent to the dissolution of the Order, and that Newcastle was one of its possessions, is an absolute falsehood". John FitzThomas Fitzgerald was Lord of Connello in 1244, when he was given grants of free chase and free warren. He was killed in the battle of Callan, which was fought near Kenmare in 1261. His infant son, Thomas, was made a ward of the Crown.

THE NEW CASTLE OF CONNELLO was first mentioned during the lordship of Thomas Fitzgerald, the son of John. On 5 July 1298 the Manor of Newcastle "contained the New Castle with buildings inside the wall, as well as those without". Thomas (1261-1298) was

succeeded by his son Maurice, in the Lordships of Decies and Desmond, as well as Connello. Records of 1306 mention Maurice as a minor and relate how custody of the castle was vested in Gerald Doronis who later granted it to Sir John de Barry of Barryroe. When Edward Bruce advanced, the Irish of Connello and those on the Geraldine manors rose in rebellion. Maurice, however, remained loyal to the Crown and his rank and status were raised from those of a feudal lord with the creation of his new title, Earl of Desmond, at Gloucester, on 22 August 1329. On 17 May 1333 he signed a declaration in French before the high altar of Christ Church, Dublin, binding himself to attend the next Parliament and to conduct himself well towards the Crown. His eldest son, Nicholas, was an idiot; some deny that he was actually Earl, and the same doubt applies to the title of his brother, John, the reputed Third Earl.

GERALD FITZGERALD (c. 1335-1398), John's son by his third wife, is better known as Gearóid Iarla. T.J. Westropp refers to him as the Fourth Earl of Desmond whereas Jocelyn Otway-Ruthven mentions him as the Third Earl in her book, *A History of Medieval Ireland* (1968). A mounted bronze figure commemorates this legendary character near what was once the entrance to the old Church of Ireland church, the outlined foundations of which can be seen between the Desmond Hall and the Square. There is some mystery concerning his death or disappearance. Some accounts say he left his camp one night and was never seen again; others state that he was slain by a personal enemy, or by an agent of the O'Brien of Thomond; and a more prosaic account claims that he died in his own house of *Caisleán Nua*. In 1370 he was imprisoned in Ennis by Brian O'Brien, but later had his son, James, fostered with the O'Briens. Gearóid Iarla is also credited with a deep knowledge of mathematics and magic, and with introducing the French tradition of courtly love into Irish poetry.

THE DESMOND HALL dates from about 1440 to 1450. This building off the town square with its "massive vaulted basement,

the window bays, with side seats, and the evident preference for cinquefoil and stepped heads, the shallow, corbelled arches, facing the great east window, and the side staircase turret", resembled that of the banquet hall of Askeaton Castle. The Desmond Hall of Newcastle West contains a fireplace dated 1638 which may have been taken from the ruins of a great house at Kilmallock. The hall was purchased in 1981 by "a number of interested groups, with a view to restoring it as a cultural centre and museum for the town".

THE CASTLE has been partly incorporated into a more modern residence but a good part of it still remains; a large section of the curtain wall; a water fosse; the bastion; one rectangular tower; one circular tower; the Desmond Hall; and the Great Hall. The two halls are separated from the rest of the castle by a modern wall. In 1866 Maurice Lenihan claimed that the carved acorns seen in some parts of the castle were emblems of the Knights Templars and dated from the earliest years of the castle.

THE GREAT HALL is much larger than the Desmond Hall but much harder to date. Its "west window and door-mouldings belong to the first half of the fifteenth century; but some of its beautiful side-lights are of earlier and rarer design ... though their mouldings and execution seem later than their pattern".

THE DESMOND ROLL OF 1583 describes the early town: "One great castle, built of square plan, a chief house of the said late Earl of Desmond ... having at each angle of the same a round tower, with various places and chambers in each tower. And there is at the south corner, on the western side of the said castle at the south part, a high square tower or peel, built for defence within the walls of the said castle. And also there were within the walls of the said castle many buildings — namely, a large hall, a large room and an excellent chamber; one garden, and in the same two fish-ponds, all of which buildings are ruined and waste. And outside the walls, and near them, are divers orchards and gardens, three acres of land". Three years later Christopher Peyton wrote a similar account of

Aerial view of Newcastle West.

Newcastle West, but called it *Castleno,* in *The Book of Survey of Thattaynted and Escheated Lands in the County of Limerick* (1586).

THE TOWN developed around the castle. It was sacked in 1302 when the church was burned in a raid that swept through the western hills and along Knockfierna. In 1315 it was totally destroyed. Its fortunes were inextricably involved with those of its overlords, the Earls of Desmond, and, at a later date, the Courtenays. The Earl of Ormond raided the Geraldine territories in 1597. He penetrated as far as Newcastle West, "whence he carried off all the cattle and other spoils that he was able to seize upon in the country. He returned home without receiving battle or opposition because at that time the Earl (of Desmond) and his relatives were in Kerry." The castle was captured by the Sugan Earl of Desmond in 1598. By then many of the Undertakers had fled into Limerick City leaving their castles "manned by servants who were careless of their defence". The castles held by Sir William Courtenay, Newcastle, Glenquin and Purtrinard were easily captured as he had "neglected to consolidate the English interest and secure the defence of his seignory". Newcastle West was retaken by the English, with hardly any opposition in 1600. Three battles were fought nearby during the reign of Elizabeth I.

THE SEIGNORY OF POLICASTRO came into existence after Sir William Courtenay was given a grant of Newcastle West, Mayne, Ballywoghan and Kilgulban on 23 September 1591, with instructions to plant English settlers on it. He "was bound to build houses for eighty families; a small enough colony to hold down a despairing and maddened population, unhinged and overturned after a long and merciless war". William failed to establish a strong English settlement here. He turned his Irish estate over to his son's care and returned to his English estates at Powderham. He and his son were dispossessed, perhaps with their own consent, and the manors reverted to the Crown until Charles I (1625-1649) regranted them to George Courtenay, William's second son, with a patent dated at Dublin 9 May 1639.

THE COURTENAY FAMILY claim descent from the hereditary Counts of Sens, from at least 836. One of them, Athon, fortified the town of Courtenay in the Isle of France during the reign of Robert the Wise. It is from this town the family surname was derived. Robert, the son of Sir Reginald de Courtenay was Baron of Oakhampton and Viscount of Devon about 1200. He later became Governor of Exeter Castle, and in 1214 he was made governor of Bridgnorth. During the War of the Roses the Courtenays sided with the House of Lancaster. The Sixth Earl of Devon was beheaded in 1462, his brother was executed in 1464, and their estate and earldom was given to Lord Stafford, who met the same fate in 1469. The restoration of Henry VI (1422-1461) to the throne in 1471 brought the Courtenay estates back to the family until the Eighth Earl fell in the battle of Tewkesbury in that year. His possessions reverted to the Yorkist supporters of Edward IV (1461 - October 1470; and March 1471 - 1483). Sir William Courtenay was descended from Hugh, the Second Earl of Devon. Hugh's sixth son, Philip, was knighted on the day before the battle of Navaret and was Richard II's

(1377-1399) representative in Ireland from 1383 to 1392. By the end of the fourteenth century this branch of the Courtenays had established their seat at Powderham Castle, Devonshire. Sir William was the fifth in succession to bear the name and title; and the eighth in descent from Sir Philip. William was a Catholic; his home was believed to contain "a dark, secret room" in which "popish priests lay concealed"; and he was denounced in the House of Commons as a Papist recusant in 1624.

GEORGE COURTENAY was more discreet than his father in his political and religious beliefs. He introduced English settlers to Newcastle West, Meane and Beauly, and made some effort to fulfil his obligations as an Undertaker. He was created a Baronet in December 1622 and was granted the constableship of Limerick Castle, which had fallen vacant on the death of his brother-in-law, Maurice Barkeley. In 1625 he received a grant to hold a Saturday market and a fair on 21 September in Newcastle; and a Wednesday market, and a fair on 24 October in Kilmeedy. George Courtenay was one of the biggest landowners in the county. He controlled and owned most of south-west Limerick. He sold off many of his holdings during the 1620s because of financial pressure, and at one time was quite anxious to leave Ireland. Thomas Wentworth may have advised Charles I (1625-1649) to regrant the estates to George Courtenay in 1639. "In consideration of the rents reserved, George Courtenay, his heirs and assigns were granted the Manor of Castlenoe, or Newcastle, with all the castles, vills, *villats,* hamlets, and hereditaments. The lands are then enumerated. [T.J. Westropp wrote], in such careless and bad spelling as to be often nearly unrecognizable, eighty-three townlands being mentioned. Then we find the castles and lands of Mene or Mahownagh and sixty-six more townlands; Beawly (the old Oughtred seignory) with its castles, including Muskrynawnane (Gardenfield in Drumcolliher) and thirty-seven other townlands, all in Conolagh Barony. These lands, with the manors, messuages [dwellings and offices with adjoining lands for household use], tofts [homesteads], tenements and tenancies, water-courses, fisheries, fish-ponds, pigeon-houses, woods, underwoods, meadows, pastures and other lands, commons, moors, mountains, royalties, minerals, quarries, &c., &c., on the said manors, vest in George Courtenay".

DURING THE CONFEDERATE WARS, Sir George Courtenay served in the defence of Limerick Castle. In his absence the English settlers in the Newcastle West region moved into the new castle in order to protect them-

River scene at Newcastle West.

selves. The fortress was "daily assaulted and besieged" from December 1641 until it was eventually surrendered to General Patrick Purcell in August 1642. In the interim the town was burned by the Confederate besiegers on Easter Monday, 14 April 1642. An attempt by the garrison to launch a counter-attack was foiled by the Sheehys. George Courtenay died in 1644 and was succeeded by his son Francis. Over the succeeding centuries the Courtenay family remained the principal landlord family in this area. Although they disposed of many large tracts of land they retained most of the Seignory of Newcastle until they sold off the greater part of their holdings, to their tenants, under the 1903 Land Purchases Act. The Courtenay family, occupied a long, irregular two-storey house, known as Courtenary Castle, within the grounds of Newcastle West Castle. The Earl opened part of his grounds to the public in the nineteenth century.

T.J. WESTROPP wrote in 1909 that at the beginning of the nineteenth century "a number of Roman bath tickets, stamped with indecent figures, were dug up in the castle". He wondered if these had anything to do with the legends of the Knights Templars! In 1827 Rev. P. Fitzgerald noted that "tradition reports that the knights used some barbarous customs which so disgusted the Irish that they put several of them to death; and the place is still shown where their remains are said to have been interred". According to legend the Knights Templars brought an "unclean thing" across many lands and seas to Newcastle West, and T.J. Westropp thought that this unamed item might have been a reference to the Roman bath tickets.

FULLER'S FOLLY is located south-east of the Desmond Castle. It bears an inscription dating its erection to 1859 although the earliest record I could find for it was in 1867, when William Fuller Hartnett (1804-1879) leased a plot of land from the Earl of Devon adjacent to the castle grounds. He erected the castellated building known as Fuller's Folly on this site. It is now occupied by architectural consultants and is situated close to the bridge alongside a pleasant, but short, riverside walk. William Fuller Hartnett had a drapery business in Bridge Street and was a personal friend of Daniel O'Connell for several years until he switched his political allegiance and support to the more radical Young Irelanders. William is still remembered locally as a larger-than-life character.

PHELAN'S MILL, downstream from, and west of the castle, is the last of a number of mills operated in Newcastle West from the earliest times. The first mill recorded on the Arra River was mentioned in the Inquisition of 1282, and was valued at 331/3 pence. In 1586 Christopher Peyton wrote of "a street called Shradegower with 1 tenement, a yard, orchard and 8 gardens with 10 acres, held by Edmond McEgower. A square mill on a parcel of the street of Shradegower called Mollen McEgower". South Quay is now the name of Shradegower Street and the mill remained in use here for over four centuries. In the 1850s it was leased to Patrick Griffin. On 25 March 1862 William Quaid took out a lease for 99 years. In 1880 he transferred his lease to Robert Quaid who subsequently sublet it to Mary Phelan in 1889. In 1910 William Phelan purchased the mill premises from the Earl of Devon, and it remained in his family until

1983. Sean Kelly wrote about the mill in 1983. "The Quaids extended the original mill premises and, at one stage, flax was carded there. The scutching pond was further upstream, past Dr. O'Brien's Bridge, and the bleaching lawn was in front of the house ... The mill was originally powered by a breast shot waterwheel ... William Phelan replaced it with a pair of turbines at the end of the 19th century ... During the War years a ton of flour per day was ground ... Grains were not mixed and one got back as flour what one gave in as grain". Corn grinding continued into the 1950s until white flour became available again. The mill stayed open as a timber mill and store until 1983.

THE POWER AND LIGHT COMPANY was established by William Phelan in 1915, when he founded the Newcastle West and District Electric Light and Power Company Limited. An electric plant was powered by the mill and the Power and Light Company remained in existence until the E.S.B. took over its function on 23 February 1935. There are three weirs west of the bridge and to the east of it a garage was actually built across the Arra River.

IN 1837 the town consisted of "four principal streets and a spacious square, the north side of which is chiefly occupied by an infantry barrack; on the south are the parish church and the castle, and the east and west sides are formed by lines of large and handsome houses. On the south side of the river, which here separates the parish from that of Monegay, are the shambles, a neat and commodious structure. A fever hospital and dispensary, which stands on an eminence near the town, has accommodations for 15 intern patients ... the bridewell contains two day-rooms, two airing-yards, and four cells. The town is a chief constabulary police station. The patent under which markets are held names Tuesday, Thursday, and Saturday; but the last only is in use. Fairs are held on 1 April, 3 May, 12 July, 20 August, 1 October and 10 December, for the sale of cattle, agricultural implements, and linen and woollen cloth. There are several establishments in the town for dying [sic] woollens, also a large ale and beer brewery, and a great number of shoe and brogue makers, all in full employment, as is also a bleaching establishment in the immediate vicinity, which occupies 8 acres and gives work to a number of men ... Coarse linen and woollen clothes, stuffs and friezes are manufactured to some extent in the surrounding district". The principal houses of the area over 150 years ago were Courtenay Castle, Springfield Castle, Glanduff Castle, Knockaderry House, Cahirmoyle, Mount Plummer, Chesterfield, Heathfield,

Castleview, Ringwood Lodge, Churchtown, Ashgrove and Glanaster. The Earl of Devon contributed a site for, and £400 towards, the erection of a Catholic church in 1828. The Church of Ireland parish church built by William Second Viscount Courtenay in 1777 has long since disappeared. Only the outline of its foundations remains. In 1840 John O'Donovan wrote of "a holy well called St. David's Well in the townland of Newcastle (or Castle Demesne) in the Earl of Devon's pleasure garden" Three years before, Samuel Lewis had written of it as "a chalybeate spring, formerly in considerable repute, and protected by a covered building which still exists". On 5 August 1858 the Christian Brothers opened a school in a former national school building which had been built for £278 in 1826 on part of the Earl of Devon's estate. In 1880 the Christian Brothers left the town.

THE TURNPIKE ROAD SYSTEM contributed towards the development of the town in a minor way during the eighteenth century. In 1709 only 70 houses and 55 town tenements were shown on a map drawn at the time of the *Moland Survey*. Turnpike roads were introduced during the reign of Charles II (1660-1685) as most of the road surfaces were then unsuitable for the heavy wagons which came into use with the growth of trade and industry. The first Irish Turnpike Act was passed in 1729. It covered the Naas road. Trustees were appointed for a term of 21 years. These men were given permission to build roads, erect toll-gates and toll-houses, and collect tolls. In 1732 the first Limerick Turnpike Act was passed. It covered the road from Newcastle through Rathkeale, Adare, Bruff and Kilmallock to Mallow. The trustees got almost unlimited credit from speculators but traffic on the roadway never matched expectations. In 1745 the trustees' lease was extended for a period of 34 years. The increase in traffic may have led to a corresponding increase in trade in the town as the market house and the market square date from the mid-eighteenth century. By the middle of the following century the turnpike system had deteriorated and in 1859 it was merged with the public road system. An old saying within the town refers to "Church Street without a church, Bishop Street without a Bishop, and Maiden Street without a maiden".

CHURCHTOWN CHURCH was badly ruined by 1840 when John O'Donovan noted a small round-headed belfry on top of the western gable. He estimated that the church might have dated from 1690.

THE CARNEGIE LIBRARY has its name and the date 1916 inscribed in stone above the doorway. The first Sinn Féin court to sit in the county, sat in the upper room of this library.

Fr. Edmund Punch was the chairman of the court and Fr. Michael Hayes was president of the West Limerick Sinn Féin Executive. More discreet locations were selected for further court sessions as the authorities had banned Sinn Féin from holding courts. The library, the homes of the O'Mahonys and Reidys in St. Ita's Road and the creamery were set on fire by the crown forces in autumn 1920 in retaliation for the wounding of an ex-serviceman by the I.R.A.. The courts continued to sit. Michael Dore, Ballysteen House, Shanagolden; John Quaid, Clonlara, Feenagh; Dan Collins, Monagea; and Seán T. Nolan, South Cappa; formed a panel of judges, while Sean Brouder and Michael J. O'Gorman acted as court clerks until they were both replaced by Bridie Kennedy, Danganbeg. Bridie retained her position until the Truce, in July 1921. Sean T. Nolan became a Cumann na Gael T.D. for West Limerick in later years. Fr. Punch became a canon; was appointed parish priest of Mungret; and became president of Limerick County Board G.A.A..

GRANGE BRIDGE was described as a "curious old bridge" over the River Deel in 1837. The spring-water supply from Kilcoleman Wells to Newcastle West flowed beneath the bed of the river. A spring well was also located inside the roadside stile. In 1642 the Confederate Irish ambushed and killed Captain John Southwell here as he was on his way to relieve the castle of Newcastle West, with forty cavalry and one hundred infantry. Grange derives its name from *Gráinseach*, the Granary. In 1840 John O'Donovan wrote that the old church on high ground about 300 yards east of the Deel, had been abandoned not long before that date as the plaster was still adhering to the walls. By then the windows and doorways had been disfigured and the graveyard had almost passed out of use.

MAHOONAGH derived its name from

Castlemahon.

Mathúmhnach, a corruption of *Magh Ghamhnach,* the Plain of the Milch Cows. In 1837 the Protestant population of Mahoonagh parish attended divine worship at Newcastle West and the Catholics had three churches within the parish at Mahoonagh, Feohanagh and on the roadside between Newcastle West and Dromcolliher. Mahoonagh village was also known as Castlemahon in 1837 and consisted of twenty-four small houses located on the eastern bank of the Deel River. "The ruins of a massive square tower, about 30 feet high, exist near Castlemahon and give name to that village. Near it is a curious circular building, with a high conical roof of stone; it was a strong fortress, erected about 1490 by the Fitzgeralds. Not far from this are the remains of the ancient church. At Mayne are traces of ancient buildings, supposed to have been ecclesiastical, though their present appearance indicates that it was a military position; they most probably formed a stronghold of the Knights Templars, and were therefore partly military and partly ecclesiastical. There is a church-yard at Aglish, but no vestige of the church, which was sometimes called Aglish

na Munni". Gilbert de Clare owned the Manor of Mahoonagh at the beginning of the fourteenth century.

CASTLEMAHON CASTLE is almost as Samuel Lewis described it over 150 years ago but the "curious circular building" near it was demolished in the 1960s. In 1642 the castle was besieged and captured by Thomas MacGibbon, a descendant of the original owner. MacGibbon was helped by an old family retainer, named Casey, who "got up early on Shrove Tuesday and went to the top of the tower, unobserved by the inmates, and whistled. He then came down, roused up the porter, Thomas Everard, and asked to be allowed out to reconnoitre. Everard complied with the request, but no sooner did Casey find the door open, than throttling the porter, he whistled again and before the alarm could be given, the Irish ambuscade was in possession and made one hundred captives". Four of these prisoners were hanged at the wind mill of Meane, one was hanged near Kilbolane Castle, and the others were released after 40 of them had been completely stripped. By 1840 no arched floors remained within the

castle and all of its windows were broken and disfigured except for a pointed one at the western end.

MAHOONABEG CHURCH was built out of small and large stones, irregularly laid. It is often claimed to be the site of St. Maedoc's Monastery as there are a number of ring forts within the region and St. Maedoc's foundation was established within a ring fort. This church was restored in 1410. Its most notable feature is a Romanesque window in the south wall. The graveyard is still in use. It is located 300 yards east of the castle.

CLONCAGH CHURCH, over three miles north-east of Mahoonagh, is located in the centre of a seven-acre, bivallate ring fort, which was later bisected by the roadway. The original church on this site was founded by St. Maedoc of Ferns. Maedoc was also known as Aedan, Aidan, Edan, Mogue, Modoc, Maidhoc, M'Aodhog and Maodhog in Ireland, and as St. De Aedesius in Brittany. He was also a disciple of St. David of Wales and died, Bishop of Ferns, in 625, or 633. Cloncagh Church was granted to the Vicars Choral of St. Mary's Cathedral, Limerick, before 1250.

233

Kilmeedy.

In 1579 it "afforded shelter to some of the distressed Irish" after the disastrous Battle of Monasteranenagh. This nave and chancel building was later used as a Protestant parish church but had become an extensive ruin by 1840.

THE CLONCAGH WELLS located near Cloncagh Church are known as St. Patrick's Well to the south-east, and Sunday's Well, to the south-west.

KILMEEDY derives its name from *Cill Míde*, the Church of *Mo Ide* or St. Ita, the prefix *Mó* being a term of endearment, affection, respect, or reverence.

KILMEEDY CHURCH was erected as a Protestant church in 1665 on the site of an earlier foundation dedicated to St. Ita and known as *Moyalthi* in 1302. In 1837 the structure had become so dilapidated that the Ecclesiastical Commissioners were anxious to rebuilt it, as it was still resorted to by the Protestant parishioners of both Clooncrew and Kilmeedy, according to Samuel Lewis. In his *Records of Ballingarry, Limerick Diocese* (1930) Rev. G.F. Hamilton, Rector of Ballingarry, writes that the church was restored in 1837. If so, only the nave was repaired as the tomb of William Hamo de Massy (1821-1848) of Glenwilliam Castle

occupied a large section of the chancel eleven years later. This church ruin is surrounded by a large graveyard which is still in use.

KNOCKADERRY derives its name from *Cnoc a' Doire*, the Hill of the Oak Grove. In 1837 the village contained 58 small indifferently built houses, with 351 inhabitants. It possessed both a national school, which catered for 50 boys and 20 girls, and a private school, in which 30 boys and 20 girls were enrolled, as pupils. Knockaderry House, the ancient seat of the D'Arcy family, was then the residence and property of J. D'Arcy Evans; Chesterfield was occupied by Major Sullivan; Dromin House was the residence of Nicholas Meade; Balliahill was the home of W. Odell; and Brook Lodge was described as "the occasional dwelling place" of the Cork-based H. Massy. Samuel Lewis made only passing references to Knockaderry Church, the foundation of which he attributed to St. Ita, and to Ballynoe Castle, which he stated was built by the Knights Templars.

FEENAGH derives its name from *Fiodhnach*, the Wooded, or Woody, Place, a description which could hardly be applied to it in 1989. In 1837 the village contained both a dispensary and a constabulary police station, and the principal seats were Heathfield,

the residence of E. Lloyd; High Mount of J. Furlong; and Feenah Cottage, the parochial house of Rev. M. Keily. Even then there was little woodland in evidence. Samuel Lewis wrote that about one-eighth of the parish of Kilmeedy, in which Feenagh was located, was under tillage and the rest was devoted to meadow and pasture, with the exception of some profitable bog, a few quarries, and about 1000 acres of mountain land. The parish also contained some large dairy farms.

A STEAM-DRIVEN THRASHER kept in John Canty's barn on his farm at Gortnagluggin, Feenagh, is still in working condition. This machine is the prime attraction on festive occasions in Feenagh, Dromcolliher and Broadford. The large complex built by the Feenagh Co-Operative Dairy and Agricultural Society Ltd., an impressive cluster of buildings, established in 1891, is nearby.

SOURCE REFERENCE NUMBERS
1 9 11 12 15 28 38 47 64 76 79 86 88 107 115 120
123 129 147 150 171 173 187 189
192 213 233 238 252 264 275

Pallas Grean

Dromkeen · Oola · Cluggin · Sarsfield's Ballyneety

PALLAS GREAN derives its name from *Palis Gréine*, the Castle or Palisade of Grian, Anye, or Aíne, the sun-goddess associated with *Cnoc Gréine*. Greane, Green, or Grean, may also be derived from *Grian*, the Sun although John O'Donovan believed that "the real meaning of the word is land when applied topographically ... that places of this name had no connection whatever with sun-worship".

THREE CIST GRAVES were discovered in a gravel pit in Corelish in the 1930s. As a general rule, short cist burials date from the Bronze Age (1750 B.C. - 500 B.C.) while the majority of the long cist burials date from after the end of the Bronze Age into early Christian times. Some few cist burials may date from the Neolithic period. These graves form a record in stone that is much earlier than the written one in which the Four Masters relate how King Cormac MacAirt fought and won a battle against the Momonians here, in 241.

THE LADY GRIAN, or Gile Gréine, according to folklore was the child of a human being and a sunbeam. When she learned of how she was conceived she committed suicide by drowning herself in Lough Graney, County Clare. Her name is commemorated in several places throughout the counties of Limerick and Clare. *Aes-Gréine*, the Folk of Grian, was the ancient name of the territory and people between Limerick City and *Cnoc Gréine*, the hill that looms over the village of Old Pallas Grean. This hill rises to a height of 864 feet, according to Samuel Lewis, who stated that basalt could be found there in 1837.

THE LIMERICK-TIPPERARY BORDER has been an area of contention from ancient times. Soon after Brian Boru's brother, Mahon, captured Cashel from the *Eoghanachta* in 964 he defeated the Vikings of Limerick at the battle of Sulchoid and sacked their city. The first action of the War of Independence took place at Solohead, County Tipperary, when the I.R.A. ambushed a gelignite patrol on 21 January 1919. A monument commemorating this event now stands in Solohead village, the Sulchoid in which Mahon defeated the Vikings almost a millennium before.

THE CORK-LIMERICK BORDER was the scene of a running fight after four Crossley tenders filled with R.I.C. and military surprised the Mid Limerick Column (I.R.A.), under the joint command of Liam Forde and Sean Carroll, as they were preparing an ambush at Shraharla on 1 May 1921. The fight continued into the following day and finished eventually at Lackelly. Paddy Starr, James Horan and Tim Hennessy were killed outright. Patrick Casey was wounded, captured, tried by drumhead court martial, and shot the following day. By then the fight had spread to Lackelly where Jim Frahill, Pat Ryan, Willie Riordan and Tom Howard of Glenbrohane were killed on 2 May, 1921. The Crown forces seem to have come through the entire affair unscathed.

THE PALLAS GREAN MOTE, Moat, or *motte,* is a fine example of the type of defensive earthwork constructed as a military fortification by the Anglo-Normans on their arrival into areas where, as new colonists, they might come into confrontation with the indigenous Irish. Geoffrey FitzRobert was the first of the Anglo-Normans to receive a grant of the lands of Greane. In 1233 Maurice Fitzgerald came into possession of Greane. In 1234 he was given permission to hold an annual fair on the feast of St. John the Baptist, and for the thirteen days following. Fairs were later held throughout the year on 1 January, 10 March, 16 October and 24 November.

THE OLD PALLAS GREAN FAIR developed from the ancient permit of 1234. Dermot O Mulryan of Cappawhite received a patent or charter which gave him control of the fair in 1782. This later passed to the O'Brien family. The Great Fair, the major event of the year, took place annually on 24 November. An office was created especially for its organiser, the Baron of Old Pallas Grean Fair, who settled any disputes or problems that arose in the course of the day. One of the advantages of being Baron was, if he were a publican, the right to keep a tavern open all night before a fair. Faction fights were a common occurrence on the fair green, particularly between the groups known as the Three Year Olds and the Four Year Olds, and the constabulary were often called out to keep the peace.

GREAN CHURCH was a collegiate church recorded as the "Free Chapel of Russell, alias Paleis" in the fifteenth century. It may have been turned over to Protestant worship after 1549 but this is not certain. A Church of Ireland church was built on the site of the older one in 1808. This was in dilapidated condition by 1837 and abandoned entirely by 1840.

PALLAS GREAN is actually two villages rather than one.

OLD PALLAS GREAN, the post-town for the parish of Greane in 1837, lies to the south of the Limerick-Tipperary road. In 1831 it contained 379 inhabitants in 61 small thatched houses. Pallas House, the Apjohn residence, stood at the head of the village, which also possessed a constabulary police station and a sub-post office.

NEW PALLAS GREAN straddles the Limerick-Tipperary road, with most of it lying to the north of that highway. The construction of the Limerick-Waterford road in the early 1800s, and the building of the railway in the 1840s, led to the development of the section that became known as New Pallas as early as 1837.

THE VILLAGE OF NICKER is located north of the road connecting New Pallas to Old Pallas. In 1837 this small village contained a Catholic Church. Lewis wrote of it as being located within the parish of Ballynaclogh or Dollardstown. Nicker is an Anglicisation of *Coiniceár*, the Irish word for a rabbit warren. The MacBriens of Coonagh had a castle here but by 1928 only the site was remembered.

THE R.I.C. BARRACKS is the most impressive building in New Pallas Grean. This was built about 1870 and remained in use as a garda station until quite recently. Bernard H. Becker visited Ireland as a special commissioner of the *Daily News* during the winter of 1880-1881. He devoted a chapter of his book to *Pallas and the Palladians:* having heard much of the outrages at Pallas, he travelled there only to discover that "the first object which catches the eye in Pallas is not a bower of ribbons and roses, but a stiff-looking police barrack. Close at hand is the railway station, another unlovely edifice, and lounging about in groups are seventy or eighty of the gloomiest and most sullen-looking people I have seen in this country ... I learn that the occasion of this general loafing is a "rent-gathering', or rather an attempt to gather rent, and that Mr. Sanders, the agent for the Erasmus Smith School Trusts, is sitting, but not in receipt of custom ... no money passes, as a matter of course, and the tenants mutter among themselves, 'nor ever will'. One neck-or-nothing friend of the people assures me that Griffith and rent and the rest of it is all 'botheration', and that Pallas folk are going to 'have their own' again, as was once said of a Stuart king, who did not get it nevertheless ... Driving in the direction of Castlegard, I pass the signs of an eviction ... as if crying to Heaven for vengeance against the oppressor. The display strikes me as entirely theatrical, for it is well known that vengeance is not left to Heaven by Pallas people, but confided to Snider bullets. The bailiffs left in charge of the house have been attacked, and yesterday, an iron hut for lodging four policemen on the disputed property was brought to Pallas station. It went no further, however, for neither horse nor cart could be got to convey any fragment of the accursed fabric to the spot required. It is expected that the district will, after this display of 'tyranny' on the part of the police, 'strike' against them and refuse to supply them with food or forage". Later in the day Becker came across "The 'Threes' and the 'Fours', not at issue with each other, but united like brothers against the common enemy. Fearful howls arise from the railway bridge and the railway station, both covered with Palladians, male and female ... brought about by the departure of Mr. Sanders, who, escorted by the police till he is safely off, rentless, but undismayed, slips away in the train". The authorities eventually managed to erect their police hut on "the land of Burke's farm" with the aid of "200 infantry, a squadron of cavalry, a demi-battery of artillery, and 70 armed constables — in all about 350 men" under the command of Colonel Humphreys whose "first care was to secure his base, the railway station, and this *point d'appui* was strongly garrisoned by the 48th. Regiment. Then the road between the station and Burke's farm was strongly patrolled — so strongly as to keep up an unbroken line of communication ... It is hardly necessary to add that no attempt at rushing or crowding the station was made by

the populace ... So the whole affair passed off quietly, and after trebling the ordinary police garrison of Pallas, the military returned to their respective quarters ... Whether the blood of the 'Threes' and 'Fours' will endure the sight of the detested hut rising on the farm of the sainted Burke remains to be seen; but it is doubtful whether the 'Boys' will attempt a *coup de main*." A new garda station has been erected behind the old station. There is little need today for a strong police presence. This new garda station contains a device known as *The Green Man* which puts callers in touch with the police in Bruff, where there is another old R.I.C. barracks similar to, but smaller than, the Pallas station.

THE BLACK AND TANS occupied the old R.I.C. barracks during the War of Independence. They flaunted a conspicuous home-made black-and-tan flag from it during the winter of 1920-1921. Early in 1921 the Tans captured an arms dump belonging to the Mid Limerick Brigade of the I.R.A., who decided to retaliate with the help of the East Limerick Brigade. An attack on the barracks was considered but abandoned because the "nature of the building, its position and defences made for difficulty of approach, and ensured a protracted fight if the defenders were to be overcome". Help from the military or police centres of Limerick City and Tipperary would probably arrive before the barracks could be captured or destroyed. The I.R.A. decided to ambush their enemies.

THE DROMKEEN AMBUSH took place three miles from Pallas at a bend in the road near Dromkeen House, just before 1.00 p.m. on 3 February 1921. Forty I.R.A. men attacked two lorries containing a total of thirteen men, five in one lorry, eight in the other, of which only two or three were regular R.I.C. men. Constables Adams, Bell, Bourke, Doyle, Foody, Hayton, Kingston, Miller, Mollaghan, Pierce and Smith were killed, two policemen managed to escape, and one I.R.A. man had his hand shattered by a bullet.

DROMKEEN derives its name from *Dro m Caoin*, the Pleasant or Delightful Ridge. During the 1950s the ballroom in Dromkeen was one of the most popular venues in provincial Ireland.

DROMKEEN CHURCH was located one mile south-west of Dromkeen station. This was the burial place of the Burgh, de Burgo or Bourke family "from time immemorial". Rev. Richard Burgh buried his first son here in 1693. In 1717 he repaired the church and placed an inscribed stone, recording his work, in one of the church walls. By 1840 the church had virtually disappeared. Today its graveyard is still in use and contains an early Christian cross slab.

DROMKEEN HOUSE is a two-storey gable-ended Georgian house, a former seat of the Bourke family. In 1836 it was in poor condition but seems to have been repaired or rebuilt by 1837 as it was then occupied by the Rev. M. Lloyd. The other principal house in the area at that time was Williamsfort, the residence of H. Croker. Dromkeen House is still occupied.

SUNDAY'S WELL, *Tobar an Domhnaigh,* was frequented into the 1830s on Saturday evenings and Sunday mornings. This was located in the townland of Curraghnaboul about half a mile north-west of Dromkeen Church.

DROMKEEN CHURCH of Ireland Church was built in 1831. Lewis described it as a neat cruciform structure with an octagonal tower crowned with pinnacles.

LINFIELD HOUSE, a large three-storey red brick house, "the fine mansion of D. Grady" in 1837, is now a partly demolished ruin.

TOBER, *Tobar na Rughilly, Tobar na Drochairigh,* possibly the Disobliging Well, was considered a holy well before 1840. East of it was a small burial-ground called *Roilig Cholium Cille,* the Graveyard of Colm's Church, *Teampull na Carraige,* the Temple of the Rock, or *Teampull Pairc na Cairrge,* the Temple of the Field of the Rock. The rock in question was *Carraic Cholium,* Colm's Rock which, like the well and graveyard, was located in the townland of Linfield. The 1928 *Ordnance Survey* maps listed the graveyard as disused. The church may have been founded in the seventh century but by 1840 no trace of the old building was visible. Samuel Lewis referred to it as Kilcolman Church.

LONGSTONE EARTH FORT derives its name from a long stone nine and a half feet high which is located in its centre. The townland later took its name from the fort. Flagstone was quarried here into modern times. Incidentally, there is a second Longstone south of Pallas Green just over the Tipperary border.

MOUNTSION was the seat of the senior branch of the White family who settled in the county during the thirteenth century. They gave their name to Ballyneety, *Baile-an-Fhaeite,* White's Town. The last member of the family to live in Mountsion lost his lands in the Cromwellian confiscations. He is believed to have followed Sarsfield into exile in France, after the second siege of Limerick, in 1691. The house underwent many alterations in the following centuries but is still occupied.

KILDUFF CASTLE is located west of the Limerick-Tipperary road. Only the northern and western walls of this tall gabled tower-house remain. Kilduff Castle may have been founded by the MacBriens. It was later held by the Hurley family from 1617 until they were transplanted into Connaught under the Cromwellian Settlement. In 1667 the castle and lands of Kilduff were given to the trustees of the Erasmus Smith Charity Schools. It was probably destroyed during the Williamite war. Ballytarsna Castle was located in the same parish as Kilduff, according to Samuel Lewis, who wrote that it was in a very ruined condition in 1837. Only the broken and disfigured remains of the foundation stones and small portions of the walls were left, possibly in Linfield townland.

OOLA derives its name from *Ubhla*, the Place of Apples; or *Ubhall* or *Abhall*, the Orchard. In 1831 Oola had 192 inhabitants in 35 houses. There was a constabulary station and a Catholic church in the village. Church of Ireland services were held in Castle Lloyd as the small Protestant community had no place of worship in the village. In 1825 some elk antlers were found near the village and a few years later (before 1837), a brazen trumpet, a spear and bronze arrowheads were discovered. The Lloyd family appeared to be the main landlord family in the vicinity. Newtown-Ellard was their seat.

CLUGGIN FAIR is best remembered for the faction fights which took place here between the Three Year Olds and the Four Year Olds. The fair took place annually on 13 May and was one of the county's most famous fairs, rivalling the fair of Pallas Grean in its heyday. The main activities were centred in Cluggin Fair Green and the Piper's Garden, two adjoining fields about one mile north-west of Oola.

CLUGGIN derives its name from an *Cloigeann*, the Skull, a round rocky hill. Cluggin Castle, Castlecluggin, *Caisleán an Chloiginn* belonged to the MacBriens of Coonagh before it passed to the Earl of Thomond. By 1840 only the castle site adjoined the townland of Cluggin.

TUOGHCLUGGIN PARISH contained the townlands of Cluggin and Castlecluggin in 1840. It had 217 inhabitants in 1831, is situated in the barony of Coonagh, and located on the border with County Tipperary. It was recorded as *Tuath an Chloiginn i gCuanachaibh*, the District of the Skull in Coonagh, as early as 1302. The old parish church, last mentioned in 1615, was levelled before 1840.

TEMPLEBREDAN PARISH is partly in the barony of Clanwilliam, County Tipperary, and partly in that of Coonagh, County Limerick. O'Donovan stated that it derived its name from *Teampull Ui Bhrighdeáin*, O'Bredan's Church, but he was unable to find any family of this name cited in documents relating to Limerick.

TEMPLEBREDAN CHURCH may have been Templebredon Church, a Franciscan friary of which only the site is remembered, in County Tipperary. It was better known as *Killeenagallive*, *Killinenallagh* or *Kyllalie*.

LIMERICK JUNCTION survived unchanged into the second half of the twentieth century. Its unusual layout earned it an international reputation as the classic Irish railway joke. The design of its platform, a long island-platform with a series of bays and crossovers, meant that every train that

Aerial view of New Pallas.

stopped here had to complete at least one reversal to reach the platform. The station was isolated from towns or villages, in fact the nearest town is Tipperary, and it is actually located in County Tipperary. In 1967 alterations eliminated the need for so many reversals and there is now a link, so that the Limerick-Dublin trains no longer have to call here.

THE GREAT SOUTHERN AND WESTERN RAILWAY came into existence in 1842 when a group of Dublin businessmen were granted leave to construct a railway line westwards, from Dublin. The company became Ireland's largest railway company, owning a total of 1,150 miles of track at its peak. The share stocks became known as *cashels* in its early years although this "Premier Line" did not build a branch line into Cashel until 1904. The company began construction in 1845. On 4 August 1846 the first trains came into operation between Dublin and Carlow. In 1847 the train steamed into Portlaoise. This was the year in which John Porter complained of the railway company's faceless administration: "A corporation of men has neither a soul to be damned, a body to be kicked or a name to be honoured". In 1848 the first train reached Thurles. On 3 July 1848 the Waterford and Limerick Railway met with the Great Southern and Western Railway at Limerick Junction. The latter company had always intended reaching Limerick City, despite the objections of the former company, and they announced plans to do so in 1857. The two companies operated jointly from Limerick to Nenagh from 1 June 1864 but eventually amalgamated. The Limerick and Ennis Railway opened in the late 1850s. This was soon followed by the Athenry and Tuam Railway, and the Athenry and Ennis Junction Railway.

PATRICK BLAKE AND JAMES O'NEILL were accused of shooting Constable Oakley in Limerick. They were arrested, tried in Dublin by court-martial, acquitted and released. They returned homewards on the evening of 20 November, 1920. They left the train at Limerick Junction. Patrick Blake, his father, and brother Michael travelled towards Limerick in a car provided by the R.I.C.. Patrick complained of the cold. Michael took off his overcoat, insisted on Patrick wearing it, and changed places in the car with his brother. An unfortunate decision. A few minutes later as the car approached Oola a number of men jumped out on the road and forced it to halt. One of them walked up to the car, put a gun to Michael Blake's head and shot him dead. James O'Neill travelled by charabanc with his mother. Just outside Limerick Junction some men boarded the

long horse-drawn vehicle and asked Jimmy O'Neill to accompany them. His bullet-riddled body was found the following day. Both men were killed by Black and Tans in civilian clothing.

CULLEN VILLAGE is located in County Tipperary but part of the old parish extends into County Limerick. In 1774 "a great number of interesting relics of remote antiquity" were found in a small bog.

LONGSTONE is located on top of the hill which overlooks Cullen. This is a ring work with a central pillarstone and is located just off the narrow road at the summit. It would be advisable for motorists to leave their cars in Cullen and walk up the hill, rather than drive.

OOLA CASTLE was destroyed by the Earl of Kildare in 1497 but was either repaired or rebuilt during the sixteenth century. It was located on an imposing site from which one can view East Limerick and the surrounding countryside. The castle, a gabled tower house was either an O'Brien or MacBrien stronghold. In 1690 Patrick Sarsfield surprised the castle in the night, blew it up, and destroyed the Williamite siege train. The castle was partly repaired by King William's forces but by 1837 it was "a stately heap of ruins, with here and there a wall nearly entire. The ruins of the church and of Oola Castle, stand close to the R.C. chapel". A concrete path by the side of Ballyneety Catholic Church leads towards the ruins which are better known today as Sarsfield's Rock, Sarsfield's Ballyneety or Ballyneety Rock. In 1976 the President of Ireland, Cearbhall O Dálaigh, unveiled a memorial to Patrick Sarsfield on this site. Near this is a commemorative plaque to P.J. Canon Lee, who was parish priest from 1958 to 1977. Only the outline of the original buildings remain, covered by earth and grass.

SARSFIELD'S ROCK entered history on the night of 11-12 August, 1690. King William's forces camped overnight on the flat ground north of the Rock, described by Begley as "a remarkable conical eminence", on their way to Limerick with a powder train, cannon and other military supplies. Patrick Sarsfield (1644-1693) intercepted them here with a 600-strong Jacobite raiding party, which was allowed into the centre of the Williamite camp when the first sentry's challenge elicited the correct password. A second challenge was met with the words "Sarsfield is the watchword — Sarsfield is the man". The raiders swept through the unsuspecting, sleeping, enemy camp. "Men were sabred and shot to death where they lay. Then Sarsfield had their cannon loaded to the muzzle, sunk in the earth and discharged, with an explosion which was heard even in the city itself". This

raid bought the Jacobite forces a little more time but by then the outcome of the war was a foregone conclusion. After their defeat at the Battle of the Boyne the Irish soldiers were still willing to fight if only the Williamites would swap kings. James II is remembered, in song and in story as a worthless figure:

Séamus a' Chaca a chaill dúinn Eire,
A leath-chos Gall, a leath-chos Gael
which translates as,
"James the Shit, who lost us Ireland,
Half-footed foreign, half-footed Irish".
One of the details often overlooked in recounting the story of Sarsfield's raid is the fact that the Jacobites raided what was essentially a civilian group under military escort. The Williamite train was mainly composed of women and children, accompanying the powder wagons to Limerick.

SARSFIELD'S RIDE, an epic two-day trip, to Ballyneety started off northwards from Limerick in order to confuse the enemy. Sarsfield's party travelled through Knockalisheen, Glennagross, Kilnacreagh, Oatfield, towards Clonlara, on to Bridgetown, Ballycorney — where a young man was taken prisoner lest he should warn the Williamites — Garraunboy, and Killaloe. Galloping O'Hogan, a *rapparee,* guided the Jacobites to a ford across the Shannon at Ballyvally, and they continued northwards into the Tountinna Mountains before turning south to meet with other *rapparees* at Labadiha Bridge or Hogan's Glen. They then made camp at Ballyhourigan Wood before moving southwards through Toor, Knockacappul, Rear Cross, Knockshanbrittas, Foilycleary, Moanvaun, Losset, Knockanavar, Toem, Clonbrick, Moanmore and Monard. Jacobite scouts met the wife of a Williamite soldier bathing her feet in a stream east of Cullen. She probably believed they were members of King William's army as she told them that the password for the night was *Sarsfield.*

DERK HOUSE was erected about 1770. This was one of the principal houses in the area in 1837. Lewis wrote that one could see the Rock of Cashel in the distance from here and that the old road used by King William on his march from Golden Bridge to Limerick was nearby. In later times Derk was the home of a Jesuit priest, Fr. Daniel Considine, a writer of spiritual pamphlets and books. The house is still occupied.

SOURCE REFERENCE NUMBERS
5 6 9 11 39 64 107 120 123 129 140 148 149 150 167 173 175 184 192 194 195 207 233 239 246

Pallaskenry

Ringmoylan · Kilcornan · Beagh · Curragh Chase

PALLASKENRY derives its name from *Pailis Chaonraighe,* the Castle, Defensive Structure or Palisade of the *Caonraighe.*

THE KENRY, *Caonraighe, Caonraí* or Tribe of *Caon,* was a name applied to the inhabitants of this area for almost two millenniums. They were ruled by the *Ui Fidhgheinte,* descendants of Eoghan Mór, King of Munster in 200 A.D., until about the middle of the tenth century when the O'Donovans assumed control of the region and ousted the *Ui Fidgeinte.* The O'Donovans had been rulers of the *U i Chairbre* prior to this and their new territory became known as *Caonraí Uí Chairbre* until Domhnall Mór O'Brien and the Anglo-Normans drove them into West Cork and Kerry during the twelfth century.

MULHOLLAND is a surname which can be traced back to the days of the *Ui Fidgeinte.* It is derived from *O Maolchallann,* the descendant of the Chief of the Kalends. Variants of this surname include Holland, Maholland, Mulholn, Mulhallen, O Mohallan, *O Maghallon* and *O Mulchallan.* Although this surname can be traced back to a branch of the *Ui Fidhgheinte,* one-time rulers of the Kenry, there are two other distinct families of the same name outside of Limerick. These are the *O Maolchallann* of Dealbna Beg, barony of Demifore, County Meath and an ecclesiastical family in Ulster who were keepers of the Bell of the Testament, or Bell of St. Patrick, from the start of the twelfth century to the end of the eighteenth century.

PALLASKENRY was described by Samuel Lewis in 1837 as a market and post-town, formerly called Newmarket, "which is one of the most improving [towns] in the county ... and comprises 115 houses, the greater number of which are well built, but covered with thatch. Petty sessions are held once a fortnight: it is a chief constabulary police station, and contains the dispensary for the barony, which has a resident physician and is open daily. The market, held on Thursday, is well attended and amply supplied with provisions". Although farming was the mainstay of the area, flax-dressing, spinning and linen weaving gave employment to many.

THE CHAPEL-RUSSELL LOAN FUND was an early nineteenth-century development grant funded by the Earl of Charleville, the County of Limerick Trustees, the London Committee, the Peasantry Society and the County of Limerick Ladies' Society, who subscribed a total of £218 between them in 1823. This money was used to promote and encourage "the spirit of industry ... The fund was lent out in small portions, sometimes in money, but more frequently in wool, flax and implements for manufacture, such as wheels, reels and looms, and is repaid by weekly instalments, in which the manufactured goods are taken at a liberal valuation. In seasons of scarcity provisions are issued, and articles for clothing and bedding occasionally". By 1836 the Trustees of the fund were able to report a profit of £76.

CHAPEL-RUSSELL PARISH was originally called *Killuragh, Kilelura, Killenalotar, Cillenalotar,* or *Killulta.* Dr. Elrington, the Church of Ireland Bishop of Limerick, created this parish in the early 1800s. Prior to that, Chapel-Russell was part of Ardcanny parish and, before 1785, was little more than an open field on which a great number of cattle were kept. The Church of Ireland parish church built in 1822 was demolished in 1958. By 1837 there was a Catholic church at White Forge and the parish also contained a Methodist church, which is now a garage. The name Chapel-Russell applied to the old Church of Killuragh, *Cill Iuragh,* the Church of the Yews, half a mile east of Pallaskenry as early as 1418. Only the graveyard now remains of this older foundation but there is a ruin called Killulta Church off the main Limerick to Askeaton road.

GERALD GRIFFIN (1803-1840) lived with his brother William, the local doctor, for almost ten years. He wrote part of *The Collegians* and his *Tales of the Munster Festivals* while residing here. In 1834 part of a golden fibula, or brooch, was found in a drain near the Church of Ireland church. This weighed 3oz. and passed into the possession of Sir Aubrey de Vere. An ancient silver dagger was also discovered about the same time in a quarry near the town.

PALLASKENRY CASTLE or Shanpallas Castle is located on Dermot O'Sullivan's land in the townland of Shanpallas. This castle was also known as *Caisleán Chaonraí* or Kenry Castle. The original name, *Sean Phailis,* was derived from the Old Wooden Palisade, one of which may have been erected here on the site of an earlier ring fort, possibly by the Anglo-Normans. Lewis claims that this castle was built by the O'Donovans and was subsequently occupied, enlarged and strengthened by the Fitzgeralds of Desmond. As the O'Donovans had left Kenry by the end of the twelfth century, it may be safe to assume that they had founded either the ring fort or the palisade from which the stone castle developed. By 1583 Shanpallas was occupied by a man responsible for another of its names, *Pallice MacWilliam Chym,* the Palisade of MacWilliam the Crooked. A great part of its walls fell in 1834. In 1840 John O'Donovan wrote that even though the south wall had fallen down to the first arch, the arch over the ground floor, the other walls were perfect. The building had been five storeys high, with six foot-thick walls reaching to a height of sixty feet and a yard, enclosed by a wall over thirty feet high in places, was located on a rock fifteen feet east of the castle. The ruins cover over half an acre of ground and are located about one mile east of Pallaskenry. They are now very ruined and overgrown but still impressive.

CAPTAIN JOHN FITZGERALD, a member of the family who once held Pallaskenry Castle, saved the life of his prince, later King Charles II, at the Battle of Naseby in 1645. After the Restoration Fitzgerald received a pension of £200 per annum from the grateful monarch.

PALLASKENRY, or the barony of Kenry, was regarded as one of the county's leading agricultural areas in 1837 when it was "most remarkable for the abundant crops and fine quality of its grain. The wheat crops are everywhere very heavy; and the produce of

Aerial view of Pallaskenry.

potatoes is about sixty barrels, in some instances one hundred barrels, of twenty-one stone each per acre".

COPESWOOD HOUSE is an agricultural college run by the Salesian Fathers, a link between the area's agricultural past and the farming methods proposed for the future.

CACKAGAY CIDER, or Cockagay Cider, was produced in great quantities in the Pallaskenry, Adare, Croom, Rathkeale and Kilpeacon regions. The name Cackagay was coined by a Clareman who made the English traveller and writer, Young, the unsuspecting butt of some Irish humour. The unknown Dalcassian assured Young that the correct name of the cider produced within the Palatinate was Cockagay Cider and Young and several other eighteenth and nineteenth century writers perpetuated the term. The joke originated because of the Palatine custom of keeping geese within the orchards and feeding them on "windfalls", apples that fell off the trees. The name was an Anglicised version of *các a' ghéidh,* the Irish for goose-droppings.

QUERN CIDER PRESSES were used in the manufacture of cider. Walter Ruttle of Fort

View, Rathkeale, remembers seeing one in his uncle's home as a child and told me that he believed Johnny Bowen of Court Matrix was the last man to use one in the Rathkeale area.

SHANNONGROVE HOUSE is an early eighteenth century house started by John Bury about 1709 and completed by his son, William in 1723. This Queen Anne residence has the Bury coat-of-arms and the date 1710 inscribed on a shield above the old front door-way. It was built in the Dutch Palladian style and may have been designed by a member of the Rothery family. It is a two storey high building, erected over a basement and is flanked by two symmetrical wings. There are four wide brick-patterned chimneys set diagonally and joined by an ornamental brick-screen, a high pitched roof and a dormered attic on this magnificent old building which has been almost continually occupied since it was built. It was restored in 1988 after having been closed, but never neglected, for a few years.

PHINEAS BURY came into possession of 5,310 acres of land in Kenry as one of the Adventurers who was allocated land under the

Cromwellian settlement. Shannongrove was then known as Killasuragh and had been the property of Edmund Fitzgerald until he was dispossessed by the Cromwellians. The Bury family lived here for almost two centuries and were prominent figures as landlords, magistrates, high sheriffs and grand jurymen within the county. In 1844 Bolton Waller purchased Shannongrove House, and the 398-acre demesne on which it was located, from the Burys. He had been a tenant of theirs for some years before this, and lived here until 1854. John Sheehy, Askeaton, bought the house in 1860 and his descendants lived here until they sold it in 1947. The Fielding, Armitage and Griffith families occupied and owned Shannongrove House until it last changed hands a few years ago. Shannongrove House is now the property of Carleton Varney, one of America's leading interior decorators.

THE SHANNONGROVE COLLAR was found in boglands belonging to the Bury family during the Williamite wars. It was never declared to be treasure trove and became a Bury family heirloom. In 1760 General

Vallancey arrived in Ireland to work in the Ordnance Survey and in the course of his travels he heard of the Bury "collar of gold". The family allowed him to weigh it and he noted that its weight equalled that of 22 golden guineas. Lieutenant-Colonel Howard Bury was the last member of the Bury family to own the Shannongrove Collar. He led the Mount Everest expedition of 1921. Before World War II Howard Bury was approached by Sir Shane Leslie and Liam S. Gógáin of the National Museum, Dublin and he showed them the family heirloom which was estimated to be 2,500 years old. In 1948 the Shannongrove Collar was presented to the Victoria and Albert Museum, London.

THE SHANNONGROVE COLUMBARI-UM is an ornamental pigeon cote which may have been built as a deliberate folly by the Burys.

THE SHANNONGROVE SCHOOL, the Charter School, or Blue School, was founded by William Bury in 1735. It was built for £5000 and was called the Blue School because of the blue clothing worn by its pupils. Boys were taught farming and various trades before being apprenticed, and girls were instructed in domestic economy as a preparation for domestic service. The boys were employed on the Bury farm during the day to bolster the school's finances. It closed in 1835.

THE RINGMOYLAN WINDMILL is a large tower-like structure located in the front garden of a modern house. This old ruin abuts on the road that leads to the quay. Its other name, the *Babby House,* was derived from a nursery which was built at the rear of the lodge at the main entrance to Shannongrove when infants were eventually accepted as pupils in the Shannongrove School. I was unable to discover why the name was apparently transferred to the ruined windmill.

RINGMOYLAN QUAY was an important harbour facility in bygone days when waterborne vessels competed for passenger and cargo traffic along the Shannon. The growth of the railways, followed by the invention of the internal combustion engine, meant that quays like this lost their former commercial importance as centres of transport. Ringmoylan Quay is directly across the river from Shannon Airport. There is an open-air swimming pool to the west of the quay, which is a popular recreational area with the local people.

BUSHY ISLAND is one of several small islands lying off Kenry. This name dates from the eighteenth century and applies to the mainland adjacent to the island, as well as to the island itself. Sir Hardress Waller had a castle on the island which was a ruin by 1655. Islandmore, *An tOileán Mór,* the Big Island, or *Oileán Mór an Ridire,* the Knight's Big Island, were the older names of this island, which was obviously a Geraldine holding, held by the Knights of Glin.

CASTLETOWN was partly an island until about 1860, when the Wallers built a retaining bank to prevent the tide-waters spreading as far as Washpool. On the part once known as the Island are the remains of a private mental hospital operated by Dr. John Peppard during the middle years of the nineteenth century.

CASTLETOWN MANOR was demolished in 1935 but a large section of its kitchen-garden wall is still visible alongside the public road not too far from Castletown Church of

Part of the estate of the Pallaskenry Agricultural College.

241

Ireland Church. The manor was reputedly built with stones from Castletown Castle, which was located a short distance away, to the north, but by 1837 little of it remained.

KILCORNAN CASTLE, Castletownwaller, Castlekenry, or Castletown Castle, developed from a Viking stronghold, the Fort of Moige, which Samuel Lewis dated to 1041. In 1164 another defensive structure was erected on the same site, possibly by the O'Donovans, but this soon fell into Anglo-Norman hands. The Fitzgeralds came into possession of the castle but lost it after the Desmond Rebellion. It appears to have been a substantial building as 600 acres of land was set aside for its deer park and 400 people sought shelter here in 1642. In 1641 it was garrisoned by Royalists but by 1642 it was in Parliamentarian hands when it was surrendered to General Purcell and his Confederate Irish forces. Kilcornan Castle was amongst the castles of Kenry recaptured by Sir Hardress Waller over a two-year period. Soldiers were garrisoned here after the Cromwellian wars and it is from this period that the name Castletownwaller dates.

SIR HARDRESS WALLER came into possession of Castletown Castle, probably as a free tenant, about 1622. In 1644 he was made Governor of Cork and served as commanding officer of the Parliamentarian forces in Munster in the absence of Lord Inchiquin. He was appointed a judge during the trial of Charles I and returned to Ireland with the rank of Major-General after the king's execution in January 1649. A relation of his, Sir William Waller, Groombridge, Kent, was also a Parliamentarian general and a regicide. After the Restoration Sir Hardress Waller lost most of his holdings around Kenry but managed to retain Castletownwaller. This may have been due to the influence of Sir Henry Ingoldsby, his father-in-law, who had supported the Stuarts. Tradition differs in relating how Sir Hardress Waller died. Some accounts claim he died as a political prisoner in Jersey; others claim that his enemies sealed him into a barrel, with inward-projecting spikes, and rolled him downhill to his death near Castletown while a third account claims that he died in bed at an advanced age. His family once boasted that they farmed from Adare to the Shannon. In 1861 one of his descendants, Rev. John Thomas Waller, Rector of Kilcornan, sparked off a series of incidents known as the "Souper Riots" by putting up anti-Catholic placards in Pallaskenry. Fifty-two people were later charged with rioting and assault.

KILCORNAN CHURCH according to Samuel Lewis, was founded by the Viking chieftain who established the Kilcornan stronghold originally known as the Fort of Moige. The name Kilcornan is derived from *Cill Churnáin,* Curnan's Church. St. Curnán Beag's feast-day on 6 January was a holiday in former times and a fair was held on it. The church ruins have all but disappeared but part of them may have been incorporated into the Waller vault. The name Kilcornan referred to the townland now known as Moige East, or Moige East Glebe, until about 1700, but was later applied to the parish. The name passed out of use for a while, replaced by Stonehall, until the 1930s.

KILCORNAN is the name today of the village which developed along the mail road which was built to connect Limerick with Tralee in the early 1800s. This is almost two miles south of Kilcornan church mentioned as *Kellchurnan* in an inquisition taken by William de Burgo in 1200-1201.

KILCORNAN CHURCH OF IRELAND PARISH CHURCH is better known as Casteltownwaller or Castletown Church. This is on the opposite side of the road to, and several hundred yards away from, the original Kilcornan Church site. In 1831 an older Church of Ireland church on this site was demolished and "a spacious and handsome edifice with a lofty embattled tower, was built entirely of hewn marble, at an expense of £1500". In 1831 the parish contained 3,840 inhabitants on 9,637 acres. The land near the Shannon was fertile and under cultivation while that towards the south was "much encumbered with stones scattered in every direction ... the principal seats are Castletown, the elegant residence of J. Waller ... Hollypark, the ancient residence of the Taylor family, now the property of Sir Aubrey de Vere, Baronet; Summerville, the ancient seat of Lord Charleville, now occupied by an agent; Castle Grey, of G. Langford, Esq.; Stonehall of E. Langford, Esq.; and Bushy Island of P. Low, Esq.. There are also many large and substantial farmhouses, and several very neat cottages ... In the R.C. divisions this parish is at the head of a union or district called Stonehall and Cappagh, comprising also the parishes of Cappagh and Nantinan; the old chapel is in the village of Stonehall, and a handsome chapel of hewn marble was built at Boherbuie in 1832 ... Near Stonehall are some very small but interesting lakes, on the shores of which are vestiges of ancient buildings".

BEAGH CASTLE looks northwards towards Shannon Airport and the Fergus Estuary. John FitzJohn Fitzgerald built the first castle here some time about 1260. It remained in his family, the Knights of Glin, until it was confiscated by the Crown in 1573. It was granted to Sir William Drury, the President of Munster. Drury hanged 400 people by "justice and mar-

tial law", including a friar and a *brehon,* before he died in 1579. A large bawn surrounds the remains of the castle, which had three arched vaults, of which only one is still complete. The ground floor is vaulted but as the building is in poor condition children should not be allowed upstairs. Loopholes can be seen in the east wall, which overlooks the pier. The structure to the west of the castle was known as the battery during the last century. As batteries or gun emplacements were erected at strategic points along the Shannon during the Napoleonic wars, it is quite possibly dating from this period. During the seventeenth century a ferry operated regularly between Beagh and County Clare. In Cromwellian times some of the transplanted Irish, given the option of choosing *Hell or Connaught,* probably embarked from here.

BEAGH derives its name from *Beitheach,* the Place Abounding with Birch Trees, but in the distant past the area west of Kenry was known as Iverus, an Anglicised version of *Uibh Rosa,* after a tribe, the *Tuath O Rosa,* who had settled here.

BEAGH CHURCH, or Iverus Church, was built on an elevated site overlooking the ancient parish of Iverus. This was one of three churches, which local tradition maintains were built by three sisters although no saint, founder or patron was remembered in 1840. The other two churches were Kileen Church, in Kilcornan parish and the church in Cappagh. In 1837 Samuel Lewis claimed that Beagh Church was founded by a Viking named Iverus in 824 but this story appears to have been long since disproved. The earliest reference to Beagh Church dates from 1237. Located in the townland of Ballyaglish, *Baile na hEaglaise,* the Townland of the Church, this ruined ecclesiastical building appeared to have been renovated prior to 1988. Its walls were in excellent condition, there was a small window and door in the south wall and the graveyard was neat and tidy. The church had few distinctive features and the concrete paths in the graveyard seemed to be of recent construction.

SAMUEL LEWIS noted in 1837 that Iverus "is embellished with many elegant houses, the chief of which are Ballysteen, the residence of E. Westropp, Esq.; Miltown of the Rev. A. Champagne; Ballynacourty, of T.E. Davenport, Esq.; Castle View of H. Ross, Esq.; and Beigh, of the Rev. G. Maxwell; besides many good farmhouses, around which are flourishing orchards. The country around Miltown is peculiarly beautiful, being highly cultivated, well fenced, and adorned with cottages and lodges". There was no Church of Ireland church in Iverus in 1837 so divine service was held in the parochial school. There was, however, a Catholic church in Ballysteen. Only the stables of Miltown House remain although it is still featured on the *Ordnance Survey* map.

CURRAGH CHASE derives its name from *Currach*, a bog. The Anglicised version, Curragh, was applied to the estate, castle and house of the Hunt family until the nineteenth century, when Sir Aubrey Vere Hunt changed his surname to de Vere and the name of the estate to Curragh Chase.

THE HUNT FAMILY were descendants of a signatory of the *Magna Carta*, a twelfth-century Earl of Oxford, and an Elizabethan courtier who was believed to have been the "true" author of Shakespeare's plays. According to the census survey of 1659 John Vere Hunt received a grant of "Curra and bog" under the Cromwellian settlement of the county. His namesake and descendant, John Vere Hunt, became a baron in 1774. As a Member of Parliament for Askeaton he voted for the Act of Union and raised two regiments of Volunteers from amongst his tenants. He had a local reputation as a nationalist because he once, jokingly, informed his militia that they were going to join the French at Ringmoylan Quay. In 1785 he founded a theatrical society at Curragh Chase with John Bateman Fitzgerald, the Knight of Glin.

SIR AUBREY DE VERE (1788-1846) was born here and educated at Harrow. He married Lord Monteagle's sister, Mary, and is remembered as a caring landlord who resided on his estate and looked after his tenants. Like his father, he was interested in the arts but wrote little until he reached his thirties. In 1822 he produced his first work, *Julian the Apostate*. He died on 28 July 1846 and his last work, *Mary Tudor*, was published posthumously in 1847. His eldest son, Stephen, succeeded to the baronetcy; travelled on, and investigated, the coffin ships; translated *Péarla an Bhrollaigh Bháin* into English as *The Snowy-Breasted Pearl*; and converted to Catholicism in 1847. When he died in 1904 the baronetcy became extinct.

AUBREY DE VERE (1814-1902) was a well-known poet during his own lifetime. He was acknowledged to be a good poet by his acquaintances, Browning, Tennyson, Thackeray and Wordsworth. Sir William Rowan Hamilton, the Astronomer Royal, in Dublin University, and Cardinals Manning and Wiseman were also close friends of Aubrey's. In November 1851 Aubrey converted to Catholicism but despite his conversion he had little else in common with the local people. He sympathised with their plight, hero-worshipped Patrick Sarsfield, approved of the Act of Union and was opposed to the Fenian and Land League movements.

CURRAGH CHASE is now a State forest complete with nature trails, a forest walk and an arboretum where specimens of shrubs and trees are cultivated. When the Hunt family came here first the area was heavily wooded. They retained and improved the woodland over the succeeding centuries. Tradition maintains that Capability Browne trained some of the Hunt workmen as landscape gardeners. In 1897 Aubrey de Vere wrote that the lake had not been there during his childhood as "at the bottom of the lawn there now spreads a lake, but at that time it was rich meadow land, divided by a slender stream, with fair green hills beyond. The pleasure ground blends insensibly with the lawns and woods". The Forest and Wildlife Service continues the work of the Hunt and de Vere families today. Curragh Chase is now a popular recreation ground with camping and caravan park facilities as well as a series of attractive picnic areas.

CURRAGH CHASE HOUSE was built on the site of a former Purcell stronghold, Curragh Castle, in the latter half of the seventeenth century. The present ruin dates from the late eighteenth century. This was a large two storey house erected over a basement. A Limerick architect designed the short adjoining front in the late 1700s, while Sir Aubrey de Vere added the longer facade about 1829. Tennyson and his son, Hallam, stayed here in 1848. The house was accidentally destroyed by fire in December 1941.

BALLYGLEAGHAN CASTLE was a Geraldine stronghold which was captured by the English in 1569. This was later retaken by the Fitzgeralds who burned it in 1580. It was the home of David Og McLoghie whose followers defeated Sir George Carew's forces in Kenry and provoked Carew into slaughtering 150 women and children at the Purcell castle in Ballyculhane. David Og was captured on Scattery Island by Turlough MacMahon on 18 December 1581, handed over to Oliver Stephenson as a prisoner, and executed in Limerick. The castle was listed as Ballyglahane in 1659 and was owned by the Knights of Glin, James II while he was Duke of York, George Beston and Lancelot Bostock before passing into the possession of William Taylor in 1703. Parts of it still survive. A turret and large flanker can be seen alongside Hollypark House, which was built on the same site.

HOLLYPARK HOUSE was built in a Georgian-Gothic style by the Taylors during the eighteenth century. The Taylor family later sold it to the de Veres and moved to *Ard Lomán*, the Height of the Bare Rocks, which they had renamed Stonehall at about the same time as they were building Hollypark House.

The name Old Stonehall is now applied to this area. In 1978 Mark Bence-Jones wrote that John Philip Cohane had restored Hollypark House which had been burned some years before.

KILLEEN PRIORY, or Killeen Abbey, in Cowpark was mentioned by Samuel Lewis in 1837 as an interesting ruin "on the new line of road, near Holly Park". This well-preserved parish church dates from the fifteenth century and resembles a defensive structure rather than a church because of its narrow windows and turret-style bell tower. It was used as a Catholic church until 1811 and was repaired under the direction of Canon Wall, during the 1930s. The stones forming the window were discovered when the ground was dug up and, with the exception of the keystone, which could not be found, replaced. The water-font is considered unusual.

KILLULTA CHURCH is believed to be one of the earliest surviving churches of its type in the county. It is known locally as the *Teampaillín* and has been dated as being no later than the eleventh century and earlier than the twelfth century by Liam de Paor and Peter Harbison. In 1905 T.J. Westropp wrote that the east end of the church with a triangular-headed window in the gable was intact but that the western gable and door had been reconstructed. Liam de Paor later remarked on the "shallow pocking produced by hammer dressing" and the "wrought masonry" which was of excellent quality. The site was used as a *cillín* or children's burial ground until 1910. It is located on rising ground to the north of the Mungret-Askeaton road.

SOURCE REFERENCE NUMBERS
9 11 13 28 44 46 47 53
64 67 86 106 120 123 129 157
184 188 192 220 238 282

Patrickswell

Attyflin · Kilpeacon · Crecora

PATRICKSWELL, *Tobar Phadraig,* was described by Samuel Lewis in 1837, under the more complete title of St. Patrick's Well. "This place derives its name from a well dedicated to St. Patrick, and still held in great veneration by the peasantry, over which has recently been placed a figure of the tutelar (sic) saint, rudely carved in stone. The village consists of one long and irregular street, and contains 89 houses, most of which are old thatched buildings, and the remainder neat, well built cottages roofed with slate and of recent erection; the mail from Limerick to Tralee passes daily through it, and a penny post to the former place has been lately established. Fairs are held on 26 February, 28 May, 16 June,14 and 20 October, and 18 December, principally for cattle and pigs; petty sessions once a fortnight; and a constabulary police force is stationed here. In the neighbourhood are several large and handsome houses with well-wooded demesnes, and numerous good farm-houses with thriving orchards, producing abundance of apples from which excellent cider is made ... The surrounding scenery is enlivened by several good houses and well-planted demesnes; the principal are Fort Etna ... and Attyflin". The main Killarney-Limerick and Cork-Limerick roads meet to the south-west of the village, becoming one highway from there into Limerick.

PATRICKSWELL RAILWAY STATION developed from the laying of two railway lines which passed through the village. In 1853 the Limerick-Foynes railway line was authorised and the first train came into operation on it in 1858. Two years later a Limerick-Cork line was authorised to connect Patrickswell and Charleville. As a result of this a railway station, or halt, was required in the village. This was located within easy reach of Attyflin House and contributed substantially to the growth of the village. It closed in 1977.

ATTYFLIN, Attyflinn, Atyfloyne, Atiflewin, Artiflony, or *Atiflewin,* derives its name from *Aít Tí Flainn* or *Atteach Flainn,* the House or Place of Flan. This Flan is believed to have been a brother of Brian Dubh O'Brien, Lord of Carrigogunnell. Folklore relates how Flan, a hospitable man and a professed infidel, became a monk when his written promise to support the monks of Monasteranenagh was thrown on a weighing scale and proved to be heavier than his more usual contribution of beef. Attyflin and Carrogogunnell are linked elsewhere in folklore. As a child T.J. Westropp heard of a malignant witch, Grana, who lit a fairy candle every night on Carrigogunnell, the Rock of the Candle, *Carraig a gCoinneal.* Anyone who saw the baleful light of this candle died. St. Patrick, protected by his faith, ascended the rock and threw the candle into the River Shannon. He saw Grana climbing towards him and jumped westwards to avoid her. She tore a huge mass of rock from the ground and threw it at him in rage. Her aim was poor. Grana's massive missile missed its target and landed in the meadows of Corcamore, where it became known as Cloughregan. Thomas Crofton Croker related this tale in his *Fairy Legends* but attributed the quenching of the candle to Regan, one of Fionn MacCumhail's warriors.

ATTYFLIN HOUSE is a Georgian residence dating from the early to middle years of the eighteenth century. It comprised four reception rooms, seven main bedrooms and three bathrooms in July 1978 when it was bought by the present owner Eamon G. Howard. The wings are lower than the central section and date from the early nineteenth century. The Westropp Arms, a lion rampant, can be seen above the front door on the external wall of the earlier house. Attyflin underwent many changes over the years. Almost all the present offices were erected before 1840 as they correspond exactly with those mapped by John O'Donovan before that date. Mountford Westropp settled in Limerick about 1657. After the Cromwellian settlement he received an unconfirmed grant of Attyflin but failed to take up possession, as its *titulado* in 1659 was named as Edward Lewis. The land was granted to James, Duke of York, later King James II, in 1660. The Countess of Orkney took out a tenancy on Attyflin and then sub-let it to Thomas Moore. The land was later forfeited when James II was ousted by William. In 1703 Mountford's son and namesake, purchased Attyflin from the Chichester House Commissioners for £760. There was then another house, which has long since disappeared, on the land, west of the present structure.

MOUNTFORD WESTROPP, also known as Mountifort or Montifort Westropp, was appointed Comptroller of Limerick Harbour for life in February 1660. He was married to Frances, the second daughter of Thomas Taylor of Ballinort, Askeaton, in 1659. He purchased Ballynamean in 1665; Kilkerin in 1671 and Drumline and Bunratty in County Clare. In 1674 he was High Sheriff of that county and was Commissioner of Clare in 1687. In 1690 his arms and horses were confiscated by the Jacobites. He was one of the Commissioners for Clare in 1697 and died in Bunratty on 10 September 1698. The Westropps of Attyflin, Carduggan, Lismehane (Fortanne), Roxborough, Coolreagh, Ross, Quinsborough, Mellon, Ballysteen, Richmond, Cork, Ardcanny, Kilkerin and India descended from Mountford. He was buried in Sixmilebridge, County Clare.

MOUNTIFORT WESTROPP of Bunratty purchased Attyflin in 1703. He was married to Elizabeth Bury of Shannongrove. He died in 1726. Elizabeth died in 1768. They had a son, John, who was High Sheriff of Limerick in 1745 and married Mary Berkeley. His line became extinct with his death in 1781 but he had devised Attyflin to his cousin, Ralph of Lismehane (Maryfort), County Clare.

RALPH WESTROPP married Mary Johnson, the daughter and co-heiress of William Johnson of Lisard. He was High Sheriff of Clare in 1771-2. In June 1806 he died and was buried at Tulla.

JOHN WESTROPP (1762-1839) of Maryfort and Attyflin, married his cousin Anna Burdett Ness of Osgodby, County York. He was High Sheriff of the county in 1798-99. He was buried at Kilpeacon.

JOHN WESTROPP (1814-1866) married Georgina Wilhelmina, daughter and co-heiress, of Col. George William Stamer of Carnelly, Clarecastle, in May 1836. She died in 1852. John married again. His second wife

Attyflin House.

Charlotte Louisa Whitehead, was also his cousin.

JOHN THOMAS MASSY WESTROPP, the eldest son of John Westropp and Georgina Wilhelmina Stamer, had property in Attyflin, Clonmoney and Doonass. He was born in 1837, served in the army and married Margaret Wilson of Rawcliffe Hall, Lancaster. She died in 1885. John died in 1903. His daughter, Mary Georgina, married Arthur White, the eldest son of Edward White of Fort Etna on 17 May 1905.

THE WESTROPP FAMILY trace their genealogical roots back to Edward de Westhorpe and his wife Johan de Manby, who were living at Brompton, York, in 1282. The family surname had changed to Westhorpe by 1421 when William Westhorpe was one of a jury that tried a claim of Whitby Abbey to certain lands. By the end of the fifteenth century the name had altered to Westropp. Captain Thomas Westropp served in the English army from 1568 to 1589. He was the first member of the family recorded in Ireland as he fought here during the "Irish War". He received a pension from Elizabeth I for the loss of his right arm and for services to the crown. Thomas returned to England, died in York in 1604, without issue, and was buried at Sutton.

THE WESTROPP FAMILY RELATION-SHIPS from the late thirteenth to the late sev-enteenth century were concentrated in England. These consisted of family surnames like de Boleby, de Manby, Linaker, Greene, Thweng, Salvyn, Wentworth, Morson, Palmes, Meynell, Witham, Conyers, Sayer, Gowerley, Lepton, Fairfax, Askwith, Laycock, Jeffryson, Wasse, Osbaldeston, and Peacock. From the seventeenth century onwards the extended Westropp family net-work expanded, particularly throughout Ireland, to include many of the more notable land-owning families of the eighteenth and nineteenth centuries. The list includes sur-names such as Taylor, Berkeley, Loftus, Atkins, Roberts, Watkins, Ross Lewin, Morony, Hickman, Keily, Macnamara, Townsend, Nugent, Molony, Sampson, Bolton, Harrison Moreland, Colclough, Thornhill, Maberly, Piercy, O'Callaghan, Kiernan, White, Crofton, Swift, Fitzgerald, Gabbett, Randall, Becher, Godsell, Bruen, Wallis, Armstrong, Anderson, Lowndes, Fulton, Freeman, Kenny, Twemlow, Hall, Bell, Woodman, Tyler, Shotton, Gibbings, Splaine, Spens, Rhoades, Need, Shaw, Hockin, Beecher, Stewart, Hughes, Exham, Beattie, Bustead, Saunders, Morgan, Anderson, Drought, Dudley, Seymour, Adams, Saunders, Odell, St. Ledger, Wilkinson, Bury, Browne, Clough, Massey, Bindon, Dawson, Vendeleur, Hobson, Ruggles-Brise Welch, Jencken, Vernon, Low, Gavin, Galwey, Collis, Minchin, Stacpoole, Lloyd, Lindsay, Gresham, O'Reilly, Finch, Lowe, Furnell, Bennett, Jones, Smith, Spaight, Ward, Lavitt, Longfield, Massy, Johnson, Evans, O'Grady, Vereker, Ormsby, M'Cree, Stamer, Rose, Keating, Jackson, Brereton, Jameson, Ness, Brady, Chapman, Wilme, Barry, Whitehead, ffrance, Barker, Crawley and Montague.

FAMOUS WESTROPP RELATIVES and in-laws included Major-General Lord Clarina; General Sir Thomas MacMahon; Sir Drury Wray; Charles Moore, Sixth Earl and First Marquess of Drogheda; George Evans, First Lord Carbery; Charles Vereker, Second Viscount Gort; Sir Hugh Dillon Massy; Alphonse, Count Danileski; and last, but not least, Thomas Johnson Westropp.

THOMAS JOHNSON WESTROPP (1860-1922) is the most renowned member of the Westropp family. He was born in Tulla, County Clare, on 16 August 1860, the son of John Westropp of Attyflin, by his second wife, Charlotte Louisa Whitehead of Uplands Hall, Lancaster. He was reared in Attyflin where he assimilated the history, folklore, myth and legends of his native country at an early age. During his life-time he visited almost every known archaeological site in Ireland; prepared notes and sketches on cook-ing places, middens, cairns, tombs, forts, cas-tles, churches and other minor monuments that would have been overlooked but for his documentation; and left a rich treasure trove of published material which is one of the prime sources used by local historians of today. His extensive family connections gave him access and entry to virtually every big house in Ireland.

MARY MORONEY of the Clare County Library brought a small hand-written notebook to my attention on 13 January 1989. Entitled *Miscellanea* it contained notes on the Westropps and related families; and had been compiled by Thomas Johnson Westropp whose name and address were inscribed on one of the inside pages; "Thomas Johnson Westropp, Springfort, Limerick, Sep. 14th 1881". He had also initialled a note underneath: "Let this book be preserved, Ap. 13 '82". From an early age he travelled throughout Ireland, recording what he could. He was a prolific writer, and a hardy traveller. His explorations covered a prodigious amount of territory long before the advent of the motorcar. His remarkable career is remembered only in the libraries and museums of Ireland.

THE O'BRIENS AND BOURKES presided over Patrickswell and the surrounding area until they were ousted by the Westropps and other English settlers. Teige O'Brien held Attyflin and Cahirduff in 1583. He sided with the Geraldines during the Desmond Rebellion and died an outlaw, his estates forfeited to the Crown. Brian Duff O'Brien surrendered his lands formally to Queen Elizabeth I in June 1584. On July 9, 1584, she confirmed him in ownership of practically all of Pubblebrien, including *Atiflewin.* Anver O'Brien of Attyflin sided with Hugh O'Donnell in 1601, and was slain in rebellion, while Aweone O'Brien of *Athiefloyn* received a pardon in the same year. Brien O'Brien laid claim to part of Attiflyn in 1633. In 1638 it was held by Conor Keown O'Brien. Margaret Stephenson, Brian Duff O'Brien's daughter, and the widow of Richard Stephenson, who was killed at Kilfinny Castle in 1642 as an "Irish papist", held Attyflin in 1655.

THE ATTYFLIN ESTATE of 1840 was dominated by "the residence of the proprietor, a commodious house newly roofed in 1817, there is a good set of offices, a garden, a well planted demesne and a splendid gate house of cut stone; on the gate is a gilt female figure, feeding an eagle." The estate contained 440 acres and 16 square perches of land which was let to five occupying tenants on a yearly lease of £1.15 an acre. County cess varied from 15 pence to 16½ pence while tithes ranged from 15 pence to 17½ pence. Farms on the estate were from one to seven acres in size. There were then 24 labourers who leased small holdings at £1.70½ pence an acre and

the remainder of the demesne was held by the proprietor. The house, gate-lodge and 230 acres were leased to Hamilton Jackson in 1851 and a further 112 acres and offices were let to John Cavanagh. The estate extended into Patrickswell. It included the houses on the southern side of the main street, of which only three were let directly by John Westropp. The others were all sublet. One of the buildings he leased directly was the old constabulary barracks, which is now a private dwelling. Mrs. Georgina White disposed of portions of the Attyflin property during her lifetime, including the houses in the village. The estate was sold to Brigadier Hewson for £10,000 in 1945 and he resold it in 1978 to the present owner Eamon Howard for £947,000. The estate then comprised the house, 337 acres, a stable yard and an extensive farmyard. The house is now an award-winning restaurant and lounge bar. It has become a favourite meeting place for the

wealthy. Members of the Arabian royal family have in the past booked the facility for business conferences etc.. There are now plans to build an eighteen-hole golf course and new functions rooms on the estate.

ANCIENT REMAINS can be found on the estate so it is more than likely that these historic structures excited the curiosity of the young T.J. Westropp. There are two *raths.* These could be described as the type of dispersed defended homesteads which dominated the Irish landscape on the eve of the Anglo-Norman invasion. One of them is nameless, with small cells and a collapsed passage, while the other, on an elevated position, is a plain circular earthwork, called Lissard, from *Lios Ard,* the High Fort. This latter site can be visited via the cut-stone arched stile which gave access to villagers working on the demesne in former times. The *kyle,* a small mound a few hundred feet southeast of Attyflin House, is believed locally to be the grave of those slain in a battle between Brian Boru and the Vikings. This was about "ten feet high and was covered with bushes, and, when dug into, contained a vast amount of fragments of bones and charred wood, also some skulls, which very soon fell to pieces and broken 'crocks' ... one 'crock' contained some flat discs of some metal, without image or superscription; no one would take them as money, and they became playthings for the children of the neighbouring villages of Patrickswell and Annagh. No weapons or bronze articles seem to have been found". There was also a well on the lands in which treasure was believed to have been hidden but when workers dredged it, all they found was mud.

FORT ETNA is an eighteenth-century house in which the gable-ended farm buildings have been treated as wings, according to Mark Bence Jones, who wrote of it in 1978. It was erected as the seat of the Peacock family, was the residence of J. Waller O'Grady in 1837, and later passed into the possession of the O'Reilly family.

MARYVILLE is similar to Fort Etna in many respects. In 1978 it was described as recently restored by its owners, the Egans.

GREENMOUNT is a large modern house designed by Donal O'Neill Flanagan in 1968 to replace the original house of the same name, which had been built as the seat of the Greene family about 1830. In 1978 it was owned by the Earl of Harrington.

KILPEACON derives its name from *Cill Beacáin,* the Church of St. Beacan, one of the six sons of Eugenius Mac Murchad of the royal house of Munster. His brothers were all church founders: Cormac of Inishmaine; Culan of Glenkeen; Emin, or Evin, of Monasterevin; Diermit of Kilmacowen; and Boedan of Kilboedain. Beacan was also known as Becan or Mo-Becoc and died in 689. The Kilpeacon Church of Ireland church may have been located on the same site as Beacan's foundation. This later building was destroyed by Whiteboys in 1762, rebuilt in 1763, and enlarged in 1820. The glebe house was rebuilt in 1817.

SIR WILLIAM KING received a grant of Kilpeacon during the reign of James I. He erected a manor adjoining Kilpeacon Castle and in 1837, Lewis noted in Kilpeacon church "a fine marble monument" commemorating Sir William King.

KILPEACON CASTLE was once a seat of Sir David Bourke who was transplanted from here so that the land could be cleared for Cromwellian settlers. Sir Edward Villiers demolished the ruins of the castle to build "a noble mansion near the site of the old house", in the early nineteenth century. This was the residence of C. Cripps in 1837 when the other principal houses were Ballyclough of E. Moroney and Leamonfield of H. Bevan. Kilpeacon House may have been designed by Sir Richard Morrison.

THE CAMP FIELD, *Bawnachumtma,* was located near Kilpeacon Castle. Some *raths* and circular fortifications were visible within this field in the 1830s. In 1821 a golden crown weiging 5 1/2 ounces, and shaped like an oyster shell was found either here or in one of the Greenhill forts. A local man had turned it up while trenching potatoes. Edward Villiers, the local landlord, sold the crown to a Dublin goldsmith for £16 or £18.90 and gave the money to the man who found it. Both Lewis and O'Donovan wrote of this area and a large *rath* or a *dún* about 350 feet in circumference on the summit of Greenhill. In the adjoining fields there were several smaller forts, surrounded by a single wall.

ST. PATRICK'S WELL in the townland of Kilpeacon was still frequented as a holy well in 1840.

KNOCKNEGAUL derived its name from *Cnoc na nGall,* the Hill of the Foreigners. The old parish church was destroyed during the war of 1641, and never repaired. The old glebe house was located near the church.

KILLONAHAN derives its name from *Cill Annacháin,* the Church of St. Onchon, or St. Onchu, whose feast-day was celebrated on 8 February. The parish church was destroyed in 1641 and never repaired. Two centuries later only part of the north wall remained and the local Church of Ireland parishioners resorted to Kilpeacon church. The nearby St. Senan's Well was the scene of a pattern up to 1820 but it dried up a few years later and the pattern ceased.

KILLONAHAN CASTLE is believed to have been built by Dermot O'Hurley in the fifteenth century.

KILLASRAGH, *Cill Lasrach,* the Church of St. Lassara, St. Lasar, St. Lassar, or St. Lassera is named after a sixth century saint whose feast-day was celebrated on 29 March. She was a nun, a niece of St. Forchera, and a student of Saint Finian and Saint Kiernan at Clonard. Her name, *Lasrach,* signified Flame. By 1840 Killasragh Church, in the townland of Ballybrinnogue South became a burial-ground for children. Another such graveyard was located in Garranroe townland. This latter *cillín* was known as *Crann Cam,* the Crooked Tree.

JOCKEYHALL was built by James Hewson in 1780. It later passed to the Dundon family. The name was probably coined by either the Hewsons or Dundons. The three townlands that existed here in earlier times were *Leaca an Mheantáin,* the Hillside of the Snipe, cov-ering the largest area of the three, *Cathair an Phollaigh,* the Fort in the Place of Holes, and *Bearna na Gaoithe,* the Windy Gap. Jockeyhall comprises part of each of these townlands which have been Anglicised to Leackinventane, Cahir Ipholloe and Bearnenaguihie. Donough O'Brien of Dooneen lived an obscure life here but he may have been the father of Conor Keown, who was in possession of Attyflin in 1638.

CRECORA derives its name from *Craobh Comhrtha,* the Sweet-scented Branch, Sweet-scented Branchy Tree or the Branch of the Sign or Token. In the early nineteenth century people used to point out a spot, 300 yards north-east of the old church, where a whitethorn bush once grew, and on which, presumably, pilgrims tied signs or tokens. Crecora took its name from this bush which may have been located close to a holy well. The old church is said to have been "destroyed in the war of 1641".

CRECORA CHURCH was badly ruined by 1840. Only the western gable and the adjoining parts of the side-walls remained standing. It appeared to have "been well built and capacious", erected out of large unquarried limestones, cement of lime and sand mortar. Lewis wrote that "many of the wealthy families of the neighbourhood have vaults in the cemetery." John Scanlan, the Colleen Bawn's murderer, was buried here. His body was not dissected in the Mulgrave Street Hospital, Limerick, as were the bodies of most criminals who had been hanged in the city. The big houses of the area in 1837 were Richmond Villa, Jockey Hall, Greenmount, Doneen, Ballymurphy and Ashfort; and there was a Catholic church, "a large modern edifice", in Crecora.

BALLINVEALA CASTLE in the south of the townland of the same name, was in a good state of preservation in 1840. This oblong ruin, located on high ground, was four storeys high with walls 50 feet high and 4 feet thick. By the time O'Donovan recorded these details only the projecting quoin stones of an adjoining building, on the western side, remained. This second building, joined to the first, was sometimes called a court.

KILLENORTY PARISH or Killenough, contained 390 inhabitants in 1831. This was located over 2 1/2 miles south-west of Patrickswell.

SOURCE REFERENCE NUMBERS
5 7 9 11 21 36 47
64 65 76 80 107 123 129
167 175 192 207 273 277

Rathkeale

Castle Matrix · Rathnaseer

RATHKEALE, the second largest town in the county, derives its name from *Rath Caola* or *Rath Gaela,* Caola's or Gaela's Fort. The town was a place of importance from an early date because of its location on the Deel river.

ST. MARY'S PRIORY may have been founded by Gilbert Harvey, for the Augustinian Canons, during the thirteenth century. Rev. John Begley wrote that it was colonised by Augustinians from Rattoo some time about 1210. Elinor Purcell made a perpetual grant of provisions to the canons in 1280. Her son, Hugh, refused to carry out her wishes after her death and was sued by the prior. They eventually came to an amicable settlement. In 1436 St. Mary the Virgin reputedly worked several miracles here and the Augustinians were allowed to grant indulgences to penitents in order to raise funds for the repair of the church. The monastery was officially suppressed in 1542 but a small community of canons may have remained here until 1581. In 1595 this, and several other monasteries, were granted to Sir Henry Wallop. By 1837 the tower and western gable were "complete, and the side walls nearly so; but the building was small and its architectural details are by no means interesting". The priory ruin is now one of the town's more notable features.

THE EARLS OF DESMOND had three strong castles in the town, one of them guarding the river passage or ford, at the time of the Desmond Rebellion. In 1579 Sir John of Desmond retreated here after his disastrous defeat at Monasteranenagh. Malbie's forces pursued the Geraldines to Rathkeale, where they plundered and burned the town. Sir John fled to Askeaton, where he was again defeated, this time by Sir George Carew. On 11 March 1580 Sir William Pelham and the Earl of Ormond met in Rathkeale, where they thought it advisable to destroy one of the Desmond castles, Castle Murison, before marching out. This was the castle that guarded the bridge and had been occupied by the Geraldines after the Battle of Monasteranenagh.

SIR WALTER RALEIGH was a mere captain in 1580 when the Queen's forces left Rathkeale to deal with the Irish and the Spanish forces who had landed at Smerwick. Raleigh distinguished himself by ambushing a number of the Irish who had collected to plunder the deserted camp. Folklore relates that the people slaughtered by Raleigh were merely sightseers who had gone to look at the camp. The Elizabethans conferred the freedom of the town on Raleigh for his action. Walter Raleigh spent a lot of time in the vicinity of Rathkeale. According to tradition, he imported potato tubers from Virginia some of which were cultivated by Edmond Southwell, who became one of Ireland's first landowners to grow potatoes. Sir Walter Raleigh's last words were addressed to his executioner, just before he was beheaded in 1618: "'Tis a sharp remedy, but a sure one for all ills". By then the potato tubers had been distributed throughout Munster, by Edmond Southwell, and the potato had been established as a regular crop.

EDMOND SOUTHWELL was one of three brothers from Suffolk who settled in the newly-planted province of Munster in the aftermath of the Desmond Rebellion. Edmond received a grant of Castle Matrix during the reign of James I (1603-1625). His brother, John, acquired Rathkeale Castle and promptly renamed it Castle Southwell. In 1616 the third Southwell, Richard, was granted a licence to keep forty taverns and to sell wine and *acqua vitae* in Limerick City. Edmond's son, Thomas, was knighted as Sir Thomas Southwell of Castle Mattress and created a baronet in 1662. He served as Sheriff of Limerick, Clare and Kerry. His son, also Thomas, was raised to the peerage as Baron Southwell in 1717. Many details of this baron's life have been forgotten but he is best remembered as the man who introduced the Palatines into the county.

THE CORPORATION OF RATHKEALE is frequently mentioned in history but little is known of its origin, charter, or constitution. It was disenfranchised by Oliver Cromwell because the town "refused his army a sufficient supply of provisions, and its privileges

were never after restored". In 1654 the town became a polling centre for the counties of Clare, Kerry and Limerick, as Cromwell proposed to introduce one hundred members for Ireland into his parliament.

IN 1837 Rathkeale was described by Samuel Lewis as "situated on the mail road from Limerick to Tralee, on both sides of the River Deel; in population it is second only to Limerick in the county; it consists principally of a single street, a mile in length, with smaller streets and lanes branching from it. The river passes through the middle of the main street, and is crossed by a bridge now in a dilapidated and dangerous state. There are several large and handsome houses, most of which are uninhabited, and a few good shops; but the town in general presents a poor and mean appearance; a number of Palatines settled in the town and neighbourhood, whose neat cottages and farm-steads form a striking contrast to most of the adjacent buildings. The market, which is large and well supplied, is held on Thursday; the fairs are on 7 February, 4 April, 1 and 19 June, 5 August, 18 September, and 18 November; those on 19 June and 18 September, which are chiefly for horses, are very much frequented; those of April and September, are for horned cattle, great numbers being sold; the remaining fairs are chiefly for sheep and pigs; all the transactions in the market and fairs are carried on in the open street. The town is a chief constabulary station ... the court-house is a large and convenient old building, but much out of repair. The bridewell is one of the largest in the county, containing three day-rooms, three airing-yards and eight cells: it is under good regulation. The fever hospital, built in 1830 near the town at an expense of £400, has accommodation for 25 intern patients; and there is a dispensary ... the parish comprises 10,705 statute acres ... five out of eight parts of the land are under tillage; two in meadow, demesnes and plantations; and one is rough pasture and marsh ... the system of agriculture is improving; the principal crops are wheat, potatoes, oats and barley, with some flax and clover. The population is almost wholly agricultural, the only manufacture being that of

Aerial view of Rathkeale.

linen on a small scale for domestic use ... a lead mine at Curraghnadaly, a mile from Rathkeale is about to be worked ... the surrounding country is embellished with numerous seats ... Beechmount ... Ballywilliam ... Mount Brown ... the glebe house ... Knocknakilla ... Rathkeale Abbey ... Wilton House ... Deansfort ... Mount Southwell ... Enniscoush ... Stoneville ... Glebe Castle ... and Castle Matrix ... In the R.C. divisions the parish is the head of a union or district, comprising also part of Kilscannell parish, and the whole of the ancient parishes of Rathnasaire and Kilcoleman. The chapel, an ancient and plain building, with a new front, is in the town; in which there are also places of worship for Wesleyans, Methodists and Independents. There are two free schools under the London Hibernian Society, and a school supported by Colonel White ... also nine private schools, in which are about 200 boys and 70 girls ... not far distant from the town are Altavilla ... Riddlestown ... Clonard ... Elm Hill ... Glenville ... Cahermoyle ... and Nantinan House".

THE RATHKEALE COIN HOARD was discovered in 1846. This consisted of over a thousand coins of Edward III (1327-1377) which may have been part of the spoils taken by the O'Briens after their victory at Monasteranenagh in 1370. A thin gold-band was also found near the town. This was one of a small group of such ornaments which could be dated to the eleventh or twelfth centuries and were generally found in Ireland or in western Scotland. In 1857 Captain Edward Hoare, a Cork antiquarian, owned this band. He published a drawing and description of it in that year.

THE CATHOLIC CHURCH was designed in a Gothic-revival style by J.J. McCarthy during Fr. James O'Shea's term as parish priest. Fr. O'Shea died in 1877. One of his predecessors, Archdeacon Michael Fitzgerald, gave his house, garden and a donation of £50 to three Christian Brothers who arrived here on 28 December 1859. They opened a school with 200 pupils on 9 January, 1860. The Brothers remained in Rathkeale until 1880. Dr. James Stritch (1644-1719) registered himself as parish priest in 1704. Despite the Penal Laws, which were still in operation, there was a harmonious relationship between the Catholic clergy and the local Protestant landowners. This relationship was disrupted, for a while, in 1748. After the death of Fr. Stritch's successor, Fr. James Moore, Henry Southwell chased away two or three priests who had been appointed as parish priests. Henry tried to have a *protégé* of his own, Fr. Charles Ryan, installed as parish priest but he was eventually persuaded to accept Fr. David Bourke.

THE CHURCH OF IRELAND CHURCH was erected in 1831 near the site of an older church and contains a monument dating from 1676. The church was built in the English style with a square tower, "embattled and crowned with crocketed pinnacles", on a gentle eminence west of the river, close to the site of Castle Southwell.

THE GLEBE HOUSE was occupied by a Protestant clergyman, Rev. C.T. Coghlan, in 1837. In 1840 O'Donovan wrote that it was still inhabited and in a good state of preservation. In 1988 it appeared to be still in good condition, was long since unoccupied, and had acquired a galvanised iron roof.

RIDDLETOWN PARK may have been designed for the Blennerhassetts by one of the Rothery family in 1730. John and Isaac Rothery were noted architects of the period, whose work is still found elsewhere, in Mount Ievers, Sixmilebridge, County Clare (c. 1730) and in Bowens Court, Kildorrery, Co. Cork (c. 1765-1775). In 1837 this three-storey house, built over a basement, was the residence of

Gerald Blennerhassett. Riddlestown Park passed, by inheritance to the Knights of Glin, who later sold it.

THE PRESENT-DAY AMERICAN QUARTER HORSE

may be descended from five Hobbie horses, a stallion and four mares, Sir Thomas Southwell sent to Sir William Berkeley, Royal Governor of Virginia, at Jamestown, in 1666. Sean O'Driscoll brought this to my attention in *The Colonial Quarter Race Horse* which was written by Alexander Mackay-Smith, and published in Richmond, Virginia in 1983.

SEAN O'DRISCOLL

has had a long and varied career. He became an artist, qualified as an architect, developed an interest in metallurgy and served in the United States Air Force during World War II. In 1945 he became the first man to engineer an escape from behind the newly-imposed Iron Curtain when he (Sean) arranged the defection of Theodore Wilhelm Schmidt. After the war he transferred to aero-space research. For a short period he served as aide to Charles Lindbergh, shortly after President Eisenhower appointed Lindbergh a brigadier-general in 1954. Sean also worked with John Wheeler, the man who first found black holes in space. John Wheeler was co-discoverer of Uranium 235 with Niels Bohr. In 1962 Eoin "Pope" O'Mahony persuaded Sean to settle in Castle Matrix. Sean's interest in Irish castles has led him into doing some research on Anglo-Norman castles of which he says there were 405 in County Limerick and a total of 2,700 throughout Ireland.

CASTLE MATRIX

may derive its name from *Caisleán Bhun Traísce* but Seán O'Driscoll, the present owner of Castle Matrix, attributes its name to an association with the Matres or Matronae. Seán believes the castle was erected on the site of a Pagan Celtic sanctuary.

THE MATRES

were triple mother-goddesses of the Pagan Celts, a type of pre-Christian Trinity. They represented the basic image of the tribal mother and their maternal aspects were of supreme importance. They were primarily concerned with maternal and sexual matters but like the *Mórrígna,* the triple raven-war-goddess, they could also be influential in battle, prognostication, and shape-shifting.

CASTLE MATRIX

Castle Matrickes, or Castle Mattress, is a fifteenth century tower house founded by the Fitzgeralds of Desmond about 1410. On 7 December 1487 James, the Ninth Earl of Desmond was murdered here by his servants. His death was instigated by one brother, and avenged by another, Maurice, who executed all of James's servants. After the Desmond Rebellion, the castle was forfeit to the Crown. Walter Raleigh carried out some repairs on the building and, according to local tradition, met the poet Edmund Spenser here. Spenser had come to Ireland as secretary to Lord Deputy Grey of Wilton in 1580. Later he became Clerk to the English Council of Munster. Spenser's barbaric views on how the Irish should be treated provoked Maurice Viscount Roche of Fermoy into proclaiming that "none of his people should have trade or commerce with Mr. Spenser". Early in the seventeenth century Edmond Southwell took up residence in the castle. In 1641 he defended it against the Confederate Irish who built forts around it and eventually captured it. This Edmond appears to have been killed in Askeaton but he was succeeded by a man of the same name, possibly his son. Edmond Southwell was mentioned in the Civil Survey of 1654 as being in possession of a castle, orchard, grist-mill and tucking-mill and in 1659 he was listed as *titulado* of Castle Matrix. Meliora Southwell married John Brown of Mount Brown in 1751.Their grandson, John Southwell Brown, renovated the castle in the 1830s and added a two-storey castellated wing, which extended as far as the bank of the River Deel but "due attention was paid to preserve its original character by its proprietor". The corner bartizans and original battlements are still intact. In 1837 the Southwell estate was a model of agricultural industry. The flour mill was "fitted up ... in the most complete manner and with the most improved machinery, which is propelled by the current of the River Deel; the mill can grind 20,000 barrels of wheat annually and gives employment to 100 persons". Castle Matrix, was unoccupied from 1931 until the early 1960s. It was repaired, renovated, and fitted with antique furniture before it was opened as the Irish International Art Centre in 1970. Castle Matrix contains a fine reference library today, in two languages, French and English, which Seán O'Driscoll uses to research the history of costume, weaponry, and art throughout the ages. The building also houses his unique collection of medieval, and older, weaponry. Sean possesses a selection of axe-heads from the crudest of Stone Age work through to the Iron Age.

THE SOUTHWELL ESTATE

entered the history of Munster as the central base from which the Palatines spread throughout Limerick and the neighbouring counties. Like the Celts, Vikings, Anglo-Normans and English before them, the Palatines made an important contribution to the culture, lifestyle, and history of the county. Their arrival in Rathkeale could be classed as the last Munster plantation although it was on a more limited scale than the plantations of the six-teenth and seventeenth centuries. The parcels of land they received were small. these new German-speaking Protestant refugees were a different breed from the English or Scottish adventurers who had profited from the previous plantations. They never interfered in the religion or politics of the native Irish. The Palatines supported the government of the day. Eventually the age-old process of assimilation turned *Gall* into *Gael.* The Palatines learned to speak the language of the countryside, Irish, as well as the language of the towns, English. Many of them became as nationalist as their Catholic neighbours and played active roles in the War of Independence. Like their ancestors, many of the Palatines today are still engaged in farming. As colonists they were a total failure. Those who remained in Ireland, like the Anglo-Normans before them, were almost totally absorbed into the native population. Only the Palatine surnames survive to mark their bearers as members of an ethnic group that is now completely Irish in outlook, thought and behaviour.

THE PALATINE SETTLEMENT IN IRELAND,

including the history of each family in Ireland, was researched and documented by Hank Jones of San Leandro, California, U.S.A., in 1965. He used data from the original records and ignored many of the family traditions because they would have changed so much in the telling over the years that their accuracy would have been suspect. For an overall picture of the Palatine history in Ireland read Walter A. Knittle's book, *18th Century Palatine Emigration* and Dr. Richard Hayes's article "The German Colony in County Limerick" which appeared in the *"North Munster Antiquarian Journal",* Volume 1, No. 2, October 1937. Hank Jones's thesis on "The Palatine Families of Ireland" surpasses all other works on the subject and is an essential guide to the Palatine surnames of Limerick. In the following charts the most commonly-used version of each surname is listed first under "Surname". The Christian name, or names, of each founder and any additional information on him/her is dealt with under "Founder(s)". Variants of each surname appear under the appropriate heading. When possible the variant in Irish appears first and in italics. The original form of the surname is given after the variant in Irish. The Southwell estate caption lists the date of each family's arrival on that estate while "Other Locations" deals with the areas to which various families moved as they spread outside the Rathkeale area. "Religion" lists the religion professed by each family on arrival in Ireland.

The restored Castle Matrix.

SURNAME	FOUNDER(S)	VARIANTS	SOUTHWELL ESTATE	OTHER LOCATIONS	RELIGION
Alton	John George Born 1669	*Altún* Altheimer Altimes	1720	Ballingirrane 1747 Ballyriggin 1761 Glenosheen 1761	Lutheran
Barkman	Abraham Born c. 1663	Berghmann Bartman	1712	New York 1765 Ballyriggin 1776 Adare 1807 Ballyorgan 1816 Glenosheen 1848	Lutheran
Barraban	Hans Wolf Born c. 1675	Barban Barrow Barrobier	—	Adare 1865	Reformed Faith
Barrer	Peter	Bear Bart Barraban	—	Ballingirrane 1747 Ballingarry - late 1700s	—
Becker	Mighel Born 1671	*Báicéir* Bekker Baker Beakir Beecher	1720	Ballingirrane 1755 New York 1764 Kilflyn 1852 Ballyorgan 1852	Reformed Faith
Benner	Paul (c. 1682-1760) Son of Henry	Bender	1715	Ballingirrane 1747	—
Bethel	Philip Bettel	Bekell	—	Limerick City - 18th century Killaloe - 18th century	Reformed Faith
Bible	John	Bible	—	Ballyorgan 1761	—
Bonus	Julius	Bonus Ponus	1720	—	Reformed Faith
Bovinizer	John Adam Born c. 1652	Bubeheiser Bovenizer Bubenhauser Bobinhefar Bobinhefer Bowenheizer	1715	 Castlematrix 1748 Ballycahane 1753 Killiheen 1755 Adare 1814	Reformed Faith
Bowen	Vandel	Boin Bohea	1720	Castle Matrix 1767 Killiheen 1776 Adare 1789	—
Bower	Kasper	Baur Bauer	1720	—	—
Bowman	Jacob	Bouman Bowerman	1715	Cooline 1764 New York 1764 Limerick City 1770 Killaloe 1790	—

SURNAME	FOUNDER(S)	VARIANTS	SOUTHWELL ESTATE	OTHER LOCATIONS	RELIGION
				Nantinan 1825 Particles 1834	
Bredhour	Israel	Bredauer Brethover Bruther	1720	Ballingirrane 1747 Canada 1766 Croagh 1825 Kiltannon 1825	Lutheran
Brough	Hans Felton	*Broc* Brough	1720	Ballywilliam 1756	—
Cave	Casimira	*Mac Dháibhidh* Cave	1720	—	—
Closterbecker	John	Closterbecker	1720	—	Lutheran
Cole	Johans Nicholas	Kole Kohl	1720	Limerick City 1741 Ballyriggin 1747 Ballyriggin 1825	—
Cooper	John	*Cúipéir* Baucher Bottcher	—	Ireland 1715	—
Corneille	Adam	Cornelius Corneal	1720	Killiheen 1755 Castle Matrix 1758 Kilscannell 1786 Adare 1811	French Hugenot
Cough	Johan Mattys	*Mac Eochadha* Kog Kough Cooke	1715	Killiheen 1720 Ballyorgan 1761 New York 1763 Kilflynn — Kilfinnane 1811	—
Crips	Hans Peter	Crips Kreps	1720	Courtmatrix	—
Crononbery	Henry	Kroniberger Cronerbery Cronsbeger	1720	Killiheen 1747 Ballyriggin 1804 Adare 1820s	—
Crow	Philip Born 1679	*Mac Conchradha* Gro	—	Everlary, Co. Cork 1720 Rathkeale 1749	Lutheran
Daube	Michael	Daube Dope Dobe Doupe	1720	Courtmatrix 1753 Nantinan 1757 Ballingirrrane 1825 Court Village 1849 Adare 1890	—
Dolmage	Johann	Dometsch Delmege Dulmage Dolmet Dollmage Dolmetcht Dolmadge	1720	Casle Matrix 1751 Ballyorgan 1761 Albany, New York 1761 West Indies 1761 Kilscannell 1760s Courtmatrix 1769 Killiheen 1830	—

SURNAME	FOUNDER(S)	VARIANTS	SOUTHWELL ESTATE	OTHER LOCATIONS	RELIGION
Embury	Andrew	Imberger	1720	Ballingirrane 1747 New York 1764	
Everett	Hartman	*Eabhróid* Ebert Everatt	1720	—	—
Felher	Charles	Felher Folker Fehler	1720	—	—
Filme	Margaret	Filme	1720	—	—
Fitzelle	Adam	Fisel Fishell Ffissel Fissel	1720	Killiheen 1753 Courtmatrix 1755 Ballyorgan 1761 Ballyriggin 1800 Oliver Estate 1814 Ballingarry —	—
Fought	Jacob	Fock Ffought	—	Mallow 1720 Castle Matrix 1752 New York 1770 Rathkeale 1787 Adare 1817	—
Glazier	Hans Jurig	*Gléasúr* Glaser Gleazer		Dublin 1720 Co. Limerick 1720s Killiheen 1753 Ballyorgan 1761 Kilscannell 1766 Bawnleigh (Tipperary) 1826	—
Grouse	George	Crouse Grouce Crause	1720	Adare 1806	—
Guyer	Johann David	Geyer Guier	1720	Ballingirrane	Huguenot
Hartwick	Caspar	Hartwick Hartrick	1720	—	—
Heavenor	Henrig and Apolonia	Herbener Hebenhorne	1720	Pallas 1747	—
Heck	Sebastian	Heck	1720	Ballingirrane 1746 Ballycahane 1753 Ballyriggin 1761 New York — Ballyorgan 1825 Kilfinnane 1828	Luterhan
Hessing	—	—	—	Limerick City 1826	—
Hibler	Anthony	—	1720	—	—

SURNAME	FOUNDER(S)	VARIANTS	SOUTHWELL ESTATE	OTHER LOCATIONS	RELIGION
Hifle	—	Hyfell Hyfle Hyphell	—	Ballycahane 1753 Pallas 1783 Ballingirrane 1825 Chapel Russell 1825 Adare 1827	—
Hoffman	Philip	Hoffman	—	Rathkeale 1720 Courtmatrix 1740s Killiheen 1740s New York 1763 Kilfinnane 1816	—
Hoopf	Hans George Born 1671	Hoppf	1720	—	—
Hoost	Jacob	Hooset	1720	—	—
Kile	—	Kite Keal	—	Ballingirrane 1802	—
Koning	Johan Joost	Konig	—	Springfield 1720	—
Latchford	—	Latchford	—	Pallas 1784 Rathkeale 1796 Adare 1836	—
Laurence	John and Margaret (born 1670)	*Labhrás* Lorentz Lawrence	1720	Ballingirrane 1747 Courtmatrix 1754 Killiheen 1758 New York 1763 Canada 1763 Nantinan 1792	Reformed Faith
Legear	Johan Adam	Lieger Le Geer Le Gear	1720	Courtmatrix 1755 Ballyorgan 1761 Kilfling (Kilflyn?) 1788 Inver Ivrossa 1812 Adare 1820	—
Lodewick	Johan Henrig	*de Léadús* Lodowick Ludwig	1720	Killiheen 1742 Rathkeale 1762 Courtmatrix 1825 Court Village 1834	Lutheran
Long	Peter John	*de Long* Long	—	County Cork 1720 Ballingirrane 1747 Ballycahane 1753 Pallas 1783 Adare 1817	—
Low	Mathew	*Mac Lughadha* Lous Lows Lokes Lowe	1720	Ballingirrane 1747 Kilfinnane Glenosheen 1825	—
Lower	Valentine	Lower Lour	1720	Courtmatrix 1743 New York 1763	—

SURNAME	FOUNDER(S)	VARIANTS	SOUTHWELL ESTATE	OTHER LOCATIONS	RELIGION
Mace	Philip	*O Miadhaigh* *Mac Con Midhe* Mace Maes Mee	—	Ireland 1715 Kilfinnane 1875	—
Meyer	—	*O Midhir* *O Mír* Myers Myer Mier Miers	—	Ireland 1715 *Droichead-Treasna* 1780 (?)	
Mick	Henry Born 1674	Mick Mich	1720	Ballingirrane 1747 Nantinan 1766	Reformed Faith Catholic 1766
Miller	John "Hans" Martin Born 1677	*Muilleóir* Miller Muller	1720	Courtmatrix 1753 Adare 1805 Killiheen 1805 New York Canada	Lutheran
Modler	Michael Born 1671	Madelaer Madler	1720	Cortmatrix 1762 Adare 1801 Limerick City 1853	Lutheran
Neizer	Hans Migel Born 1661	Nasar Neyser Neazor Mezar	1720	Kilcornan 1770 Ballycahane 1776 Pallas 1784	Lutheran
Passe	Katherine	Passe Puff	1720	—	—
Piper	Hans Peter Born 1652	*Piobar* *Piobart* *Piobaire* Pfeifer Pifer Pipper Pepper Peppard	1715	Killiheen 1753 Ballingirrane 1776	Lutheran
Puff	Andreas	Poffe Poff Passe ?	1720 ?	Ireland 1715 Courtmatrix 1744 New York 1763 Kerry 1834	—
Richardt	Christopher	*Mac Risteáird* Richard Richards	1720	—	—
Rodenbecker	Johann	Rodenberger Roderberger Rhodenbecker	1720	Killiheen 1755 Nantinan 1766	—

SURNAME	FOUNDER(S)	VARIANTS	SOUTHWELL ESTATE	OTHER LOCATIONS	RELIGION
Rose	Peter Rosine or Johan Christopher Rose	*De Rús* *Rós* Rosine Rose Ross	—	Nantinan 1731 Kilscannell 1746 Ballingirrane 1747 Ballycahane 1753 America 1765 Rathkeale 1766 Adare —	—
Ruckle	"John" Caspar	*De Riodal* *Riodal* Roogall Ruttle Ruddle	1720	Ballingirrane 1747 Nantinan 1754 New York 1764 Newpark 1776 Ballycahane 1776 Pallas 1783 Adare —	
Rynard	Conrad	*Raghnard* Reynhard Rhinehardt Rinhart	1720	Limerick City 1728 Killiheen 1755 Graigue 1795 Adare 1795	—
Ryner	Johan Pieter	Reiner	1720	Limerick City 1738	
St. John	Elias Sohn Philip Sohn	*De Suingean* *Suingean* Sohn Singeon Son John Shon	1720	Ballingirrane 1747 Canada — Adare 1832	—
Schmidt	Andrew and Sophia	*Mac an Ghobhann* *O Gabhann* Schmidt Smythe	1720	Effin 1776 Adare 1793	—
Shallas	Peter Born 1671	Schalosch	1720	—	Reformed Faith
Sheaffer	Andrew	Sheafer	1720	—	—
Shearman	Ann	*Searman* Shearman	1720	—	—
Shimmell	Johann Nicholaus	Schimell Shimmel	1720	New York 1763 Killiheen 1769	—
Shire	Hans Adam	Schyer	1720	Killiheen 1742 Courtmatrix 1755 New York 1764 Barrigone — Adare 1827	—
Shoemaker	Batholomew Born 1668	Schumacher	1720	Ballingirrane 1747 Bohercullane 1761 Particles 1771 Glenosheen — Kilfinnane —	Lutheran

SURNAME	FOUNDER(S)	VARIANTS	SOUTHWELL ESTATE	OTHER LOCATIONS	RELIGION
Shoneweiss	John Born 1661	Shonweiss Shonewise Shoenweiss	1720	—	Reformed Faith
Shouldice	Elizabeth	Schides Shoreldis Shouldize Sholdis Shouldis Shouldish Shouldes	1720	Ballyorgan 1761 New York 1771 Killiheen 1776 Adare 1800	—
Siebard	Felton or Valentine	Siebard Seibert	1720	—	—
Singer	John	Singer	1720	—	—
Smeltzer	Christopher	Smelser	1720	Ballingirrane 1747	—
Sparling	George	Sperling	1720	Killiheen 1747 America 1763 Adare 1776 Ballynahill 1776 Ballingirrane 1785 Askeaton 1815 Newcastle 1821 Kilcooly 1826	
Sperling	Stuffle	von Sperling Sperling	—	Ireland 1701	—
Steepe	Hans Peter	Steepe	1720	Nantinan 1759 Ballyriggin 1761 Castle Oliver — Kilfinnane 1888	—
Steevell	John	Steevell	1720	—	—
Stork	Hans Henrig Born 1664	Stork Stark	1720	Killiheen 1755 Ballingirrane 1755 Ballyriggin 1761 Kilscannell 1766 Adare 1776 Ballyorgan 1817 Thomastown 1831	Lutheran
Strough	Johan Born 1679	Strauch Stroud Strouch Strowch	1720	Ireland 1715 Courtmatrix 1751 Killiheen 1753 Reeus 1758 Ballyorgan 1761 Glenosheen —	—

SURNAME	FOUNDER(S)	VARIANTS	SOUTHWELL ESTATE	OTHER LOCATIONS	RELGION
Switzer	Johan Jacob of Assenheim	*Suitséir* Schweitzer	1720	Courtmatrix 1746 Tipperary — Dublin — Killiheen 1761 Ballingirrane 1775 Adare 1776 Castle Matrix 1776 Canada — Kilpeacon 1834	Luterhan
Teskey	Jacob Born 1659	Teske	1720	Killiheen 1755 Courtmatrix 1755 Ballingirrane 1776 Tarbert 1826 Kilscannell 1830 America 1846 Adare 1849 Curraheen 1935	Lutheran
Tettler	Johan Jacob	Dedler Detlor	1720	Ballingirrane 1747 Ballycahane 1753 America 1756 New York 1763 Kilflynn 1797	—
Tyse	Mattys	Tys Twiss	—	Ireland 1715 Wexford 1720	—
Ushelbaugh	John	Usselbach Urshelbach	1720	Balligirrane	—
Vogler	—	Vogeler	—	Limerick City 1726	—
Williams	—	MacUilliam	—	America 1765 Kilflynn — Ballingarry 1787	—
Wolf	George	Wolf (Not to be confused with an older Limerick family, *De Bhul* or Woulfe)	— (Ballinalagha)	Ireland 1715 Wexford 1720 Duckstown 1825	—
Young	Nicholas Born 1688	Jung	1720	Ballingirrane 1747 Glenosheen 1761	Lutheran
Youngman	Henry	Young Jung	1720	Killiheen 1755	—
Zigler	Heinrich Born 1668	Ziegler	1720	—	Reformed Faith

THE PALATINES were mainly German-speaking Protestant refugees who later adopted the Methodism of John Wesley and propagated their new beliefs throughout Limerick, Ireland, America and Canada. They were a tolerant people and, although their convictions were sincere, they never became proselytisers. In 1709 they concealed Catholic refugees within their ranks when Queen Anne announced her intention to return Catholic families to the Palatinate. After the Palatines settled in Ireland many of them merged with the general population while others rose to prominence. The Switzer and Dolmage families became the most influential of the Irish-based settlers but several others became more famous abroad.

JACOB BARKMAN (1755-1838) fought in the American Revolution. Captain Charles Oliver detailed a Palatine yeoman named Bartmann to flog Patrick "Staker" Wallis through the streets of Kilfinnane prior to his execution for his part in "procuring the assassination of Chas. S. Oliver".

AGNES BENNER (1731-1832) was married twice, first to Peter Lawrence of Killiheen and secondly to Peter Miller (1740-1819). She settled in St. Armand, Quebec and was very involved in American Methodism and the United Empire Loyalists.

THE METHODIST EPISCOPAL CHURCH was influenced by the Heck, Embury and Ruckel families. Paul Heck (1730-1792) and Barbara Ruckel (1734-1804) established the first Methodist society in colonial America with Philip Embury.

"LONG ANNE" TESKEY (1765-1880) was the last of the German-speaking Palatines. She outlived all her contemporaries and died at the age of 115 years. Another Teskey, Sarah Teskey of Curraheen, died at the age of 102 years in 1935.

JOHN RIDER (1648-1769) was recorded in The Freeman's Journal on 14 January 1769 as having lived to the age of 121 years. Originally known as Hans Rieter, he had settled in Wexford rather than Limerick.

PEADAR STEEPE of Ballyhargan was an active member of the East Limerick Brigade of the I.R.A. during the Troubles.

THE WEST LIMERICK BRIGADE of the I.R.A. was composed of five battalions that functioned within, and outside, the West Limerick region. This brigade operated in parts of Kerry and its members took part in attacks on the Brosna R.I.C. barracks. On 10 March 1920, during the Rathkeale Fair, Sergeant George Neazor of the R.I.C. was killed and Constable Doyle was wounded, in Ward's Hotel, when they refused to hand over their arms to an I.R.A. raiding party. SEAN FINN commanded the West Limerick Brigade of the I.R.A. in 1919. His officers were Garrett McAuliffe, Newcastle West; James Colbert, Monelena, Athea; Paddy Roche; Jim Liston, Castlemahon; Mossie Hartnett, Tournafulla; Con Foley, Broadford; Jimmy Halpin, Pallaskenry; and J.T. O'Connor, Ballyhahill. Sean Finn organised escape routes for the men who took part in the Soloheadbeg Ambush and the Knocklong Rescue. Sean was later killed in action at Ballyhahill on 30 March, 1921.

WILLIAM JOYCE, Lord Haw-Haw, in one of his war-time propaganda broadcasts denigrated the Irish army of the day by stating that "they couldn't even drive the Sheridans out of Rathkeale".

KILCOLMAN CHURCH had virtually disappeared by 1840, when only a side wall built of large field-stones, cemented with lime and sand mortar, remained. The graveyard was still in use at that time.

BALLYALLINAN CASTLE was built by the O'Hallinan family but it was later occupied by gallowglasses, the MacSheehys, on behalf of their overlords, the Earls of Desmond. Dermot O'Connor captured Ballyallinan Castle from Rory MacSheehy in 1600 but was forced to surrender it after a siege.

BALLYALLINAN CHURCH, Teampall Beinid, the Church of Beinid is east of the castle. By 1840 only the side walls and part of the east gable was intact. O'Donovan believed that St. Beinid could have been another name for St. Benedict.

ST. BEINID'S WELL, Tobar Beinid, St. Benedict's Well, and St. Bernard's Well may be one and the same. O'Donovan noted that St. Beinid's Well was thirty yards south-west of Teampall Beinid and made only a vague reference to St. Bernard's Well in Ballyallinan North. Patrick Hogan in Holy Wells of Ireland (1980) wrote that pilgrims visited St. Bernard's Well on 20 August and Good Friday's seeking cures for rheumatism, lameness, and sore eyes. These pilgrims used to leave pins and nails as votive offerings. Sometimes nails were driven into an ash tree above the well, possibly in memory of the crucifixion. Ballyallinan is four miles south-west of Rathkeale.

RATHNASEER CHURCH derives its name from Rath na Saer, the Fort of the Artificers or Workmen. This is an ancient nave and chancel church two miles south of Rathkeale. The western gable had been completely destroyed by 1840 but the eastern gable has survived and contains a round-topped window.

RATHNASEER CASTLE was a Geraldine castle. This building was only 35 feet high a century and a half ago when an arched floor could be seen over the ground floor.

LISNACOLLA CASTLE was built by the MacSheehys, who were introduced into this part of the country by the Seventh Earl of Desmond in 1420. This castle was also known as Liosnacoille or Woodfort Castle and was the seat of the MacSheehys after they had been appointed the Earl's constables. It is four miles west of Rathkeale.

MAC SHEEHY, is derived from Mac Sítheach, the Son of Sitheach or the Peaceful. Sítheach was a great-grandson of Domhnall, from whom the Scottish MacDonnells took their name. The MacSheehy surname is also rendered as Sheehy, M'Shihy, M'Shiehie and M'Shee. The name was first recorded in Ireland when the MacSheehys took part in a fratricidal battle between two O'Connor factions near Ballysodare, County Sligo, in 1367. During the fourteenth, fifteenth and sixteenth centuries they served as mercenaries, or gallowglasses throughout the length and breadth of Ireland.

CLONARLA CASTLE in the parish of Dundonnell was demolished in the 1830s so that T. Fitzgerald Massey could build a new mansion, Clonarla, on the site. By 1837 only a few fragments of the castle survived. The only other house of note in the parish in the same year was the seat of Gerald Blennerhassett, Riddlestown, on the banks of the River Deel. Dundonnell parish contained 476 inhabitants on 1239 statute acres in 1831.

SOURCE REFERENCE NUMBERS
9 10 11 44 48 75 76 105
107 120 123 129 135 150 192 195
198 223 233 238 264 282

BIBLIOGRAPHY * Asterisk denotes source containing unpublished material.

1. Ahern, Richard, "A History of the Christian Brothers in Limerick", *The Old Limerick Journal.* Autumn 1987.
2. *Aviation of the Shannon,* Irish Air Letter Publication. 1985.
3. Barry, Jim, *Flying the North Atlantic — A History in Photographs,* 1987.
4. Barry, J. Grene, "Notes on Bourchier Castle and New Church, Lough Gur." *The Journal of the Royal Society of Antiquaries of Ireland.* Part 2. Vol. XXXIII. 1903.
5. Barry, T.B., *The Archaeology of Medieval Ireland..* London and New York. 1987.
6. Becker, Bernard H., *Disturbed Ireland — Being the Letters Written during the Winter of 1880-81,* London, 1881.
7.* Beggan, G., "The Story of Attyflynn, Its House and Demesne in the Barony of Pubblebrien and the County of Limerick", Private circulation, unpublished.
8. Begley, Rev. John, *The Diocese of Limerick. Ancient and Medieval.* Dublin, 1906.
9. Begley, Rev. John. *The Diocese of Limerick from 1691 to the Present Time,* Dublin, 1938. *The Diocese of Limerick in the 16th and 17th Centuries,* Dublin, 1927.
10.* Behan, Niall, "The Palatines", unpublished.
11. Bence-Jones, Mark, *Burke's Guide to Country Houses, Ireland.* London, 1978.
12. Benedictine Monks, The, *The Book of Saints. A Dictionary of Servants of God Canonised by the Catholic Church: extracted from the Roman and other Martyrologies.* Compiled by the Benedictine Monks of St. Augustine's Abbey, Ramsgate, 1921.
13. Bord Fáilte. *Limerick and Tipperary North 1980/1981.* Published in association with Shannonside Tourism Organisation.
14. Boland, S.J., "Fr. John Creagh in the Kimberleys", *Old Limerick Journal - Australian edition,* No. 23, Spring 1988.
15. Brady, Anne M., and Brian Cleeve, *A Biographical Dictionary of Irish Writers.* Gigginstown, 1985.

16. Bromage, Mary C., *De Valera and the March of a Nation,* London, 1956.
17. Browne, Kevin J., *Eamon de Valera & the Banner County,* Dublin, 1982.
18.* Browne, Tony, "Houses and Families of Limerick City and County", unpublished.
19. Burke, Sir Bernard, *A Genealogical and Heraldic History of the Landed Gentry of Great Britain and Ireland.* London, 1894.
20. Burke, Sir Bernard, *A Genealogical and Heraldic History of the Peerage and Baronetage, the Privy Council, Knightage and Companionage.* London, 1912.
21. Burke, Sir Bernard, *A Genealogical and Heraldic History of the Landed Gentry of Ireland.* London, 1912.
22. Cappagh Handball Club, *Souvenir Booklet issued for the Official Opening of the new Handball Court at Cappagh, Co. Limerick, 1969.*
23. Carbery, Mary, *The Farm by Lough Gur,* London, 1937. Cork, 1973.
24. Carew, Sir George, *Pacata Hibernia or A History of the Wars in Ireland during the Reign of Queen Elizabeth especially within the Province of Munster under the government of Sir George Carew and compiled by his direction and appointment.* (Edited and with an introduction and notes by Standish O'Grady), London, 1896.
25. Castleconnell Guild, Irish Countrywomen's Association. *Castleconnell, Co. Limerick. A Walking Tour and Historical Notes.* 1987.
26. Central Statistics Office. *Census 86. Local Population Report. No. 19 County Limerick (excluding Limerick County Borough). Population by age, sex, marital status and household. Composition in towns, D.E.D.'s, urban and rural districts.* Government publications sale office. November 1987.
27. Central Statistics Office, *Census 86, Local Population Report. No. 24 Limerick City Borough - Population by age, sex, marital status and household composition.* Government publications. December 1987.
28. Chambers's, *Shorter English Dictionary,* Edinburgh & London, 1955.
29. Clarke, Philip, Brian Jackman, Derrick Mercer and Clive Crook, *The Sunday times — 1000 Days Out in Great Britain and Ireland,* London, 1981.
30. Clark, William Smith, "The Limerick Stage 1736-1800". Part One. *The Old Limerick Journal.* Winte, 1981.
31. Clark, William Smith, "The Limerick Stage 1736-1800". Part Two. *The Old Limerick Journal.* Summer 1982.
32. Cleeve, Brian, *Dictionary of Irish Writers (Fiction),* Cork, 1966. *Dictionary of Irish Writers. (Non-fiction),* Cork, 1969.
33. Corporation of the City of Limerick, *Limerick. Treorán Oifigiúil do Luimneach. Official Guide to the City of Limerick,* 1988.
34. Cottle, Basil, *The Penguin Dictionary of Surnames.* London, 1978.
35. Craig, Maurice and the Knight of Glin, *Ireland Observed, a Guide to the Buildings and Antiquities of Ireland,* Cork, 1970.
36. Crone, John S., *A Concise Dictionary of Irish Biography,* Dublin, 1928.
37. Cronin, Seán, *Irish Nationalism. A History of its Roots and Idealogy,* 1980.
38. Cussen, John, "William Fuller Hartnett and Fuller's Folly", *The Annual Observer,* Newcastle West, December 1984.
39. Cussen, Robert, "Caleb Powell, High Sheriff of County Limerick, 1858, sums up his Grand Jury". *North Munster Studies, Essays in Commemoration of Monsignor Michael Moloney.* Edited by Etienne Rynne, 1967.
40. Danaher, Patricia, "An Uphill Battle for People of Southill", *The Irish Press,* 6 October, 1987.
41. Daniel Glyn, *The Megalith Builders of Western Europe,* London, 1962.
42. De Breffny, Brian, Rosemary ffolliott, and George Mott, *The Houses of Ireland. Domestic Architecture from the Medieval Castle to the Edwardian Villa,* London, 1984.
43. De Breffny, Brian, and George Mott, *The Churches and Abbeys of Ireland ,* London, 1976.
44. De Breffny, Brian and George Mott *Castles of Ireland,* London, 1977.
45. De Valera, Ruaidhri, and Seán O Nualláin, *Survey of the Megalithic Tombs of Ireland. Volume IV.*

Counties Cork, Kerry, Limerick, Tipperary, Stationery Office, Dublin. 1982.

46. De Vere, Aubrey, *Recollections of Aubrey de Vere*, New York and London, 1897.

47. Dinneen, Rev. Patrick S., *Foclóir Gaedhilge agus Beárla — An Irish-English Dictionary*, Dublin, 1927.

48. Dolley, Michael, "The Mediaeval Coin-Hoards of Thomond", *North Munster Antiquarian Journal*, Volume XII, 1969.

49. Dolley, Michael, and William O'Sullivan, "The Chronology of the first Anglo-Irish Coinage". *North Munster Studies*. (Edited by Etienne Rynne), Limerick, 1967.

50. Dolley, Michael, *Anglo-Norman Ireland. c. 1100-1318*, Dublin, 1972.

51. Doran, Patrick F., "The Hunt Museum", *North Munster Antiquarian Journal*, Volume XX, 1978.

52. Dowd, Rev. J., *St. Mary's Cathedral, Limerick*, Limerick, 1899.

53. Duane, Mary, "Mount Trenchard", *North Munster Studies*, (Edited by Etienne Rynne), Limerick, 1967.

54. Duffy, Paul, "A Limerick Pawnshop Farthing". *North Munster Antiquarian Journal*, Volume XXV, 1983.

55. Egan, Fr. Batholomew, *Franciscan Limerick, the Order of St. Francis in the City of Limerick*, Limerick, 1971.

56. Fallon, Niall, *The Armada in Ireland*, 1978.

57. Fanning, Thomas. "Two Cross-Inscribed Stones from Reask, Co. Kerry, at Adare Manor", *North Munster Antiquarian Journal*, Volume XIV, 1971.

58. Feeley, Pat, "The Rockite Uprising in Co. Limerick — 1821". *The Old Limerick Journal*, Autumn, 1987.

59. Feeley, Pat, "Aspects of the 1904 Pogrom", *The Old Limerick Journal*, Summer 1982.

60. Fitzgerald, Patrick, "Late Michael Geoghegan", *Ballyguiltenane Rural Journal*, Christmas 1982 and New Year Edition.

61. Fitzgibbon, Constantine, "A Visit to Limerick — 1952", *The Old Limerick Journal*, Summer 1982.

62. Fitzgibbon, Constantine, *The Irish in Ireland*, London, 1983.

63. Fitzgerald, Rev. P., and J.J. M'Gregor, *The History, Topography and Antiquities of the County and City of Limerick with a preliminary view of the History and Antiquities of Ireland*, Volume II, Limerick, London, 1827.

64. Fógra Fáilte, Official Guide. *Limerick City and County*. The National Tourist Publicity Organisation for Ireland, Dublin.

65. Frost, James, *The History and Topography of the County of Clare, 1893*. Cork, 1978.

66. Gallagher, Thomas, *Paddy's Lament — Ireland 1846-1847. Prelude to Hatred*, Dublin, 1985.

67. Gaughan, J. Anthony, *The Knights of Glin, A Geraldine Family*, Dublin, 1978.

68. Gilhooly, John T., *Stair Chaisleán Ui gConaing Atháin. The Annals of Castleconnell and Ahane since Prehistoric Times*, Castleconnell, 1988.

69. Gleeson, Dermot F., *A History of the Diocese of Killaloe*, Part 1, 1962.

70. Gleeson, Willie W., "City of Commerce", *The Old Limerick Journal*, Summer 1982.

71. Gleeson, Willie W., "R.I.C. and the Black and Tans", *Limerick Leader*, Saturday, 27 March, 1982.

72. Gleeson, W.W., "The Brazen Head", *The Old Limerick Journal*, Autumn 1981.

73. *Glin Castle, Co. Limerick*. Limerick.

74. Green, Alice Stopford Green, *Irish Nationality*, London.

75. Green, Jonathon, *Famous Last Words*, London, 1979.

76. Gwynn, Aubrey, and R. Neville Hadcock, *Medieval Religious Houses Ireland*, London, 1970. Reprinted 1988.

77. Hall, Mr. and Mrs. Samuel Carter, *Hall's Ireland — Mr. & Mrs. Hall's Tour of 1840*, London, 1841. Reprinted 1984.

78. Hamilton, Frank, *Limerick in Days gone By ... A Guide to the olde cittie. A Walk through Thomondgate, the Parish and Johnsgate*, Limerick, 1978.

79. Hamilton, Rev. G.F., *Records of Ballingarry. Limerick Diocese*. Limerick, 1930.

80. Hannan, Kevin. "A Forgotten Limerick Genius", *The Old Limerick Journal*. Autumn 1987.

81. Hannan, Kevin, "Garryowen", *The Old Limerick Journal*. December 1979.

82. Hannan, Kevin, "How Plassey Got Its Name", *The Old Limerick Journal*. December 1979.

83. Hannan, Kevin. "The Sandmen", *The Old Limerick Journal*, Autumn 1981.

84. Hannan, Kevin. "The Irishtown", *The Old Limerick Journal.*, Spring 1982.

85. Hannan, Kevin. "St. Michael's", *The Old Limerick Journal*, Winter 1981.

86. Harbison, Peter. *Guide to the National Monuments in the Republic of Ireland including a selection of other monuments not in State care*, Dublin, 1970.

87. Harbison, Peter. *Pre-Christian Ireland. From The First Settlers to the Early Celts*, London, 1988.

88. Hartnett, Michael. "Newcastle West — 1970". *The Old Limerick Journal*, Winter 1986.

89. Haydn, J.A. *Misericords in St. Mary's Cathedral, Limerick*, (Revised by Rev. M.J. Talbot), Limerick, 1969.

90. Healy, James N., *Irish Ballads and Songs of the Sea*, Cork, 1967.

91. Herbert, Robert. "Castleconnell and its Spa", *North Munster Antiquarian Journal*, Vol. V. No. 4, 1948.

92. Herbert, Robert. *Worthies of Thomond. A Compendium of Short Lives of the Most Famous Men and Women of Limerick and Clare to the present day*, Limerick, 1944.

93. Herity, Michael, and George Eogan. *Ireland in Prehistory*, London, 1977.

94. Hewson, Michael, "Emigration to the 'North American Colonies' from the Port of Limerick in 1841", *North Munster Antiquarian Journal*, Volume XXIII, 1981.

95. Hinchy, P. "Longford Bridge", *The Lough Gur & District Historical Society Journal*, St. Patrick's Day 17th March 1986.

96. Hogan, Robert, *Dictionary of Irish Literature*, Dublin, 1980.

97.* Honan, Joseph S., "The Real Irish", unpublished manuscript, Clare County Library, Ennis. 1989.

98.* Honan, Joseph S., "Men of Stature — Collins, Griffith and O'Higgins", unpublished manuscript. Clare County Library, Ennis.

99. Howard, Leonard. "The Penal Laws in Limerick 1670-1684" *North*

Munster Antiquarian Journal. Volume XII, 1969.

100. Hull, Eleanor, *A Text Book of Irish Literature* second impression, Dublin, 1910.

101. Hyman, Louis. *The Jews of Ireland from Earliest times to the year 1910* ,(reprint) Shannon, 1972.

102. Ireland, Aideen, "An Eighteenth Century Map of Ash Hill, Kilmallock", *North Munster Antiquarian Journal,* Volume XXV, 1983.

103. Jackson, Robert Wyse, *The Story of Limerick,* Cork, 1973.

104. Jehovah's Witnesses. *1988 Yearbook of Jehovah's Witnesses,* Pennsylvania, 1987.

105.* Jones, Hank, "The Palatine Families of Ireland". California, thesis 1965, unpublished.

106. Jones, Joan Wynne, *The Abiding Enchantment of Curragh Chase — A Big House Remembered,* 1983.

107. Joyce, P.W. Joyce, *The Origin and History of Irish Names of Places,* Dublin, 1913.

108. P.W. *A Smaller Social History of Ancient Ireland,* Second Edition, 1908.

109. Keane, Edward, "St. Patrick's Journey through West Limerick". *North Munster Studies. (*Edited by Etienne Rynne), 1967.

110. Keane, John. "Limerick Breweries", *The Old Limerick Journal,* Autumn 1981.

111. Keating, Barry, "The Dromcolligher Cinema Tragedy", *The Annual Observer,* Newcastle West, July 1980.

112. Keating, Tim. "Three Townlands", *Ballyguiltenane Rural Journal,* 1986.

113. Kee, Robert, *The Green Flag. A History of Irish Nationalism,* London, 1972.

114. Kelly, M.J. and C. *Illustrated Guide to Lough Gur, Co. Limerick,* Revised Edition, 1985.

115. Kelly, Sean, "Phelan's Mill", *The Annual Observer,* Newcastle West, June 1983.

116. Kemmy, Jim. *The Granary,* Limerick City Library, Limerick, 1987.

117. Kemmy, Jim. "How Garryowen got its name Owen's Garden. Famous Limerick Gardens — III", *Old Limerick Journal,* Autumn 1981.

118. Kemmy, Jim, "The Death of a Cabin-Boy", *The Old Limerick Journal,* Winter 1981.

119. Kemmy, Jim, "The Siege of Clampett's Bow", *The Old Limerick Journal,* December 1979.

120. Killanin, Lord, and Michael V. Duignan, *Shell Guide to Ireland,* London, Revised Edition, 1967.

121. Kilroy, Roger and McLachlan, *Illuminated Limericks,* London, 1982.

122. Langan, John, *Ecclesiastical History of Ireland,* 1824.

123. Lenihan, Maurice, *Limerick; Its History and Antiquities, ecclesiastical, civil and military, from the earliest ages, with copious historical, archaeological, topographical, and genealogical notes and illustrations; maps, plates, and appendices, and an alphabetical index, etc. Compiled from the ancient annals, the most authentic ms. and printed records, recent researches, etc., etc..* Dublin, 1866.

124. Leo, Marie, "Ballingirlough", *Lough Gur and District Historical Society Journal,* 1983.

125. Leo, Marie. "Grange", *The Lough Gur and District Historical Society Journal,* St. Patrick's Day 17th March 1986.

126.* Leonard, Denis. "Notes on the Inner City Development Project", unpublished.

127.* Leonard, Denis. "Notes on the Limerick Civic Trust", unpublished.

128.* Leonard, Denis M. "Notes on Limerick Jewish History", unpublished, (Limerick Civic Trust. Labour History Workshop).

129. Lewis, Samuel. *A Topographical Dictionary of Ireland,* London, 1837.

130. Limerick City Trust, *Limerick. An Appreciation,* Limerick, 1987.

131. Limerick Civic Trust, *Limerick Street Antiquities,* Limerick, 1986.

132. *Limerick Christmas Gazette,* 1987, "Recalling the day that Limerick's city centre came to a standstill — Todd's Great Fire, August 25, 1959".

133. "Limerick Quakers", *The Clare Champion,* Friday, 16 September, 1988.

134. Lilburn, Hugh, *Presbyterians in Limerick ,* Limerick, 1946.

135. Logan, Patrick, *The Holy Wells of Ireland,* Gerrard Cross, Bucks., 1980.

136. Longfield, Ada Kathleen, *Anglo-Irish Trade in the Sixteenth Century,* London, 1929.

137. Lovett, Phil. "The Wellesley Bridge", *The Old Limerick Journal.* Winter 1981.

138. Lovett, Phil. "The Development of the Port of Limerick in the 19th century". *The Old Limerick Journal,* Spring 1982.

139. Lucas, A.T., "A Horizontal Mill at Knocknagranshy, Co. Limerick". *North Munster Antiquarian Journal,* Volume XII, 1969.

140. Lundon, Thomas, *A History of KIlteely-Dromkeen.*

141. Lydon, J.F., "Reviews and Short Notices", *Annual Report of the I.C.H.S., 1962-3. (*A report approved on 30 May 1963 at the Conference of Irish Historians held at Magee University College), Derry.

142.* Lynch, Dr. Patricia A., "The European Connections of two Irish writers: Maria Edgeworth and Kate O'Brien": A paper presented to the Triennial Conference of the International Association for the Study of Anglo-Irish Literature, the New University of Ulster at Coleraine, July 1988 (unpublished).

143. Lynch, P.J. "Obituary. Patrick Weston Joyce, LL.D., M.R.I.A." *Journal of the North Munster Archaeological Society. In continuation of the Journal of the Limerick Field Club,* Vol. III. No. 2, January 1914.

144. Lyons, F.S.L., *Charles Stewart Parnell.* London, 1977.

145. Lysaght, Paddy, *The Feale from its source to the sea,* Pallaskenry, 1987.

146. Macardle, Dorothy, *The Irish Republic — A documented chronicle of the Anglo-Irish conflict and the partitioning of Ireland, with a detailed account of the period 1916-1923 with a preface by Eamon de Valera,* Dublin, 1951.

147. McAuliffe, John, "The Deel — Past and Present", *The Annual Observer,* December 1984.

148. Mac Bradaí, Yann Philippe, the genealogist, discovered the Sarsfield-Princess of Wales connection in 1982. This was published simultaneously in *The Limerick Leader, Irish Press, Evening Press* and *Cork Examiner* on 15 January 1983. Further royal lineage discoveries re Princess of Wales, the Duchess of York and their consorts were published in 1986, 1987 & 1988 in *Sunday Tribune, Limerick Leader &*

149. McCarthy, Major J.M., "Dromkeen Ambush. An action of the Black and Tan period". *An Cosantóir*, Dublin, 1943.

150. MacCarthy, Colonel J.M., Editor *Limerick's fighting story — From 1916 to the truce with Britain",* Tralee.

151. McCormack, W.J., Editor, "A Chronology of Sheridan le Fanu's life" in *Uncle Silas* by Sheridan le Fanu, Oxford, 1981.

152. McCormick, Donald, *The Hell-Fire Club — The story of the amorous Knights of Wycombe,* London, 1958. Reprinted, 1975.

153. MacCurtain, Margaret, *Tudor and Stuart Ireland,* Dublin, 1972.

154. MacEoin, Uuinseann, *Survivors. The story of Ireland's struggle as told through some of her outstanding living people recalling events from the days of Davitt, through James Connolly, Brugha, Collins, de Valera, Liam Mellows, and Rory O'Connor, to the present time,* 1980. Third Edition, revised and enlarged 1987.

155. McEvoy, Dermot, "Scandal at Bruff". A series of three articles published between September 1980 and Spring 1981 in *The Old Limerick Journal.* (Edited by Jim Kemmy).

156. MacLeod, Catriona, "The Statue of Our Lady of Limerick: A gift in reparation". *North Munster Studies,* (Edited by Etienne Rynne). Limerick, 1967.

157. MacLysaght, Edward, *Irish Life in the Seventeenth Century.* Reprinted Shannon, 1969.

158. MacLysaght, Edward, *The Kenmare Manuscripts,* The Irish Manuscripts Commission, *Coimisiún Lámhscríbhinní na hÉireann,* Government Publications Office, 1942.

159. MacLysaght, Edward, *The Surnames of Ireland,* Third Edition, Dublin, 1978.

160. MacMahon, Tony, "Studiisque Asperrima Belli", *The Old Limerick Journal,* Autumn 1981.

161. MacMahon, Tony, "The Evolution of Local Government", *Old Limerick Journal,* Spring 1982.

162. McNamara, Tom, "Knockainey in Ancient Times", *The Lough Gur & District Historical Society Journal,* March 1987.

163. McNamara, Tom. "Evolution of a civilisation", *The Lough Gur & District Historical Society Journal,* March 1986.

164. MacNeill, Maire, *The Festival of Lughnasa — A study of the survival of the Celtic Festival of the beginning of harvest.* Dublin, 1982.

165. MacSpealáin, Gearóid. "Notes on place-names in the City and Liberties of Limerick", *North Munster Antiquarian Journal,* Vol. III. No. 2, Autumn 1942.

166. MacSpealáin, Gearóid, "Place Names of County Limerick. Barony of Coshlea". *North Munster Antiquarian Journal.* Vol. 5. No. 4, 1948.

167. MacSpealáin, Gearóid, (F.G. Spencer), "Some Interesting Place-names in County Limerick", *North Munster Antiquarian Journal,* Vol. III. No. 3, Spring 1943.

168. Marrinan, Sean, "The Ball at Roxborough House, 1895", *North Munster Antiquarian Journal,* Volume XXVI, 1984.

169. Marrinan, Sean, "Dickens in Limerick, 1858", *North Munster Antiquarian Journal,* Volume XXIV, 1982.

170. Maxwell, Constantia, *Irish History from Contemporary Sources (1509-1610),* London, 1923.

171. Meghen, P.J., "Turnpike roads in Co. Limerick", *The Old Limerick Journal,* Winter 1986.

172. Mitchell, G.F., "Antiquities. The Rudiments, 1785-1840", *The Royal Academy, a bicentennial history, 1785-1985,* Dublin, 1985.

173. Moody, T.W. & F.X. Martin, *The Course of Irish History,* Cork, 1984.

174. Mulcahy, Mary. "Herbertstown", *Lough Gur and District Historical Society Journal,* 1983.

175. Mulligan, Fergus, *One Hundred and Fifty Years of Irish Railways,* Dublin, 1983.

176. Murphy, Charlotte M. *Limerick City — An Architectural Guide,* Shannon, 1986.

177. Murphy, Charlotte, "The Limerick to Killaloe Canal", *The Other Clare,* Volume 8, Shannon, 1984.

178. Ní Chinnéide, Síle, "A Journal from Cork to Limerick in December 1790", *North Munster Antiquarian Journal.* Volume XIV, 1971.

179. Nash, Ogden, Edward Lear, Charles Barsotti, Dean Walley, and others, *New Comic Limericks, Laughable Poems,* (Edited by Ivanette Dennis and illustrated by Louis Marak), 1969.

180. National Parks and Monuments Service, *Visitor's Guide. King John's Castle, Limerick.*

181. Newman, Rev. Jeremiah, "John McEnery — Limerick priest Palaeontologist 1796-1841" *North Munster Studies,* (Edited by Etienne Rynne), Limerick, 1967.

182. O'Brien, Conor, *From Three Yachts,* Revised Edition, 1949.

183. O'Brien, Ivar, *O' Brien of Thomond — the O'Brien's in Irish history 1500-1865,* Chichester, 1986.

184. O'Connell, James, *The Meaning of Irish Place Names,* Belfast, 1979.

185. O'Connor, G.B. *Elizabethan Ireland. Native and English,* Dublin.

186. O'Connor, John, *Mungret, History and Antiquities,* 1971.

187. O'Connor, Patrick J., *Exploring Limerick's past. An historical geography of urban development in city and county,* Newcastle West, 1987.

188. O Corrbuí, Máirtín. *Kenry, The Story of a Barony in County Limerick.*

189.* O Dálaigh, Brian, "An early nineteenth century painting of Ennis", *The Other Clare,* Volume 10, 1986, (published). "A History of an O'Brien stronghold c. 1210-1626", (unpublished).

190. O'Donnell, Patrick D., *The Irish Faction Fighters of the 19th century,* Tralee, 1975.

191. O'Donoghue, D.J., *The Geographical Distribution of Irish Ability,* 1906.

192. O'Donovan, John. *Ordnance Survey Letters — Limerick,* 1840.

193.* O'Donovan, Reenie. "Notes on Kilrush Church," Unpublished. Prepared for a lecture on that site on Wednesday 31 August, 1988, to the Shannon Archaeological and Historical Society).

194. O'Dwyer, Michael. "Three East Limerick Fairs", *North Munster Studies,* (Edited by Etienne Rynne), Limerick, 1967.

195. O'Farrell, Padraic, *Who's Who in the Irish War of Independence 1916-1921,* Cork, 1980.

196. O'Farrell, Padraic, *Shannon Through Her Literature,* Cork, 1983.

197. * O'Flaherty, Eamon, "Urban Politics and Municipal Reform in eighteenth

century Limerick", unpublished.

198. O Floinn, Raghnall, "A Gold Band, found near Rathkeale, Co. Limerick", *North Munster Antiquarian Journal*, Volume XXV, 1983.

199. O'Grady, Desmond, "Shawn-a-Scoob", *The Old Limerick Journal*, December 1979.

200. O'Kelly, Michael J. "A Survey of the Antiquities in the Barony of Small County, County Limerick", *North Munster Antiquarian Journal*, 1942.

201. O Kelly, Michael J. "A Survey of the Antiquities in the Barony of Small County, County Limerick", Part II, *North Munster Antiquarian Journal*, Spring 1943.

202. O'Kelly, Michael J.. "Knockea, Co. Limerick", *North Munster Studies*, Limerick, 1967.

203. O'Leary, David. "The Glin river and its course", *Ballyguiltenane Rural Journal*, 1986.

204.* O'Mahony, Chris, and Mary Pyne, *"Family History in Limerick"*, unpublished.

205. O'Riordan, Manus, "Anti-Semitism in Irish Politics", *Dublin Jewish News*, March-April 1979.

206. O'Riordan, Manus, "The Sinn Fein tradition of anti-Semitism:- from Arthur Griffith to Sean South" published in *The Irish Jewish Year Book 1984-1985* under the title of "Anti-Semitism in Irish politics".

207. O'Riordáin, Seán P., *Antiquities of the Irish Countryside*, London and New York, Reprinted 1984.

208. O'Sullivan, John. *A History of the Church in Killagholehane and Broadford*, August 1988.

209. O'Sullivan, Michael, "The Kenmare [Browne] estate", *The Lough Gur & District Historical Society Journal*, March 1987.

210. O'Sullivan, Michael. "Geoffrey de Marisco", *The Lough Gur and District Society Journal*, St. Patrick's Day 17th March 1986.

211. O'Sullivan, Thomas F., "The City of Limerick in the 17th century — A Topographical study". *Tercentenary Commemoration of the Cromwellian Siege of Limerick 1651-1951*, Limerick, 1951.

212. O Tuama, Seán, *An Duanaire. 1600-1900: Poems of the Dispossessed, (*Curtha i Láthair ag Seán O Tuama, with translations into English verse by Thomas Kinsella), 1981.

213. Otway-Ruthven, A.J., *A History of Medieval Ireland*, London, 1968.

214. Petrie, George, *The Ecclesiastical Architecture of Ireland — An Essay on the origin and uses of the Round Towers of Ireland*, Dublin, 1845.

215. Pierce, Thomas, "The Stephensons: Sixty Years of Limerick History. *North Munster Studies. (*Edited by Etienne Rynne), Limerick, 1967.

216. Place, J.A., and Joe MacMahon. "The Lax Weir", *Limerick Chrismas Gazette*, 1988.

217. Quane, Michael, "Kildimo Seminary, Co. Limerick, 1808-1817", *North Munster Antiquarian Journal*. Volume XV, 1972.

218. Quilty, Pat, (Editor), *The Lough Gur & District Historical Society Journal*. St. Patrick's Day, 17th March, 1987.

219. Quinlan, Michael, "Patrickswell graveyard", *The Lough Gur and District Historical Society Journal*, St. Patrick's Day, 17th March, 1986.

220. Read, Charles A., *The Cabinet of Irish Literature, Selections from the works of the chief poets, orators, and prose writers of Ireland*, London, 1902.

221. Roche, Richard, *The Norman Invasion of Ireland*, Dublin, 1979.

222. Ronan, Myles V., *The Reformation in Ireland under Elizabeth 1558-1580*, London, New York, Toronto, 1930.

223. Ross, Anne, *Everyday Life of the Pagan Celts*, London, 1970.

224.* Ruttle, Walter. "Notes on the Palatines", unpublished. (Lecture on Palatine history delivered to Newcastle West Archaeological and Historical Society, 1 February 1989).

225. Ryan, P.J. "The Royal Irish Constabulary", *The Old Limerick Journal*, Summer 1982.

226. Ryan, Des, "The Jews of Limerick", Part Two, *The Old Limerick Journal*.

227. Ryan, P.J., "Some Local Industries". *The Old Limerick Journal*, Autumn 1981.

228. Rynne, Etienne, "John Daly and the Bard of Thomond", *North Munster Antiquarian Journal*, Volume XIX, 1977.

229. Rynne, Etienne. "A Late Medieval Casket from Knockmore, Co. Clare — Discussion". *North Munster Antiquarian Journal*, Volume XIV, 1971.

230. Sanderson, Edgar, *A History of the British Empire, (*New Edition. Extended and revised), London, 1909.

231. Scott, George. "Some unrecorded finds of gold ornaments, from the counties of Limerick,Clare and Tipperary". *Journal of the Limerick Field Club*, 1905-1907.

232. Seoighe, Mainchín, *A Walking Tour of Historic Limerick*, Shannonside Tourism, 1982.

233. Seoighe, Mainchín, *Portrait of Limerick*, London, 1982.

234. Seoighe, Mainchín, "The Stepping Stones", *The Lough Gur and District Historical Society Journal*. St. Patrick's Day, 17th March, 1987.

235. Seoighe, Mainchín, *Dromin and Athlacca. The story of a rural parish in Co. Limerick*, Limerick, 1978.

236. Seoighe, Mainchín, "Loingeas Lochlannch i Loch Gair", *The Lough Gur and District Historical Society Journal*, St. Patrick's Day, 1986.

237. Seoighe, Mainchín, *De Valera and Bruree*, Bruree, 1985.

238. Seoighe, M., *The Limerick Guide — Official Irish Tourist Board Guide to County Limerick*. Bórd Fáilte — Irish Tourist Board Publication.

239. Shannonside, the Mid-Western Regional Tourism Organisation, *Sarsfield's Ride, Marcaíocht an t Sairséalaigh*, Limerick Leader.

240.* Sheaff, Nicholas, "Historical Survey of the Chamber of Commerce premises, 96 O'Connell Street, Limerick", unpublished.

241. Sheehy, Maurice, *When the Normans came to Ireland*, Cork, 1975.

242.* Shee-Twohig, Elizabeth, "Excavation ring fort at Croom, Co. Limerick", *North Munster Antiquarian Journal*, Volume XIX, 1977 (Published). Shee-Twohig, Elizabeth, and Liam Irwin, "Notes on Sluggery Ring Fort", unpublished.

243. Shell, Irish, and B.P.. *The Shannon Guide — A navigational pilot, fishing and touring guide*. (Edited by John A Dowling, John Weaving,

Dom Roche and Eric Erskine).
November 1962 to April 1963.

244. Simms, J.G., "The Siege of
Limerick, 1690", *North Munster
Studies*, (Edited by Etienne Rynne),
Limerick, 1967.

245. Smyth, Alfred P., *Scandinavian
York and Dublin, The History and
Archaeology of two related Viking
kingdoms*, Volume II, Dublin, 1987.

246. Spellissy, Sean, and John O'Brien,
Clare, County of Contrast, 1987.

247. Spellissy, Seán, "Scattery Island",
Clare Association Yearbook 1987.

248. Stalley, Roger. *The Cistercian
Monasteries of Ireland*, London,
1987.

249. Stalley, R.A., *Architecture and
Sculpture in Ireland 1150-1350*,
Dublin, 1971.

250. Stewart, Dolly, "The Goose's
Corner", *The Old Limerick Journal*,
December, 1979.

251. Sykes, Christopher Simon, *The
Knights' Tale* [Knights of Glin].

252. Sykes, J.B., Editor, *The Concise
Oxford Dictionary of Current
English — based on the Oxford
English Dictionary and its supple-
ments*, Oxford, 1976.

253. Taisce, An. *Adare — A short guide
to the village*, Limerick, 1976.

254. Talbot, Rev. M.J., *A Pictorial Tour
of Limerick Cathedral*.

255. Talbot, M.J., Very Rev., *The
Monuments of St. Mary's
Cathedral, Limerick*, Limerick,
1976.

256. Talbot, The Very Reverend Michael
J., "The Memorial to Prior Johannes
Ffox in St. Mary's Cathedral,
Limerick", *North Munster Studies*,
(Edited by Etienne Rynne),
Limerick, 1967.

257. Tankard, Peter M., "The Tankards of
Tankardstown: Flemish or Norman?"
*North Munster Antiquarian
Journal*, Volume XXVII, 1985.

258. Tierney, Mark, O.S.B. *Glenstal
Abbey. A Historical Guide*, Glenstal
Abbey, 1980.

259. *Tipperary and Limerick Recorder*,
"The Hill of Ballybrood", Saturday,
15 January, 1927, and Saturday 25
June 1927.

260. Wallace, Martin, *100 Irish Lives*,
London, 1983.

261. Wallace, Patrick F., "The
Organisation of pre-railway public

transport in counties Limerick and
Clare", *North Munster Antiquarian
Journal*, Volume XV, 1972.

262. Walsh, Larry, "A flint javelin-head
from Kilmacow wedge-tomb,
Knockfeerina, Co. Limerick",
*North Munster Antiquarian
Journal*, Volume XXVI, 1984.

263.* Walsh, Larry, *Historic Limerick —
The City and its Treasures*, The Irish
Heritage Series: 45. Dublin, 1984.
(Published). *"Notes on Limerick
City Museum"*, unpublished.

264. Warwick, *The Warwick English
History a sketch of the development
of England and the Empire from 55
B.C. to the present time*, London.

265. Weir, Anthony, *Early Ireland — A
Field Guide*, Belfast, 1980.

266. Weir, Hugh W.L., *Historical
Genealogical Architectural Notes
on some Houses of Clare*, Whitegate,
1986.

267. Weir, Hugh W.L., *O'Brien People
and Places*, Whitegate, 1983.

268. Westropp, T.J. "The Assembly Places
of Oenach Cuirbre and Sid Asail at
Monasteranenagh, County
Limerick". *Proceedings of the
Royal Irish Academy*, Dublin,
London, 1919-1920.

269. Westropp, T.J., "Ancient Castles of
County Limerick", *Proceedings of
Royal Irish Academy*, Vol. 26,
Section C, 1906-1907.

270. Westropp, T.J., "Ancient Places of
Assembly in the Counties of
Limerick and Clare", *Journal of the
Royal Society of Antiquaries of
Ireland*, Volume XLIV, 1919.

271. Westropp, T.J., *The Antiquities of
Limerick and its neighbourhood*,
Dublin, 1916.

272. Westropp, Thomas J., "Notes on
Askeaton, County Limerick. Part II
— The History after 1579, *Journal
of the Royal Society of Antiquaries
of Ireland*, Part 2 — Vol. XXXIII,
30th June, 1903.

273. Westropp, T.J., "Carrigogunnell
Castle and the O'Briens of
Pubblebrian, in the County of
Limerick", Part I and Part II,
*Journal of the Royal Society of
Antiquaries of Ireland*, 1906.

274. Westropp, Thomas Johnson,
"Cromwellian Account Books,
Limerick", *The Journal of the
Royal Society of Antiquaries of
Ireland*, Part 2 — Vol. XXXVI, 30th
June, 1906.

275. Westropp, T.J., *The Desmond

Castle, Newcastle West, Co.
Limerick, The Journal of the Royal
Society of Antiquities of Ireland*,
1909-1910.

276. Westropp, Thomas J., "St. Mary's
Cathedral, Limerick: Its Plan and
Growth". *The Journal of the Royal
Society of Antiquaries of Ireland*,
Part 2, Volume VIII, Fifth series,
June 1898.

277.* Westropp, Thomas J., "Miscellanea",
notes, unpublished, 1881.

278. Whelan, Frank, *Cappagh — A
Sense of History*.

279. White, Rev. P., *History of Clare and
the Dalcassian Clans of Tipperary,
Limerick, and Galway*, Dublin, 1893.

280. Woodham-Smith, Cecil., *The Great
Hunger 1845-1849*, London, 1962.

281. Woulfe, Rev. Patrick, "Names and
Surnames in County Limerick",
*Journal of the North Munster
Archaeological Society*, 1919.

282. Woulfe, Rev. Patrick, *Sloinnte
Gaedheal is Gall, Irish Names and
Surnames*, Dublin, 1923.

283. Wyndham Quin, Lieut-Commander
Valentine, *Notes on the History of
Adare*, Limerick, 1934.

284. Younger, Calton, *Ireland's Civil
War*, London, 1968.

FACES INDEX

FACES INDEX

Greyhound Racing 70, 214
Grierston Bog 178, 215
Groody River 73
Grove, The, Ballingarry 113
Gun-Running 168, 169

Hagstown 220
Haldon Hill, Battle of 181
Hamilton's Tower 183
Ham, Limerick 60
Hanging Gardens, William Roche's, Limerick 45, 46
Hay Market, Limerick 61
Headrace, The 144
Heathfield House 232, 234
Hell-Fire Club Premises, Askeaton 107
Henry Street, Limerick 183
Herbertstown 185, 217, 219
Hermitage, The, Castleconnell 143
Hero's Grave, Ballynagallagh 220
Hiberno-Norse Coins 93
High Mount House 234
High Spirits 194, 195
Hobson's Choice, Limerick 48
Hollypark House 242, 243
Holohan Stone, Mungret Abbey 222
Holy Trinity Church, Dromin 110
Horses 21, 214, 250
Hospital 189, 192, 219
Hospital Abbey 191, 192
Hospital Church 191, 192
Hospital of St. John of Jerusalem 189
Houndscourt 201
House of Industry, Limerick 77, 79
Howth 169
Hunger Strike 79, 177
Hunt Collection, Plassey 28
Hunting 214
Hunt Museum, Plassey 101

Inch St. Lawrence 127
Inghean Bhaoith's Church, Glenquin 204
Inner City Development Plan, Limerick 18
Interpretative Centre, Lough Gur 218
Irish Railway Joke 237, 238
Irishtown, Limerick 35, 36, 37, 38, 39, 40, 41, 42, 43
Iron Age 165, 198, 250
Island House 142
Islandmore House, Croom 148
Iverus 242, 243

Jerusalem 60, 189, 190, 223
Jesuit Church, Limerick 48
Jewish History 55, 115
Jockeyhall 247
John O'Grady Monument, Limerick 62
John Street, Limerick 38

Kelpie 169
Kenmare Castle, Hospital 191
Kenmare, County Kerry 191

Kenry 181, 239, 240
Kerry Beagle 214
Kerry, County 15, 182, 203, 230
Kerrykyle 88
Kilballyowen House 119
Kilbeheny 179
Kilbeheny Church 179
Kilbigly Church 124
Kilbolane Castle 233
Kilbradran Church 173
Kilbreedy 212
Kilbreedy Major Church 212, 215
Kilbreedy Minor Church 212
Kilbroney Church 109, 110
Kilcaskin 162
Kilcoleman Wells 232
Kilcolman Church 260
Kilcolman Parish 174
Kilcoora Church 160
Kilcornan 242
Kilcornan Castle 242
Kilcornan Church 242
Kilcosgrave Castle 173
Kilcosgrave House 173
Kilcosgrif House 173
Kilcruig 201
Kilcullane Castle 187
Kilcullane Church 187
Kilcullane House 187
Kilcurley Church 195
Kilcurley House 195
Kildacolam Castle 193
Kildacolam Church 193
Kildacolam Townland 193
Kildimo 193
Kildimo Court 193
Kildimo Seminary 193
Kilduff Castle 236, 237
Kilfergus Church 182, 183
Kilfergus Parish 180, 182, 183
Kilfinnane 196, 197, 198
Kilfinnane Castle 197
Kilfinnane Education Centre 198
Kilfinnane Moat 197
Kilfinny Castle 156, 246
Kilfinny Church 156
Kilflyn Parish 201
Kilfrush 215
Kilfrush Castle 215
Kilfrush Church 215
Kilfrush House 215
Kilkeedy Churches 147
Kilkeedy Parish 147
Killaliathan Church 157, 158
Killaliathan Parish 158
Killaloe, County Clare 37
Killanure 127
Killasragh 247
Killasragh Church 247
Killeaney Wood 180
Killeedy 202
Killeedy Castle 203

Killeedy Church 203
Killeely 80
Killeenagarriff 102
Killeenagarriff River 102
Killeen Priory, Cowpark 243
Killenorty Parish 247
Killenough Parish 247
Killila Church 160
Killila (Mount Plummer) 160
Killocia 206
Kill Teidhill 188
Killulta Church 239 243
Killulta Parish see Chapel-Russell Parish
Killuragh Church 239
Killuragh Parish see Chapel-Russell Parish
Kilmacanearla Church 116
Kilmacluana Church 131
Kilmacow 131
Kilmacow Church 116
Kilmacow Flint Javelin-Head 116
Kilmacow Wedge-Shaped Gallery Grave 116
Kilmallock 37, 190, 206, 207, 208, 209, 210, 229
Kilmallock Barracks 119, 210
Kilmallock Gate, Adare 95
Kilmallock Town Walls 208
Kilmeedy Church 234
Kilmeedy 234
Kilmoylan Church 173, 174
Kilmoyle House, Limerick 78
Kilmurry, Caherconlish 127
Kilmurry Parish 101
Kilnamona Hill 116
Killonahan Church 247
Killonahan 247
Killonahan Castle 247
Kilpeacon 247
Kilpeacon Castle 247
Kilpeacon Church 247
Kilpeacon Church of Ireland Church 247
Kilquan Church, Cahir Hill 199
Kilrush, 78
Kilrush Church, 78
Kilrush, County Clare 167
Kilscannell 91
Kilshane Abbey 116
Kilteely 111, 118
Kilteely Catholic Church 188
Kilteely Hill 188
Kinard 180
Kincora, County Clare 19
Kingdom Hall 43
Kingdom of Thomond 16
King's Castle, Kilmallock 207
King's Gate, Westminster 190
King's Island, *Inis Sibtond, Inis Uibhtonn, Odin's Island, Odensey* 11, 15, 16, 28
King John's Castle, Limerick 15, 16, 17, 18, 37, 231
Kingstown, County Dublin 169
Kinsale, County Cork 182
Knockabooley 174